VALERIUS M

Memorable Deeds and Sayings

VALERIUS MAXIMUS

Memorable Deeds and Sayings

One Thousand Tales from Ancient Rome

Translated, with Introduction, by

HENRY JOHN WALKER

Hackett Publishing Company, Inc.
Indianapolis/Cambridge

For further information, please address:

Hackett Publishing Company, Inc.
P.O. Box 44937
Indianapolis, IN 46244-0937

www.hackettpublishing.com

Cover photograph by Fred Voetsch, Acclaim Images
Cover design by Abigail Coyle
Text design by Jennifer Plumley
Composition by Professional Book Compositors, Inc.
Printed at Sheridan Books, Inc.

Library of Congress Cataloging-in-Publication Data

Valerius Maximus.
    [Factorum et dictorum memorabilium libri IX. English]
    Memorable deeds and sayings / Valerius Maximus ; translated, with introduction, by
Henry John Walker.
        p. cm.
    ISBN 0-87220-675-0 — 0-87220-674-2 (pbk.)
    1. Rome—Social life and customs—Early works to 1800.   2. Rome—Civiliza-
tion—Early Works to 1800.   3. Didactic literature, Latin—Translations into English.
4. Exempla—Translations into English.   5. Anecdotes—Early works to 1800.
I. Walker, Henry John, 1959–.   II. Title.

DG78.V3513 2004
937'.02—dc22   2003056867

The paper used in this publication meets the minimum requirements of
American National Standard for Information Sciences—
Permanence of Paper for Printed Library Materials,
ANSI Z39.48-1984

In ricordo del 20 settembre 1993

quando a li miei occhi apparve prima
la gloriosa donna de la mia mente.

TABLE OF CONTENTS

BOOK FOUR

BOOK FIVE

BOOK SIX

ACKNOWLEDGMENTS

I would especially like to thank three people for helping me to produce this book: my editor, Deborah Wilkes, for supporting this translation of Valerius Maximus and guiding me throughout its production with her excellent advice; my reader, Professor Joseph Pucci, for doing such a wonderful job and making my translation readable; and Lorelei Purrington of Bates College, for her generous assistance with the final version.

I would also like to thank my colleagues at Bates College, Laurie O'Higgins, Lisa Maurizio, and Margaret Imber, for their support, friendship and kindness; James Barrett and Ramachandran Bharath at Colby College for their lively lunch breaks; my wife, Nikky Singh, for accompanying me through the entire process; and my family back home, Mammy, Jofie, Charlie, and Mary Rose, my little nieces and nephews, and the great dog Pip, who has seen two generations of my family pass by, "and is now ruling over the third."

Last, but not least, I must ever give thanks and praise to "the glorious lady of my thoughts" whose incarnation and birth mark the beginning of her new life and mine—Sarah Walker.

INTRODUCTION

Valerius Maximus finished this great collection of almost one thousand stories[1] from the Roman world in A.D. 31. Apart from the fact that he was a close friend of a consul,[2] we know almost nothing about Valerius: he has effaced himself completely behind his collection of stories. The period in which he lived and wrote was the beginning of a new era for Rome and indeed for the west in general. The Roman Republic had been destroyed with horrifying bloodshed, and the age of the emperors had begun. Western history would be dominated by monarchs for the next nineteen centuries.[3] The beginning of this long era of domination was a very disturbing time, when the future looked bleak and people were cut off from their past. Valerius recorded these stories because they provided a link with that past—they preserved the moral values of the Republic. They are great stories, of course, but he did not want the Romans to read them just for fun; he also wanted his readers to absorb the values represented by these stories, to turn to them for moral guidance and to use them as models of behavior. His readers did not disappoint him; the Romans eagerly adopted his book as a moral code from the time it was written. And people kept turning to his stories long after the Roman emperors had disappeared and other monarchs had taken their place. His stories continued to provide his readers with a more noble code of behavior in a world of universal servility.[4]

Fortunately, we do not need Valerius to teach us how to live. We have gradually developed our own traditions of liberty, patterns of democratic behavior, and role models. We have Gandhi and Mandela as well as Brutus the Liberator and Cato of Utica.[5] But it is hard to resist the appeal of a man who can tell one thousand tales, and nobody else could tell us what it felt like to be an ancient Roman, what the

---

[1] I come up with a different number every time I try to count them, but there are approximately 960 stories.

[2] A consul was similar to a modern-day president (see consul in the Glossary). The friend of Valerius was Sextus Pompeius, consul in A.D. 14. For more on their friendship, see the end of the next section in this Introduction.

[3] In the middle of the century, the Roman poet Lucan wrote about the death of the Republic and predicted with gloomy accuracy, "From now on till the end of time, we are slaves."

[4] At the end of Shakespeare's *Hamlet*, the prince's friend, Horatio, pays an extraordinary tribute to the values of the Roman Republic when he contrasts its tradition of freedom with the atmosphere in Denmark and declares, "I am more an antique Roman than a Dane." Once a large enough number of people were converted to Horatio's views, and chose *en masse* to act like ancient Romans, the French Revolution and American Revolution were all but inevitable.

[5] These men were the first and last great Republicans in Rome. Brutus founded the Republic in 509 B.C., and Cato committed suicide in 46 B.C. rather than live under a dictator.

ancient Romans really believed, what their private world was like, and what they did when nobody was watching. We no longer feel any need to act like ancient Romans, but when we open this book, we enter their world.

One Thousand Tales from Ancient Rome

The stories of Valerius Maximus give us a unique insight into how the Romans behaved every day, how they felt about almost every issue you could imagine, and what characteristics they most admired in people. We also learn a lot about their brutality and their nastiness, characteristics that are politely ignored by most Roman authors. Valerius tells us openly how the Romans would treacherously kill foreign enemies[6] and ruthlessly massacre political opponents.[7] He does not romanticize imperialism, and he does not gloss over the bloodshed of the civil wars in which the Republic had perished. The very fact that he presents us with a whole series of these gruesome stories makes their effect all the more powerful. We cannot brush them aside as aberrations; the Romans acted at times with great cruelty, and they did not mind hearing about such behavior. Valerius gives us a picture of the Romans that is probably closer to the ugly one we find in a book like *The Rotten Romans*;[8] it is not a very romantic picture, but it is an honest one.

The Romans went through great political changes, but the last century of the Republic was also an era of great social mobility. This phenomenon had obviously captured the imagination of the Roman public, and Valerius records thirty-four stories dealing with this theme. He devotes one chapter to stories about poor people and outsiders who made it to the top of society[9] and another chapter to stories of people from aristocratic families who made a mess of their lives.[10] In yet another chapter, he looks at the issue of social mobility in itself[11] and includes under this heading both men of the aristocracy, who were irresponsible in their youth, and men from poor backgrounds, who didn't have much opportunity in life. As far as Valerius is concerned, how the young noblemen reform their characters later in life is no less remarkable than the rise of the poor young men to positions of great power. So he is remarkably free of snobbery. He attributes success to a person's character and dismisses social status as a trick of fortune.[12] This makes

---

[6]See 9:6,2–4 (Book 9: Chapter 6, Roman Stories 2–4).

[7]Valerius describes a massacre of opponents in 9:2,1–4. His descriptions of individual executions in 9:13,2–3 are particularly disturbing, though Valerius himself feels no pity for the victims.

[8]Deary 1994. I would like to thank my daughter, Sarah, for drawing my attention to this work.

[9]See 3:4.

[10]See 3:5.

[11]6:9.

[12]Speaking of a man who rose to become governor of Asia, Valerius says, "his former way of earning a living was to be blamed on fortune whereas his present rise in status was to be attributed to his own character" (6:9,7).

Valerius very unusual among Roman authors. Normally the issue of social mobility is raised only to give the writer an opportunity to indulge in satire and to sneer at the new elite. Valerius is one of few authors to record these changes with impartiality, and his balanced stories give us a much truer sense of how it was perceived than the snobbish satires from the same era.

Valerius also brings us into the private world of the ancient Romans. Sometimes he gives us wonderfully intimate and moving insights into people we knew only as famous public figures. He does not explain the political goals of the Gracchus brothers, but he does record their mother's wonderful words about her children. A very pretentious lady who kept showing off her expensive jewelry came to visit the Gracchus' mother, Cornelia. She endured this display of wealth until her children came home and then declared to her guest, "These are my jewels."[13] Again, Valerius does not lecture us on Socratic philosophy, but he does tell us how Socrates made a hobbyhorse out of a reed and played around with his sons.[14] And Valerius notes that this does not detract from the reputation of Socrates; on the contrary, it is precisely because "no part of wisdom was hidden from him" that Socrates could behave in this very human way. Valerius records lots of other stories that show real affection among parents and children,[15] and they are in direct contradiction with the usual image we have of the Roman father as a harsh and brutal patriarch. There is, of course, some truth to this stereotype of the all-powerful and abusive father, and Valerius cites some memorable examples,[16] but his own feelings on the subject are quite clear. Even when he records these stories about murderous, tyrannical patriarchs, he declares that insofar as they behave with strictness and severity, they are no longer acting like fathers.[17] The real fathers are the indulgent ones. As Valerius remarks, this is the kind of father we find in comedies,[18] but it is a pleasant surprise to discover that you could also have found a father like this in the streets of Rome.

Women, of course, were generally confined to a secluded world of which we see so little in other authors' works. The stereotype we usually get is of the well-behaved woman who would gladly face death rather than dishonor,[19] who gets married and loyally stands by her husband.[20] In this case, the stereotype seems to reflect the reality, and we get little in Valerius' book to contradict it. He even holds up the Indian custom of suttee as a model for all women to follow and expresses

---

[13]See 4:4,pref.

[14]See 8:8,ext.1 (Book 8: Chapter 8, Foreign Story 1). The abbreviation "ext." stands for "externus," meaning "foreign." This abbreviation appears before the number of each Foreign Story.

[15]See 5:7, 9, and 10.

[16]See 5:8.

[17]Speaking of Brutus the Liberator, who had to sentence his own sons to death for treason, Valerius says, "He left the role of a father so that he could play the part of a consul" (5:8,1).

[18]"The previous fathers were as gentle as fathers in a comedy" (5:8,pref.).

[19]See 6:1,1–4 and 6:1,ext.1–3.

[20]See 6:7.

his unbounded admiration for this practice. He tells us that if a man dies in India his favorite wife must join him on the funeral pyre. According to Valerius, this unfortunate woman is always delighted and jumps with joy onto the flames of her husband's funeral pyre.[21] At the end of this gruesome narrative, he gives a list of brave nations and declares that these women who burn themselves alive surpass the men of all these nations in courage. It is perhaps some small consolation to us that these models of feminine courage were situated at a safe distance from the Roman world, but the implied attitude toward women is found throughout the work of Valerius. There are some stories about women who were not so well behaved, but the stories are recorded to warn everyone that such women will inevitably receive horrible punishments for their harmless deviations.[22] There is, however, an interesting chapter on women lawyers,[23] something we rarely hear of in ancient Rome, but Valerius predictably goes out of his way to denounce them. So we do see something of the private lives of Roman women in his book, but they behave with a suspect conformity to the stereotype we find elsewhere and, disappointingly, we learn little new about them from Valerius.

Another aspect of private life that was carefully concealed in ancient Rome was homosexuality. We rarely hear of homosexual relationships in Rome, except between a master and a slave, which was the only such relationship permitted by law. But Valerius reveals that male homosexuality[24] was found in the Roman army and in high society. In the case of the army, all the stories of Valerius involve a high-standing military figure taking advantage of his status to seduce a young man of free birth.[25] The seducer is severely punished in each of these stories, which is not so surprising given the ruthless way in which discipline was enforced in the Roman army. In one case, however, the seducer claims that his freeborn partner regularly sold his body for money. This defense would be pointless unless the jury believed that soldiers frequented male prostitutes, and the jury did in fact accept the seducer's version of the facts,[26] but it punished him anyway. When we turn to high society, on the other hand, the consequences are less serious. One nobleman is, admittedly, jailed for seducing another nobleman's son, but it sounds like a case of rape.[27] But in the other cases[28] there are no legal consequences. In fact, Valerius

---

[21]See 2:6,14.

[22]See 6:3,6–12.

[23]See 8:3.

[24]He doesn't mention female homosexuality, but gay women do appear in the works of other Roman writers of the first century A.D. The writers were all men and usually denounced gay women for their masculinity.

[25]See 6:1,10–12.

[26]Valerius remarks that the tribunes (see tribune of the plebs in the Glossary), who were asked to intervene in this case, did not want soldiers "to *pay* for pleasures at home" (6:1,10), which shows that his payment of the young man had been accepted as a fact by the court.

[27]See 6:1,7.

[28]See 9:1,8 and 9:12,8.

tells us of a party thrown for an aristocratic consul in which a young nobleman, who is mentioned by name, prostitutes himself as part of the entertainment.[29] Valerius does not focus on the phenomenon of homosexuality by devoting an entire chapter to it, but he does make us aware that it was a powerful undercurrent in Rome.

The political beliefs of ordinary Romans are rarely mentioned in the works of ancient authors. What was their personal reaction to the leaders who tried to make Rome a more democratic society? Valerius gives us an insight into this grassroots tradition. He tells a touching story about a man who got into trouble simply because he kept in his home a picture of the recently murdered radical, Saturninus.[30] Valerius reveals that the Roman public felt a deep, personal loyalty to the memory of these reformers and that it could easily be led astray by anyone who claimed a relationship with one of its benefactors.[31] In one story recorded by Valerius, we learn that a man who claimed to be the grandson of Marius was able to draw as big a crowd as Caesar himself.[32] In other authors' works, we hear of fickle mobs that are easily fooled and led astray, but Valerius makes it clear that the poorer Romans had a definite idea of the direction in which they would like to be led. He uncovers a whole tradition that revered the memory of these reforming political leaders, even though he himself shares the prejudices of the propertied classes and mentions this populist tradition only to denounce it.

Although he shares the attitudes of the aristocracy to some extent, Valerius records several anecdotes that reveal the dreadful contempt to which poorer Romans were subjected by the Roman elite. In one story, Scipio Aemilianus, who is generally regarded as a very humane man by historians, tells an assembly of the plebs[33] that its members are all ex-slaves and barely deserve to call Italy their homeland.[34] In two stories that reflect a similar attitude on the part of the main characters, Scipio Nasica mocks a poor man because his working-class hands are so rough,[35] and the aristocratic Claudia wishes more of the Roman populace had been killed off in the First Punic War.[36] These stories put a human face on the great political battles of the Roman Republic, and they bring us much closer to the people of Rome than the speeches of Cicero. The plebeians to whom Valerius introduces us are much less well-behaved, and the nasty reactions of the exasperated aristocrats in these stories reveal that the misbehavior of the crowds could not be dismissed or ignored so easily. Other authors might create the impression that politics was an upper-class sport in which Roman aristocrats played against each

---

[29]See 9:12,8.

[30]See 8:1,damn.3.

[31]Various imposters appeared claiming to be long-lost sons of populist leaders such as Tiberius, Gracchus, Marius, and Clodius. The Roman crowds adored these imposters. (See 9:7,1–2 and 9:15,1–4.)

[32]See 9:15,1.

[33]See assembly—tribal and plebs, plebeian in the Glossary.

[34]See 6:2,3.

[35]See 7:5,2.

[36]See 8:1,damn.4.

other, but from Valerius we learn that the Roman people were players as well, they had a game plan of their own, and even the most powerful leaders of Rome were threatened by them.

Valerius introduces us to a new Rome. Most of his stories focus on the aristocracy, but we learn about obscure aspects of their life; other stories focus on obscure people, the ordinary citizens of Rome. Valerius himself may have belonged to the second category, but he had a unique insight into the first one. He mentions himself only twice in stories that involve his friend Sextus Pompeius, who was consul in A.D. 14. One of them tells us how Valerius went to the Roman province of Asia with his friend, who was going there to govern the province around A.D. 25. While they were traveling to Asia, they spent some time touring the islands of Greece, where they witnessed a touching case of euthanasia.[37] The other story tells us about when Sextus Pompeius died and that many people were jealous of Valerius because he was friendly with such an important person.[38] This suggests that Valerius was far from being an aristocrat himself and that he should not have dared to befriend one. But that is all we know about Valerius Maximus, apart from the fact that he wrote this book.[39] He is just an ordinary Roman who belongs to the mainstream of ancient Rome and enables us to enter it.

How Valerius Organized His Book

Valerius had to put an enormous amount of work into writing his book, and it must have taken him at least a decade to complete it.[40] In his Preface (in Book 1) he says that he wanted to save others from the trouble of doing so much research. He studied Cicero and Livy as well as Varro and other ancient authors whose works have disappeared. But we do not have to follow him in this laborious task: for his readers in ancient Rome and for his readers today, Valerius created a shortcut to Roman civilization. He organized his thousand stories in what he hoped would be a reader-friendly way. The entire work is divided into nine books (ancient Roman books were quite short), and the books are subdivided into chapters. Each of these chapters deals with a specific topic, and contains several stories that illustrate this topic. So, if you want to know how some Romans got on with their parents, you don't have to study all of ancient history and figure it out yourself. You merely have to turn to Book 5: Chapter 8, which deals with the topic of "Fathers Who Were Severe with Their Children," and read the stories there.[41]

---

[37]See 2:6,8.

[38]See 4:7,ext.2.

[39]Another work on Roman first names was also attributed to him, but we don't know who wrote it.

[40]He started Book 6 before A.D. 29 (see 6:1,1) and he finished Book 9 at the end of A.D. 31 (see 9:11,ext.4).

[41]But this is only one side of the story. Some Roman parents were very nice indeed, and Valerius tells us about them in 5:7.

After he has told us a few Roman stories on a particular topic, Valerius then goes on to tell us some foreign stories. Almost all of these foreign stories come from the Greeks, and most of them are about famous kings and philosophers. Valerius includes foreign stories because he wants to show that Roman values are not peculiar to Rome itself. These values are universally valid and are the natural culmination of ancient civilization. All the great leaders and philosophers of the world were merely preparing the way for the Roman world. The most moral and the most intelligent people living in foreign countries agree with the Romans on every important issue; the purpose of the foreign stories, therefore, is not to show respect for other cultures but to reinforce the superiority of the Romans. We can see this from his attitude toward Greeks in general: although some very exceptional Greeks may be suitable as role models, the Greeks as a race are boastful,[42] compulsive liars,[43] and corruptly decadent.[44] When he turns from Roman stories to foreign ones, he frequently tells us that there are far more Roman examples of such virtuous behavior.[45] A story about a good Greek is a rare thing indeed, but a story about a good Roman merely illustrates the normal behavior of Romans in general.

Valerius also makes it clear to us that the foreign stories are less important than the Roman ones. He tells us that the foreign stories are included for the sake of variety:[46] they are there to amuse us; they do not deserve the serious attention we might give to Roman stories.[47] Indeed, the very fact that he includes the foreign stories is in itself a tribute to the natural honesty of the Romans, which forces them to be more than fair to foreigners.[48] Since the foreign stories often predate the Roman ones, there was a potential danger that this might make the Romans look bad. It might look as if the Romans were merely imitating foreigners, but Valerius admits this possibility in one case only—the case of intellectual activity. "Since the dedication of the Greeks has greatly encouraged our own, it should get the reward it deserves in the Latin language."[49] Romans typically went out of their way to acknowledge that the Greeks were doubtless better than they were when it came to frivolous activities such as literature and art, but when it came to the serious business of life, when it came to strength of character and ruling the world, the Romans were vastly superior. Admittedly, Romans could imitate the Greeks if they decided to pursue a career in the arts but that was considered something of a comedown. Valerius is horrified that Gaius Fabius Pictor would have chosen to win glory as an artist instead of pursuing a career in Roman government like the other members of his family.[50] Apart from the frivolous cases of art and literature,

---

[42]See 3:2,22.

[43]See 4:7,4 (at the end of the story).

[44]See 9:1,5.

[45]See 2:7,6; 6:3,ext.1 and 7:2,ext.1.

[46]See 2:10,ext.1 and 3:8,ext.1.

[47]See 6:9,ext.1.

[48]See 4:3,ext.1 and 4:7,ext.1.

[49]See 8:7,ext.1.

[50]See 4:3,9.

which are Greek topics, the only story that really matters is the story of Rome. Valerius may have devoted a considerable portion of his work to foreign stories, but these stories only play a supporting role in the great drama of world civilization, a role that serves only to enhance the glory of the main characters in this drama—the Romans.

Why Valerius Wrote His Book

It is a good thing for us that Valerius wrote his book and that we still have it, because nobody else could have given us such an honest and intimate view of the Romans. But why did the Romans themselves want to read such a book, and why did Valerius write it?

To answer this, we shall have to take a closer look at the world Valerius lived in. By the time Valerius was working on this book, it was quite obvious that Rome had entered a new stage in its history. Almost a century beforehand, in 49 B.C., Caesar had declared himself dictator, and that was the end of the Republic. Patriotic Republicans had rebelled against Caesar, but they were defeated in a series of disheartening battles that were fought between 48 and 45 B.C. The Republicans avenged themselves by assassinating Caesar in 44 B.C., but they were defeated once again by Antony and Augustus in 42 B.C., and most of them were brutally massacred by the victors. Eventually Antony and Augustus grew to hate each other, and after getting rid of Antony, Augustus became the first Roman emperor in 27 B.C. Augustus spent the rest of his life promising to restore the Republic, but by the time he died in A.D. 14, the Romans were no longer waiting for the return of the Republic. Augustus had been a very subtle tyrant, but the new emperor, Tiberius (A.D. 14–37), made it abundantly clear to his subjects that they were now living under a monarchy and that the days of the Roman Republic and its aristocratic Senate were gone forever. It was clear that the emperors were here to stay, and Valerius' Preface reflects this new realization.[51] It is the first in a long series of groveling dedications to mighty kings and emperors, written by humble authors and placed at the beginning of their works. His embarrassing servility sets the tone for the next nineteen centuries.

But the Romans had lost more than their liberty; their political leadership had perished along with the Republic. The new regime could not bring itself to trust the remnants of the old nobility from the old city, and there weren't enough of them to go around anyway, since most of them had died in the wars and massacres of Augustus. So the emperor had to draw his administrators from a new class of men who were born into more modest families from Italy and the provinces. These new men had not inherited the cultural knowledge and values of the Roman political elite; they had to acquire these traits, and they had to do it quickly. They had to learn how to present themselves in public in a way that would not embarrass their imperial benefactor and his new regime. They had to learn how to speak in public in a way that would show they were legitimate representatives of the

---

[51]See 1:1,pref.

Roman Empire and all it stood for. They had to appropriate a culture that was not theirs by right of birth and live up to the standards set by the old republican elite and its supercilious descendants, some of whom were still around to remind the new administrators of their lowly origins.[52]

The work of Valerius Maximus was tailored to meet the social anxieties and insecurities of the people who belonged to this new administrative class. Valerius enabled them to project a good image of themselves in society. If they were not quite sure how to judge a situation, they could now refer to an example set by one of the great names from the old Republic. In a sense, Valerius was showing them how to be successful imposters, but he started a game that has gone on for two thousand years. The history of the west has been dominated by people claiming to be the inheritors of Roman tradition. The aristocrats of the Republic did not have to make any such claims; they didn't need a book by Valerius Maximus to tell them about the great deeds and sayings of their ancestors. By the time they reached adolescence, they probably would have screamed if anyone had mentioned the great Cornelius family again. But men like Pontius Pilate, the famous but not very successful governor of Judaea,[53] were in a very different situation. They did not inherit these old stories and patterns of behavior from their ancestors; they had to learn them, and Valerius came along to teach them. He was not just telling them good stories to amuse them; he was supplying them with examples to which they could refer and models that they should follow or avoid. His supply of one thousand stories met a real demand in the Roman world in which he lived.

Valerius Maximus through the Ages

The demand for Valerius' stories did not go away. Every generation was anxious about its distance from the golden days of the Republic, when noblemen knew instinctively how a Roman ought to behave. And every generation wanted a quick way of acquiring that instinctive knowledge. The manuscripts of Valerius Maximus were copied again and again. In fact, the public later demanded an even shorter route to the world of the Republic, but it was still the route of Valerius. Two authors wrote abridged versions of the *Memorable Deeds and Sayings,* and these abridgments survive to the present day. One was produced by Julius Paris (at the end of the fourth century A.D.) and the other by Nepotianus (in the fifth century A.D.). The very fact that these two works were written makes it clear that Valerius was regarded as the most reliable authority on the disappearing world of ancient Rome.

Valerius' work remained popular after the fall of the Roman Empire and was a bestseller throughout the Middle Ages and the Renaissance period.[54] His book and

---

[52]Valerius' book was "a sort of reference book for would-be gentlemen, a rising class of entrepreneurs and *arrivistes* who needed quick exemplary history to provide a sort of 'instant ancestry.'" Kraus 2000, 455.

[53]Pontius Pilate was eventually dismissed by his superior, the governor of Syria, for brutally overreacting to a protest movement by the Samarians.

[54]Carter 1975, 49; Conte 1994, 38.

the Bible were the two most influential ancient books during these eras,[55] and more manuscripts of them survive than of any other prose work.[56] Both the Bible and *Memorable Deeds and Sayings* were regarded as ancient history, but they were not just valued as historical works. There is a curious parallel between the moral stories of the Old Testament or the use of parables in the New Testament and the exemplary stories[57] of Valerius Maximus. These sacred and secular stories were recorded not to produce an accurate description of the past but to provide moral guidance and show people how to live their lives, and this is how they were read up until the Enlightenment. People read the Bible to provide themselves with spiritual guidance in their inner lives, and they read Valerius Maximus to provide themselves with practical guidance in their secular lives. Valerius showed them how they too could behave like Romans. As late as the seventeenth century, in the famous "Delphin" edition[58] of Valerius Maximus, the editor urged the son of Louis XIV to read the work carefully because it would teach him how to become a great king.[59]

The prestige of Valerius Maximus (and of the Bible, too, for that matter) went down in the eighteenth century, and during the nineteenth century Valerius' work was attacked for failing to live up to the standards of "scientific history," the foundation of all knowledge in that age.[60] This attack was perfectly justified, and Valerius would not have denied it. He states quite openly in the Preface of his work that only a madman would try to write history in his day and age.[61] Valerius was not trying to be a historian; his goals were very different. We can see how great the difference is by considering one among many criticisms directed against him. At the beginning of the twentieth century, a scholar denounced Valerius because "he relates omens and miracles in a spirit of unquestioning superstition."[62] The scholar was absolutely right, but Valerius did not want to question Roman beliefs nor deconstruct Roman values. He wanted to record them exactly as they were and pass them on to the next generation, and that is what makes him so important for us today. Ironically, it is his very refusal to perform a historical critique of Roman ideals that makes Valerius Maximus such a valuable historical source for the worldview of the Romans.

---

[55]Niebuhr 1849, Vol. 2, p. 93.

[56]Bloomer 1992, p. 2.

[57]Valerius himself calls his stories "examples" (*exempla*).

[58]The "Delphin" editions were a series of works by Latin authors produced for the son of Louis XIV.

[59]Cantel 1823, pp. 1–3.

[60]Summarizing the attitudes of that century of scholarship, Duff remarks, "He takes few steps towards scientific history" (Duff 1931, p. 74). The culmination of such destructive criticism is Carter's brilliantly satirical account of Valerius Maximus (Carter 1975, *passim*).

[61]"What person in his right mind would hope that he could record the course of Roman and foreign history, which has been treated by previous writers in an elegant style, and do so either with greater attention to detail or with more striking eloquence?" (1:1,pref.).

[62]Duff 1931, p. 72.

Valerius accurately preserved for us the very bland version of the Romans' past that the Romans wanted to hear. It is narrow and nationalistic, and it shows no interest in political or social analysis; it is saturated with the prejudices of the propertied classes in Rome, because these were the real Roman people as far as he was concerned.[63] Strictly speaking, his stories are not history at all; they are the kind of patriotic myths that people always like to hear and that politicians have never ceased to tell. The work of Valerius is indeed, as one modern scholar says, "a *Reader's Digest* shortcut to Roman history,"[64] but that is nothing to sneer at. The *Reader's Digest* does, after all, reveal how ordinary Americans and Britons feel about the world. It differs a great deal from the academic view and it may not be a view we would like people to hold, but we ignore these beliefs at our peril. The men who read Valerius Maximus realized the power of such beliefs; it was the very reason that they resorted to his work in the first place. If they wanted to be respected, they had to imbue their own deeds and sayings with those values, and they had to uphold them in their public life.

Martin Bloomer, the first scholar in modern times to write a serious analysis of Valerius Maximus, summarizes Valerius' achievement as "a new generation's appropriation of Roman noble culture."[65] This formula explains exactly what Valerius Maximus was doing and why his work remained so popular for so many centuries. After all, everyone who takes any interest in ancient Rome automatically joins yet another new generation that appropriates the culture of the Roman nobility. Valerius Maximus' writings make this appropriation easier for us, as they made it easier for his own contemporaries. It is an extraordinary advantage for us that we can still have access to the imaginary world of the ancient Romans, a world preserved by a man whose own life is completely unknown to us, because Valerius chose to pass that world intact onto us, rather than impose the stamp of his own personality upon it.

Works Cited in Introduction.

Bloomer, W. Martin. 1992. *Valerius Maximus and the Rhetoric of the New Nobility.* Chapel Hill: University of North Carolina Press.

Cantel, Pierre Josephe, S. J. 1823. Epistula. In *Valerius Maximus: Factorum Dictorumque Memorabilium Libri Novem,* edited by Johann Kapp. London: A. J. Valpy.

Carter, C. J. 1975. Valerius Maximus. In *Empire and Aftermath: Silver Latin II,* edited by T. A. Dorey. London: Routledge & Kegan Paul.

Conte, Gian Biagio. 1994. *Latin Literature: A History.* Translated by Joseph B. Solodow. Baltimore, MD: The Johns Hopkins University Press.

[63]See 2:3,1 where Valerius explicitly contrasts "the people" and "men without property." In his view, the latter are not part of "the people."

[64]Carter 1975, p. 49.

[65]Bloomer 1992, p. 12.

Deary, Terry. 1994. *The Rotten Romans*. London: Scholastic Children's Books.

Duff, J. Wight. 1931. *A Literary History of Rome in the Silver Age*. New York: Charles Scribner's Sons.

Kraus, S. 2000. "The path between truculence and servility." In *Literature in the Greek ad Roman Worlds*. Edited by Oliver Taplin. Oxford: Oxford University Press.

Niebuhr, Barthold Georg. 1849. *Lectures on the History of Rome*. Vol. 2, edited by Leonhard Schmitz. London: Taylor, Walton, and Maberly.

NOTE ON THE
TRANSLATION

Valerius Maximus is a challenging author to translate, largely because of his periodic style.[1] He loves to produce long, complicated sentences that demonstrate his mastery of the Latin language. Often he fits an entire story into one long, intimidating sentence. I have not tried to follow him along this path: I have cut his sentences into two or three parts, replaced pronouns with nouns, and altered the format of proper names in the interest of clarity. When Valerius makes minor slips of the pen I have often corrected them without pointing this out in a footnote.[2] My translation is, therefore, a relatively free one, but I hope that I have made it a readable one.

In the case of certain famous Romans (whose names appear in the Glossary at the back of this book), I have standardized their names throughout. For example, Valerius refers to Gaius Julius Caesar sometimes as Julius and sometimes as Caesar; I have called him Caesar throughout.

I have also provided English equivalents for all Latin terms, except officials of the Roman government (such as consuls) and ancient coins (such as denarii). All the Latin terms I have used are in the Glossary at the back of this book.

My translation is based on Kempf's edition of Valerius Maximus in the Teubner Series.[3]

[1]Shackleton Bailey's translation for the Loeb Classical Library in 2000 was the first to appear in English since the seventeenth century. He stretches the English language to its limits in order to provide a remarkable version that closely replicates the style of Valerius Maximus.

[2]I have done this consistently when Valerius gets someone's first name wrong.

[3]*Valerii Maximi Factorum et Dictorum Memorabilium Libri Novem*, edited by Karl Friedrich Kempf. Leipzig, Germany: Teubner, 1888.

THRACE

Philippi

ILLYRIA

MACEDONIA

EPIRUS

THESSALY

AEGEAN SEA

ACARNANIA

Artemisium

Thermopylae

EUBOEA

AETOLIA

Delphi

PHOCIS

Chalcis
Eretria

BOEOTIA

Thebes

ACHAEA

Marathon

Megara

ELIS

ARCADIA

Corinth

Athens

Salamis

ATTICA

Mantinea

ARGOLIS

Epidaurus

Argos

MESSENIA

Cycladic Islands

Sparta

LACONIA

| 0 | 20 | 40 | 60 | 80 | 100 miles |

CRETE

Greece

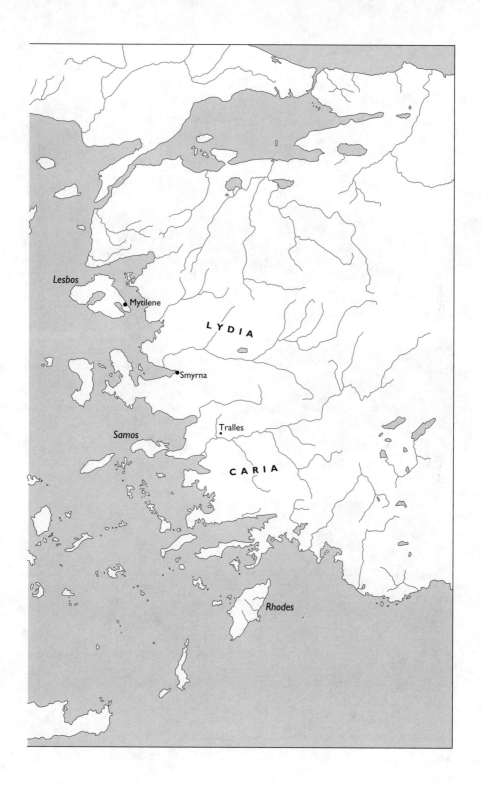

Lesbos

●Mytilene

L Y D I A

●Smyrna

Tralles
●

Samos

C A R I A

Rhodes

TRANSPADANA

VENETIA

Mediolanum

River Po

Placentia

LIGURIA

AEMILIA

UMBRIA

ETRURIA

River Tiber

Lake
Trasimene

CORSICA

Veii
Rome

SARDINIA

*TYRRHENIAN
SEA*

*Aegates
Islands*

0 20 40 60 80 100 miles

Italy

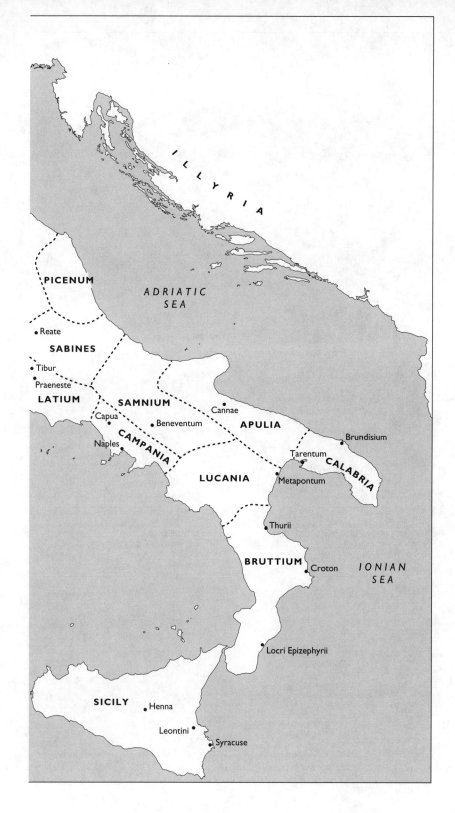

ILLYRIA

ADRIATIC
SEA

PICENUM

• Reate

SABINES

• Tibur

Praeneste •

LATIUM

SAMNIUM

Capua •

• Beneventum

CAMPANIA

Naples •

Cannae

APULIA

Brundisium •

Tarentum •

CALABRIA

LUCANIA

Metapontum •

• Thurii

BRUTTIUM

• Croton

IONIAN
SEA

• Locri Epizephyrii

SICILY

• Henna

Leontini •

• Syracuse

Roman Empire

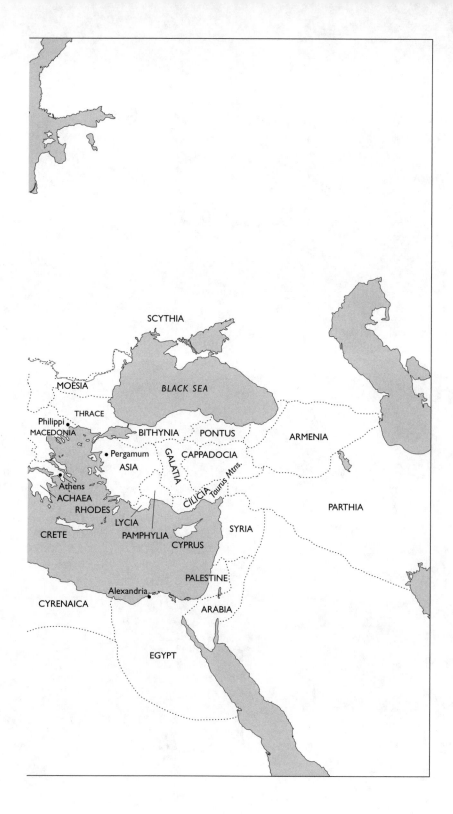

SCYTHIA

MOESIA

THRACE

Philippi •
MACEDONIA

BLACK SEA

BITHYNIA

PONTUS

ARMENIA

• Pergamum

GALATIA

CAPPADOCIA

ASIA

Athens •

ACHAEA

RHODES

CILICIA

Taurus Mtns.

PARTHIA

LYCIA

CRETE

PAMPHYLIA

CYPRUS

SYRIA

PALESTINE

Alexandria •

CYRENAICA

ARABIA

EGYPT

BOOK ONE

Preface

[To the Emperor Tiberius][1]
Many of the deeds and sayings from the city of Rome and from foreign nations are well worth recording. Other authors have dealt with these stories at great length, but this makes it impossible to learn about them in a short period of time, so I have decided to make a selection of them from the most famous writers. I have arranged the stories in such a way that readers who want to find historical precedents would be spared the trouble of spending a lot of time on research. I had no desire to include everything. Who could collect the achievements of all time within a modest number of volumes? What person in his right mind would hope that he could record the course of Roman and foreign history, which has been treated by previous writers in an elegant style, and do so either with greater attention to detail or with more striking eloquence?

To sanctify this work, therefore, I call upon you, our emperor, the true savior of our country. Both gods and men are united in their wish that every sea and land should be under your control. With heavenly foresight, you kindly nourish the virtues that I shall speak of, and you severely punish every vice. In the old days public speakers quite rightly began their speeches with a prayer to Jupiter Best and Greatest, and the most outstanding poets started off with a prayer to some god. I am only a minor writer, so I am even more justified in seeking the protection of your favor. Our faith in the other gods derives from popular belief, but our faith in your divinity comes from your living presence and is as sound as our faith in the stars of your father and your grandfather.[2] The extraordinary brightness of those stars has added a glorious brilliance to our religion. The other gods came to us from heaven, but the Caesars are our gift to heaven. And since it is my intention to start off with the worship of the gods, I shall briefly discuss its nature.

---

[1]Tiberius was emperor from A.D. 14 to 37.

[2]The emperor Augustus adopted Tiberius as his son, which would make Julius Caesar his grandfather by adoption. Comets had appeared in the sky after the deaths of Caesar and Augustus and were interpreted as signs of their divinity. Caesar was declared a god in 42 B.C., and Augustus in A.D. 14.

Chapter 1. Religion

Respect for Religion
Roman Stories[3]

1. 1. Our ancestors organized the regular annual festivals by means of the traditional science of the pontiffs; they guaranteed success in public affairs through the observations of the augurs; they interpreted the predictions of Apollo from the books of the seers; and they averted evil portents by the rites of the Etruscans.[4] It has been our ancient custom to resort to religious rites such as prayer when we want to entrust some matter to the gods; a religious vow when we have to request something;[5] a formal thanksgiving when we have to repay the gods; a search for favorable signs, either from animal organs or from lots, when the future has to be ascertained;[6] and sacrifice when we want to perform a solemn rite. We also use sacrifice to avert evil when portents are reported or places are struck by lightning.

Our ancestors were very eager not just to preserve religious observance but even to expand it, so when the state was already very powerful and prosperous, the Senate voted to send ten sons from their foremost families to the various peoples of Etruria, so that the young men might learn the Etruscan science of ritual.

Our ancestors had from the very beginning worshiped Ceres in the Greek manner, so in choosing a priestess of Ceres, they brought Calliphana in from Velia, even though that city had not yet obtained the right of Roman citizenship. They wanted the goddess to have a priestess trained in her ancient rituals.[7]

Our ancestors had a very beautiful temple for this goddess in the city, but when, during the Gracchan troubles, they were warned by the Sibylline Books to placate Most Ancient Ceres, they sent the committee of ten to propitiate her at Henna, since they believed that this place was the origin of her cult.[8]

[3]Roman stories are simply referred to by their number, so the first story would be 1:1,1 (Book 1: Chapter 1, Roman Story 1).

[4]The pontiffs supervised the national religion and organized the religious calendar; the augurs observed the behavior of birds to determine the future; the books of the seers were the Sibylline Books, a collection of prophecies given to the last king of Rome, Tarquin the Proud (534–510 B.C.), and the "rites of the Etruscans" were the rites of the Etruscan diviners. See Glossary for more on pontiffs, augurs, sibyls, and diviners.

[5]By means of a "religious vow" (*votum*), a Roman would promise some gift (such as a sacrifice or a statue) to a god or goddess in exchange for some favor. As soon as the favor was granted, he had to present the gift. Such gifts are known as votive offerings.

[6]The Etruscan diviners predicted the future by examining the organs of sacrificial victims. The Senate used to cast lots to discover whom the gods wanted to govern a province or command an army (see 1:5,3), but there were also permanent lottery oracles, such as the oracle of Fortune at Praeneste (see 1:3,2).

[7]A special law was passed making Calliphana a Roman citizen in 96 B.C. Velia was a Greek city in Lucania (southern Italy).

[8]Henna was an ancient Sicilian city that predated even the arrival of the Greeks to that island. Tiberius Sempronius Gracchus (tribune of the plebs, 133 B.C.) was murdered in 133

Our generals likewise often went all the way to Pessinus after gaining a victory so as to fulfill their religious vows to the Mother of the Gods.[9]

1. 2. When the consul Postumius, who happened to be the flamen of Mars, wanted to go to Africa and fight a war there, the chief pontiff, Metellus, forbade him to leave the city under pain of a fine, because he did not want Postumius to abandon his religious duties. Although Postumius was the supreme executive officer, he yielded to the authority of religion. Postumius felt he could not safely engage in a Martial struggle if he deserted the rituals of Mars.[10]

1. 3. We must praise the religious respect shown by his twelve fasces, but we must praise even more the obedience of twenty-four fasces in a similar matter.[11] In a letter sent from his province to the college of augurs, Tiberius Gracchus[12] told them that he had been reading books about public sacrifices. These books made him aware that the augural tent had been wrongly set up during the consular elections, which he himself had organized. When the augurs reported this matter to the Senate, the Senate ordered Gaius Figulus to return to Rome from Gaul and Scipio Nasica to return to Rome from Corsica. Both men had to resign their consulships.[13]

1. 4. Similarly, during periods when very different wars were going on, Publius Cloelius Siculus, Marcus Cornelius Cethegus, and Gaius Claudius were ordered, and indeed forced, to resign their priesthoods, because they had carried the animal organs toward the altars of the immortal gods in a careless manner.[14]

1. 5. While Quintus Sulpicius was performing a sacrifice, his miter fell off his head; for this he was deprived of his priesthood.[15]

B.C. The committee of ten (see Glossary) probably went to Henna in 132 B.C., after the Slave War in Sicily had ended.

[9]The black stone of the Great Mother of the Gods (Cybele) was brought to Rome from Pessinus (in Asia Minor) in 204 B.C., but some Romans still went to Pessinus itself to worship the goddess in her hometown.

[10]Aulus Postumius Albinus was both consul and flamen of Mars in 242 B.C., during the First Punic War. Lucius Caecilius Metellus (cos, 251 B.C.) was chief pontiff from 243 B.C. until his death in 221 B.C.

[11]The twelve fasces were the symbol of a consul (Aulus Postumius Albinus); the twenty-four were therefore the symbol of the two consuls (Gaius Marcius Figulus and Publius Cornelius Scipio Nasica Corculum).

[12]Tiberius Sempronius Gracchus (cos, 177 B.C.) was governor of Sardinia in 162 B.C.

[13]Gaius Marcius Figulus and Publius Cornelius Scipio Nasica Corculum had been elected consuls for 162 B.C. After resigning they were replaced by two other men.

[14]Publius Cloelius Siculus had been appointed king of sacrifices in 180 B.C., but it is not known when he was forced to resign. Gaius Claudius had to resign as flamen of Jupiter in 211 B.C. during the Second Punic War. Marcus Cornelius Cethegus (cos, 204 B.C.) resigned as the flamen of Jupiter in 223 B.C. during a war against the Gauls of northern Italy.

[15]Quintus Sulpicius had to resign as flamen in 223 B.C.

Because the cry of a mouse was heard in the middle of a sacrifice, the dictator Fabius the Delayer and his master of the horse Gaius Flaminius had to resign their offices.[16]

1. 6. To these cases we must add the following story. The chief pontiff, Publius Licinius, decided to have a vestal virgin flogged to punish her for being careless in watching over the eternal fire one night.[17]

1. 7. On the other hand, when a pupil of the chief virgin, Aemilia, allowed the fire to go out, the goddess Vesta[18] kept the young woman safe from all criticism. Pleading with the goddess, the young woman placed the best linen garment she possessed on the hearth, and the fire suddenly came back to life.

1. 8. It is not surprising that the gods have constantly watched over us, and have had the kindness to protect and expand our empire, since we seem to pay careful attention to the tiniest details of religious observance. It must not be imagined that our state ever allowed its eyes to wander from the strictest observance of religious ceremonies. After Marcus Marcellus had conquered Clastidium and later Syracuse, he held his fifth consulship and wanted to consecrate a temple to Honor and Courage in fulfillment of religious vows he had made in public.[19] The college of pontiffs forbade this, and ruled that a single temple could not properly be dedicated to two gods. They argued that if some portent occurred in the temple, it would be impossible to distinguish which of the two gods would have to be placated by a sacrifice. They also pointed out that it was not the custom for sacrifices to be offered to two gods, except in the case of some well-established divine pairs. As a result of this ruling by the pontiffs, Marcellus had to set up statues of Honor and Courage in separate temples. The prestige of this very distinguished man did not deter the college of pontiffs, nor did the additional expense incurred deter Marcellus—he followed the proper procedure in his religious observances.

1. 9. It might seem that all these illustrious consuls overshadow Lucius Furius Bibaculus, and that he should hardly be set up as an example next to Marcellus. But he is not to be deprived of his fame as a man whose character was both dutiful and religious. When he was a praetor, Bibaculus was ordered to carry the sacred shields by his father, who was the master of the college of Salian priests,[20] and the praetor's six lictors had to march in front of him.[21] The praetor obeyed, although

---

[16]Fabius the Delayer (cos, 233 B.C.) and Gaius Flaminius (cos, 223 B.C.) resigned in 221 B.C.

[17]Publius Crassus Licinius Dives (cos, 205 B.C.) had been appointed chief pontiff in 212 B.C. This incident occurred in 206 B.C. It was considered disastrous to allow the eternal fire of Rome to go out.

[18]Vesta was the goddess of fireplaces, especially the eternal fire of Rome.

[19]Marcus Claudius Marcellus (cos, 222 B.C.) had conquered Clastidium (in Liguria, northern Italy) during his first consulship in 222 B.C. and Syracuse when he was governor of Sicily in 211 B.C. He held his fifth consulship in 208 B.C.

[20]Lucius Furius Bibaculus was a praetor and his father Furius Bibaculus was the chief Salian priest some time between 227 and 218 B.C. The Salian priests used to perform an ancient war dance with sacred shields.

[21]A praetor was accompanied by six attendants called lictors.

by virtue of his public office, he was exempt from carrying out this duty. Our state has always held that everything should be considered secondary to religion, even in cases where it also wanted to demonstrate its respect for men who held the highest offices. As a result its magistrates did not hesitate to perform menial tasks during religious rituals. These men felt that they would be good masters over human affairs only if they had been good and faithful servants to the power of the gods.

1. 10. The same sentiments were also to be found in the hearts of private citizens. When our city was captured by the Gauls, the flamen of Quirinus and the vestal virgins were carrying sacred objects, sharing the burden among them. They crossed the Wooden Bridge and were beginning to go up the hill that leads to the Janiculum,[22] when they were spotted by Lucius Albanius, who was bringing his wife and children in a wagon. The religion of the state meant more to him than his personal feelings for his family, so he ordered them to get off the wagon. He put the virgins and their sacred objects on the wagon, abandoned his previous journey, and brought them all the way to the town of Caere. The people there welcomed the sacred objects with the greatest veneration. A testimony of our gratitude for their hospitality and kindness survives to this very day: we adopted the term "ceremonies" for sacred rites at that time, because the people of Caere had faithfully honored our rites when the Republic was shattered, just as they had done when it was flourishing. That dirty farmyard wagon had come just in time to carry our sacred objects, and its glory equals and perhaps surpasses the glory of our most brilliant triumphal chariot.[23]

1. 11. During the same crisis of our Republic, Gaius Fabius Dorsuo provided a memorable example of respect for religion. Although the Gauls were besieging the Capitol, he refused to let this interfere with the traditional sacrifice of the Fabian family.[24] So he tucked up his toga following the ritual of Gabii,[25] carried the sacred objects on his hands and shoulders, walked past the enemy checkpoints, and made his way to the Quirinal hill. When he had completed the entire ritual in the traditional manner, he returned to the Capitol like a man who had conquered the army of his conquerors.

1. 12. In the consulship of Publius Cornelius and Baebius Tamphilus our ancestors showed great scruples in their respect for religion.[26] When farm-hands were digging rather deeply in a field under the Janiculum belonging to a scribe called Lucius Petillius, they found two stone chests. An inscription on one revealed

[22]The Wooden Bridge (*Pons Sublicius*) went from Rome to the northern side of the Tiber, where the Janiculum hill stood.

[23]The Gauls captured Rome in 390 B.C. The sea-port of Caere (in Etruria, western Italy) had always been friendly to Rome. The fanciful etymology deriving the word "ceremony" from Caere works a little better in Latin, where ceremony is spelled "caerimonia."

[24]Gaius Fabius Dorsuo was one of the pontiffs in 390 B.C. but in performing this ritual on the Quirnal hill in Rome he was carrying out his religious duty as a member of the Fabius family.

[25]Gabii was a city in Latium.

[26]Publius Cornelius Cethegus and Marcus Baebius Tamphilus were consuls in 181 B.C.

that it contained the body of Numa Pompilius.[27] In the other were found seven Latin books about the law of the pontiffs, and as many Greek books about the discipline of philosophy. They ordered that the Latin books should be preserved with the greatest care, but they felt that the Greek ones might in some way tend to undermine religion. Following Senate instructions, the city praetor, Quintus Petillius, ordered the sacrificial attendants to make a fire and burn the books in public.[28] The men of those days did not want to retain anything in this state that might take people's minds away from the worship of the gods.

1. 13. The duumvir[29] Marcus Atilius, had a book containing the secrets of public ritual entrusted to his safekeeping. He was bribed by the Sabine Petronius and gave him the book so that Petronius could make a copy of it. King Tarquin condemned Atilius to be sewn into a sack and thrown into the sea.[30] Long afterward, this type of punishment was prescribed by law for parricides. And rightly so, because a crime against parents and a crime against the gods should receive the same punishment.

1. 14. But in these matters that relate to the maintenance of religious belief, I suspect that Marcus Atilius Regulus[31] surpassed everyone. He had been brilliantly victorious, but had been reduced to the wretched status of prisoner of war by the treacherous tactics of Hasdrubal and the Spartan commander Xanthippus.[32] Regulus was sent as a messenger to the Roman Senate and People to ask that several young Carthaginians be released in exchange for him, just one elderly man. Instead, he advised the Romans against the exchange and went back to Carthage, though he was quite aware that he was returning to a cruel people who were understandably antagonistic to him. He did so because he had sworn to the Carthaginians that he would go back to them if their prisoners of war were not released. Certainly, the immortal gods could have curtailed the ferocious savagery of the Carthaginians, but the gods allowed them to behave in their usual manner so that the glory of Atilius would be all the more conspicuous. In the Third Punic War the gods would exact a just revenge for the cruel torture of this most religious soul by wiping out their city.

1. 15. The Senate of our state is so much more respectful toward the gods! After the defeat at Cannae,[33] it decreed that women should not stay in mourning

---

[27]Numa Pompilius was the second king of Rome (715–673 B.C.) and was believed to have invented most of its religious rituals.

[28]Quintus Petillius Spurinus (cos, 176 B.C.) was city praetor in 181 B.C.

[29]Originally a committee of two, (the duumvirs) looked after the Sibylline Books. The committee grew larger as time went by. (See Sibyl and committee of ten in the Glossary.)

[30]Tarquin the Proud was the last king of Rome (534–510 B.C.).

[31]Marcus Atilius Regulus (cos, 267 B.C.) was tortured to death in 255 B.C. during the First Punic War.

[32]Throughout the First Punic War, Hasdrubal, son of Hanno, commanded the Carthaginian soldiers and Xanthippus commanded the mercenaries recruited from Greece to fight on the Carthaginian side.

[33]The Roman disaster at Cannae (in Apulia, southern Italy) took place in 216 B.C. during the Second Punic War.

beyond three hundred days, so that they could carry out the rituals of Ceres.[34] The greater part of our Roman manpower was lying dead in that accursed and frightful place, so no household was free from grief. The mothers, daughters, wives, and sisters of the men who had recently been killed were therefore obliged to wipe away their tears, lay aside their mourning garb, put on white clothing, and offer incense on the altars. Their constancy in upholding religion made the gods too ashamed to commit any further cruelties against our race, since we could not be diverted from the worship of the gods even by the harshness of our misfortunes.

Neglect of Religion
Roman Stories

1. 16. People believed it was because of the anger of Juno that the consul Varro fought so disastrously against the Carthaginians at Cannae.[35] When, as aedile, he was organizing the games in the circus, he had stationed a young male actor of exceptional beauty on the carriage of Jupiter Best and Greatest.[36] This misdeed was remembered several years later and atoned for with sacrifices.

1. 17. People also say that Hercules exacted a vengeance that was both severe and conspicuous when his cult was insulted. The Potitius family was in charge of Hercules' cult, and Hercules himself had granted this hereditary right to them. Following the orders of the censor Appius, the Potitius family transferred Hercules' cult to lowly slaves owned by the state. As a result, all the young men of the family (there were more than thirty of them) were wiped out within a year. The great name of Potitius was reduced to twelve households and almost disappeared. Appius, for his part, was struck blind.[37]

1. 18. Apollo was also a strict defender of his own divinity. When the Romans defeated Carthage, his statue was stripped of its golden garment, so he made sure that the sacrilegious hands were cut off and discovered among the fragments of his garment.[38]

1. 19. Apollo's son, Aesculapius,[39] was just as effective in avenging himself when his cult was insulted. Turullius, Antony's prefect, cut down a large part of a sacred grove belonging to his temple in order to build ships for Antony.[40] While

---

[34]Ceres was the goddess of grain and her festival was celebrated by women.

[35]Gaius Terentius Varro (cos, 216 B.C.) was one of the Roman commanders at Cannae, but he managed to get back alive.

[36]Gaius Terentius Varro (cos, 216 B.C.) had been an aedile in 221 and 220 B.C. Juno was always jealous of Jupiter, who would have been attracted by Varro's young actor.

[37]Appius Claudius Caecus (cos, 307 B.C.) was censor in 312 B.C. when the state took over Hercules' cult. His last name, Caecus, means "blind."

[38]Carthage was sacked by the Romans in 146 B.C.

[39]Aesculapius was the god of medicine.

[40]This temple of Aesculapius was located on the Greek island of Cos. Decimus Turullius (tyrannicide, 44 B.C.) served as a prefect in Antony's navy in 31 B.C.

Turullius was performing this wicked task, Antony's forces were utterly defeated.[41] Augustus commanded that Turullius be put to death, and the god revealed his divine powers by having him dragged into the very place he had desecrated.[42] The god made sure that Augustus' soldiers killed him there rather than anywhere else. By his death, Turullius paid the penalty for those trees he had already cut down and guaranteed that the trees still standing would be protected from such a violation. The god thereby increased the extraordinary devotion that his worshipers had always felt for him.

1. 20. Quintus Fulvius Flaccus did not escape with impunity when, as censor, he took marble tiles from the temple of Juno Lacinia and removed them to the temple of Equestrian Fortune that he was building in Rome.[43] It is said that after this misdeed he was never mentally sane again. In fact, he died in the greatest mental anguish after hearing that of his two sons who were fighting in Illyria, one had been killed and the other seriously wounded.[44] The Senate was shaken by his misfortune, and it had the tiles brought back to Locri.[45] By the very considerate piety of its decree, it undid the wicked deed of the censor.

1. 21. The Senate was, by heavens, equally just in punishing the wicked greed of a legate of Scipio Africanus, Pleminius, who plundered the treasury of Proserpina.[46] The Senate ordered that Pleminius be brought in chains to Rome, but before he could defend himself he died of a horrible disease in prison. The Senate also ordered that the goddess recover her money; in fact, it even doubled the amount.

Respect for Religion and Neglect of Religion
Foreign Stories[47]

1. ext. 1. As far as the crime of Pleminius was concerned, the conscript fathers rightly avenged the goddess;[48] but when it came to the violent avarice of King Pyrrhus,[49] it was actually the goddess who defended herself powerfully and effectively. Pyrrhus forced the Locrians to give him a large sum of money from the treasury of Proserpina. He was sailing with this evil plunder on board when a violent

[41]Antony was defeated at the sea battle of Actium (on the west coast of Greece) in 31 B.C.

[42]Augustus put Turullius to death in 30 B.C.

[43]Quintus Fulvius Flaccus (cos, 179 B.C.) was censor in 174 B.C. when he took the tiles from Juno Lacinia's temple.

[44]Quintus Fulvius Flaccus hanged himself after the death of his son in 172 B.C.

[45]Juno Lacinia's temple was at Croton (in Bruttium, southern Italy), not at Locri Epizephyrii.

[46]Quintus Pleminius was a legate in the army of Scipio Africanus in 205 B.C. He was in charge at Locri Epizephyrii (in Bruttium, southern Italy) in 205 B.C., where he robbed the temple of Proserpina (goddess of the dead).

[47]When referring to foreign stories, the abbreviation "ext." is used. The first story in this section would be 1:1,ext.1 (Book 1: Chapter 1, Foreign Story 1).

[48]The senators were called the conscript fathers (see Glossary). The goddess is Proserpina.

[49]King Pyrrhus of Epirus robbed the temple of Proserpina at Locri Epizephyrii in 276 B.C.

storm suddenly dashed him and his entire fleet onto the shore near the temple of the goddess. Proserpina's money was found safe on the shore and restored to the protection of her most holy treasury.

1. ext. 2. King Masinissa did not behave in this way.[50] The prefect of his navy landed on Malta and, behaving just like Pyrrhus, he took enormous ivory tusks out of the temple of Juno and brought them to the king as a gift. When the king discovered where they had come from, he had them brought back to Malta on a quinquerime[51] and replaced in the temple of Juno. They were inscribed with a statement in his own language, declaring that the king had received them in all innocence and had gladly returned them to the goddess. This deed was typical of Masinissa's spirit rather than his Punic origins.[52]

1. ext. 3. But why should a man's character be judged by his race? Masinissa was brought up in a barbarous society, but he rejected sacrilege as something utterly foreign to him. Dionysius, although he was born in Syracuse, took great pleasure in making funny remarks about his many acts of sacrilege, which we shall now review.[53]

After he plundered the temple of Proserpina at Locri, and as he was sailing over the deep sea with favorable winds, he laughed and said to his friends, "Do you see what a pleasant voyage is granted by the immortal gods themselves to sacrilegious men?"[54]

He took away a very heavy gold cloak from the statue of Olympian Jupiter. The statue had been presented with this cloak by the tyrant Gelon from his share of the booty captured from the Carthaginians.[55] Dionysius threw a woolen cloak onto the statue instead and said, "A gold cloak is heavy in the summer and cold in the winter, but a woolen one is more suited to both times of the year."

He ordered the golden beard to be removed from the statue of Aesculapius at Epidaurus. The reason he gave was that it was not right for Apollo, Aesculapius' father, to be seen without a beard and for Aesculapius himself to be seen with one.[56]

He took silver and golden tables from the temples. Since these bore the usual Greek inscription stating that they belonged to the good gods, he declared that he was availing himself of the gods' goodness.

He used to take the golden victories and dishes and garlands that statues often hold in their outstretched hands. He would say that he was accepting them as a

---

[50]Masinissa was king of Numidia (modern Algeria) from 209 to 149 B.C. He was a Roman ally.

[51]A quinquerime was a large warship.

[52]Punic is another word for Carthaginian. The Romans hated the Carthaginians, but there was no ethnic connection between the Numidians and the Carthaginians.

[53]Dionysius I was tyrant of Syracuse from 405 to 367 B.C. The Romans would expect him to behave better than a "barbarian" from north Africa.

[54]This temple of Proserpina in southern Italy was frequently plundered (see 1:1,21 and 1:1,ext.1).

[55]Gelon was tyrant of Syracuse from 485 to 478 B.C. and had defeated the Carthaginians in 480 B.C.

[56]The chief temple of Aesculapius was at Epidaurus (in southern Greece).

gift, not stealing them, and he argued that it was very stupid to beg the gods for good things, and then to refuse to accept them when the gods handed them to you.

Dionysius got away with this during his own lifetime, and he never paid the penalty he deserved, but he did pay for it after his death through the disgrace of his son. When the gods avenge themselves, their wrath proceeds at a slow pace; they make up for this delay by the severity of their vengeance.[57]

1. ext. 4. Timasitheus, the ruler of the Liparae Islands, made sure that he would not incur the wrath of the gods.[58] He adopted an exemplary course of action that benefited him as well as his entire country. His people used to engage in piracy, and they happened to seize from a ship at sea a very heavy golden dish, which the Romans had dedicated as a tithe of their spoils to Pythian Apollo.[59] The people were eager to divide it among themselves, but when he discovered …

[End of Story as recorded by Julius Paris: … he had it brought all the way to Delphi.][60]

1. ext. 5. [Story as recorded by Julius Paris: When Alexander captured Miletus, his soldiers burst into the temple of Ceres of Miletus to plunder it. The goddess struck them blind by throwing a flame at them.]

[Story as recorded by Nepotianus: Alexander the Great captured Miletus. When his soldiers entered the temple of Ceres, they were struck blind so that they would not see the mysteries that are known to women alone.][61]

1. ext. 6. [Story as recorded by Julius Paris: The Persians were forced onto Delos with their thousand ships, but in dealing with the temple of Apollo, their hands were reverential, not rapacious.]

[Story as recorded by Nepotianus: The Persians landed on Delos with their thousand ships. Delos' wealth could have enticed the conquerors to plunder, but out of respect to the god, they refrained from taking any booty.][62]

1. ext. 7. [Stories as recorded by Julius Paris: The Athenians expelled the philosopher Protagoras because he had dared to write that in the first place he did not know whether the gods existed, and secondly, if they did exist, he did not know what they were like.

The same people condemned Socrates because he seemed to be introducing a new religion.

---

[57]Dionysius II succeeded his father as tyrant of Syracuse, but he was deposed twice (357 and 344 B.C.) and ended his days as a schoolteacher in Corinth.

[58]Timasitheus was a pirate king in the Liparae Islands (off the north coast of Sicily).

[59]The Roman envoys were bringing this golden dish to Apollo's temple in Delphi in 394 B.C. to thank him for their victory over Veii (in Etruria, western Italy).

[60]The rest of Chapters 1–4 (apart from the very last story of Chapter 4) is missing from the manuscripts. We have to rely on the summaries of Valerius Maximus made by Julius Paris at the end of the fourth century A.D. and Nepotianus during the fifth century A.D.

[61]King Alexander the Great of Macedonia captured Miletus (a Greek city on the west coast of Asia Minor) in 334 B.C.

[62]The Persians occupied the holy Greek island of Delos in 479 B.C. during their war against Greece.

They tolerated Phidias when he said that the statue of Minerva should be made of marble rather than ivory, since its splendor would last longer, but when he added that it would also be cheaper, they ordered him to be quiet.]

[Stories as recorded by Nepotianus: The philosopher Protagoras was expelled by the Athenians and his books were burned in public, because he had written that it could not be known whether the gods existed, and if they did exist, it could not be known what they were like.

Socrates was condemned in the same city because he had sometimes argued against their religion.

Phidias, a sculptor in ivory, said that images of the gods could be made out of marble at a lower cost, but the Athenians ordered him to make the statue out of ivory.][63]

1. ext. 8. [Story as recorded by Julius Paris: Diomedon was one of the ten commanders at the battle of Arginusae who won a victory for the Athenians but a condemnation for themselves. When he was being led to the punishment he did not deserve, the only thing he said was that the sacred vows he himself had publicly made for the safe return of the army should be carried out.]

[Story as recorded by Nepotianus: Among the same people, Diomedon, one of their ten leaders, was being led to execution after winning a battle; he asked that the sacred vows he had made on behalf of the army should be carried out.][64]

1. ext. 9. [Story as recorded by Julius Paris: After Brennus, the leader of the Gauls, entered the temple of Apollo at Delphi, he took his own life by the will of the god.]

[Story as recorded by Nepotianus: After a series of victories, Brennus the king of the Gauls reached Delphi itself, and human power was no longer able to offer any resistance to him. The local farmers sought the protection of Apollo, and the god prophesied that he would be on their side and that the shining white girls would fight against the Gauls. Brennus and his entire army were lost in a snowstorm.][65]

Chapter 2. False Religiosity

Roman Stories

2. 1. [Story as recorded by Julius Paris: Numa Pompilius wanted the Roman people to be devoted to religion, so he led them to believe that he used to meet with the goddess Egeria at night, and that it was on her advice he established rituals that would especially please the gods.]

[63]Protagoras was banished from Athens in 415 B.C. Socrates was put to death in 399 B.C. Phidias was attacked for impiety in 432 B.C.

[64]The Athenians won the sea battle of Arginusae (off the west coast of Asia Minor) in 406 B.C., but the generals were put to death for failing to bury the dead.

[65]Brennus attacked Greece in 280 B.C. and was defeated at the holy city of Delphi in 278 B.C. The "shining white girls" of the prophecy are the snowflakes.

[Story as recorded by Nepotianus: Numa Pompilius realized that the Romans had been brutalized by their endless wars, so he taught them how to worship the gods. To make it easier for him to domesticate the Romans, he made up the story that he met regularly with the nymph Egeria and that she was his teacher. This increased his prestige among his savage people.][66]

2. 2. [Story as recorded by Julius Paris: Scipio Africanus would not take part in public or private business without first having spent some time in the temple of Capitoline Jupiter. This led people to believe that he was the son of Jupiter.]

[Story as recorded by Nepotianus: Scipio Africanus would not take part in public or private business without first spending a long time in the temple of Capitoline Jupiter; only then could anyone visit him.][67]

2. 3. [Story as recorded by Julius Paris: Whenever Sulla intended to fight a battle, he would embrace in the sight of his soldiers a little statue of Apollo that he had taken from Delphi. He would beseech the god to fulfill his promises.]

[Story as recorded by Nepotianus: When intending to do battle, Sulla would humbly pray in the sight of his soldiers to a statue of Apollo that he had taken from Delphi. He would beseech the god to fulfill his promises, and he gave the impression that he relied on this statue before starting a war.][68]

2. 4. [Story as recorded by Nepotianus: Marius used to keep a Syrian priestess in his camp, and he claimed that he followed her advice in all his undertakings.][69]

2. 5. [Story as recorded by Julius Paris: Quintus Sertorius used to bring a white doe through the harsh hills of Lusitania. He claimed that she used to advise him what to do and what not to do.]

[Story as recorded by Nepotianus: Sertorius had a white doe in his Spanish army, and he persuaded those barbarians that she was his adviser.][70]

Foreign Stories

2. ext. 1. [Story as recorded by Julius Paris: Every ninth year, Minos, the king of Crete, used to go away into a high cave that was considered sacred according to an ancient religious tradition. He would stay in it and then proclaim laws as if they had been handed on to him by Jupiter, who he alleged was his father.][71]

---

[66]Numa Pompilius was the second legendary king of Rome (715–673 B.C.).

[67]Scipio Africanus had started this practice by the time he became commander of the Roman army in Spain in 210 B.C.

[68]Sulla plundered the Greek holy city of Delphi in 87 B.C. during the war against King Mithridates VI of Pontus.

[69]This Syrian priestess, who was called Martha, attached herself to Marius in 102 B.C.

[70]Quintus Sertorius had been governor of Nearer Spain in 83 B.C. He was invited back by the Lusitanians (in modern Portugal) to become their leader against the Romans in 80 B.C. This was when he acquired his magic doe.

[71]Minos was a mythical king of Crete. The story may refer to an ancient ritual requiring a king to renew his sacred power every nine years.

2. ext. 2. [Story as recorded by Julius Paris: When Peisistratus was recovering the dictatorship he had lost, he pretended that Minerva was leading him back to the citadel. He paraded in front of him an unknown woman called Phya, who was decked up to look like the goddess, and deceived the Athenians.][72]

2. ext. 3. [Story as recorded by Julius Paris: Lycurgus convinced the very level-headed state of Sparta that the laws he was making had been drawn up on the advice of Apollo.][73]

2. ext. 4. [Story as recorded by Julius Paris: Zaleucus claimed to be acting on the authority of Minerva, and was considered the shrewdest man among the Locrians.][74]

Chapter 3. Superstitious Cults

Roman Stories

3. 1. [Story as recorded by Julius Paris: The new custom of Bacchic rituals was introduced here, but it started turning toward dangerous madness and was suppressed.]

[Story as recorded by Nepotianus: Bacchanalian mysteries took place in Rome. But when men and women got together at nighttime and went wild, this foreign cult was abolished in a huge bloodbath of its followers.][75]

3. 2. [Story as recorded by Julius Paris: Lutatius Cerco, the man who finished off the First Punic War, was prevented by the Senate from resorting to the lottery oracle of Fortune at Praeneste. They judged that the government of the Republic should rely on its ancestral auspices, not on foreign ones.]

[Story as recorded by Nepotianus: There was a rumor that Lutatius Cerco, the man who finished off the First Punic War, wanted to cast lots and pick them up at random in the temple of Fortune at Praeneste. When the Senate learned of this, it forbade him to consult a foreign oracle and rely on its answers. The envoys and aediles sent to deliver this message were ordered to bring him back to Rome for punishment if he had consulted the oracle already. The Senate's action was very beneficial and made his auspices reliable Roman ones. By starting off from the altars of his own country, he was able to devastate the very prosperous Aegates Islands right before the eyes of the Carthaginians.][76]

---

[72]Peisistratus was an Athenian tyrant who started his second reign with this trick in 556 B.C.

[73]Lycurgus, the legendary lawgiver of Sparta (in southern Greece), supposedly lived in the ninth century B.C.

[74]Zaleucus was the lawgiver of Locri Epizephyrii (in southern Italy) around 650 B.C.

[75]Women left their homes to take part in the cult of Bacchus, but the Senate passed a decree against the cult in 186 B.C. The decree authorized a horrifying witch-hunt.

[76]Quintus Lutatius Cerco was consul in 241 B.C. when peace was made with Carthage, but the battle of the Aegates Islands (off the west coast of Sicily) was won the previous year.

3. 3. [Story as recorded by Julius Paris: During the consulship of Marcus Popillius Laenas and Gnaeus Calpurnius, the praetor for foreigners, Gnaeus Cornelius Hispanus, issued an edict ordering the Chaldaeans to leave the city and Italy within ten days. The praetor felt that they deceived frivolous and silly people with their dishonest interpretation of the stars and cultivated a money-making air of obscurity with their lies. The Jews had tried to corrupt Roman values with their cult of Jupiter Sabazius, so the praetor forced them to go back to their home.]

[Story as recorded by Nepotianus: Cornelius Hispanus expelled the Chaldaeans from the city and ordered them to leave Italy within ten days to prevent them from making money out of their foreign science. The Jews had tried to pass their religion on to Romans, so Hispanus expelled them from the city and demolished their private altars in all public places.][77]

3. 4. [Story as recorded by Julius Paris: The Senate decided that the temples of Isis and Serapis should be demolished, but none of the workers dared to touch the temples. The consul Lucius Aemilius Paullus took off his official striped toga, grabbed an axe, and smashed in the doors of that temple.][78]

Chapter 4. The Auspices[79]

Preface

[Preface as recorded by Nepotianus: It is well known that the city of Rome was founded with the help of the auspices. Remus was the first to receive the auspices— he saw six vultures; Romulus was later, but he saw twelve vultures. So Romulus had a stronger claim than Remus, since Remus based his claim on his auspices being earlier, but Romulus on his being greater.][80]

Roman Stories

4. 1. [Story as recorded by Julius Paris: King Lucius Tarquin wanted to add some units to the cavalry units that Romulus had enrolled after taking the auspices,

---

[77]Gnaeus Calpurnius Piso and Marcus Popillius Laenas were consuls, and Gnaeus Cornelius Scipio Hispanus was praetor for foreigners in 139 B.C. The Babylonians (Chaldaeans) were experts in astrology; the Jews had been making converts.

[78]The famous Lucius Aemilius Paullus was consul in 182 and 168 B.C., but Shackleton-Bailey suggests that this story might be about Lucius Aemilius Lepidus Paullus (cos, 50 B.C.).

[79]The word "auspices" literally means "bird sightings" or "bird watchings" (from *avis,* "bird," and *spicere,* "to sight, to watch"). Before starting anything important, the Romans would "take the auspices," in order to find out whether the gods approved of it. They "took the auspices" by examining the behavior of birds in flight or of chickens eating.

[80]Romulus founded the city of Rome in 753 B.C. and was the first of its legendary kings. Remus was his twin brother.

but he was prevented from doing so by the augur Attius Navius. Tarquin angrily asked him whether the thing he was thinking about was possible. When Attius took the auspices and replied that it was, Tarquin ordered him to cut a whetstone with a razor. Attius brought a whetstone, and by carrying out that incredible task, he made the power of his science clear to the king.]

[Story as recorded by Nepotianus: King Lucius Tarquin was planning to add some units to the ones that Romulus had set up, but the augur Attius Navius said that the gods should be consulted first. The king ordered him to find out whether the thing he had in mind was possible. After consulting the gods, the augur replied that it was possible. "I want you," said the king, "to cut a whetstone with a razor." Without the slightest delay, the augur did so. From then on the trustworthiness and prestige of augurs remained very high in Rome. A statue was set up to Navius, showing him with his whetstone and razor.][81]

4. 2. [Story as recorded by Julius Paris: Tiberius Gracchus was making preparations for his revolution, and at dawn he asked for the auspices at his home. He got a very sad response, because as he was going out the door, he knocked his foot so badly that he broke his toe. Then three crows cawed against him, knocked a part of a roof tile off, and threw it down in front of him. After he ignored all these signs, he was thrown down from the Capitol by Scipio Nasica, the chief pontiff, and died after being struck by a piece of a bench.]

[Story as recorded by Nepotianus: When Tiberius Gracchus was going up for election as tribune, he consulted the sacred chickens at his home, and they opposed his going to the Campus Martius. When he went on obstinately, he soon knocked his foot outside the door so badly that he broke a joint. Then three crows flew in his face with ill-omened caws, started fighting among themselves, and in doing so knocked a tile down before his feet. When he consulted the gods on the Capitol he received similar auspices. He had behaved badly as a tribune, so he was killed by Scipio Nasica: first he was struck with a piece of a bench, then he was killed with a wooden club. The plebeian aedile, Lucretius, ordered that his body, and the bodies of those who were killed with him, be left unburied and thrown into the Tiber.][82]

4. 3. [Story as recorded by Julius Paris: During the First Punic War Publius Claudius wanted to fight a naval battle, and he asked for the auspices in the traditional way of our forefathers. When the man in charge of the sacred chickens replied that they were not coming out of their cage, Claudius ordered them to be thrown into the sea, saying, "Since they do not want to eat, let them drink!"]

[81]This story is about Tarquin the Elder, the fifth of Rome's legendary kings (616–579 B.C.). The units were used both as army units and as voting units (see unit—army and unit—voting in the Glossary).

[82]Tiberius Sempronius Gracchus (tribune of the plebs, 133 B.C.) was a populist politician. He and his supporters were murdered by a lynch gang of senators led by Publius Cornelius Scipio Nasica Serapio (cos, 138 B.C.). This conservative politician was also the chief pontiff from 141 B.C. until his death in 132 B.C. The plebeian aedile for 133 B.C. was Lucretius Vespillo.

[Story as recorded by Nepotianus: During the First Punic War, Publius Claudius, a headstrong man, consulted the sacred chickens. When someone said that the chickens were not eating, which was a bad omen, he replied, "Let them drink!" and ordered that they be thrown into the sea. Shortly after that, he lost his fleet off the Aegates Islands. This was a great disaster for our Republic and for Claudius himself.][83]

4. 4. [Story as recorded by Julius Paris: The fellow consul of Publius Claudius, Lucius Junius, ignored the auspices and lost his fleet in a storm. Junius avoided the disgrace of being convicted by taking his own life.][84]

4. 5. [Story as recorded by Julius Paris: The chief pontiff, Metellus, was heading for Tusculum when two crows flew into his face as if they were trying to stop his journey. They barely managed to make him go back home. The following night, the temple of Vesta caught on fire. While the fire was going on, Metellus went right through the flames, grabbed the statue of Pallas, and saved it.]

[Story as recorded by Nepotianus: As the chief pontiff, Metellus, was heading for the region of Tusculum, two crows clearly tried to stop him, but he ignored the augury and continued with his journey. Then the birds started to claw and peck at each other. Metellus was astonished and went back to Rome. On the following night, he snatched the statue of Pallas from a fire.][85]

4. 6. [Story as recorded by Julius Paris: The imminent death of Cicero was foretold by the auspices. He was in his holiday home near Caieta and before his very eyes a crow hit the pointer of his sundial and knocked it out of its place. Immediately afterward, it headed toward him and held the border of his toga in its beak until a servant announced that the soldiers had arrived to kill him.]

[Story as recorded by Nepotianus: Our own Cicero, after he had been put on the death list, was hiding in the region of Caieta, and Antony was hunting him down. A crow knocked the iron pointer that shows the hours so hard with his beak that he broke it off; then the crow grabbed Cicero's toga and pulled at it. At that very moment, his assassins rushed toward him.][86]

4. 7. [Story as recorded by Julius Paris: Marcus Brutus had led the remnants of his army out against Augustus and Antony when an eagle flew from each of the two camps. After the eagles had fought each other, the one that had come from the side of Brutus flew away after being badly mawled.]

---

[83]Publius Claudius Pulcher (cos, 249 B.C.) lost most of the fleet in a disastrous attack on Drepanum (on the west coast of Sicily near the Aegates Islands) during the First Punic War (264–241 B.C.). The sacred chickens were no laughing matter in Rome (see auspices in the Glossary), and he narrowly escaped being convicted for treason.

[84]Lucius Junius Pullus (cos, 249 B.C.) lost his fleet off the south coast of Sicily.

[85]Lucius Caecilius Metellus (cos, 251 B.C.) was chief pontiff from 243 to 221 B.C. The statue of Pallas had supposedly been brought to Rome from Troy by Aeneas, the mythical ancestor of the Romans, so it was very sacred indeed. The temple of Vesta also held the eternal fire of Rome.

[86]Cicero was murdered by order of Antony in 43 B.C. when the triumvirs massacred their political opponents. Caieta was on the coast of Latium.

[Story as recorded by Nepotianus: Marcus Brutus, the partner of Cassius, was forewarned about the outcome of the civil war. An eagle flew from each of the confronting camps, and the two came together over the plain where Brutus did battle and fought each other. The winner went back to Augustus, while the one that had flown from the side of Brutus was put to flight.][87]

Foreign Stories

4. ext. 1. [Story as recorded by Julius Paris: King Alexander wanted to build a city in Egypt, but the architect Deinocrates had no chalk, so he drew a plan of the future city with barley. A huge crowd of birds emerged from a nearby lake and ate up the barley. The Egyptian priests interpreted this to mean that the city would be able to support a large population of settlers with its food supply.][88]

4. ext. 2.[89] King Deiotarus used to take the auspices before doing almost anything, and his life was saved by the appearance of an eagle.[90] When he saw it, he refused to make use of a particular house. On the following night, that house collapsed, and its ruins lay flat on the ground.

Chapter 5. Omens[91]

Roman Stories

5. 1. The observation of omens has some connection with religion since people believe that these things do not happen by chance but are caused by divine providence.

Omens had an important effect when the city had been devastated by the Gauls.[92] The Conscript Fathers were deliberating whether they should move to Veii or rebuild our city walls. At that moment, some cohorts were returning from guard duty, and their centurion happened to shout in the assembly place, "Standard-bearer, set up the standard; this is the best place for us to stay."[93] When it

---

[87]The tyrannicides Marcus Junius Brutus and Gaius Cassius Longinus led the armies of the Republic at Philippi (in eastern Macedonia) in 42 B.C. Their armies were defeated by Augustus and Antony and the two Republican leaders committed suicide.

[88]Alexandria (in Egypt) was founded by King Alexander the Great in 331 B.C. after he conquered Egypt. Its architect was Deinocrates.

[89]With this story, we return to the original manuscript of Valerius Maximus and no longer have to rely on the summaries of Julius Paris or Nepotianus.

[90]Deiotarus was king of Galatia (in Asia Minor) from 52 B.C. until his death in 40 B.C.

[91]In this chapter, Valerius restricts the term *omen* to refer only to spoken remarks that predict the future. The only exception is Roman Story 5, where the ass uses sign language.

[92]The Gauls captured Rome in 390 B.C.

[93]A centurion commanded a unit (about 60 men). A cohort contained six units, but cohorts were not used until the Second Punic War.

heard these words, the Senate declared that it accepted the omen, and it removed all traces of its plan to move to Veii. These few words determined their choice of a home for what would eventually be the greatest of empires! I think the gods must have felt it was not right that the Roman nation, which had begun with the most favorable auspices, should change its name and turn into the city of Veii; or that the glory of their famous victory should be granted to the ruined city recently defeated by them.[94]

5. 2. The man who brought about this glorious achievement, Camillus,[95] prayed that if any one of the gods thought that the Roman people were too successful, then he should be allowed to satisfy that god's jealousy by some personal misfortune. He suddenly slipped and fell down, and it seemed that this omen was referring to the judicial conviction that later ruined him.[96] The victory and the holy prayer of this very distinguished man have rightly competed for glory. Because a man who wants to promote the good of his country and a man who wants to deflect its evils toward himself are equally brave.

5. 3. And what of the memorable omen that came to the Consul Lucius Paullus![97] It fell to him by lot to wage war against King Perseus.[98] He went back home from the Senate house and kissed his little daughter Tertia, who was a very small girl at that time. He noticed that she was sad, and he asked her why she had that face on her. She answered that Persa was dead. A puppy that the girl adored had died, and its name was indeed Persa. Paullus seized the omen and from that chance statement he acquired almost certain hope of a very glorious triumph.[99]

5. 4. Caecilia, the wife of Metellus, early in the night, in the old-fashioned way, was looking for an omen for her sister's adult daughter, and she herself provided the omen. She had been sitting in a little temple waiting for a long time, but she heard nothing that would suit her purpose. The young woman grew tired of standing for so long and asked her maternal aunt to let her sit down for a while. She replied, "You are welcome to take my place." These words were inspired by kindness, but they were a clear omen of what would happen. For Caecilia died not long after, and Metellus married the young woman I am talking about.[100]

5. 5. There is no doubt that Gaius Marius saved his life by observing an omen.[101] When he was declared a public enemy by the Senate, he was brought to

---

[94]Veii had been sacked by the Romans so it would have been humiliating to move there in 390 B.C.

[95]The dictator Marcus Furius Camillus sacked Veii in 396 B.C.

[96]Camillus was exiled in 391 B.C. for allegedly stealing some of the booty from Veii.

[97]Lucius Aemilius Paullus (cos, 182 B.C.) was consul for a second time in 168 B.C. when the war against King Perseus of Macedonia broke out.

[98]The Senate would cast lots to decide which consul would command the army. The lots supposedly revealed the will of the gods.

[99]Paullus defeated King Perseus at Pydna in 168 B.C. and celebrated a triumph over him in 167 B.C.

[100]All three characters in this story were members of the aristocratic Caecilius Metellus family.

[101]Marius had to flee for his life in 88 B.C. when Sulla marched on Rome.

the house of Fannia at Minturnae and held in custody there.[102] He saw an ass being offered food, but the ass ignored it and ran toward water. He felt that the providence of the gods had presented him with this as a sign for him to follow, and he was in general very skilled at interpreting religious signs. He induced the crowd, which had gathered together to help him, to have him brought to the sea. He quickly got onto a small ship, sailed to Africa, and escaped Sulla's conquering army.

5. 6. When Pompey the Great was defeated by Caesar at the battle of Pharsalus, he sought safety in flight, and ordered the fleet to sail to the island of Cyprus, so that he could gather some forces there. Pompey landed at the town of Paphus, where he saw a magnificent house on the shore. He asked the helmsman what its name was, and he replied that it was called Katobasileia (the Palace of the Underworld). These words destroyed the little bit of hope he had left. But he did not hide his feelings: he turned his eyes away from the building, and moaning aloud, he revealed the sorrow which this dreadful omen had caused him.[103]

5. 7. Marcus Brutus, after carrying out the assassination, was warned by an omen of the predestined end he richly deserved. After that evil deed he was celebrating his birthday, and when he wanted to recite some Greek poetry, his mind led him to recite this particular Homeric line:

But dreadful fate and the son of Leto killed me.

At the battle of Philippi, that very god, chosen by Augustus and Antony as their watchword, turned his weapons against Brutus.[104]

5. 8. Fortune also tweaked the ear of Gaius Cassius with a fitting remark. The Rhodians begged him not to deprive them of all their statues of the gods, and Fortune made him reply that he had left the Sun behind. She wanted to magnify his insolence as a rapacious victor by the arrogance of his words. When he was shattered by his defeat in Macedonia, Fortune forced him to leave not just the statue of the Sun, which was the only thing he had conceded to the pleading Rhodians, but in truth the light of the sun itself.[105]

5. 9. It is also worth noting the omen under which the consul Petillius died while waging war in Liguria.[106] When he was attacking a mountain, which was

[102]Marius had helped Fannia out with her marital problems in the past (see 8: 2,3). Minturnae was on the coast of Latium.

[103]Pompey was defeated by Caesar at Pharsalus (in northern Greece) in 48 B.C. The bad omen came true, because Pompey was murdered soon afterward in Egypt.

[104]Marcus Junius Brutus (tyrannicide, 44 B.C.) was defeated at Philippi (in Macedonia) by Augustus and Antony in 42 B.C. Brutus committed suicide after the battle. Apollo (the son of Leto) was the patron god of the triumvirs.

[105]Gaius Cassius Longinus (tyrannicide, 44 B.C.) plundered Rhodes to supply the Republican army before the battle of Philippi in 42 B.C. He committed suicide after the battle. The colossal statue of the Sun in Rhodes was one of the seven wonders of the world.

[106]Quintus Petillius Spurinus (cos, 176 B.C.) died fighting against the Ligurians of northern Italy near Mutina (modern Modena).

called Letum (death), he encouraged his soldiers by saying, "Today I shall definitely get Letum." By fighting somewhat carelessly, he confirmed his chance utterance by his own death.

Foreign Stories

5. ext. 1. Two foreign cases of this type can appropriately be added to our national ones. When the people of Priene begged for help against the Carians, the Samians, inspired by arrogance, sent them the Sibyl as a joke instead of sending a fleet and an army. The people of Priene interpreted this as a protection given by the gods, and gladly received her. She correctly predicted what was destined to happen, so they felt she had led them to victory.[107]

5. ext. 2. When Apollonia was losing a war against the Illyrians, its citizens begged the Epidamnians to help them. The Epidamnians said that they were sending the river near their walls, called the Ajax, to their assistance. The people of Apollonia did not regret replying, "We accept this gift." They assigned the first place in the battle line to the river as if it were their leader. Contrary to all expectations, they defeated the enemy, and they attributed their success to the omen. Then they sacrificed to the river Ajax as a god, and they decided that from then on they would make it their leader in every battle.[108]

Chapter 6. Prodigies[109]

Preface

Our theme also requires us to give an account of prodigies that have occurred, whether favorable or unfavorable.

Roman Stories

6. 1. When Servius Tullius[110] was just a little boy, the people in his household saw with their very own eyes a flame flickering around his head as he was sleeping. Tanaquil, the wife of king Ancus Marcius, was amazed at this prodigy, and although

---

[107]Priene and Samos were both Greek states, so Priene would naturally expect Samos to help them against the native Carians. All three were on or near the western coast of Asia Minor (modern Turkey).

[108]Once again we have two Greek states that we would expect to combine forces against the native Illyrians. All three were on the eastern coast of the Adriatic Sea.

[109]Valerius uses the term *prodigy* to refer to an unnatural event that foreshadows the future.

[110]Servius Tullius was the sixth of the legendary kings of Rome (578–535 B.C.).

Servius was the son of a slave woman, Tanaquil brought him up as her own son and raised him to the glory of royal power.[111]

6. 2. Another flame had an equally happy result—the flame that shone from the head of Lucius Marcius while he was making a speech to his men.[112] He was the commander of the two armies that had been disheartened by the deaths of Publius and Gnaeus Scipio in Spain.[113] The soldiers were fearful until they saw this apparition, but it encouraged them to regain their usual fortitude. As a result, they killed thirty-eight thousand of the enemy, took a large number prisoner, and captured two camps full of supplies from Carthage.

6. 3. In the long and bitter war against Veii, the Romans confined the people of Veii within the walls of their city but were unable to capture the city.[114] This delay seemed equally intolerable to the besiegers and the besieged, but by a remarkable prodigy the immortal gods showed the Romans a path to the victory they longed for. All of a sudden, the Alban Lake rose beyond its normal water level, although its volume had not been increased by rain from heaven nor added to by the flooding of any river.[115] Envoys were sent to the Delphic oracle to find an explanation for this mystery, and they brought back the instructions of the oracle: the Romans should release the water of that lake and flood the fields; by this means, Veii would come under the power of the Roman people. But even before our envoys made this report, a diviner from Veii had been captured by our men (since we had no seers of our own), and when he was brought into the camp, he had told them what the future would be.[116] The Senate had been advised by two predictions, occurring almost simultaneously, so it followed the dictates of religion and gained control of the enemy city.

6. 4. The story that follows had a very successful outcome. Sulla was consul during the Social War, and when he was sacrificing in front of the general's headquarters in the territory of Nola, he suddenly saw a snake that had slid out from the bottom of the altar.[117] After seeing this, he followed the encouraging advice of the diviner Postumius, and at once he led the army out to fight and captured the

[111]Tanaquil was actually the wife of the fifth king, Tarquin the Elder (616–579 B.C.), not of the fourth king, Ancus Marcius (640–617 B.C.).

[112]Lucius Marcius Septimius was a military tribune in 211 B.C., serving against the Carthaginians in Spain under Publius Cornelius Scipio (cos, 218 B.C.) and his brother Gnaeus Cornelius Scipio Calvus (cos, 222 B.C.).

[113]Lucius Marcius Septimius was chosen by the men to lead them after the Scipio brothers had died in battle. (See 2:7,15 and 8:15,11.)

[114]Rome and Veii (in Etruria) had been rivals throughout the fifth century B.C. The final war between them lasted ten years (405–396 B.C.).

[115]The supernatural flooding of the Alban Lake (in Latium, near Rome) occurred in 398 B.C., two years before the fall of Veii.

[116]Being an Etruscan city, Veii would naturally have a diviner at its disposal.

[117]Sulla was a legate during the Social War (the war against the Italians) from 90 until 89 B.C. He was a consul in 88 B.C. after the war. Nola was in Campania (western Italy).

strongest camp of the Samnites.[118] This victory was the starting point of his progression to the wide-ranging power he would wield in the future.

6. 5. The prodigies that occurred in our city at the first outbreak of war during the consulship of Publius Volumnius and Servius Sulpicius were also very remarkable.[119] A cow changed from its normal lowing to human speech and terrified those listening with this unusual portent. Pieces of meat came scattering down like a shower of rain and most of the pieces were snatched up quickly by birds; the rest stayed on the ground for several days, but did not give off a bad smell or show any visible signs of decay.

It was believed that portents of the same kind occurred during another national emergency.[120] A six-month-old boy shouted out "Triumph!" in the cattle market. Another boy was born with the head of an elephant. In Picenum there was a shower of stones. In Gaul a wolf took a sentry's sword from its scabbard. In Sardinia two shields sweated blood. At Antium bloody ears of corn fell into the baskets of the reapers. In Caere water flowed mixed with blood.[121]

It was also generally accepted that during the Second Punic War a cow belonging to Gnaeus Domitius said, "Beware, Rome!"[122]

6. 6. Gaius Flaminius was created consul without taking the auspices. When he was ready to fight against Hannibal at Lake Trasimene, he ordered that the standards be pulled up, but his horse slipped and he was thrown over its head and landed flat on the ground. He was not at all inhibited by this prodigy, and when his standard-bearers said that the standards could not be moved from where they stood, he threatened to punish them unless they dug the standards out at once. If only he had paid the penalty for this rashness by his own misfortune and not by a disastrous defeat for the Roman people! Because in that battle, fifteen thousand Romans were killed, six thousand were captured, and ten thousand were forced to run away. The consul was slain in the fight, but Hannibal searched for his body and buried it properly; indeed, Hannibal had done his best to bury the Roman Empire.[123]

[118]The Samnites lived in central Italy and were the greatest rebels against Rome.

[119]A war against the hill tribes of Latium started in 461 B.C. when Publius Volumnius Amintinus Gallus and Servius Sulpicius Camerinus Cornutus were consuls.

[120]These prodigies occurred in 217 B.C. during the Second Punic War. The Romans suffered a major defeat that year at Lake Trasimene (see 1:6,6).

[121]The cattle market was in Rome, Picenum was in eastern Italy, Gaul means Cisalpine Gaul (northern Italy), Antium was on the coast of Latium (south of Rome), and Caere was in Etruria (north of Rome).

[122]This prodigy actually occurred when Gnaeus Domitius Ahenobarbus was consul in 192 B.C., at the beginning of the war against Syria. It has no connection with the Second Punic War.

[123]Hannibal, the Carthaginian leader in the Second Punic War, was the greatest threat Rome ever faced. He launched an invasion of Italy in 218 B.C. and defeated the Romans in several major battles. The Roman defeat at Lake Trasimene took place in 217 B.C. when Gaius Flaminius was consul.

6. 7. In his insane perseverance, Gaius Hostilius Mancinus followed the headlong rashness of Flaminius. As this consul was about to go off to Spain, the following prodigies occurred.[124]

He wanted to make a sacrifice at Lavinium, but when the sacred chickens were released from their cage, they ran off into nearby woods, and although they were searched for with the greatest diligence, they could not be found.[125]

He reached the Port of Hercules on foot, and as he was going on board his ship there, these words from no human speaker came to his ears: "Wait, Mancinus."[126]

He was terrified by this, so he turned back and headed for Genoa, and when he had gone onto a boat there, an exceptionally large snake was seen and then disappeared from sight.

So the number of these prodigies equaled the number of his disasters: an unfortunate battle, a shameful peace treaty, and a deplorable handover.[127]

6. 8. The rashness of this very careless man is less surprising when compared with the tragic end of a very respected citizen, Tiberius Gracchus. It was foretold by a prodigy, though he failed to plan ahead and evade it. When he was consul, he made a sacrifice in Lucania, and two snakes slid up from a concealed location, ate the liver of the victim he had sacrificed, and returned to their hiding place.[128] Because of this event, he started the sacrifice all over again, but the same prodigy occurred. After he had killed yet a third victim, he carefully guarded its organs, but could neither stop the snakes sliding up nor prevent them from escaping. Although the diviners said that this prodigy referred to the general's life, Gracchus did not take precautions against the schemes of his treacherous friend, Flavus.[129] This friend led Gracchus to a place where the Carthaginian commander, Mago, was hiding with a band of soldiers, and the unarmed Gracchus was killed.[130]

6. 9. The fact that they were both consuls in the same year, made similar mistakes, and died in the same way, brings me from Tiberius Gracchus to a story about Marcellus.[131] He was inflamed with pride because he had captured Syracuse and had been the first to force Hannibal to flee (in front of the walls of Nola).[132] He worked very hard to destroy the Carthaginian army in Italy or to expel it from

---

[124]Gaius Hostilius Mancinus was consul in 137 B.C. and was defeated by the Numantines in Spain.

[125]Lavinium was near the coast of Latium.

[126]The Port of Hercules is now called Monaco.

[127]The Senate refused to ratify his peace treaty and handed him over to the Numantines in 136 B.C.

[128]Tiberius Sempronius Gracchus (cos, 215 B.C.) was consul again in 213 B.C. but this event occurred in 212 B.C. when he was commanding the Roman army in Lucania (southern Italy).

[129]Flavus was a Roman ally in Lucania who changed sides and joined the Carthaginians.

[130]Mago commanded the Carthaginian army in south Italy. He ambushed Gracchus in 212 B.C.

[131]Tiberius Sempronius Gracchus (cos, 215 B.C.) and Marcus Claudius Marcellus (cos, 222 B.C.) had been consuls together in 215 B.C.

[132]Marcellus captured Syracuse in 212 B.C. and had raised morale after the great Roman disaster at Cannae when he drove the Carthaginians away from Nola (in Campania) in 216 B.C.

Italy, and by means of a solemn sacrifice, he tried to ascertain the will of the gods. The first victim that fell before the brazier was found to have no lobe on its liver; the next had a double lobe on its liver. After inspecting them, the diviner reported with a sad face that he did not like the look of these organs since the propitious one only appeared after the defective one. Although he was warned in this way not to attempt anything risky, Marcus Marcellus dared to go out on the following night with a few men to reconnoitre. He was surrounded by a large number of enemy soldiers in Bruttium, and the grief caused by his death was as great as the loss inflicted on his country.[133]

6. 10. The consul Octavius was alarmed by a dreadful omen, but he was quite unable to avoid it. The head of Apollo's statue fell off by itself, and it stuck into the ground in such a way that it could not be removed. Octavius was in violent disagreement with his fellow consul, Cinna, and he assumed that this event represented his own death. He was frightened by the portent, but his life did come to the sad end it had predicted; only then could the immovable head of the god be dislodged from the earth.[134]

6. 11. At this point we cannot get away with passing over in silence the case of Marcus Crassus, which must be counted among the most serious defeats of the Roman Empire.[135] Before this great disaster he was bombarded by a large number of very obvious portents. When he was about to lead his army out of Carrhae against the Parthians, he was given a black cloak, although it is customary to give a white or purple cloak to those going off to battle. The soldiers gathered sadly and silently at his headquarters, though they should have been running and shouting eagerly, in accordance with the old custom. One of the eagle-standards could hardly be pulled up by the senior centurion; the other was extracted with great difficulty, and then as it was being carried it turned of its own accord in the opposite direction. These prodigies were considerable but that defeat was even more so: all those beautiful legions were destroyed, all the standards were captured by the enemy, and the great glory of the Roman army was trampled underfoot by the cavalry of the barbarians; the father's face was spattered with the blood of his son, who was a young man of excellent character; among the corpses piled up in random heaps lay the body of the general, left there to be torn apart by birds and beasts.[136] I should have liked to speak more calmly, but what I have recorded is the truth. This is how the gods flare up when their warnings have been ignored; this is how human plans are reproved when they exalt themselves over the plans of the gods.

---

[133]Marcellus was consul again in 208 B.C. when he was killed in an ambush by Hannibal in Bruttium (southern Italy).

[134]Gnaeus Octavius (cos, 87 B.C.) drove Lucius Cornelius Cinna (cos, 87 B.C.) from Rome, but he was murdered when Marius and Cinna marched on Rome later in 87 B.C.

[135]Marcus Licinius Crassus Dives (cos, 70 B.C.) was governor of Syria in 53 B.C. when he launched his disastrous campaign against the Parthian Empire (modern Iran and Iraq).

[136]Crassus died along with his son at Carrhae (on the eastern border of Syria).

6. 12. Pompey had also been warned abundantly by almighty Jupiter not to go ahead and face the ultimate risk of a war with Caesar.[137] When he marched out from Dyrrachium,[138] Jupiter threw thunderbolts against his army, swarms of bees concealed his standards, a sudden sadness afflicted the spirits of his soldiers, the entire army panicked at night, and sacrificial victims fled from the very altars. But the invincible laws of destiny did not allow his mind to judge those prodigies correctly, although in general he was far removed from any folly. He made light of them, and thus in the space of one day he lost his great prestige, his wealth, which was greater than that of the highest ranking private person, and all those honors that starting as a young man he had accumulated to the envy of others.

It is widely known that on that day statues of their own accord turned their backs in the temples of the gods; war cries and the clanging of weapons were heard in Antioch and Ptolemais, and the sound was loud enough to make everybody run to the city walls; the sacred drums sounded out from the inner sanctuaries of the temples in Pergamum; a green palm tree shot up to its full height from the cracks of the pavement under Caesar's statue in the temple of Victory at Tralles. It is clear from these things that the power of the gods favored the glory of Caesar and wanted to end the errors of Pompey.[139]

6. 13. In veneration of your altars and your most holy temples, o divine Caesar,[140] I pray that your spirit will be propitious and favorable, and that your caring protection will allow the misfortunes of these great men to disappear from view behind the precedent set by your own misfortunes. For we have all heard of that day when you sat on a golden throne, wrapped in a purple robe, because you did not want people to think you were rejecting this honor that the Senate had created and was bestowing upon you with so much enthusiasm.[141] Before you presented yourself to the view of the eager and expectant citizens, you devoted some time to that supernatural world you were soon to join. After sacrificing a choice bull, you did not find a heart among its organs, and Spurinna the diviner replied that this sign concerned your life and plans, since both of these were contained in the heart. Then suddenly, those men burst forth to assassinate you, but although they wanted to remove you from among the living, they actually added you to the company of the gods.

---

[137]Pompey led the armies of the Republic against Caesar in 48 B.C.

[138]Dyrrachium was on the coast of Illyria. Both armies headed east and met at Pharsalus (in Thessaly) where the Republican armies were defeated.

[139]Antioch and and Ptolemais were in Syria. Pergamum and Tralles were in the province of Asia.

[140]Caesar was declared a god in 42 B.C.

[141]The Senate was about to grant Caesar royal honors (a purple robe and throne) on the day he was assassinated (March 15, 44 B.C.).

Foreign Stories

6. ext. 1. My account of national stories about such prodigies must end with this one, because if I continued with Roman stories, I might seem to be inappropriately changing from the heavenly realm back to private homes. Therefore, I shall touch on some foreign stories. Since they appear in the middle of a Latin work, they will not be so impressive, but they can bring some pleasant variety to it.

It is a definite fact that when Xerxes led his army against the province of Greece, an army mare gave birth to a hare.[142] This type of portent revealed the outcome of his mighty expedition. He had overrun the sea with his fleets and the land with his infantry forces, but he was forced to retreat in terror like that timid animal and go back to his own kingdom.

Xerxes had finally and with great difficulty managed to go through Mount Athos,[143] and even before he destroyed Athens, he was planning to invade Sparta. While he was dining, a wondrous prodigy occurred: when wine was poured into his cup, it turned into blood, not once or twice, but three times. The magi were consulted about this, and they warned him to refrain from his undertaking.[144] And if there had been any trace of common sense in his insane mind, he would have realized that he had already received abundant warnings about Leonidas and the Spartans.[145]

6. ext. 2. When Midas, the one who ruled over Phrygia, was a boy, some ants piled up grains of wheat in his mouth as he was sleeping.[146] His parents asked what was the meaning of this prodigy, and the augurs replied that he would be the richest of all men. And their prediction was not an empty one, since Midas surpassed almost all kings in his excessive wealth. The gods had granted him a trivial gift when he was a baby in a cradle, but they made up for it later with treasure houses full of gold and silver.

6. ext. 3. I would rightly and properly prefer the bees of Plato to the ants of Midas.[147] Those ants were a sign of a fading and fragile happiness, but Plato's bees were a sign of complete and eternal happiness when they placed honey into the lips of the little boy sleeping in his cradle. When they heard about it, the interpreters of prodigies said that extraordinary sweetness and eloquence would flow from his mouth. I personally think that those bees did not feed on Mount Hymettus, with its sweet-smelling thyme, but that the divine muses inspired the bees to feed on their own Mount Helicon, which blossoms with every kind of learning, so that the bees could pour the sweet food of eloquence into Plato's great mind.[148]

---

[142]King Xerxes I of Persia launched his unsuccessful invasion of Greece in 480 B.C.

[143]Xerxes cut a passage through Mount Athos (in northern Greece).

[144]The magi were Persian priests.

[145]King Leonidas of Sparta tried to hold the Persians back at Thermopylae in 480 B.C., but the entire Spartan force was wiped out.

[146]The semilegendary King Midas of Phrygia (west Asia Minor) lived around 700 B.C.

[147]Plato was born in 427 B.C.

[148]Mount Hymettus (in Attica) was famous for its honey. Mount Helicon (in Boeotia, central Greece) was the home of the muses.

Chapter 7. Dreams

Roman Stories

7. 1. But since I have mentioned how sleep brought riches to Midas and learning to Plato, I shall tell how the sleep of many people has been troubled by visions that revealed the truth. What better place could I start from than the most sacred memory of the divine Augustus? His doctor, Artorius, was sleeping on the night before the day when Roman armies fought against each other on the plains of Philippi.[149] Minerva appeared to him and told him that although Augustus was afflicted with a serious illness, Artorius should advise him not to avoid the upcoming battle on the grounds of bad health. When Augustus heard this, he commanded his men to carry him into battle on a stretcher. While he was there, watching over things and overexerting himself to gain victory, his camp was captured by Brutus.[150] How can we avoid thinking that the gods arranged this? They did not want a man who was already destined for immortality to experience the destructive force of fortune, since that would be unworthy of his heavenly spirit.

7. 2. The mind of Augustus was naturally quick and subtle in judging every situation, but he paid particular attention to the dream of Artorius because of what had happened recently in his own family. He heard how Calpurnia, the wife of his father, the divine Caesar, had seen a vision in her sleep during the last night that he had spent on this earth.[151] She had seen him lying in her bosom, covered with wounds, and she was really terrifed by this frightful dream. She begged him continually to keep away from the Senate house on the following day.[152] But he did not want people to think that he would base his actions on a woman's dream, so he went off to hold that Senate-meeting during which those murderers laid their violent hands on him.

It is not right to compare a father and a son in any matter, especially when they have both attained the rank of gods, but Caesar had already won the path to heaven by his achievements, whereas Augustus still had a long series of good deeds to perform on this earth. The gods wanted Caesar simply to know about the transformation he would soon undergo, but they wanted Augustus to delay his transformation into that higher status; in this way, the heavens would have a new glory in Caesar and the promise of another in Augustus.[153]

7. 3. Here is another dream that was quite amazing and had a glorious outcome. On the same night, the two consuls, Publius Decius and Titus Manlius

---

[149]Augustus defeated the Republican army at Philippi (in Macedonia) in 42 B.C.

[150]In the first battle of Philippi (October 42 B.C.) the Republican leader, Marcus Junius Brutus, managed to capture the camp of Augustus.

[151]Caesar adopted Augustus in his will, who from then on referred to him as his father. Calpurnia had this dream on the night before March, 15 44 B.C.

[152]Caesar was assassinated in the Senate house.

[153]Caesar started a new fashion, because it became standard practice to declare every emperor a god on his death.

Torquatus, had this dream during the Latin War, which was a serious and dangerous war.[154] They were in their camp not far from the foot of Mount Vesuvius
when a vision appeared to each of them in his sleep.[155] It predicted that one side
had to yield its commander to the gods of the Underworld and to Mother Earth,
whereas the other side had to yield its army to them. If the leader of one side dedicated the enemy forces and also himself to those gods his side would win.[156] On
the following day, the consuls tried to appease the gods by sacrifice to see whether
the prediction could be evaded, but they promised to obey it if it proved to be a
genuine warning from the gods. The organs of the sacrificial victims confirmed
the dream. The consuls arranged it between themselves that if one wing of the
army began to experience difficulties, its commander would save our country from
its fate by sacrificing his own life. Neither commander shrank back from this
arrangement, but fate demanded the life of Decius.

7. 4. The following is another dream that likewise involved the state religion.
During the Plebeian Games,[157] a householder had punished his slave with a flogging, tied him to a yoke, and led him to the executioner through the Circus
Flaminius just before the procession was beginning.[158] Jupiter appeared to Titus
Latinius, a member of the plebs, in his sleep and instructed him to tell the consuls
that Jupiter had not been pleased with the dancer who had preceded the recent
games in the circus. If the consuls did not atone for this matter by carefully starting
the games all over again, a very serious disaster would befall the city.

Latinius was afraid that he might get into trouble if he bothered the supreme
executive power with his religious scruples, so he kept silent. Immediately afterward, his son was suddenly afflicted with a violent illness and died. Latinius was
asked in his sleep by the same god whether he had paid a harsh enough penalty for
neglecting his commands. But Latinius kept to his plan, and wasted away physically. Finally, he followed the advice of his friends and was brought on a stretcher
into the presence of the consuls and from there to the Senate. There he explained
all that had happened to him, and then, to the astonishment of all, he recovered his
physical strength and returned home on foot.

7. 5. We should not cover up the following story in silence either. Cicero was
expelled from the city through the schemes of his enemies.[159] He was staying at a

---

[154]Titus Manlius Imperiosus Torquatus (cos, 347 B.C.) and Publius Decius Mus (cos, 340
B.C.) were consuls together in 340 B.C. In the Latin War the Romans fought against the
peoples of Latium and Campania.

[155]The Latins and Campanians were defeated near Mount Vesuvius (in Campania).

[156]This ritual dedication of oneself as a sacrifice to the gods of the Earth and the Underworld was called a *devotio*.

[157]This incident occurred during the Great Games (not the Plebeian Games) in 489 B.C.
The Great Games were held every September in honor of Jupiter and included chariot races.

[158]Gaius Flaminius built his racecourse (the Circus Flaminius) in 220 B.C. so the Great
Games of 489 B.C. must have been at a different circus.

[159]Publius Clodius Pulcher (aedile, 56 B.C.) sent Cicero into exile in 58 B.C.

country house in the plain of Atina,[160] and when his mind was deep in sleep, he dreamt that he was wandering through a deserted region that had no roads. Marius came up to him dressed in the outfit of a consul and asked him why he was going around aimlessly with such a sad face. When Marius heard of the misfortune that was afflicting Cicero, he took Cicero's right hand, presented him to his nearest lictor, and had the lictor escort Cicero to the monument built by Marius himself, explaining that Cicero would find hopes of a happier fortune there. And that is how things turned out, for it was in the temple of Jupiter built by Marius that the Senate decree allowing Cicero to return was passed.[161]

7. *6.* The awful misfortune that awaited Gaius Gracchus was revealed plainly and openly to him while he was sleeping. When Gaius was deep in sleep, he saw the ghost of his brother, Tiberius, telling him there was no way Gaius could evade the evil fate that had ended his own life.[162] Many people heard this story from Gracchus before he took up the tribunate during which he died just like his brother.[163] Coelius, a reliable Roman historian, writes that this story had reached his ears while Gaius was still alive.[164]

7. *7.* The following story outdoes the fearful apparition in the dream I have just mentioned. The forces of Antony were crushed at Actium, and Cassius of Parma, who had followed his party, fled to Athens.[165] In the early part of the night, he was sleeping in bed, his mind exhausted with worries and cares, when he had a dream. A huge man was coming toward him—he was dark skinned and he had an unkempt beard and long hair. When Cassius asked who he was, he replied, "*kakos daimon*" (evil spirit). Cassius was terrified at the horrible sight and the frightening name, so he called to his slaves and asked whether they had seen anyone of such a description entering or leaving his bedroom. They assured him that nobody had come there, so he went back to sleep again, and the same vision came before his mind. By now he was wide awake, so he had a lamp brought in and ordered the slaves not to leave him. A very short space of time remained between this night and his execution, a punishment inflicted on him by Augustus.[166]

---

[160]Atina was in Lucania (southern Italy). Cicero stayed there before going into exile in Macedonia.

[161]Cicero was recalled in 57 B.C. after a year of exile. The Senate often met in temples, but Marius built the temple of Courage, not the temple of Jupiter.

[162]Gaius Sempronius Gracchus (tribune of the plebs, 123 B.C.) was the brother of the populist politician, Tiberius Sempronius Gracchus, who had been murdered by a lynch mob of senators while serving as a tribune of the plebs in 133 B.C.

[163]Gaius Sempronius Gracchus was a tribune of the plebs in 123 and 122 B.C. He was murdered in 121 B.C.

[164]Lucius Coelius Antipater wrote a history of the Second Punic War around 120 B.C.

[165]Augustus defeated Antony at the battle of Actium (on the west coast of Greece) in 31 B.C. Both Augustus and Antony had been supporters of Caesar, whereas Cassius of Parma had been one of the tyrannicides in 44 B.C.

[166]Augustus put Cassius of Parma to death in 30 B.C.

7. *8.* Haterius Rufus, a Roman equestrian, was warned by a dream that gave him what I might call a very accurate sketch of his future, as was proved by its outcome.[167] A gladiator fight was being put on in Syracuse, and in his sleep he saw himself being stabbed forcefully by a retiarius. On the following day, he told the dream to the people sitting next to him at the spectacle. It so happened that right beside the equestrian's seat, a retiarius was brought on with a murmillo. When the equestrian saw his face, he told these people that this was the retiarius who killed him in his dream, and he wanted to go away from there at once. They got rid of his fear by their talk but brought about the wretched man's death. The retiarius forced the murmillo into that place and threw him down, and while he was trying to strike the murmillo as he lay there, he ran Haterius through with a sword and killed him.[168]

Foreign Stories

7. *ext. 1.* Hannibal also had a dream that was as accurate in its prediction as it was hateful to the Roman race; not just his waking hours but even his sleep itself was hostile to our empire.[169] He had a dream that conformed to his plan and his wishes, in which he imagined that a rather tall young man, of human appearance, had been sent to him by Jupiter as his guide in the invasion of Italy. At first Hannibal obeyed the young man's warning and followed his footsteps without turning his eyes in any other direction. However, the natural human inclination to examine forbidden things soon made him look behind, and he saw a serpent of enormous size rushing quickly and flattening whatever came in its way; behind it he saw clouds bursting with a huge crash of the heavens and daylight hidden in the shadows of darkness. He was astonished and asked what the prodigy was and what it signified. His guide replied, "You see the destruction of Italy; be silent now, and leave the rest to the secrets of fate."

7. *ext. 2.* Alexander, the king of Macedonia, had been well warned by a vision seen in his sleep to guard his life more carefully, if only fortune had been willing to supply him with the sense to evade the danger to his life.[170] In his dream he learned about the deadly handiwork of Cassander before he felt it when he was murdered. Alexander imagined that he was being killed by Cassander although he had never seen him. After some time went by Alexander saw Cassander in person, and the vision that had frightened him that night was there before his eyes. After he discovered that Cassander was Antipater's son,[171] Alexander recited a Greek

---

[167]The equestrians were the Roman business elite.

[168]A retiarius was a gladiator who fought with a net and a trident, and a murmillo was a gladiator who was armed with a helmet and a sword. Perhaps this retiarius had managed to capture the murmillo's sword.

[169]Hannibal had this dream just before he left Spain to invade Italy in 218 B.C.

[170]Alexander the Great of Macedonia died in 323 B.C.

[171]Antipater governed Macedonia while Alexander the Great was conquering the world, but they had a disagreement in 324 B.C. and Alexander dismissed him. Cassander visited Alexander on his deathbed in Babylon to plead on his father's behalf.

verse that makes light of belief in dreams, and he cast his suspicions about poisoning far from his mind. But it is believed that the poison had already been prepared for him and that he died at the hands of Cassander.

7. *ext. 3.* The gods were much kinder in the case of the poet Simonides, for they reinforced the lifesaving warning he received in his sleep with the gift of sound commmon sense.[172] His ship had landed on some coast, where there was a body lying unburied, and he had provided it with a proper burial. He was warned by that corpse not to sail on the following day, so he stayed behind on dry land. The people who had set sail from there were overwhelmed by a storm at sea right before his eyes. He was happy that he had chosen to stake his life on a dream rather than on a ship. He kept this kindness in mind and immortalized it in a very elegant poem. He built a better and more lasting tomb for the dead man in the minds of men than the grave he had dug for him on the lonely and unknown sands.

7. *ext. 4.* Another vision in sleep that came true was the one of King Croesus.[173] First it filled his mind with great fear and then with sorrow as well. He had two sons, and he dreamt that Atys, the son who had exceptional quickness of mind and physical gifts, the one who was destined to succeed him as king, had been killed by a weapon. Being a concerned father, Croesus stopped at nothing in his efforts to evade the cruel disaster that he had been warned about. The young man had regularly been sent out to fight in battle; now he was kept back at home. He used to have an arsenal filled with many weapons of every kind; Croesus ordered that it be taken away from him. He went around with friends who wore swords; now they were forbidden to go near him. In spite of this, destiny created a way for this sad event to happen.

An enormously large boar was destroying the cultivated fields of Mount Olympus[174] and killing lots of country people. They begged the king to help them deal with this unusual misfortune. The king's son forced his father to send him to destroy the beast; this was somewhat easier for him since the king's fears focused on the cruel danger posed by a sword, not by a tusk. But while they all eagerly concentrated on killing the boar, fortune, determined to bring about the inevitable violent deed, caused a spear that had been thrown at the beast to turn toward the king's son. Indeed, fortune especially wanted one particular man to bloody his hands with this evil killing, the very man whom the king had appointed as his son's guardian. This man had come as a suppliant to Croesus, after polluting himself by an unintentional killing, and Croesus out of respect to the gods of hospitality had purified him of the murder with a sacrifice.[175]

7. *ext. 5.* Indeed, Cyrus the Elder is no small proof of the invincible necessity of fate. His maternal grandfather, Astyages, tried in vain to evade the outcome of

[172]Simonides of Ceos, the lyric poet, lived from about 550 to 470 B.C.

[173]Croesus was king of Lydia (in west Asia Minor) from 560 until 546 B.C.

[174]This is Mount Olympus in Asia Minor, not the famous Mount Olympus in Greece.

[175]It was an ancient custom to harbor suppliants, even if they had committed a murder.

two dreams foretelling that Cyrus was destined from birth to rule over all of Asia.[176] In his sleep Astyages had seen his daughter, Mandane, flood all the peoples of Asia with her urine, so he married her off to a Persian of modest means rather than to some very prominent Mede, lest the royal power might go over to that family. And when Cyrus was born, Astyages ordered that he be exposed, because during his sleep he had a similar dream in which a vine grew from the genitals of Mandane, and it kept growing until it overshadowed every part of his kingdom. But he only frustrated himself by trying with his human schemes to obstruct the fortune of his grandson, which had been predestined by the judgment of the gods.

7. *ext. 6.* When Dionysius of Syracuse was still restraining himself and behaving like a private citizen,[177] a woman of noble birth from Himera dreamt in her sleep that she ascended to heaven, and while there she visited the homes of all the gods.[178] Then she noticed a very strong man, with blond hair and freckles on his face, who was tied up in iron chains and lying beneath the throne and feet of Jupiter. She asked the young man acting as her guide in her tour of heaven who this person was, and she heard that he was the awful destiny of Sicily and Italy, and that once he was freed from his chains, he would be the ruin of many a city. She told everyone about this dream the following day. Later, an evil stroke of fortune that attacked the liberty of Syracuse and the lives of the innocent released Dionysius from the custody of heaven and sent him like a thunderbolt against their peace and tranquillity. The woman spotted him in the middle of a crowd that rushed out dutifully to see him as he entered the gates of Himera, and she shouted out that this was the man she had seen in her dream. The tyrant learned of this, and that was the reason he got rid of her.

7. *ext. 7.* The mother of the same Dionysius had a dream that was safer for her. While she bore Dionysius in her womb, she dreamt that she gave birth to a little satyr. She consulted an interpreter of prodigies, and he realized that her son would be the most famous and powerful man of the Greek race, and that is exactly what happened.

7. *ext. 8.* On the other hand, Hamilcar, the Carthaginian general, while he was besieging Syracuse, believed he heard a voice in his sleep declaring that he would dine in that city on the following day.[179] So he joyfully prepared his army for battle, as if the gods had promised victory to him. But a dispute arose between the Carthaginians and their Sicilian allies, and in the meantime the Syracusans made a sudden attack, captured his camp, and dragged him in chains through the gates of their city. He was deceived by his overconfidence rather than by his dream, because he did dine in Syracuse, but he was the city's captive, not, as he had anticipated, its conqueror.

---

[176]Astyages was the last king of Media (northern Iran). He was overthrown by Cyrus the Great, founder of the Persian Empire, who reigned from 559 to 529 B.C.

[177]Dionysius I was tyrant of Syracuse from 405 to 367 B.C.

[178]Himera was on the north coast of Sicily. It was obliterated by the Carthaginians in 409 B.C.

[179]This episode occurred in 296 B.C. when King Agathocles of Syracuse was fighting against the Carthaginians.

7. ext. 9. Alcibiades also foresaw his wretched end in a dream that was all too true.[180] In his sleep he had seen himself covered with his girlfriend's cloak. After he was killed and left there unburied, his body was covered with that very cloak.

7. ext. 10. The next dream may be a bit long, but it is too convincing for me to leave it out. Two Arcadian friends were traveling together and arrived at Megara.[181] One went to stay with a family acquaintance; the other paid to stay at an inn. The one who was staying at the house saw his friend in a dream, and his friend was begging him to come to his aid because he was trapped by the treacherous innkeeper. His friend could be saved from this imminent danger if he came quickly. He was alarmed by this vision, jumped out of bed, and tried to get to the inn where his friend was staying. By some accursed fate, he gave up his humanitarian plan as if it had been pointless, went back to bed, and fell asleep again. Then his friend appeared to him again badly wounded and begged him to avenge his death at least, since he had not bothered to save his life. His friend had been murdered by the innkeeper, and the body had been put on a cart and covered with dung, and was being brought to the city gate at that very moment. He was struck by the constant pleading of his friend and ran at once to the city gate. There he found the cart that had been pointed out in his dream, and he led the innkeeper off to be executed.

Chapter 8. Miracles[182]

Preface

Many strange things happen in the daytime to people who are wide awake, just as they do in the dark, when people are wrapped up in a cloud of dreams. It is hard to tell where these things have come from or how they occur, so it would be right to call them miracles. There is a great heap of them, but this is the first one that comes to my mind.

Roman Stories

8. 1. The Roman dictator, Aulus Postumius, and the Tusculan leader, Mamilius Octavius, were fighting fiercely at Lake Regillus, and for a long time neither army was retreating.[183] Then Castor and Pollux appeared as champions of the Roman side and completely routed the enemy forces.

---

[180]Alcibiades, the erratic Athenian leader, was murdered in Asia Minor in 404 B.C.

[181]Arcadia was an inland region of the Peloponnese (southern Greece); Megara was on the isthmus that joins southern and northern Greece.

[182]A "miracle" literally means anything that is amazing. Unlike a prodigy, it does not necessarily reveal the future.

[183]Aulus Postumius Albus Regillensis defeated the Latins at the battle of Lake Regillus in 499 or 496 B.C.

A similar thing happened in the Macedonian War.[184] Publius Vatinius, a citizen of Reate, was going to Rome at night, and he thought he saw two very handsome young men come toward him riding on white horses.[185] They announced that on the previous day, King Perseus had been captured by Paullus.[186] He revealed this to the Senate and was thrown into jail for insulting the majesty and dignity of the Senate with such a silly story. But a letter from Paullus revealed that Perseus had indeed been captured on that day, so Vatinius was released from prison, and on top of that he was rewarded with a plot of land and exempted from military service.

There was yet another time when people realized that Castor and Pollux had been watching out for the empire of the Roman people. They were seen washing off sweat from themselves and from their horses at the pool of Juturna, and their temple near this stream was unlocked and opened by no human hand.[187]

8. 2. But let us continue with other gods who also favored this city with their divine power. Our citizens had been devastated by a plague for three years in a row, and we saw that neither divine mercy nor human devices would put an end to this great and lasting misfortune. But by carefully inspecting the Sibylline Books, the priests discovered that we could not recover our usual health unless Aesculapius were brought here from Epidaurus.[188] Since this was the only remedy that was destined to help us, we sent envoys there, confident that our request would be granted since our prestige was already very great throughout the world.

We were not deceived in our expectation. We were offered assistance as eagerly as we had requested it. The Epidaurians immediately led the Roman envoys to the temple of Aesculapius, which is five miles outside their city, and they very kindly invited the envoys to feel free to take anything from the temple that they thought might be beneficial to our country. The god himself went along with their ready kindness, and he gave his divine approval to the words of these mortals, as we can see from what ensued.

There is a snake that the Epidaurians rarely saw, but whenever they did, it always brought some great blessing upon them and they worshiped it as a form of Aesculapius. It started to slide through the most crowded parts of the city with kindly eyes and in a gentle manner, and for three days everyone saw it and devoutly admired it. Then the snake clearly revealed its eager longing for a more glorious home, because it made its way to the Roman trireme. The sailors were terrified at this unusual sight, but the snake continued on its way up to the place where the tent of the envoy, Quintus Ogulnius, was located, and there it very calmly curled

---

[184]The Romans fought the Third Macedonian War from 172 to 167 B.C.

[185]Reate was in the Sabine region (central Italy). The heavenly twins, Castor and Pollux, usually appeared on horseback.

[186]King Perseus of Macedonia was defeated by Lucius Aemilius Paullus (cos, 182 B.C.) at the battle of Pydna in 168 B.C.

[187]Juturna was the nymph of a spring near Lavinium.

[188]The chief temple of Aesculapius (the god of medicine) was in Epidaurus (in southern Greece). The snake of Aesculapius was brought to Rome in 292 B.C.

itself up into several coils.[189] At this, the envoys felt they had achieved what they had hoped for, so they expressed their gratitude, learned about the cult of the snake from local experts, and joyfully set sail.

After a safe voyage, they landed at Antium.[190] The snake, which had stayed still on the ship up until now, slid forward to the entrance of the temple of Aesculapius, and curled itself around a very tall palm tree that stood over a myrtle bush with lots of spreading branches. For three days it was given its customary food, and the envoys were very worried that it might refuse to go back onto the ship. But after enjoying the hospitality of the temple at Antium, the snake allowed itself to be brought to our city. When the envoys landed on the banks of the Tiber, the snake swam across to the island where the temple was dedicated.[191] As soon as it arrived, it put an end to the crisis that it had been brought here to remedy.

8. 3. Juno was equally glad to move to our city. When Furius Camillus captured the city of Veii, he ordered some soldiers under his command to remove the statue of Juno Moneta, which was venerated with extraordinary devotion in that place, and bring it to our city.[192] As the soldiers were trying to remove the statue from its temple, one of them jokingly asked the goddess whether she wanted to go to Rome, and she replied that she did. When they heard these words the soldiers were astounded and put an end to their joking. They now believed that they were not just carrying a statue but bringing the goddess Juno herself from heaven. They joyfully placed her in that part of the Aventine hill where we can still see her temple today.[193]

8. 4. A statue of Feminine Fortune stands at the fourth milestone on the Latin Way, and it was consecrated along with its temple when Coriolanus' mother pleaded with Coriolanus and stopped him from destroying our city.[194] It was generally believed that the statue spoke the following words, not once but twice: "You were pious in donating me, ladies, and you were pious in dedicating me."

8. 5. Valerius Publicola had expelled the kings, and during his consulship he waged war against the people of Veii and the Etruscans.[195] They wanted to restore Tarquin to his ancient throne, and the Romans were trying to hold onto the liberty they had recently won.[196] Tarquin and the Etruscans were fighting with success on the right wing, when they suddenly panicked. Although they were winning, they

---

[189]Quintus Ogulnius Gallus (cos, 269 B.C.) led the special delegation to Epidaurus.

[190]Antium was south of Rome on the coast of Latium.

[191]The temple of Aesculapius was on the Insula Tiberina (Tiber Island) in the middle of the river in Rome.

[192]The dictator Marcus Furius Camillus captured Veii in 396 B.C. and brought this statue of Juno Regina (not Juno Moneta) to Rome.

[193]The temple of Juno Regina was built on the Aventine hill in 392 B.C.

[194]Gaius Marcius Coriolanus, the disgruntled Roman leader, was dissuaded from attacking Rome by his mother, Veturia, and his wife, Volumnia, in 488 B.C.(see 5:2,1 and 5:4,1).

[195]Publius Valerius Publicola (cos, 509 B.C.) defeated a coalition of Etruscan cities, including Veii, in the first year of the Republic, 509 B.C.

[196]The last king of Rome, Tarquin the Proud, was expelled in 509 B.C.

started to run away, and what is more, they spread their panic to the soldiers from Veii and brought them along with them in their flight. People came up with a miracle to explain this occurrence; a loud voice had suddenly come from the nearby forest of Arsia, and people claim that it was Silvanus shouting something like these words:[197] "Etruscan losses will be greater by one, and the Roman army will emerge victorious." When the number of bodies was sorted out, it provided an extraordinary proof that these words were true.

8. 6. Well now, should I not commemorate the help that Mars gave to the Romans in winning a war? The people of Bruttium and Lucania had a violent hatred for the city of Thurii and were trying to destroy it with all their might; but our consul, Gaius Fabricius Luscus, was especially eager to protect it from harm.[198] From each side the armies came together at a particular place, and it was doubtful how things would turn out. The Romans were afraid to start the battle, when an exceptionally tall young man started telling them to take courage. As he noticed that they were still rather unenthusiastic, he grabbed a ladder, went right through the enemy lines, reached their camp, put the ladder up against their palisade, and climbed over it. Then he shouted out in a loud voice that he had taken the first step to victory. This drew our soldiers there to capture the enemy camp, and the forces from Lucania and Bruttium had to rush to defend it; the two armies clashed and wore themselves out in an indecisive battle. But by the force of his exploits, this same man enabled the Romans to defeat the enemy and slaughter them or make them captive: twenty thousand were killed, five thousand were made captive, including Statius Statilius, the commander of both national armies, and twenty-three military standards were taken.

On the following day, the consul honored those men who had served him exceptionally well, but he said he was reserving the rampart crown for the man who had surprised the enemy camp. When no one was found to claim this award, they came to the conclusion that father Mars had been among them to help his people. There were many clear pieces of evidence to support this belief, but the one that proved it was a helmet decorated with two crests that had covered the god's head. Fabricius decreed a public thanksgiving to Mars and when it took place the soldiers, wearing laurels and full of high-spirited joy, bore witness to the help they had received from the god.

8. 7. I shall now tell a story that was well known in its own age and came down to later generations. Aeneas brought the national gods from Troy and placed them in Lavinium.[199] His son Ascanius brought them from there to Alba, a city he had founded himself, but they went back to their old shrine.[200] Since people might

---

[197]Silvanus was a god of the forests. The forest of Arsia was between Rome and Veii.

[198]Gaius Fabricius Luscinus was consul in 282 B.C. Thurii was a Greek city in Bruttium (southern Italy).

[199]Aeneas was a hero of Troy (on the coast of Asia Minor), and the Romans regarded him as their ancestor. They believed they still had his statue of the goddess Pallas (see 1:4,5), which they took from Lavinium (near the coast of Latium).

[200]Alba Longa was the ancient religious center of Latium before the Romans destroyed it.

have suspected that this was done by human means, the gods were brought back to Alba, but they revealed their will by going to Lavinium once again. I am aware that people are usually very skeptical when they consider stories about those who with their merely mortal eyes and ears have seen the immortal gods move or heard them speak. But the story I am telling is not a new one; it has been handed down and told over and over again, so its authors should command our belief. These events have been consecrated by the most glorious works of our literature, and it is my duty to accept them as the truth.

8. 8. Since I have mentioned our city and the origins of our state, its glorious offspring, the divine Caesar, comes to mind. Gaius Cassius can never be mentioned without reminding us of his murderous crime against our state, and when he was fighting with great determination at the battle of Philippi, he saw the divine Caesar.[201] Caesar looked more venerable than a mere mortal, he was wearing a purple military cloak, and with a menacing look on his face he spurred his horse straight on toward Cassius. Cassius was terrified at this sight, and ran away from his enemy, after shouting out at him, "What more can I do, if killing you was not enough?" Indeed, Cassius, you did not kill Caesar, because it is impossible for any god to die. You merely violated the mortal body he was temporarily using, and by so doing you earned yourself the hostility of a god.

8. 9. Pompey the Great had been treacherously murdered by King Ptolemy, and Lucius Lentulus was sailing past the shore where his body was being cremated with bits of wood from a broken-up boat.[202] He saw the funeral pyre that Fortune herself should have been ashamed of, and although he was unaware of what had happened, he said to his fellow soldiers, "For all we know, they might be cremating Pompey in that fire." The fact that he spoke these divinely inspired words is a miracle.

8. 10. Those were the words of a human spoken by chance, but the following words were practically spoken by the god Apollo himself, and the way they foretold the death of Appius confirms our trust in the Pythia's ability to predict the truth.[203] The civil war started when Pompey, following a course that was deadly to himself and bad for our state, broke off his friendship with Caesar.[204] Appius was eager to know how this serious civil war would end. He exploited his rights as a governor[205]—he was in charge of Achaea—and forced the priestess of the Delphic tripod[206] to go down to the deepest part of the holy cave. In that place, people who consult the oracle get clear responses, but the overdose of divine inspiration

---

[201]Gaius Cassius Longinus (tyrannicide, 44 B.C.) commanded one of the Republican armies at the battle of Philippi in 42 B.C.

[202]After being defeated by Caesar at Pharsalus, Pompey went to Egypt in 48 B.C. where he was murdered by order of King Ptolemy XIII. Lucius Cornelius Lentulus Crus (cos, 49 B.C.) had fought for Pompey and the Republicans at Pharsalus.

[203]The Pythia was the prophetess of Apollo at Delphi.

[204]The civil war started in 49 B.C., when Caesar marched from Gaul into Italy.

[205]Appius Claudius Pulcher (cos, 54 B.C.) was governor of Achaea (Greece) in 48 B.C.

[206]The Pythia sat on a sacred tripod when she was prophesying.

is deadly to the priestess who gives the responses. The virgin was filled with the force of the divine spirit caught inside her, and in a frightening voice, she chanted what was destined to happen, though her words to Appius were obscure and ambiguous: "This war," she said, "has nothing to do with you, Roman: you will possess the Hollows of Euboea." He thought he was being warned by Apollo not to get involved in the war, so he retired to the region lying between Rhamnous, a well-known part of Attica, and Carystus, on the sea of Chalcis; this region is called the Hollows of Euboea.[207] He died of a disease before the battle of Pharsalus was fought, and by being buried in the Hollows, he possessed them just as the god had predicted.[208]

8. 11. The following events are also considered as miracles. When the sanctuary of the Salian priests was burnt down, nothing was recovered intact apart from the augural staff of Romulus.[209]

The statue of Servius Tullius [was completely unharmed when the temple of Fortune burned down].[210]

[The statue of Quinta Claudia] was set up in the entrance of the temple of the Mother of the Gods.[211] The temple was destroyed by fire twice, first in the consulship of Publius Scipio Nasica and Lucius Bestia,[212] and again in the consulship of Marcus Servilius and Lucius Lamia,[213] but the statue stood there on its plinth and was untouched by the flames.

8. 12. The funeral pyre of Acilius Aviola also provided our state with cause for astonishment. He was believed to be dead by his doctors and servants, and after he had been laid out at his home for some time, he was brought out for cremation. When the flames reached his body, he shouted out that he was still alive, and he called to his tutor for help—the tutor was the only person who had stayed there—but Acilius was already engulfed in the flames and he could not be rescued from his fate.[214]

It was generally held that Lucius Lamia, a former praetor, also spoke out on his funeral pyre.[215]

---

[207]Chalcis was on the west coast of Euboea, where the island almost touches the Greek mainland, and Carystus was on the south tip of Euboea. Rhamnous was on the east coast of Attica, facing Euboea.

[208]Pompey and the Republicans were defeated at Pharsalus in 48 B.C.

[209]The Salian priests were priests of Mars who did a sacred war-dance.

[210]A few words (the ones in square brackets) are missing from the manuscript, but they are in the abridged version made by Julius Paris (at the end of the fourth century A.D.). The statue of Servius Tullius (the sixth king of Rome) was miraculously unharmed when the temple of Fortune burned down in 213 B.C.

[211]Quintia Claudia had received the sacred stone of the Mother of the Gods from the hands of Publius Cornelius Scipio Nasica (cos, 191 B.C.) when he brought it to Rome in 205 B.C.

[212]Publius Cornelius Scipio Nasica Serapio and Lucius Calpurnius Bestia were consuls in 111 B.C.

[213]Marcus Servilius and Lucius Aelius Lamia were consuls in A.D. 3.

[214]A tutor (paedagogus) was a slave who looked after a young boy, and the bond between them was often a strong one.

[215]Lucius Aelius Lamia was a praetor in 43 and 42 B.C.

Foreign Stories

8. ext. 1. What happened to Er from Pamphylia makes the previous stories less extraordinary. Plato writes that Er fell in battle and was left lying among the other war dead for ten days. He was taken from there, and two days later, when they put him on the funeral pyre, he came back to life and told them about the extraordinary things he had seen while he was dead.[216]

8. ext. 2. Since we have moved on to foreign stories, here is something that happened to a very learned man in Athens. He was hit on the head by a stone, and he could remember everything very vividly, but the one thing he forgot was literature, which had been his special passion. It was a dreadfully cruel blow to the mind of this afflicted man; it was almost as if his sensibilities had been carefully examined with the intention of wounding him where his greatest happiness lay and where the injury would be the most bitter to him. It carried the exceptional learning of this man away for a hateful burial. If he was destined not to enjoy the fruits of his studies, it would have been better for him never to have gone near them, than to have tasted their sweetness and then lost it.

8. ext. 3. The story of what happened to the next person is even more tragic: Nausimenes was an Athenian, and his wife came across her son and daughter having sex together. Horrified at the sight of this unexpected atrocity, she was struck dumb and was unable to cry out then or speak ever again. The pair paid for their sexual misbehavior by taking their own lives.

8. ext. 4. That was how Fortune cruelly took away someone's voice, but the next story tells how she kindly gave someone a voice. Echecles, an athlete from Samos, was dumb.[217] He had won a victory, but they tried to deprive him of the honor and prize he had earned. He was so fired up with indignation that he broke out into speech.

8. ext. 5. Gorgias of Epirus was brave and famous, and his birth was remarkable.[218] During his mother's funeral, he slipped out from her womb, and his unexpected cries made the people carrying her bier stop. This was a new sight for his country, a baby that had practically been born and cradled on his mother's funeral pyre. At the very same moment in time, a woman gave birth after she had died, and a boy had a funeral before he was yet born.

8. ext. 6. A man wanted to kill Jason of Pherae,[219] but the wound he gave him was sent from heaven by Fortune. He treacherously struck Jason with a sword, burst an abscess that none of the doctors could heal, and relieved Jason of a deadly affliction.

8. ext. 7. Simonides was equally beloved by the immortal gods, since they saved his life from imminent danger and removed him from harm.[220] He was dining at

---

[216]Plato tells this story in Book 10 of the *Republic*. Pamphylia was on the south coast of Asia Minor.

[217]Samos was a Greek island off the west coast of Asia Minor.

[218]Epirus is modern Albania.

[219]Jason of Pherae united all of Thessaly under his rule (374–370 B.C.)

[220]Simonides of Ceos (550–470 B.C.) was a Greek poet.

8. ext. 18. Why did these things happen to the children of all-powerful kings, to a very famous king, to a poet of brilliant talent, to very learned men, to a man of no importance? Even Nature herself, that creative artist of all things good and bad, could not provide us with an answer to this nor to the following questions.

Why does Nature favor the wild goats born on Crete so much? When they are wounded with arrows she practically guides them with her own hands toward the herb called ditammy, which helps to cure them; and she enables the goats to expel the arrows and their poison as soon as they have eaten that herb.

Whereas all other animals in all other places have to refresh themselves every day by drinking water, why has Nature enabled goats on the island of Cephallenia to satisfy their thirst for most of the year by opening their mouths and gulping down breezes from the sky?[238]

Why did she allow the temple of Juno Lacinia in Croton to have an altar with ashes that are never stirred, no matter what winds may be blowing?[239]

And finally, why did she want one stream in Macedonia and another in the region of Cales to have the properties of wine, so that men get drunk on it?[240]

But it is my duty to record these things and not to be astonished at them. I know that Nature rightly demands the freedom to act as she pleases since she has the endless task of bringing everything into existence.

8. ext. 19. Since I have been touching on things that go beyond the normal, I should also mention the snake that Livy talks about in such detail and with such style.[241] He says that in Africa, near the river Bagradas, there was a snake so huge that it was able to prevent the army of Atilius Regulus from using the river.[242] It snatched up many soldiers in its huge mouth, and crushed many others to death in the coils of its tail. It could not be wounded by throwing spears at it; finally it was attacked from all sides with giant catapults and succumbed to the blows of the heavy rocks raining down on it. That snake was a more terrifying sight to all our cohorts and legions than Carthage itself. It polluted the river with its blood and the surrounding region with the noxious smell of its body lying there. The Romans had to move their camp from that place. Livy notes that the hide of the beast was sent to our city and measured one hundred and twenty feet.

---

[238]Cephallenia was an island off the west coast of Greece.

[239]Juno Lacinia's temple was on the promontory of Lacinium near Croton (southern Italy).

[240]Cales was a city in Campania.

[241]The famous historian, Livy (59 B.C–A.D. 17), wrote a 142-volume history of Rome.

[242]The river Bagradas flowed between Carthage and Utica. The African campaign of Marcus Atilius Regulus in the First Punic War lasted from 256 to 255 B.C.

BOOK TWO

Preface

I have examined the rich and powerful realm of nature, and I shall now turn my pen toward the ancient and remarkable customs of our own city and of other nations: we must find out what were the origins of the happy life we now lead under the best of emperors, and by looking toward them, we may in some way benefit the morals of our own age.[1]

Chapter 1. Ancient Customs [of the Roman Family]

1. 1. Our ancestors never did anything without first taking the auspices, not only in public matters but even in private ones. Because of this custom, an auspex still takes part in our marriage ceremonies, but he is no longer required to take the auspices. Nevertheless, his name recalls the old custom.[2]

1. 2. Women used to dine with men, but women sat whereas men reclined. This custom, derived from the way people ate, has had an effect on our religion: at the banquet in honor of Jupiter, the god is invited to dine on a couch, whereas Juno and Minerva are invited to dine on chairs.[3] Our era has kept this severe practice more diligently on the Capitol than in private homes, presumably because it is more important to maintain discipline among goddesses than among women.

1. 3. Women who had restricted themselves to one marriage were honored with the garland of modesty: our ancestors felt that the heart of a married woman was especially incorruptible and trustworthy if she refused to leave the bedroom in which she had lost her virginity, but they believed that to have experienced many marriages was a sign of legalized promiscuity.

1. 4. No divorce took place between a wife and her husband from the origins of the city to its 520th year.[4] The first man to divorce his wife was Spurius Carvilius,

---

[1]The "best of emperors" is, of course, Tiberius, who was emperor at the time Valerius was writing this book.

[2]*Auspex,* which literally means a "bird watcher," is a less common term for "augur." At a wedding, the "auspex" was simply the man who witnessed the ceremony. (See augur and auspices in the Glossary.)

[3]The Banquet of Jupiter (*Epulum Iovis*) took place on September 13 each year at the triple temple of Jupiter, Juno, and Minerva on the Capitol.

[4]The first divorce took place in 231 B.C., which strictly speaking was the 523rd year of Rome, but Valerius has rounded the year off to the nearest decade.

and he did it because she was barren. Although his motive seemed reasonable, he was criticized nonetheless, because people felt that even his desire for children should not have been put before loyalty to his spouse.[5]

1. 5. Our ancestors wanted to safeguard a married woman's honor with a fortress of modesty, so if anyone summoned a married woman to court, he was not allowed to touch her body.[6] Thus her dress was left untainted by the touch of another man's hand.

Long ago, the use of wine was unknown to Roman women, presumably to prevent them from falling into any disgrace.[7] The first step toward lack of restraint starts with father Liber, and drinking usually leads to illicit sexual behavior.[8] The modesty of women, however, was not rough and severe, and it was tempered by an honorable sort of charm—they had, after all, indulgent husbands, an abundance of gold, and quite an amount of purple clothes—and they carefully dyed their hair with ashes to a golden red color to make themselves look more attractive. In those days women did not have to fear the gaze of men who break up other people's marriages. The sense of mutual respect in both sexes guaranteed that what married women saw and how they were seen was honorable.

1. 6. If ever some argument arose between a man and his wife, they would go to the shrine of the goddess Viriplaca, which is on the Palatine.[9] There each of them spoke in turn, said whatever they wanted to, put aside their dispute, and went home reconciled. It is said that the goddess was given this name because she placates husbands. She should definitely be venerated and, in my opinion, honored with special and choice sacrifices, since she is the guardian of our day-to-day domestic peace. Although the yoke of marriage is based on equal affection, the goddess, by her very name, gives masculine dignity the respect it deserves from women.

1. 7. That was the sort of respect that existed between spouses. Well, is it not clear that the same kind of respect existed in other relationships? I want to show how great its force was from a small piece of evidence: for a long time a father would not bathe with an adult son, nor a father-in-law with his daughter's husband. It is obvious, therefore, that they paid the same sort of religious respect to relations by blood or by marriage as they did to the immortal gods themselves, since they thought it no less wrong to be naked within those very sacred family ties than to be naked in some sacred space.

1. 8. Our ancestors also established a formal banquet called the Caristia. Only relatives by blood and by marriage could take part in it. If any quarrel had arisen

[5]Spurius Carvilius Maximus Ruga was consul in 234 B.C.

[6]The Laws of the Twelve Tables (passed in 451 and 450 B.C.) gave a plaintiff the right to seize the defendant and drag him to court, but apparently this applied only to male defendants.

[7]See 6:3,9 where a Roman murdered his wife for drinking wine.

[8]Liber ("free") was the Roman name for Bacchus, the Greek god of wine.

[9]Viriplaca means "husband placater" (from *vir,* "husband," and *placare,* "to placate"). The Palatine was a hill in Rome.

among these close relatives, it was resolved at these ritual banquets where everyone was in good spirits and had come to promote reconciliation.[10]

1. 9. Young people used to shower thoughtful honors on the elderly, as if all the older men were shared by the young as their fathers. That is why, on days when the Senate was in session, young men would invariably escort one of the Conscript Fathers, who was a relative or a friend of their father's, to the Senate house. The young men stayed there beside the doors until they could be of service to the senator by escorting him back home. Their voluntary guard duty gave those young men the physical and mental strength to take up active service on behalf of the state. From this training in hard work and modesty, they taught others those virtues that they themselves would soon display.

Whenever young men were invited to a dinner, they would carefully inquire who was to be at the party; they did not want to rush ahead and sit down before some older man arrived. When the table was cleared, they allowed the older men to stand up and leave first. From this it is clear that even at dinnertime young men were accustomed to speaking very rarely and always modestly in the presence of older men.

1. 10. Older men used to write songs that dealt with the famous deeds of men before their time, and they sang them at parties to the sound of the flute. This made the young men all the more eager to rival those deeds. What could be more splendid, and also more useful than this rivalry? The young men paid due respect to old age; and the old men, who had come to the end of their career, gave support and encouragement to the young men who were just starting off on a life full of activity. How could I choose a place like Athens, or some Greek school, or some foreign studies over our own type of upbringing? This upbringing produced the great men of the Camillus, Scipio, Fabricius, Marcellus, and Fabius families. But I do not want to bore you by naming every single celebrity in our empire's history right now, so I shall simply say that this upbringing produced the most famous gods in heaven, our divine Caesars.[11]

Chapter 2. Ancient Customs [of the Roman Senate]

2. 1. Our ancestors were filled with such love for their country that for many centuries no senator revealed the secret debates of the Conscript Fathers. The only

---

[10]The Caristia was a family reunion celebrated every year on February 22. It was, therefore, somewhat similar to the American festival of Thanksgiving, and its name actually derives from the Greek word *kharistia,* which means "thanksgiving."

[11]The most famous members of the aristocratic families mentioned here were Marcus Furius Camillus (dictator, 396 B.C.), who captured Veii; Scipio Africanus, who defeated Hannibal; Scipio Aemilianus, who destroyed Carthage and Numantia (in Spain); Gaius Fabricius Luscinus (cos, 282 B.C.), who fought against King Pyrrhus; and Marcus Claudius Marcellus (cos, 222 B.C.) and Fabius the Delayer, both of whom fought against Hannibal. The "divine Caesars" were Caesar and Augustus.

one to do so was Quintus Fabius Maximus, and he did it by accident. Fabius was going away to the countryside, and while he was going there he met Publius Crassus, who was heading back home to the city.[12] Fabius told him about the declaration of the Third Punic War, which had been discussed at a secret meeting of the Senate.[13] He remembered that Crassus had been elected as a quaestor three years before that, but did not realize that Crassus had not yet been enrolled in the senatorial order by the censors.[14] This was the only way in which people could enter the Senate house, even if they had held a high public office. But although Fabius had made an honorable mistake, he was severely reprimanded by the consuls: they did not want anyone to undermine the importance of secrecy, which is the best and most reliable bond uniting those who govern a country.

As a result, when Eumenes, the king of Asia, a man who really loved our city, announced to the Senate that Perseus was getting ready to wage war against the Roman people, nobody was allowed to find out what he had said or what the Fathers had replied until it became known that Perseus had been captured.[15]

The Senate house was the profound and trustworthy heart of our state, fortified on all sides with a palisade of healthy secrecy. When senators passed its threshold, they put private affections aside, and fell in love with our state. So you would have thought that nobody (I don't even want to say one person) had heard what had in fact been entrusted to the ears of many men.

2. 2. Magistrates[16] long ago behaved with great respect for their own rank and for the sovereignty of the Roman people, as can be seen from the following story. Many facts prove that they upheld its dignity, and one is their adamant insistence that they should always speak Latin exclusively in replying to Greeks. In fact, the magistrates even forced Greeks to speak through an interpreter, which got rid of that rhetorical fluency they are so good at, and they forced the Greeks to do so not only in our city, but also in Greece and Asia. Their intention was, of course, to make the Latin language honored and respected in every nation. Those good old magistrates were not behind in their literary education, but they believed that in every matter the Greek cloak should bow to the Roman toga, and they felt it would be disgraceful if the might and prestige of the empire were to be sacrificed to the sweet attractions of literature.[17]

[12]Quintus Fabius Maximus Servilianus (cos, 142 B.C.) was senior to Publius Licinius Crassus Dives Mucianus (cos, 131 B.C.).

[13]The Third Punic War started in 149 B.C.

[14]Publius Licinius Crassus Dives Mucianus had been a quaestor in 152 B.C. but was not yet a member of the Senate in 149 B.C.

[15]Eumenes II was king of Pergamum (which later became the Roman province of Asia) from 197 to 158 B.C. The Third Macedonian War lasted from 172 to 167 B.C. King Perseus was captured (see 5:1,8) and died in Italy (see 5:1,1c).

[16]The term *magistrate* referred to any of the major elected officials in Rome (see Glossary).

[17]The Romans probably decided to impose Latin as the language of international diplomacy in 282 B.C. after a Roman envoy had been insulted by the Tarentines for his poor Greek (see 2:2,5).

2. 3. So we must not accuse you of rustic severity, Marius, or condemn you for refusing to polish up your public speaking. You were an old man, you had been crowned twice with laurels, you were renowned for the trophies won over the Numidians and Germans.[18] As a conqueror you refused to polish yourself up with the eloquence of a conquered nation. I am sure you refused because you did not want to desert our ancestral customs so late in life by devoting your mind to this foreign intellectual exercise.

So who opened the door to this practice of making speeches in Greek, which deafens our senators? In my opinion, it was the rhetorician Molon, the man who inspired Cicero in his studies. It is well established that he, before any other foreigner, was heard in the Senate without using an interpreter. He did deserve this honor, since he had helped the most powerful master of Roman eloquence.[19]

The city of Arpinum is remarkably fortunate, whether you consider its most arrogant despiser of literature or its richest source of literary works.[20]

2. 4. Our ancestors strictly upheld the custom that nobody should come between a consul and his nearest lictor, even if someone happened to be accompanying the consul on public business. Only a consul's son, provided he was just a little boy, had the right to walk in front of his father. Quintus Fabius Maximus had been consul five times; he had held supreme power long beforehand and was now an old man.[21] His son, who was consul, invited him to walk in front, between him and a lictor, because he did not want his father to be pushed about by the crowd of hostile Samnites with whom they were going to parley.[22] But the custom I mentioned was upheld so strictly that Fabius Maximus refused to do this.

Fabius was also sent to Suessa by the Senate as a legate to his son, who was consul.[23] He noticed that his son had come outside the walls of the town to greet him, but he was indignant that out of eleven of the lictors, not one had ordered him to get down from his horse, so he remained sitting on it in a rage. When his son realized this, he ordered the nearest lictor to attend to this matter.[24] As soon as he heard these words, Fabius obeyed his son and said, "My son, I was not being

---

[18]Marius celebrated triumphs over King Jugurtha of Numidia in 104 B.C. and over the Germans in 101 B.C.

[19]Molon came from Rhodes and taught Cicero rhetoric from 79 to 77 B.C.

[20]Both Marius and Cicero came from Arpinum (in Latium).

[21]The father is Quintus Fabius Maximus Rullianus, who held five consulships between 322 and 295 B.C. and two dictatorships ("supreme power") in 315 and 313 B.C. He and his son were heroes of the Samnite Wars.

[22]The son is Quintus Fabius Maximus Gurges (cos, 292 B.C.).

[23]This story is about a completely different father and son who lived a century later: Fabius the Delayer and his son Quintus Fabius Maximus (cos, 213 B.C.). The father was serving as legate under his son. There were two places called Suessa in Latium, but this meeting actually took place in Suessula (in Campania, western Italy).

[24]Like all consuls, the son was attended by twelve lictors, but the first eleven were intimidated by the great Fabius. Even the chief lictor, who had the privilege of standing next to the consul, did not dare to challenge Fabius until the son ordered him to do so.

disrespectful toward your high rank, but I wanted to find out whether you knew how a consul should behave. I am well aware of the respect that is owed to a father, but in my judgment, public institutions are more important than personal respect."

2. 5. I have told of the glorious deeds of Quintus Fabius, and now some men of remarkable self-possession come to mind. They were sent as envoys by the Senate to demand reparations from Tarentum.[25] They were seriously insulted there, and one of them even had urine thrown at him. When they were presented at the theater, which is the Greek custom, they carried out their duties as envoys, saying exactly what they had been told. They did not complain about the insults to which they had been subjected, because they did not want to say anything that was not included in their instructions. Respect for our ancient customs was deep-rooted in their hearts, and it could not be dispelled by the profound resentment they felt because of the insults they had received. O city of Tarentum, you certainly put an end to your enjoyment of your riches! You were the envy of others because you had enjoyed such affluence for such a long time, you were puffed up with the splendor of your immediate good fortune, and you were full of disdain for a rugged but reliable courage that depended on itself alone, but all the time you were rushing blindly and madly onto the all-powerful sword of our empire.

2. 6. But I must move away from the decadent and abandoned morals of Tarentum and turn to the very strict customs of our ancestors. Long ago, the senators would regularly assemble at the place that is called the Senaculum today.[26] The senators did not wait for an edict before assembling there, so they could rush from the Senaculum straight to the Senate house if they were summoned.[27] They thought that a person had a dubious reputation as a citizen if he did not carry out his duty to the Republic by himself but rather had to be ordered to do it. If a man is forced to do something by a superior, that goes to the credit of the one who gives the order rather than the man who carries it out.

2. 7. I must also recall that the tribunes of the plebs were not allowed to enter the Senate house; seats were placed for them outside the doors.[28] The tribunes used to examine the decrees of the Fathers very carefully, and if they disapproved of any of the decrees, they would not allow them to be passed into law. The letter C used to be written at the bottom of ancient Senate decrees, and this mark meant

---

[25]This embassy went to Tarentum in 282 B.C. It led to the war against King Pyrrhus of Epirus.

[26]A Senaculum was a place where the Senate met, and there were three such places in Rome. Valerius is referring to the main Senaculum beside the Senate house.

[27]The consul would issue an edict to call a meeting of the Senate. Valerius says that in the good old days, the senators would already be waiting at the Senaculum just in case a meeting was called.

[28]The tribunes of the plebs were supposed to protect ordinary Romans from their aristocratic magistrates, whereas the Senate consisted entirely of former magistrates. See magistrate and tribune of the plebs in the Glossary.

[29]The Latin for "recommend" is *censere,* hence the letter C.

[30]The quaestors (see Glossary) were in charge of government finances.

that the tribunes had also recommended those decrees.[29] Although the tribunes were always vigilant on behalf of the plebs and preoccupied with restraining the power of the magistrates, they still allowed the state to provide the magistrates with silver vessels and golden rings; by these marks of distinction the tribunes hoped to make the prestige of the magistrates all the more splendid.

2. 8. But if the dignity of the magistrates was increased, they had to adhere to very strict standards of self-denial. When they sacrificed victims, the animal organs were taken to the quaestors of the treasury and put on sale.[30] The sacrifices of the Roman people brought honor to the immortal gods and self-restraint to mortal men, so at these very altars our generals learned to keep their hands clean. They valued self-denial so much that if a governor had been honest in administering a province, his debts were often paid off by the Senate. The senators saw that while these men were away, they had maintained the prestige of the state and the glory of the Senate, so they felt that it was unfair to the governors and dishonorable for the Senate if these men lost rank when they came home.

2. 9. Twice every year the young men of the equestrian order would fill the city for a display of their skills, and both these displays had been established by great men.

The custom of holding the Lupercalia was started by Romulus and Remus to express their joy when their grandfather, King Numitor of Alba Longa, allowed them to found a city under the Palatine Hill, where they had been reared.[31] Faustulus, the man who had reared them, encouraged them to start the Lupercalia, and Evander the Arcadian had previously consecrated this spot.[32] Goats were killed at a sacrifice, and the shepherds got carried away by the cheerful banquet and the plentiful supply of wine. The shepherds were then divided into two teams, tied the skins of the sacrificial victims around their waist, and jokingly chased anyone they met. This merry event is commemorated in the annual calendar of festivals.

It was Quintus Fabius, on the other hand, who started the custom that the equestrians should ride past on the ides of July wearing purple cloaks.[33]

This was the Quintus Fabius who had been censor with Publius Decius.[34] Political strife had flared up when the lowest classes had gained control of the assembly, so he ended the trouble by enrolling the entire mob that lived near the Forum into four tribes only, which he called the Urban Tribes.[35] He had made a name for himself earlier by his military exploits, but this deed saved the state and earned him the name of Maximus.

---

[31]The Lupercalia festival was held every year on February 15.

[32]Faustulus was the poor shepherd who saved the infants Romulus and Remus from death. Evander was from Arcadia (southern Greece) and had built a settlement on the future site of Rome.

[33]The colorful Review of the Equestrians took place every year on July 15.

[34]Quintus Fabius Maximus Rullianus (cos, 322 B.C.) and Publius Decius Mus (cos, 312 B.C.) were censors together in 304 B.C.

[35]The city population had been distributed among all thirty-one tribes, each of which had one electoral vote. By restricting the city population to the four old urban tribes, Rullianus ensured that they could only influence four electoral votes.

Chapter 3. Ancient Customs [of the Roman Army]

3. 1. We have to praise the modesty of the people too.[36] They tirelessly exposed themselves to the hardships and dangers of military service, and thereby made sure that their generals would not be forced to ask men without property to take the military oath.[37] Such men were suspect because of their extreme poverty, and the people did not trust them with weapons granted by the state.

This old tradition had been in force for a long time and was well established by then, but Marius abolished it by enlisting men without property as soldiers. He was a magnificent Roman citizen in all other respects, but he was aware that he was new to the political world and he had no great love for its old traditions. Besides, he knew that if the army legions kept up this old tradition of rejecting men from the lower classes, some commentator who envied his achievements might likewise reject Marius himself because he was a lower-class general. So he decided that the old snobbish way of recruiting the Roman army should be abolished, because such a rejection of the poor might ultimately lead people to reject his own glorious achievements.[38]

3. 2. The tradition of training soldiers in handling weapons was started by the consul Publius Rutilius, who was consul with Gnaeus Mallius.[39] There was no precedent set up by any previous general for Rutilius to follow, so he summoned trainers from the gladiatorial school of Gaius Aurelius Scaurus. That is how the finer arts of evading or inflicting blows became second nature to our legions. Rutilius created a fine mixture of skill with courage and courage with skill, so that their skill became braver under the impact of their courage, while their courage became more prudent by their acquisition of skill.

3. 3. The idea of using lightly armed troops was invented in wartime when our general, Fulvius Flaccus, was besieging Capua.[40] The Campanian cavalry kept on making attacks, and our cavalry were unable to stand up to them since ours were fewer in number.[41] The centurion, Quintus Navius, chose some men with agile bodies from the infantry, armed each of them with seven short spears with curved heads, and gave them a small shield for protection. He taught them to jump up quickly behind a man on horseback, and then quickly slide off again. Dropping these foot soldiers from the horses in the middle of a cavalry battle would make it easier for them to use their weapons effectively against both the men and the horses of the enemy. This strange new type of fighting was the one thing that helped us

---

[36]By the "people," Valerius means the property-owning classes among the Romans, who preferred to join the army themselves rather than allow the poor to bear arms.

[37]Citizens without property (see Glossary) were a specific social group in the Roman census.

[38]Marius allowed men without property to join the army when he was consul in 107 B.C.

[39]Publius Rutilius Rufus and Gnaeus Mallius Maximus were consuls in 105 B.C.

[40]Quintus Fulvius Flaccus was consul in 212 B.C. and started the siege of Capua (in Campania).

[41]The Campanians sided with the Carthaginians in the Second Punic War.

to counteract the underhanded behavior of the Campanians. Its inventor, Navius, was decorated for his deeds by his commander.

Chapter 4. Ancient Customs [of the Roman Theater]

4. 1. We must now step from army customs to the camp of the city—in other words, the theater. It often produces rowdy armies, and although it was intended for the worship of the gods and the delight of the public, it pollutes these religious and entertaining elements with the blood of civilians. Peace must blush to see men behave like this for the sake of theatrical fantasies.[42]

4. 2. Theatrical performances were started by the censors Messalla and Cassius,[43] but Publius Scipio Nasica brought in a law to auction off all the equipment belonging to their theater.[44] There was even a Senate decree declaring that nobody could set up seats in the city itself or within a mile of it, and that nobody could watch the games sitting down. Presumably the Senate wanted the natural manliness of the Roman nation to be well known so that we should stand even when relaxing our minds.

4. 3. For 558 years the Senate mingled with the people at the games. But the aediles Atilius Serranus and Lucius Scribonius ended this practice when they were organizing the games for the Mother of the Gods.[45] They followed a proposal of Scipio Africanus and had separate seats for the Senate and the people.[46] This deed alienated the hearts of the common people and seriously undermined Scipio's popularity.

4. 4. I shall now start from the beginning and explain why the games were instituted. During the consulship of Gaius Sulpicius Peticus and Gaius Licinius Stolo,[47] an unbearably virulent plague broke out, and it kept our state from warfare because we were so overwhelmed by our internal domestic problems. Eventually it seemed that we would find more help in discovering some new way of honoring the gods than in any human devices. Hymns were composed to placate the gods in heaven, and people took the time to listen to them.

---

[42]There were often violent riots at the theater.

[43]Marcus Valerius Messalla (cos, 161 B.C.) and Gaius Cassius Longinus (cos, 171 B.C.) started to build the first permanent stone theater when they were censors together in 154 B.C.

[44]Publius Cornelius Scipio Nasica Corculum (cos, 162 B.C.) got the Senate to demolish the stone theater in 151 B.C.

[45]Valerius is calculating (a little inaccurately) from the legendary foundation date of Rome, 753 B.C. Aulus Atilius Serranus (cos, 170 B.C.) and Lucius Scribonius Libo were aediles in 194 B.C.

[46]Scipio Africanus created this seating arrangement when he was consul in 194 B.C.

[47]Gaius Sulpicius Peticus and Gaius Licinius Stolo were consuls in 364 B.C.

Up until that time people had been happy with the spectacle in the circus that Romulus celebrated for the first time when the Romans had abducted the Sabine maidens; Romulus called this festival the Consualia.[48] But people always start off with something small and follow it up persistently, so the young people added actions to these lyrics that were full of respect toward the gods and jokingly moved their bodies in a clumsy and awkward way.

And that is what led people to bring in a performer from Etruria.[49] His graceful agility was an ancient skill of the curetes and also of the Lydians, which is where the Etruscans came from originally.[50] It was a delightful novelty for the Romans to see and it won them over. Since a performer was called *ister* in Etruscan, they gave the name *histrio* to a stage actor.

After that, the theatrical art gradually moved on to stage medleys,[51] and the poet Livius was the first to get spectators used to the idea of having plays with a plot.[52] He used to act in his own plays, but he was called back for too many encores by the public and lost his voice. So he got a slave to speak and a flute player to play while he acted out the part in silence.

The Atellan farces were brought in from the Oscans;[53] this type of entertainment was kept within bounds by Italian puritanism, so it does not have a bad reputation. People who act in it are not expelled from their tribe or forbidden to join the army.[54]

4. 5. Since the origin of the other games is obvious from their names, it does not seem unreasonable to explain how the Secular Games began, since their origin is not so well known.[55] The city and its territory were being devastated by a great plague, and Valesius, a rich man who lived in the country, had two sons and a daughter whose illness was driving even the doctors to despair. He was going to the fireplace to get hot water for them, and he went on his knees and begged the family Lares to transfer the danger from his sons onto his own head.[56] Then a voice came saying that he could save them if he would bring them at once down the

[48]The Consualia were held every year on August 21 and December 15. The festival took place in the Circus Maximus and included chariot races.

[49]After the digression about the Consualia, Valerius has come back to 364 B.C. when Etruscans were brought in to perform on stage.

[50]The curetes were sacred dancers in Crete, and the Lydians were a people from the west coast of Asia Minor. The Romans believed that the Etruscans came originally from Lydia.

[51]The stage medley (*satura*) was a song and dance routine.

[52]Lucius Livius Andronicus put on his first play in 240 B.C.

[53]Atellan farces were an ancient Italian institution, involving stock characters who reappeared in each farce. The Oscans were the peoples of south and central Italy.

[54]Other actors were subject to these penalties.

[55]The Secular Games were celebrated about once every century. The most recent Secular Games had been held by Augustus in 17 B.C.

[56]The family Lares were spirits who looked after the home. They were worshiped at the family fireplace.

river Tiber to Tarentum.[57] Once he got there he would cure them with water taken from the altar of Father Dis and Proserpina.[58]

Valesius was very confused by this prediction, since he was being told to go on a long and dangerous journey by sea. But doubtful hope was better than definite anxiety, so he brought the children to the banks of the Tiber at once—he lived in a farmhouse near the village of Eretum, in the Sabine region—and setting off for Ostia by boat, he landed at the Campus Martius early in the night.[59] The sick children were thirsty and he wanted to help them. There was no fire on the ship, but the captain said he could see smoke nearby, and he told Valesius to get off at Tarentum, for that was the name of the place. Valesius eagerly grabbed a cup, filled it with water from the river, and was already feeling much happier as he brought the cup to the place the smoke was coming from. He felt sure that he was hot on the trail and that he was close to the remedy granted by the gods. He found smoldering ground there rather than the remains of a fire, but he held firmly to his omen, picked up a few scraps of firewood that he was lucky enough to find there, and kept blowing on them until he produced a flame. With this, he heated the water and gave it to the children to drink. They drank it, fell into a wholesome sleep, and were suddenly released from the grip of this long-term illness.

They told their father that in their sleep they had seen some god or other wiping their bodies all over with a sponge. The god instructed them that dark victims should be sacrificed at the altar of Father Dis and Proserpina and that banquets for the gods and nighttime games should be celebrated there, because it was from there that the drink was brought to them. Valesius had seen no altar in that place, so he thought he was being asked to set one up there, and he went off to the city to buy an altar. He left men behind to build the foundations, and told them to dig down until they reached a firm substratum. They followed their master's orders, but when they had dug up the earth and reached a depth of twenty feet, they found an altar bearing an inscription to Father Dis and Proserpina. A slave reported this to Valesius, and when he heard about it, he gave up the idea of buying an altar, and sacrificed black-skinned victims (which were called "dark" victims in the old days) at Tarentum. He celebrated games and banquets for the gods for three nights in a row, since that is how many children of his had been freed from danger.

Valerius Publicola, who was our first consul, was eager to help his fellow citizens, and followed the example of Valesius.[60] On behalf of the state, he made

---

[57]Tarentum was in Calabria (southern Italy), so Valesius would have to go there by sea, but it later turns out that the mysterious voice was talking about a different place called Tarentum.

[58]Dis and Proserpina were the gods in charge of the Underworld.

[59]Eretum was in the Sabine region, on the border with Latium. Eretum was upriver from Rome and Ostia was at the mouth of the Tiber, so Valesius would pass by Rome on his journey downriver to the sea. The Campus Martius ("Plain of Mars") was a large field lying between the city walls and the river Tiber.

[60]Publius Valerius Publicola (cos, 509 B.C.) organized the Secular Games when he was consul again in 504 B.C.

sacred vows at the same altar, slaughtered black-skinned bulls to Dis and black-skinned cows to Proserpina, and held banquets for the gods and games for three nights. Then the altar was buried underground, just as it had been originally.

4. 6. As people grew richer, the sacred games followed fashion by becoming more luxurious.[61] This trend led Quintus Catulus to imitate the luxury of Campania, so he became the first man to cover the seating area with an awning to shade the spectators.[62]

Pompey was ahead of everyone else in counteracting the summer heat by having water run down through channels.[63]

Claudius Pulcher decorated the backdrop in a variety of colors; before that, it used to be covered with panels that had nothing painted on them.[64]

Gaius Antonius put a silver border around the entire backdrop, Petreius put a gold one, and Quintus Catulus put an ivory one.[65]

The Lucullus family made the stage revolve, and Publius Lentulus Spinther decorated it with silver stage properties.[66]

Originally the parade had worn red tunics, but Marcus Scaurus had them wear costumes of the most refined type.[67]

4. 7. The first gladiatorial show at Rome was held in the Forum Boarium[68] during the consulship of Appius Claudius and Marcus Fulvius.[69] Marcus and Decimus, the sons of Brutus Pera, put on this show at the funeral of their father to honor his ashes.[70]

Athletic contests were first put on through the generosity of Marcus Scaurus.[71]

[61]In Rome, theatrical and sporting events took place during religious festivals, so all games were sacred.

[62]Quintus Lutatius Catulus (cos, 78 B.C.) celebrated games in 69 B.C. when he dedicated the reconstructed temple of Jupitor on the Capitol.

[63]Pompey built the first permanent stone theater in Rome. He dedicated it with sumptous games in 55 B.C.

[64]Gaius Claudius Pulcher (cos, 92 B.C.) was an aedile when he celebrated games in 99 B.C.

[65]These politicians celebrated games with theatrical performances when they were praetors. Gaius Antonius Hybrida (cos, 63 B.C.) was praetor in 66 B.C., Marcus Petreius was praetor in 64 B.C., and Quintus Lutatius Catulus (cos, 78 B.C.) was praetor in 81 B.C.

[66]These politicians celebrated games when they were aediles. Lucius Licinius Lucullus (cos, 74 B.C.) and Marcus Terentius Varro Lucullus (cos, 73 B.C.) were aediles in 79 B.C.; Publius Cornelius Lentulus Spinther (cos, 57 B.C.) was an aedile in 63 B.C.

[67]Marcus Aemilius Scaurus celebrated these games when he was an aedile in 58 B.C.

[68]The Forum Boarium was beside the Tiber.

[69]Appius Claudius Caudex and Marcus Fulvius Flaccus were consuls in 264 B.C.

[70]Decimus Junius Pera had been consul in 266 B.C.

[71]Marcus Aemilius Scaurus was aedile in 58 B.C.

Chapter 5. Ancient Customs [of Roman Society]

5. 1. Nobody had seen a gilded statue in our city or in any part of Italy until Manius Acilius Glabrio set up an equestrian statue to his father in the temple of Pietas.[72] He had dedicated the temple himself during the consulship of Publius Cornelius Lentulus and Marcus Baebius Tamphilus,[73] when his prayers had been granted and he had defeated King Antiochus at Thermopylae.[74]

5. 2. For many centuries, the civil law was kept secret and was included with the rituals and ceremonies of the immortal gods, so it was known to the pontiffs alone. Then Gnaeus Flavius, a scribe and the son of a freed slave, was elected curule aedile, to the great indignation of the nobility.[75] He made the civil law public and displayed the calendar of festivals to almost everyone in the Forum.

Flavius once went to visit his fellow aedile, who was sick. The bedroom was packed with a crowd of nobles, and they would not make room for him to sit down. So Flavius ordered his state chair to be brought in and sat on that. He upheld his status as a public official and took revenge on their contempt.

5. 3. Investigations into poisoning were unknown in Roman custom and law, but they began when it was revealed that several married women had committed this crime. They were secretly and treacherously killing their husbands with poison, but they were exposed by the testimony of one slave girl. Some of them were tried and sentenced to death; the number reached 170.[76]

5. 4. The guild of flute players usually draws attention to itself in the Forum. While others are carrying on serious public and private business, the flute players have their faces covered with a mask, wear multicolored clothes, and play their music. Here is how they won this freedom to do as they please.

In accordance with an ancient custom, flute players could eat in the temple of Jupiter, but one day they were forbidden to do this.[77] They were very angry and went off to Tibur.[78] The Senate was not happy that sacred rites would have to be conducted without their services, so it sent envoys to the people of Tibur and asked them to bring the flute players back to the temples of Rome as a favor to the

---

[72]Manius Acilius Glabrio (cos, 154 B.C.) inaugurated the temple of Pietas and raised a statue to his father, Manius Acilius Glabrio (cos, 191 B.C.) in 181 B.C.

[73]Publius Cornelius Cethegus and Marcus Baebius Tamphilus were consuls in 181 B.C.

[74]Valerius is confused. It was the father, Manius Acilius Glabrio (cos, 191 B.C.), who defeated King Antiochus the Great of Syria in 191 B.C. and promised to build the temple, but the son, Mancius Acilius Glabrio (cos, 154 B.C.), who carried out his father's promise and built it.

[75]Gnaeus Flavius was curule aedile in 304 B.C.

[76]The consuls Gaius Valerius Potitus and Marcus Claudius Marcellus carried out this witch-hunt in 331 B.C.

[77]The flute players were expelled from the temple of Jupiter by the censors in 312 B.C.

[78]The flute players went off to Tibur (modern Tivoli, in the hills west of Rome) in 311 B.C. and were brought back the same year.

Senate. The flute players refused to change their minds, so the people of Tibur pretended to hold a holiday banquet, wore the flute players out with wine and sleepiness, and had them brought to our city on wagons.

Their ancient privilege was restored to the flute players, and they were given the right to act the fool. The reason they wear masks is that they are ashamed of the trick played on them when they were drunk.

5. 5. The simple eating habits of people long ago are a sure sign of their kindness and self-restraint. It was no disgrace for the greatest men to lunch and dine in the open air. They certainly did not have the types of banquet that would embarrass them if ordinary people saw them. They were so intent on self-restraint that they had porridge more often than bread, and that is why the thing we call a cake at sacrifices is made out of wheat flour and salt, why the inner organs of sacrificial victims are sprinkled with wheat flour, and why we put porridge in front of the sacred chickens when we are looking for the auspices. People long ago kept the gods happy by offering first fruits and little portions from what they ate themselves, and their offerings were all the more effective because they were so simple.

5. 6. People long ago generally paid homage to the gods in the hope that the gods would confer benefits on them, but they worshiped Febris in her temples in the hope that she would do them less harm.[79] Some of her temples survive to this day; there is one on the Palatine, another in the square with the monuments of Marius,[80] and a third at the top of the Long Street. Any remedies that had been applied to the bodies of sick people were brought to these temples. These remedies had been invented to soothe the mental torment that people go through, but they had some basis in experience. On the whole, people looked after their health by hard work, the surest and most reliable protection against illness. Their simple way of life was more or less the mother of their good health; it was hostile to luxurious banquets, unfavorable to excessive drinking, and opposed to overindulgence in sexual pleasure.

Chapter 6. Ancient Customs [of Foreign Countries]

6. 1. The state of Sparta was very close to our ancestors in its austerity, and it held the same principles as they did. In keeping with the very strict laws of Lycurgus,[81] the state for a long time prevented its citizens from looking to Asia, because they might be captivated by its enticements and fall into a decadent way of life. The Spartans had heard that luxury and excessive spending and all kinds of unnecessary pleasures derived from that place, and that the Ionians were the first to invent the custom of wearing perfume and garlands at parties and having dessert

[79]Febris was the goddess of fever.

[80]These monuments were trophies celebrating the victories of Marius.

[81]Lycurgus was the legendary lawgiver of Sparta.

afterward, which are significant incitements to decadence. The Spartans took pleasure in hard work and endurance, so it is not at all surprising that they did not
want the firm muscles of their country to be made soft and weak by the corruption of foreign pleasures. They saw that it was much easier to move from virtue to
decadence than from decadence to virtue. Their own leader, Pausanias, showed
that their fears were not unfounded.[82] He had performed the greatest deeds, but as
soon as he gave himself up to the ways of Asia, he lost all shame and his courage
was undermined by the effeminate lifestyle of that place.

    6. 2. The army of that state would never go into battle until the men had urged
themselves on and heated up their spirits with the sound of flutes playing an
anapestic rhythm.[83] The lively and repeated sound of that beat encouraged them to
attack the enemy forcefully. They used to wear red tunics in battle to disguise and
hide the blood from their wounds, not that the sight of the wounds would terrify
them, but it might make the enemy a little more confident.

    6. 3. The Spartans had extraordinary spirit and courage in war; the Athenians
come next because they exercise such good sense in peacetime. In Athens, idle
men, drooping with apathy, are hauled off like criminals from their hiding places
to the Forum, and they are accused of behavior that is disgraceful even if it is not
a serious crime.[84]

    6. 4. In the same city, the revered council of the Areopagus would diligently
investigate what each Athenian citizen did and how he supported himself with his
work.[85] This made people follow the path of honor, because they recollected that
they would have to explain their way of life.

    6. 5. The same city of Athens first introduced the custom of honoring good
citizens with a garland when it tied together two small branches of olive and put
them around the head of the famous Pericles.[86] This was an admirable custom,
whether you would choose to look at what they did or the person they honored.
Such honors are the most effective incitement to virtue, and Pericles above all others deserved to be the first to be presented with such a reward.

    6. 6. Well, what about this Athenian law? It is well worth mentioning! If a
freed slave is proved to be ungrateful by his former master, he is deprived of his
right to freedom! "I will no longer regard you as a citizen since you so wickedly
underestimate this great honor," the law says, "and I cannot be brought to believe
that you will be any good to our city since I see that you are so bad to your household. Go away now and be a slave again since you did not know how to live as a
free man."

---

[82]Pausanias was the Spartan general who defeated the Persians in 479 B.C., but he was later
condemned and put to death for intriguing with the Persians.

[83]The anapestic rhythm consists of two short beats followed by one long beat: di-di-dum.

[84]This law was attributed to the Athenian lawgiver, Solon, who was archon in 594 B.C.

[85]The council of the Areopagus lost these powers in 461 B.C.

[86]Pericles was the leading democratic politician in Athens from about 460 B.C. until his
death in 429 B.C.

6. 7. The Massilians have the same custom to the present day.[87] They are quite remarkable for their austere way of life, their adherance to old ways, and their love for the Roman people. They allow a slave's freedom to be revoked three times, but if they find out that the same slave has cheated his master three times, they think he should not be helped after making a fourth mistake. It is his own fault if he loses his rights because he has exposed himself to that risk too many times.

The same state of Massilia was a keen guardian of strict morality. It would not allow mimes to be shown on the stage, because their plots consist, for the most part, of sexual activity and it did not want people to get into the habit of looking at such scenes in case they might feel they were free to imitate them.

The city closes its gates against all those charlatans who try to support a lazy lifestyle by pretending to be religious. It thinks that such false and deceptive cults should be done away with.

Since the founding of Massilia, there has been a sword in the place where criminals are executed. The sword is eaten away with rust and can hardly function, but it shows how the Massilians preserve everything that has been handed down by ancient tradition even in the smallest details.

The Massilians have two chests lying before the city gates; one is for the bodies of free men, the other is for the bodies of slaves. The bodies of the dead are carried on a wagon to the place of burial without any wailing or lamentation. Mourning is confined to the day of the funeral, and it ends with a sacrifice in the home and a banquet for friends and relatives: What is the point in giving in to human sorrow or resenting the gods because they do not want to share their immortality with us?

In that city, a poison made from hemlock is kept by the state, and it is given to anyone who has explained to the Six Hundred (that is the name of their senate) why he wants to die. They hold an inquiry with manly kindness, and they do not allow anyone to end his life casually, but if someone has a good reason for leaving this life, they give him a quick way of dying. In this way, people who have been too unfortunate or too fortunate end their lives in a way that has been approved. Each of these circumstances gives them reasonable grounds for ending their lives— the unfortunate ones do not want their misery to last, the lucky ones do not want their good fortune to desert them.

6. 8. I think this custom of the Massilians does not come from Gaul; it comes from Greece and from there it was brought to Massilia.[88] I think this because on my journey to Asia with Sextus Pompeius, I noticed that they have the same custom on the island of Ceos when I came to the town of Iulis.[89] It happened by chance that a woman who was of the highest rank but very elderly had explained to her fellow citizens why she had to leave this life, so she decided to end it now

[87]Massilia was in southern Gaul (modern Marseille).

[88]Massilia was founded by Greek colonists.

[89]Sextus Pompeius (cos, A.D. 14) was governor of Asia in A.D. 25. Valerius mentions his friend again at 4:7,ext.2. This story of their trip to Ceos (an island near Attica) is the only personal one that Valerius includes in his entire work.

with poison. She considered it very important that Pompeius was there since his presence would make her death more glorious. Being blessed with every virtue and renowned for his kindness, that great man could not reject her pleas. He went up to her and made a lovely speech that flowed from his mouth as if it were a rich fountain of eloquence. For a long time he tried in vain to dissuade her from the plan she had formed, but in the end he allowed her to carry out her objective. She was over ninety years old, but her mind and body were in excellent condition.

Her couch, as far as I could tell, was made up more elegantly than it would be on a normal day, and as she lay on it, she propped herself up with her elbow and spoke: "Sextus Pompeius, may the gods I am leaving (rather than the ones I am heading for!) repay your kindness in urging me to stay alive and in agreeing to witness my suicide.[90] I have always experienced the good side of Fortune's face, and I don't want to be forced to experience her grim side simply because I long to see the light. So I am giving up the remaining period of my life in exchange for a good ending, especially since I shall be leaving two daughters and a crowd of grandchildren after me."

She urged her family to love one another, divided her fortune among them, and entrusted her elder daughter with the cult of her soul and the rituals of her family. Then with her right hand, which did not shake, she took the cup in which the poison had been prepared. She poured libations to Mercury and called upon his divine power to give her an easy journey and escort her to the better region of the Underworld.[91] She eagerly gulped down the fatal potion, and from time to time she told us which parts of her body were becoming stiff. When she told us that the stiffness was now getting close to her vital organs and to her heart, she asked her daughters for their hands so that they could carry out their last obligation to her by closing her eyes. We Romans were astounded by this unusual sight, but when she sent us away, our eyes were filled with tears.

6. 9. But I must return to the people of Massilia, which is where I was before I went off on this digression. Nobody with a weapon is allowed to enter their city, and there is a man on the spot who takes any weapon, keeps it safe, and returns it when the owner is leaving the city. They are very hospitable, and they want to be kind to visitors, but they want to keep themselves safe too.

6. 10. When someone has left the walls of Massilia behind they run into the old custom of the Gauls. Tradition has it that the Gauls will lend you money, but you will have to pay back the loan in the Underworld. They do this because they are convinced that human souls are immortal. I would call them fools, if these men in their breeches did not have the same belief as Pythagoras in his Greek cloak.[92]

---

[90]The gods she is leaving are the cheerful Olympian gods. The gods she is heading for are the sinister gods of the Underworld.

[91]Mercury was the god of travel and commerce, and he escorted the dead to the Underworld.

[92]Breeches were considered typical of Gaul. Pythagoras, the sixth century thinker, was as famous for his religious beliefs, which included reincarnation, as for his mathematical genius.

6. 11. So the philosophy of the Gauls is greedy and based on making a profit, but that of the Cimbrians and Celtiberians is lively and brave.[93] They jump for joy when they are at war, because they will leave this life in a glorious and happy way, but they lament when they are sick, because they will die in a disgusting and miserable way. The Celtiberians even think it is a disgrace to survive a battle when their leader dies since they promised to protect him with their lives. You would have to praise the resoluteness of both these peoples, because the Cimbrians and Celtiberians believe that they must bravely uphold the security of their country and the spirit of loyalty among fellow soldiers.

6. 12. One of the tribes in Thrace rightly expects people to admire their wisdom in celebrating people's births with tears and their funerals with rejoicing.[94] They do not follow the theories of any learned men, but they have discovered the true nature of our human condition. All creatures naturally want to stay alive, but this often makes them act disgracefully and endure humiliations. Let us get rid of this desire, and we shall discover that the end of our life is considerably more happy and blessed than its beginning.

6. 13. So the Lycians are quite right to put on a woman's dress whenever they have to go into mourning.[95] They will be struck by the incongruity of the clothes and this will make them all the more ready to cast aside their silly grief.

6. 14. But why should I praise men for being so very brave and practical? Consider the women of India. It is their ancestral custom that several women should be married to one man, and when he dies they have a competition to decide which of them he loved the most. The winner jumps for joy, and she is led off by her happy-faced friends and relatives. She flings herself on top of her husband's funeral pyre, and she is burned alive on it beside her husband's body as if she were the happiest of women. The wives who lost the competition stay on in this life in sadness and grief.[96]

Proclaim the courage of the Cimbrians to all, add on the loyalty of the Celtiberians, join the courageous wisdom of the Thracians to that, attach the clever way of dispelling grief that the Lycians have invented; in spite of all this, you will not admire any of them more than the funeral pyre of the Indians and the faithful wife who climbs onto it as if it were a marriage bed, carefree in the face of death.

6. 15. Next to the glory of these women I shall put the disgraceful behavior of the Phoenician women. The contrast will make their behavior seem all the more disgusting. There is a temple of Venus at Sicca, where respectable ladies get together, and then they go off to make money and amass a dowry by degrading their

---

[93]The Cimbrians came from Denmark and marched on Italy in 101 B.C. The Celtiberians lived in eastern Spain and resisted the Romans from 197 to 133 B.C.

[94]Thrace (modern Bulgaria) was regarded as a wild and warlike country.

[95]Lycia was on the south coast of Asia Minor.

[96]The Indian custom of burning widows alive is called *suttee* and incidents still occur, even though it has been illegal for almost two centuries.

bodies. It is, of course, by means of such dishonorable unions that they intend to enter the honorable union of marriage.[97]

6. 16. The Persians had a very admirable custom. They would not see their children until the children reached the age of seven. This enabled them to endure the loss of their little ones with resignation.

6. 17. We should not even criticize the kings of Numidia if, in accordance with the custom of their nation, they refused to kiss any human being.[98] Everyone agrees that whatever is placed in a high and exalted position should be free of any humble or everyday associations, and thus it will be all the more venerable.

Chapter 7. Military Discipline

Preface

I come now to the chief glory and mainstay of the Roman Empire, a characteristic that has fortunately been preserved intact and unchanged to the present day: the strong bond of military discipline. The serene and quiet enjoyment of blessed peace rests in its protective embrace.

Roman Stories

7. 1. Scipio Aemilianus won his grandfather's title by destroying Carthage.[99] He was then sent to Spain during his consulship to crush the insolent pride of the city of Numantia, which had grown worse through the fault of our previous commanders.[100] The minute he entered the camp, he made a proclamation that everything the soldiers had acquired for their pleasure should be confiscated and removed. It is a definite fact that a huge number of peddlers and camp followers, as well as two thousand prostitutes, had to leave the camp then. Our army, terrified of death, had recently disgraced itself by making a dishonorable treaty, but once it was cleared of this filthy and shameful scum, its courage was roused and revived. Numantia had been so fierce and confident, but now our army burned it down, destroyed its buildings, and razed it to the ground.[101] The wretched surrender by

---

[97]Sicca was a Phoenician colony in north Africa, between Carthage and Numidia. Temple prostitutes were found in sanctuaries of the Phoenician goddess Astarte (Venus).

[98]Numidia was a kingdom in north Africa (modern Algeria).

[99]Scipio Aemilianus was the grandson (by adoption) of Scipio Africanus. He received the title of Africanus after destroying Carthage in 146 B.C. (his full name was, therefore, Publius Cornelius Scipio Aemilianus Africanus).

[100]Scipio Aemilianus was consul (for the second time) in 134 B.C. He went to Spain to crush the city of Numantia and complete the conquest of the country.

[101]Scipio Aemilianus destroyed Numantia in 133 B.C. (see 3:2,ext.7 and 7:6,ext.2).

Mancinus was proof that our military discipline had been neglected,[102] and the splendid triumph of Scipio Aemilianus was a reward for its restoration.[103]

7. 2. Metellus followed the principles of Scipio Aemilianus.[104] During his consulship he took command of our army in Africa, which had been ruined in the war against Jugurtha by the excessive indulgence of Spurius Albinus.[105] With all the resources at his command, Metellus struggled to restore the sort of discipline that the army used to have long ago. Rather than dealing with particular aspects of the problem, he solved the whole problem at once and restored military discipline to its former condition. He immediately removed all peddlers from the camp, and he forbade the sale of cooked food. When the army was marching, he did not allow any soldiers to use slaves or pack animals; they had to carry their own equipment and food themselves. And he kept changing the location of his camp. He always had the camp properly protected with a palisade and ditch, as if Jugurtha was constantly nearby.

What progress did he make by restoring the self-restraint of his soldiers and making them work hard again? The answer is obvious. He defeated the enemy over and over again, and he raised lots of trophies, whereas the Roman soldiers had never managed to see Jugurtha on the run when they had serving been under a self-seeking general.

7. 3. Commanders did a lot for military discipline when they ignored family ties and did not hesitate to uphold and punish their relatives for infringements against it, even though this brought disgrace on their own family. For example, during the war against the runaway slaves in Sicily, the consul Publius Rupilius expelled his own son-in-law Quintus Fabius from the province because, through his negligence, Fabius had lost the citadel of Tauromenium.[106]

7. 4. The consul Gaius Aurelius Cotta had to cross over to Messana to take the auspices again, and he put a relative of his, Publius Aurelius Pecuniola, in charge of the siege of Lipara.[107] But when Pecuniola made a blunder, let the siege earthenwork go on fire, and almost allowed our camp to be captured, Cotta had him flogged with the rod and forced him to continue his military service as a simple foot soldier.

7. 5. The censor Quintus Fulvius Flaccus expelled from the Senate his own brother, Fulvius, with whom he shared an inherited property. The censor did this

---

[102]Gaius Hostilius Mancinus had surrendered to the Numantines in 137 B.C. (see 1:6,7).

[103]Scipio Aemilianus celebrated a triumph in Rome in 132 B.C.

[104]Quintus Caecilius Metellus Numidicus (cos, 109 B.C.) commanded the Roman army in Numidia from 109 to 107 B.C.

[105]Under Spurius Postumius Albinus (cos, 110 B.C.) the Roman army had been defeated by King Jugurtha of Numidia.

[106]The consul Publius Rupilius brought the First Slave War in Sicily to an end in 132 B.C. Quintus Fabius Maximus Eburnus (cos, 116 B.C.) served under him as quaestor. Tauromenium was on the east coast of Sicily.

[107]Gaius Aurelius Cotta was consul and Publius Aurelius Pecuniola was a military tribune in 252 B.C. during the Sicilian campaign of the First Punic War. Lipara was off the north coast of Sicily, whereas Messana was on the northeast corner of Sicily.

because his brother had had the nerve to send the legion, in which he served as military tribune, back home without being ordered to do so by the consul.[108]

These stories do not deserve to be told so briefly, but I am being urged on by even greater ones. What could be so difficult a task as to force someone to return home in disgrace, even though you belong to the same family and share the same ancestral death masks;[109] or to humiliate someone and have him flogged with the rod, even though both of you have the same name and family and are united by a long and ancient relationship; or to turn the glare of a censor against your own dear brother?

If we were to give just one of these stories to each of the most famous states, they would consider themselves entitled to boast about their great military discipline.

7. 6. But our city has spread all kinds of extraordinary stories across the entire world. The axes of our generals are found dripping with their own blood, because no breach of military order must go unpunished. When these axes come out of the camp our reaction is mixed: in public we find them impressive but in private we find them tragic, so we are not sure whether it is our duty to congratulate the generals first or to commiserate with them. My mind is, therefore, unsettled when I recall your stories, Postumius Tubertus and Manlius Torquatus, the strictest over-seers of military behavior. I can see that I shall be overwhelmed by the weight of your well-deserved reputations, and that I shall reveal the shortcomings of my talent rather than give a fair representation of your qualities.

You, Postumius, had a son, Aulus Postumius, and you wanted him to carry on your family and the rites of your household gods: when he was a charming baby, you cuddled him in your arms and gave him kisses; when he was a boy, you taught him to read and write; when he was a young man, you taught him to fight; he was upright and brave, he loved you and his country equally. But when you were dictator, he rushed forward from his position, relying on his own initiative rather than waiting for your orders, and he defeated the enemy.[110] He had won, but you ordered him to be beheaded with an axe; you were his father, but you had the strength to say the words that would put this command into effect. But I know for certain that however bright the day was, your eyes were covered in darkness, and that you were unable to look on as the extraordinary command that required such courage was carried out.

Your case was similar, Torquatus. You were consul during the war against the Latins when your son was challenged by Geminus Maecius, the commander of the Tusculans, and went over to fight against him without letting you know. He won a glorious victory and was bringing back his spectacular spoils when you ordered a lictor to seize him and slaughter him in the way we kill a sacrificial victim. You

---

[108]Quintus Fulvius Flaccus (cos, 179 B.C.) was censor in 174 B.C. His brother, Marcus Fulvius Flaccus, had served as a military tribune in 180 B.C. during the war against the Ligurians.

[109]Roman families kept ancestral death masks (see Glossary) in the home.

[110]Aulus Postumius Tubertus was dictator in 431 B.C. during a war against the Aequians, who lived east of Latium.

felt that it was better for a father to do without a brave son than for our fatherland to do without military discipline.[111]

7. 7. Well, do we not think that the dictator Lucius Quinctius Cincinnatus showed great spirit after he had defeated the Aequiculi and sent them under the yoke?[112] At that time, he forced the consul Lucius Minucius to resign, because the same enemy had besieged his camp.[113] Cincinnatus felt that Minucius was unworthy of the highest executive office, because he had kept himself safe not by his courage but by a ditch and a palisade, and he had not been ashamed to have Roman soldiers cooped up behind barricaded gates and trembling with fear. The twelve fasces symbolize the highest executive office and the highest honor conferred by the Senate, the equestrian order, and the entire plebs. Latium and the might of all Italy are ruled by their command, but they were battered and broken by the criticism of the dictator and yielded to him. To prevent the glory of the army from being insulted with impunity, the consul, who has the power to punish every crime, was punished himself.

It was with such propitiatory offerings, if I may describe them as such, that we used to appease your divinity, o Mars, father of our empire, whenever we deviated in any way from your auspices. We used to offer you the disgrace of our relatives and our in-laws and our brothers, the death of our sons, the degrading resignation of our consuls.

7. 8. The story that follows is of the same type. When Papirius was dictator, his master of the horse, Quintus Fabius Rullianus, acted against his orders and led the army into battle.[114] Fabius returned to the camp, but even though he had defeated the Samnites,[115] the dictator was unmoved by his courage, his success, or his noble birth; he ordered that the rods be readied and Fabius stripped. What an extraordinary sight! This man was Rullianus, he was the master of the horse, and he was victorious, but he handed himself over to the lictors who ripped his clothes apart and stripped him. The lictors were getting ready to lacerate him with their flogging, to open up the wounds he had received in the battle with a brutal beating, and to cover with blood the honor he had just won by his splendid victories. At this point, the army pleaded with Papirius, and Fabius was given the opportunity of fleeing to the city, but he asked the Senate for help in vain: Papirius persevered relentlessly in demanding that Fabius be punished. So Rullianus' father, who had

---

[111]Titus Manlius Imperiosus Torquatus was consul and his son, Titus Manlius Torquatus, was a prefect in his army in 340 B.C. when the Latin War started. Tusculum (modern Frascati) was in Latium, not far from Rome.

[112]It was the custom to humiliate defeated soldiers by making them crawl under a wooden bar called the yoke.

[113]Lucius Minucius Esquilinus Augurinus (cos, 458 B.C.) was defeated in a battle against the Aequian hill tribes on the borders of Latium; Lucius Quinctius Cincinnatus (cos, 460 B.C.) was appointed dictator and saved the day.

[114]Lucius Papirius Cursor (cos, 326 B.C.) was dictator and Quintus Fabius Maximus Rullianus (cos, 322 B.C.) was his master of the horse in 325 B.C. during the Second Samnite War.

[115]The Samnites lived in central Italy.

been dictator himself and had held three consulships, was obliged to bring the matter before the people and humbly beg the tribunes of the plebs to intervene on his son's behalf.[116] Even this could not restrain the harsh severity of Papirius. Finally, Papirius was induced to stop by the entire body of citizens and by the tribunes of the plebs themselves, but he swore that he was giving up the punishment as a concession not to Fabius but to the people and the power of the tribunes.

7. 9. When Lucius Calpurnius Piso was consul and fighting a war against the runaway slaves in Sicily, his cavalry prefect, Gaius Titius, was surrounded by a crowd of enemy soldiers and surrendered his weapons to them.[117] Piso inflicted the following kinds of disgrace on his prefect: he ordered Titius to remain at the general's headquarters from morning until night throughout the whole period of his military service wearing a toga with the edges cut off, an unbelted tunic, and no shoes. The consul did not allow Titius to socialize with the men or to use the baths; he also took away the horses from the cavalry units Titius had commanded and transferred them to the auxiliary units of sling throwers.

The great disgrace they had inflicted on their country was punished by their own disgrace, and Piso did it to produce the following effect: these soldiers had longed so much to save their lives that they had allowed runaway slaves, who deserved crucifixion, to set up trophies over them. Although they were free citizens, they had not been ashamed when they were forced by the hands of slaves to go under the disgraceful yoke, so now they would find out that life too can be bitter, and even if they had once dreaded death like women, they would soon long for it like men.

7. 10. Quintus Metellus was no less harsh than Piso.[118] When he was fighting at Contrebia, Metellus stationed five cohorts to hold a position, but they were driven from it by enemy forces.[119] He ordered them to win back that position at once, not because he hoped they could possibly regain the position they had lost, but because he wanted to punish them for their bad conduct in the previous engagement by exposing them to certain danger in the following one. He even made a proclamation that if any one of them ran away and headed for the camp, he should be killed as if he were an enemy soldier. This harsh reaction cowed the soldiers, but even though they were physically exhausted and their minds were full of despair for their lives, they managed to overcome the fact that the terrain put them at a disadvantage and that the enemy outnumbered them. Compulsion is a very effective way of hardening weak-willed men.

7. 11. Quintus Fabius Maximus was in the same province, and he was anxious to crush and undermine the ferocious spirit of that nation.[120] He was very kind by

[116]Marcus Fabius Ambustus, the father of Rullianus, had been consul in 360, 356, and 354 B.C. and dictator in 351 B.C.

[117]Lucius Calpurnius Piso Frugi was consul and Gaius Titius was the prefect in charge of the allied cavalry in 133 B.C. during the First Slave War in Sicily.

[118]Quintus Caecilius Metellus Macedonicus was consul in 143 B.C. and commanded the army against the Celtiberians in Spain.

[119]Metellus eventually captured Contrebia in 142 B.C. (see 7:4,5).

[120]Quintus Fabius Maximus Servilianus was governor of Farther Spain in 141 B.C. when he committed these atrocities.

nature, but he forced himself to put aside his merciful character for the time being and to adopt a harsh and severe policy. If he captured anyone who had deserted from the Roman garrison to the enemy, he had their hands cut off. As they went around with their mutilated arms, they made the others too terrified to desert. By cutting off the hands of rebels from their bodies and throwing them on the ground that was covered with their blood, he proved to the others that they should not dare to do likewise.

7. *12.* Nobody could have been kinder than Scipio Africanus. Nevertheless, to strengthen military discipline, he felt he would have to adopt some of that bitter cruelty that was so foreign to his nature. We can see this from what happened when he had defeated Carthage.[121] Africanus had got all those who had deserted to the Carthaginians from our armies under his power again, but he punished the Roman deserters much more harshly than the Latin ones.[122] He looked upon the Romans as slaves who had run away from their native land, so he crucified them. He looked upon the Latins as disloyal allies, so he beheaded them. I will not go into this matter any further, because it was something Scipio did, and because it is not right to gloat over Romans who suffered the punishment of a slave however much they deserved it. Especially since I can now move on to tell stories in which no Roman blood is shed.

7. *13.* After Scipio Aemilianus had put an end to the Carthaginian empire, he threw non-Roman deserters to wild animals when he was giving shows for the people.[123]

7. *14.* Lucius Paullus, when he had defeated King Perseus, threw foreigners guilty of the same offense on the ground and had them trampled to death by elephants.[124] This was a very useful example, if I may be permitted to judge the actions of excellent men in all humility and without being blamed for my insolence. Military discipline requires a harsh and abrupt style of punishment since military strength lies in armed force; if such force deviates from the right path, it will destroy a commander unless he destroys it first.

7. *15.* Rather than the measures taken by individuals, it is now time for me to mention the measures taken by the entire Senate to maintain and protect the traditions of the army.

The Carthaginians had destroyed the two armies of Publius and Gnaeus Scipio in Spain.[125] Lucius Marcius, their military tribune, took the scattered remains of these armies and with extraordinary courage made them into a fighting force. The soldiers elected him as their commander, and he wrote to the Senate about what he had done, starting his letter with these words, "Lucius Marcius, Propraetor."

---

[121]Scipio Africanus defeated the Carthaginians in 201 B.C.

[122]The word "Latin" refers to Rome's Italian allies in general (not just allies from Latium).

[123]Scipio Aemilianus razed Carthage to the ground in 146 B.C. At his triumph, he put on games that must have included the spectacle of wild animals mauling deserters.

[124]Lucius Aemilius Paullus (cos, 182 B.C.) defeated King Perseus of Macedonia in 168 B.C.

[125]Publius Cornelius Scipio (cos, 218 B.C.) and his brother Gnaeus Cornelius Scipio Calvus (cos, 222 B.C.) died fighting in Spain in 211 B.C. during the Second Punic War.

The Conscript Fathers did not like his use of this title, because commanders are appointed by the people, not by the soldiers.[126] This was a critical and dangerous time, since the Republic had suffered an enormous loss, so the Senators might have felt it was all right to humor military tribunes, especially since this one had succeeded in restoring the entire state to its proper status. But no disaster and no merit were more important than military discipline.

The senators remembered the proud severity their ancestors had displayed in the war against Tarentum.[127] The forces of the Republic had been shaken and worn down in that war, but then King Pyrrhus voluntarily handed over a large number of captured Roman citizens to the Senate.[128] The Senate decreed that those captives who had served in the cavalry would have to fight among the infantry, while those who had been in the infantry would be transferred into the auxiliary units of slingers; none of the captives could pitch his tent inside the camp, or protect the place he had been assigned outside the camp with a palisade or ditch, or have a tent made of skins. The Senate offered the soldiers the chance of returning to their previous status in the army if anyone brought back two sets of armor captured from the enemy. These soldiers were nothing more than disgusting little gifts sent by Pyrrhus, but after they had been humiliated by these punishments, they were transformed into his most relentless enemies.

The Senate unleashed its anger in a similar way against those who had deserted the Republic at Cannae.[129] By a stern decree, it had relegated them to a status worse than death when it received a letter from Marcus Marcellus asking for permission to use them for the siege of Syracuse.[130] The Senate wrote back that those men did not deserve to enter a Roman camp, but that it would allow Marcellus to do whatever he thought might benefit the Republic, provided that none of those men would be granted leave, be presented with any military decoration, or enter Italy as long as any enemy soldiers remained in the country. That is how much courageous men hate the spineless.

Well, how badly the Senate took it when his soldiers allowed the consul Quintus Petillius to be killed while he was fighting with great courage against the Ligurians![131] Since these soldiers had not exposed themselves to the weapons of the enemy to save their general's life, the Senate decided that the legion's service for that year should be discounted and that the soldiers should receive no pay. The

---

[126]The illegal promotion of Lucius Marcius Septimius is mentioned again at 1:6,2 and 8:15,11.

[127]The war against King Pyrrhus of Epirus started off as a dispute between his ally Tarentum and Rome.

[128]The Romans were defeated by Pyrrhus in 280 and 279 B.C.

[129]The Roman disaster at Cannae took place in 216 B.C. during the Second Punic War.

[130]The Roman soldiers who had escaped from Cannae were exiled to Sicily for the duration of the war ("a status worse than death"). Marcus Claudius Marcellus (cos, 222 B.C.) besieged Syracuse in 213 B.C.

[131]Quintus Petillius Spurinus was consul in 176 B.C. when he died fighting the Ligurians (see 1:5,9).

decree of that eminent body was an impressive and enduring monument to Petillius, and it allowed his ashes to rest in peace since they had been glorified by his
death in battle and by his vindication in the Senate house.

In the same spirit, the Senate rejected Hannibal's offer when he gave them the
opportunity of buying back six thousand Roman prisoners of war that he had in his
camp.[132] They realized that this huge crowd of armed young men could not have
been captured so disgracefully if they had been prepared to die honorably. I do not
know which was the greater disgrace for them: that their country had so little confidence in them that it did not care whether they fought for it, or that Hannibal had
so little fear of them that he did not care whether they fought against him.

The Senate has been strictly vigilant in upholding military discipline on many
occasions, but I suspect that the following instance may have been the most spectacular one. Our soldiers had occupied Rhegium in violation of the rules of war,
and when their commander, Vibellius, had died, they had acted on their own initiative and appointed his scribe, Marcus Caesius, as their new general.[133] The Senate threw the soldiers in jail, and even though Marcus Fulvius Flaccus, a tribune of
the plebs, warned the Senate not to punish Roman citizens contrary to the customs of our ancestors, the Senate persisted in carrying out its decision.[134] But to
ensure that its enforcement would cause less resentment, the Senate ordered that
five hundred of these soldiers be flogged with the rod and beheaded each day and
that nobody give burial to their bodies or mourn them.

Foreign Stories

7. ext. 1. The Conscript Fathers were mild in their behavior if we care to consider the brutality of the Carthaginian Senate in carrying out military business. If
its commanders planned a war badly, the Senate had them crucified, even if luck
made the campaign turn out well. The Carthaginian Senate attributed the good
outcome to the help of the immortal gods and the bad management to the commanders alone.

7. ext. 2. Clearchus, the commander of the Spartans, used to maintain military
discipline by a famous saying of his.[135] He was constantly drumming it into his
soldiers' heads that they ought to be more frightened of their commander than of
the enemy. Clearchus was clearly warning them that they would pay for it with
their lives if they hesitated to risk their lives in battle.

They were not surprised to be told this by their commander since they recalled
the tender words of their mothers to them as they went off to battle, warning the
men to come back to their mother's eyes alive and with their shield or be carried

---

[132]Hannibal had captured these Roman soldiers after Cannae in 216 B.C.

[133]These soldiers had been sent to protect Rhegium in 282 B.C. They had taken over the
city instead, and a Roman army was sent to expel them in 270 B.C.

[134]Marcus Fulvius Flaccus (cos, 264 B.C.) was a tribune of the plebs in 270 B.C.

[135]In 401 B.C. Clearchus led an army of Spartan mercenaries who fought in a war between
two Persian princes.

back dead and on their shield.[136] This was the watchword the Spartan soldiers received within the walls of their own home before going out to fight.

We have done enough by merely considering foreign stories since we can take legitimate pride in the much larger number of stories with far happier endings from our own country.

Chapter 8. The Right to Triumph

Preface

By vigorously maintaining military discipline, the Roman Empire became the master of Italy; it gained power over many cities, great kings, and mighty nations; it opened up the straits of the Black Sea; it broke through the barriers of the Alps and the Taurus Mountains and occupied them; and although it had started off in the tiny cottage of Romulus,[137] it became the leader of the entire world. Since all triumphs result from military discipline, my next topic is to start talking about the right to triumph.[138]

Roman Stories

8. 1. Some generals wanted triumphs to be decreed in their honor after they had fought minor battles. To counteract this, it was stipulated by law that nobody could have a triumph unless he had killed five thousand enemy soldiers in one battle. Our ancestors felt that the honor of our city would be enhanced not by the number of our triumphs but by their glory. To prevent this splendid law from being turned into a dead letter by men who were eager for laurels, it had to be backed up by another law, which was proposed by the tribunes of the plebs, Lucius Marius and Cato of Utica.[139] It penalized generals who, in their letters to the Senate, would dare to falsify the number of enemy soldiers who had been killed in battle or the number of our citizens who had been lost. The law ordered our generals, as soon as they had entered the city, to swear in the presence of the city quaestors that they had written truthfully about each of these numbers to the Senate.

8. 2. After mentioning these laws, it will be timely to bring up a trial in which a question over the right to triumph arose between two very famous men and was

---

[136]If a soldier ran away, he would first get rid of his heavy shield; a real Spartan could never run away, so he had to fight and die with his shield.

[137]A hut made of straw was preserved on the Palatine Hill, and the Romans believed it was the cottage in which Romulus was reared.

[138]A triumph was a victory parade from the Campus Martius to the Capitol. The conquering general rode in a chariot and wore a crown of laurel branches.

[139]Lucius Marius and Cato of Utica were tribunes of the plebs in 62 B.C. Their law was probably directed against Pompey, who returned to Rome from the east in that year.

discussed in detail. The consul Gaius Lutatius and the praetor Quintus Valerius had destroyed an important Carthaginian fleet near Sicily.[140] On these grounds, the Senate decreed a triumph honoring the consul. But when Valerius wanted a triumph decreed in his honor too, Lutatius said this should not be done because it would make the lesser magistrate equal to the greater one by honoring each of them with a triumph. The argument went on relentlessly, and Valerius challenged Lutatius by legally guaranteeing that the Carthaginian fleet had been destroyed under his (Valerius') leadership. Lutatius did not hesitate to accept the challenge.[141] They agreed that Atilius Calatinus would act as their judge,[142] and Valerius made the following argument before him: throughout the battle, the consul had lain crippled on a stretcher, and he himself had carried out all the functions of a general.

Before Lutatius could start making his case, Calatinus said, "I want to ask you the following question, Valerius. If you held opposite views about whether you should fight or not, which should have the greater weight, what the consul ordered or what the praetor ordered?" Valerius replied that he was not disputing that the decision of the consul would have priority. "Well then," said Calatinus, "if you had received opposite auspices, whose auspices would you go by?" "Once again," replied Valerius, "it would be the consul's." "In that case," Calatinus said, "since I have agreed to arbitrate between you about your commands and your auspices, and since you admit that Lutatius is your superior in both cases, I have no grounds for further hesitation. Therefore, Lutatius, even though you have remained silent so far, I judge in your favor."

The judge had acted admirably, in not allowing time to be wasted on a matter that was so obvious. Lutatius had the stronger case since he was firmly upholding the rights of the highest executive office, but Valerius was not wrong either, because he was seeking a reward for a brave and successful fight, even if he was not legally entitled to it.

8. 3. What would you do with Gnaeus Fulvius Flaccus? The honor of a triumph is sought after so much by other people, but when the Senate decreed one in his honor because he fought so well, he ignored and rejected it. He presumably foresaw exactly what would happen to him. When he went into the city, he was at once tried before a public court and condemned to go into exile, so if he did commit any offense against religion by his insolence, he paid for it by this punishment.[143]

---

[140]Gaius Lutatius Catulus (cos, 242 B.C.) and Quintus Valerius Falto (cos, 239 B.C.) defeated the Carthaginians at the Aegates Islands (off the west coast of Sicily) in March of 241 B.C. At the time of the battle Lutatius was still a consul, and Valerius a praetor.

[141]Each side has made a legal guarantee (called a *sponsio*) that his version of the facts is correct; if his version is wrong, then he has to pay his opponent a sum of money mentioned in the guarantee.

[142]Aulus Atilius Calatinus (cos, 258 B.C.) had a lot of prestige because he had already been a consul (twice) and a censor.

[143]Gnaeus Fulvius Flaccus was a praetor in 212 B.C. and was badly defeated by Hannibal. He went into exile to avoid being sentenced to death for treason. Naturally, he was never offered a triumph. Valerius may be confusing him with his brother, Quintus Fulvius Flaccus, who was consul in 212 B.C. and appears in the next story.

8. 4. Quintus Fulvius and Lucius Opimius were much wiser. When Fulvius captured Capua, and when Opimius forced the people of Fregellae to surrender, they asked the Senate for the right to hold a triumph.[144] Each of them was proud of his achievements, but neither was granted his request. The Conscript Fathers were not motivated by jealousy (at no point did they allow such a sentiment to enter the Senate house), but they were very strict in upholding the law, which stipulated that a triumph should be decreed if territory had been added to the empire, not if the Roman people had merely recovered their previous possessions. The difference between adding something new and restoring something lost is as great as the distance that separates the beginning of a good deed from the ending of an injustice.

8. 5. In fact, the law I am talking about was upheld so rigidly that a triumph was not decreed for Scipio Africanus when he won back the two provinces of Spain, or for Marcus Marcellus when he captured Syracuse, since they did not hold any executive office when they were sent to fight those campaigns.[145] So we are to think well of men who seek any kind of glory whatsoever, men who capture some uninhabited mountain regions or the figureheads of pirate galleys, and then rush off to pluck laurel branches that earn them little respect; but when a man tore Spain away from the Carthaginian Empire, or cut off Syracuse, the head of Sicily, we were unable to get triumphal chariots ready for them. And for what men did we refuse this? For Scipio Africanus and Marcellus, whose names alone are as good as an eternal triumph. They were renowned for their deeds of true unwavering courage, and the survival of our country rested on their shoulders. The Senate did, of course, want to see these men crowned, but it thought they should wait for more proper laurels.

8. 6. I shall add the following detail to these stories. When a general is about to hold a triumph, it is the custom that he should invite the consuls to dinner and then ask them to refrain from coming. This ensures that on the day he has his triumph, nobody at the banquet will hold a higher rank than he.

8. 7. Even if someone had performed glorious deeds that greatly benefited the Republic during a civil war, he was not proclaimed a general on that account, no public thanksgivings were decreed, and he did not hold an ovation or a triumph complete with a chariot. Such victories might have been necessary, but it was felt that they were always tragic since they had been won by shedding the blood of our own people, not the blood of foreigners. So it was with regret that Nasica murdered Tiberius Gracchus, and that Opimius murdered Gaius and his followers.[146]

---

[144]Quintus Fulvius Flaccus (cos, 237 B.C.) took Capua in 211 B.C. (see 3:2,ext.1 and 3:8,1). Capua had sided with the Carthaginians in the Second Punic War. Lucius Opimius (cos, 121 B.C.) destroyed Fregellae (in Latium) in 125 B.C. Fregellae had rebelled briefly against Rome.

[145]Scipio Africanus won Spain from the Carthaginians in a campaign that lasted from 210 to 206 B.C. Marcus Claudius Marcellus captured Syracuse after a long siege that went on from 213 to 211 B.C. These two men had been given special military commands because of their personal abilities, but as Valerius points out, they did not hold any executive office.

[146]Publius Cornelius Scipio Nasica Serapio (cos, 138 B.C.) led the crowd that murdered Tiberius Sempronius Gracchus (tribune of the plebs, 133 B.C.) and his supporters in 133

When Quintus Catulus had annihilated his fellow consul, Marcus Lepidus, and all his rebel forces, he showed very restrained joy on his return to the city.[147]

Gaius Antonius, who defeated Catiline, had his men clean their swords before returning to their camp.[148]

Lucius Cinna and Marius had greedily drunk the blood of their fellow citizens, but they did not go to the temples and altars of the gods immediately afterward.[149]

Sulla won many civil wars, and his victories were very cruel and arrogant.[150] When he had reached the height of his power and was celebrating his triumph, the procession included representations of many cities in Greece and Asia, but there was no representation of any town with Roman citizenship.[151]

It is unpleasant and tiresome to go on any longer about these wounds to our Republic. The Senate did not grant laurels to a man, nor did any man want to receive laurels, if a part of our state was in tears at his victory. But men eagerly stretch out their hands to receive the oak leaves, the crown that is granted to those who have saved the lives of their fellow citizens. The doorposts of the emperor's palace are eternally and gloriously triumphant in possessing that honor.[152]

Chapter 9. The Disapproval of the Censors

Preface

After discussing the strong bond of army discipline and the careful maintenance of military order, the idea naturally suggests itself that I should move on to the censorship, which is our master and guardian in peacetime. Through the courage of our generals, the financial resources of the Roman people have grown to extraordinary affluence, but our honesty and self-restraint are subjected to the strict supervision of the censors, and their activity has as important an effect as our glorious deeds in war. What is the use in achievements overseas if we live bad lives at home? Cities may be sacked, nations may be overrun, kingdoms may be seized,

---

B.C. (see 2:8,7 and 5:3,2e). Lucius Opimius (cos, 121 B.C.) organized the lynching of Gaius Sempronius Gracchus (tribune of the plebs, 123 B.C.) and his supporters in 121 B.C. (see 4:7,2; 6:8,3; and 9:4,3).

[147]Quintus Lutatius Catulus and Marcus Aemilius Lepidus had been consuls in 78 B.C. Lepidus marched on Rome in 77 B.C., and Catulus defeated him near the city. Lepidus managed to escape to Sardinia.

[148]Gaius Antonius Hybrida was consul in 63 B.C. Catiline started a rebellion that year, but Antonius defeated him in northern Etruria in 62 B.C.

[149]Lucius Cornelius Cinna was consul in 87 B.C. when he and Marius massacred Sulla's supporters.

[150]Sulla marched on Rome twice (88 and 82 B.C.) and massacred his political opponents.

[151]Sulla celebrated his triumph over King Mithridates VI of Pontus in 81 B.C.

[152]Augustus received this crown of oak leaves in 27 B.C. for ending the civil wars.

but if a sense of duty and shame does not exist in our public life and in our Senate house, then all the wealth we have accumulated, even if it reaches heaven itself, will not rest on a stable foundation. It is, therefore, important to know and recall the actions of those who have held the office of censor.[153]

Roman Stories

9. 1. The censors Camillus and Postumius ordered any men who had reached old age without marrying to pay a sum of money into the treasury as a penalty.[154] They were liable to a second penalty if they dared in any way to complain about this very just rule and were denounced in the following way:

> Nature has laid this law down that just as you were born, so you should beget children. If you had any sense of shame, you would see that by rearing you, your parents have obliged you to pay this debt off by rearing grandchildren for them. Furthermore, you have had the good fortune to enjoy a long grace period for performing this duty, but you have allowed those years to go by without earning the name of husband and father. So you must go now and pay that tough fine, which will go to benefit people with large families.

9. 2. The censors Marcus Valerius Maximus and Gaius Junius Brutus Bubulcus were equally severe in a similar kind of investigation.[155] They expelled Lucius Annius from the Senate, because after he had married a young woman, he divorced her without getting a council of friends together to advise him. I suspect that his offense was greater than the one I spoke of above. Those bachelors simply rejected the sacred rite of marriage, but this man unlawfully abused it. The censors were, therefore, perfectly justified when they decided he did not deserve to be in the Senate.

9. 3. Cato the Censor was equally justified when he expelled Lucius Flamininus from the Senate.[156] Flamininus had condemned someone in his province to death and beheaded him, but he had chosen the date of the execution to please some woman he was in love with by letting her see it.[157] Cato could have been held back by his respect for the consulship that Flamininus had held, or by the prestige of his brother, Titus Flamininus;[158] but he was a censor and he was Cato,

---

[153]Two censors were elected to hold a census every five years. They also supervised public morality. They had the power to demote a citizen to a lower social class, or even deprive him of his voting rights, if he had misbehaved in some way. They could likewise expel a man from the Senate.

[154]Marcus Furius Camillus (dictator, 396 B.C.) and Marcus Postumius Albinus Regillensis were censors in 403 B.C.

[155]Marcus Valerius Maximus Corvinus (cos, 312 B.C.) and Gaius Junius Bubulcus Brutus (cos, 317 B.C.) were censors in 307 B.C.

[156]Cato was famous for his severity as a censor in 184 B.C., which is why he was always known as "Cato the Censor." Lucius Quinctius Flamininus had been consul in 192 B.C.

[157]His province was Liguria (northern Italy).

[158]His brother was the famous Titus Quinctius Flamininus (cos, 198 B.C.).

which made him a model of severity twice over. Cato decided that Flamininus should be censured all the more because he had disgraced the grandeur of the highest office with such a low deed and because he hadn't shown any concern that his ancestral death masks would be associated both with the surrender of King Philip and with a prostitute enjoying the sight of human bloodshed.[159]

9. 4. What am I to say about the censorship held by Fabricius Luscinus?[160] Every age has told and will tell again in the future how he refused to allow Cornelius Rufinus to stay in the senatorial order.[161] Rufinus had acted splendidly during his two consulships and his dictatorship, but he had bought silver vessels weighing ten pounds, and Luscinus felt this was decadent and would set a bad example. By Jove, I think that the literature of our age is overawed when it is obliged to carry out the task of recording such strictness; it is afraid that people will think it is recording events in a city quite different from ours. It is hard to believe that within the same urban boundary ten pounds of silver were once considered an outrageously extravagant amount for a man to possess but are now looked down upon as a sign of great poverty.

9. 5. The censors Marcus Antonius and Lucius Flaccus expelled Duronius from the Senate because when he was tribune of the plebs, he had vetoed a law that had been introduced to restrict spending on banquets.[162] The remarkable reason for his expulsion was that Duronius had insolently mounted the rostra to make the following speech:

> Citizens, a bridle has been forced upon you that cannot be endured in any way. You have been bound and restricted by the bitter chains of slavery: a law has been proposed that commands you to be frugal. Let us veto this law that is covered with the rust of the harsh old days: What is the point in freedom if you cannot ruin yourselves in luxury when you want to?

9. 6. Well, let us now present a pair of men who were joined as partners under a yoke of courage and shared the same high offices but quarreled because they were both ambitious men. Claudius Nero and Livius Salinator were the strong torso of our Republic during the Second Punic War, and they were uncompromising in carrying out their duties as censors.[163] When they were reviewing the equestrian units (to which they themselves belonged because they were still young

---

[159]Titus Quinctius Flamininus (cos, 198 B.C.) had defeated King Philip V of Macedonia in 197 B.C.

[160]Gaius Fabricius Luscinus (cos, 282 B.C.) was censor in 275 B.C.

[161]Publius Cornelius Rufinus (cos, 290 B.C.) had fought successful campaigns against the Samnites and King Pyrrhus of Epirus.

[162]Marcus Antonius (cos, 99 B.C.) and Lucius Valerius Flaccus (cos, 100 B.C.) were censors in 97 B.C. Marcus Duronius was a tribune of the plebs some time between 102 and 97 B.C.

[163]Marcus Livius Salinator (cos, 219 B.C.) and Gaius Claudius Nero (cos, 207 B.C.) were censors in 204 B.C. They had defeated the Carthaginians in 207 B.C. at the battle of the Metaurus river in Umbria (eastern Italy).

enough) they came to the Pollia Tribe.[164] The crier read the name of Salinator, but he was doubtful whether he should summon him or not. Nero noticed this hesitation and ordered the crier to summon his fellow censor and make him sell his horse[165] because Salinator had been convicted by a court of the people.[166] Salinator inflicted the same penalty on Nero, and his justification was that Nero had been dishonest in pretending to be reconciled with him.[167]

If one of the gods had told these men that the long, glorious lines of ancestral death masks in their families would one day join together in the birth of the emperor who keeps us all safe, these men would have put aside their quarrels and united in the closest bond of friendship. They had saved our country themselves, and they would leave it behind for their common descendant to preserve.[168]

Salinator did not hesitate to relegate thirty-four tribes to the status of nonvoting citizens because they had convicted him and then elected him consul and censor.[169] The pretext he put forward was that by doing both these things, they must necessarily have been guilty either of recklessness or of perjury. He only left one of the tribes free of censure, the tribe of Maecia, because they had voted that he deserved neither to be convicted nor to hold public office. What kind of a rigid and strong-minded character should we think Salinator had? The adverse verdict in his trial could not compel him, and his election to the greatest public offices could not entice him to behave more leniently in carrying out his duties to the Republic.

9. 7. A good large part of the equestrian order, four hundred young men, had to endure censure with patience. They had been ordered to complete a series of fortifications in Sicily, but had done nothing about it, so Manius Valerius and Publius Sempronius deprived them of their state horses and put them among the nonvoting citizens.[170]

9. 8. The censors were very strict in punishing disgraceful cases of cowardice. Marcus Atilius Regulus and Publius Furius Philus deprived the quaestor Lucius Metellus and many Roman equestrians of their state horses and put them among the nonvoting citizens, because after the disastrous battle of Cannae, they had sworn that they would join Metellus in abandoning Italy.[171]

---

[164]These were both the cavalry units in which equestrians served and also the voting units in which they voted. See unit—army and unit—voting in the Glossary.

[165]If an equestrian had to sell his horse, he was thereby demoted from the cavalry to the infantry.

[166]Salinator had been condemned for his handling of the war against the Illyrians in 219 B.C.

[167]Their hostility and reconciliation are dicussed at 4:2,2.

[168]The emperor Tiberius was a member of the Claudius and Livius families, since his parents were Tiberius Claudius Nero (praetor, 42 B.C.) and Livia Drusilla (who later married Augustus).

[169]A nonvoting citizen (see Glossary) was the lowest class of Roman citizen.

[170]Manius Valerius Maximus Messalla (cos, 263 B.C.) and Publius Sempronius Sophus (cos, 268 B.C.) were censors in 252 B.C. while the First Punic War was being fought in Sicily.

[171]Marcus Atilius Regulus (cos, 227 B.C.) and Publius Furius Philus (cos, 223 B.C.) were censors, and Lucius Caecilius Metellus was a quaestor in 214 B.C. Metellus had suggested leaving Italy after Cannae in 216 B.C.

These censors also severely censured those men who had fallen into Hannibal's hands, and were then sent by him as representatives to the Senate to arrange an exchange of prisoners, but had stayed on in the city even though they failed to get what they requested. The censors were severe because they felt that it was typical of the Roman nation to keep its word, and because one of the censors denouncing their falsehood was Marcus Atilius Regulus whose own father thought it better to die suffering the worst tortures than to deceive the Carthaginians.[172]

These censors had thereby moved from civilian life to army life, where they wanted our men neither to fear the enemy nor to deceive him.

9. 9. Two cases of the same type follow, and once I have added them to the others, that will be enough.

Gaius Geta was expelled from the Senate by the censors Lucius Metellus and Gnaeus Domitius but later he was elected censor himself.[173]

Marcus Valerius Messalla had likewise been punished with a censure, but afterward he gained the position of censor.[174]

Their former disgrace made their sense of honor all the keener: their shame at what happened inspired them to strive with all their strength and show their fellow citizens that they deserved to be rewarded with the censorship rather than punished by it.

Chapter 10. Prestige

Preface

The prestige of famous men acts as a sort of private censor. It does not have lofty tribunals or public attendants at its disposal, but it succeeds in winning respect. It slips into people's minds, introducing itself in an easy and pleasant manner, disguising itself as celebrity. You would be quite right in calling it a long-term and happy office, even if it is not a government office.

Roman Stories

10. 1. What greater honor could be paid to a consul than the honor that was given to Metellus when he was on trial? He was pleading his case on a charge of misgovernment, and his financial records were requested by the prosecutor and

---

[172]The father of the censor Regulus was the famous Marcus Atilius Regulus (cos, 267 B.C.) who was tortured to death by the Carthaginians in 255 B.C. He likewise had been sent back to arrange an exchange of prisoners but urged the Roman Senate to reject the exchange.

[173]Lucius Caecilius Metellus Diadematus (cos, 117 B.C.) and Gnaeus Domitius Ahenobarbus (cos, 122 B.C.) were censors in 115 B.C. Gaius Licinius Geta (cos, 116 B.C.) became censor in 108 B.C.

[174]Marcus Valerius Messalla (cos, 161 B.C.) was censor in 154 B.C.

circulated among the jury so that they could inspect a particular entry.[175] The entire jury kept their eyes from looking at the records, because they did not want it to be thought that they had any doubts about what was entered in them. The jury believed that the proof that he had administered his province honestly was to be read in the life of Quintus Metellus rather than in his financial records. They felt it was not right that the integrity of such a great man should be judged from a little bit of wax and a few letters of the alphabet.[176]

10. 2. But is it any wonder that his fellow citizens paid Metellus the honor he deserved, since even our enemies did not hesitate in honoring Scipio Africanus? During the war he was waging against Rome, the soldiers of King Antiochus captured the son of Africanus.[177] The king received the son with great honors, presented him with royal gifts, and quickly sent him back to his father without being asked to, although at that very time he was being expelled from the territory of his kingdom by Africanus.[178] But although he was a king and had been harmed by Africanus, he preferred to show his respect for the prestige of that great man than to avenge his own troubles.

While Africanus was staying at his villa in Liternum, several pirate chiefs happened to come at the same time to see him.[179] He thought that they were coming to attack him, so he positioned a group of his own slaves on the roof to defend the house, and his mind was occupied with making preparations for beating off the pirates. When the pirates noticed this, they sent away their soldiers, threw down their weapons, went up to his door, and shouted out that they had come not to threaten Scipio's life but as admirers of his courage; they wanted to see and meet the great man as it would be like a gift from heaven to them: "So he was in no danger and he should not object to our getting a look at him." When his slaves told Scipio about this, he ordered them to unbolt the doors and let the pirates in.

The pirates paid homage to his doorposts, as if they were some very sacred altar or holy temple, and they eagerly grabbed Scipio's right hand and kissed it for a long time. In his hall they placed gifts of the kind that are usually offered to the immortal gods and they went back to their homes delighted that they had been so lucky as to see Scipio.

---

[175]Quintus Caecilius Metellus Numidicus (cos, 109 B.C.) was a provincial governor in 111 B.C. and army commander in Numidia from 109 to 107 B.C. His trial for misgovernment could have dealt with either of these commands. It must have occurred in 110 or 106 B.C.

[176]The Romans kept records on wax-covered tablets. The letters were scratched into the wax with a metal pen.

[177]Lucius Cornelius Scipio (praetor, 174 B.C.), the son of Scipio Africanus, fought in the war against King Antiochus the Great of Syria in 190 B.C.

[178]Scipio Africanus served in the war against Antiochus as a legate under his brother, Scipio Asiaticus. Although his brother got all the glory and the title Asiaticus, Scipio Africanus was the one who really defeated Antiochus.

[179]Liternum was on the coast of Campania. Scipio Africanus retired there (5:3,2b) after being put on trial in 184 B.C. (see 3:7,1e).

What could be more noble, what could be more gratifying than this product of his prestige? He soothed the anger of an enemy king by the admiration the king had for him, he saw pirates elated at the sight of his presence. If the stars ever glide down from the sky and present themselves to human beings, they will not receive greater veneration than he did.

10. 3. This happened to Scipio Africanus while he was still alive, but the following happened after Aemilius Paullus had died. When his funeral was taking place, the leading men of Macedonia happened to be staying in Rome on a diplomatic mission, and they shouldered his funeral bier of their own free will.[180] This will seem even more significant if one realizes that the front of that bier was decorated with symbols of his triumph over Macedonia. What a great honor they paid to Paullus! For his sake, they were not afraid to carry the proof of the defeat of their own nation in full view of the crowd. This spectacle gave his funeral the appearance of a second triumph. Macedonia revealed your glory to our city twice over, Paullus, with its booty when you were alive and with its shoulders when you had met your end.

10. 4. No small honor was paid to the prestige of your son, Scipio Aemilianus, either, whom you gave in adoption because you wanted him to glorify two families.[181] When he was a very young man, he was sent by the consul Lucullus from Spain to Africa to get help; the Carthaginians and King Masinissa asked him to make peace between them and treated him like a consul and general.[182] Carthage did not know what its destiny was to be: by the kindness of gods and men, that good-looking young man, who was just starting his life, was being reared to bring about the destruction of that city.[183] The title Africanus had been granted to the Cornelius family earlier because one of them had captured Carthage; it would be granted to them again because another Cornelius would destroy Carthage.[184]

10. 5. What is more wretched than being convicted; what is more wretched than being exiled? The tax collectors conspired to ruin Publius Rutilius, but they

---

[180]Lucius Aemilius Paullus (cos, 182 B.C.) had defeated King Perseus of Macedonia in 168 B.C. See 4:3,8 and 5:1,8. Paullus died in 160 B.C.

[181]Lucius Aemilius Paullus (cos, 182 B.C.) placed one of his sons for adoption by Publius Cornelius Scipio (augur, 180 B.C.), who was the childless son of Scipio Africanus. The adopted child thereby became Scipio Aemilianus.

[182]Lucius Licinius Lucullus (cos, 151 B.C.) was governor of Spain in 150 B.C. He sent Scipio Aemilianus, who was serving under him as a legate, to get war elephants from King Masinissa of Numidia. The king was engaged in a border dispute with Carthage at the time. Scipio Aemilianus would have been about thirty-five years old.

[183]The border dispute between Carthage and Masinissa led almost immediately to the Third Punic War (149–146 B.C.), which ended with the complete destruction of Carthage by Scipio Aemilianus.

[184]The title Africanus had been granted to Scipio Africanus at his triumph over Hannibal in 201 B.C. Scipio Aemilianus received the same title at his triumph over Carthage in 146 B.C. (see 2:7,1).

did not have the power to undermine his reputation.[185] When he was going off to Asia, all the cities of that province sent representatives to meet him and prepare for his arrival. In this case, one might more correctly describe it as a triumph rather than an exile.

10. 6. When Marius reached the bottom of his worst misfortunes, he too was saved in this critical period of his life by virtue of his prestige. Marius was locked up in a private house at Minturnae, and a government slave, who was a Cimbrian by race, was sent to kill him.[186] The Cimbrian drew his sword and held it up, but he could not bear to attack Marius, even though Marius was an old man, unarmed, and covered in filth. The Cimbrian was blinded by the glory of that man, threw down his sword, and ran away from there astonished and terrified. Obviously the disastrous defeat of the Cimbrians came before his eyes, and the annihilation of his defeated nation crushed his spirits.[187] The immortal gods also thought it unjust that Marius had destroyed an entire nation but would be killed by one man from it. The people of Minturnae, for their part, were completely captivated by his prestige, and though Marius was now completely crushed and the dreadful workings of fate had him trapped, these people kept him safe.[188] The savage victory of Sulla did not intimidate them, although the character of Marius himself might have deterred them from saving Marius.

10. 7. Cato of Utica was greatly admired for his brave and honest lifestyle. Against the wishes of the consul Caesar he spent an entire day speaking against the tax collectors in the Senate house.[189] Because of this, Caesar ordered a lictor to bring him off to jail. But the Senate respected Cato so much that the entire body had no hesitation in accompanying Cato there. This reaction led Caesar's divine spirit to give up its resolution.

10. 8. Cato of Utica was watching the Floral Games, which the aedile Messius had put on, and the crowd was too ashamed to request that the mime girls take off their clothes.[190] Favonius, a very close friend of Cato's, was sitting beside him, and he told Cato about this.[191] Cato left the theater so that his presence would not interfere with what normally went on during such spectacles. As he was leaving,

---

[185]While serving as a legate in Asia in 97 B.C., Publius Rutilius Rufus (cos, 105 B.C.) had tried to protect the provincials from abuses by the equestrian tax collectors. A vindictive equestrian jury found him guilty of misgovernment and banished him to Asia in 92 B.C.

[186]Marius was declared a public enemy when Sulla marched on Rome in 88 B.C. Minturnae was on the coast of Latium. The house in which Marius was detained belonged to an old friend of his called Fannia (see 1:5,5 and 8:2,3).

[187]Marius had defeated the Cimbrians in 101 B.C.

[188]The people of Minturnae helped Marius escape to Africa (see 1:5,5).

[189]Caesar was consul in 59 B.C., and he supported the equestrian tax companies in their efforts to renegotiate their tax contracts. Cato of Utica, as usual, did everything he could to obstruct powerful men like Caesar.

[190]Cato of Utica had just returned from Cyprus. Gaius Messius was aedile in 55 B.C.

[191]Marcus Favonius (praetor, 49 B.C.) later fought for the Republic at Pharsalus (48 B.C.) and Philippi (42 B.C.).

the crowd loudly applauded him and then went back to their usual theatrical plea-sures. By this they revealed that they paid more respect to the prestige of this one man than they claimed for themselves as a whole.

Was it his wealth, his political power, or his triumphs that they respected? He was a man with very little inherited wealth, his character was rigidly austere, he had only a modest number of clients, his home was closed to intrigue, he had just one ancestral death mask on his father's side, and his demeanor was far from charming, but his moral integrity was impeccable in every way. This is why anyone who wants to describe an excellent, upright citizen must define him as a "Cato."

Foreign Stories

10. ext. 1. We shall have to give a little bit of space to foreign stories. If we sprinkle them among stories from our own country, they will create some pleasant variety. Harmodius and Aristogeiton had tried to free Athens from tyranny,[192] and when Xerxes defeated that city, he brought their statues back to his kingdom.[193] After a long period of time, Seleucus had them brought back to their original location.[194] The statues stopped at the city of Rhodes, and its citizens invited the statues to a public banquet and even placed them on the couches of the gods. Nothing could be more blessed than the reputation of these two men, which created so much respect for a little lump of bronze.

10. ext. 2. What great honor was paid in Athens to Xenocrates, a man renowned for his intelligence and likewise for his upright character![195] He was called to give testimony and he went up to the altar to swear that everything he had said was the truth, as is the custom in that state. The entire jury stood up and proclaimed that he should not have to take an oath. They would not exempt themselves from this obligation when they gave their verdict later, but they felt that they had to make this concession to his honest character.

---

[192]Harmodius and Aristogeiton assassinated the brother of the tyrant Hippias in 514 B.C. They had meant to get the tyrant himself.

[193]King Xerxes I of Persia occupied Athens in 480 B.C.

[194]Seleucus I Nicator was king of Syria from 305 to 281 B.C.

[195]Xenocrates was the head of Plato's Academy from 339 to 314 B.C.

BOOK THREE

Chapter 1. Innate Characteristics

Preface

I shall now discuss the cradle (as it were) and the first beginnings of virtue. I shall show how certain personalities revealed their innate characteristics and gave a foretaste of the way in which they would, as time went by, attain the highest reaches of glory.

Roman Stories

1. 1. When he was just a boy, Aemilius Lepidus went off to battle, killed an enemy soldier, and saved the life of a fellow citizen.[1] This memorable deed is recalled in a statue set up on the Capitol by decree of the Senate. The statue is wearing the locket and striped toga of a boy.[2] The Senate thought it would be unfair to consider him too young for this honor since he had shown he was old enough for courageous deeds. Lepidus anticipated the responsibility of adulthood by the speed with which he started fighting bravely. He won double glory from this battle, although at his age he should hardly have been allowed even to see a battle. The shields of the enemy, their swords drawn from the scabbards, the spears flying everywhere, the thunder of their cavalry charges, and the impact when the armies come together—these things can even strike considerable terror into mature young men; but in the midst of all this, a boy from the Aemilius family was brave enough to seize spoils and earn a crown.

1. 2. Cato of Utica was not lacking in the same spirit when he was a boy.[3] He was being reared in the house of Marcus Drusus, his maternal uncle, who was a tribune of the plebs.[4] Some Latins had come together to ask Drusus about getting Roman citizenship,[5] and Quintus Poppaedius, the leading man of Latium and a friend of Drusus, asked Cato to help the allies in getting around his uncle.[6] With a

---

[1] Marcus Aemilius Lepidus (cos, 187 B.C.) performed this exploit during the Second Punic War when he was only fifteen years old.

[2] All freeborn boys wore a special locket (called a *bulla*) and a toga with a purple stripe along its edge.

[3] Cato of Utica was only four years old in 91 B.C.

[4] Marcus Livius Drusus (tribune of the plebs, 91 B.C.) supported the Italians in their campaign for full citizen rights.

[5] Here, as elsewhere, Valerius refers to Rome's Italian allies as Latins.

[6] Quintus Poppaedius Silo was an Italian activist.

stern look on his face, Cato said he would not do it. He was asked again and again, but he kept to his decision. Then Poppaedius brought Cato up to a high part of the house and threatened to throw him down if he would not give in to his request, but even this could not move Cato from his decision. So Poppaedius was forced to make this remark, "Let us be glad, my fellow Latins and allies, that this boy is so small, because when he becomes a senator, we will not even be allowed to hope for Roman citizenship." At this tender age Cato's personality had already adopted the dignity of the entire Senate house, and his determination dismayed the Latins who wanted so much to get their hands on the right to Roman citizenship.

When Cato of Utica was still wearing the striped toga of a boy, he went to pay his respects to Sulla.[7] There he saw the heads of outlawed political enemies that had been brought into Sulla's living room, and he was shocked by this horrifying sight.[8] He asked his tutor (whose name was Sarpedo) why nobody could be found to assassinate so ruthless a tyrant. Sarpedo replied that people did not lack the will to do so but rather the opportunity, as Sulla had a large number of bodyguards to keep him safe. Cato begged Sarpedo to give him a sword and pointed out that he could easily kill Sulla since he usually sat on Sulla's couch. His tutor had to admire Cato's spirit, but he was horrified at his proposal. From then on, he always searched the boy before bringing him to Sulla.

Nothing could be more admirable than this: a boy found himself in the headquarters of a brutal regime, but he was not afraid of the conqueror, even though Sulla was at that very time murdering consuls, populations of entire cities, whole legions, and the greater part of the equestrian order. If you had put Marius himself in that place, he would quickly have started making plans for his own escape rather than planning to assassinate Sulla.[9]

1. 3. Sulla's son, Faustus, was in school and praised his father for making a death list of political enemies, and he threatened to do the same as soon as he was old enough. His schoolmate, Gaius Cassius, punched him with his fist. That fist should not have disgraced itself by assassinating a public leader.[10]

Foreign Stories

1. ext. 1. We must have something Greek now, so here is a story about the famous Alcibiades. I cannot tell whether his virtues or his vices did more damage to his country; he deceived his fellow citizens with his virtues and destroyed them with his vices.[11] When Alcibiades was just a boy, he went to see his maternal uncle

---

[7]Cato of Utica was thirteen years old in 82 B.C., when Sulla became dictator.

[8]The dictator Sulla massacred his political enemies in 82 B.C.

[9]Marius was Sulla's great rival.

[10]Ironically, Faustus Cornelius Sulla, a dictator's son, died fighting for the Republic against a dictator in 46 B.C. His schoolmate Gaius Cassius Longinus was the future tyrannicide.

[11]Alcibiades was a promising but erratic Athenian leader. He defected to the Spartans in 415 B.C. but came back to Athens again in 407 B.C.

Pericles.[12] He found Pericles sitting sadly on his own, and he asked Pericles why he looked so troubled. Pericles said that by authority of the state, he had built the Propylaea of Minerva, which is the gateway to the citadel.[13] He had spent a vast sum of money on that work, and he could not figure out how he was going to explain his management. That is why he was so troubled. "Well," said Alcibiades, "why don't you figure out instead how you could avoid explaining it?" So that most eminent and practical man, having failed to come up with a plan of his own, adopted the boy's plan. Pericles kept the Athenians occupied in a war with their neighbors, and they did not have the time to demand any explanations from him.[14] But Athens should consider whether she should complain about Alciabiades or take pride in him, since to this very day she cannot make up her mind and decide whether she hates him or admires him.

Chapter 2. Courage

Preface

Now that we have revealed how virtue starts off and develops, we shall continue with its fulfillment. Its greatest force and most effective strength are found in courage.

Romulus, founder of our city, I am well aware that you should come first in this type of glorious activity, but allow me, I beg you, to run ahead and tell one story before I come to yours. Even you will have to honor it, since it was by virtue of this deed that your glorious work, Rome, did not fall to pieces.

Roman Stories

2. 1. The Etruscans were rushing over the Wooden Bridge to attack our city, but Horatius Cocles took his stand on the last part of the bridge.[15] Fighting tirelessly, he held back the entire enemy army until our men could chop down the bridge behind his back. When he saw that our country had been relieved from immediate danger, Horatius jumped into the Tiber wearing his armor. The immortal gods were amazed at his courage and kept him safe and sound. He was not shaken by his fall from that height, he did not sink under the weight of his armor, he was not swept under by a whirlpool, and he was not even harmed by the spears

[12]Pericles led Athens from about 460 B.C. until his death in 429 B.C.

[13]The Propylaea on the Athenian Acropolis was finished in 432 B.C.

[14]This is a curious explanation for the outbreak of the Peloponnesian War (between Athens and Sparta).

[15]Horatius Cocles was the hero of the battle against Lars Porsenna and the Etruscans in 508 B.C. The Wooden Bridge (*Pons Sublicius*) crossed from Rome to the northern (Etruscan) side of the Tiber.

that were coming at him from all directions. In the end, he swam to safety. All his fellow citizens and all his enemies had their eyes glued on this one man: his enemies were stunned with admiration and his fellow citizens were caught between joy and fear.

This one man separated two armies that were engaged in a very bitter fight, as he fought back one army and defended the other. In short, this one man protected our city with his shield as effectively as the Tiber does with its waters. This is why the Etruscans could say as they went away, "We defeated the Romans, but we were defeated by Horatius."

2. 2. The story of Cloelia makes me abandon my original plan. She performed a daring deed at about the same time, and definitely against the same enemy and in the same river Tiber. She had been given as a hostage to Porsenna along with some other young women, but she escaped the enemy watchmen at night.[16] She rode off on a horse, swam across the river quickly, and freed herself from bondage and our country from fear. Although she was a young woman, she was a beacon of courage to grown men.

2. 3. Now I am getting back to Romulus. He was challenged to single combat by Acro, the king of Caenina.[17] Although Romulus believed that his army was superior both in the number of its men and in their courage, and although it was safer for him to fight with his whole army than to fight alone, he preferred to seize an omen of victory by the work of his own right hand. And Fortune did not betray his brave decision. Acro was killed, the enemy was routed, and Romulus brought back rich spoils to Jupiter Feretrius from this battle.[18] That should be enough for this story, because the courage of Romulus has been consecrated by the religion of the state and does not need the praise of a private citizen.[19]

2. 4. The next man after Romulus to consecrate those spoils to the same god was Cornelius Cossus. When he was master of the horse[20] he came up against the leader of Fidenae in battle and killed him.[21] Romulus showed his greatness in starting this new type of honor, and Cossus also acquired great honor for having the courage to imitate Romulus.

---

[16]Cloelia came from an aristocratic family. A statue of her on horseback stood on the Sacred Way in Rome. Lars Porsenna was an Etruscan king who attacked Rome in 508 B.C.

[17]Caenina was a Latin town and it attacked the Romans to avenge the abduction of Latin women by the Romans.

[18]Rich spoils (*spolia opima*) were items taken from the body of an enemy commander. The spoils had to be won by a Roman general who fought an enemy commander in single combat. This happened only twice in the history of the Republic (see 2:2,4 and 2:2,5).

[19]After his death, Romulus was worshiped as the god Quirinus.

[20]Aulus Cornelius Cossus (cos, 428 B.C.) was master of the horse in 426 B.C., but he must have won the rich spoils when he was consul in 428 B.C.

[21]Cossus won rich spoils by killing Lars Tolumnius, king of Veii in Etruria. Fidenae was a Latin city on the border with Etruria and allied with Veii. Lars Tolumnius was the leader of this alliance, not of Fidenae itself.

2. 5. We should not keep the story of Marcus Marcellus separate from the previous stories. He had such energy and spirit that he attacked the king of the Gauls near the Po, although the king was protected by a huge army whereas Marcellus had only a few horsemen. Marcellus killed the king, stripped him of his armor, and dedicated it to Jupiter Feretrius.[22]

2. 6. Titus Manlius Torquatus, Valerius Corvus, and Scipio Aemilianus showed the same sort of courage in a similar kind of fighting. The first two challenged the enemy leaders and killed them, but because they had performed these deeds under the auspices of their general, they did not present their spoils as an offering to Jupiter Feretrius.[23]

Scipio Aemilianus was fighting in Spain under the command of Lucullus, and when they were besieging Intercatia, a powerful city, he was the first to climb over its walls.[24] There was nobody in that army with such nobility, innate spirit, or future achievements, and nobody whose personal safety should have been spared or taken into consideration above his. But in those days all the most illustrious young men would face the greatest danger and hardship to expand or protect our country. They felt it would be a disgrace if they were superior to others in status but inferior to them in courage. That is why Aemilianus requested to go on this mission whereas everyone else was trying to avoid it because it was a difficult one.

2. 7. In addition to the previous stories, the following great example of courageous action comes to us from the old days. The Romans had been defeated by the army of the Gauls, and they retreated to the Capitol and the citadel.[25] Since everyone could not stay on these hills, the Romans were forced to adopt the plan of leaving the older people in the lower part of the city so that the young men would find it easier to defend the remnants of our territory. But even in its most wretched and sorrowful time, our state did not forget its courage. Those who had held public office opened their doors and sat on their state chairs with the emblems of the offices they had held and the priesthoods they had acquired. At the hour of their death, they wanted to hold onto the glory and distinction of their previous life and to encourage the ordinary people to endure their misfortunes with greater fortitude.

At first, the sight of our leading men filled the enemy with respect, because they were moved by our strange behavior, by the splendor of our robes, and by the nature of our courage. But they were Gauls after all, and they had won a battle, so who could doubt that they would soon turn from admiration to laughter and every

---

[22]Marcus Claudius Marcellus was consul in 222 B.C. when he won rich spoils by killing Viridomarus, the commander of the Gauls, at the battle of Clastidium (in Liguria, northern Italy).

[23]Titus Manlius Imperiosus Torquatus (cos, 347 B.C.) and Marcus Valerius Corvus (cos, 348 B.C.) were just military tribunes when they defeated a commander of the Gauls in single combat (Torquatus in 361 B.C. and Corvus in 349 B.C.).

[24]Scipio Aemilianus served as a military tribune in Spain under the consul Lucius Licinius Lucullus in 151 B.C. Intercatia was in northern Spain.

[25]The Gauls defeated the Romans in 390 B.C. They occupied Rome apart from the citadel, which was on the top of the Capitol hill.

kind of mockery? Marcus Atilius did not wait for them to insult him, so when a Gaul ruffled Atilius' beard, Atilius gave him a violent blow on the head with his staff. Raging with pain, the Gaul rushed to kill him, and Atilius even more eagerly offered himself up to death. Courage does not know how to act as a captive, it does not know the disgrace of submission, it feels that yielding to Fortune would be more dreadful than any death, so it thinks up new and impressive ways of dying, if indeed a man whose life ends in this way could be described as dying.

2. 8. Now we must acknowledge the claim to glory that our young Romans have earned. The consul Gaius Sempronius Atratinus was fighting without much success against the Volscians at Verrugo.[26] Our battle line was already yielding, and our young horsemen were afraid it might be routed. So they dismounted from their horses, formed themselves into infantry units of one hundred men, and rushed at the enemy army. They dislodged the enemy and took up position on a nearby hill. This made the Volscians turn all the force of their attack against these men, and it gave our legions a respite that saved them and restored their spirits. The enemy was already thinking about raising trophies, but they had to leave when night put an end to the fighting, and they were not quite sure whether they were leaving in victory or in defeat.

2. 9. The young men of the equestrian order were also very active when the master of the horse, Fabius Maximus Rullianus, was fighting a war against the Samnites.[27] Their astounding courage saved Fabius from being convicted for wrongfully engaging his forces in battle. Papirius Cursor was setting out for the city to take the auspices again, so he put Fabius in charge of the camp and told him not to lead the army into battle. In spite of this, Fabius joined battle with the enemy, but he was reckless as well as unlucky in doing so, and there is no doubt that he was losing the battle. But the young men, who were of the highest character, took the bridles off their horses, urged them on violently with their spurs, and charged against the Samnites. Their stubborn determination snatched victory from the hands of the enemy and restored to our country a man who had every prospect of becoming a truly great citizen.

2. 10. What physical strength our foot soldiers had when they swam out, stood firmly on the slippery seabed as if it were dry land, and dragged back to the shore the Carthaginian ships that were quickly escaping as the oarsmen rowed frantically![28]

2. 11. A soldier of the same period became equally famous. He was at the battle of Cannae, when Hannibal crushed our Roman forces but did not break our spirit.[29] Because of his wounds, the soldier's hands were useless for holding a weapon. But as a Numidian was trying to strip off his armor, our soldier clung to

---

[26]Gaius Sempronius Atratinus was consul in 423 B.C. Verrugo was a fortress of the Volscians who lived in southern Latium. The consul was later put on trial for endangering his men.

[27]Lucius Papirius Cursor (cos, 326 B.C.) was dictator, and Quintus Fabius Maximus Rullianus (cos, 322 B.C.) was his master of the horse, in 325 B.C., during the Second Samnite War (326–304 B.C.).

[28]The next story shows that this incident must have occurred during the Second Punic War.

[29]Hannibal defeated the Romans badly at Cannae (in Apulia, southern Italy) in 216 B.C.

his neck and mutilated his face by biting off his nose and ears.[30] He died as he was inflicting these bites that fully avenged him. If you put aside the unhappy outcome of that battle, you will see how much braver was the man who died than the man who killed him. Even in victory the Carthaginian was at the mercy of the dying man, and this was some consolation to our soldier; at the last moment of his life, the Roman was able to avenge himself.

2. 12. The spirit of that soldier was exceptionally manly in adversity, as was the spirit of the general I am going to tell you about. When Publius Crassus was fighting a war against Aristonicus in Asia,[31] he was captured between Elaea and Smyrna by some Thracian soldiers, for Aristonicus had a large number of Thracians in his army.[32] Crassus did not want to fall into the hands of Aristonicus, so he thought up a way of seeking death that would enable him to avoid that dishonor. He took the rod that he used to control his horse and stuck it into the eye of one of the barbarians. Enraged by the violent pain, the barbarian plunged his dagger into Crassus' side, but in avenging himself, the barbarian freed the Roman general from the disgrace of losing prestige. Crassus showed Fortune that he did not deserve to be so deeply insulted by her. She had set up a cruel trap against his liberty, but he had cleverly and bravely broken away from it; she had handed him over to Aristonicus, but he had brought himself back to honor.

2. 13. Metellus Scipio had the same way of thinking.[33] The party of his son-in-law, Pompey, had failed to hold out in Africa. Metellus Scipio headed for Spain with the fleet, but when he noticed that the ship he was sailing on had been captured by the enemy, he ran his sword through his abdomen.[34] As he was lying on the poop deck, he heard Caesar's soldiers asking where the general was and he replied, "The general is doing just fine." That was all he managed to say, but it was enough to prove the moral courage that has earned him glory for all time.

2. 14. Utica is a monument to the glorious end of your life, Cato.[35] More glory than blood flowed from your courageous wounds. Without flinching you threw yourself on your sword, and you proved to the human race that for honest men, honor without life should be more precious than life without honor.

---

[30]Some Numidians (from North Africa) fought for the Carthaginians.

[31]Aristonicus, an illegitimate son of a former king, organized a rebellion against the Romans in 133 B.C.

[32]Publius Licinius Dives Crassus Mucianus (cos, 131 B.C.) was captured by Aristonicus in 130 B.C. Elaea and Smyrna were on the west coast of Asia Minor. The Thracians were from modern Bulgaria.

[33]Quintus Caecilius Metellus Pius Scipio Nasica (cos, 52 B.C.) commanded the Republican army in Africa (47–46 B.C.).

[34]He killed himself after being defeated in 46 B.C. by Caesar at Thapsus (in the province of Africa).

[35]Cato of Utica heard about the defeat of the Republicans at Thapsus and committed suicide at Utica (both cities were in the province of Africa) in 46 B.C. His suicide was regarded as a moral victory by Republicans who referred to him as "Cato of Utica." Normally, such titles were only given to generals who had celebrated a triumph over their enemy.

2. 15. Cato's daughter had a spirit that was far from womanly. On the night preceding the day of the horrible deed, her husband Brutus told Porcia about the plan
he had devised for assassinating Caesar.[36] When Brutus went out of her bedroom,
she asked for a barber's knife claiming she wanted to clip her nails, but she cut herself
with it as if it had slipped by chance. The slave girls screamed, and this brought
Brutus back into her room. He started to scold her for trying to do a barber's task.
Then Porcia whispered to him, "This was not an accident, but given our present circumstances, it is a clear proof of my love for you; I wanted to see how easy it would
be to kill myself with a sword if things did not turn out as you had planned."

2. 16. Cato the Censor, the ancestor from whom the Porcius family is derived,
was more fortunate than his descendant. An enemy soldier was attacking him with
great force on the battlefield when Cato's sword fell out of its scabbard. He noticed it was gone and spotted it under a crowd of fighting soldiers with enemy feet
all around it. He took it back so calmly that you would think he had not grabbed
it because he felt himself in great danger, but had picked it up because he felt no
fear.[37] The enemy was so astonished when they saw this that they humbly came to
him the following day begging for peace.[38]

2. 17. I shall have to include courageous actions in civilian life along with all
these military exploits, because courage deserves the same praise whether it is displayed in the Forum or in an army camp. When Tiberius Gracchus was tribune of
the plebs he won the masses over by giving them lavish handouts.[39] He had the
Republic under his control, and he went around in public saying that the Senate
should be abolished and the plebs should govern alone. The consul Mucius
Scaevola summoned a meeting of the Conscript Fathers in the temple of Public
Trust, and they were trying to decide what should be done in this crisis. They all
voted that the consul should defend the Republic with armed force, but Scaevola
said he would not use force at all.[40] Then Scipio Nasica spoke: "Since the consul,
by following the letter of the law, is going to bring about the destruction of the
Roman Empire and of all our laws, I volunteer as a private citizen to act as your
leader in carrying out your wishes." Then he wrapped his left hand in the hem of
his toga, raised his right hand, and proclaimed, "Those who want to save our Republic should follow me." By these words, he got rid of any hesitation on the part
of law-abiding citizens, and he forced Gracchus and his criminal factions to pay
the penalty they deserved.[41]

---

[36]Porcia, the daughter of Cato of Utica, married Marcus Junius Brutus (praetor, 44 B.C.) in
45 B.C. She committed suicide after the Republican defeat at Philippi in 42 B.C.

[37]It was not Cato the Censor but his son Marcus Porcius Cato Licinianus who performed
this exploit at the battle of Pydna in 168 B.C.

[38]The commander at the battle of Pydna was Lucius Aemilius Paullus (cos, 182 B.C.), not
Cato the Censor or his son.

[39]The populist Tiberius Sempronius Gracchus was tribune of the plebs in 133 B.C.

[40]Publius Mucius Scaevola (the pontiff) was consul in 133 B.C.

[41]Publius Cornelius Scipio Nasica Serapio (cos, 138 B.C.) led a group of senators who
lynched Tiberius Gracchus and his supporters.

2. 18. Saturninus, a tribune of the plebs; Glaucia, a praetor; and Equitius, who had been elected tribune of the plebs for the following year, stirred up a major revolutionary movement in our state.[42] The masses were aroused and nobody stood up to them. Marius was holding his sixth consulship,[43] and Marcus Aemilius Scaurus first urged him to defend our laws and liberty with armed force and then ordered armor to be brought for himself.[44] When it was brought he put it on, even though his body was weak and dilapidated with extreme old age. Leaning on a spear, he stood before the door of the Senate house, and although he had only a little bit of life left in him, he made sure that the Republic would not die. His determination inspired the Senate and the equestrian order to exact revenge from the rebels.

2. 19. Let us now present a man who was once the shining glory of military and civilian life, one who is now the shining glory of the stars, the divine Caesar, the clearest image of true courage.

The Nervians were making a fierce attack with a huge crowd of men, and Caesar saw that his battle line was beginning to give way. He grabbed a shield from a soldier who was not fighting with much spirit, held it before himself, and started to fight with great energy. His courage was infectious and inspired the entire army, and although their luck had been running out, his divine enthusiasm turned the battle around.[45]

In another battle, the standard bearer of the Mars Legion had turned around to start a retreat. Caesar grabbed him by the throat and turned him in the opposite direction, and pointing to the enemy with his right hand said, "Where do you think you are going? That's where the men we're fighting against are." With physical force he cured that one soldier of his cowardice, but his strong words cured all his legions. They were getting ready to surrender, but he showed them how to win.[46]

2. 20. Let us move on now to a deed of courage by a mere human being. Hannibal was besieging Capua, where the Roman army was stationed.[47] Vibius Accaus was the prefect of a Paelignian cohort, and he threw their standard over the Carthaginian palisade.[48] He pronounced a curse on himself and his fellow soldiers if they would allow the enemy to keep the standard. He was the first to run out to try to get it back, and his cohort followed behind.

---

[42]Lucius Appuleius Saturninus (tribune of the plebs, 103 B.C.), Gaius Servilius Glaucia (praetor, 100 B.C.), and Lucius Equitius seized the Capitol with their supporters in 100 B.C.

[43]Marius was holding his sixth consulship in 100 B.C.

[44]Marcus Aemilius Scaurus (cos, 115 B.C.) induced the Senate to declare a state of emergency during which Saturninus, Glaucia, and Equitius were lynched.

[45]Caesar performed this exploit during his campaign against the Nervians of Belgium in 57 B.C.

[46]This incident occurred during his campaign against the Republicans in Africa (47–46 B.C.).

[47]This incident occurred in 212 B.C. when Hanno was attacking Beneventum, and the Romans succeeded in capturing his camp. Valerius is confused here: Hannibal was over 100 miles away in Tarentum and Capua was actually a Carthaginian ally at this time.

[48]The Paelignians were Roman allies from central Italy.

When Valerius Flaccus,[49] the tribune of the Third Legion, saw this, he turned to his men and said, "As far as I can see, we have just come here to look at other people's courage, but I do not want our nation to have the shame of seeing Romans coming second to Latins in glory. I, at any rate, want to die with honor or succeed with courage, and I am ready to rush forward on my own."[50] When he heard this, the centurion Pedanius grabbed his standard, held it in his right hand and said, "This is going with me now inside the enemy palisade, so if you don't want to have it captured, you'll have to follow me."[51] He burst into the Carthaginian camp with it, bringing the entire legion along with him. Shortly before this, Hannibal had high hopes that he would seize Capua, but the reckless courage of these three men did not even allow him to keep his own camp.

2.21. Quintus Occius was in no way inferior to these men in courage. People used to call him Achilles because of his bravery. I do not want to go through the rest of his deeds, but the two stories I am about to relate will make it abundantly clear what a great soldier he was. He was a legate under the consul Quintus Metellus, and he went off to Spain and fought under him in the Celtiberian War.[52]

It so happened that Occius had set up his table for lunch when he was challenged to fight by a young man of the enemy nation. Occius got up from the table and secretly ordered that his armor and horse be brought outside the palisade; he was afraid that Metellus might stop him if he heard. The Celtiberian insolently rode up against him, but Occius chased him and killed him. He stripped his body and, jumping with joy, brought the spoils back to the camp.

Occius was also challenged to single combat by Pyresus, who was the most noble and courageous of all the Celtiberians, but Occius forced him to surrender. The young man was very hot-blooded, but he felt no shame in surrendering his sword and army cloak to Occius, even though both armies were looking on. On the contrary, he asked that they should form a bond of friendship whenever peace would be restored between the Romans and the Celtiberians.

2.22. We cannot overlook Acilius, either. He was a soldier in the Tenth Legion and was fighting on Caesar's side in a naval battle.[53] He grabbed onto a ship from Massilia with his right hand, but it was cut off. He then grabbed the stern with his left hand, and did not stop fighting until the ship was captured and sunk.

This exploit is not as well known as it deserves to be. But the Greeks are very good at singing their own praises, and when Cynegeirus of Athens was similarly relentless in pursuing the enemy, the Greeks advertised this deed in their literature and made sure that all future generations would remember it.[54]

---

[49]Lucius Valerius Flaccus (cos, 195 B.C.) was a military tribune in 212 B.C.

[50]Here, as elsewhere, Valerius refers to Rome's Italian allies as Latins.

[51]Pedanius was the senior centurion of the Third Legion, and Valerius Flaccus, as military tribune, was his commanding officer.

[52]Quintus Occius served as a legate under the consul, Quintus Caecilius Metellus Macedonicus, in 143 B.C. at the start of the Third Celtiberian War (143–133 B.C.).

[53]Massilia remained loyal to the Republic and was attacked by Caesar in 49 B.C.

[54]Cynegeirus had his hand cut off and died fighting the Persians at Marathon in 490 B.C.

2. 23. Acilius won glory in a naval battle, but Marcus Cassius Scaeva comes next. He won glory in a land battle and served as a centurion under the same general as Acilius.[55] He had been put in charge of a fort, and was fighting to hold it. Justuleius, a prefect of Pompey, was struggling with all his might and using a large number of soldiers to capture him, but Scaeva killed every soldier who came near him.[56] He did not take one step backward, and he was still fighting when he fell onto the huge pile of bodies he had created. It became apparent then that he had wounds to his head, shoulder, and thigh; his eye was knocked out; and his shield was pierced with 120 blows.

That is the sort of discipline that inspired the soldiers in the camp of the divine Caesar. One of his soldiers kept attacking the enemy after he had lost his right hand, the other after he had lost an eye. The first was victorious after his loss, the second was not really defeated in spite of his loss.

I do not know in which realm of nature I should express greater admiration for the deeds of your indomitable spirit, Scaevius. Your courage was so outstanding that you have left us all wondering whether the exploits you performed at sea or the words you spoke on land reveal more courage. Caesar was not content with confining his achievements to the shores of the Atlantic Ocean, so he went to war again and laid his heavenly hands on the island of Britain.[57] You, Scaevius, were there with four other soldiers, crossing by boat over to a rock. This rock was near an island that the enemy was holding with a huge military force. But the tide went out, and the water between the rock and the island was turned into dry land, which made it easy to cross from one to the other. A huge crowd of barbarians rushed across, and while the other soldiers returned to the mainland using the boat, you stayed there alone, guarding the position and not moving away from it.

Spears were flying at you from every direction, and on every side the enemy was struggling to get at you. With your right hand you sent as many spears into the bodies of your enemies as five soldiers could throw in a whole day's fighting. In the end, you drew your sword and pushed back the most daring of the enemy, sometimes knocking them back with your shield, at other times attacking them with your sword. If they had not actually seen you, the Romans and the Britons would never have believed the sight before their eyes. The enemy soldiers were exhausted, but after this they were so angry and embarrassed that they had to make a last effort. You had already been wounded in the thigh with a spear, you had been hit on the face with a heavy stone, your helmet had been battered to pieces by the blows it received, and your shield had disintegrated with all the holes in it. You decided to risk your life in the sea, and although you were weighed down with your breastplate and back armor, you swam across the waves that you had colored with the blood of the enemy.

---

[55]Scaeva served under Caesar during the civil war (49–45 B.C.).

[56]Justuleius was a prefect in Pompey's army and defended Dyrrachium (on the coast of Illyria) against Caesar in 48 B.C.

[57]Caesar attacked Britain in 55 and 54 B.C.

You deserved the highest praise for using your weapons to good effect, but when you saw your general, you apologized to him for losing them [since you had come back without your shield].[58] You were a great soldier in battle, but you were even greater in upholding the discipline demanded of a soldier. Caesar was an excellent judge of courage, and he honored your words and your deeds too by promoting you to the rank of centurion.

2. 24. As far as the exceptional courage of soldiers is concerned, it would be proper to conclude these Roman stories by recalling the exploits of Lucius Siccius Dentatus.[59] You would probably think that his exploits and the honors he received for them go beyond anything you could believe, but the most reliable historians, including Marcus Varro, have gone out of their way to assert the truth of these events in their works.[60] They record that Siccius Dentatus fought in 120 battles, and he had such mental and physical strength that he seems to have played a major role in winning every battle. He took back thirty-six spoils from the enemy, a number that includes the spoils of eight men who challenged him to single combat and fought him with both armies looking on; he saved the lives of fourteen citizens, snatching them from death at the last moment; and he had forty-five wounds on his chest but none on his back. He followed the triumphal chariots of his generals nine times, and he drew the attention of all our citizens with his display of numerous military decorations: 8 golden crowns were carried before him, 14 civic crowns, 3 turreted crowns, 1 siege crown,[61] 83 torque collars, 160 armbands, 18 spears, and 25 metal discs. That was enough military decoration for a legion, not to mention a soldier.

Foreign Stories

2. ext. 1. A bloodbath at Cales, involving a large number of victims, also evoked great admiration. Fulvius Flaccus was in that town, and he wanted to avenge the betrayal of Rome by Campania, so he summoned the leading men of Campania into his presence and sentenced them to death.[62] But he received letters from the Senate forcing him to halt the execution of these men. Then Gaius Vibellius Taurea, a Campanian, of his own accord handed himself over to Fulvius and, speaking as loudly as he could, said, "Fulvius, you are filled with such longing to shed our blood; why do you hesitate to use your bloody axe against me? Then

---

[58]The missing words in the square brackets are recorded in the abridgment of Julius Paris (written at the end of the fourth century A.D.).

[59]Lucius Siccius Dentatus was an army legate until his death in 449 B.C.

[60]Marcus Terentius Varro (117–27 B.C.) wrote six hundred volumes of learned and literary works.

[61]A civic crown was given to a soldier who had saved the life of a fellow soldier; the turreted crown, to the soldier who first scaled the walls of an enemy city; and the siege crown, to a soldier who raised a siege.

[62]Capua fell to Quintus Fulvius Flaccus (cos, 237 B.C.) in 211 B.C. He arrested its leading senators and sent them to Cales (in northern Campania).

you could boast that you ordered the execution of a man who is much braver than you are." Fulvius said he would gladly have done so, but he was prevented by the Senate's instructions. "But the Conscript Fathers have not given me any orders," said Vibellius, "so look at this: you will see me performing an exploit that will be a happy sight for your eyes, but far too great for your mind to grasp." And at once, he killed his wife and children and threw himself on his sword. What kind of man should we think he was? Through his own death and the death of his family, he wanted to show that he would rather denounce the cruelty of Fulvius than benefit from the clemency of the Senate.

2. ext. 2. Well, what a passionate spirit Darius had! He was freeing Persia from the base and cruel tyranny of the magi, and he knocked one of them down in a dark room and threw the full weight of his body on top of him.[63] A comrade of his in this glorious deed was reluctant to strike the magus, because he was afraid that while he was aiming at the magus he might also wound Darius himself. But Darius said, "Your concern for me should not make you nervous about using your sword; you should feel free to run your sword through both of us, as long as this fellow dies right now."

2. ext. 3. At this point, the famous Spartan, Leonidas, comes to mind. Nothing could be braver than his determination, his exploits, his death. He stood with three hundred fellow citizens at Thermopylae and opposed all of Asia.[64] Xerxes was oppressing the land and the sea, and he did not terrorize only human beings. He even threatened Neptune with chains and the sky with darkness,[65] but he was driven to the depths of despair by the obstinate courage of Leonidas. Unfortunately, the wicked treachery of the local inhabitants deprived Leonidas of the tactical advantage afforded by that place, which had been a great help to him. But rather than desert the position he had been placed in by his country, Leonidas chose to die fighting. He was very cheerful as he urged his men on to the battle in which they would all die, and he told them, "Enjoy your lunch, my fellow soldiers. We'll have dinner in the Underworld." He had given them notice that they were to die, but it was as if he had promised them victory, for the Spartans obeyed his words without any misgivings.

2. ext. 4. Othryades fought and died splendidly, and he made the region of Thyrea greater in fame than in size. By writing a few letters with his own blood, he snatched victory from the enemy. This bloody inscription on the trophy he erected almost after he was dead brought victory to his own country.[66]

---

[63]The magi were Persian priests, and they supported Bardiya (king of Persia in 522 B.C.). Darius claimed that the king was merely a priest pretending to be Bardiya. Darius killed Bardiya and made himself king in 521 B.C.

[64]King Leonidas of Sparta held the narrow pass of Thermopylae (in northern Greece) against King Xerxes I of Persia in 480 B.C.

[65]Xerxes threw chains into the sea when a storm damaged his fleet, and he boasted that his arrows would block out the sun.

[66]Sparta and Argos (both were states in southern Greece) fought over the border region of Thyrea around 550 B.C. Orthryades was the last soldier on the battlefield, and he won a technical victory for Sparta by raising a trophy.

2. ext. 5. The courage of the Spartans produced extraordinary results, but the next story tells of their sad decline. Epaminondas was the great joy of Thebes and the first man to defeat Sparta.[67] His successful battles at Leuctra and Mantinea shattered the ancient military glory of Sparta and the morale of its citizens, who had never been defeated until that time.[68] A spear went right through Epaminondas, he was running short of blood, and he had difficulty breathing.[69] His men were trying to revive him, but he asked them first whether his shield was safe, and then whether the enemy had been completely defeated. He discovered that things were exactly as he had hoped, and this is what he said:

> My fellow soldiers, this is not the end of my life, but the beginning of something better and greater. Your friend Epaminondas is being born, because that is what it means to die like this. I see that Thebes, under my leadership and auspices, has become the leading state in Greece while the brave and proud city of Sparta lies crushed by our arms. Greece has been freed from a cruel tyranny. I don't have a family, but I am not dying childless, because I am leaving two wonderful daughters behind me, Leuctra and Mantinea.

He ordered them to pull the spear out of his body, and he died with a happy look on his face, as if the gods had allowed him to enjoy his victories to the full and he had entered the gates of his native city alive.

2. ext. 6. Theramenes of Athens also revealed a very steadfast mind when he was forced to die in the city jail. By order of the Thirty Tyrants, he was given poison to drink, and he swallowed it down without flinching.[70] As a joke, he took the little that was left over, and threw it on the ground, making it splash loudly. Beaming at the government slave who had given him the poison, he said, "This is a toast to Critias; make sure you bring this cup to him at once." Critias was the most ruthless of all the Thirty Tyrants.[71] Suffering death with such ease is indeed the same as liberating oneself from death. And that is how Theramenes departed this life, dying as if he were in bed at home. His enemies thought that they had punished him, but he felt that his life had merely come to its natural end.

2. ext. 7. Theramenes acquired manliness from his reading and his education, but Rhoetogenes of Numantia managed to learn the same virtue from the schoolmistress (as it were) of his nation, ferocity.[72]

---

[67]Thebes was the capital of Boeotia (in central Greece), and Epaminondas was its leader.

[68]Epaminondas defeated the Spartans in 371 B.C. at Leuctra (in Boeotia), and in 362 B.C. at Mantinea (in Arcadia, southern Greece).

[69]Epaminondas died on the battlefield of Mantinea.

[70]The Thirty Tyrants overthrew the democracy of Athens and governed the state from 404 to 403 B.C. Theramenes was a moderate member of the Thirty.

[71]Led by the extremist Critias, the Thirty Tyrants put Theramenes and other political opponents to death in 403 B.C.

[72]Rhoetogenes killed himself when his city was destroyed by Scipio Aemilianus in 133 B.C. The fall of Numantia (in northern Spain) completed the Roman conquest of Spain.

Rhoetogenes surpassed all his fellow citizens in nobility, wealth, and political position, and when the state of Numantia was crushed and destroyed, he went around everywhere gathering fuel for a fire. Then he set fire to his building complex, which was the most beautiful one in that city. Immediately after that, he drew his sword and put it on the ground in front of everyone. He ordered the men to fight in pairs, so that he could cut the throat of the loser and throw the body on top of the burning house. He applied this strict rule for dying, killed them all off, and finally plunged into the flames himself.

2. ext. 8. I shall now refer to the fall of a city that was equally hostile to Rome. When Carthage was captured, Hasdrubal's wife attacked him for failing in his duty to her, because he had been content with asking Scipio Aemilianus to save only his life.[73] Their children agreed to die with her, so she took them along, holding them by the hand on either side, and jumped into the inferno of her burning city.

2. ext. 9. Next to that story of a woman's courage I shall put the equally brave death of two young women. A dreadful civil war broke out in Syracuse, and the entire family of King Gelon was massacred in broad daylight.[74] His family was reduced to his only daughter, Harmonia, who was not yet married. Their enemies rushed in to kill her, but her nurse got a young woman of the same age, dressed her up in royal robes, and exposed her to the swords of their enemies. Even when she was being murdered, the young woman did not reveal her true status. Harmonia was filled with admiration at her courage, and she could not bear to survive such a loyal friend. So she called the murderers back, told them who she was, and got them to kill her. The first young woman lost her life because she hid a deception; the second young woman lost her life because she revealed the truth.

Chapter 3. Endurance

Preface

Because she inspires splendid deeds in men and women, Courage draws attention to herself. She urges Endurance to go out in public, since Endurance also has strong roots and is full of the same noble spirit. They resemble each other so closely that you would think Endurance was either the sister or the daughter of Courage.

---

[73]Scipio Aemilianus destroyed Carthage in 146 B.C. at the end of the Third Punic War. Hasdrubal was the Carthaginian general throughout the war.

[74]Gelon never actually became king of Syracuse, because he died before his father. Gelon's son, Hieronymus, was king when the entire family was wiped out in 214 B.C.

Roman Stories

3. 1. What could fit in more closely with the stories I have just told than the exploit of Mucius? He was very angry that the Etruscan king, Porsenna, was subjecting our city to a long, harsh war.[75] He secretly entered Porsenna's camp, armed with a sword, and tried to kill him while he was sacrificing at an altar. But he was caught in the middle of his attempt to carry out this brave and patriotic deed. Mucius did not invent some excuse for being there, and by his amazing endurance, he showed how little he feared torture. I think he must have been annoyed with his right hand, because it had been of no use to him in assassinating the king, so he stuck it into a brazier, and let it burn to a cinder. That certainly drew the attention of the immortal gods; they had never seen such an offering brought to their altars before. Even Porsenna forgot about the danger he had escaped, and he was forced to admire Mucius rather than think about revenge. "Go back to your own people, Mucius," said the king, "and tell them that you tried to take my life from me, but I gave your life back to you." Mucius didn't go down on his knees to thank him for his kindness. He was more upset that Porsenna was still alive than glad that he himself was alive. He returned to the city and won the eternally glorious name of Scaevola.[76]

3. 2. Pompeius was also a man of admirable courage. He was once carrying out his duties as an envoy when he was intercepted by King Gentius.[77] The king ordered him to reveal the Senate's plans, but Pompeius put his finger into a lamp that was lit and burned it off. His endurance struck the king, and it made him give up his hopes of getting anything out of Pompeius by torture. It also made him very eager to win the friendship of the Roman people.

I do not want to investigate any more stories of this type from Rome, because I might be forced to remind people of the hateful civil wars. So I am content with those two Roman stories, which did honor to our most celebrated families and involved no sorrows to our state. I shall now add some foreign stories.

Foreign Stories

3. ext. 1. In keeping with an ancient Macedonian custom, boys from the noblest families would assist King Alexander when he was sacrificing.[78] One of them picked up an incense burner and stood before Alexander. A burning coal fell onto his arm. His flesh was burning so badly that the smell reached the noses of the bystanders. But the boy kept his agony quiet and held his arm out rigidly, because he did not want to disturb Alexander's sacrifice by throwing the incense burner down or crying out inauspiciously. The king was delighted with the endurance of

---

[75]The exploit of Gaius Mucius Cordus Scaevola occurred in 508 B.C. when Lars Porsenna was attacking Rome. (See 3:2,1 and 3:2,2 for more heroic exploits in this war.)

[76]Scaevola meant "the Left-handed Man."

[77]King Gentius of Scodra (in Illyria) supported King Perseus of Macedonia in his war against Rome (172–167 B.C.). Pompeius went on an embassy to King Gentius in 168 B.C.

[78]Alexander the Great was king of Macedonia from 336 to 323 B.C.

this boy, but he wanted to be absolutely sure of his steadfastness. So he deliberately made the sacrifice last longer, but even this did not make the boy change his behavior. If Darius had gotten a look at this extraordinary event, he would have known that soldiers from such stock were invincible, since they were endowed with such great courage from a tender age.[79]

But there is also a heroine who fights with energy and determination in the warfare of the mind; she is powerful because of her learning, and she is a priestess in the sacred rites of knowledge: her name is Philosophy. Once you have welcomed her into your heart, she gets rid of every dishonorable and worthless feeling, she strengthens your character with a fortress of real virtue, and she makes you overcome fear and sorrow.

3. ext. 2. I shall start off with Zeno of Elea.[80] He was very astute in his observation of nature and very keen to inspire young people to use their minds properly. People trusted his teachings because he could point to his own upright behavior. Zeno could have enjoyed a life of peace and freedom in his own country, but he left it and went to Agrigentum, which was miserably oppressed by a tyrant.[81] Zeno had so much confidence in his own talents and character that he thought he could cure a tyrant, even one like Phalaris, of his insane ferocity. But he discovered that Phalaris had gotten into the habit of acting like a tyrant, and that this habit was more important to Phalaris than sound advice.[82]

Zeno therefore set all the young men of noble family in that city afire with the desire to free their country. Word of this reached the tyrant's ears, so he summoned the people to gather in the public square and began to torture Zeno with every kind of device, asking him repeatedly who his colleagues in this plot were. But Zeno did not reveal a single name; instead, he cast suspicion on the closest and most loyal friends of the tyrant. He kept rebuking the people of Agrigentum for their cowardice and lack of spirit, and this struck them so forcefully that they suddenly had a change of heart and stoned Phalaris to death. One old man had been put on the rack, but he did not beg for mercy or cry out piteously; instead, he bravely encouraged an entire city to change its mind and its fortune.

3. ext. 3. There was a philosopher of the same name who had plotted against the life of the tyrant Nearchus.[83] He was being tortured as a punishment and also to make him betray his colleagues. He mastered the pain but was still eager for

---

[79]Darius III, the last king of Persia, reigned from 335 to 330 B.C. He lost his empire to Alexander the Great.

[80]The philosopher Zeno of Elea lived in the fifth century B.C. Elea was a Greek city in Lucania (southern Italy).

[81]Agrigentum was a city on the south coast of Sicily.

[82]Phalaris ruled Agrigentum from 570 to 554 B.C. and was notorious for torturing his enemies (see 9:2,ext.9). Phalaris died before Zeno of Elea was born, so it looks as if Valerius has confused some story about a victim of Phalaris with the story of Zeno and another tyrant (see 3:3,ext.3).

[83]This is the real story about the fifth-century philosopher Zeno of Elea (in Lucania, southern Italy).

some revenge, so he said he had a secret and that it would be very advantageous for the tyrant to hear it. They loosened the rack, and when he saw that it was the right moment for his trick, he took the tyrant's ear in his teeth and did not let go until he lost his life and the tyrant lost that part of his body.

3. ext. 4. Anaxarchus displayed similar endurance when he was being tortured by Nicocreon, the tyrant of Cyprus.[84] No amount of physical force could stop Anaxarchus from torturing the tyrant in turn by lashing him with the harshest insults. Finally, the tyrant threatened to cut his tongue out, but he said, "You effeminate young man, even this part of my body will not come under your power." And at once, he bit his own tongue off with his teeth, chewed it up, and spat it at the tyrant's face which was exploding with rage. That tongue had astonished everyone who heard it lecturing, and it won the admiration of King Alexander above all.[85] It had explained the structure of the earth, the form of the sea, the movements of the constellations, and the nature of the entire universe in the most brilliant and eloquent way. But it was almost more glorious at its end than in the days of its prime, because that brave end proved that its actions were as glorious as its teachings. It may have left Anaxarchus while he was still alive, but it made his death more splendid.

3. ext. 5. The tyrant Hieronymus exhausted his torturers for nothing when he used them on Theodotus, a very dignified man.[86] The whips would have broken, the lyre-torture strings would have gone slack, the rack would have gone loose, the burning metal plates would have gone cold before anyone could make Theodotus reveal the names of his colleagues who plotted to kill the tyrant. Instead, he falsely incriminated the tyrant's right-hand man, who was the axis around which the entire tyrannical system had revolved, and Theodotus thereby deprived the tyrant of his most loyal protector. By virtue of his endurance, Theodotus did not just keep quiet about his secrets; he even managed to get revenge for the torments he endured. Hieronymus may have enjoyed torturing an enemy, but he stupidly lost an ally.

3. ext. 6. It is believed that the Indians train themselves in endurance with great persistence. There are even some Indians who spend their entire life going around naked; at some times they toughen their bodies up in the frozen snow of the Caucasus Mountains,[87] at others they go through flames without so much as a groan. Their contempt for pain wins them considerable fame, and they are honored as sages.[88]

3. ext. 7. All these things were achieved by people with lofty and learned souls, but the mind of a slave came up with the following deed, which is no less admirable. A barbarian slave was upset with Hasdrubal for killing his master, so he

---

[84]Anaxarchus of Abdera (on the south coast of Thrace) was a philosopher who lived from 380 to 320 B.C. Nicocreon was tyrant of Cyprus from 330 to 310 B.C.

[85]Anaxarchus had accompanied Alexander the Great during his conquest of Asia.

[86]Hieronymus was king of Syracuse from 215 to 214 B.C. Theodotus survived his ordeal, and the entire royal family was massacred in 214 B.C. (see 3:2,ext.9).

[87]The "Indian Caucasus" is the Hindu Kush range.

[88]The Indians who go around naked are Hindu or Jain ascetics.

attacked him suddenly and killed him.[89] The slave was caught and subjected to every kind of torture but steadfastly persisted in showing on his face the pleasure he had gotten from his revenge.

Virtue is not snobbish about allowing people to approach her; if lively minds have been inspired by her, she allows them to come right into her home. She does not consider a person's social status when she decides to be generous or niggardly with her favors. Instead, she offers them to all people alike, and she judges you by your desire for virtue rather than by your social rank. When you come for her goods, she lets you calculate the proper weight, so you can take away with you however much your character can bear. That is why it happens that people born in humble circumstances rise to the highest rank, whereas people born of a family with the most noble ancestral death masks fall into some disgrace or other and turn the light handed down by their ancestors into total darkness. These things are made clearer by stories that illustrate them. I shall start off with people who changed to a higher status, because they provide wonderful material for a story.

Chapter 4. People Who Were Born in Humble Circumstances but Ended Up Famous

Roman Stories

4. 1. A country cottage was the birthplace of Tullus Hostilius, and he spent his youth looking after livestock; but he spent his adult years ruling the Roman kingdom and doubling its size, and his old age was exceptionally distinguished and glowed with the highest degree of prestige.[90]

4. 2. Although Tullus is a great example of extraordinary advancement, he was still a local man. But when fortune brought Tarquin to our city to take over the kingdom of Rome, he was an outsider because he was Etruscan, and even more of an outsider because he was born in Corinth.[91] People looked down on him because he was the son of a businessman, and they were ashamed of him because his father had been a refugee. But by working hard, he became very successful and inspired admiration rather than resentment. He expanded our territory, he advanced the worship of the gods by creating new priesthoods, he increased the size of the Senate, he improved the equestrian order, and—to summarize all his glorious achievements—his brilliant qualities insured that this state would not regret having borrowed a king from its neighbors rather than choosing one from its own people.

---

[89]Hasdrubal commanded the Carthaginian army in Spain from 228 B.C. until he was murdered by a Spanish slave in 221 B.C.

[90]Tullus Hostilius was the third of Rome's legendary kings (673–641 B.C.).

[91]Tarquin the Elder was the fifth of Rome's kings (616–579 B.C.). Tarquin's father was a businessman from Corinth in southern Greece, but he gave his son an Etruscan name.

4. 3. Fortune demonstrated her power to an exceptional degree in the case of Tullius by making him a king even though he had been born a slave in this city.[92] He even had the fortune to enjoy the longest reign, completing four purification ceremonies[93] and celebrating three triumphs. In short, the inscription on his own statue is ample proof of where he had come from and where he got to, because it joins together his servile name and his royal title.[94]

4. 4. Varro also made extraordinary progress in rising from his father's butcher shop to the consulship.[95] Fortune thought it would be a very minor achievement to present the twelve fasces[96] to a man who had been reared on the earnings of this low trade, so she outdid herself by giving him Lucius Aemilius Paullus as his fellow consul. She poured her favors on Varro so lavishly that she brought him back safe to the city, although he was responsible for destroying the army of the Roman people at Cannae, whereas she allowed Paullus to die, although he had been opposed to the idea of starting the battle. She even got the Senate to come out in front of the city gates and thank Varro for wanting to come back, and she also extorted a dictatorship from the Senate for this man who had brought about our disastrous defeat.[97]

4. 5. Marcus Perperna was quite a disgrace to the consulship, since he held it before he was even a citizen.[98] But in fighting wars he was a far better general for our Republic than Varro had been. He took King Aristonicus prisoner and avenged the defeat of Crassus;[99] but if he triumphed in this life, he was condemned under the Papian law after he died.[100] His father had exercised the rights of a Roman citizen even though he was not entitled to, so the Sabellians put the father on trial and deported him to his original home.[101] This cast a shadow on the reputation of Marcus Perperna; his consulship must have been a false one, his command a smoke screen, and his triumph a failure, since he had wrongfully acquired them as an immigrant in a city that was not his own.

---

[92]Servius Tullius was the sixth king of Rome (578–535 B.C.)

[93]Servius Tullius was said to have started the practice of taking a census. The census always concluded with a purification ceremony.

[94]Servius Rex would literally mean "slave king."

[95]Gaius Terentius Varro was consul with Lucius Aemilius Paullus in 216 B.C., the year of the Roman disaster at Cannae.

[96]A consul was accompanied by twelve attendants carrying fasces (bundles of sticks symbolizing the power of the state).

[97]Varro never became a dictator (see 4:5,2).

[98]Marcus Perperna was consul in 130 B.C.

[99]Publius Licinius Dives Crassus Mucianus (cos,131 B.C.) had been defeated by Aristonicus of Pergamum in 130 B.C. (see 3:2,12), but Perperna captured Aristonicus later that year.

[100]Perperna died overseas in 129 B.C. and never celebrated a triumph. The Papian law (passed in 65 B.C.) expelled all non-Italians from Rome, but a similar law had been passed in 126 B.C. and perhaps that was when Perperna's father was expelled from Rome.

[101]Sabellian is a generic name for all the peoples of central and southern Italy.

4. 6. The rise of Cato the Censor, on the other hand, should have been prayed for by our state.[102] His family was unknown in Tusculum, but he made it one of the most famous in Rome. He enhanced the beauty of Latin literature, strengthened military discipline, advanced the prestige of the Senate, and produced the family from which our great glory, Cato of Utica, arose.[103]

Foreign Stories

4. ext. 1. We must add a few foreign stories to our Roman ones. Socrates was judged the wisest of men not only by the general consensus of the human race but also by the oracle of Apollo.[104] His mother, Phaenarete, was a midwife, and his father, Sophroniscus, was a stonemason, but Socrates rose to the most brilliant radiance of glory. Not that he didn't deserve to. In his time, the most learned men were wasting their minds in pointless controversies: they were trying to measure the size of the sun, the moon, and other stars, using long-winded proofs that had no solid basis, and they even had the nerve to try to grasp the nature of the entire universe. Socrates was the first to turn his attention away from these deviations into ignorance. He forced himself to examine the deepest secrets of the human condition and the feelings that are hidden away in our hearts. If virtue is to be valued in itself, then he above all others taught us how to live.[105]

4. ext. 2. Even in their own day, nobody knew who Euripides' mother was, or Demosthenes' father, but almost every scholar writes that Euripides' mother sold vegetables and Demosthenes' father sold knives. And yet, what could be more spendid than the dramatic power of Euripides or the rhetorical power of Demosthenes?[106]

Chapter 5. People Who Had Famous Parents but Came Down in the World

Preface

The second part of my undertaking follows, and it deals with the ancestral death masks of illustrious men that have been obscured, for I shall now tell of those who came down in the world from the splendor of their ancestors. These

---

[102]Cato the Censor was the son of a farmer from Tusculum (modern Frascati) in Latium.

[103]Cato of Utica was revered as a Republican hero for choosing to commit suicide in 46 B.C. rather than submit to Caesar (see 3:2,14).

[104]Socrates lived from 469 B.C. to 399 B.C. One of his friends consulted the Delphic oracle and was told that nobody was wiser than Socrates.

[105]Socrates was the first philosopher to concentrate on ethics rather than scientific speculation.

[106]Euripides, the Athenian playwright, lived from 480 to 406 B.C., and Demosthenes, the Athenian orator, lived from 383 to 322 B.C.

monsters came from noble families, but they wallowed in a disgusting mire of spineless vice.

Roman Stories

5. 1. What could be more monstrous than Scipio, the son of Africanus? He was born into such a glorious household but allowed himself to be captured by a tiny group of King Antiochus' soldiers.[107] He had the two splendid titles of his father and uncle before him. His father had already won his title by defeating Africa, and his uncle was well on the way to acquiring his title, since he had reconquered most of Asia.[108] It would therefore have been better for the son of Africanus to take his own life than to give up his hands to be chained, beg for his life, and receive it as a favor from his enemy. But Scipio Asiaticus was soon to defeat that enemy and lead him home in a triumph that would gladden the eyes of gods and men.

The same son of Africanus was a candidate for the praetorship, but when he went to the Campus Martius, he looked disgraceful with his white toga covered in dirt stains.[109] If his father's scribe, Cicereius, had not used his influence to help him out, it seems unlikely that the son of Africanus would ever have won this public office from the people.[110] What is the difference between losing an election and bringing the praetorship home in this way? His relatives felt that he was degrading the praetorship, so they made sure that he would not dare to set up court or give judgment. They even took his ring off his finger, because it had a cameo of Africanus on it. Good gods, how did you allow such darkness to emerge from such lightening?[111]

5. 2. Quintus Fabius Maximus Allobrogicus was renowned as a citizen and a general,[112] but what a spoiled, decadent life his son Quintus Fabius Maximus led! Even if we ignore all his other vices, we can still fully expose his disgraceful character by the following story. The city praetor, Quintus Pompeius, decreed that he should not be allowed to inherit his father's property.[113] Throughout the entire city, nobody could be found to condemn that decree. People were angry at the

---

[107]Lucius Cornelius Scipio (praetor, 174 B.C.), the son of Scipio Africanus, was captured in 190 B.C. by Antiochus the Great of Syria.

[108]Scipio Africanus received the title Africanus after defeating Carthage in 201 B.C.; his brother, Scipio Asiaticus, received the title Asiaticus in 189 B.C. after defeating Antiochus the Great of Syria in 190 B.C. (see 2:10,2).

[109]Elections took place in the Campus Martius ("Plain of Mars"), a large field between the city walls and the river Tiber.

[110]With the help of Gaius Cicereius, Lucius Cornelius Scipio became a praetor in 174 B.C. (see 4:5,3). Gaius Cicereius himself became a praetor in 173 B.C.

[111]The censors for 174 B.C. expelled Lucius from the Senate.

[112]Quintus Fabius Maximus Allobrogicus (cos, 121 B.C.) defeated the Allobroges (in southern France). As a result, Provence was added to the Roman Empire.

[113]Quintus Pompeius Rufus (cos, 88 B.C.) was the city praetor in 91 B.C. The city praetor was responsible for cases between two Roman citizens.

idea that the son would waste all that money on his vices, since it should have been used to advance the splendor of the Fabius family. His father had been too kind in making him his heir, so the state was strict in depriving him of his inheritance.

5. 3. Clodius Pulcher had the favor of the plebs, but this tough man became infatuated with Fulvia,[114] and his military glory came under a woman's command.[115]

Their son, Pulcher, apart from the fact that he had been spineless and effete in his youth, was notorious because of his mad love for a prostitute of the lowest kind. An embarrassing kind of death put an end to his life. He greedily wolfed down a pork belly and sacrificed his life to his base, disgusting lack of self-control.[116]

5. 4. In a truly great generation of talented and distinguished citizens, Quintus Hortensius reached the highest level of influence and eloquence.[117] His grandson Hortensius Corbio led a life that was more abject and obscene than that of any prostitute. In the end, he prostituted his tongue to satisfy the lust of all the male customers in the brothel as vigilantly as his grandfather had used his tongue to defend the civil rights of his fellow citizens in the Forum.

Chapter 6. Illustrious Men Who Humored Themselves in Their Dress or in the Rest of Their Lifestyle with Greater Freedom than the Customs of Our Ancestors Would Allow

Preface

I notice that I have started off in a very dangerous direction; so I am going to stop myself now, because if I keep going on about shipwrecked lives of this kind, I shall get caught up in worthless gossip. So I shall turn around and leave those ugly specters to wallow in the quagmire of their own disgrace. It is better to tell about illustrious men who humored themselves by making slight innovations in their dress or in some other area of their lifestyle.

Roman Stories

6. 1. Scipio Africanus spent some time in Sicily planning the destruction of Carthage and trying to find a good procedure for expanding the size of his army

---

[114]The Latin actually says "his dagger stuck to Fulvia's dress," which Freudians will enjoy.

[115]This is the populist Publius Clodius Pulcher (aedile, 56 B.C.). His wife, Fulvia, later married Antony, so she was always vilified in imperial propaganda.

[116]The younger Clodius Pulcher must have had some redeeming characteristics, because he managed to become a praetor and an augur.

[117]Quintus Hortensius Hortalus (cos, 69 B.C.) was Cicero's great rival as an orator.

and transporting it over to Africa.[118] While he was carrying out the plans and preparations for this great undertaking, he spent time in the gymnasium, and he wore a Greek cloak and Greek sandals.[119] This did not make him any slower in attacking the Carthaginian army, and I suspect that it made him even more eager to attack. When people have lively and energetic minds like his, they will take action even more vigorously after they have allowed themselves some relaxation. I suspect he thought he would become more popular with our allies if he showed his approval for their lifestyle and their daily visits to the gymnasium.[120] He himself only went to the gymnasium after he had exhausted himself with a heavy load of long, hard work, and after he had forced his body as a whole to prove how tough it was by engaging in constant military activity. The army was his work; the gymnasium was his relaxation.

6. 2. We can see the statue of Scipio Asiaticus on the Capitol, wearing a Greek cloak and Greek sandals. He presumably wanted his statue to look like this because he had occasionally gone around dressed in such clothes.[121]

6. 3. When Sulla was a general, he did not think it any disgrace to walk around Naples wearing a Greek cloak and Greek sandals.[122]

6. 4. Gaius Duilius was the first Roman to win a naval triumph over the Carthaginians.[123] Whenever he attended a state banquet, he used to go home from the dinner by torchlight, with a flute player and a lyre player going ahead of him. That was how he recalled his famous military success in his celebrations at night.

6. 5. Papirius Maso carried out his official duties to the state with great success, but he was not granted a triumph by the Senate.[124] So he came up with the idea of holding a triumph by himself on the Alban Mount[125] and set an example for others in the future; and whenever he was present at a public spectacle, he would wear myrtle instead of the usual laurel crown.[126]

---

[118]Scipio Africanus was consul and also governor of Sicily in 205 B.C. He launched his invasion of Africa from Sicily in 204 B.C.

[119]His Greek lifestyle was considered a little eccentric for a military commander.

[120]Most of the Sicilian cities were founded by Greeks, so they would have had a gymnasium.

[121]Scipio Asiaticus was the brother of Scipio Africanus.

[122]Sulla was a legate in the Roman army (not a general) when he served in southern Italy (90–89 B.C.). Naples was a Greek city in Campania.

[123]When he was consul in 260 B.C., Gaius Duilius defeated the Carthaginian navy at the battle of Mylae (on the north coast of Sicily).

[124]Gaius Papirius Maso defeated the Corsicans during his consulship in 231 B.C., but he was refused a triumph by the Senate.

[125]The sanctuary of Jupiter Latiaris on the Alban Mount was the old religious center of the Latins. Several Roman generals celebrated triumphs there at their own expense.

[126]A laurel crown was a symbol of victory for athletes, soldiers, and poets, and it was used at official triumphs. The myrtle crown was used for less important military celebrations such as an ovation (at which the general walked rather than riding in a chariot) or a triumph on the Alban Mount.

6. 6. Here is a practice of Marius that was almost insolent. After his triumphs over Jugurtha and the Cimbrians and Teutons,[127] he always drank from a huge goblet with handles, because it was said that Father Liber used this kind of cup when he returned from Asia and celebrated his triumph over India.[128] By the very way Marius drank his wine, he was drawing a comparison between his victories and those of Liber.

6. 7. When Cato of Utica was a praetor,[129] he conducted the trials of Marcus Scaurus[130] and others who came before him, without putting on any tunic underneath but simply wearing his striped toga alone.

Chapter 7. Self-confidence

Preface

These stories and others like them reveal that men of courage allowed themselves some liberty in going against custom. But in the stories I shall tell below, it will be noticeable how much self-confidence those men always have.

Roman Stories

7. 1. Publius and Gnaeus Scipio and the greater part of their army had been wiped out in Spain by the Carthaginians.[131] All the nations of that province became allies of Carthage, and none of our leaders dared to go there to remedy the situation. However, Scipio Africanus, though only twenty-four years old, promised that he would go. His confidence gave the Roman people hope of recovery and victory.[132]

7. 1a. Scipio Africanus kept up his confidence when he came to Spain itself. He was besieging Badia, and when people came before his tribunal, he ordered them to appear before him again on the following day in a temple that was inside the city walls of the enemy. He quickly gained possession of the city, and at the very time and place he had promised, he set up his state chair and judged their cases. Nothing could be more noble than his confidence, more truthful than his

---

[127]Marius celebrated his triumph over Jugurtha in 104 B.C. and his triumph over the Cimbrians (from Denmark) and Teutons (from Germany) in 101 B.C.

[128]In Greek myth, Dionysus (Liber) had conquered India.

[129]Cato of Utica was a praetor in 54 B.C.

[130]Marcus Aemilius Scaurus (praetor, 56 B.C.) was governor of Sardinia in 55 B.C. He was prosecuted in 54 B.C. for misgoverning Sardinia.

[131]The brothers Publius Cornelius Scipio (cos, 218 B.C.) and Gnaeus Cornelius Scipio Calvus (cos, 222 B.C.) were defeated and killed in Spain in 211 B.C.

[132]Scipio Africanus was the son of Publius and took over the army in Spain in 210 B.C.

advance notice, more effective than his quick action, and more grand than his dignity.[133]

7. *1b.* Scipio was just as high-spirited and successful in crossing to Africa. He brought his army over from Sicily, even though the Senate forbade him to do this. If he had not followed his own counsel in this matter, but had obeyed the wishes of the Conscript Fathers, nobody would ever have discovered how to finish off the Second Punic War.[134]

7. *1c.* Scipio matched this confidence after he had landed in Africa. Two spies sent by Hannibal were caught in his camp, and when they were brought before him, Scipio did not punish them or interrogate them about the plans or military strength of the Carthaginians. On the contrary, he made sure they were escorted around all his army units, and he asked them whether they had been able to get a good look at everything they were told to spy on. Then he served them lunch, fed their pack animals, and sent them back safe. Scipio's confident spirit undermined the morale of the enemy before he destroyed their army.[135]

7. *1d.* Let's turn to his actions at home, which also revealed his exceptional confidence. Scipio Asiaticus was ordered in the Senate house to account for 4,000,000 sesterces from the money of Antiochus that he had received.[136] Lucius produced the book in which all his receipts and expenses were recorded, and he could have used it to refute the accusation by his enemies. But Scipio Africanus tore it up instead. He was outraged that anyone would call into question any official action that he had authorized as a legate.[137] He even went on to make the following speech:

> Conscript Fathers, I may have been a subordinate officer acting under someone else's authority, but I will not give an account of those four million sesterces to the treasury. I made that treasury richer by two hundred million sesterces when I was in command and acting under my own auspices, and I do not think that people have grown so malicious as to make you question my innocence. After all, when I made the whole of Africa yield to your power, I did not bring anything back from Africa that I might call my own, apart from the title of Africanus. The treasures of Carthage did not make me greedy, the treasures of Asia did not make my brother greedy; we are both much richer in resentment from others than in money for ourselves.[138]

---

[133]Scipio Africanus commanded the Roman army in Spain from 210 to 206 B.C.

[134]Scipio Africanus crossed over to Africa in 204 B.C. (see 3:6,1).

[135]This incident occurred just before the battle of Zama, which ended the war in 202 B.C.

[136]The Petillius brothers, who were tribunes of the plebs in 187 B.C., demanded an investigation into the accounts of Scipio Asiaticus (see 5:3,2c).

[137]The investigation was really an attack against Scipio Africanus, who had acted as his brother's legate during the war against King Antiochus the Great of Syria. Cato the Censor probably instigated the Petillius brothers to attack Scipio Asiaticus.

[138]The case against Scipio Asiaticus was reopened in 184 B.C., and he almost went to jail (see 5:3,2c and 8:1,damn.1).

The entire Senate approved of his resolute defense, and also of the following action of his. Some money had to be withdrawn from the treasury for purposes vital to the state. The quaestors were afraid to open the treasury, because this seemed to be against the law. Scipio Africanus demanded the keys as a private citizen, opened the treasury, and made the law bow to the public good. What gave him this confidence was his awareness that he had obeyed all the laws.

7. *1e.* I shall never get tired talking about the deeds of Scipio Africanus over and over again; after all, he never got tired performing good deeds of this type. Marcus Naevius, a tribune of the plebs,[139] or as some people say, the two Petillius brothers,[140] summoned him to appear before the people. A huge crowd accompanied Scipio to the Forum; he went up to the rostra,[141] placed his triumphal crown on his head, and spoke: "On this day, citizens, I forced the arrogant city of Carthage to submit to our terms: so it would be right for you to come along with me to the Capitol and offer our thanksgiving."

These were splendid words, and the effect they produced was just as glorious. As he went up to the couch of Jupiter the Greatest and Best, he was accompanied by the whole Senate, the entire equestrian order, and all of the plebs. As a finale, the tribune of the plebs had to hold his trial before the people without the people being there, and he had to stay alone and abandoned in the Forum, making a fool of himself with his false accusations. He could not endure the shame, so he went on to the Capitol himself and changed from Scipio's accuser to his greatest admirer.

7. *2.* Scipio Aemilianus shared his grandfather's spirit to a remarkable degree. He was besieging a well-fortified city, and some of his men suggested he should spread booby traps with metal spikes around its walls and lay down leaden sheets with nails sticking out over every river crossing. This would make it impossible for the enemy to break out suddenly and make a surprise attack on our garrison. Aemilianus replied that a man could not desire to capture a city and at the same time fear its citizens.[142]

7. *3.* Wherever I turn in recalling memorable deeds, I am forced to stick with the Scipio family, whether I want to or not. At this point, how could I leave out Scipio Nasica, a man who became famous for a statement that revealed his confident spirit? The price of grain was going up, and Gaius Curiatius, a tribune of the plebs, brought the consuls before a public meeting.[143] He kept pressing the consuls to propose to the Senate that it buy grain and send envoys overseas to complete this purchase. Since this project was not a good idea, Scipio Nasica wanted to put a stop to it, so he started speaking against it. At this, the plebs heckled him, and he

[139]Marcus Naevius (tribune of the plebs, 184 B.C.) was the man who attacked Scipio Africanus. Cato the Censor was probably behind this attack.

[140]Quintus Petillius and Quintus Petillius Spurinus (tribunes of the plebs, 187 B.C.) had attacked Scipio Asiaticus (see 3:7,1d and 5:3,2c).

[141]The rostra was the speaker's platform at the assembly place in the center of Rome.

[142]This story refers to Scipio Aemilianus' siege of Numantia (in Spain) from 134 to 133 B.C.

[143]Publius Cornelius Scipio Nasica Serapio was consul, and Gaius Curiatius was tribune of the plebs, in 138 B.C.

said, "Be quiet, citizens, I have a much better understanding of what is good for the Republic than you do." When they heard these words, they fell into a respectful silence, and they gave greater consideration to his prestige than to their own food supply.

7. 4. The spirit of Livius Salinator should be remembered for all time. He had destroyed Hasdrubal and the Carthaginian army in Umbria,[144] and he was told that there were some Gauls and Ligurians[145] from that army wandering around in small groups without any commanders or battle standards; so it would be easy to crush them with a small force. Livius answered that they should be spared, because the enemy needed to have some messengers of their own to report this great disaster back to them.

7. 5. That showed determination in battle, but the following story shows a determination in peacetime that is no less admirable; it was displayed by the consul Lucius Furius Philus in the Senate.[146] Quintus Metellus and Quintus Pompeius were former consuls and bitter enemies of his.[147] Philus was eager to head off to Spain, which was the province he had been allotted, but they were continually raising objections, so he forced them to go with him as his legates. This was not just bold and confident but almost foolhardy! These men hated him bitterly, but he dared to have them constantly by his side. One can hardly rely on one's friends on such a mission, but he did not mind choosing his assistants from among his enemies.

7. 6. If anyone likes his deed, they can hardly be displeased with the behavior of Lucius Crassus, who was renowned for his eloquence in the days of our forefathers.[148] He was governing the province of Gaul after his consulship when Gaius Carbo, whose father he had convicted, came there to spy on his administration of the province.[149] Crassus did not expel Carbo from the province; on the contrary, he even gave him a place on his tribunal, and he did not make a decision on any case without consulting him first. So the bitter and impetuous Carbo did not get anything out of his trip to Gaul, apart from discovering that his father had been guilty and had been sent into exile by a completely honest man.

7. 7. Cato the Censor had often been summoned by his enemies to defend himself in court, but he was never convicted of any crime.[150] In the end, he had so much confidence in his innocence that when they brought him before a public

---

[144]Marcus Livius Salinator was consul in 207 B.C. and defeated Hasdrubal (Hannibal's brother) at the battle of the Metaurus (a river in Umbria, eastern Italy).

[145]The Ligurians and the Gauls had allied themselves with Hannibal.

[146]Lucius Furius Philus was consul in 136 B.C.

[147]Quintus Caecilius Metellus Macedonicus (cos, 143 B.C.) and Quintus Pompeius (cos, 141 B.C.) had served previously in Spain.

[148]Lucius Licinius Crassus (cos, 95 B.C.) was governor of Cisalpine Gaul (northern Italy) in 94 B.C.

[149]The son, Gaius Papirius Carbo Arvina (praetor, 83 B.C.), had not yet held any political office. The father, Gaius Papirius Carbo (cos, 120 B.C.), had committed suicide after being convicted in 119 B.C. (see 6:5,6).

[150]Cato the Censor was put on trial forty-four times.

inquiry, he requested Tiberius Gracchus as his judge, even though he differed from him to the point of hatred in his views on governing the Republic.[151] Cato's determination put an end to the constant harassment by his enemies.

7. *8.* Marcus Scaurus had the same fortune, enjoyed an old age that was just as long and healthy, and had the same spirit. He was accused at the rostra of taking a bribe from King Mithridates to betray the Republic,[152] and this was how he made his case:

> Citizens, it is unfair that I have lived my life among one set of people but should have to defend it before a different set of people; but I shall be so bold as to ask you a question, since most of you were not there to witness my actions when I was carrying out my public offices: Varius Severus from the Sucro claims that Aemilius Scaurus was bribed by a king and betrayed the empire of the Roman people;[153] Aemilius Scaurus claims that he had nothing to do with such an offense. Which of the two do you believe?

The people were deeply impressed by this, and by shouting continuously they made Varius give up his completely insane accusation.

7. *9.* Marcus Antonius, an eloquent speaker, took the opposite course; he proved his innocence not by refusing to plead his case but by doing so gladly. He was setting off for Asia as its quaestor and had already gotten as far as Brundisium.[154] A letter informed him that he was being charged with a sexual offense before the praetor Lucius Cassius,[155] whose tribunal was so harsh that it was known as the Hazard of the Accused.[156] Antonius could have avoided the trial by appealing to the Memmian law, which exempted a man from trial while he was overseas on the Republic's business, but he rushed back to the city. By this decision, so full of fine confidence, Antonius won a speedy acquittal and departed with even greater honor.

7. *10.* Here are some splendid cases of public confidence. In the war we fought against Pyrrhus,[157] the Carthaginians without being asked sent a fleet of 130 ships

---

[151]Tiberius Sempronius Gracchus (cos, 177 B.C.) had married the daughter of Scipio Africanus, and Cato the Censor hated the Scipio family.

[152]Marcus Aemilius Scaurus (cos, 115 B.C.) had been sent (around 100 B.C.) on an embassy to King Mithridates VI of Pontus. Scaurus was later accused of treason by Quintus Varius Severus Hybrida (tribune of the plebs, 90 B.C.).

[153]The Sucro was a river in Spain, so Scaurus was suggesting that Severus Hybrida was not a real Roman.

[154]Marcus Antonius (cos, 99 B.C.) was quaestor for Asia in 113 B.C. He was Mark Antony's grandfather. Brundisium (modern Brindisi), on the east coast of Calabria, was the main harbor for anyone traveling east.

[155]Lucius Cassius Longinus Ravilla (cos, 127 B.C.) was appointed as a special prosecutor (not a praetor) in 113 B.C. to investigate the case of three vestal virgins who had been accused of sexual misconduct.

[156]The word "hazard" (*scopelus*) means a hazard to navigation, such as an underwater rock.

[157]The Romans fought against King Pyrrhus of Epirus from 280 to 275 B.C.

to Ostia to protect the Romans.[158] The Senate decided it should send envoys to tell the commander of the Carthaginians that the Roman people undertook only wars that it could fight with its own soldiers; so the Carthaginians should bring their fleet back to Carthage.

Several years later, when the forces of the Roman empire had been depleted at Cannae, the Senate had the courage to send military reinforcements to Spain. At that very time, Hannibal was battering the Capena gate with his army, but the Senate ensured that the property where the enemy camp was located should not be sold at a lower price than it would have fetched before the Carthaginians occupied it.[159] If people behave like this in bad times, doesn't it mean that they are shaming cruel Fortune into helping them?

7. 11. A huge distance lies between them, but we shall cross from the Senate to the poet Accius.[160] It will, however, be more suitable to move from him to foreign stories, so let us bring him forward. Caesar Strabo, a most distinguished and successful man, used to go to the guild of poets, but Accius would never stand respectfully when Caesar Strabo entered.[161] Accius was not unaware of Caesar Strabo's prestige, but he was confident that if anyone were to judge them by their literary output, he would prove to be a considerably better writer. So nobody accused Accius of being arrogant, because in that guild the competition was over books rather than ancestral death masks.

Foreign Stories

7. *ext. 1.* Euripides did not even seem arrogant in Athens when the people asked him to remove a sentence from one of his tragedies, but he went onto the stage and said he wrote plays to educate the people, not to learn from them.[162] One has to admire such confidence, which accurately weighs its true value and demands its rights but avoids being contemptuous or arrogant.

The response he gave to the tragic poet Alcestis must also be commended.[163] Euripides was complaining to Alcestis that he had been able to produce no more than three verses in three days, and that this had required an enormous amount of effort on his part. Alcestis boasted that he had written a hundred verses with ease. "But there is a difference," said Euripides, "because yours will last for only three

---

[158]The Carthaginians sent this fleet to help Rome in 278 B.C. Ostia, at the mouth of the Tiber, was the harbor for Rome.

[159]Hannibal had defeated the Romans at Cannae (in Apulia, southern Italy) in 216 B.C. These actions occurred in 211 B.C. when Hannibal advanced as far as Rome itself. The Capena gate was in the walls of Rome on the road to Capua.

[160]Lucius Accius was a famous Roman playwright who wrote tragedies. He lived from about 170 to 90 B.C.

[161]Gaius Julius Caesar Strabo Vopiscus (aedile, 90 B.C.) wrote plays in his spare time.

[162]Euripides, the Athenian playwright, lived from 480 to 406 B.C.

[163]This Alcestis is unknown; perhaps Valerius got the name wrong.

days, whereas mine will last for all time." The numerous writings of Alcestis rushed off and barely finished the first lap on the racecourse of human memory, whereas the work of Euripides was composed in a careful style and will voyage on-ward for all time, its sails filled with the winds of glory.

7. *ext. 2.* I shall add another story from the Athenian stage. Antigenidas the flute player had a pupil who made great progress but was not successful in winning the approval of the public.[164] So when everybody was listening, Antigenidas said to the pupil, "Play for me and for the Muses." When art has achieved perfection, it can, of course, do without the artificial charms of Fortune, because it does not lose its legitimate self-confidence. Art knows what praise it deserves, and if it does not receive that praise from others, it still records the praise as received in its own private judgment.

7. *ext. 3.* When Zeuxis had completed his painting of Helen, he did not feel like waiting around to find out how people were going to react to it.[165] Instead, he added the following verses at once:

> It is no disgrace that the Trojans and well-greaved Achaeans
> Endure misfortunes for a long time on behalf of such a woman.[166]

Was the painter so proud of his artistic skill that he thought it had grasped all the beauty that Leda could give birth to in heaven, or that Homer could express with his divine genius?[167]

7. *ext. 4.* Phidias made a playful allusion to the poetry of Homer in a striking statement. He had finished his statue of Olympian Jupiter, the most outstanding and marvelous work produced by the hand of man.[168] A friend asked Phidias what he had in mind when he captured the face of Jupiter in his ivory portrait, which looked as if Phidias had gotten it from heaven itself. Phidias replied that he had used the following verses as his guide:

> The son of Kronos spoke and bowed with his dark brow:
> His divine locks flowed down from the immortal head
> Of the king, and he made great Olympus shake.[169]

7. *ext. 5.* The bravest commanders do not allow me to linger any longer on these frivolous stories. His fellow citizens were angry with Epaminondas,[170] and to

---

[164]Antigenidas was a flute player from Thebes in the fourth century B.C.

[165]Zeuxis was a painter from southern Italy who lived in the fifth century B.C. The painting of Helen was in the temple of Juno Lacinia at Croton (in Bruttium, southern Italy).

[166]The quotation is from Homer, *Iliad* 3: 156–7.

[167]Leda was Helen's mother.

[168]Phidias was an Athenian sculptor who lived in the fifth century B.C. He completed the statue of Zeus (Jupiter) at Olympia (in southern Greece) in the 430s B.C.

[169]The quotation is from Homer, *Iliad* 1: 528–30.

[170]Epaminondas was the leader of Thebes (in central Greece) in the fourth century B.C. (see 3:2,ext.5).

insult him they put him in charge of constructing roads in their city (that was the lowest public duty there). He took on the job without the slightest hesitation and assured them he would take care that the work was done beautifully and quickly. The remarkable way he carried out his duty changed it from being the lowest task to the most distinguished and coveted honor in Thebes.

7. *ext. 6.* When he was an exile at the court of King Prusias, Hannibal advised the king to fight a battle.[171] The king said that this was not what the sacrificial entrails foretold. "You don't say?" said Hannibal, "Do you want to trust a lump of veal rather than a veteran commander?"

If you simply count the words, he spoke briefly and abruptly; but if you judge the sense, he spoke profusely and powerfully. He had snatched the provinces of Spain from the Roman people; he had brought the powerful regions of Gaul and Liguria under his power; he had forced a way through the peaks of the Alps by an extraordinary crossing; he had burnt Lake Trasimene horribly into our memories; he had made Cannae into the most famous monument of Carthaginian victory; he had occupied Capua; he had destroyed Italy.[172] Hannibal poured out all these achievements in front of that man. And he was not going to tolerate it if his glorious achievements, proved over such a long period of time, were rejected in favor of a liver from a single sacrificial victim. And indeed, as far as planning military tactics or judging military campaigns is concerned, the mind of Hannibal would have outweighed all the little sacrificial fires and altars of Bithynia, even if Mars himself were to judge the matter.

7. *ext. 7.* The following statement by King Cotys was also full of noble spirit.[173] When he learned that the Athenians had awarded him with citizenship, he replied, "I too shall award them the rights of my nation." He equated Thrace with Athens, because if he valued Thrace less in this exchange of favors, it might be thought that he had a low opinion of his own origins.

7. *ext. 8.* Both Spartans in the following stories gave noble answers. The first was criticized by someone because he went into battle although he was lame. He replied that it was his intention to fight, not to run away.[174]

The other was told by someone that the sun was always blocked out by the arrows of the Persians. He replied, "That's good news: we shall fight in the shade."[175]

A man from that city had the same kind of spirit; a foreign friend of his was showing off the high and thick walls of his native city, and the Spartan said, "If

---

[171]Some time after 190 B.C., Hannibal was banished from Carthage and fled to King Prusias I of Bithynia (see 5:3,ext.1).

[172]Hannibal conquered Spain and then crossed the Alps in 218 B.C. to invade Italy. He defeated the Romans at Trasimene (217 B.C.) and Cannae (216 B.C.), and he won Capua over to his side.

[173]Cotys was king of Thrace (modern Bulgaria) from 383 to 360 B.C.

[174]Agesilas II (king of Sparta, 399–360 B.C.) made this remark.

[175]King Leonidas I of Sparta said this at Thermopylae in 480 B.C.

you raised those walls for women, you acted well; but if you raised them for men, you acted shamefully."[176]

Chapter 8. Determination

Preface

We have finished our discussion about the heart that is open, high-spirited, and full of confidence, so we are more or less obliged to perform the remaining task of depicting determination. When people are confident that they have grasped a situation properly and justly in their mind, it naturally happens that if anyone disparages their decision after they have acted upon it, they will defend that decision fiercely, and if anyone tries to stop them before they act upon it, they will put that decision into effect immediately.

Roman Stories

8. 1. When I search for stories to illustrate my chosen subject and look around everywhere, the thing above all others that comes before my eyes is the determination of Fulvius Flaccus. Capua had been taken in by the deceptive promises of Hannibal, and it had wickedly agreed to betray Rome in exchange for gaining control over Italy. Flaccus took the city by force, winning a splendid victory, and he rightfully condemned the behavior of his enemies.[177] The Campanian Senate had been responsible for that wicked decree, and he decided to wipe it out completely. He put the senators in chains and held them in two different prisons, at Teanum and Cales,[178] intending to carry out his decision to punish them after he had finished some public business that seemed more immediately necessary.

But a rumor went about that the Roman Senate had issued a more merciful decree, and Flaccus was afraid that these evil Campanians might escape their proper punishment. He galloped at full speed to Teanum by night and killed the men who were being held there; then he went off at once to Cales to finish the job off relentlessly. The prisoners were already tied to the stake when a letter arrived from the Conscript Fathers attempting in vain to save the Campanians. Flaccus kept the unopened letter in his left hand, ordered the lictor to carry out his legal duty, and did not open the letter until it was too late to follow its instructions. His determination was even more glorious than his victory, because if you analyzed his glory and judged him by its separate parts, you would find that he was greater for punishing Capua than for capturing it.

[176]This remark was attributed to various Spartan kings. The walled city they insulted was Corinth.

[177]Capua had sided with Hannibal after the Roman defeat at Cannae (216 B.C.). Quintus Fulvius Flaccus (cos, 237 B.C.) took Capua in 211 B.C.

[178]Teanum and Cales are in Campania, to the north of Capua.

8. 2. His determination was remarkable in its severity, but the determination that Fabius the Delayer never tired of showing was remarkable in its loyalty to our country. Fabius paid out of his own money to ransom captured soldiers from Hannibal and was never repaid by the state; but he did not mention this.[179] When Fabius was dictator, the Senate granted equal powers to Minucius, his master of the horse; but he kept silent.[180] Fabius was persecuted by many other insults too; but he never changed his attitude or allowed himself to be angry with the Republic. That's how devoted he was in his love for his fellow citizens.

Well? Didn't Fabius show the same determination in waging war? The Roman Empire had almost been destroyed at the battle of Cannae, and it seemed that it would barely be able to raise an army. Fabius thought it would be better to baffle and evade Carthaginian attacks rather than fight against them in a pitched battle.[181] He was harassed by the frequent threats of Hannibal, and even though he was often presented with deceptive opportunities of success, he never deviated from his plan to save our country, even when he would only be risking a minor engagement. His most difficult task was that in every situation he had to master any feelings of exasperation or excessive confidence. So it looks as if Scipio Africanus and Fabius were equally important in saving our city, Scipio by fighting battles, and Fabius by evading them. Scipio destroyed Carthage by his quick actions, and Fabius, by his delaying tactics, prevented Rome from being destroyed.[182]

8. 3. The following story will make it clear what wonderful determination Gaius Piso showed when he was consul during a period of great unrest for the Republic.[183] Marcus Palicanus was a very rebellious man, and he had won the support of the people with his deadly flattery. The people were trying to bring the ultimate disgrace on the consular elections by granting that most distinguished position to him even though his disgusting behavior deserved some special kind of punishment rather than any public office.[184] And the tribunes were there like Furies to inflame the bewildered masses; when the masses were running wild, the tribunes gave their support; when the masses were calming down again, the tribunes fired them up with their speeches. Our state was in this pitiful and shameful condition, and Piso was almost forcefully dragged by the tribunes to the rostra. From all sides they pestered him, asking him whether he would officially declare Palicanus consul, if Palicanus won the votes of the people. At first Piso replied that he did not

---

[179]Fabius the Delayer ransomed the prisoners in 217 B.C. (see 4:8,1).

[180]Fabius the Delayer was dictator, and Marcus Minucius Rufus (cos, 221 B.C.) was his master of the horse, in 217 B.C., after the Roman defeat at Lake Trasimene.

[181]It was because of these tactics that he became known as Fabius the Delayer (*Fabius Cunctator*).

[182]Scipio Africanus led the Romans to victory in Spain (206 B.C.) and Africa (202 B.C.).

[183]Gaius Calpurnius Piso was consul in 67 B.C.

[184]Marcus Lollius Palicanus (praetor, 69 B.C.) declared himself a candidate during the election campaign of 67 B.C. As tribune of the plebs in 71 B.C., Palicanus had fought to restore the veto power of the tribunes.

think the Republic was so lost in the dark that it would sink to this level of degra-
dation. Then, as they persisted in harassing him and saying, "Well, what if the Republic has sunk so low?" he said, "I will not declare him consul." By this abrupt
response, Piso took the consulship away from Palicanus even before he could win
it. Piso disregarded all their terrible threats and would not alter the splendid in-
flexibility of his mind.

8. 4. Metellus Numidicus had the same kind of determination, and it enabled
him to withstand a political storm that was an insult to his character and prestige.
He realized what the tribune of the plebs, Saturninus, was aiming for with his
deadly schemes and, if they were not resisted, what damage his schemes would
cause to the Republic once they emerged.[185] Metellus chose to go into exile rather
than support the laws of Saturninus.[186] Could anyone be called more determined
than this man? Rather than give up his principles, he put up with losing his native
land, where he enjoyed the highest level of esteem.

8. 5. I would not put anyone above him, but I would still feel entitled to compare Quintus Scaevola the Augur with him.[187] Sulla had dispersed and destroyed
the party of his opponents, occupied the city, and intimidated the Senate with his
army.[188] He was carried away by his desire to have Marius declared a public enemy
as quickly as possible. Nobody dared to go against his wishes, and Scaevola was the
only one who refused to express an opinion when asked about this issue. Sulla
started threatening him aggressively, but Scaevola spoke out: "You can show me
those troops of soldiers that you have placed all around the Senate house; you can
threaten me with death over and over again; but I am an old man, and I have only
a short while to live. You will never get me to declare Marius a public enemy just
to save myself, because Marius saved this city and Italy."[189]

8. 6. What have women got to do with public meetings? If you keep to the
customs of our ancestors, the answer is nothing whatsoever. But when peace in
our country is being tossed around by stormy waves of rebellion, the influence of
ancient custom is swept aside, and what violence forces people to do is more important than what modesty suggests and urges them to do. For this reason, I shall
not put your story in a bad light, Sempronia, sister of Tiberius and Gaius Gracchus,
wife of Scipio Aemilianus, or say that you behaved inappropriately in meddling
with the serious affairs of men. I shall honor your memory by telling how you did
not let down your eminent family when the tribune of the plebs brought you out
in front the people in a time of great upheaval.

---

[185]Lucius Appuleius Saturninus was tribune of the plebs in 100 B.C. His "deadly scheme"
was merely a law about redistributing conquered land.

[186]Quintus Caecilius Metellus Numidicus (cos, 109 B.C.) was the only senator who refused
to uphold the land law of Saturninus. He chose exile instead.

[187]Quintus Mucius Scaevola the Augur (cos, 117 B.C.) died shortly after this (88 B.C.).

[188]Sulla was consul in 88 B.C. He marched on Rome and outlawed many of his political opponents, including Marius.

[189]Marius had saved Rome by defeating the Teutons (in 102 B.C.) and Cimbrians (in 101 B.C.).

You were forced to stand in a place where even the leaders of our state look noticeably uneasy: the most powerful men were intimidating you with their grim faces and making threats against you; the ignorant mob was shouting out at you; and the entire Forum was fanatically trying to make you kiss Equitius, as if he were the son of your brother Tiberius, because they wrongfully wanted him to be acknowledged as a member of the Sempronius family. Who knows what gloomy corner that monster was dragged out of, but he had the accursed arrogance to claim a relationship with complete strangers. You, however, put an end to his efforts.[190]

8. 7. The luminaries of our city will not feel resentful if the courage of a centurion is displayed in the midst of their extraordinary brilliance.[191] Humble people should of course respect the distinguished, but people of noble birth should likewise cherish good qualities in an unexpected person, rather than looking down on him. Should Titius be excluded from this set of stories?[192] While he was standing on guard in Caesar's army, he was taken prisoner by soldiers escorting Scipio.[193] He was told that his only chance of saving his life was to agree to become a soldier of Pompey, the son-in-law of Scipio. He did not hesitate in replying, "Thank you, Scipio, but I do not need to live on those terms." He had no ancestral death masks, but what a noble soul he was![194]

8. 8. Maevius, a centurion of the divine Augustus, upheld the same principles of determination. He had fought exceptionally well on many occasions during the war against Antony, but he was caught by the enemy in a surprise ambush and brought before Antony in Alexandria.[195] The centurion was asked what should be done with him, and he said, "Tell them to put me to death, because neither the favor of sparing my life nor the punishment of ending it could induce me to stop being a soldier of Augustus or to start being yours." Because he was so determined in his contempt for life, he was granted it all the more easily: Antony rewarded his courage by letting him live.

Foreign Stories

8. ext. 1. There are many more Roman stories of this type, but we just have to avoid overdoing it. So I shall allow my pen to glide over to foreign stories now. Blassius must hold first place in these stories, since nothing could be more obstinate

---

[190]Lucius Equitius was a populist leader and claimed to be a son of the populist Tiberius Sempronius Gracchus (tribune of the plebs, 133 B.C.). See 9:7,1 and 9:15,1. Equitius probably wanted Sempronia to support him during the election campaign of 100 B.C.

[191]Centurions were promoted from ordinary soldiers, so their background was humble.

[192]Lucius Titius was a military tribune (not a centurion) in Caesar's army in north Africa from 47 to 46 B.C.

[193]Quintus Caecilius Metellus Pius Scipio Nasica (cos, 52 B.C.) commanded the Republican army in north Africa from 47 to 46 B.C.

[194]Titius was captured and put to death in 46 B.C.

[195]Antony and Cleopatra were defeated at Actium (in western Greece) in 31 B.C., and they withdrew to Egypt. Alexandria was the capital city of Egypt.

than his determination. His native city, Salapia, was occupied by a Carthaginian garrison, and he wanted to win it back to the Roman side.[196] He had a rival, Dasius, who disagreed with him bitterly and passionately about how their state should be governed, and anyway Dasius was wholeheartedly committed to his friendship with Hannibal. But Blassius could not carry out the plan he had in mind without the aid of Dasius, so he took the risk of trying to get Dasius to help him, though it was more a case of wishful thinking than of any real hope of success. Dasius immediately told Hannibal everything Blassius had said, and he even added a few details that would make him look better and make his opponent look worse.

Hannibal ordered the two of them to come before him, so that Dasius could prove his charge and Blassius could defend himself. The case was going on before Hannibal's tribunal, and everyone was looking on, absorbed by the trial, when it happened that some more urgent business had to be dealt with. So Blassius without letting it show on his face started whispering to Dasius, urging him to support the Roman side rather than the Carthaginian one. Then Dasius shouted out that Blassius was trying to incite him against Hannibal, in the very presence of the commander himself. But everyone thought this was unbelievable, because it had been picked up by the ears of only one man and was being alleged against Blassius by his enemy, so even though Dasius was telling the truth, he didn't convince anyone. But not long afterward, the marvelous determination of Blassius won Dasius over, and Blassius handed over to Marcellus both Salapia itself and the five hundred Numidians who were there to garrison the city.[197]

8. ext. 2. The Athenians had gone against Phocion's advice, and had succeeded in spite of this, but Phocion persisted in standing by his views.[198] At a public meeting, he said that he was delighted with their success, but that his plan had still been a much better one; he did not retract his own correct interpretation simply because the bad plans of another person had happened to turn out well; he felt that the other person's plans had been luckier, but his own had been wiser. And indeed chance makes people inclined to rash behavior when it helps a bad plan to succeed; it gives this unexpected assistance so that it can later cause even greater harm.

The character of Phocion was quiet, forgiving, and openhearted, a proper balance of every charming quality. Everybody quite rightly agreed in thinking that he should be honored with the name of Phocion the Good. Determination seems by nature to be a rather rigid virtue, but it flows gently in someone so mild-hearted. Socrates, on the other hand, had a mind that was surrounded by a wall of manliness, so he has provided us with a rather more rugged example of persistence.

8. ext. 3. The entire state of Athens had flown into a most unjust and ferocious rage, and it harshly sentenced to death the ten praetors who had destroyed the

---

[196]Salapia was on the west coast of Apulia (southern Italy). It sided with Hannibal after the battle of Cannae (216 B.C.).

[197]Marcus Claudius Marcellus (cos, 222 B.C.) regained Salapia in 210 B.C.

[198]Phocion was an Athenian general who advocated peace with Macedonia. This story might refer to the unexpected success of the Athenians in freeing Byzantium from Macedonia from 341 to 340 B.C.

Spartan navy at Arginusae.[199] At that time Socrates happened to be one of the officials who were responsible for drawing up the decrees of the plebs.[200] He decided that it would not be right for so many men who had behaved so admirably to be sacrificed to an outburst of hatred for no justifiable reason. He stood resolutely opposed to the rash desires of the mob, and the loud shouting at the meeting and their excited threats against him could not force him to grant his approval to their mass hysteria. Because of his opposition, the mob was prevented from getting its wishes by the lawful route, so it went ahead and polluted its hands with the unlawful murder of the praetors. Socrates was not afraid to let his own death be an eleventh one caused by this outburst of madness in his frantic country.

8. ext. 4. The next story does not have the same kind of splendor, but it can be considered an equally clear test case of determination. Ephialtes was an effective public speaker and clearly a trustworthy man in Athens. He was ordered by the state to prosecute several men. Among the men he was obliged to denounce was Demostratus, who had an exceptionally good-looking son called Demochares. Ephialtes' heart was passionately attached to this young man. In the public office he had been allotted, Ephialtes was an aggressive prosecuter, but in the realm of his private feelings, he was a pitiable defendant. When the young man came to beg him to be more lenient in pursuing his father's case, Ephialtes could not bear to send him off or to look at him, as Demochares pleaded and groveled at his knees. Ephialtes covered his face, and weeping and moaning he allowed the young man to make his pleas, but in spite of this he was strictly honest in prosecuting Demostratus and getting him convicted. I don't know whether his victory won him more praise or more torment, because before he could ruin the guilty man, Ephialtes had to defeat himself first.[201]

8. ext. 5. But Dion of Syracuse surpassed him as a model of self-discipline. Dion had complete trust in Heraclides and Callippus, but some people warned him against them, saying he should be more careful since they were plotting against him.[202] He replied that he would prefer to leave this life than to be terrified of a violent death and to equate friends with enemies.

8. ext. 6. The story that follows is illustrious because the subject matter is remarkable in itself and the man responsible for it is very famous. Alexander, the king of Macedonia, had completely crushed the extraordinary empire of Darius in

---

[199]The Athenians won the battle of Arginusae (off the west coast of Asia Minor) in 406 B.C. By "praetors" Valerius means the ten generals who were elected in Athens every year.

[200]By "plebs" Valerius means the people of Athens. The people could not vote on any decree unless it had first been approved by the council, and Socrates was a member of the council in 406 B.C.

[201]These three men are unknown, though there was a famous democratic politician in fifth-century Athens called Ephialtes.

[202]Heraclides was Dion's rival, but they were joint rulers of Syracuse from 356 to 354 B.C. Callippus murdered Dion in 354 B.C. and ruled Syracuse.

a famous battle.[203] The weather in Cilicia was scorching, traveling was uncomfortable, and Alexander was very hot, so he jumped into the river Cydnus, which flows through Tarsus and is famous for its clear waters.[204] Immediately afterward, his muscles went numb and his limbs went dead and lost sensation from the shock of the ice-cold water. The entire army was paralyzed with anxiety, and Alexander was brought into the city, which was near the camp. He lay sick at Tarsus, and the hopes of his imminent victory wavered in accordance with the progress of his illness. Some doctors were called in; they consulted with each other conscientiously and started looking for some cure that would save his life. Their discussions pointed to one medicine, and his doctor, Philip—he was a friend and colleague of Alexander—prepared it with his own hands and gave it to him.[205] A letter suddenly arrived from Parmenio,[206] warning the king to look out for a plot by Philip, since the doctor had been bribed by Darius. After Alexander had read the letter, he drank down the medicine without the slightest hesitation and handed the letter over to Philip so that he could read it. The immortal gods gave Alexander a very fitting reward for his loyal trust in his friend, for they did not allow this false accusation to obstruct the restoration of his health.

[203]Alexander the Great of Macedonia had defeated King Darius III of Persia in 334 B.C. at the river Granicus (in northwest Asia Minor).

[204]Tarsus was the capital city of Cilicia (on the south coast of Asia Minor). Alexander was there in 333 B.C., shortly before his final victory over the Persians.

[205]Philip of Acarnania was Alexander's personal doctor.

[206]Parmenio was Alexander's best general.

BOOK FOUR

Chapter 1. Moderation

Preface

I shall turn to the most beneficial aspect of the human spirit: moderation. It does not allow our minds to go astray if we suddenly lose control of ourselves or are taken by a rash impulse. This is why moderation is never attacked by the fangs of criticism and always enjoys a wealth of praise. So moderation should review the effects of its influence on famous men.

Roman Stories

1. 1. I shall begin with the birth of our highest public office. Valerius won the name of *Publicola* (devoted to the people) because he had such great respect for the prestige of the people. After the kings were expelled, the entire force of their regime and all its insignia were subsumed under the consulship. When Valerius saw that all of this had been handed over to him, his sense of moderation made him tone down the offensive arrogance of his public office and adopt a more acceptable demeanor instead, so he removed the axes from his fasces, and he always lowered the fasces before the people at public meetings.[1] He also reduced the number of his fasces by half, by voluntarily taking on Spurius Lucretius as his fellow consul, and since Lucretius was the older of them, he gave orders that the fasces should be presented to him first.[2] He proposed a law at the centuriate assembly that forbade a magistrate to flog or put to death a Roman citizen without giving him the right to appeal to the people.[3] To make our state more free, he gradually undermined his own power. What about the fact that he demolished his own house because it had been built on a height and gave the appearance of a fortress? He may have ended up with a house that was lower down, but wasn't his glory all the higher?

1. 2. I do not really like leaving Publicola behind, but I want to move on to Furius Camillus. Even when he rose from the lowest humiliation to the highest

---

[1] The fasces symbolized the state: a bundle of sticks united into one body. The axes (attached to the bundle) symbolized the state's right to inflict capital punishment.

[2] Publius Valerius Publicola and Spurius Lucretius Tricipitinus were consuls in 509 B.C. (the first year of the Republic).

[3] The centuriate assembly elected consuls and made laws. It consisted of the Roman people grouped in voting units (see unit—voting in the Glossary).

[4] Marcus Furius Camillus (dictator, 396 B.C.) had been exiled in in 391 B.C. Ardea was in Latium, near the coast.

political power, he kept his sense of moderation. He was in exile at Ardea when our city was captured by the Gauls, and his fellow citizens went to ask him for help.[4] But Camillus would not go to Veii to take command of the army until he had been assured that the government had gone through all the customary legal formalities in appointing him dictator.[5] The triumph of Camillus over Veii was splendid,[6] his victory over the Gauls was extraordinary,[7] but that hesitation of his was far more remarkable. It is a very much more difficult task to overcome oneself than an enemy, and neither to run away too quickly when things go badly nor to be too demanding and overly happy when things go well.

1. 3. Marcius Rutilus Censorinus matched Furius in his moderation. When he was elected censor for the second time, he summoned the people to a public meeting.[8] There he criticized them in the strictest words he could manage, because they had granted him this power twice. Their ancestors had decided that the term of this office should be restricted, because its power was too great. Both Censorinus and the people had acted correctly: he by showing them that they should be moderate in entrusting men with political power, and they by entrusting themselves to a moderate man.

1. 4. Well, what a great consul Lucius Quinctius Cincinnatus proved to be![9] The Conscript Fathers wanted to extend his term of office, not just because of his extraordinary achievements, but also because the people were trying to reelect the same men as tribunes for the next year. Neither of these things was legally possible, and Cincinnatus rejected both. In this way he restrained the extremism of the Senate and at the same time he shamed the tribunes into following his example. This single individual ensured that our most distinguished order and our people would be free from the reproach of having acted unjustly.

1. 5. Fabius Maximus noticed that he himself had held the consulship five times, and that his father, grandfather, great-grandfather, and ancestors had held it on many occasions.[10] During the elections, when people were unanimous in electing his son as consul, Fabius used all his might in arguing with the people that they should give the Fabius family a break from this office. It was not that he lacked faith in his son's qualities—in fact, his son was a remarkable man—but he did not want the highest power to be held by one family all the time. What could be more effective or more powerful than the moderation of this man, which even overcame the feelings of a father, which are considered all-powerful?

[5]Camillus was worried that it might be unconstitutional for an exiled Roman to hold public office. He wanted to be properly appointed as dictator by the Senate and people.

[6]Camillus had captured Veii in 396 B.C., so it was a Roman city when the Gauls attacked in 390 B.C.

[7]Camillus drove the Gauls from Rome in 390 B.C.

[8]Gaius Marcius Rutilus Censorinus (cos, 310 B.C.) was censor for the second time in 265 B.C.

[9]Lucius Quinctius Cincinnatus was consul in 460 B.C.

[10]This could be Quintus Fabius Maximus Rullianus (cos, 322 B.C.) or Fabius the Delayer (cos, 233 B.C.). Each of these men held five consulships.

1. 6. Our ancestors felt very grateful to Scipio Africanus and intended to reward him, so they tried to glorify his great achievements with matching honors.[11]
They wanted to raise statues to him in the assembly place, at the rostra,[12] in the
Senate house, and even in the temple of Jupiter Best and Greatest; they wanted to
add his image dressed in its triumphal gear to the couches of the gods on the Capitol; they wanted to present him with an unending consulship throughout all the
years of his life and with a perpetual dictatorship. But he did not allow them to
grant him any of these honors either by a referendum of the plebs or by a decree
of the Senate. So he showed his greatness in refusing these honors just as he had
shown it in earning them.

Scipio Africanus showed the same strength of mind in defending the cause of
Hannibal before the Senate, when Hannibal's fellow citizens had sent representatives accusing him of stirring up political trouble among them.[13] Africanus argued
that the Conscript Fathers should not meddle with the political affairs of the
Carthaginians, and by his profound moderation he showed his consideration for
the safety of Hannibal and the status of Carthage. He was content to act as their
enemy only to the point of defeating them.[14]

1. 7. Marcus Marcellus was the first man to show us that Hannibal could be defeated and that Syracuse could be captured.[15] During his consulship, some Sicilians
came to the city to complain about him, but Marcellus did not call a Senate meeting about the matter. His fellow consul, Valerius Laevinus, happened to be away,
and Marcellus thought this might make the Sicilians rather nervous about making
their complaints.[16] When Laevinus returned, Marcellus took the initiative in rec-
ommending that the Sicilians be admitted before the Senate, and he bore their
complaints against him with equanimity. Laevinus then ordered them to leave, but
Marcellus forced them to stay, so that they could be present while he defended
himself. After that, when both sides had made their final arguments, he followed
the Sicilians as they left the Senate house, so that the Senate would feel more at
ease in reaching a decision. When their complaints were disproved, the Sicilians
humbly begged him to accept them as his clients, and he kindly agreed. Finally,
when he obtained Sicily by lot, he handed the province over to his fellow consul.[17]
It would be impossible to praise Marcellus in enough different ways, because he
himself showed such moderation toward our allies at so many new, different levels.

---

[11]Scipio Africanus defeated Hannibal in 202 B.C.

[12]The rostra was the speaker's platform in the assembly place.

[13]In 195 B.C., Hannibal's political enemies in Carthage tried to turn the Romans against him
by claiming that he was plotting with King Antiochus the Great of Syria.

[14]The Senate rejected the advice of Scipio Africanus, and Hannibal was exiled from
Carthage (see 3:7,ext.6 and 9:2,ext.2).

[15]Marcus Claudius Marcellus (cos, 222 B.C.) drove Hannibal back in 216 B.C. and captured
Syracuse in 212 B.C. (see 1;6,9).

[16]Marcellus was consul with Marcus Valerius Laevinus in 210 B.C.

[17]In 209 B.C., Laevinus was governor of Sicily and Marcellus commanded an army in southern Italy.

1. 8. How admirable also was the behavior of Tiberius Gracchus! He was a tribune of the plebs,[18] and he was openly hostile to Scipio Africanus and Scipio Asiaticus. Bail had been granted to Asiaticus, but he was not able to pay it, so the consul ordered him to be taken away to the public jail.[19] Asiaticus appealed to the whole body of tribunes, but none of them wanted to intercede on his behalf, so Gracchus withdrew from his fellow tribunes and wrote up a decree. Nobody had any doubt that his written words would be biased because of his anger against Asiaticus. But Gracchus first swore that he had not become friends with the Scipios, and then read out his decree, which went something like this: "Since Lucius Cornelius Scipio[20] on the day of his triumph had driven enemy commanders before his chariot and had thrown them into prison, it was unworthy and foreign to the dignity of the Republic for Scipio himself to be sent to the same prison; therefore, Gracchus would not allow this to happen." The Roman people were happy to learn that they had been mistaken in their opinion of Gracchus, and they paid his moderation the praise it deserved.

1. 9. Gaius Claudius Nero must also be included among these other models of exceptional moderation. He had shared with Livius Salinator the glory of destroying Hasdrubal.[21] Nevertheless, Nero chose to follow on horseback behind Salinator at his triumph, rather than to hold a triumph of his own, even though the Senate had decreed a triumph for him too. Nero did this because the battle had been fought in Salinator's province. So Nero did have a triumph without his own chariot, and it was all the more glorious in that people not only praised the victory of Salinator, but they praised Nero's moderation as well.

1. 10. We cannot allow ourselves to be silent about Scipio Aemilianus.[22] He had served as a censor and was performing the rites of purification at the end of his census: and at the sacrifice of the boar, the ram, and the bull, the scribe was reading the customary prayer from the official book, in which the immortal gods are asked to make the circumstances of the Roman people better and greater. Scipio Aemilianus said, "Our circumstances are good and great enough; so I pray that the gods will keep them safe forever." And at once he ordered that the hymn in the official book be changed in this way.

Since then, the censors have used this modest form of prayer in the rites of purification at the end of their census. Scipio Aemilianus wisely saw that it was right to pray for the expansion of the Roman Empire when triumphs were requested

---

[18]Tiberius Sempronius Gracchus (cos, 177 B.C.) was tribune of the plebs in 184 B.C.

[19]Marcus Naevius (tribune of the plebs, 184 B.C.) reopened an old case against Scipio Asiaticus (see 3:7,1d).

[20]The full name of Scipio Asiaticus was Lucius Cornelius Scipio Asiaticus.

[21]Marcus Livius Salinator (cos, 219 B.C.) was consul again in 207 B.C. with Gaius Claudius Nero (cos, 207 B.C.). They defeated Hasdrubal (Hannibal's brother) at the battle of the Metaurus (a river in Umbria, eastern Italy).

[22]Scipio Aemilianus was a censor in 142 B.C.

within the seventh milestone,[23] but once it had acquired the greater part of the entire world, it would be greedy to demand anything further, and the empire would be more than happy if it lost nothing of what it already possessed.

His moderation was equally apparent when he was acting in his official capacity as a censor. Scipio Aemilianus was reviewing the equestrian units, and when he had summoned Gaius Licinius Sacerdos and saw him coming before him, he said that he knew Sacerdos had perjured himself after taking a solemn oath. So if anyone wanted to accuse Sacerdos, they could use Scipio as a witness. But nobody came up to perform this task, so Scipio said, "You may lead your horse on, Sacerdos, and evade the censor's black mark. I do not want people to think that I was playing the roles of accuser, witness, and judge in your case."[24]

1. 11. The same spirit of moderation was noticeable in Quintus Scaevola, an outstanding man.[25] He was summoned as a witness for the prosecution, and he gave replies that seemed to undermine seriously the case of the accused. As he was going away, he added that the jury should accept his testimony only if other witnesses corroborated it, since it would set a very bad precedent if a man were to perish on the testimony of a single witness. In this way he had proper regard for his own religious scruples, and he also gave sound advice that would serve the common good.

1. 12. I realize that I am compressing great citizens and their great deeds and statements into very short and limited descriptions. But I have to speak briefly about subjects that are great both in quality and in quantity, and I am overwhelmed by the countless number of people and deeds, and by the glory of these outstanding subjects, so I cannot achieve both quality and quantity. Anyway, my original plan was not to give each of these topics the praise it deserves, but merely to record all of them. So two glorious men of our country, Macedonicus and Numidicus, both from the Metellus family, will be so kind as to allow me to depict them in a cursory manner.

Metellus Macedonicus had a very bitter argument with Scipio Aemilianus. Their dispute started off with their rivalry in achievement, but it turned into a serious and publicized enmity.[26] In spite of this, when he heard people shouting that Scipio had been killed, Metellus Macedonicus rushed into the street and with a sad face and disturbed voice said, "Come quickly, come quickly, citizens! The defenses of our city have been knocked down. While Scipio Aemilianus was sleeping in his home, some evil men murdered him." [27]

---

[23]Valerius means that Rome was once so small that a place less than seven miles away counted as enemy territory, and would be a legitimate object of a Roman triumph.

[24]If an equestrian passed the censor's review successfully, he was told to lead his horse on. Otherwise, he was commanded to sell his horse and thereby lost his status as an equestrian.

[25]This is probably Quintus Mucius Scaevola the Pontiff (cos, 95 B.C.).

[26]Quintus Caecilius Metellus Macedonicus (cos, 143 B.C.) had conquered Macedonia in 148 B.C., and Scipio Aemilianus had destroyed Carthage in 146 B.C. and finished the conquest of Spain in 133 B.C.

[27]Scipio Aemilianus died suddenly and mysteriously in 129 B.C.

O Republic, you were unhappy at the death of Scipio Aemilianus and yet happy with the humane and public-spirited grief of Metellus Macedonicus! At the same moment, the Republic realized what a great leader it had lost and what type of leader it still retained. Metellus Macedonicus also told his sons to carry the funeral bier of Scipio Aemilianus on their shoulders, and in addition to this honor paid at his funeral, he added the following verbal one, that they would never again be able to render this service to a greater man. What became of all those arguments in the Senate house? What became of their many disagreements at the rostra? What became of those battles, which barely remained civilian, between these great citizens and leaders? All those things were, of course, eliminated by moderation, a virtue we should regard with exceptional respect.

1. 13. Metellus Numidicus had been banished from his country by the populist party, and he went into exile in Asia.[28] He happened to be watching a public spectacle there in Tralles[29] when he received a letter stating that the Senate and people were unanimous in granting him the right to return to our city. But he did not leave the theater until the show was over, and he did not in any way reveal his joy to the people sitting next to him but kept his great happiness hidden inside himself. Everyone agrees that his expression was the same both when he was banished and when he was allowed to return. By virtue of his moderation and his strength of mind, he always maintained a middle course in good times and bad.

1. 14. I have praised a long list of families for this virtue, but the Porcius family cannot be bypassed in silence as if it had no share in this glory. Cato of Utica shows me that this cannot be allowed, and he relies on a great proof of exceptional moderation. Cato was extremely diligent and scrupulous in bringing the money from Cyprus to our city.[30] Because of this service, the Senate proposed a measure officially recognizing Cato as a candidate in the elections for praetor, even though he was out of turn. But Cato himself did not allow this, saying that it would be unfair if they made such a decree in his favor, since they had never made one like it for anyone else. He did not want them to make a change in his case, so he thought it would be better to risk the erratic behavior of the electorate than to take advantage of the Senate's generosity.[31]

1. 15. Now, as I am trying to move over to foreign stories, Marcus Bibulus, a man of the topmost rank who held the highest public offices, grabs hold of me.[32] While he was spending time in the province of Syria, he discovered that his two sons, both of them exceptionally talented, had been killed by the soldiers of

[28]Quintus Caecilius Metellus Numidicus was exiled from 100 to 98 B.C. (see 3:8,4).

[29]Tralles was an inland city in the province of Asia.

[30]Cato of Utica was the quaestor in charge of the annexation of Cyprus (58–56 B.C., see 4:3,2).

[31]Cato terminated his candidacy during the election campaign of 56 B.C. He eventually became a praetor in 54 B.C.

[32]Marcus Calpurnius Bibulus (cos, 59 B.C.) was governor of Syria in 50 B.C.

Gabinius in Egypt.[33] Their killers were put in chains and sent to Bibulus by Queen Cleopatra, so that he could take whatever vengeance he pleased on them for this dreadful tragedy.[35] No greater favor could have been offered to a man in sorrow, but he forced his grief to give way before his moderation. He ordered that the men who had butchered his own flesh and blood be sent back unharmed to Cleopatra at once, saying that the power of punishing those men should belong not to him but to the Senate.

Foreign Stories

1. ext. 1. Archytas of Tarentum[35] was immersing himself deeply in the teachings of Pythagoras at Metapontum,[36] and after a long time and a lot of hard work, he had grasped the entire work of that philosophy. After he returned to his homeland and began to look over his rural estate, he realized that it had been ruined and destroyed by the neglect of his overseer. Glaring at the man who had behaved so badly toward him, he said, "I would have punished you if I had not been so angry with you." He preferred to let him go unpunished, rather than in anger to punish him more harshly than would have been right.

1. ext. 2. The moderation of Archytas was too generous; Plato's was more restrained. He flew into a violent rage at the offense of a slave, but since he was afraid that he himself might not be able to fix on a proper punishment, he handed over the task of ascertaining the penalty to his friend Speusippus.[37] Plato thought it would be a disgrace for him if he made the offense by a slave and the punishment by Plato earn equal disapproval.

So I am not at all surprised that he was consistently moderate in dealing with his pupil Xenocrates.[38] He had heard that Xenocrates had made many disrespectful remarks against him; without the slightest hesitation, Plato refused to consider this accusation. His informer kept insisting with a convincing look on his face, and he asked Plato why he didn't trust him; Plato replied that it was not believable that he should like someone so much and not be liked by him in return. Finally, the malicious fellow, who was trying to stir up trouble between friends, resorted to taking an oath. Plato did not want to argue about whether he was perjuring himself, so he declared that Xenocrates would never have said such things unless he

---

[33]Aulus Gabinius (cos, 58 B.C.) sent soldiers to Egypt in 55 B.C. to put down a rebellion and keep King Ptolemy XII Neos Dionysos in power. These were the soldiers who later murdered the sons of Bibulus (in 50 B.C.).

[34]Cleopatra VII (who later intrigued with Caesar and Antony) had become queen of Egypt in 51 B.C.

[35]Archytas of Tarentum (in Calabria, southern Italy) was a Pythagorean philosopher. He lived from about 430 to 350 B.C.

[36]Pythagoras moved to Metapontum (in Lucania, southern Italy) in 510 B.C. and died there.

[37]Speusippus was Plato's nephew and succeeded him as head of the Academy (348–339 B.C.).

[38]Xenocrates eventually became the third head of the Academy (339–314 B.C.).

had felt that they would be of some good to Plato. You would think that Plato's soul had spent its lifetime not in a mortal body but wearing a suit of armor in the citadel of heaven; it fought invincibly and beat off all attacks by human vices, and it kept every aspect of virtue safely enclosed in its lofty embrace.

1. ext. 3. Dion of Syracuse is by no means to be compared with Plato if we judge them by their writing, but when it comes to showing moderation, he set a more impressive example. He had been expelled from his homeland by the tyrant Dionysius and went to Megara.[39] He wanted to meet privately with Theodorus, the leader of that city, but he was not admitted to his house; he was kept waiting outside the door for a long time, and he said to a friend, "We must bear this patiently. Perhaps we ourselves, when we were at the height of our power, behaved somewhat like this." By his serene wisdom, he made being an exile easier for himself.

1. ext. 4. We must take up the story of Thrasybulus at this point. The savagery of the Thirty Tyrants had forced the Athenian people to leave their own home— the people led a miserable life wandering all over the place—but Thrasybulus strengthened them both in spirit and with weapons and brought them back to their homeland.[40] After liberty was restored, he made his famous victory even more glorious by his renowned moderation: a referendum of the plebs forbade anyone to mention what had happened in the past. This dismissal from memory, which the Athenians call an "amnesty," brought their shattered and declining state back to its previous condition.[41]

1. ext. 5. The following story is no less worthy of admiration. Stasippus of Tegea had a relentless rival in the state government, who was an honest and distinguished man in other respects.[42] His friends were encouraging Stasippus to remove or get rid of this man by any means whatsoever, but Stasippus said he would not do it. A good citizen occupied this position to look after their country, and Stasippus did not want a bad or dishonest one to take it instead; he preferred to be violently attacked by his opponent rather than have his country deprived of an exceptional spokesman.

1. ext. 6. Pittacus also had a heart that was endowed with moderation. The poet Alcaeus persistently attacked him with all his bitter hatred and powerful talent. But when his fellow citizens made Pittacus their tyrant, Pittacus only reminded Alcaeus what he could do if he wanted to destroy Alcaeus.[43]

---

[39]Dion was exiled from Syracuse by the tyrant Dionysius II. Dion remained in exile from 367 to 357 B.C. Megara is on the isthmus that joins northern Greece to the Peloponnese (southern Greece).

[40]Thrasybulus overthrew the regime of the Thirty Tyrants in 403 B.C.

[41]The Athenian people ("the plebs") declared an amnesty in 403 B.C. for all political crimes committed by the regime of the Thirty Tyrants.

[42]Stasippus of Tegea (in Arcadia, southern Greece) was a pro-Spartan politician in the fourth century B.C. Most Arcadians hated Sparta.

[43]Pittacus ruled Mitylene (on the island of Lesbos, off the west coast of Asia Minor) for ten years (590–580 B.C.) and banished his aristocratic opponents, including the poet Alcaeus.

1. ext. 7. The mention of this man reminds me that I should talk about the moderation of the Seven Sages.[44] In the region of Miletus[45] some fishermen were drawing a net and a certain man bought their catch. A very heavy tripod made of gold was pulled out of the net, and an argument arose, with the fishermen claiming that they had sold only the fish they had caught and the buyer saying that he had bought whatever they were lucky enough to catch. Because it was such an unusual occurrence and because such a large sum of money was involved, the decision was referred to the entire people of that state. The people decided that they should consult Apollo at Delphi to find out which of the men should be awarded the table. The god replied that it should be given to the man who surpassed the others in wisdom, and these were his words:

"Who is the first of all in wisdom? I declare that the tripod is his."

So the people of Miletus agreed that they should give the table to Thales.[46] He handed it over to Bias,[47] Bias handed it over to Pittacus, Pittacus gave it to another man, and so on through the entire circle of the Seven Sages, until it finally came to Solon;[48] and Solon handed over the honor and prize for the greatest wisdom to Apollo himself.

1. ext. 8. I must also bear witness to the moderation of Theopompus, the king of Sparta.[49] He set up the custom in Sparta of electing ephors, to counterbalance the power of the kings at Sparta just as the tribunes of the plebs counterbalance the power of the consuls at Rome.[50] His wife told him that as a result of his actions he would be leaving his sons in a weaker position, and Theopompus said, "The position in which I leave them will be weaker but more permanent." An excellent answer indeed. In the final analysis, a government is permanent only if it imposes limits on its own power. By restraining the monarchy within the limits of the law, Theopompus distanced it from absolutism but moved it all the closer to the good will of its subjects.

1. ext. 9. When Scipio Asiaticus withdrew and forced Antiochus to confine his kingdom to the region beyond the Taurus Mountains, he deprived Antiochus of the province of Asia and the peoples next to it.[51] The king thanked the Roman people in all sincerity, because they had relieved him from governing a region that

---

[44]The Seven Sages were seven statesmen and thinkers of the sixth century B.C. The list varies but always includes the four wise men in this story.

[45]Miletus was on the west coast of Asia Minor.

[46]Thales of Miletus was a philosopher around 585 B.C.

[47]Bias of Priene (near Miletus on the west coast of Asia Minor) was a statesman around 500 B.C.

[48]Solon was archon of Athens in 594 B.C.

[49]Theopompus was king of Sparta from 720 to 675 B.C.

[50]The five ephors had the power to fine or imprison the kings at Sparta.

[51]Scipio Asiaticus defeated Antiochus the Great of Syria in 190 B.C. The Taurus Mountains are between Turkey and Syria, so Antiochus lost the equivalent of all of modern Turkey.

was too large, and because he could be content with a kingdom of moderate dimensions. Indeed, nothing is so glorious or splendid that it does not require restraining by moderation.

Chapter 2. People Who Used to Be Enemies but Came Together as Friends or In-Laws

Preface

These stories have been glorified by many famous authors, so let us turn to the extraordinary way in which the human mind changes from hatred to goodwill. I shall certainly be happy to describe these things with my pen: if we feel happy when we see a wild ocean turn into a calm one, or a cloudy day turn into a clear one, if we experience the greatest joy when war turns into peace, then we must celebrate the removal of bitter hostility and tell stories about it with joy.

Roman Stories

2. 1. Marcus Aemilius Lepidus had been consul twice and was the chief pontiff; and the splendor of his public positions was matched by his dignified way of life. He had a long-standing and very bitter hostility toward Fulvius Nobilior, a man who was equally distinguished. But as soon as they were elected censors, Lepidus left his hostility behind in the Campus Martius.[52] He felt that it would not be right for them to disagree because of a private dispute, since they would be joined together in the highest public office. Their contemporaries approved of this wise decision, and ancient writers of history have handed down the story for us to admire.

2. 2. Those historians did not want future generations to be unaware of the glorious decision by Livius Salinator to put an end to his quarrels. He was burning with hatred against Nero when he went into exile, since Nero's testimony had been particularly damaging to him.[53] But after Salinator was recalled from exile and his fellow citizens elected Nero to the consulship with him,[54] Salinator forced himself to forget his own nature, which was a very bitter one, and his grievance, which was a very serious one. He felt that if he persisted in being disagreeable while sharing this powerful position with his colleague, and if he showed himself to be a relentless enemy, he would be acting like a bad consul. His change to a quieter state of mind brought about the salvation of our city and of Italy in a harsh

---

[52]Marcus Aemilius Lepidus (cos, 187 B.C.) was censor in 179 B.C. with Marcus Fulvius Nobilior (cos, 189 B.C.) Elections took place in the Campus Martius.

[53]Marcus Livius Salinator (cos, 219 B.C.) had gone into voluntary exile after being convicted of misconduct during the Illyrian War.

[54]Salinator was consul again in 207 B.C. with Gaius Claudius Nero (cos, 207 B.C.).

and difficult period of time. By relying on the united force of their courage, they destroyed the terrifying armies of Carthage.[55]

2. 3. There is a famous case of enmity being laid aside in the story of Scipio Africanus and Tiberius Gracchus.[56] They still hated each other when they came to a ritual banquet, but when they left it, they were united both in friendship and by marriage: Scipio was not just content with following the advice of the Senate and making friends with Gracchus at the Banquet of Jupiter on the Capitol;[57] he even betrothed his daughter Cornelia to him on the spot.

2. 4. This type of kindness was especially noticeable in the case of Cicero. When Aulus Gabinius was accused of misgovernment, Cicero defended him with all his might, even though when Gabinius was consul, he had expelled Cicero from the city.[58] Publius Vatinius had always been hostile to Cicero's political success, but Cicero still protected him during two state trials.[59] Nobody accused Cicero of being shallow; on the contrary people praised him, because it is far nobler to overcome a grievance by doing good than to retaliate and keep the mutual hatred alive.

2. 5. Cicero's behavior seemed so admirable that even his greatest enemy, Publius Pulcher, did not hesitate to imitate it. Pulcher had been accused of sacrilegious adultery by three men of the Lentulus family, but when one of them was accused of electoral bribery, Pulcher protected him and spoke on his behalf.[60] Looking at the jurymen and the praetor and the temple of Vesta,[61] he decided to act as a friend to Lentulus, even though Lentulus had once made such hostile speeches against him in their presence when he was trying to ruin Pulcher's life by making a disgusting accusation against him.

2. 6. Caninius Gallus behaved admirably when he was on trial and also when he was prosecutor. Gallus convicted Gaius Antonius but married Antonius' daughter;[62] Gallus was convicted by Marcus Colonius but chose Colonius to administer his property.

---

[55]Nero and Salinator defeated the Carthaginians at the river Metaurus (in Umbria, eastern Italy).

[56]Tiberius Sempronius Gracchus (cos, 177 B.C.) and Scipio Africanus were reconciled in 184 B.C. after Gracchus had saved Scipio Asiaticus from jail (see 4:1,8).

[57]The Banquet of Jupiter (*Epulum Jovis*) took place on the Capitol every year on September 13.

[58]Aulus Gabinius (cos, 58 B.C.) had supported the banishment of Cicero (58–57 B.C.), but when Gabinius came home from Syria in 54 B.C. and was accused of misgovernment, Cicero defended him.

[59]Cicero defended Publius Vatinius (cos, 47 B.C.), a former legate of Caesar, in 54 B.C.

[60]Publius Clodius Pulcher (aedile, 56 B.C.) had been tried in 61 B.C. for adultery with Caesar's wife during a religious festival. His three accusers were Lentulus Crus (cos, 49 B.C.), Lentulus Marcellinus (cos, 56 B.C.), and Lentulus Niger (praetor by 61 B.C.).

[61]The temple of Vesta was at the opposite end of the Forum from the assembly place, where the court would have met.

[62]In 59 B.C. Lucius Caninius Gallus (tribune of the plebs, 56 B.C.) prosecuted Gaius Antonius Hybrida (cos, 63 B.C.).

2. 7. The lifestyle of Caelius Rufus may have been degenerate, but the compassion he showed toward Quintus Pompeius has to be admired.[63] Pompeius had been ruined by Caelius in a state trial,[64] and later Pompeius' mother, Cornelia, refused to hand over landed property that had been bequeathed to Pompeius. Pompeius sent letters begging Caelius for help, and Caelius defended him in his absence with determination. Caelius read out the letter from Pompeius in court, as evidence of his dire need, and used it to undermine Cornelia's wicked greed. Because of the extraordinary kindness behind such deeds, we cannot ignore them, even when someone like Caelius performs them.

Chapter 3. Self-denial and Self-control

Preface

It is with great care and particular enthusiasm that I have to tell how famous individuals have used their judgment and reason to keep their hearts free from the almost insane attacks of desire and greed. A household, a state, a kingdom will easily survive on a permanent basis provided that the desire for sexual pleasure and money wins the least power there. Wherever those true curses of the human race infiltrate themselves, injustice prevails, disgrace runs rampant, violence makes its home, and wars are born. Let us voice our approval and commemorate the character of people who have opposed these dreadful vices.

Roman Stories

3. 1. Scipio Africanus was only twenty-four years old when he destroyed the city of New Carthage in Spain,[65] and for him this was an omen that the greater city of Carthage would be captured.[66] He gained possession of many hostages, whom the Carthaginians had kept locked up in that city, including a young, unmarried woman of extraordinary beauty. But although Scipio was a young man and unmarried and had conquered her country, as soon as he discovered that she was from a distinguished Celtiberian family and that she had been betrothed to Indibilis, the greatest nobleman of that race, he summoned her parents and fiancé and handed her over to them without raping her. He took the money he had received for the young woman's ransom and added it to her dowry. His self-restraint and generosity put Indibilis under a moral obligation to him, so Indibilis won the

---

[63]Marcus Caelius Rufus (praetor, 48 B.C.) was politically opposed to Quintus Pompeius Rufus (tribune of the plebs, 52 B.C.).

[64]Caelius prosecuted Pompeius in 51 B.C. and had him exiled.

[65]Scipio Africanus captured New Carthage in 209 B.C.

[66]Carthage was destroyed by his adopted grandson, Scipio Aemilianus, in 146 B.C.

hearts of the Celtiberians over to the Romans and responded to the good deeds of Scipio with the gratitude they deserved.[67]

3. 2. Just as Spain witnessed the self-denial of this man, so Epirus, Achaea, the Cycladic islands, the coastal region of Asia Minor, and the province of Cyprus witnessed Cato of Utica's.[68] He took on the task of bringing back money from Cyprus, but he kept his mind completely free from both lust and avarice, though he had ample opportunity for both kinds of misbehavior. Royal treasures were under his control and all those Greek cities, which were hothouses of pleasure, were necessary stopping points throughout his entire voyage. Munatius Rufus, his constant companion during his mission in Cyprus, speaks of this in his writings.[69] I do not focus on the testimony of Rufus: Cato's glory relies on its own self-evidence, because both self-restraint itself and Cato were born from the same womb of Nature.

3. 3. Drusus Germanicus was the exceptional glory of the Claudius family and a rare paragon of his country.[70] And more than all this, the greatness of his achievements, considering his age, wonderfully matched those of his august step-father and brother, the divine lights of our state.[71] It was well known that he restricted his sexual pleasures to those he enjoyed with his beloved wife. By her famous deeds, Antonia,[72] though she was a woman, surpassed the men of her family in glory, and she repaid her huband's love with her exceptional loyalty to him. After his death,[73] although she was beautiful and in the prime of her life, she lived with her mother-in-law rather than remarrying.[74] Together in one bed, Antonia let her youthful vigor waste away while the other woman grew old as she went through widowhood. Let their bedroom mark the culmination of these stories.

3. 4. Now let us pay attention to men whose minds never paid any attention at any time to amassing wealth. Gnaeus Marcius was a young man of patrician family, and a famous descendant of King Ancus.[75] He got his extra name (Coriolanus) from the Volscian town of Corioli, which he had captured.[76] After he had carried out deeds of notable courage, he was praised in front of the army by the consul Postumus Cominius in a studied speech.[77] Coriolanus was presented with every military award, sixty acres of land, his choice of ten captured soldiers, and as many horses with equipment, a herd of one hundred cattle, and as much silver as he

---

[67]The Celtiberians lived in eastern Spain. They resisted Roman conquest until 133 B.C.

[68]Cato of Utica was sent to annex Cyprus (58–56 B.C.)

[69]Munatius Rufus was a Stoic philosopher.

[70]Nero Claudius Drusus Germanicus was the younger brother of the emperor Tiberius.

[71]His august stepfather was the Emperor Augustus.

[72]Antonia was Antony's daughter.

[73]Drusus died in 9 B.C.

[74]Antonia's mother-in-law was the empress, Livia Drusilla.

[75]Ancus Marcius was the fourth king of Rome (640–617 B.C.)

[76]Gnaeus Marcius Coriolanus had captured Corioli in 493 B.C.

[77]Postumus Cominius Auruncus was consul in 493 B.C.

could carry away. But he refused to accept any of these awards apart from the freedom of one prisoner, who was a family friend, and a horse that he himself could
use in battle. His spirit of moderation was so strict that you couldn't tell whether
he was more to be praised for choosing these prizes or for refusing those ones.

3. 5. Manius Curius was the most rigid model of Roman frugality and the
most perfect example of courage.[78] When the Samnite envoys were brought in to
see him, he was sitting on a rustic bench beside the fireplace and taking his dinner
from a wooden bowl; you can imagine the kind of meal it was from its presenta-
tion. He thought nothing of the wealth of the Samnites, but they were amazed at
his poverty. They had brought him a huge amount of gold presented by their
state, and speaking kindly they invited him to accept it, but he burst out laughing
and said at once, "You have been sent on a pointless, not to mention stupid, mission; tell the Samnites that Manius Curius would rather rule over rich men than
become a rich man himself; take away that expensive gift, which was invented to
do mischief to men, and remember that I cannot be defeated in battle or corrupted by money."

When Curius had driven King Pyrrhus out of Italy, he did not touch a single
thing from the royal plunder but used it to enrich our army and city.[79] The Senate
decreed that the people should get five acres of land each, and that he should get
thirty, but he did not take more than the people had been assigned. He felt that a
man would not be a good citizen of the Republic if he was not content with what
had been granted to all the other citizens.

3. 6. Fabricius Luscinus felt the same way.[80] In his day, he held the highest
offices and exercised the greatest influence in the entire state, but his income was
no more than that of the poorest man. The entire Samnite people were his clients,
and they sent him ten thousand copper coins, five pounds of silver, and ten slaves,
but he sent the lot back to Samnium. By virtue of his self-restraint, he was extremely rich even though he had no money, and he had enough people attending
to him even though he had no slaves, because what made him rich was not possessing a lot but wanting just a little. So his home may have been empty when it
came to copper and silver and slaves from Samnium, but it was full of the glory he
had won from that nation.

The prayers of Fabricius were in keeping with his rejection of these gifts. He went
as an envoy to Pyrrhus,[81] and in the king's palace he heard Cineas of Thessaly[82]
talking about someone in Athens who was renowned for his philosophy. This
philosopher claimed that people should not do anything unless it brought them

---

[78]Manius Curius Dentatus defeated the Samnites when he was consul in 290 B.C.

[79]Curius was consul again in 275 B.C. and defeated King Pyrrhus of Epirus.

[80]Gaius Fabricius Luscinus (cos, 282 B.C.) triumphed over the Samnites when he was consul
again in 278 B.C.

[81]Fabricius went on this embassy to King Pyrrhus of Epirus in 280 B.C.

[82]Cineas of Thessaly was a diplomat employed by King Pyrrhus.

pleasure.[83] Fabricius treated this statement as monstrous, and at once he prayed the gods to inflict that philosophy on Pyrrhus and the Samnites. Athens may boast of its learning, but a wise man would prefer the religious horror of Fabricius to the teachings of Epicurus. And this is proved by what happened: the city that valued pleasure above all lost its mighty empire, whereas the city that took pleasure in hard work seized that empire; Athens was unable to maintain its liberty, whereas our city even had the power to grant liberty to others.

3. 7. One would be right in thinking that Sextus Paetus, who had the extra name of Catus ("the wise"), was a student of Curius and Fabricius.[84] When he was consul, the Aetolian nation sent envoys to him bringing him silver vessels of every kind, which were very heavy and made with wonderful artistry.[85] These envoys had gone to congratulate him previously and had reported home that they had seen earthenware vessels on his table. But Catus advised them not to imagine that self-control was like poverty and needed donations; then he ordered them to leave with their parcels. How right he was to prefer our native goods to Aetolian luxuries! If only later ages had been content to follow the example of frugality he set! Where have we come to now? You can hardly stop slaves turning up their noses at crockery that a consul was not embarrassed to use in those days.

3. 8. When Paullus had defeated King Perseus,[86] he used the riches of Macedonia to end the ancient and traditional poverty of our city. As a result, the Roman people freed themselves for the first time from the burden of paying property taxes.[87] But Paullus did not make his own household richer in any way. He felt he had done very well for himself if other people got the money from his victory and he got the glory.

3. 9. Quintus Fabius Gurges, Numerius Fabius Pictor, and Quintus Ogulnius endorsed this view of his.[88] They were sent on a delegation to King Ptolemy,[89] and they took all the gifts that he had privately given them and donated them to the treasury, even before they reported to the Senate about their mission. They clearly believed that men who acted on state business should not gain anything from it apart from the glory of having carried out their duties properly. But here is a real indication of the kindness of the Senate and the conscientious discipline of our ancestors: everything the envoys had placed in the treasury was given back to them, not just by decree of the Conscript Fathers but also with the permission of the people; the quaestors quickly distributed these goods to each of the envoys. In the case of these goods, the generosity of Ptolemy, the self-denial of the envoys,

---

[83]The renowned philosopher was Epicurus (341–270 B.C.).

[84]Sextus Aelius Paetus Catus was consul in 198 B.C.

[85]The Aetolians (in northern Greece) were allies of Rome during the Second Macedonian War (200–196 B.C.).

[86]Lucius Aemilius Paullus (cos, 182 B.C.) defeated King Perseus of Macedonia in 168 B.C.

[87]The property tax (*tributum*) was abolished for Roman citizens in 167 B.C.

[88]Quintus Fabius Maximus Gurges (cos, 292 B.C.), Numerius Fabius Pictor (cos, 266 B.C.), and Quintus Ogulnius Gallus (cos, 269 B.C.) went as envoys to Egypt in 273 B.C.

[89]Ptolemy II Philadelphus was king of Egypt from 282 to 246 B.C.

and the fairness of the Senate and people received the approval they deserved for their part in this good deed.

3. 10. The facts themselves prove that Calpurnius Piso imitated the self-restraint shown by the two men of the Fabius family and by Ogulnius with a similar type of praiseworthy behavior.[90] When he was consul, Piso had freed Sicily from the serious war waged by the runaway slaves. He followed the usual custom of generals and rewarded those men who had performed especially useful services for him. Among them was his own son, who had fought very bravely on several fields. He decorated him with a golden crown weighing three pounds, but only in name, because he said it would be wrong for a public official to use state funds in paying for something that would come to his own family. So he promised that he would leave the young man the same amount of gold in his will, so that his son could receive the honor in public from him as a commander but the monetary prize in private from him as a father.

3. 11. Come, now, if some famous man nowadays were to use goatskins as blankets, govern Spain with the help of three slaves, spend only 500 asses[91] on his voyage to his overseas province, and be content with the same food and wine as the sailors, wouldn't he be thought an unfortunate fellow? But Cato the Censor bore these conditions with complete equanimity, because he had always been happy with frugality, and he kept to this type of lifestyle with the greatest of pleasure.[92]

3. 12. Many years later, Cato of Utica was no match for this old-fashioned self-restraint, since he was born in a state that was already rich and delighting in luxuries. Nevertheless, when he was fighting in the civil wars and bringing his son with him, he kept twelve slaves, more than Cato the Censor had had but less than was normal according to the very different fashion of his times.[93]

3. 13. My heart is thrilled to go through these stories about our greatest men. Scipio Aemilianus, after two famous consulships and the same number of triumphs, which had been especially glorious for him, carried out his duties on a delegation with the help of seven slaves. I suspect he might have been able to acquire many more slaves than this from the plunder of Carthage and Numantia,[94] but he preferred to have the glory of his achievements go to himself and the plunder go to his country. As a result, when he was making his way through allied and foreign nations, they counted not his slaves but his victories, and they judged him not by the amount of gold and silver he had, but by his grandeur.[95]

[90]Lucius Calpurnius Piso Frugi was consul in 133 B.C. during the First Slave War in Sicily (135–132 B.C.).

[91]The as was a Roman coin (see Money—Roman in the Glossary).

[92]Cato the Censor fought against the Spaniards when he was consul (in 195 B.C.)

[93]Cato of Utica was a Republican commander from 49 B.C. until his suicide in 46 B.C.

[94]Scipio Aemilianus destroyed the African city of Carthage in 146 B.C. and the Spanish city of Numantia in 133 B.C.

[95]Scipio Aemilianus visited Roman allies in the eastern Mediterranean in 140 B.C.

3. 14. Self-restraint has been discovered in the hearts of the entire plebs on many occasions, but it will be more than enough to tell two stories, which are separated by a long period of time.

When the terror inspired by his attack was dissipating, and his army from Epirus was losing its spirit, Pyrrhus wanted to buy the goodwill of the Roman people, since he was unable to undermine their courage.[96] So he brought almost all of his sumptuous royal treasure to our city. But although his envoys brought gifts of great value and of every variety—gifts that men and women could enjoy—around to people's houses, no door was opened to receive any gift. Pyrrhus was a high-spirited rather than effective defender of the insolence of the Tarentines,[97] but I wonder whether the real glory for defeating him belongs to the moral qualities of our city.

In the whirlwind that Marius and Cinna launched against the Republic, the admirable self-denial of the Roman people was seen once again.[98] Marius and Cinna handed over the houses of the men they had put on their death list so that the lower classes could loot them, but nobody was found who would reach for this plunder at the cost of grieving their fellow citizens. Every single person kept away from those houses as if they were sacred temples. This compassionate self-restraint of the plebs was indeed a silent denunciation of the cruel victors.

Foreign Stories

3. ext. 1. We must not begrudge foreigners or fail to commemorate them for the same praiseworthy qualities. Pericles, the Athenian leader, had Sophocles, the writer of tragedies, as one of his fellow praetors.[99] They were busy with their public duties when a young freeborn man went by, and Sophocles praised his good looks in exaggerated language. Pericles criticized his lack of self-control and said that a praetor should keep his hands away from monetary profit, but he should also keep his eyes away from lustful gazing.

3. ext. 2. When Sophocles was getting old, someone asked him whether he was still sexually active. "The gods forbid!" he said, "I am so glad to have escaped from that because it felt like a mad tyranny."[100]

3. ext. 3. People have told us that Xenocrates practiced equal self-denial in his old age.[101] The story that follows is no small proof of this view. During an all-night festival, Phryne, a well-known prostitute at Athens, lay down beside him

[96]King Pyrrhus of Epirus offered the Romans generous peace terms in 280 B.C. after he had failed to win a quick victory.

[97]Pyrrhus supported Tarentum in its dispute with Rome (see 2:2,5).

[98]Lucius Cornelius Cinna (cos, 87 B.C.) and Marius took over Rome in 87 B.C. and massacred their political opponents.

[99]Praetor here means an Athenian general (*strategos*). Pericles and Sophocles were generals in 440 B.C.

[100]Plato tells this story in the first book of the *Republic*.

[101]Xenocrates was head of Plato's Academy from 339 to 314 B.C.

when he was drunk on wine.[102] She had made a bet with some young men that she would be able to undermine his self-control. He did not push her away verbally or physically, and he let her stay on his lap as long as she wanted, but when he let her go, she had not achieved her goal. This act of self-restraint was the result of a mind imbued with philosophy, but the little prostitute made a very witty remark. The young men laughed at her, because although she was so beautiful and so elegant, she had been unable to win over the heart of a drunken old man with her charms. They demanded the amount that had been agreed on, since they had won the bet. But she replied that she had made a bet with them about a man, not about a statue. Could anyone give a more truthful and accurate account of Xenocrates' self-restraint than the one that was made by that little prostitute herself?

In spite of her beauty, Phryne could not undermine the resolute self-restraint of that man in any way. Well? Could King Alexander[103] have shaken it with his riches? You would think that he too had been tempting a statue and had failed in the same way. He had sent envoys to Xenocrates with several talents.[104] Xenocrates brought the envoys into the Academy and entertained them in his usual style (that is, a modest one) and with very small helpings. On the following day, they asked him who they should pay the money to. "What!" he said, "Didn't you realize from yesterday's dinner that I don't need any?" So the king wanted to buy the friendship of the philosopher, but the philosopher did not want to sell his friendship to the king.

3. ext. 4. Alexander may have acquired the reputation of being unconquerable, but he was unable to conquer the self-restraint of Diogenes the Cynic.[105] Alexander went up to Diogenes as he was sitting in the sun and urged Diogenes to tell him if there was anything he wanted. Diogenes happened to be sitting on the sidewalk, and although people called him scruffy, he was a man of strong moral character, so he said, "We can talk about other things later, but for now I would like you to stop blocking the sunlight." This was the meaning behind those words: Alexander is trying to unseat Diogenes with his riches, but it will be easier for Alexander to unseat Darius with his armies.

Diogenes was at Syracuse, rinsing vegetables, when Aristippus said to him, "If you would agree to flatter Dionysius, you wouldn't have to eat those." And Diogenes answered, "You've got it wrong. If you would agree to eat them, you wouldn't have to flatter Dionysius."[106]

---

[102]Phryne was a famous Athenian prostitute who modeled for statues of Aphrodite.

[103]Alexander the Great, king of Macedonia (336–323 B.C.).

[104]A talent was 6,000 drachmas (see money—Greek in the Glossary).

[105]Alexander the Great met the Cynic philosopher, Diogenes of Sinope (412–323 B.C.), in Corinth in 336 B.C.

[106]The philosopher Aristippus of Cyrene (430–355 B.C.) spent his last years in Sicily. Dionysius II was tyrant of Syracuse (367–357 and 346–344 B.C.).

Chapter 4. Poverty

Preface

We discover that children are a married woman's greatest jewels from the following story in one of the books of collected anecdotes by Pomponius Rufus. A lady from Campania was a guest at the house of Cornelia,[107] the mother of the Gracchus brothers, and she was showing off her jewels, which were the most beautiful ones in that era. Cornelia kept her talking until her children came back from school, and then she said, "These are my jewels."[108]

A man who longs for nothing obviously has everything, and even more securely than a man who owns every possession. The ownership of possessions tends to fade away, but the enjoyment of a sound mind is not subject to the attacks of misfortune. So what is the point in regarding wealth as the highest point of happiness or poverty as the lowest level of misery? The happy appearance of the rich is filled with lots of inner bitterness whereas the rather scruffy look of the poor is enriched with firm and lasting advantages. But this will be made clearer by real people than by words.

Roman Stories

4. 1. The monarchy was abolished because of the excessive arrogance of Tarquin, and Valerius Publicola started off the consulship with Junius Brutus.[109] After that, Publicola held three consulships that were very popular with the Roman people. By carrying out many great deeds, he added to the glory of his ancestral death masks, but at the same time this star of the consulship did not leave enough money behind to pay for his own funeral when he died. So his funeral had to be paid for with public funds. It would be pointless to probe the poverty of this great man by discussing it any further. It is abundantly clear how little he must have possessed during his lifetime if he could not afford a funeral bier and pyre when he died.

4. 2. Can we imagine how distinguished Menenius Agrippa must have been if the Senate and plebs chose him as the man to make peace between them?[110] He must, of course, have been as distinguished as a man should be if he saves the state. But he was so poor when he died that he would have had to do without the honor

---

[107]Cornelia was the daughter of Scipio Africanus and had married Tiberius Sempronius Gracchus (cos, 177 B.C.).

[108]Cornelia's daughter married Scipio Aemilianus, but her sons died horribly (see 1:4,2 and 6:8,3).

[109]Tarquin the Proud (the last king of Rome) was expelled in 509 B.C. Lucius Junius Brutus and Publius Valerius Publicola were the first consuls.

[110]Agrippa Menenius Lanatus (cos, 503 B.C.) persuaded the plebs to come back to Rome in 494 B.C.

of a burial if the people had not contributed a penny[111] each toward his funeral. But when our state had been divided by dangerous civil strife, it wanted to be united by the hands of Agrippa, because it realized that although they may have been poor hands, they were clean ones. When he was alive he had no property to report to the census, but after his death we still enjoy his magnificent legacy today, the social unity of Rome.

4. 3. I must confess, however, that there was silver in the homes of Gaius Fabricius and Quintus Aemilius Papus, the leading men of their era.[112] Each of them had a dish for the gods and a salt cellar, but Fabricius was more elegant because he chose to put a little pedestal made of horn under his dish. Papus behaved rather assertively when he inherited those items, because he decided on account of their religious significance that he would not get rid of them.

4. 4. What about those incredibly rich men who were called from their ploughs to become consul? Was it for pleasure that they turned over the barren and baked soil of Pupinia?[113] Was it for amusement that they drenched themselves in sweat to break up huge sods of clay? No, the truth is that although the Republic used them as generals in times of danger, the poverty of their estates forced them to live (why should I hesitate to call things by their true name) like farmhands.

4. 5. The men who had been sent by the Senate to summon Atilius so that he could take command over the Roman people found him sowing seed.[114] But those hands worn away with farmwork guaranteed the survival of our state and destroyed the enormous armies of our enemies. His hands had recently been guiding a pair of oxen at the plough, but now they held the reins of a triumphal chariot; and when they laid down the ivory staff, they were not embarrassed to return to the rustic handle of his plough. Atilius can console the poor, but even more so can he teach the rich that their frantic acquisition of wealth is not necessary for one who desires true glory.

4. 6. Atilius Regulus had the same name and family and was our greatest glory and our greatest loss in the First Punic War.[115] He was exhausting the resources of the insolent Carthaginians with his many victories in Africa when he learned that because of his fine achievements, his command was being extended for another year.[116] He wrote to the consuls that the overseer for his small farm of five acres in Pupinia had died. A hired laborer had seized his opportunity, stolen a farm tool, and disappeared from the place. So Regulus asked the consuls to send another man to succeed him as commander, because otherwise his wife and children would

---

[111]The Latin has "sextans"—a tiny coin worth one sixth of an as (see money—Roman in the Glossary).

[112]Gaius Fabricius Luscinus (cos, 282 B.C.) and Quintus Aemilius Papus (cos, 282 B.C.) fought successful wars against various Italian peoples.

[113]Pupinia was in Latium between Rome and Tusculum (modern Frascati).

[114]Gaius Atilius Regulus (cos, 257 B.C.) defeated the Carthaginian navy in 257 B.C.

[115]Marcus Atilius Regulus (cos, 267 B.C.) was tortured to death by the Carthaginians (see 1:1,14) in 255 B.C. during the First Punic War (264–241 B.C.).

[116]Regulus commanded the Roman army in Africa during 256 and 255 B.C.

have no way of feeding themselves on the abandoned farm. When the Senate learned of this from the consuls, it ordered that the farm of Atilius be rented out to a tenant farmer at once, that his wife and children be provided with food, and that the stolen goods be replaced using public funds. That is how highly our treasury valued the example Atilius had set by his courage, which Romans will take pride in for all time.

4. 7. The estates of Lucius Quinctius Cincinnatus were equally enormous: he possessed a farm of five acres, and he had lost two of these in paying a fine, because he had used them to guarantee a friend's debt to the treasury. He had also used his income from this farm to pay a fine for his son Caeso, who had not appeared in court to defend himself.[117] But Cincinnatus went on ploughing his three acres and not only retained his dignity as head of the family but was even offered a dictatorship.[118] Nowadays a citizen thinks he is living in straitened circumstances if his house alone occupies as much space as the entire farm of Cincinnatus occupied.

4. 8. What about the Aelius family? How rich they were! There were sixteen members of the Aelius family who lived at the same time in a small little house,[119] in the place where the Monuments of Marius now stand.[120] They also had one farm in the region of Veii, so its owners were more numerous than the number of men needed to work on it. They had a special seating area for the spectacles at the Circus Maximus and the Circus Flaminius.[121] These seats had been presented to them by the state for their courage.

4. 9. The same family did not have a gram of silver until Paullus, after defeating Perseus, presented his son-in-law, Quintus Aelius Tubero, with five pounds of silver from the booty.[122] I will not point out that the leader of our state gave his daughter in marriage to a man whose family was visibly short of money. Paullus himself died in such poverty that if the farm, which was the only thing he left after him, had not been sold, his wife would have had no way of getting her dowry back.

It was the character of men and women that counted in our state, and in all matters the respect paid to people was gauged according to their moral qualities. Their qualities won them military commands, created marriage alliances, and prevailed above everything in the Forum and behind the walls of their private homes. Each man strove to advance his country, not his private affairs, and preferred to be a poor man in a rich empire rather than a rich man in a poor one. This glorious principle received the following reward: money could not buy the respect that was

[117]Lucius Quinctius Cincinnatus (cos, 460 B.C.) had to pay up when his son was fined in 461 B.C.

[118]Cincinnatus was called from his humble farm to be made dictator in 458 B.C.

[119]The Aelius Tubero family were living together like this in the early second century B.C.

[120]The Monuments of Marius were trophies of his military victories.

[121]The Circus Maximus (in the valley between the Palatine and Aventine hills) and the Circus Flaminius (in the Campus Martius) were the biggest and oldest racetracks in Rome.

[122]Quintus Aelius Tubero (tribune of the plebs, 177 B.C.) married Aemilia, the daughter of Lucius Aemilius Paullus (cos, 182 B.C.). Tubero had served as a legate under Paullus in 168 B.C., when Paullus defeated King Perseus of Macedonia.

rightly given to moral qualities, and the state came to the assistance of illustrious people who were poor.

4. 10. During the Second Punic War, Gnaeus Scipio wrote to the Senate from Spain asking it to send someone to replace him,[123] since he had an unmarried daughter who had reached adulthood and she could not get a dowry without him. The Senate did not want the Republic to lose a good commander, so it took on the role of a father. The Senate consulted with the wife and relatives of Scipio, settled on a dowry, supplied that sum from the treasury, and gave the young woman in marriage. The size of the dowry was 40,000 asses, which enables us to gauge not only the generosity of the Conscript Fathers but also the nature of old family fortunes. Those fortunes were so modest that Tuccia, the daughter of Caeso, seemed to have brought an enormous dowry to her husband in bringing him 10,000 asses, and Megullia earned the nickname of Dotata (dowried), because she had entered her husband's home with 50,000 asses.[124] Through its generosity, the Senate also protected the daughters of Fabricius Luscinus and Scipio from getting married without a dowry, since their family fortunes had no funds to their credit apart from the richest glory.[125]

4. 11. Marcus Scaurus records how small an inheritance he received from his father in the first volume of his three-volume autobiography. He says that he was left only six slaves and that his entire fortune was 35,000 sesterces. The spirit of the future leader of the Senate was raised on that sum of money.[126]

We ought, therefore, to consider these examples, and to take consolation in them, since we never stop complaining about our lack of money. We would see no silver, or a very small amount of it, few slaves, five acres of barren soil, funerals in families that cannot afford to pay for them, and daughters lacking a dowry; but we would also see extraordinary consulships, wonderful dictatorships, and countless triumphs. So why do we revile a modest income as if it were the principal misfortune of the human race, complaining about it day and night? Such an income nursed the men of the Publicola, Aemilius, Fabricius, Curius, Scipio, and Scaurus families and other strong men of equal courage with its small but reliable breasts. We should lift up our hearts instead, and if our spirits have been crushed by concentrating on money, we should restore them by recalling the old days. By the little cottage of Romulus,[127] and by the humble buildings of the old Capitol, and by the eternal hearth of Vesta, content with earthenware vessels even now, I swear that no riches could be preferred to the poverty of such men.

[123]Gnaeus Cornelius Scipio Calvus (cos, 222 B.C.) served in Spain from 217 until his death in 211 B.C.

[124]Caeso Tuccius, his daughter Tuccia, and Megullia Dotata are otherwise unknown.

[125]Valerius tells us about the poverty of Fabricius at 4:3,6 and the daughter of Scipio Calvus at 4:4,10.

[126]Marcus Aemilius Scaurus (cos, 115 B.C.) was leader of the Senate from 115 B.C. until his death in 88 B.C.

[127]The Romans were sentimental about the straw hut of Romulus (see 2:8,pref).

Chapter 5. Modesty[128]

Preface

It seems appropriate to move on now from poverty to modesty: this is what taught truly just men to neglect their private possessions and to desire that those of the state should be as splendid as possible; it deserves to have temples raised and altars consecrated to it, just as we have them for the heavenly gods; because it is the begetter of every honorable intention, the guardian of the most solemn obligations, the teacher of innocence; it is dear to our near ones, it is pleasing to strangers, and it presents a favorable appearance in every place and at every time.

Roman Stories

5. 1. But let us turn from its praises to its achievements. From the foundation of our city to the consulship of Scipio Africanus and Tiberius Longus, there was no separate seating for the Senate and the people when they watched the games.[129] In spite of this, no member of the plebs ever brought himself to sit in front of the Conscript Fathers at the theater: the respect shown in our state was so scrupulous.

Their respect was clearly illustrated one day when Lucius Flamininus had to stand at the very back of the theater. He stood there because he had been removed from the Senate by Cato the Censor and Lucius Flaccus,[130] even though he had already held the office of consul and was also the brother of Titus Flamininus, who had defeated Macedonia and Philip.[131] But the entire audience forced Lucius to move up to the place his rank deserved.

5. 2. Terentius Varro shattered the Republic by carelessly starting the battle of Cannae.[132] His sense of shame would not allow him to accept the dictatorship that had been offered to him by the entire Senate and people, and by this refusal he atoned for his culpability in that great disaster. He caused people to attribute the battle to the anger of the gods, and his modesty to his own good character. And so, on the inscription under his death mask, refusing a dictatorship brought more honor to him than holding one brought to other men.

5. 3. But let us move on to a glorious consequence of this sense of respect. People were outraged when Fortune brought Lucius Scipio and Gaius Cicereius, the son and scribe of Scipio Africanus, onto the Campus seeking election as

---

[128] *Verecundia* (modesty) is what makes a person show consideration and respect toward other people. I've used the words "modesty" and "respect" to translate it in this chapter.

[129] Scipio Africanus and Tiberius Sempronius Longus were consuls in 194 B.C. The censors for that year reserved special seats for the Senators.

[130] Cato the Censor and Lucius Valerius Flaccus were censors in 184 B.C. They expelled Lucius Quinctius Flamininus (cos, 192 B.C.) from the Senate (see 2:9,3).

[131] His brother, Titus Quinctius Flamininus (cos, 198 B.C.), had defeated Philip V of Macedonia in 197 B.C.

[132] Gaius Terentius Varro (cos, 216 B.C.) survived the Roman disaster at Cannae in 216 B.C.

praetors.[133] When ordinary people discussed the matter, they criticized Fortune for her utter madness in bringing together the offspring and client of such a great man to fight against each other in an election. But Cicereius turned their criticism of Fortune into praise for his character: when he saw that he was winning against Lucius Scipio in all the voting units, he went down from the voting area, threw aside his whitened toga, and started to canvass for his rival. Cicereius felt it was better to lose the praetorship out of respect for the memory of Scipio Africanus than to win it for himself. His modesty was well rewarded: Lucius Scipio won the office then, but people congratulated Cicereius instead.

5. 4. We shall not leave elections just yet. Lucius Crassus was seeking election as consul, and was obliged, like all other candidates, to go around the Forum pleading with the people.[134] But he could never be brought to do so in the presence of Quintus Scaevola, a most wise and distinguished man, and his own father-in-law. Crassus used to ask Scaevola to go away so he could devote his time to this silly business.[135] The respect Crassus had for that man's status was greater than the regard he had for his own candidacy.

5. 5. Pompey the Great had been defeated by Caesar at the battle of Pharsalus,[136] and on the following day he entered Larisa,[137] where the entire population of that town went out to greet him, but he said, "Go and perform this service for the victor." I would have said that he did not deserve to be defeated, if he had not been defeated by Caesar; clearly he was well mannered when disaster struck him; he was no longer able to use his status, so he acted on his sense of modesty instead.

5. 6. It was often apparent how strong this sense of modesty was in Caesar too, and his last day made it clear.[138] He had been outrageously wounded by the daggers of several traitors, but at the very moment when his divine spirit was departing from his mortal body, not even those twenty-three wounds could prevent him from following the rules of modesty: for he pulled down his toga with both hands to cover the lower part of his body as he fell. This is not the way that men die; this is the way that immortal gods return to their home.

Foreign Stories

5. ext. 1. I shall include the following story with the foreign ones, because it occurred before Etruria obtained Roman citizenship.[139] There was a young man

---

[133]This election campaign took place on the Campus Martius in 175 B.C. Lucius Cornelius Scipio won and became a praetor in 174 B.C. Gaius Cicereius became a praetor in 173 B.C.

[134]This election campaign was in 96 B.C. Lucius Licinius Crassus won and was consul in 95 B.C.

[135]Quintus Mucius Scaevola the Augur had been consul himself in 117 B.C.

[136]Caesar defeated Pompey and the Republicans at Pharsalus (in Thessaly) in 48 B.C.

[137]Larisa was also in Thessaly.

[138]Caesar was stabbed to death in the Senate house on March 15, 44 B.C.

[139]Etruscans got Roman citizenship in 265 B.C.

of exceptional beauty in that region, and his name was Spurinna. His extraordinary beauty was turning the eyes of many illustrious women, and he felt that he was earning the suspicion of their husbands and relatives because of this. So he disfigured his beautiful face with wounds, for he preferred to be ugly and have people trust his integrity rather than allow his beauty to incite lust in others.

5. ext. 2. There was a very old man at Athens, and when he went to see the shows at the theater, not one of the citizens offered him a seat, but by chance he came near the Spartan envoys. They were moved by the man's age and showed their respect for his white hairs and his years by standing up for him, and they offered him a seat among themselves in the most honorable place. When the people saw this happen, they applauded loudly in approval of this respect shown by a foreign city. They say that one of the Spartans then remarked, "So, the Athenians do know what is right; they just don't bother doing it."

Chapter 6. Love in Marriage

Preface

I shall proceed from a mild and gentle feeling to an equally honorable one, though it is more passionate and exciting. I shall bring before the reader's eyes certain pictures, as it were, of legitimate love to be contemplated with the most profound veneration. We shall go through the achievements of the strong trust built up between spouses. These deeds are hard to imitate, but it is useful to learn about them, because when one pays attention to extraordinary achievements, one should not be ashamed to perform minor ones.

Roman Stories.

6. 1. A male and female snake were caught in the house of Tiberius Gracchus, and he was informed by a diviner that if he let the male go, his wife would die shortly afterward, but if he let the female go, he himself would die.[140] He followed the version of the prophecy that saved his wife rather than himself, and he ordered the male to be killed and the female to be let go. As he witnessed the death of that snake before him, he was enduring the vision of his own death. So I do not know whether I should call Cornelia more fortunate in having such a husband or more wretched in losing him.

As for you, Admetus, king of Thessaly, you have been found guilty of a harsh and cruel deed by the great judge.[141] You allowed your wife to sacrifice her life for

---

[140]Tiberius Sempronius Gracchus (cos, 177 B.C.) was married to Cornelia (see 4:2,3 and 4:4,pref.), the daughter of Scipio Africanus.

[141]In Greek myth, Admetus, king of Pherae, persuaded his wife, Alcestis, to die in his place. "The great judge" is public opinion.

yours, and when she had ended her life in a voluntary death so that you would not die, you dared to face the daylight! You had, of course, attempted to abuse the kindness of your parents before that![142]

6. 2. Gaius Plautius Numida was a victim of cruel Fortune, but even though he was also a member of the senatorial order, he was a lesser man than Gracchus.[143] Still, he was equally exemplary in this kind of love. When he heard of his wife's death, he could not control his grief and drove a sword through his chest. Then his servants intervened and prevented him from finishing off his plan. They bandaged him up, but as soon as he got the chance, he tore the bandages off and opened up the wound, and with his relentless right hand he tore his life, which was afflicted with grief and bitterness, from his own chest and abdomen. By this very violent death, he showed what a great marital flame he had hidden in his heart.

6. 3. Marcus Plautius also had the same name and love.[144] By order of the Senate, he was bringing an allied fleet of sixty ships back to Asia, and he landed at Tarentum. His wife, Orestilla, who had followed him there, was afflicted with an illness and died. He carried out her funeral and placed her on the pyre, and while performing the rite of anointing her and kissing her, he took out his sword and threw himself upon it. His friends placed him just as he was, wearing his toga and shoes, beside the body of his wife; then they applied the torches and cremated the pair of them together. Their tomb was set up there—it can still be seen at Tarentum—and it is called the tomb "of the two lovers." If the dead have any feelings, I have no doubt that Plautius and Orestilla entered the Underworld with their faces beaming, since they were partners in death. Indeed, when love is both very great and very honorable, it is far better to be united by death than separated by life.

6. 4. The similar feelings of Julia,[145] the daughter of Caesar, were well known. During the elections for the aedileship,[146] she saw that the clothes of her husband, Pompey the Great, had been brought back from the Campus spattered with blood. Terrified by the thought that he had been murdered, she had a blackout and collapsed. She was pregnant, and the sudden shock to her mind and the serious physical pain made her have a miscarriage. This was indeed a great disaster for the entire world, because its peace would not have been disrupted by the insane ferocity of all those civil wars if only the friendship of Caesar and Pompey had remained intact through the bond of a child related to both of them.

6. 5. Every age will honor your chaste passion with the admiration it deserves, Porcia, Cato of Utica's daughter.[147] When you realized that your husband, Brutus, had been defeated and killed at Philippi, you did not hesitate to swallow burning coals, since nobody would give you a sword.[148] Though you had the heart of a

[142]Admetus had previously asked his parents to die for him, but they refused.

[143]Gaius Plautius Numida was a senator around 100 B.C.

[144]Marcus Plautius Hypsaeus was a prefect in the navy (84–83 B.C.).

[145]Julia married Pompey in 59 B.C.

[146]Pompey was consul in 55 B.C. and presided over election campaigns at the end of the year.

[147]Porcia, Cato of Utica's daughter, was married to Marcus Junius Brutus (the tyrannicide).

[148]Porcia committed suicide after the Republicans were defeated at Philippi in 42 B.C.

woman, you imitated the manly death of your father. But I wonder whether yours was braver, since he died in a normal way, but you died from a new kind of death.[149]

Foreign Stories

6. ext. 1. There are also stories of pure love from foreign lands, and they have not been hidden in the dark and left unknown, so it will be enough to have mentioned a few of them. It is easy to show how much the Carian queen, Artemisia, missed her husband, Mausolus, after death had taken him away from her, by considering the magnificence of the special honors of every kind that she paid him and of the monument she erected, which even became one of the Seven Wonders.[150] But why should you list those honors or talk about that famous tomb, since she herself wanted to become a living and breathing tomb for Mausolus, according to those writers who say that she sprinkled the ashes of her dead husband into a potion and drank it down herself?

6. ext. 2. Queen Hypsicratea gave full rein to her feelings of love for her husband, Mithridates. For his sake, she took delight in changing her exceptionally beautiful appearance to make herself look like a man. She cut her hair short and got used to a horse and weapons, so that it would be easier for her to share in his troubles and dangers. Indeed, even when he was defeated by Pompey and had to flee through savage tribes, she was physically and mentally indefatigable in following him.[151] Her exceptional loyalty was the greatest consolation and most delightful respite to Mithridates in his setbacks and difficulties. He felt that since his wife stayed with him throughout his exile, he had his home and household gods with him in his wanderings.

6. ext. 3. But why should I examine Asia, the endless and empty lands of the barbarians, their hideouts among the inlets of the Black Sea? The most splendid and glorious city of all of Greece, Sparta, displays an exceptional case of a wife's loyalty before our eyes, an amazing action that deserves to be compared with all the glorious deeds of that state.

The Minyans were descended from the famous group of comrades that followed Jason, and their ancestors were born on the island of Lemnos.[152] Several centuries went by, and the Minyans remained there as if it were their permanent home, but then they were forcibly expelled by the Pelasgians.[153] The Minyans needed outside help, so they occupied the highest peaks of the mountains of

---

[149]Cato of Utica had committed suicide in 46 B.C.

[150]King Mausolus of Caria died in 353 B.C., and Artemisia erected the famous Mausoleum as his tomb. Caria was on the west coast of Asia Minor.

[151]King Mithridates VI of Pontus was defeated and expelled from his kingdom by Pompey in 66 B.C.

[152]In Greek myth, Jason's companions (the Argonauts) landed on Lemnos, where the women had killed all the men. The Argonauts slept with the women, and their descendants were the Minyans.

[153]The Pelasgians were a mythical people who had lived in Greece before the Greeks came.

Taygetus as refugees.[154] The Spartan state had great respect for the sons of Tyndareus[155]—and that pair of brothers, who were destined for the stars, had shone out among those sailors of noble fame—so it led the refugees down and included them under its laws and privileges. But the Minyans repaid this great kindness by harming the city that had deserved so well of them, and trying to take it over. So they were locked up in the public prison while awaiting execution. The Minyans were due to suffer this penalty during the night, according to the ancient Spartan custom, but their wives, who belonged to noble Spartan families, induced the guards to let them in so that they could speak with their husbands who were about to die. The women went into the prison, exchanged clothes with their husbands, and then enabled the men to escape with veils over their heads as if they were distraught women. At this point, what more can I say than that those women deserved to be married to Minyans?

Chapter 7. Friendship

Preface

Let us now look at the strong and powerful bond of friendship, which is in no way inferior to the power of a relationship by blood. It is even more secure and tested in that the latter is created by our fortune at birth and is the work of mere chance, whereas friendship is created by an individual's free choice and is based on sound judgment. So you could more readily escape blame in turning away from a relative than from a friend, because if you break up with a relative you will not always be accused of injustice, whereas if you break up with a friend you will always be accused of fickleness. A man's life would be empty if it were not protected by the friendship of others, so he should not lightly acquire such an essential support, and once he has found true friendship, he should not cast it aside.

Friends who are truly loyal are discovered in hard times especially, because whatever one gets then comes entirely from an affection that will last. The attention paid to fortunate people comes from flattery rather than affection, and it is definitely suspect, since it always demands more than it gives. In addition there is the fact that men whose luck has broken down are more in need of the support of their friends, either for protection or for consolation. When people's affairs are happy and prosperous, they do not need the support of their fellow humans so much, since they are spoiled by the support of the gods. As a result, the recollection of posterity clings more tenaciously to the names of those who did not desert their friends in hard times than to those who befriended people living in prosperity. Nobody mentions the friends of Sardanapallus,[156] but Orestes is almost more

---

[154]Mount Taygetus was near Sparta.

[155]The sons of Tyndareus were the heavenly twins, Castor and Pollux.

[156]Sardanapallus is the Latin name for Ashurbanipal, king of Assyria from 669 to 630 B.C.

famous because of his friend Pylades than because of his father, Agamemnon.[157]
The friendship shown to prosperous people wastes away in sharing their pleasures
and luxuries, whereas the partnership of Orestes and Pylades went through difficult
and harsh circumstances but came out shining from the very fact of experiencing
those misfortunes. But why should I mention these foreign stories when I could
use ones from home instead?

Roman Stories

7. 1. It was felt that Tiberius Gracchus had been a traitor to his country, and
not without reason, since he had put his own political power above its security.[158]
Nevertheless, it is worth discovering how constant and loyal a friend Gaius Blossius
of Cumae was to him, even in his very wicked schemes.[159] Gracchus had been declared a public enemy, he had suffered the death penalty, he had been deprived of
the honor of burial, but in spite of this he did not lose the affection of his friend.

The Senate ordered the consuls Rupilius and Laenas to take action in the traditional way of our ancestors against those who had supported Gracchus.[160] The
consuls relied especially on the advice of Laelius,[161] and when Blossius came before him to clear himself and use his friendship with Gracchus as an excuse,
Laelius said, "Well, what if Gracchus had asked you to set the temple of Jupiter
Best and Greatest on fire? Would you have followed his wishes, on account of that
friendship you are so proud of?" Blossius replied, "Gracchus would never have
given that order."

He had gone far enough, or perhaps even too far, because he had dared to defend the man's character, which the entire Senate had agreed in condemning. But
what followed was much more daring and much more dangerous. Harassed by the
constant interrogations of Laelius, Blossius stuck to his point without flinching,
and he replied that he would have done even this if Gracchus had given the word.

Who would have thought that Blossius was unprincipled if he had kept quiet
about this? Who would not have thought that he was actually a wise man if he had
spoken as the circumstances of that time required? But Blossius did not want to
save his own life by honorable silence or by circumspect speech, lest he might in
any way betray the memory of his unfortunate friend.

[157]In Greek myth, Orestes killed his mother, Clytemnestra, but Pylades remained his loyal
friend. Agamemnon was the commander of the Greeks in the Trojan War.

[158]Tiberius Sempronius Gracchus (tribune of the plebs, 133 B.C.) was murdered by his political opponents.

[159]His loyal friend, Gaius Blossius, was a Stoic philosopher from Cumae (on the coast of
Campania).

[160]Publius Popillius Laenas and Publius Rupilius were consuls in 132 B.C. and started a
witch-hunt against the supporters of Gracchus.

[161]Gaius Laelius Sapiens (cos, 140 B.C.) held no public office in 132 B.C. He was helping the
consuls as an ordinary senator.

7. 2. Equally strong cases of loyal friendship are found in the same household: when the schemes of Gaius Gracchus had already been put down and his career was ruined, when all the members of his conspiracy were being hunted down every-where, when he was devoid of any helpers, he had just two friends, Pomponius and Laetorius, who protected him by putting themselves in danger while hostile weapons rushed at him from every direction.[162]

To make it easier for Gracchus to escape, Pomponius fought very ferociously for a long time at the Triple Gate and held back a group of soldiers that was rush-ing after Gracchus. Pomponius could not be dislodged from his position alive, and it was only when the soldiers had finished him off with multiple wounds that they were able to cross over his dead body; I think he was still resisting them even after his death.[163]

Laetorius on the other hand stood firmly on the Wooden Bridge, and with his high spirits he held the bridge until Gracchus could cross over.[164] When he was overwhelmed by the force of their numbers, he turned his sword upon himself and suddenly jumped into the depths of the Tiber. On that bridge, Horatius Cocles had once revealed his affection for our entire country, and now Laetorius displayed the same kind of affection toward a single friend, and gave up his life as well.[165]

What great soldiers the Gracchus brothers would have had on their side if only they had been content to follow the path of their father or their maternal grand-father![166] How vigorous and steadfast Blossius and Pomponius and Laetorius would have been if they had taken part in the trophies and triumphs of those men! They had, after all, been such enthusiastic supporters of the mad schemes of Gracchus, and they had kept to their friendship even if it was an ill-omened one. But however tragic these stories may be, they stand out all the more clearly as models of loyal friendship.

7. 3. If future generations judged Lucius Reginus by the standards he should have upheld in carrying out his official duties, they would rightly tear him to shreds with their abuse; but if they judged him by his loyalty to his friends, they would rightly let him rest in that excellent harbor—an admirable conscience.[167] When Reginus was a tribune of the plebs, Caepio was thrown into jail because people felt it was his fault that our army had been destroyed by the Cimbrians and Teutons.[168]

---

[162]The Senate massacred the followers of Gaius Sempronius Gracchus (tribune of the plebs, 123 B.C.) in 121 B.C.

[163]Pomponius Rufus fought at the Triple Gate, which was right beside the river Tiber.

[164]Laetorius fought at the Wooden Bridge which was just upstream from the Triple Gate.

[165]Horatius Cocles had held the Wooden Bridge against Lars Porsenna and the Etruscans in 508 B.C. (see 3:2,1).

[166]Their father, Tiberius Sempronius Gracchus (cos, 177 B.C.), had defeated the Celti-berians and the Sardinians. Their maternal grandfather, Scipio Africanus, had won the Second Punic War.

[167]Lucius Antistius Reginus was a tribune of the plebs in 103 B.C.

[168]Quintus Servilius Caepio (cos, 106 B.C.) had been badly defeated by the Cimbrians and Teutons in 105 B.C. He was found guilty of mishandling the war and imprisoned in 103 B.C.

Out of respect for their close and long-standing friendship, Reginus freed Caepio from the public jail. But he was not content to have gone just this far as a friend; he even went into exile with Caepio. What a great and invincible divinity you are, Friendship! On one side the Republic was holding Reginus back with her hand, on the other side your hand was dragging him off; but although the Republic was asking him to remain an inviolable officer, and you were condemning him to exile, your authority was so persuasive that he chose this punishment over his public office.

7. 4. That achievement of yours was amazing, but the one that follows was even more admirable. Remember how far you drew out the loyal affection of Volumnius toward his friend without causing any harm to the Republic! Volumnius was born of an equestrian family, and had been a close friend of Marcus Lucullus.[169] Since Lucullus had supported the party of Brutus and Cassius, Antony had put him to death. Volumnius was perfectly free to escape, but he stayed by his friend's body, and he went so far in his weeping and groaning that his excessive loyalty brought about his own death.

Because of his noticeable and persistent weeping, Volumnius was brought before Antony. When he stood in Antony's presence, he said, "General, order me to be brought at once to the body of Lucullus and killed there: I should not stay alive after he has been killed, since I was the one who advised him to embark on this ill-fated campaign."

What could be more loyal that this affection? Volumnius made the death of his friend more bearable by incurring the hatred of his enemy; he jeopardized his own life by accusing himself of instigating his friend; and in order to make his friend more pitiable, he made himself more hated.

Antony was only too ready to oblige him. Volumnius was brought where he wanted to go, eagerly kissed the hand of Lucullus, took up his head, which had been cut off and was lying there, and pressed it to his breast. Then he lowered his neck and offered it to the victor's sword.

Let Greece speak of Theseus, who supported Pirithous in his wicked lust and ventured into the realm of Father Dis: only a silly man would tell such stories, only a foolish man would believe them.[170] To see the blood of friends flowing together, wounds joined with wounds, and death attached to death—these are the real proofs of Roman friendship, whereas those other stories are the monstrous lies of a race that is only too ready to make things up.

7. 5. Lucius Petronius deservedly claims his share of credit here: those who perform equally daring deeds in honor of friendship must get an equal share in its glory. Petronius was born of a very humble family, but through the kindness of Publius Caelius he rose to the equestrian order and had a splendid military career.[171] He did

---

[169]Marcus Licinius Lucullus fought on the Republican side at Philippi in 42 B.C.

[170]In Greek myth, Theseus went with his friend Pirithous into the Underworld (the kingdom of Dis). Pirithous was hoping to abduct Proserpina (queen of the Underworld).

[171]An equestrian (see Glossary) had to possess 400,000 sesterces. Publius Caelius must have helped Petronius get this money.

not get a chance to show his gratitude to Caelius in happy circumstances, but he proved it with great loyalty under circumstances that Fortune decided would be unfavorable.

The consul Octavius put Caelius in charge of Placentia,[172] but the city was captured by Cinna's army.[173] Caelius was already quite old and suffering from bad health, so he went to Petronius for help in ensuring that he would not be taken alive by the enemy. Petronius tried in vain to deflect him from his plan, but since Caelius persevered in his request, Petronius killed him and then joined him in death. The man who had enabled him to rise through all the stages of his distinguished career was lying there dead, and Petronius did not want to live after him. Self-respect brought about the death of the one, and loyalty brought about the death of the other.

7. 6. Servius Terentius must be included with Petronius, though he was not destined to die on behalf of his friend—something he wanted to do. Terentius should be judged by his good intentions, not by their failed outcome, because insofar as it was in his power, he himself would have died and Decimus Brutus would have evaded the risk of death.[174]

Brutus was fleeing from Mutina when he discovered that the horsemen sent by Antony to kill him had arrived.[175] Brutus tried to hide himself somewhere in the dark to save his life from the punishment it deserved, but the horsemen burst into the place. Terentius told a loyal lie, and was helped by the dark, because he pretended that he was Brutus and offered up his body for the horsemen to butcher. But he was recognized by Furius, who had been given the duty of punishing Brutus, so Terentius was not able to prevent the execution of his friend by dying himself.[176] Fortune forced him to live against his will.

7. 7. Let us turn from this grim and severe aspect of unwavering friendship to its happy and calm side. Let us call friendship away from places that were completely full of weeping and groaning and killing, and let us place it in a happy home, which is where friendship deserves to be: a place shining with charm and dignity and an abundance of wealth. Arise, then, from the place that people believe is assigned to the souls of upright men, Gaius Laelius over here, and Marcus Agrippa over there! Because both of you possessed steadfast minds and enjoyed favorable omens, you, Laelius, won the greatest friend among men, and you, Agrippa, won the greatest friend among gods.[177] And bring forward into the light

---

[172]Publius Caelius was a prefect, serving under Gnaeus Octavius (cos, 87 B.C.). Placentia (modern Piacenza) was in Aemilia (northern Italy).

[173]Lucius Cornelius Cinna, the other consul in 87 B.C., marched on Rome and massacred his opponents.

[174]Antony ordered the murder of Decimus Junius Brutus Albinus (the tyrannicide) in 43 B.C.

[175]Mutina (modern Modena) was in Aemilia (northern Italy).

[176]Furius murdered Brutus Albinus (see 9:13,3).

[177]Gaius Laelius Sapiens (cos, 140 B.C.) was a close friend of the great man, Scipio Aemilianus, and Marcus Vipsanius Agrippa (cos, 37 B.C.) was a close friend of the great god, Augustus.

along with you the entire crowd of happy people who follow your lead and are weighed down with glory and rewards as veteran soldiers of genuine loyalty. Your steadfast minds, your energetic services, your invincible secrecy, your constant vigilance and kind watchfulness on behalf of the status and safety of your friends, and furthermore the rich rewards of these actions—when future generations see all of this, they will be both more willing and more scrupulous in striving to uphold the laws of friendship.

Foreign Stories

7. ext. 1. My mind is captivated by these national stories, but the honesty of the city of Rome urges me to tell of good deeds by foreigners. Damon and Phintias, who had both been initiated into the rites of the Pythagorean way of life, were joined together in a completely loyal friendship. Dionysius of Syracuse[178] wanted to kill Phintias, but he granted him some time to go home and organize his affairs before his death, and Damon did not hesitate to offer himself to the tyrant as a hostage on behalf of his friend. Phintias, who had just had his neck under the sword, was freed from the risk of death, and Damon, who could have lived on in safety, put his head under that same sword. So everyone, especially Dionysius, was looking forward to seeing how this strange and exciting event would turn out.

Later, as the day that had been fixed drew nearer and Phintias was not returning, everyone blamed his reckless supporter for being such a fool. But Damon claimed that he had nothing to fear when it came to his friend's loyalty. At one and the same time, the deadline fixed by Dionysius and the man who had agreed to that deadline arrived. The tyrant was amazed at the courage of both men, and he canceled the punishment out of respect for their loyalty. Furthermore, he asked them to accept him into their partnership as a friend who would earn this third place by returning their kindness.

Is the power of friendship this great? It could create contempt for death, it could override the pleasure of staying alive, it could make cruelty gentle, it could turn hatred into love, it could change punishment into reward. It deserves almost the same veneration that we pay to the rites of the immortal gods. The survival of our state depends on those rites, but our survival as private people depends on the power of friendship. And if the temples are the sacred homes of the gods, then the loyal hearts of humans are like temples filled with the sacred spirit of friendship.

7. ext. 2. King Alexander realized that this was the case. He captured the camp of Darius,[179] and with his favorite friend Hephaestion at his side[180] he came to speak to the relatives of Darius, who were all in the camp. The mother of Darius was cheered up by his arrival and lifted up her head from the ground where she

[178]This could be Dionysius I or his son Dionysius II (tyrants of Syracuse in the fourth century B.C.).

[179]Alexander the Great captured the camp of Darius III of Persia after the battle of Issus in 333 B.C.

[180]Hephaestion was Alexander's closest friend. Later, they both married daughters of Darius.

had lain prostrated. Since Hephaestion was more impressive in height and appearance, she bowed down before him in the Persian way, greeting him as if he were Alexander. When her mistake was pointed out, she was absolutely terrified and tried to find words with which to excuse herself. But Alexander said to her, "There is no need to get upset just because of a name: he is Alexander too." Which man should we congratulate first? The man who was prepared to say this or the man who had the good fortune to hear it? Alexander was a most magnanimous king, and he had already conquered the entire world by his victories or was soon to do so, but in these few words he shared himself with his friend. Oh, what a gift those famous words were, bringing equal glory to the giver and the receiver!

I have good reason to respect the gift of friendship in my own private life, since I have benefited from the affection that a very famous and learned man showered upon me. And I am not nervous that it would be inappropriate for me to say that my friend Pompeius is like Alexander,[181] since Alexander himself felt that his friend Hephaestion was actually another Alexander. I would in fact be guilty of a very serious crime if I went through these stories of loyal and kind-hearted friendship without mentioning Pompeius at all. He showed me an affection like that of the most doting parents, and his affection enhanced the happy occasions of my life and diminished the sad ones. If my material circumstances are comfortable, that is only because he went out of his way to improve them; he made me more secure against misfortune; he made my intellectual career more brilliant and more exciting by his guidance and patronage.

The loss of my excellent friend has gratified the envy of certain people, presumably because my happiness tormented them. It is not my fault that they envy me, because I shared my influence, such as it was, with anyone who wanted to make use of it, but there is no happiness modest enough to evade the fangs of envy. Where could you hide away from certain people, or with what supplication could you win them over, to stop them becoming happy and elated over the misfortune of another, as if it were their own good fortune? They are made rich by the losses of others, wealthy by their disasters, and immortal by their deaths. But the best avenger of their arrogance is the uncertainty of the human condition; it will determine how long they will mock at the misfortunes of others before experiencing some misfortunes of their own.

Chapter 8. Generosity

Roman Stories

8. 1. My work dutifully wandered off course and dwelled on my personal sorrows, but it must be brought back on track, and I must take the time to speak

---

[181]Sextus Pompeius (cos, A.D. 14) was a close friend of Valerius Maximus. They went to Asia together (see 2:6,8).

of generosity. There are two very admirable sources of this virtue, good judgment and honorable kindness: because only when it arises from these sources does it strike a balance. The amount of the gift itself does produce gratitude, but its timeliness makes this gratitude considerably stronger: to the price of the gift is added the priceless factor of the right circumstances.

Many centuries ago, this factor made the small sum of money spent by Fabius the Delayer earn him admiration up to the present day. He had received prisoners of war from Hannibal at a price they had agreed on. When the Senate did not provide this money, Fabius sent his son into the city to sell the only farm in their possession and paid the proceeds to Hannibal at once.[182] If you calculate this sum mathematically, it was very small, since the property he sold was only five acres of land, and what is more, this land was in Pupinia; but if you consider the spirit of the man who paid it, this sum was greater than all the money in the world: he preferred to lose his ancestral property than have his country lose its honor. He deserves all the more praise for doing this, because to strive beyond one's powers is a clearer indication of genuine enthusiasm than to take it easy and stay within them. The second man gives what he is able to, the first man gives even more than he is able to.

8. 2. A woman called Busa, who lived at the same time and was the richest woman in the region of Apulia, should rightly be acknowledged for her generosity, but her extraordinary wealth could not be compared with the straitened circumstances of the Fabius family. Within the walls of Canusium, she was admittedly very kind in feeding around ten thousand of our citizens, who had survived the battle of Cannae.[183] But although she was generous to the Roman people, she looked after her own financial status; whereas Fabius, in honor of his country, moved from poverty into real destitution.

8. 3. The generosity of Quintus Considius became well known; it set a very good example and was of considerable benefit to himself. The mad behavior of Catiline had caused such confusion in the Republic that even rich people could not pay back the money they owed their creditors, since his rebellion had depressed the prices of property.[184] Considius had lent out 15,000,000 sesterces, but he did not allow his agents to demand payment of either the principle or the interest from his debtors. Insofar as he could, he lessened the bitterness of the public disorder by his calm behavior as a private citizen. In a remarkably obliging way, he asserted that he would profit from his own money, not from the blood of his fellow citizens. People nowadays who really enjoy doing business love to bring bloodstained money back home, but they would learn how disgraceful their joy and exultation are if they did not think it beneath themselves to read carefully the Senate decree thanking Considius.

---

[182]Fabius the Delayer was dictator in 217 B.C. when he ransomed the prisoners and sent his son, Quintus Fabius Maximus (cos, 213 B.C.), to sell the family farm.

[183]Canusium was a city in Apulia, near Cannae. The survivors of the battle gathered there.

[184]As part of his revolutionary program (63–62 B.C.), Catiline promised a cancellation of all debts.

8. 4. It seems to me that the Roman people must be complaining against me for some time now, because although I have been researching the generosity of individuals, I have not mentioned their generosity: after all, the greatest glory of the Roman people lies in the spirit they have shown toward kings and city-states and nations, and the glory of every famous deed is rejuvenated if it is told again and again. When our people had captured Asia in a war, they handed it over to king Eumenes as a permanent gift,[185] believing that the empire of our city would be more exalted and glorious if it chose to present the richest and most beautiful part of the world as a gift to others rather than keep it as a source of profit to itself. This gift brought even greater benefits than our victory itself, because to annex such a huge territory might make others envious, but to present such a huge gift could not fail to win us glory.

8. 5. In truth, no literary work could give the heavenly spirit of Roman generosity the praise it deserves. After the defeat of Philip, king of Macedonia, when all of Greece was gathered together for the Isthmian Games, a trumpet gave the sign for everyone to be silent, and Titus Quinctius Flamininus ordered a herald to read out the following proclamation:[186] "The Senate and people of Rome, and their general, Titus Quinctius Flamininus, order that all the cities of Greece that were under the rule of King Philip should be free and pay no tribute." When they heard these words, the people were overwhelmed by their great and unexpected joy, and at first they did not make a sound, not being able to believe that they had really heard those words. But when the herald repeated the proclamation, they filled the heavens with loud, joyous shouts, and it is a well-established fact that the birds flying overhead were so astonished that they fell from the sky in terror. A man of great spirit might have freed that number of prisoners of war from slavery, but the Roman people granted freedom to that number of the most famous and wealthy cities.

It is important for the majesty of the Roman people that we should recall not only the gifts that they have kindly given to others but also their gratitude when they received gifts from others: the Roman people are admired for practicing goodness in the first case, and for rewarding it in the second.

Foreign Stories

8. ext. 1. When King Hiero of Syracuse heard about the disastrous defeat of the Romans at Lake Trasimene,[187] he sent seventy thousand bushels of wheat, fifty thousand bushels of barley, and two hundred forty pounds of gold as a gift to our city. He was not unaware of the self-respect of our ancestors, which might have

---

[185]After they had defeated King Antiochus the Great of Syria in 190 B.C., the Romans granted a large part of his territory to their ally, King Eumenes II of Pergamum.

[186]Titus Quinctius Flamininus (cos, 198 B.C.) proclaimed the independence of the Greek states at the Isthmian Games (in 196 B.C.).

[187]Hiero II (king of Syracuse from 269 to 215 B.C.) was a Roman ally in the Second Punic War. The Romans had been badly defeated by Hannibal at Lake Trasimene in 217 B.C.

prevented them from accepting the gold, so he presented it in the form of a statue of Victory to force them to accept his generosity on religious grounds. He was a generous man first in wanting to send the gift, and then in making sure that it would not be sent back.

8. ext. 2. I shall tell about Gillias of Acragas, who is widely known to have had practically the heart of generosity itself.[188] He had exceptional wealth, but he was much richer in his spirit than in his possessions and was always preoccupied with giving money away rather than getting it for himself. So much so, in fact, that his house was treated as a factory of generosity: from the wealth of his house, buildings for the use of the general public were erected, spectacles were offered to please the eyes of the people, splendidly sumptuous banquets were given, and extra supplies of grain were provided during shortages.

These gifts were made to the general public, but he also made private grants to maintain people who were suffering from lack of money, he provided dowries for young women who were crushed by poverty, and he helped out people who were shaken by some sudden disaster. He gave a warm welcome to guests both in his city home and in his country houses, and his guests were always sent away laden with gifts of all kinds. Indeed, on one occasion when five hundred horsemen from Gela were forced onto his property by a violent storm, he fed and clothed them all.[189]

Why go on? You would have said that his heart was not just the heart of a kind human being but that of the goddess Fortune herself, when she is in a good mood. So whatever Gillias possessed was like the common possession of all men. The state of Acragas as well as the neighboring regions prayed night and day for his good health and success.[190] Compare on the other hand those treasure chests that are locked and bolted relentlessly: Would you not think that the money he spent was worth a lot more than the money those chests guard?

---

[188]Gillias (other authors call him Tellias) lived in the fifth century B.C. Acragas is the Greek name for Agrigentum (on the south coast of Sicily).

[189]Gela (also on the south coast of Sicily) was an ally of Acragas against the Carthaginians.

[190]Gillias committed suicide in 406 B.C. when the Carthaginians captured Acragas.

BOOK FIVE

Chapter 1. Kindness and Compassion

Preface

What more suitable companions could I provide for generosity than kindness and compassion,[1] since they aim at the same kind of glory? The first of these is shown to those who are poor, the second to those who are in trouble, the third to those whose luck has turned against them. And though you would not know which to praise the most, it seems to me that the one that derives its name from an actual god must surpass the others in our approval.[2]

Roman Stories

1. 1a. Before anything else, I shall record the exceptionally kind and forgiving actions of our Senate. When Carthaginian representatives came to our city to ransom their prisoners of war, the Senate refused the money and handed over the young Carthaginians, who numbered 2,743.[3] What a huge army of enemy soldiers it allowed to get away, what a large sum of money it rejected, what a big number of Carthaginian crimes it forgave! I think the representatives themselves must have been astonished and said to themselves, "Oh, how generous the Roman nation is; they should be compared with the gods for kindness! Oh, how lucky our mission was too; it surpassed our hopes! We have received a favor that we ourselves never would have granted."

1. 1b. The following story is no small proof of the Senate's kindness. Syphax had once been a very powerful king of Numidia, but he died a prisoner in Tibur.[4] The Senate decreed that he should be given a state funeral, so it not only granted him his life but also honored him with a proper burial.

1. 1c. It showed similar compassion in the case of Perseus. He had been banished to Alba, was confined there, and died.[5] The Senate sent a quaestor to give

---

[1]Generosity was the last topic in Book 4, and Valerius regards kindness and compassion as being lesser virtues that follow along after it.

[2]The Latin word for generosity is *liberalitas,* which according to Valerius "derives its name from an actual god," Liber (the god of wine). In fact, both *liberalitas* and the god Liber derive their names from the word *liber,* which means "free."

[3]The Senate released only two hundred Carthaginian prisoners, and that was after Carthage had surrendered in 201 B.C.

[4]Syphax was king of western Numidia (in north Africa), who joined the Carthaginians in 204 B.C. He was captured in 203 B.C. and died in 201 B.C. Tibur (modern Tivoli) was in Latium.

[5]The Romans banished King Perseus of Macedonia to Alba (in Latium) in 167 B.C.

him a state funeral, because it would not allow his royal remains to lie there without being honored.

1. 1d. Those services were performed for enemies who had been unfortunate and whose lives had come to an end; the following were done for friends who were fortunate and still alive. When the Macedonian War was over, our general Paullus sent Misagenes, the son of Masinissa, back to his father along with the horsemen that he had brought to help the Romans.[6] But the fleet was scattered in a storm, and Misagenes was carried to Brundisium in critical condition.[7] When the Senate heard about this, it immediately ordered a quaestor to go there and see to it that the young man would be provided with accommodation and given everything he might need for his recovery; that all expenses incurred by the young man himself and his retinue would generously be paid for; and that ships would be provided so that he could return to Africa with his men in proper safety. The Senate ordered the quaestor to pay each of the horsemen a pound of silver and 500 sesterces. This timely and attentive kindness of the Conscript Fathers would have ensured that even if the young man had died, his father would have borne his loss with greater resignation.

1. 1e. When our Senate heard that Prusias, the king of Bithynia, had come to congratulate it on its victory over Perseus, it sent the quaestor Lucius Cornelius Scipio to Capua to meet him.[8] The Senate decreed that the best possible house in Rome should be rented for the king, and that both he and also his retinue should be supplied with provisions at public expense. The entire city bore the expression of a kind friend in welcoming the king. Prusias had come as a close friend of ours, and he returned to his kingdom with twice as much good feeling toward us.

1. 1f. Even Egypt managed to benefit from the kindness of Rome. Its king, Ptolemy, had been deprived of his throne by his younger brother.[9] He had come to Rome to seek our help, with a very small number of slaves and dressed very shabbily, and he was staying in the house of an artist from Alexandria.[10] When this was reported to the Senate, it summoned the young man and made the most elaborate apologies imaginable for not following our ancestral custom of sending a quaestor to meet and welcome him officially. The Senate explained that it had behaved in this way not from any lack of respect, but because his arrival had been so sudden and secretive. The senators immediately escorted him from the Senate house to the state guest house, and they urged him to get out of his rags and fix a day when he would come before the Senate. Indeed, the Senate even saw to it that

---

[6]Masinissa (king of Numidia, 209–149 B.C.) sent his son, Misagenes, to fight for Lucius Aemilus Paullus (cos, 182 B.C.) against King Perseus of Macedonia.

[7]Misagenes was on his way home in 168 B.C. when he had to stop at Brundisium (on the coast of Calabria, southern Italy).

[8]Prusias II (king of Bithynia, in Asia Minor, 181–149 B.C.) came to Rome to offer his congratulations in 167 B.C. Capua was in Campania (western Italy).

[9]Ptolemy VI Philometor (king of Egypt, 180–145 B.C.) was expelled from Egypt in 164 B.C. by his own brother, the future Ptolemy VIII Euergetes II Physcon.

[10]Alexandria was the capital of Egypt, built by Alexander the Great in 331 B.C. (see 1:4,ext.1).

a quaestor gave him a grant of money every day. Through this series of favors, the Senate gradually lifted him up from the ground and restored him to his royal splendor, and it made him overcome his fears about his own misfortunes by placing his hopes in the support of the Roman people.[11]

1. 2. But I shall now turn from the Conscript Fathers as a whole to individual senators. During the First Punic War, the consul Lucius Cornelius had captured the town of Olbia.[12] The Carthaginian commander, Hanno, had died fighting very bravely for that town, so Cornelius laid out the body in his own tent and gave him a splendid funeral. He had no hesitation in performing the funeral rites of an enemy by himself, since he believed that his victory would avoid the envy of gods and humans only if it was the kindest one possible.

1. 3. What can I say about Quinctius Crispinus?[13] Even the most powerful emotions, anger and pride, could not shake his gentle nature. He had very kindly welcomed Badius of Campania into his own home as a guest, and he had taken the greatest care in helping him to get over an illness. After the wicked defection of Campania,[14] he was challenged to single combat by Badius during a battle, but although Quinctius was considerably superior to him both in physical strength and in personal courage, he chose to rebuke his ungrateful friend rather than defeat him.

"What are you doing, you madman?" he said, "What perverse desire is leading you astray? Was it not enough for you to share in the treacherous madness of your state? Did you have to fall into your own private madness? Obviously, Quinctius is the only Roman you would love to use your wicked weapons against, even though you owe some respect and gratitude to my household, which saved your life! The bonds of friendship and the gods of hospitality, which are sacred to our people but empty words to hearts like yours, prevent me from entering into single combat against you. In fact, if the two armies were rushing against each other, and my shield had knocked you down by chance, and I recognized it was you, I would have pulled my sword back from your neck. So let it be your shame that you wanted to kill your host; it will not be said against me that I killed my guest. Find someone else to end your life; my upbringing has saved you."

The heavenly gods gave each one what he deserved, since Badius was cut down in that battle, whereas Quinctius came out of it renowned for his extraordinary fighting.

1. 4. What a famous and memorable model of compassion Marcus Marcellus was! We have to acknowledge this! After Marcellus had captured Syracuse,[15] he stood on its citadel to look down from this viewpoint at the plight of that city, which had once been so powerful but now was devastated. But when he saw its sad condition, he could not keep back his tears. If someone who did not recognize him had seen Marcellus, they would have thought that this victory was someone

---

[11] The Senate sent envoys to Egypt to restore Ptolemy VI Philometer in 163 B.C.

[12] Lucius Cornelius Scipio (cos, 259 B.C.) defeated Hanno at Olbia (on Sardinia).

[13] Titus Quinctius Crispinus was serving in the Roman cavalry when this incident took place near Capua in 212 B.C.

[14] Campania had joined the Carthaginians after the Roman disaster at Cannae in 216 B.C.

[15] Marcus Claudius Marcellus (cos, 222 B.C.) captured Syracuse (in Sicily) in 211 B.C.

else's. So, city of Syracuse, you had some grounds for self-satisfaction in the midst of your great disaster, because even if you were not destined to survive intact, your fall was softer under such a gentle conqueror.

1. 5. When Quintus Metellus was fighting the Celtiberian War in Spain, he besieged the city of Centobriga.[16] He had already moved up the battering ram, and it seemed that he would soon knock down the only section of the wall that could be destroyed, but he chose kindness over immediate victory. Rhoetogenes had defected to him, and the people of Centobriga placed his sons in front of the Roman battering ram. Metellus did not want the boys to be killed in this cruel way before their father's eyes, and even though Rhoetogenes himself said that even the death of his boys should not stop Metellus sacking the city, Metellus called off the siege. This compassionate deed may not have captured the walls of this one city, but it did capture the hearts of all the cities of Celtiberia with the result that Metellus did not need very many sieges to bring the Celtiberians back under the power of the Roman people.[17]

1. 6. The kindness of Scipio Aemilianus was spectacular and widely known. After the sack of Carthage,[18] he sent letters around to all the cities of Sicily telling them to send representatives to get back the works of art that the Carthaginians had stolen from their temples,[19] and to make sure these works were put back in their former homes. A kind deed that was welcomed by both gods and humans!

1. 7. That deed was matched by the following kind action of the same man.[20] His quaestor was selling prisoners of war by auction and sent a young man of extraordinary beauty and noble bearing to Scipio. When he discovered that the young man was from Numidia, had been left an orphan at the death of his father, had been brought up in the home of his maternal uncle Masinissa, and though underage had joined this campaign against the Romans without Masinissa's consent, Scipio decided he would have to forgive the young man's error and pay proper respect to the friendship of a king who was very loyal to the Roman people.[21] So Scipio presented the young man with a ring and a golden brooch, a broad-striped tunic, a Spanish cloak, and a fully equipped horse. He also provided the young man with horsemen as an escort and sent him to Masinissa. Scipio believed that the greatest reward for his victory would be to return their works of art to the gods and their flesh and blood to humans.

---

[16]Quintus Caecilius Metellus Macedonicus (cos, 143 B.C.) fought the Celtiberians of eastern Spain in 142 B.C.

[17]Quintus Caecilius Metellus Macedonicus fought against the Celtiberians as consul in 143 B.C. and as governor of Nearer Spain in 142 B.C.

[18]Scipio Aemilianus destroyed Carthage in 146 B.C.

[19]Carthage had conquered most of Sicily in the fourth and third centuries B.C.

[20]The kind action described in this story was performed by Scipio Africanus, not Scipio Aemilianus.

[21]Scipio Africanus sent the boy back from Spain to Numidia (in north Africa) in 209 B.C. Masinissa was not yet a Roman ally, but this generous action by Africanus later convinced him to join the Romans in 206 B.C.

1. 8. When praising people for this type of behavior, we have to mention Lucius Paullus.[22] Perseus within a brief moment of time had changed from king to prisoner, and when Paullus heard that Perseus was being brought before him, he went up to Perseus wearing the full uniform of a Roman general. When the king tried to prostrate himself before his feet, Paullus lifted him up with his right hand and, speaking in Greek, told him to take courage. Paullus invited him into his tent and requested him to sit by his side at his council meetings; he also felt that Perseus deserved a place of honor at his table. Show anyone the battle in which Perseus was defeated and the series of events I have described, and they will have trouble deciding which spectacle delights them more: because if it is an extraordinary achievement to defeat an enemy, it is no less admirable to know how to pity his misfortunes.

1. 9. The kindhearted behavior of Lucius Paullus reminds me that I must not ignore a compassionate action by Pompey. Tigranes, the king of Armenia, had himself waged major wars against the Roman people, and he had also used his power to protect the bitter enemy of our city, Mithridates, when Mithridates was driven from Pontus.[23] Pompey did not allow Tigranes to lie in supplication before him for a long time,[24] and instead raised his spirits with kind words and requested him to put his crown, which he had thrown off, back on his head. Pompey made some specific demands of Tigranes and then restored him to his former status, believing that it was equally noble to destroy kings and to create them.[25]

1. 10. What a splendid example Pompey was in showing kindness to others; what a tragic example he was in hoping to find kindness from others! He had placed the royal symbol on the forehead of Tigranes, but his own head was stripped of its three triumphal crowns,[26] and it found no place of burial in a world that had just recently belonged to it. Instead, it was cut from his body, deprived of cremation, and brought as a hideous gift that revealed the treachery of the Egyptians and moved Pompey's conqueror to pity:[27] because when Caesar saw it, he forgot that he was Pompey's enemy and appeared as Pompey's father-in-law again; he shed tears over Pompey both on his own behalf and on his daughter's;[28] and he saw to it that his head was cremated with lots of precious perfumes. If the heart of our divine leader had not been so gentle, the head of the man who had only shortly before been considered the mainstay of the Roman Empire—that is how fortune turns human affairs upside down—would have lain there unburied.

---

[22]Lucius Aemilius Paullus (cos, 182 B.C.) defeated King Perseus of Macedonia at Pydna in 168 B.C.

[23]King Tigranes II of Armenia had given shelter to King Mithridates VI of Pontus in 71 B.C.

[24]Pompey invaded Armenia in 66 B.C., and Tigranes surrendered to him.

[25]Tigranes stayed on as king, ruling Armenia from 95 to 56 B.C.

[26]Pompey had celebrated triumphs over the Numidians (79 B.C.); over the Spaniards (71 B.C.); and over the pirates, Mithridates VI of Pontus, and Tigranes II of Armenia (61 B.C.)

[27]Pompey was murdered in Egypt in 48 B.C., by order of King Ptolemy XIII of Egypt, who hoped that this would please Caesar.

[28]Julia, Caesar's daughter, had been married to Pompey. She had died in 54 B.C.

When Caesar heard about Cato of Utica's death,[29] he said that he envied Cato's renown and that Cato had envied his, but he kept Cato's fortune safe for Cato's children. And indeed, if he had saved Cato, that would have been no small part of the divine achievements of Caesar.[30]

1. 11. The mind of Antony was not immune to such kindhearted behavior: he gave the body of Marcus Brutus to a freed slave of his for burial, and to make the cremation more honorable, he ordered the freed slave to dress the body in its military cloak, since he put aside all hatred in judging his dead enemy.[31] When Antony discovered that his former slave had stolen the military cloak, he was enraged and punished him immediately, but said this to him first: "What? Didn't you know what man's burial I had entrusted you with?" The plains of Philippi were glad to see his brave and loyal victory, but they were not displeased to hear those words of noble indignation either.

Foreign Stories

1. ext. 1. The telling of that Roman story leads me on to Macedonia, because I am compelled to proclaim the merits of Alexander. Just as his courage in war earned him boundless glory, so his compassion won him extraordinary affection. While he was marching through all the nations in his tireless progress, he was caught by a winter storm in a certain place.[32] He was sitting on a high seat near the fire when he noticed an elderly Macedonian soldier who was paralyzed by the exceptional cold. Taking into consideration their ages rather than their fortunes, Alexander went down and, with those hands that had destroyed the might of Darius, he took the old man who was bent over with the cold and put him on his own seat: people remarked that for the Persians it would have been a capital offense to sit on the royal throne, but for this old man it saved his life. So is it any wonder that his men thought it a pleasure to serve for so many years under a commander who valued the safety of a common soldier more than his own dignity?

Alexander succumbed to no human being but to nature and fortune, and although he was wasting away through the violence of his illness, he still lifted himself up on his elbow and held out his hand to all those who wanted to touch it.[33] And what man would not have run to kiss that hand, which was already being seized by death? It was more lively in its kindness than in its actual life force, but it was still strong enough to be grasped by the men of a huge army.

1. ext. 2. The next man's kindness did not have the same force, but the story I

---

[29]Cato of Utica committed suicide in 46 B.C. rather than live under a dictator.

[30]Caesar tried to win over his former enemies through his policy of clemency.

[31]Antony defeated the Republicans at Philippi (in Macedonia) in 42 B.C., and Marcus Junius Brutus (the tyrannicide) killed himself.

[32]Alexander the Great of Macedonia spent the winter of 327 B.C. in Sogdiana (modern Uzbekistan).

[33]As Alexander lay dying in the summer of 323 B.C., his men filed passed him to say goodbye.

shall tell about Peisistratus, the Athenian tyrant, deserves to be remembered.[34] A young man was burning with love for the unmarried daughter of Peisistratus, went up to her, and kissed her in public. Peisistratus' wife urged him to punish the young man with death, but he replied, "If we kill people who love us, what will we do to people who hate us?" Those words were so noble that nobody would believe they had come from the mouth of a tyrant.

That was how Peisistratus tolerated a wrong done to his daughter, but the way he tolerated a wrong done to himself was even more admirable. While he was having dinner, he was subjected to nonstop abuse by his friend Thrasippus. But Peisistratus kept his thoughts and his words so far from anger that you would have thought he himself was a mere attendant and the man shouting at him was a tyrant. When Thrasippus was going away, Peisistratus was worried that he was leaving the party early because he had become frightened of what he had done, so he began pleading with Thrasippus in a friendly way to keep him there. Thrasippus, carried away by a fit of drunken violence, spat in his face, but even this did not succeed in rousing Peisistratus to punish him. In fact, Peisistratus even restrained his own sons, who were longing to avenge their father's wounded dignity. On the following day Thrasippus wanted to punish himself by taking his own life, but Peisistratus came to him, gave his word that he would continue to value him as a friend, and dissuaded him from his plan. If Peisistratus had done nothing else that deserved to be honored by history, these deeds alone would have won him the most favorable attention of posterity.

1. ext. 3. King Pyrrhus was equally gentle in spirit. He had heard that some people had been speaking very disrespectfully about him at a banquet in Tarentum.[35] He summoned the people who had taken part and he asked them whether they had said the things that had reached his ears. Then one of them said, "The things that have been reported to you were only a game and a joke compared with the things that we would have said about you if the wine hadn't run out." His excuse for their drunken behavior was so witty and his truthful confession was so open that the king's anger changed to laughter. By his compassion and self-restraint, he ensured that the people of Tarentum thanked him when they were sober and blessed him when they were drunk.

When Roman envoys were coming toward Pyrrhus' camp to ransom prisoners of war from him, his high-minded kindness made him send Lycon of Molossia to meet them and make sure they arrived safely. Pyrrhus himself rode outside the gate in his regalia to give them an honorable welcome. His successes and achievements did not turn his head and make him ignore his sense of duty toward people who at that very time were fighting a war against him.

1. ext. 4. At the end of his days, Pyrrhus received a well-deserved reward for his kind nature.[36] He had made an ill-omened attack on the city of Argos, and

[34]Peisistratus was tyrant of Athens from 560 to 527 B.C.

[35]King Pyrrhus of Epirus came to help Tarentum (on the south coast of Italy) fight against the Romans from 280 to 275 B.C.

[36]Pyrrhus died in 272 B.C., fighting in Argos (southern Greece) against King Antigonus Gonnatas of Macedonia.

Alcyoneus, the son of king Antigonus, had cut off his head and joyfully brought it to his father, as if he were bringing him a splendid trophy of victory.[37] Antigonus had also taken part in the battle, fighting for the hard-pressed Argives, but he criticized the young man for taking unrestrained pleasure in the sudden fall of such a great man and for ignoring the role of chance in human affairs. Antigonus took the head of Pyrrhus from the ground and covered it with the hat, which, like all Macedonians, he wore on his own head; then Antigonus replaced the head on the body of Pyrrhus, and made sure it was given a most honorable cremation. Furthermore, Helenus, a son of Pyrrhus, was his prisoner of war, so Antigonus brought Helenus before him, requested him to look and think like a king, gave him the bones of Pyrrhus in a golden urn, and had him bring them home to Epirus to Alexander, the brother of Helenus.[38]

1. ext. 5. The Samnites had sent our army, including the consuls, under the yoke[39] at the Caudine Forks,[40] but the Campanians welcomed our army with respect as it entered their city; and even though our army was deprived not only of its arms but even of its clothes, the Campanians treated it as if it were victorious and were displaying spoils taken from the enemy. With great kindness, they immediately presented the insignia of office to the consuls, gave clothes, arms, horses, and food supplies to the soldiers, and undid the deprivation and disgrace of this Roman defeat. If the Campanians had maintained the same attitude toward our empire against Hannibal, they would not have given our fierce axes grounds for savage revenge.[41]

1. ext. 6. Since I have mentioned our most bitter enemy, I shall end the section at hand with Hannibal's acts of kindness toward the Roman nation. Aemilius Paullus had been killed at Cannae, and Hannibal searched out his body and, insofar as he could, did not allow it to lie there unburied.[42]

When Tiberius Gracchus was caught in an ambush by the Lucanians, Hannibal arranged a funeral for him with the greatest honors, and he handed his bones over to our soldiers to bring them back to our homeland.[43]

Marcus Marcellus was killed in the territory of Bruttium while he was spying on the arrangements of the Carthaginians with more eagerness than common

---

[37]The text here is a little garbled and speaks of a "champion" and someone "being in difficulties." I have omitted these words from my translation.

[38]Alexander II was King of Epirus after the death of Pyrrhus.

[39]The Samnites (in central Italy) humiliated the defeated Romans by making them crawl under a wooden bar called the yoke.

[40]The Samnites defeated the Romans at the Caudine Forks in 321 B.C. The Caudine Forks was a mountain pass on the border between Samnium (central Italy) and Campania (western Italy).

[41]The Campanians sided with Hannibal in 216 B.C., and their leaders were beheaded by the Romans in 211 B.C. (see 3:8,1 and 3:2,ext.1).

[42]The consul, Lucius Aemilius Paullus, died at Cannae in 216 B.C.

[43]Tiberius Sempronius Gracchus (cos, 215 B.C.) died in Lucania (southern Italy) in 212 B.C. (see 1:6,8).

sense. Hannibal honored him with a proper funeral, presented the body with a Carthaginian cloak and a laurel crown, and put it on a pyre.[44]

So the sweetness of kind behavior even penetrates the savage hearts of barbarians, softens the grim and cruel eyes of enemies, and curbs the insolent pride of victory. It is not hard and difficult for kindness to find a quiet path between enemy weapons, between drawn swords clashing against each other. Kindness overcomes anger, conquers hatred, and mingles enemy blood with tears for the enemy. It even led Hannibal to speak admirable words when he decided what funeral honors should be paid to Roman leaders. In fact, the funerals of Paullus and Gracchus and Marcellus brought him even more glory than his victories over them, since he had deceived them with Carthaginian guile but honored them with Roman gentleness. But you brave and loyal spirits, you did not get a funeral you would be ashamed of: it might have been more desirable to have died in your country, but it was even more splendid to die for your country; and if you lost the glory of a proper funeral through bad luck, you won it back through your courage.

Chapter 2. Gratitude

Preface

I wanted to set before you expressions of gratitude and deeds of ingratitude so that by comparing them you would gauge the true value of virtue and vice and thereby reward them appropriately. But since they differ so much in their contrary goals, they should also be separated in my writing, and the one that deserves praise should take its place before the one that deserves blame.

Roman Stories

2. 1. I shall start off with deeds from public life. When Marcius,[45] in his efforts against his own country, had already moved a huge army of Volscians up to the gates of the city and was threatening the Roman Empire with death and darkness, his mother, Veturia, and his wife, Volumnia, pleaded with him and did not allow him to bring his wicked deeds to completion.[46] In honor of these women, the Senate issued the most generous decrees glorifying the entire body of married women: it ordained that men would have to make way for women in the street, thereby acknowledging that a woman's dress had done more to save the Republic than a man's weapons; and it added the new distinction of a headband to the old one of earrings. The Senate

---

[44]Marcus Claudius Marcellus (cos, 222 B.C.) died in Bruttium (southern Italy) in 208 B.C. (see 1:6,9).

[45]Gnaeus Marcius Coriolanus had been exiled from Rome in 491 B.C. and had joined the Volscians (in southern Latium).

[46]Veturia and Volumnia persuaded Coriolanus not to attack Rome in 488 B.C. (see 5:4,1).

also allowed women to use purple clothing and gold trimmings. In addition to this, it had an altar erected to Feminine Fortune in the place where Coriolanus had been won over by the entreaties of the women, and by this specially devised cult, the Senate proved how greatly it appreciated the benefit it had received.[47]

The Senate revealed the same spirit in the days of the Second Punic War. When Capua was being besieged by Fulvius,[48] there were two Campanian women who could not get their kind feelings for Rome out of their minds. They were Vestia Oppia, a married woman with a family, and Cluvia Facula, a prostitute, and the first sacrificed every day for the well-being of our army, while the second never failed to supply the Roman prisoners of war with food. When Capua was defeated, our Senate restored their freedom and property to these women, and declared that it would be happy to give them any further reward they might request. It is remarkable that the Conscript Fathers would have the time to thank two very ordinary women during our great celebrations, not to mention that they thanked them so eagerly.[49]

2. 2. What incident could reveal gratitude more clearly than those young Roman men who voluntarily presented themselves to take the military oath during the consulship of Nautius and Minucius?[50] The young men wanted to come to the aid of the people of Tusculum whose territory had been invaded by the Aequians,[51] because a few months previously the Tusculans had defended the empire of the Roman people with the greatest loyalty and courage.[52] This was unheard of before, that an army conscripted itself rather than let it appear that their country was lacking in gratitude.

2. 3. There was a striking case of great public gratitude toward Fabius the Delayer.[53] After governing the Republic very well during five consulships, he died, and people competed with each other in contributing money to ensure that his funeral procession would be all the greater and more spectacular. Let anyone dare to laugh at rewards for courage after seeing that the burials of brave men are happier than the lives of cowards.

2. 4. While Fabius was still alive, he was thanked in a most glorious way. By a referendum of the plebs, his master of the horse, Minucius, was given equal power with Fabius, who was dictator, something that had never been done before.[54] The army was divided between the two men, and Minucius fought with his army alone against Hannibal in Samnium. He was foolish to have started this battle, and it would

---

[47]The temple of Feminine Fortune was four miles south of Rome on the Latin Way (see 1:8,4).

[48]Quintus Fulvius Flaccus (cos, 237 B.C.) besieged Capua from 212 to 211 B.C.

[49]The two women were praised at a Senate meeting in 210 B.C.

[50]Lucius Minucius Esquilinus Augurinus and Gaius Nautius Rutilus were consuls in 458 B.C.

[51]Rome defended Tusculum against the Aequians in 459 B.C. and again in 458 B.C. The Aequians came from the Sabine region of central Italy.

[52]Tusculum (modern Frascati), in Latium, had helped Rome in 460 B.C.

[53]Fabius the Delayer died in 203 B.C., after being consul five times between 233 and 209 B.C.

[54]Fabius the Delayer was elected dictator in 217 B.C., with Marcus Minucius Rufus (cos, 221 B.C.) as his master of the horse.

have had a disastrous outcome had he not been saved when Fabius came to the rescue. Minucius himself addressed Fabius as father, and he wanted his legions to salute Fabius as their patron; he laid aside the burden of a shared command, and, as was only proper, he subordinated the office of master of the horse to that of dictator. By expressing his gratitude in this way, he corrected the error of the foolish mob.

2. 5. Minucius, indeed, behaved as admirably as Quintus Terentius Culleo, who was born of a praetorian family and was an exceptionally distinguished member of the Senate.[55] Culleo set an excellent example during the triumph of Scipio Africanus by following his chariot wearing a cap of liberty on his head, because he had been captured by the Carthaginians and freed by Africanus.[56] With the Roman people looking on, he quite rightly acknowledged the benefit he had received from the man who had given him back his freedom, by treating him as his patron.[57]

2. 6. When Flamininus held his triumph over King Philip, not just one man but two thousand Roman citizens accompanied his chariot wearing caps of liberty.[58] They had been captured during the Punic Wars[59] and had been living as slaves in Greece, but through his own efforts Flamininus rounded them up and restored them to their former status. The general won twice as much glory by presenting his country with the spectacle of the enemies he had defeated and the citizens he had rescued. And the rescue of those citizens was also twice as welcome to everyone, both because there were so many of them and because they showed such gratitude in regaining the liberty for which they had longed.

2. 7. Metellus Pius' constant love for his exiled father earned him his extra name, Pius, which was as famous for his tears as the names of others were for their victories.[60] When he was consul, he did not hesitate to canvass the people on behalf of Quintus Calidius, who was a candidate for the praetorship,[61] because when Calidius was tribune of the plebs, he had passed a law restoring Metellus' father to citizenship.[62] In fact, Metellus always referred to Calidius as the patron of his house and family. This behavior did not in any way detract from his leadership of the state, which was never in any doubt, because it was gratitude, not submissiveness,

---

[55]Quintus Terentius Culleo (praetor, 187 B.C.) was a veteran of the Second Punic War. "Praetorian family" means that one of his ancestors was a praetor.

[56]Scipio Africanus celebrated his triumph over Carthage in 201 B.C.

[57]When a master freed a slave and presented him with the cap of liberty, the master became the former slave's patron, so Culleo is acting like a former slave toward Scipio Africanus.

[58]Titus Quinctius Flamininus celebrated his triumph over King Philip V of Macedonia in 194 B.C.

[59]The Second Punic War (218–201 B.C.) had ended recently.

[60]Quintus Caecilius Metellus Pius was consul in 80 B.C. His father, Quintus Caecilius Metellus Numidicus (cos, 109 B.C.), had been exiled in 100 B.C. (see 3:8,4).

[61]Metellus Pius helped Quintus Calidius in the election campaign of 80 B.C., and Calidius did in fact become a praetor in 79 B.C.

[62]Calidius was a tribune of the plebs in 98 B.C. when he recalled Metellus Numidicus from exile.

that made him value his own extraordinary prestige less than the great favor he had received from a man who was far inferior to him.

2. 8. The gratitude felt by Marius was not just exceptional but overpowering too. When two cohorts from Camerinum[63] showed amazing courage in holding back the violent assault of the Cimbrians,[64] he rewarded them with Roman citizenship on the very battlefield, though that was against treaty regulations. He came up with an honest and extraordinary excuse for this action by saying that in the midst of all the noise of the fighting, he had been unable to hear the details of the civil law. That was certainly a time when it was more appropriate to defend the laws than to listen to them.

2. 9. In their competition for glory, Sulla always follows closely in the steps of Marius. When Sulla was dictator, he uncovered his head, rose from his chair, and descended from his horse in honor of Pompey, who was just a private citizen.[65] Sulla declared at a public assembly that he was glad to do this because he bore in mind that when Pompey was eighteen years old, he and his father's army had helped Sulla's side.[66] Pompey received many honors, but I wonder whether he received anything greater than this one, that the greatness of his services forced Sulla to forget his true nature.[67]

2. 10. On these splendid heights, we shall have to make some space for the gratitude of the lowest classes. The praetor Marcus Cornutus was contracting for the funeral of Hirtius and Pansa by order of the Senate.[68] Those engaged in the funeral business promised they would provide the use of their equipment and their own labor free of charge, since these two men had died fighting for the Republic. By asking Cornutus repeatedly, they got him to agree that they would also be granted the task of providing the funeral trappings at the nominal charge of one sesterce.[69] Their low legal status increases rather than diminishes the glory of their deed, because they disdained to make a profit even though their entire lives were devoted to nothing else than making a profit.

With all due respect to their ashes, I hope the kings of foreign nations will allow me to speak of them right after that despised group.[70] But either I had to leave that group out, or I had to put them at the end of my national stories. Since I did not want the honorable deeds of even the lowest people to fall into oblivion,

---

[63]Camerinum was a city in Umbria (eastern Italy).

[64]Marius defeated the Cimbrians (from Denmark) in northern Italy in 101 B.C.

[65]When Pompey landed in Italy in 83 B.C., Sulla greeted him in this way. This was just before Sulla's dictatorship (82–79 B.C.)

[66]Pompey's father, Gnaeus Pompeius Strabo (cos, 89 B.C.), had defended Rome against the army of Marius in 87 B.C.

[67]According to his "true nature," Sulla was a bloodthirsty tyrant (see 3:1,2).

[68]Gaius Vibius Pansa Caetronianus and Aulus Hirtius were consuls in 43 B.C. They died fighting against Antony. Marcus Caecilius Cornutus (praetor, 43 B.C.) took over after their death.

[69]See money—Roman in the Glossary.

[70]Funeral directors were despised because they belonged to the lower classes and made money out of death.

I gave them a separate place of their own, so that they would not seem joined to the Roman stories or placed above the foreign ones.

Foreign Stories

2. ext. 1. When Darius was still a private citizen, he was charmed by a cloak owned by Syloson of Samos,[71] and he gazed at it so longingly that Syloson offered it to him spontaneously and indeed eagerly. When he took over the throne, Darius revealed how much gratitude had developed in his heart for this gift: he handed over the entire city and island of Samos to Syloson for his own use.[72] Darius honored not the economic value of the gift but the way Syloson had taken the opportunity to be generous, and he took into account the circumstances of the man who had given the gift rather than the circumstances of the man who had received it.

2. ext. 2. King Mithridates also showed himself to be splendid in his gratitude. When Leonicus, who had fiercely defended the king's life, was captured by the Rhodians in a naval battle,[73] Mithridates exchanged all his enemy prisoners of war for him. He felt it was better to be swindled by his greatest enemies than not to show gratitude to a man who deserved it so well.

2. ext. 3. The Roman people were generous in the huge gift they gave to King Attalus by presenting him with Asia.[74] But Attalus was grateful too in his fair-minded will, which bequeathed the same Asia to the Roman people.[75] It would be impossible to praise the generosity of the Roman people or the way in which Attalus appreciated their goodness to him in words that would equal in number the magnificent cities that had been granted to him in a friendly spirit, or given back by him in a grateful one.

2. ext. 4. But I wonder whether the heart of King Masinissa, more than anyone else's, was filled with the marks of a grateful spirit. Through the services of Scipio Africanus, his kingdom had been generously expanded,[76] and right to the end of his life (the immortal gods allowed Masinissa to live to a ripe old age) he retained the memory of that famous gift with unwavering loyalty.[77] As a result, not only Africa but all nations knew that he felt a stronger friendship for the Cornelius family and for the city of Rome than he did for himself.

---

[71]Syloson was the brother of Polycrates, the ruler of Samos (an island off the west coast of Asia Minor).

[72]Darius I was king of Persia from 521 to 486 B.C. After Polycrates of Samos was put to death (see 6:9,ext.5), Darius gave the island to Syloson.

[73]King Mithridates VI of Pontus attacked Rhodes in 88 B.C.

[74]After defeating Antiochus the Great of Syria in 190 B.C., the Romans gave the western half of Asia Minor to King Eumenes II (not Attalus) of Pergamum in 188 B.C.

[75]King Attalus III of Pergamum, who died in 133 B.C., bequeathed his enlarged kingdom to the Romans. This territory became the province of Asia.

[76]After defeating the Carthaginians, Scipio Africanus presented King Masinissa of Numidia with much of their territory in 201 B.C.

[77]Masinissa was one hundred years old when he died in 148 B.C. (see 8:13,ext.1).

Although he was hard hit by Carthaginian attacks and could barely guarantee the safety of his own kingdom, Masinissa was completely willing to hand over a large and good part of the Numidian army to Scipio Aemilianus,[78] because Aemilianus was the grandson of Africanus, and Masinissa gave more consideration to the favor he had received long ago than to his present danger. Aemilianus had been sent there by the consul Lucullus to ask for help and to lead those troops back to him in Spain.[79]

When Masinissa was growing old, he left the great wealth of his kingdom to his sons, who were fifty-four in number; and as he was beginning to fail on his bed, he wrote a letter begging Manius Manilius, who was the governor in charge of Africa, to send Scipio Aemilianus, who was serving in the governor's army at that time.[80] Masinissa felt that his death would be happier if he gave up his last breath and gave his last commands while holding Scipio's right hand. But realizing that his death would come before Scipio arrived, he gave the following instructions to his wife and children: they should respect only one people in the world—the Romans, and only one family within the Roman people—the Scipios; they should keep everything just as it was for Aemilianus; they should use him as their judge in dividing the kingdom; whatever Aemilianus decided, they should uphold it as sacred and unchangeable, just as if Masinissa himself had specified it in his will. In all these various tasks, Masinissa's tireless career of loyalty lasted until he reached the age of one hundred.[81]

By these examples and others like them, the kindness of the human race is nourished and grows. These are the torches, these are the goads that make the human race burn with desire to help others and win their respect. The greatest and most splendid wealth is the respect a man can earn from the wide range of good deeds he has happily done for others. Since I pay a religious devotion to such people, I shall now speak of those who neglect this virtue, to attack them and to make virtue more appreciated.

Chapter 3. Ingratitude

Roman Stories

3. 1. The senators tore the father of our city to pieces in the Senate house,[82] though he had placed them in the highest rank of honor; and they did not think it a crime to take the life of a man who had given immortal life to the Roman Empire.

---

[78]Masinissa handed over his war elephants to Scipio Aemilianus in 150 B.C.

[79]Scipio Aemilianus served as a military tribune under Lucius Licinius Lucullus (cos, 151 B.C.) in Spain in 150 B.C.

[80]Manius Manilius (cos, 149 B.C.) was in charge of Africa in 148 B.C. Scipio Aemilianus served under him as a military tribune.

[81]Scipio Aemilianus divided the kingdom among three sons of Masinissa.

[82]The usual story was that Romulus disappeared in a storm and was proclaimed a god, but there was also this more gruesome version of his death.

That was indeed a rough and savage generation, and even the profound respect of later ages was not able to conceal the fact that it had stained itself horribly with the blood its founder.

3. 2a. A natural remorse on the part of our state followed this crime of minds that had fallen into ingratitude. Furius Camillus had been very successful in expanding the power of Rome and very steadfast in maintaining it.[83] But he was not able to ensure his own safety in our city, even though he had guaranteed its security and increased its prosperity. He was brought to trial by Lucius Appuleius, a tribune of the plebs, for embezzling booty from Veii, and by a harsh and, so to speak, iron-hearted verdict, he was sent into exile.[84] All this happened at the very time he lost his son, an excellent young man, so Camillus should have been consoled with sympathy rather than burdened down with new misfortunes. But his country ignored the extraordinary achievements of this great man and added the condemnation of the father to the funeral of his son. Someone might object that the tribune of the plebs had complained that 15,000 asses were missing from the treasury, so that was what his fine was set at. But the Roman people did not deserve to lose such a leader for such a sum of money!

3. 2b. I am still shaking with outrage at that story, but another outrageous story comes to mind. The Republic was not only battered and broken down by the fighting in the Second Punic War, but it was almost short of blood and dying, when Scipio Africanus made it the conqueror of Carthage.[85] But his fellow citizens repaid his glorious deeds with unjust treatment and made him live in an obscure village and a deserted marshland.[86] He did not bear in silence his resentment at this voluntary exile when he went down to the Underworld, because he ordered them to write on his tomb, "Ungrateful fatherland, you do not even have my bones." What could be more undeserved than his expulsion, more justified than his complaint, more reasonable than his revenge? He refused his ashes to his fatherland, which he had prevented from falling into ashes. This was the only punishment that the ungrateful heart of the Roman city received from Scipio, but it was indeed a greater punishment than the violence of Coriolanus:[87] he struck his country with fear, but Scipio struck it with shame. He could not even bring himself to complain about his country—that is how steadfast he was in his true loyalty—until after his death.

3. 2c. What happened to his brother could, I suppose, have been some consolation to him after these experiences. His brother defeated King Antiochus, added Asia to the empire of the Roman people, and held a splendid triumph—and that is precisely why he was accused of embezzlement and sent to jail![88]

---

[83]Marcus Furius Camillus (dictator, 396 B.C.) captured Veii (in Etruria) in 396 B.C.

[84]Lucius Appuleius had Camillus exiled in 391 B.C.

[85]Scipio Africanus defeated the Carthaginians in 202 B.C.

[86]Scipio Africanus was prosecuted in 184 B.C. (see 3:7,1e). He died shortly afterward in Liternum (on the coast of Latium).

[87]After being exiled in 491 B.C., Gnaeus Marcius Coriolanus joined Rome's enemies (see 5:4,1).

[88]Scipio Asiaticus defeated Antiochus the Great of Syria in 190 B.C., but he was prosecuted in 187 B.C. (see 3:7,1d) and was almost sent to jail in 184 B.C. (see 4:1,8).

3. 2d. Scipio Aemilianus was in no way inferior to his grandfather in courage, but he was in no way more fortunate in his end, either. He had removed from this world two cities that threatened the Roman Empire, Numantia and Carthage,[89] but at home he met up with a man who took his life, and he never found anyone in the Forum to avenge his death.[90]

3. 2e. Who is unaware that Scipio Nasica earned as much glory in politics as both Scipio Africanus and Scipio Aemilianus earned in arms? He was the man who prevented the strangulation of the Republic when Tiberius Gracchus got his accursed hands around its throat.[91] But he too had to withdraw from public life because his fellow citizens had judged his merits so unfairly. He went to Pergamum ostensibly as an envoy but spent the remainder of his life there, and did not miss his ungrateful country.[92]

3. 2f. I have dwelt on the same family, but I have not yet finished with the grievances of the Cornelius clan. Publius Lentulus was a very famous citizen who truly loved the Republic. He had bravely and loyally fought back the evil schemes and forces of Gaius Gracchus on the Aventine and was seriously wounded.[93] His reward for fighting that battle, which had maintained the law, public order, and liberty in their rightful condition, was that he was forbidden to die in our city. Malicious abuse forced him to accept from the Senate a grant of free travel, and he called a public meeting in which he asked the immortal gods never to let him return to his ungrateful people. He set off for Sicily, and by staying there resolutely, he made his prayer come true.[94] So five members in a row of the Cornelius family were notorious examples of their country's ingratitude.

3. 2g. At least their withdrawals from public life were voluntary. But when Ahala was master of the horse and killed Spurius Maelius, who was aiming at royal power, the penalty he paid for defending the liberty of his fellow citizens was exile.[95]

3. 3. The mind of the Senate and people is roused up like a sudden storm, so it must be subjected to moderate criticism, but the ungrateful deeds of individuals must be cut to pieces with unrestrained indignation. Such individuals were free to make their own decision, since they could weigh each alternative rationally, but they chose treachery over loyalty. What shower, what storm of words, could properly

[89]Scipio Aemilianus destroyed Numantia (in Spain) in 133 B.C. and Carthage (in Africa) in 146 B.C.

[90]Scipio Aemilianus died suddenly and mysteriously in 129 B.C. (see 4:1,12).

[91]Publius Cornelius Scipio Nasica Serapio (cos, 138 B.C.) led the senators who murdered the populist tribune of the plebs, Tiberius Sempronius Gracchus, in 133 B.C. (see 3:2,17).

[92]The Senate sent him off in 132 B.C. to organize the new province of Asia (formerly the kingdom of Pergamum). He died there in that year.

[93]In 121 B.C. Publius Cornelius Lentulus (cos, 162 B.C.) attacked the supporters of Gaius Sempronius Gracchus (tribune of the plebs, 123 B.C.). The Aventine hill was in the southern part of Rome.

[94]Popular hatred inspired Lentulus to depart for Sicily in 120 B.C.

[95]Gaius Servilius Ahala was master of the horse when he killed the populist Spurius Maelius in 439 B.C. (see 6:3,1c).

rain down on the wicked head of Sextilius? When he had been prosecuted on a very serious charge, Caesar Strabo had defended him eagerly and successfully.[96] Later, when Cinna published his death list,[97] Caesar Strabo was a fugitive and was forced by his dreadful circumstances to ask Sextilius to return the favor, so he begged Sextilius for protection on his property at Tarquinii.[98]

But Sextilius felt no horror as he dragged Caesar Strabo away from the sacred bonds of his treacherous table and the altars of his evil household and handed him over to the ferocious victor to be slaughtered. Imagine if a former accuser had been turned into his suppliant by a change in political fortunes and had gone down on his knees to beg Sextilius for this tragic assistance. Even then it would have been cruel to reject him; for if the wrongs they have done make us hate people, their misfortunes make us sympathize with them. But Sextilius with his own hand betrayed not his accuser but his defender to the savage violence of his enemy. If Sextilius did this through fear of death, he did not deserve to live; if he did it in hope of a reward, he most certainly deserved to die.[99]

3. 4. I shall turn to another deed of ingratitude that matches this one. At the request of Marcus Caelius,[100] Cicero defended Gaius Popillius Laenas, from the region of Picenum,[101] with an eagerness that was no less effective than his eloquence, and although Popillius was uncertain about the outcome of his shaky case, Cicero restored him safely to his home. This same Popillius had never been harmed by Cicero, either in word or in deed, but when Cicero's name appeared on the death list,[102] Popillius went up to Antony without being asked and requested that he be sent to track Cicero down and murder him.[103] When Popillius was granted the role of carrying out this revolting task, he danced with joy and ran off to Caieta.[104] Apart from the fact that Cicero was a man of great public distinction, he had also shown great enthusiasm in carrying out the major task of saving the life of Popillius, so he deserved his respect as a private friend. But Popillius ordered him to bare his throat, quickly cut off the head of the master of Roman eloquence, and amputated the hand made famous in peacetime. Popillius did this calmly and serenely, and then eagerly returned to the city with his burden as if he were carrying rich

[96]This man is Gaius Julius Caesar Strabo Vopiscus (aedile, 90 B.C.), who was an amateur poet (see 3:7,11).

[97]Marius (cos, 107 B.C.) and Lucius Cornelius Cinna (cos, 87 B.C.) took control of Rome in 87 B.C. and massacred their political opponents. They also published a death list of their opponents and rewarded anyone who murdered an opponent on that list.

[98]Sextilius is unknown. Tarquinii was a city near the coast of Etruria (western Italy).

[99]Caesar Strabo was murdered in 87 B.C.

[100]Marcus Caelius Rufus (praetor, 48 B.C.) was a friend of Cicero.

[101]Picenum was in eastern Italy.

[102]Antony and Augustus published a death list of their political enemies in 43 B.C. and rewarded anyone who brought in the head of an enemy.

[103]Gaius Popillius Laenas was a military tribune in 43 B.C. when he murdered Cicero.

[104]Cicero was staying at Caieta on the coast of Latium.

spoils.[105] As Popillius carried his wicked burden, it never occurred to him that he was carrying the head of the man who had once made a speech to save his head. Words are not powerful enough to criticize this monster, since we do not have another Cicero to lament the sad fate of Cicero in a worthy manner.

3. 5. I do not know how I should speak of you, Pompey the Great. I look upon the extent of your good fortune, which once filled every land and every sea with its splendor, and then I recall that its downfall was greater than anything I could attempt to describe in my writing. But even if I did not mention it, people's minds would recall with some disapproval that Gnaeus Carbo had been killed on your orders, even though he had helped you fight for your father's estate in the Forum when you were a very young man.[106] By his death you showed more regard for the power of Sulla than for your own sense of honor.[107]

Foreign Stories

3. ext. 1. But I do not want foreign cities to gloat over these confessions of our ingratitude. The number of our generals and armies that Hannibal slaughtered to ensure the security and victory of the Carthaginians was so great that even if he had killed a similar number of ordinary enemy soldiers, he would have won great glory. But the Carthaginians still took it into their heads to banish him from their sight.[108]

3. ext. 2. Sparta produced nobody who was greater or did more good than Lycurgus.[109] It is said, after all, that when he consulted the oracle, Pythian Apollo[110] responded that he did not know whether to include Lycurgus among men or gods. But neither the exceptional uprightness of his life, nor his loyal devotion to his country, nor the laws he had developed to preserve it could protect him from experiencing the hostility of his fellow citizens. He was often pelted with stones, he was thrown out of the Forum on one occasion, he even had his eye knocked out, and finally he was banished from the country itself. What can you expect from other cities, when even the city that earned such a great reputation for steadfastness and self-control and austerity behaved so ungratefully toward the man who had deserved so well of it?

3. ext. 3. Take Theseus away from the Athenians, and Athens would be nothing, or at least not so famous.[111] His fellow citizens used to live scattered in villages, but he brought them together into one city and gave the form and appearance of a

---

[105]Rich spoils were taken from an enemy commander (see 3:2,3; 3:2,4; and 3:2,5).

[106]Gnaeus Papirius Carbo (cos, 85 B.C.) had supported Pompey after the death of Pompey's father in 86 B.C.

[107]Sulla was dictator in 82 B.C. when he sent Pompey to kill Carbo.

[108]Hannibal was exiled by his political opponents in 195 B.C. (see 4:1,6).

[109]The legendary Lycurgus supposedly lived in the ninth century B.C.

[110]Pythian Apollo refers to the oracle of Apollo at Delphi. The oracles were revealed by a priestess called the Pythia.

[111]Theseus was a mythical king who united the territory of Athens into a state.

great state to a people who lived apart from each other as people do in rural areas. When he was barely an adolescent, he rebelled against the savage orders of the mighty King Minos;[112] he suppressed the unbridled arrogance of Thebes;[113] he came to the aid of the children of Hercules;[114] and wherever there was any monster or villain, he destroyed it with the courage of his spirit and the strength of his right hand. But he was banished from Athens, and Scyros, an island less significant than the exiled man himself, held his bones when he died.[115]

Solon passed such glorious and beneficial laws for the Athenians that if they had been content to use them permanently, they would have held onto their empire forever;[116] he won for them the island of Salamis, which was like an enemy outpost threatening their security from nearby;[117] he saw the rise of the tyranny of Peisistratus and was the only man who dared to say openly that it should be crushed by force.[118] But he spent his old age as an exile in Cyprus, and it was not his fate to be buried in the country he deserved so well of.[119]

The Athenians would have behaved well toward Miltiades if they had sent him into exile immediately after he had defeated three hundred thousand Persians at Marathon, but instead they made him die chained up in a prison.[120] In my view, they should have felt they had been quite cruel enough to the man who had deserved so well of them. But on the contrary, after they had forced him to die in this way, they did not allow his body to be buried before they handed his son Cimon over to be put in chains too. This son of a great leader who was himself destined to be the greatest leader of his age was thus able to boast that the only inheritance of his father's he had benefited from was his chains and his prison![121]

Aristides was the standard by which justice was measured in the whole of Greece, and he was also an exceptional example of self-discipline, but he was ordered to depart from his country. How lucky Athens was that, after his exile, it was able to find any good man or patriotic citizen, since moral integrity departed with Aristides![122]

[112]King Minos demanded victims from Athens to feed the Minotaur, but Theseus killed the Minotaur.

[113]Theseus forced the Thebans to allow their enemies to bury their war-dead.

[114]The children of Heracles had come to Athens for help.

[115]Scyros was a small island off the east coast of Greece.

[116]Solon passed his code of laws in 594 B.C.

[117]The Athenians conquered Salamis around 600 B.C.

[118]Peisistratus was tyrant of Athens from 560 to 527 B.C.

[119]Rather than live under Peisistratus, Solon went to Cyprus in 560 B.C. He died there in the following year.

[120]Miltiades won the battle of Marathon in 490 B.C. He was tried for treason in 489 B.C. and died in the same year.

[121]Cimon dominated Athenian politics from 479 to 461 B.C. He was exiled in 461 B.C.

[122]Aristides "the Just" was exiled in 482 B.C. He was recalled in 480 B.C. and was an important politician from then until his death in 468 B.C.

Themistocles is the most famous case of a man who suffered from the ingratitude of his country. He had made it secure, famous, rich, and leader of Greece, but he experienced such hostility there that he felt he had to appeal to Xerxes for pity, even though he had destroyed Xerxes shortly before and Xerxes owed him no pity.[123]

Although Phocion was well endowed with the qualities that are thought to be most effective in winning men over—compassion and generosity—he was almost put on the rack by the Athenians. It is certain that after he died, no piece of Attic earth could be found to throw over his bones, since he had been expelled from that land in which he had once lived and been the best of citizens.[124]

So why shouldn't we call it mass hysteria when there is a general consensus to punish the greatest virtues as if they were the most serious crimes and to repay good deeds with ill-treatment? Such behavior should be viewed as intolerable everywhere, but particularly so in Athens, a city where one could take legal action against ungrateful people, and rightly so. Because whoever fails to show proper gratitude to someone that has deserved well of them undermines the system of giving and receiving favors, without which human existence would hardly be possible. Don't the Athenians deserve harsh criticism? They had the fairest laws but the most unfair personalities, and they chose to follow their characters rather than their laws. If divine providence could have enabled those excellent men, whose misfortunes I have just related, to appeal to the law punishing ingratitude and to bring their country to court before another state, would they not have made the clever and talkative people of Athens fall silent and speechless by the following accusation?

> Your rival households and huts scattered throughout rural areas have become the mainstay of Greece; Marathon shines out with its trophies over the Persians;[125] Salamis and Artemisium are considered the shipwrecks of Xerxes;[126] your walls, which were destroyed by mighty armies, have risen up again, more beautiful than ever. Where did the men who brought about these achievements live? Where do they lie now? Answer us! Why, you ungratefully forced Theseus to be buried on a tiny rocky island, and Miltiades to die in jail, and Cimon to wear his father's chains, and the conquering Themistocles to embrace the knees of the enemy he had conquered, and Solon, along with Aristides and Phocion, to flee from their homes. And in the meantime, while our ashes are disgracefully and tragically scattered abroad, you keep the ashes of Oedipus, who was polluted by the murder of his father and by marriage with his mother.[127] You even honor his ashes with an altar and worship them with holy offerings on the Are-

---

[123]Themistocles defeated King Xerxes I of Persia at Salamis in 480 B.C. Themistocles was exiled in 472 B.C. and eventually sought asylum in Persia, when a new king, Artaxerxes I, came to the throne in 465 B.C.

[124]Phocion was favorable to Macedonia, the enemy of Athens. He was put to death in 318 B.C.

[125]Miltiades won the battle of Marathon (on the east coast of Attica) in 490 B.C.

[126]Themistocles won the sea battles of Artemisium (on the north coast of Euboea, an island off the east coast of Greece) and Salamis (an island near Athens) in 480 B.C.

[127]Actually, it was Theseus who welcomed Oedipus to Athens.

opagus, the revered place where gods and mortals disputed,[128] and on the exalted acropolis of your guardian goddess, Minerva.[129] That's how much you value the bad deeds of foreigners over the good deeds of your own people. So read the law that binds you under oath, and since you were unwilling to pay us the rewards you owed us for deserving so well of you, you shall have to pay us the proper compensation for the harm you have done us.

Their ghosts are silent, constrained by the inexorable laws of fate. But the tongues of those who are free to speak out will not conceal their criticism of you, Athens, since you never appreciate good deeds.

Chapter 4. Loyalty to Parents[130]

Preface

Let us leave aside the ungrateful and talk about considerate people instead. It is much better to devote our attention to something that is admirable than something that is hated. So let us deal with you now, you stories about everything that lucky parents could wish for, you stories about offspring who were born under happy auspices. You will make people happy to have had children and eager to have more.

Roman Stories

4. 1. Coriolanus was a man of the highest courage and the deepest wisdom, and he deserved the very best from our Republic. He was devastated by the disgrace of an extremely unjust condemnation and fled to the Volscians, who were enemies of Rome at the time.[131] Qualities like his are highly valued in every land. He had gone to the Volscians simply to find a place of refuge, but within a short while he attained the highest public office there. His fellow Romans had refused to accept him as a general who would have saved them, but it turned out that they were forced to see him as a leader who almost brought about their destruction. He defeated our armies on several occasions, and by means of his victories he gradually built a path for the Volscian army that led right up to the walls of our city. The Roman people, who had been so arrogant in misjudging their own good

---

[128]The Areopagus was a hill in Athens where murder trials took place. In Greek myth, the gods had participated in the trial of Orestes on the Areopagus.

[129]The temple of Athena (Minerva) was on the acropolis.

[130]Valerius calls this chapter "Loyalty to Parents, Brothers, and Country" and has no titles for Chapters 5 and 6. I have divided the title among the three chapters.

[131]Gaius Marcius Coriolanus was exiled in 491 B.C. and joined the Volscians (in southern Latium).

fortune, who had shown no compassion for Coriolanus when he was on trial, were now forced to fall at his knees, when he was no more than an exile.

Envoys were sent to plead with him, but they achieved nothing. Then the priests with their sacred headbands were sent to him, but they likewise came back without any results. The Senate was astounded, the people were terrified, and men and women alike wept at the thought of their inevitable ruin. At that point, Veturia, the mother of Coriolanus, dragging his wife, Volumnia, and his children along with her, went off toward the camp of the Volscians.[132] When her son saw her, he said, "O my country, you have dissolved and overcome my anger by using this woman to plead for you. Although you have richly deserved my hatred, I release you out of respect for her womb." And at once, he freed the territory of Rome from the army of its enemy. His heart had been full of resentment at the injury he had received, full of hope at the victory he was about to attain, full of shame at the task he was going to abandon, full of fear of the death penalty, but his sense of duty emptied his heart of all these things and occupied it completely. The sight of his mother alone changed a dreadful war into a wholesome peace.

4. 2. The same sense of duty powerfully affected Scipio Africanus, when he had barely started the years of his adolescence, and it gave him the strength to come to his father's aid in battle with the courage of a real man.[133] When his father was consul and fighting an ill-fated battle against Hannibal at the river Ticinus, he was wounded critically, but his son rushed in to save him.[134] The young man was unsure because of his age, he was inexperienced in warfare, and the outcome of this unlucky battle was enough to frighten even the most experienced warrior, but none of these things deterred him. He was deservedly honored with a crown and won twice as much glory, because he had saved the man who was both his general and his father from the very jaws of death.

4. 3. The citizens of Rome have only heard about those exemplary deeds, but they have witnessed the following deed with their own eyes. Pomponius, a tribune of the plebs, had summoned Lucius Manlius Capitolinus to a trial before the people,[135] on the grounds that in his eagerness to grasp a chance of winning a war he had stayed in office beyond the term permitted by law; and he also accused Capitolinus of abusing his son, a very talented young man, by making him work on the farm and by keeping him away from public affairs. After Torquatus, the young man in question,[136] heard about this, he set off for the city at once, and at dawn he made his way to Pomponius' house. Pomponius thought Torquatus had

[132]Valerius also tells the story of Veturia at 1:8,4 and 5:2,1.

[133]Scipio Africanus was seventeen years old in 218 B.C.

[134]Publius Cornelius Scipio (cos, 218 B.C.) was the father of Scipio Africanus. Hannibal defeated the Romans at the river Ticinus (modern Ticino), which flowed through Transpadana (northern Italy).

[135]Marcus Pomponius was tribune of the plebs in 362 B.C. when he prosecuted Lucius Manlius Capitolinus Imperiosus (dictator, 363 B.C.).

[136]The son was Titus Manlius Imperiosus Torquatus (cos, 347 B.C.). For his childhood on the farm, see 6:9,1.

come to reveal the misdeeds of his father, by whom he had been treated with undue harshness. He therefore ordered everyone to leave the room, believing that Torquatus would give his evidence more freely if there were no onlookers. This gave the young man the perfect opportunity for what he had planned. He took out a sword, which he had concealed on his person, and by means of the most terrifying threats, he forced the tribune to swear that he would abandon the case against his father. As a result, Capitolinus did not have to appear in court. A sense of duty is always admired, even when it is felt toward kind parents; but Torquatus deserves even greater praise, because although his father was quite a brutal man, he still came to his rescue. He was moved to respect his father, not by any kindness or affection that had been shown to him, but by his own natural feelings alone.

4. 4. Marcus Cotta showed a similar sense of duty. On the very day that he first wore his adult toga, he came down from the Capitol and immediately sought out Gaius Carbo, who had condemned his father.[137] He took legal proceedings against Carbo and ruined him in court.[138] This magnificent deed revealed his character and showed how this young man would develop.

4. 5. The influence of his father was equally powerful over Gaius Flaminius. When he was tribune of the plebs, Flaminius had brought in a law under which the territory conquered from the Gauls would be divided into individual allotments, but he did this against the will of the Senate, which fought against the measure.[139] Flaminius vigorously resisted the pleas and threats of that body, and he was not even deterred by the army that was drafted against him, in case he should persevere in his views. But when he was standing at the rostra and putting the measure to the vote, his father grabbed him by the shoulder. Crushed by the power of this private citizen, Flaminius came down from the rostra, and nobody raised the slightest murmur against him for deserting the assembly he had summoned.[140]

4. 6. These were great achievements of a manly sense of duty, but I wonder whether the deed of the vestal virgin Claudia was not even more powerful and high-spirited than all of these. While her father was celebrating a triumph,[141] she noticed that a tribune of the plebs was trying to drag him violently from his triumphal chariot. With extraordinary speed, she ran in between the two men and prevented this abuse of power, which was inspired by political hatred. As a result, the father had his triumphal procession up to the Capitol, but his daughter had her own triumph to the temple of Vesta. And it was hard to tell which of them won the greater praise: the man who had victory by his side or the daughter with her sense of duty.

---

[137]In 70 B.C., Gaius Papirius Carbo (praetor, 62 B.C.) had prosecuted the father, Marcus Aurelius Cotta (cos, 74 B.C.).

[138]Carbo was in the east until 59 B.C. When Carbo returned, he was prosecuted by the son, who was also called Marcus Aurelius Cotta.

[139]The son, Gaius Flaminius (cos, 223 B.C.), was a tribune of the plebs in 232 B.C.

[140]The land law was passed eventually in the same year. His father, also called Gaius Flaminius, never held political office.

[141]Appius Claudius Pulcher (cos, 143 B.C.) was refused a triumph but celebrated one in spite of the Senate.

4. 7. Forgive me, ancient hearths, and grant me pardon, eternal fires, if the theme of my work moves on from your most sacred temple to a place in the city that is a necessary evil and far from pleasant. For the value placed on a sense of duty is high and cannot be diminished by the harshness of fortune or one's low estate. In fact, if its circumstances are wretched, its value is made all the more evident.

A freeborn woman appeared before the praetor's court and was found guilty of a capital offense. The praetor handed her over to the prison manager to be jailed and executed.[142] When she arrived there, the man in charge of the prison was moved by pity for her and did not strangle her immediately. He also allowed her daughter to visit her, but the daughter was carefully searched to make sure she was not bringing any food with her. He imagined that his prisoner would eventually die of starvation. When several days went by, however, he started to wonder how it was that the mother was surviving for so long. He observed the daughter more carefully, and he realized that she was taking out her breast and lessening the pangs of her mother's hunger with her own milk. He was amazed at this strange spectacle, so he reported it to the prison manager, the prison manager reported it to the praetor, the praetor reported it to the committee of jurymen, and her sentence was commuted. Where does the sense of duty not penetrate? What does it not think up? Even in jail, it invented a novel way of saving a mother's life. What could be so extraordinary, what could be so unheard of, as the tale of a mother being breast-fed by her own daughter? Someone might think that this action was against the laws of nature; but in fact, to honor one's parents is the greatest law of nature.

Foreign Stories

4. ext. 1. The same consideration should apply to the dutiful actions of Pero. Her father, Mycon, when he was a very old man, suffered the same misfortune and was likewise sent to jail. Pero took his head to her breast and nursed him, as if he were a baby. When people look at a painting of this deed, they are amazed and cannot take their eyes away. As they admire the representation in front of them, the reality of what happened so long ago is brought back to life. In the silent depiction of those human forms, they believe they can see living and breathing bodies. But the human mind will inevitably have the same experience if the even more effective art of painting in words stimulates it to visualize such ancient deeds as if they had just occurred.

4. ext. 2. I certainly do not want to cover you up in silence, Cimon.[143] You did not hesitate to pay for your father's burial by voluntarily suffering imprisonment.[144] Even if you later happened to emerge as a very great man, both as a citizen and as a leader, you won even greater glory in jail than you did in government. Other

[142]There were three prison managers (*triumviri capitales*) in Rome, and they were responsible for prisons and executions.

[143]This is the famous Cimon, leader of Athens from 479 to 461 B.C.

[144]Cimon's father was Miltiades, who died in 489 B.C. (see 5:3,ext.3).

virtues merely earn a lot of admiration, but a sense of duty wins an enormous amount of love as well.

4. ext. 3. I shall also commemorate you, brothers whose courage was nobler than your social status. Although you were born in Spain in very humble circumstances, you won glory by the honorable way in which you died, because you paid back your parents for raising you by sacrificing your lives on their behalf. The Paciaecus family had promised 12,000 sesterces to the person who would assassinate Etpastus, who was dictator of that country and had killed their father. You agreed on condition that the money would be given to your parents after you were executed. You not only dared to perform a famous deed; you also made it more complete by actively seeking a courageous death. Your hands brought about revenge for the Paciaecus family, a fitting punishment for Etpastus, financial support for your parents, and a glorious end for yourselves. You are still alive today, even in the grave, because you preferred to look after your parents' old age than look forward to your own.[145]

4. ext. 4. Two other pairs of brothers, Cleobis and Biton, and Amphinomus and Anapius, are better known. The first pair are renowned because they physically carried their mother so that she could take part in the rites of Juno.[146] The second pair are well known because they carried their father and mother on their shoulders through a blazing fire.[147] But neither pair was ready to die in order to save their parents' lives.

4. ext. 5. I would not like to take away from the glory of the Argives or belittle the glorious deeds on Mount Aetna. But I want to move the light of fame up to a dutiful deed that is rather obscure because it remains unknown. I am glad to bear witness to the piety of the Scythians. When Darius made repeated attacks against their land with all the resources of his realm, they gradually retreated before him until they had reached the most remote and deserted regions.[148] Speaking on his behalf, the envoys of Darius asked the Scythians when they would stop running away and start fighting instead. They replied that they did not possess any cities or agricultural land to fight for, but when Darius reached the tombs of their ancestors, he would discover how well the Scythians could fight. By this single very pious statement, this frightfully barbarous race redeemed itself from any charge of savagery. The first and best teacher of duty is Nature herself. She does not need to use any spoken words or written works; through her own silent power, she pours love for parents into the hearts of children. What good does education do us? It makes our characters more polished; it does not make them better. For true goodness is born inside us; it is not manufactured.

---

[145]In spite of this memorable deed, nothing further is known about these people.

[146]Cleobis and Biton were from Argos, and their mother was a priestess of Hera there.

[147]Amphinomus and Anapius saved their parents from an eruption of a volcano, Mount Aetna, and were worshiped as heroes in Sicily.

[148]Darius I of Persia conquered Thrace (modern Bulgaria) in 512 B.C. The Greeks thought his ultimate goal was to conquer Scythia (modern Ukraine).

4. ext. 6. Those people wander around in wagons, hide themselves in secret parts of the forests, and live like animals by tearing cattle to pieces: Who taught them to give such an answer to Darius? Who else but that goddess who also taught the son of Croesus, who was incapable of speech, to cry out suddenly in order to save his father's life.[149] Cyrus had captured Sardis, when one of the Persian soldiers, not recognizing his victim, was rushing in like a madman to kill Croesus.[150] It was as if the boy forgot what fortune had denied him from the day he was born. He shouted to the soldier that he should not kill King Croesus and made him pull back the sword, which was almost stuck into his father's throat. Until that time, the boy had been mute, but he acquired the power to speak when his father's life was at stake.

4. ext. 7. The same kind of affection armed a young man from Pinna called Pulto with extraordinary strength of mind and body during the Italian War.[151] His city was under siege, and he was in charge of its gates. His father was a prisoner of war, and the Roman general made him stand where the son could see him and ordered the soldiers to take out their swords and stand around the father.[152] He then threatened to kill the father unless the son would allow him to pass through and attack the city. But the young man was so affected that he single-handedly rescued his father from the hands of the enemy. He should be renowned twice over for his sense of duty: he saved his father's life and did not betray his country.

Chapter 5. Loyalty to Brothers

Preface

Next in rank to the affection toward parents comes the fondness of brothers for each other. It is rightly felt that the first bond of love is created by receiving many great favors from another person, and it should likewise be judged that the next bond of love is created by receiving those favors along with another person. How full of sweetness that memory is: I lived in the same womb before I was born, I spent the time of my infancy in the same cradle, I called the same people my parents, they made the same eager prayers on my behalf, I took the same pride in our ancestral death masks! A wife is dear, children are sweet, friends are pleasant, in-laws are well liked, but our fondness for those people we come to know later should never detract from the first one we felt.

---

[149]Croesus was the last king of Lydia (in western Asia Minor). He ruled from 560 to 546 B.C.

[150]Cyrus the Great of Persia captured Sardis (the capital of Lydia) in 546 B.C.

[151]Pinna (in the Sabine region, central Italy) sided with the Romans in their war against the Italians (90 to 89 B.C.).

[152]Pinna was besieged and captured by the Italians, so the enemy leader would have been an Italian general, not a Roman one.

Roman Stories

5. 1. I say this with Scipio Africanus to back me up. He was tied to Laelius by a very close friendship, but he still humbly begged the Senate not to deprive his brother of his allotted province by transferring it to Laelius.[153] He promised to go to Asia and serve as a legate under Scipio Asiaticus,[154] even though he was older and Scipio Asiaticus was younger; he was very brave, and his brother was un-warlike; he excelled in glory, and his brother had won no fame; and more important than all else, his brother had not yet won the name of Asiaticus, whereas he had already won the name of Africanus.[155] And so, he acquired a most glorious title and presented his brother with another glorious title; he got a purple robe for the African triumph and gave his brother one for the Asian triumph; and he was considerably greater in serving his brother than his brother was in commanding him.

5. 2. The consul Marcus Fabius defeated the Etruscans and the people of Veii in a famous battle,[156] and though the Senate and people had eagerly offered him a triumph, he declined to accept it, because his brother, Quintus Fabius, a former consul,[157] had died fighting with great bravery in that battle. How great should we think the bond of brotherly love in his heart was, if it could undo the great brilliance of this distinguished honor?

5. 3. That story did honor to the old days, but the next one does honor to our own age, which has had the good fortune to witness a brotherly love that glorified the Claudius family and now glorifies the Julius family.[158] Our emperor and father, Tiberius, had a very strong natural love in his heart for his brother, Drusus.[159] After defeating our enemies,[160] Tiberius had come to Ticinum to embrace his parents, when he learned that the health of Drusus, who was in Germany, was in a serious and dangerous condition, and that he might not live. He was panic-stricken and rushed away immediately. He obviously made the journey in wild haste, almost in a single breath, since he crossed the Alps and the Rhine riding day and night, changing his horse repeatedly, and then was happy to carry out a journey of two

---

[153]Scipio Asiaticus and Gaius Laelius were consuls in 190 B.C. They cast lots to decide which of them would go to Asia to fight against Antiochus the Great of Syria. Scipio Asiaticus won the lottery to go to Asia, but the Senate was not sure he would win against Antiochus.

[154]Scipio Africanus did, in fact, serve as a legate in Asia under Scipio Asiaticus in 190 B.C.

[155]Scipio Africanus had celebrated a triumph over the Carthaginians and received the title Africanus in 201 B.C. Scipio Asiaticus received his triumph and the title Asiaticus in 189 B.C.

[156]Marcus Fabius Vibulanus (cos, 483 B.C.) was consul again in 480 B.C. and defeated the army of Veii (a city in Etruria near Rome).

[157]Quintus Fabius Vibulanus (cos, 485 B.C.) died fighting in 480 B.C.

[158]The emperor Tiberius and his brother, Drusus, belonged to the Claudius family at the time of this event (9 B.C.), but Tiberius was later adopted into the Julius family (in A.D. 9).

[159]Nero Claudius Drusus (cos, 9 B.C.) was fighting the Germans on the river Elbe.

[160]Ticinum (modern Pavia) was in Transpadana (northern Italy). Tiberius went there to see his mother, Livia Drusilla, and his stepfather, Augustus. He had been fighting in Pannonia (modern Hungary) and Dalmatia (on the east coast of the Adriatic Sea).

hundred miles through a barbarous region that had only recently been pacified, with Namantabagius as his sole guide and companion.[161] But while he was going through great hardship and danger, and managing without human company, the most sacred power of loyalty, and the gods, who favor the highest virtues, and Jupiter, the most faithful guardian of the Roman Empire, were with him all the time.

Drusus was too close to death to be thinking about his duties to others, and had already lost his mental vigor and physical strength, but at the very moment that separated his life from death, he ordered his legions to advance in full uniform to meet his brother and hail him as general. Drusus also gave orders that a general's tent should be set up for his brother to the right of his own one, and he wanted his brother to have the status of consul and general. Thus he gave way before his brother's prestige and at the same time went away from this life. I know for certain that no other example of brotherly love could appropriately be placed beside theirs than the love of Castor and Pollux.[162]

5. 4. But it will certainly not be displeasing to the most famous generals in all of history if the loyalty of an ordinary soldier toward his brother is added to this part of my book. This soldier was serving in Pompey's army when he killed in close combat a soldier of Sertorius who was attacking him fiercely during a battle.[163] When he was stripping the body as it lay there, he discovered that it was his own brother. He complained loudly for a long time against the gods for granting him this evil victory, brought the body near the camp, covered it with an expensive garment, and placed it on a funeral pyre. Then he set it alight with a torch, and immediately afterward, he stuck the sword he had killed him with through his own breast, lay down over the body of his brother, and cremated himself in the same fire. He should have lived, since he was innocent, having acted in ignorance, but he preferred to consider his own sense of loyalty rather than the forgiveness of others, and he did not fail to join his brother in death.

Chapter 6. Loyalty to One's Country

Preface

Loyalty to the close bonds of blood has done its bit; it now remains for loyalty to one's country to display itself. To its majesty, even the authority of parents, which is equal to that of the gods, subjects its power; even the affection among brothers yields quietly, willingly, and with good reason, because the Republic can survive unharmed when a home is destroyed, but the destruction of a city necessarily

---

[161]The "barbarous region" is all of Germany between the Rhine and the Elbe, which was briefly a part of the Roman Empire (12 B.C.–9 A.D.).

[162]The heavenly twins, Castor and Pollux, were renowned for their brotherly love.

[163]Pompey fought in Spain against the army of the Roman rebel, Quintus Sertorius (praetor, 83 B.C.) from 76 to 71 B.C.

brings down with it the homes of all its citizens. But what is the point in trying to grasp this feeling in mere words, since some people have shown the extent of its power by giving up their lives for it?

Roman Stories

6. 1. Brutus, our first consul, galloped on the battlefield against Arruns, the son of the exiled King Tarquin the Proud.[164] They threw their spears at the same time, and each of them suffered a mortal wound and lay there lifeless. So I would rightly note that liberty came to the Roman people at a very high price.

6. 2. When the earth caved in and a huge gaping hole suddenly appeared in the middle of the Forum, an oracle declared that the hole could be filled only by the thing that gave strength to the Roman people. Curtius was a very noble young man, both in spirit and by birth, and he understood that the oracle was referring to our city's supremacy in courage and warfare. So he put on his military uniform, mounted his horse, and, applying his spurs vigorously, rode headlong into that chasm.[165] All the citizens eagerly threw grain over Curtius to honor him, and at once the earth went back to its original condition.[166] In later times many glorious events have shone out in the Roman Forum, but no story is known today that is more famous than this one about the loyalty of Curtius toward his country. He holds first place in glory, but I shall place a similar deed next to his.

6. 3. When the praetor Genucius Cipus[167] was marching out of the city gate wearing his general's uniform, a strange type of prodigy occurred that had never been heard of before. Things like horns suddenly grew out of his head, and an oracle declared that he would become king if he went back to the city. To prevent this from happening, he imposed a voluntary and lifelong exile on himself. As far as real glory is concerned, his patriotism should rightly place him above the seven kings. To commemorate his patriotism, a bronze representation of his head was set into the gate where he went out, and it is called the Little Bronze Gate, because small coins were called "little bronzes" long ago.[168]

6. 4. It would be hard to imagine anyone winning greater glory in this matter than Genucius, but the praetor Aelius comes second to him.[169] While he was administering justice, a woodpecker sat on his head. The diviners declared that if he spared the woodpecker's life, the family of Aelius would be very fortunate but the Republic would be in a wretched condition, whereas if he killed it, the

[164]Lucius Junius Brutus (cos, 509 B.C.) died fighting against the Etruscans. Arruns Tarquinius was the son of Tarquin the Proud, the last king of Rome.

[165]Marcus Curtius sacrificed himself to the gods of the Underworld in 362 B.C.

[166]The Lacus Curtius ("pond of Curtius") marked the spot in the Forum.

[167]Nothing else is known about Genucius Cipus, but this must be an old legend.

[168]The Little Bronze Gate (porta rauduscula) was in the walls of Rome on the road to Ostia.

[169]Nothing else is known about the legendary Gaius Aelius Tubero, apart from the fact that he lived before 216 B.C., the year in which the battle of Cannae was fought.

opposite would happen in both cases. At once, in the presence of the Senate, Aelius killed the woodpecker with his own teeth. His family lost seventeen men of exceptional courage at the battle of Cannae; the Republic with the passage of time rose to the highest imperial glory. Of course, Sulla and Marius and Cinna laughed at such exemplary behavior and thought it foolish.[170]

6. 5. Publius Decius Mus was the first member of his family to reach the consulship.[171] During the Latin War,[172] he saw that the Roman line was giving way and was almost broken, so he offered his life as a sacrifice to the infernal gods in exchange for the survival of the Republic. At once he spurred his horse on and rushed into the middle of the enemy army, seeking deliverance for the Republic and death for himself. He caused great carnage and fell covered with enemy spears. From his wounds and blood, our unexpected victory emerged.

6. 6. He would be the only example of such a general if he had not produced a son who matched him in spirit.[173] While the son was holding his fourth consulship, he followed his father's example and offered himself as a sacrifice to the infernal gods in the same way. He fought with equal vigor, and by the same kind of death he restored the failing and ruined forces of our city.[174] So it is hard to decide whether the Roman state derived more benefit from these leaders of the Decius family while it still had them or when it lost them, since by living, they prevented it from being defeated, and by dying, they ensured that it would be victorious.

6. 7. Scipio Africanus did not die for the Republic, but his wonderful courage ensured that the Republic would not die. After our city was crushed by the defeat at Cannae, it seemed no more than an easy prey for the victorious Hannibal, and for this reason the remnants of our shattered army were discussing a plan for abandoning Italy, developed by Lucius Metellus.[175] Scipio was a very young military tribune, but he took out his sword, and, threatening to kill anyone who disobeyed, he forced all the men to swear that they would never leave their country. He not only displayed the greatest patriotism himself, but he also recalled that spirit back to the hearts of men who were beginning to lose it.

6. 8. Come on, let us turn from these individuals to the whole population— what great love for their country was shared by all and inflamed the entire state! When the treasury was exhausted by the Second Punic War and did not even have enough funds to cover the cult of the gods, the business community on its own initiative approached the censors and urged them to give them contracts as if the

---

[170]Marius and Lucius Cornelius Cinna (cos, 87 B.C.) attacked Rome and massacred their political opponents in 87 B.C. Sulla did the same in 82 B.C.

[171]Publius Decius Mus was consul in 340 B.C. when he sacrificed himself to the gods of the Underworld.

[172]The Romans fought against the rest of Latium from 340 to 338 B.C.

[173]Publius Decius Mus (cos, 312 B.C.) was consul for the fourth time in 295 B.C. when he sacrificed himself to the gods of the Underworld.

[174]Rome was fighting a war against the Samnites of central Italy in 295 B.C.

[175]Lucius Caecilius Metellus (quaestor, 214 B.C.) and Scipio Africanus were with the Roman survivors from Cannae in 216 B.C. Scipio Africanus was nineteen years old at the time.

Republic were rolling in money. The businessmen promised that they would pay for everything themselves and would not ask for an as back until the war was over.[176]

In addition, the masters of the slaves that Sempronius Gracchus had liberated for fighting so bravely at Beneventum did not bother to demand compensation from the general.[177]

In the army, furthermore, no horseman, no centurion asked to be paid his salary. Men and women contributed whatever gold or silver they possessed, and boys likewise contributed their symbols of free birth[178] to keep the treasury afloat during those difficult times. Nobody even wanted to take advantage of the Senate's offer that anyone who made such gifts would be freed from the burden of paying the property tax; on the contrary, they all paid that tax with great eagerness.[179]

They were aware that after the capture of Veii—when gold had to be sent to Apollo at Delphi to pay the tithe that Camillus had promised the god, and there was no way of buying it—the married ladies had contributed their jewelry to the treasury;[180] and they had also heard that the thousand pounds of gold, which was owed to the Gauls in exchange for their lifting the siege of the Capitol, had been paid for with the married ladies' jewelry.[181] Urged on by their own inclinations and by the examples set by these women long ago, they felt that they should leave nothing undone.

Foreign Stories

6. ext. 1. There are also foreign cases of the same conduct. When the region of Attica had been weakened by a huge enemy army and was being destroyed by fire and sword, the Athenian king, Codrus, despaired of human resources and turned to the oracle of Apollo at Delphi.[182] He sent envoys to find out how he could shake off that dreadful war. The god replied that it would come to an end if the king died at the hands of the enemy. Word of this spread not only through all of Athens but also in the camp of the enemy, and as a result the enemy commander ordered that nobody should do physical harm to Codrus. When Codrus discovered this, he took off his royal insignia, put on the clothes of a slave, went up to a

---

[176]The business community made this offer to the censors in 214 B.C. The as was a Roman coin (see money—Roman in the Glossary).

[177]Tiberius Sempronius Gracchus (cos, 215 B.C.) had created an army of slaves in 216 B.C. When the slaves defeated the Carthaginians in 214 B.C. at Beneventum (in Samnium, central Italy), Gracchus gave them their freedom.

[178]All freeborn boys wore a special locket (called a *bulla*).

[179]These generous offers were also made to the censors of 214 B.C.

[180]Marcus Furius Camillus (dictator, 396 B.C.) captured Veii. The promised offering of gold was sent to Apollo at Delphi in 394 B.C.

[181]The Gauls demanded one thousand pounds of gold before they would leave Rome in 390 B.C.

[182]Codrus was the last of the legendary kings of Athens. He sacrificed his life during an invasion by the Peloponnesians (southern Greeks).

group of enemy soldiers who were collecting fodder, attacked one of them with a sickle and forced the soldier to kill him. The king's death ensured that Athens would not die.

6. ext. 2. The spirit of Thrasybulus derived from the same fountain of patriotism.[183] He wanted to free the city of Athens from the horrible regime of the Thirty Tyrants[184] and was attempting this enormous task with a small group of men. When one of his associates asked him, "How much gratitude will Athens owe you for restoring her liberty?" he replied, "May the gods grant that I will seem to have paid Athens all the gratitude I owe her." The spirit in which he acted made his famous abolition of the tyranny even more glorious.

6. ext. 3. The courage of Themistocles made him the conqueror of the Persians, but the injustice of his country made him their commander.[185] Nevertheless, to avoid attacking his own country, he started a sacrifice, drew the bull's blood into a dish, and drank it down; then he fell dead before the very altar as a glorious sacrifice to patriotism.[186] His famous death ensured that Greece would not need another Themistocles.

6. ext. 4. The following is a story of the same type. There was a long-standing dispute between Carthage and Cyrene about the extent of their territories.[187] In the end, they decided to send a group of young men out from each city at the same time, and the place where they met would be considered the boundary between the two peoples. But two Carthaginian brothers from the Philaenus family treacherously got around this arrangement, and by starting before the appointed time and walking quickly, they advanced the Carthaginian border by quite a distance. When the young men of Cyrene discovered this treachery, they complained about it for a long time, but finally they tried to counteract the injustice by imposing a harsh condition: they declared that the boundary would be legally valid only if the Philaenus brothers agreed to be buried alive there. But what happened did not match their expectations: without delay the brothers gave themselves up to be buried in the ground by the people of Cyrene.[188] The brothers wanted the extent of their country rather than the extent of their own lives to be increased, and they now rest in peace having expanded the Punic empire with their efforts and their corpses.

Where are the high walls of proud Carthage? Where is the glory of its harbor, famous on every sea? Where is its fleet, feared on every shore? Where are all its armies? Where is its mighty cavalry? Where is that pride, which was not content with the vast region of Africa? Fortune handed all those things over to the two

---

[183]Thrasybulus led the democrats who liberated Athens in 403 B.C.

[184]The regime of the Thirty Tyrants lasted from 404 to 403 B.C.

[185]Themistocles defeated the Persians at Salamis in 480 B.C. but was exiled from Athens in 472 B.C. (see 5:3,ext.3). He settled down in the Persian empire in 464 B.C.

[186]Themistocles died in Persia in 459 B.C.

[187]Cyrene (modern Libya) was the next state east of Carthage (modern Tunisia).

[188]The altars of the Philaenus brothers (*arae Philaenorum*) marked the border between Carthage and Cyrene. These altars were actually grave mounds.

Scipios:[189] but even the destruction of their country has not extinguished the memory of the extraordinary deed of the Philaenus brothers. So except for virtue, there
is no other form of immortality that can be won by the heart and hand of a mortal.

6. ext. 5. Their patriotism was full of youthful spirit. Aristotle, on the other hand,
was at the end of a life and although he lived in complete academic ease, he was barely
keeping his wrinkled old body alive, but he watched over his country's well-being
with great vigor.[190] His country had been flattened to the ground by the enemy
army, but while he was lying in bed in Athens, he had his city rebuilt by the very
Macedonian hands that had demolished it. The defeat and destruction of the city by
Alexander is not as famous an achievement as its restoration by Aristotle.[191]

It is therefore clear that men of generous and unstinting patriotism have arisen in
every social class and in every age group. The convergence of these amazing stories,
which are renowned throughout the world, testifies to this sacred law of nature.

Chapter 7. The Love and Indulgence of Parents toward Their Children

Preface

Let the indulgence of parents toward their children now spread its sails of devotion and gentleness: and sailing on with a healthy wind, may it carry along a
pleasant cargo of sweetness with it.

Roman Stories

7. 1. Fabius Rullianus had completed five terms as consul with the greatest of
glory, and he had done all that life and virtue could demand.[192] In spite of this, he
did not object to serving as a legate under his son, Fabius Gurges, and to going out
and finishing off a war that was difficult and dangerous.[193] It was almost as if he was
going to fight without his body and rely on his mind alone: on account of his extreme old age, he was more suited to resting in bed than struggling on the battlefield. But he took the greatest pleasure in riding on horseback behind the
triumphal chariot of his son, whom he himself had once carried as a little boy in

---

[189]Scipio Africanus defeated Carthage in 202 B.C., and Scipio Aemilianus obliterated the
city in 146 B.C.

[190]Aristotle lived in Athens from 335 B.C. until his death in 322 B.C., but his hometown was
Stagira (in northern Greece).

[191]Stagira had been destroyed by Philip II of Macedonia in 349 B.C., but it was rebuilt by
Alexander the Great.

[192]Quintus Fabius Maximus Rullianus had been consul five times between 322 and 295 B.C.

[193]Quintus Fabius Maximus Gurges was consul in 292 B.C., and Rullianus served under him
as a legate in a war against the Samnites of central Italy (see 2:2,4).

his own triumphs. And he was regarded not as someone who had joined that glorious procession, but rather as the man who had brought it about.[194]

7. 2. The family rank of Caesetius, a Roman equestrian, was not so spectacular, but his kindness was as great.[195] After Caesar had defeated all foreign and domestic enemies,[196] he ordered Caesetius to disown his son, because this son, while serving as tribune of the plebs, and aided by his fellow tribune Marullus,[197] had stirred up hatred against Caesar by suggesting that Caesar had been trying to make himself king.[198] But Caesetius dared to make the following reply: "You will tear all my sons away from me, Caesar, before I would denounce or reject a single one of them." He had, however, two other sons of the highest character, and Caesar promised that he would gladly grant them advancement in their status. Even though the extraordinary compassion of a godlike prince kept this father safe, who would not think that Caesetius had taken a superhuman risk by refusing to yield to a man to whom the entire world had submitted?

7. 3. But I suspect that Octavius Balbus had a more impetuous and passionate love for his son.[199] The father was put on the death list of the triumvirs but had sneaked out of his house by the back door.[200] He was well on the way to escaping when he heard his neighbors shouting, incorrectly, that his son was being brutally murdered inside. So he threw himself toward the death he had just escaped and handed himself over to be killed by the soldiers. Of course, he valued that moment, in which he happened beyond all hope to see his son safe, more than his own safety. How miserable were the eyes of that young man, which had to see the father who loved him so much dying in this way because of him!

Foreign Stories

7. ext. 1. But to turn to things that are more pleasant to hear: Antiochus, the son of King Seleucus, fell madly in love with his stepmother, Stratonice.[201] Realizing that he was burning with a wicked passion, he tried to hide this unnatural and traumatic love with a natural discretion. These conflicting feelings contained within the

---

[194]Rullianus took part in his son's triumph over the Samnites in 291 B.C.

[195]As an equestrian, the father would not have held political office.

[196]Caesar defeated the last of the Republicans in Spain in 45 B.C.

[197]The son, Lucius Caesetius Flavus, was a tribune of the plebs with Gaius Epidius Marullus in 44 B.C.

[198]These two tribunes removed a crown from a statue of Caesar and prosecuted Romans who had saluted Caesar as king.

[199]The father, Gaius Octavius Balbus, had celebrated the death of Caesar in 44 B.C., but he was not one of the tyrannicides.

[200]Balbus was one of the victims when the triumvirs Antony and Augustus massacred their political opponents in 43 B.C.

[201]Seleucus I Nicator was king of Syria from 323 to 281 B.C. His son, Antiochus I Soter, was king from 281 to 261 B.C.

same flesh and bones, and the struggle between his extraordinary desire and his exceptional modesty, reduced his body to a skeleton. He himself was lying in bed, looking like a corpse; his friends were crying; his father was devastated with grief at the approaching death of his only son and was contemplating his future childlessness. The entire dwelling looked more like a funeral home than a palace.

But Leptines the mathematician (or, as some people say, Erasistratus the doctor) banished this cloud of sorrow by his foresight. He was sitting beside Antiochus, and he noticed that whenever Stratonice entered, the young man would go red all over and his breathing would become quicker, but when she left, he would grow pale and the rapid breathing would slow down again. So he observed the young man more closely and discovered the truth: when Stratonice was entering the room, and again when she was leaving, he surreptitiously held the young man's arm, and from his pulse rate, which was quicker in the first case and slower in the second, he discovered what illness the young man was suffering from. He revealed this to Seleucus at once. The king did not hesitate to hand over this wife, whom he loved very much, to his son. He wrote off the fact that the young man had fallen in love as a blow from fortune; but he attributed the fact that he had been prepared to repress this love, even to the point of death, to the young man's modesty. Let us put before our minds this old king who loved his wife: it will soon become clear how many things and what difficult things the kindness of fatherly affection has overcome.

7. *ext. 2.* Whereas Seleucus surrendered his wife to his son, Ariobarzanes handed over the kingdom of Cappadocia to his son, in the presence of Pompey.[202] When Ariobarzanes mounted Pompey's tribunal, and at his invitation sat on the state chair, he saw that his son was placed in the clerks' section, a position beneath his dignity. Ariobarzanes could not bear to look at his son placed so far beneath him, so he left his seat immediately, took off his crown, placed it on his son's head, and started urging him to move to the place that he had just left. The young man burst into tears and started shaking all over, the crown slipped off, and he could not go where he was ordered. And though it almost goes beyond what people believe to be true, the man who surrendered his kingdom was quite happy, whereas the one receiving it was grief-stricken. Their extraordinary argument would never have ended if Pompey had not added his personal command to the wishes of the father. He proclaimed the son king, commanded him to take the crown, and forced him to sit on the state chair.

---

[202]Ariobarzanes I Philoromaios was king of Cappadocia (on the south coast of Asia Minor) from 92 to 62 B.C. Pompey reorganized the entire region of western Asia in 62 B.C. The son, Ariobarzanes II Philopator, became king that year.

Chapter 8. Fathers Who Were Severe with Their Children

Preface

The previous fathers were as gentle as fathers in a comedy; the following fathers were harsh, like fathers in a tragedy.

Roman Stories

8. 1. Lucius Brutus was as glorious as Romulus, because Romulus founded our city, whereas Brutus founded Roman liberty.[203] His sons tried to reestablish the tyranny of Tarquin, which he himself had abolished.[204] Brutus was the head of state and ordered that his sons be captured, flogged in front of his platform, tied to a stake, and beheaded with an axe. He left the role of a father so that he could play the part of a consul; and he preferred to live without children, than fail to avenge the Republic.

8. 2. Cassius followed his example. His son, Spurius Cassius, was tribune of the plebs and had been the first to introduce a land law.[205] By many other populist actions, he had won over the affections of the people, who were greatly attached to him. After he laid down that office, his father held a family meeting of friends and relatives at his house, accused his son of aiming at royal power, and found him guilty. He ordered that his son be flogged and put to death; then he consecrated his son's personal property to Ceres.[206]

8. 3. Titus Manlius Torquatus had won exceptional esteem because of his many outstanding achievements, and he was also very learned in civil law and in pontifical rites.[207] He felt, however, that he did not even require a family council in a similar affair. Through its envoys, Macedonia had sent complaints to the Senate about his son Decimus Silanus, who had governed that province.[208] Torquatus asked the Conscript Fathers not to reach any decision in this matter until he himself had investigated the case of the Macedonians and his son. He received the complete approval not only of that distinguished body but also of the Macedonians who had come to make the complaints. He held an investigation and tried the case in his own house by himself. For the space of two full days he paid attention to each side, and on the third day, after he had carefully listened to all the witnesses, he pronounced the following judgment: "Since it has been proved to me

---

[203]Romulus was the founder and first king of Rome; Lucius Junius Brutus was its first consul in 509 B.C.

[204]Tarquin the Proud was the last king of Rome. The sons of Brutus were part of a plot to restore the king.

[205]The son, Spurius Cassius Vecellinus (cos, 502 B.C.), was consul for the third time in 486 B.C. when he introduced a law giving land to the poor.

[206]Vecellinus was put to death in 485 B.C. Ceres was the goddess of grain.

[207]The father, Titus Manlius Torquatus (cos, 165 B.C.), was also one of the pontiffs.

[208]The son, Decimus Junius Silanus Manlianus, was governor of Macedonia in 141 B.C.

that my son Silanus accepted bribes from our allies, I declare him to be unworthy of the Republic and my house, and I order him to depart from my sight at once." Stricken by this severe sentence of his father, Silanus could no longer bear to look upon the light of day and hanged himself that night.[209]

Torquatus had played the part of a stern and scrupulous judge, the Republic had received its due, and Macedonia had received its revenge. Even a strict father might have been affected by the suicide of his mortified son, but Torquatus did not attend his son's funeral, and at the very time that the funeral procession was taking place, he made himself available to those clients who wished to consult him. For he realized that he was sitting in that very living room where the death mask of the great Torquatus Imperiosus was placed, a man renowned for his severity.[210] And one thought kept recurring to this very practical man: that the death masks of one's ancestors, with a list of their achievements, were deliberately placed in the most conspicuous part of the house to ensure that their descendants would not just read about their merits but would go on to imitate them.

8. 4. Marcus Scaurus was the leading light and glory of our country.[211] When the Roman cavalry were defeated by a Cimbrian attack at the river Athesis, they abandoned the consul, Catulus, and fled to Rome in terror.[212] Scaurus sent a messenger to his son, who had taken part in this disorderly flight, and the messenger told him that Scaurus would have been much happier to find the body of his son dead on a battlefield than to have seen him guilty of such a disgraceful desertion. So, if there was any self-respect whatsoever left in his heart, he should avoid the sight of the father he had disgraced. The son remembered the days of his youth, and how Scaurus had often made it clear to him what kind of son he deserved to have and what kind of son he would be compelled to disown. So when the young man received his father's message, he was forced to use his sword more bravely against himself than he had ever used it against the enemy.[213]

8. 5. Aulus Fulvius, a man of senatorial rank, stopped his son, who was going off to battle, just as forcefully as Scaurus had insulted his son, who was running away from it. The young man shone out among his contemporaries because of his character, his literary gifts, and his good looks. For some perverse reason, he became friends with Catiline and was impetuously rushing off to join his camp.[214] He was halfway there when his father intercepted him and put him to death. His last words to his son were that he had begotten him not to fight for Catiline against his country, but rather for his country against Catiline. He could have kept him

---

[209]Silanus committed suicide when he returned from his province in 140 B.C.

[210]Titus Manlius Imperiosus Torquatus (cos, 347 B.C.) had put his son to death for disobeying orders on the battlefield in 340 B.C. (see 2:7,6).

[211]Marcus Aemilius Scaurus (cos, 115 B.C.) was leader of the Senate from 115 B.C. until his death in 88 B.C.

[212]Quintus Lutatius Catulus was badly defeated by the Cimbrians (from Denmark) in 102 B.C. The river Athesis (modern Adige) was in Venetia (northern Italy).

[213]The son, Aemilius Scaurus, was a legate in 102 B.C.

[214]Lucius Sergius Catilina (praetor, 68 B.C.) started a rebellion in 63 B.C.

locked up inside the house until the madness of the civil war was over: but that would have been spoken of as the action of a concerned father, whereas what he actually did is renowned as the deed of a severe one.

Chapter 9. The Lenience of Parents toward Children Who Were under Suspicion

Preface

But I want to tell of fathers with gentler natures, and to blend their clemency into my work to counterbalance the impetuous and harsh severity of the ones I have mentioned. So I shall put stories of fathers who showed forgiveness beside those stories of fathers who exacted punishment.

Roman Stories

9. 1. Lucius Gellius had held every high public office including the censorship when he discovered very serious and substantiated allegations against his son, that he had slept with his stepmother and planned to kill his father.[215] He did not, however, rush off suddenly to avenge himself; instead, he invited almost the entire Senate to take part in his family council, where he revealed his suspicions and gave the young man the opportunity of defending himself.[216] After examining the case closely, he acquitted his son, and this was both the family council's verdict and his own. If he had been carried away in a fit of anger and had rushed off to vent his rage on his son, he would have committed a great crime rather than punishing one.

9. 2. Quintus Hortensius was the glory of Roman oratory in his day, and he showed remarkable tolerance in dealing with his son.[217] Hortensius had such deep misgivings about his son's disrespectful behavior, and he hated his degenerate lifestyle so much, that he was going to make his sister's son, Messalla, his heir.[218] When he was defending Messalla on a charge of electoral bribery, he told the jurymen that if they condemned Messalla, he would have nothing left apart from the kisses of his grandsons to console him.[219] This statement, which he even included in the published version of the speech, showed that he considered his son to be a mental torment rather than a joy to him. But he did not want to undermine the natural order of things, so he left his son as his heir, not his grandsons,

---

[215]The father was Lucius Gellius Publicola (cos, 72 B.C.).

[216]The son, who had the same name, was Lucius Gellius Publicola (cos, 36 B.C.).

[217]The father, Quintus Hortensius Hortalus (cos, 69 B.C.), was Cicero's great rival in oratory. His son was Quintus Hortensius (praetor, 45 B.C.).

[218]The nephew of Hortensius Hortalus was Marcus Valerius Messalla Rufus (cos, 53 B.C.).

[219]Messalla was prosecuted for bribery in 51 B.C.

and restrained his wounded feelings. While living, he testified to the young man's real character, but in death he gave due honor to his flesh and blood.[220]

9. 3. Quintus Fulvius, a man of noble birth and great prestige, did the same, but his son was considerably more vile. Fulvius asked the Senate for help, begging them to send a prison manager to search out his son, who was suspected of trying to kill his father and was in hiding. When his son was arrested by order of the Conscript Fathers, Fulvius did not censure him; he actually wanted him to inherit everything on his death. Fulvius made the son he had begotten his heir, not the son he had learned about from experience.[221]

9. 4. Next to the compassionate actions of these great men I shall place the decision of an obscure father who thought about things in a strange and unusual manner. When he discovered that his son was plotting against his life, he could not get it into his head that his own flesh and blood would go so far as to commit such a crime. So he took his wife aside and pleaded with her not to keep him in the dark any longer but to reveal whether the young man had been another woman's baby or one that she herself had conceived with another man. By her emphatic assertions under oath, she convinced him not to have any suspicions of that kind.

The father took his son to a remote place, gave him a sword that he had hidden on his person, and offered him his throat to cut, assuring him that there was no need of any poison or hired assassin to carry out the death of his father. This action had no gradual effect; it gave the young man a sudden shock and filled his heart with honest intentions. At once he threw the sword away and said, "I want you to live now, Father, and if you are kind enough to allow me to make this prayer, I even want you to live on after me. The only thing I ask is that my love for you should not seem less valuable because it arises from repentance."

O wilderness, stronger than the ties of blood; o forests, more peaceful than the home; o sword, more convincing than parenthood; o gift of freely offered death, more effective than the gift of life![222]

Chapter 10. Parents Who Bravely Endured the Deaths of Their Children

Preface

We have written of those fathers who patiently put up with the injustices of their children; let us now record those who bravely endured the deaths of their children.

---

[220]Hortensius Hortalus died in 50 B.C.

[221]Fulvius and his son have never been identified.

[222]This "obscure father" and his son have never been identified.

Roman Stories

10. 1. While he was a pontiff, Horatius Pulvillus was dedicating a temple to Jupiter Best and Greatest on the Capitol.[223] He was holding the temple's doorpost and was in the middle of pronouncing the ritual words when he heard that his son had died. But he did not remove his hand from the doorpost, because he did not want to interrupt the dedication of such an important temple. He refused to turn his attention from the state religion to his private sorrow, because he did not want people to think that the role of a father was more important for him than that of a pontiff. He set a glorious example, but the one that follows is no less splendid.

10. 2. Aemilius Paullus was the embodiment of a most fortunate father and later of a most wretched one. He had four sons of remarkable beauty and exceptional character. He deprived himself of two by having them adopted into the Cornelius and Fabius families;[224] Fortune took the two remaining sons away from him. One of them died four days before his father's triumph; the other was seen by all in the triumphal chariot but died three days later.[225] Paullus had once had so many children that he could give them away; now he was suddenly left alone without any children. In the speech he made before the people about his actions, he left no one in any doubt about the mental courage with which he had borne his misfortunes, especially in this final statement that he added to the speech:

"We were in a period of great prosperity, my fellow citizens, and I was afraid that Fortune might have some harm in store for us, so I prayed to Jupiter Best and Greatest and Queen Juno and Minerva that if any harm was threatening the Roman people, they should direct it entirely against my family instead.[226] So all is well: by answering my prayers, they saw to it that you should pity my misfortunes instead of my lamenting yours."

10. 3. I shall add one more national story, and then I shall allow my narrative to wander off into stories of foreign sorrows. When Quintus Marcius Rex was sharing the consulship with Cato,[227] he lost a boy who was very respectful, had great prospects, and—what magnified the misfortune in no small way—was his only son. He felt that his life was ruined and destroyed by the death of his son, but he controlled his sorrow by his deep wisdom. So he was able to leave the young man's funeral pyre and go at once to the Senate house and, since it was his legal duty to preside over its meeting on that day, he convened the Senate. If he had not known how to endure his sorrows bravely, he could not have divided this single

[223]Marcus Horatius Pulvillus was a consul and a pontiff in 509 B.C. The temple he dedicated was the most important temple to Jupiter in the Roman world.

[224]Lucius Aemilius Paullus (cos, 182 B.C.) was the biological father of Quintus Fabius Maximus Aemilianus (cos, 145 B.C.) and Scipio Aemilianus.

[225]The two other sons of Aemilius Paullus were still boys when they died in 167 B.C. This was the year of his triumph over King Perseus of Macedonia.

[226]These three gods shared the temple of Jupiter that was dedicated in 509 B.C. (see 5:10,1).

[227]Quintus Marcius Rex was consul in 118 B.C. with Marcus Porcius Cato (Cato the Censor's grandson).

day between his duties as an ill-starred father and a diligent consul, failing in neither of them.

Foreign Stories

10. ext. 1. The Athenian leader, Pericles, was deprived of two remarkable adolescent sons within four days.[228] On the very days of their deaths, he addressed public meetings, he had the same expression as always on his face, and his speech was in no way subdued. He even managed to wear a garland on his head, as usual, not wanting his private grief to interfere with ancient customs in any way. So it is not without reason that his great moral courage won him the nickname of Olympian Jupiter.

10. ext. 2. As far as the Socratic school of philosophy is concerned, Xenophon was second only to Plato in his rich and fertile style.[229] When he was performing a traditional sacrifice, he learned that the elder of his two sons, who was called Gryllus, had died at the battle of Mantinea.[230] But he did not think this was any reason to interrupt the divine ritual he had started, and he thought it would be enough simply to take his garland off. He asked how his son had died, and when he heard that he had died fighting with great courage, he put the garland back on his head and declared before the gods to whom he was sacrificing that he derived more joy from the courage of his son than bitter sorrow from his death. Another man would have removed the sacrificial victim, knocked down the altar, drenched the incense with his tears, and thrown it away. But the body of Xenophon was unmoved in its piety; his mind stayed firm in its wise determination; and he felt that giving way to his sorrow would be sadder than the actual disaster he was told about.

10. ext. 3. Anaxagoras must not be forgotten, either.[231] When he heard about the death of his son, he said, "What you have told me is nothing unexpected or unusual: I always knew that someone born from me would be mortal." His courage spoke these words that were inspired by the most useful principles. If someone listens to them attentively, he will be aware that if we have children, we should remember that nature determines at the very same moment both when they should receive life and when they should give it up. And that since nobody dies, unless they have lived, it follows that nobody can live, unless they will die.

---

[228]The two sons of Pericles died in the Athenian plague of 430 B.C.

[229]Xenophon was an Athenian writer and a follower of Socrates.

[230]Xenophon was unhappy with Athenian democracy and moved to Sparta in 396 B.C. His son died fighting for Sparta at Mantinea (in Arcadia, southern Greece) in 362 B.C.

[231]Anaxagoras was a philosopher from Clazomenae (on the west coast of Asia Minor). He moved to Athens around 460 B.C. and spent most of his life there.

BOOK SIX

Chapter 1. Chastity

Preface

From what place should I summon you, Chastity, the chief support of men and women? You live in the fires of Vesta, which have been consecrated by ancient religious custom;[1] you keep watch over the couch of Juno on the Capitol;[2] you are constantly on guard at that pillar of the Palatine, the august household and sacred marriage bed of Julia;[3] the lockets of boyhood are under your protection;[4] the beauty of youth is kept pure by its respect for your divinity; the dress of a lady is respected because it is under your guardianship; so come and acknowledge these actions that you yourself have brought about.

Roman Stories

1. 1. Lucretia is the champion of Roman chastity, but by a nasty mistake of Fortune her manly spirit was allotted the body of a woman. She was violently forced to have sex with Sextus Tarquinius, the son of King Tarquin the Proud.[5] In the most earnest language she complained about her ill-treatment before a council of her family, and then she killed herself with a sword that she had brought there hidden in her clothes. Her brave suicide led the Roman people to replace the monarchy with government by consuls.[6]

1. 2. Lucretia could not bear the disgrace after she had been abused. But Verginius, a man from a plebeian family but with the spirit of a patrician,[7] did not even spare his own flesh and blood in order to make sure that his household would not be afflicted with such a disgrace. Appius Claudius, the decemvir,[8] relying on the power of his office, kept demanding to have sex with Verginius' unmarried

---

[1]Vesta, the goddess of the fireplace, was a virgin goddess.

[2]Juno was the goddess of marriage and was worshiped with Jupiter in his temple on the Capitol.

[3]Livia Drusilla, the wife of Augustus, was renamed Julia Augusta when Augustus died in A.D. 14.

[4]All freeborn boys wore a special locket (*bulla*).

[5]The rape and suicide of Lucretia took place in 510 B.C.

[6]The first year of the Republic was 509 B.C.

[7]Lucius Verginius was a tribune of the plebs in 449 B.C.

[8]The decemvirs were appointed to codify the laws of Rome. Appius Claudius Crassus Inregillensis Sabinus (cos, 471 B.C.) was the leader of the decemvirs.

daughter, so Verginius led his daughter into the Forum and killed her, preferring to be the murderer of a chaste girl, rather than the father of an abused one.

1. 3. Pontius Aufidianus, a Roman equestrian, was endowed with an equally strong spirit. When he discovered that his daughter's tutor allowed Fannius Saturninus to enjoy her virginity, Aufidianus was not content with putting the wicked slave to death; he also killed his daughter. Rather than celebrate a disgraceful wedding for her, he held a tragic funeral.[9]

1. 4. What about Publius Maenius? How strictly he behaved as a guardian of chastity! Maenius put to death a freedman of whom he was very fond, because he discovered that the freedman had given a kiss to his daughter, who was already of marriageable age. It would certainly have been possible to view this misconduct as a minor lapse rather than sexual abuse. But Maenius considered it important to instill the discipline of chastity in the as yet malleable sensibility of his daughter, by this cruel punishment. By this harsh example he taught her that she should bring to her future husband not only a virginity that was intact but even lips that were untouched.[10]

1. 5. Quintus Fabius Maximus Eburnus had carried out the highest public offices with great splendor, and he finished off his career with a dignified censorship.[11] Fabius made his son pay the penalty for a chastity that was dubious, and Fabius himself paid the penalty for punishing his son by voluntarily going into exile and avoiding the sight of his country.[12]

1. 6. I would have said that this former censor was too fierce, if I did not see that Publius Atilius Philiscus, who had been forced by his master to sell his body when he was a boy, was later so strict a father.[13] He killed his own daughter because she had disgraced herself by having premarital sex. How sacred should we consider chastity was in our state, where we observe that even the peddlers of lust turned out to be such severe punishers of it?

1. 7. The following is the story of an outstanding man and a memorable deed. When Marcus Claudius Marcellus was a curule aedile, he summoned Gaius Scantinius Capitolinus, a plebeian aedile, to appear before the people, because Scantinius had approached the son of Marcellus for sexual favors.[14] Scantinius claimed that he could not be forced to appear because he held an office that was sacrosanct.[15] He begged the tribunes for protection, but the entire body of tribunes said they would not intervene to prevent this trial about chastity from taking place. So Scantinius

---

[9] The people in this story have not been identified.

[10] The people in this story have not been identified.

[11] Quintus Fabius Maximus Eburnus (cos, 116 B.C.) was censor in 108 B.C. when he put his son to death for sexual misbehavior.

[12] Eburnus was, in fact, prosecuted and banished in 104 B.C. for murdering his son.

[13] Slaves were expected to render sexual services and could be forced to work as prostitutes.

[14] Marcus Claudius Marcellus (cos, 222 B.C.) was a curule aedile and Gaius Scantinius Capitolinus was a plebeian aedile in 226 B.C. (see aedile in the Glossary).

[15] A plebeian aedile was under the protection of the tribunes of the plebs.

was brought to trial, and he was found guilty on the sole testimony of the man he had solicited. It is well established that the young man refused to speak and kept his head bent to the ground after he had been brought onto the stand, and that his embarrassed silence was very effective in assuring his vengeance.[16]

1. 8. Metellus Celer was also harsh in punishing lecherous inclinations. He prosecuted Gnaeus Sergius Silus before the people for promising money to a married woman, and he had him convicted on this basis alone.[17] Silus was brought before the court not for his deeds but for his intentions, and his desire to do wrong did him more harm than his not having carried it out did him good.

1. 9. The assembly of the people was harsh in that case; the Senate house, in the following one. Titus Veturius was the son of that Veturius who had made a disgraceful treaty during his consulship and was therefore handed over to the Samnites.[18] When Titus Veturius was still a very young man, he was forced by the ruin of his family and his serious debts to sell himself to Publius Plotius as a slave.[19] He was flogged by Plotius, because he refused to have sex with him, and he brought a complaint before the consuls. When the consuls informed the Senate about the matter, it ordered Plotius to be sent to prison: it wanted the chastity of any member of the Roman race to be protected, no matter what his status happened to be.

1. 10. What wonder is it that all the Conscript Fathers unanimously voted this way? Gaius Cornelius had finished up a military career of great bravery, and because of his courage his generals had rewarded him four times with the honor of being the senior centurion of his legion. But Gaius Pescennius, a prison manager, had Cornelius clapped in irons for having sexual relations with a young man of free birth.[20] Cornelius appealed to the tribunes, and though he did not deny the sexual relationship, he said he was prepared to make a legal guarantee[21] that the young man had openly and unreservedly sold his body for cash, but the tribunes refused to intervene. So Cornelius was forced to die in prison: the tribunes of the plebs did not think that our Republic should make deals with brave men so that they could pay for pleasures at home by facing danger overseas.

1. 11. The story of this lecherous centurion's punishment is followed by the story of the equally disgraceful end of a military tribune, Marcus Laetorius Mergus. Cominius, a tribune of the plebs, summoned him before the people because

---

[16]The Scantinian law, forbidding homosexual relations with a freeborn male, was supposedly passed as a result of this case.

[17]Gnaeus Sergius Silus was prosecuted in 88 B.C. by the aedile Quintus Caecilius Metellus Celer (cos, 60 B.C.). Serious cases were judged by an assembly of the people.

[18]The father, Titus Veturius Calvinus (cos, 334 B.C.), was defeated by the Samnites at the Caudine Forks in 321 B.C.

[19]A man could be enslaved if he failed to pay off his debts. This practice of debt slavery was abolished at the end of the fourth century B.C.

[20]Gaius Pescennius was a prison manager (*triumvir capitalis*) in 149 B.C.

[21]In making a legal guarantee (*sponsio*), a person made a statement, put down a sum of money, and had to pay it to the legal opponent if the guaranteed statement was false.

he had approached his adjutant for sexual favors.[22] Laetorius could not bear his guilty feelings, and before the date of the trial he punished himself by exile and then death. He had paid the penalty that nature required, but even though he was dead, he was found guilty on that charge of sexual immorality by the verdict of the entire plebs. The army standards, the consecrated eagles, and that most reliable guardian of the Roman Empire, our strict military discipline, followed him all the way into the Underworld, because although he should have been his adjutant's role model in virtue, he had tried to become the corrupter of his integrity.

1. 12. This army spirit led the general, Marius, to declare that Gaius Lusius had been justifiably killed by Gaius Plotius, even though Lusius was the son of Marius' own sister and a military tribune, whereas Plotius was just a common soldier. The reason was that Lusius had dared to approach Plotius for sexual favors.[23]

1. 13. But I want to run briefly through those who followed their own anger rather than the laws of the state in upholding sexual morality. Sempronius Musca caught Gaius Gellius in adultery and flogged him with a lash; Gaius Memmius caught Lucius Octavius in the same way and gave him a beating; Carbo Attienus was caught by Vibienus and castrated, as was Pontius by Publius Cerennius. The man who caught Gnaeus Furius Brocchus handed him over for his slaves to rape. These men incurred no punishment for giving way to their anger.[24]

Foreign Stories

1. ext. 1. I shall add some foreign stories to these national ones. There was a Greek woman called Hippo, who was captured by an enemy fleet, and threw herself into the sea to preserve her chastity by dying. Her body was washed ashore at Erythrae; it was buried where the land touches the waves and is covered by a mound to this day.[25] But the glory of her moral integrity has been handed down for all time, and Greece makes it more vivid every day by celebrating it with the highest praise.

1. ext. 2. That was a story of an impetuous reaction, but the following is a story about chastity where the reaction was premeditated. The consul Gnaeus Manlius had destroyed part of the military forces of the Galatians on Mount Olympus, and he had captured the rest.[26] The wife of the chieftain Orgiago was a woman of extraordinary beauty, and she was forced to have sex with the centurion who had been ordered to guard her. When they came to the place where the centurion,

---

[22]Marcus Laetorius Mergus was prosecuted by Lucius Cominius some time between 312 and 290 B.C.

[23]Gaius Lusius served as military tribune in Gaul under his uncle, Marius, in 104 B.C.

[24]The men in this story have not been identified, but the punishments were not unusual.

[25]Erythrae was on the west coast of Asia Minor.

[26]Gnaeus Manlius Vulso attacked the Galatians (who lived in central Asia Minor) when he was consul in 189 B.C. The Mount Olympus mentioned here was in Galatia; it is not the famous Mount Olympus in Thessaly.

through a messenger, had told her relatives to bring the money for her ransom, the centurion started weighing the gold, and while his mind and eyes were occupied with this task, she spoke out in her native language and ordered the Galatians to kill him. When they had killed the centurion and cut off his head, she took the head in her hands, went to her husband, threw the head at his feet, and told him all about her ill-treatment and her revenge. Could anybody say that anything apart from the body of this woman had fallen into the power of the enemy? Her spirit could not be defeated nor her chastity overcome.

1. ext. 3. The wives of the Teutons begged the victorious Marius to send them as a gift to the vestal virgins, and they declared that they intended to avoid sleeping with men just like those virgins.[27] When Marius did not grant this request, they took their own lives the following night by hanging themselves. The gods were good to us in not giving this spirit to their husbands on the battlefield, because if those men had wished to imitate the courage of their wives, they would have made the trophies of our Teutonic victory unlikely.

Chapter 2. Frank Statements and Actions

Preface

The frankness of a strong will can be witnessed from its statements and its actions alike, but although I would not provoke such frankness, I would not try to stop it if it came along of its own accord. It is halfway between a virtue and a vice; it deserves praise if it restrains itself in a beneficial way, but it deserves reproach if it goes further than it should. It is more pleasing to the ears of the mob than acceptable to the mind of any wise person, since it is protected more often by the tolerance of others than by its own foresight. But since it is my intention to deal with every aspect of human life, I shall record it with my usual honesty and judge it fairly.

Roman Stories

2. 1. After Privernum had been captured and the men who had incited it to rebel had been killed, the Senate was still burning with indignation as it discussed what course it should take concerning the rest of the town's inhabitants.[28] Their survival depended on luck, which could have gone either way, since they were at the mercy of conquerors who were also angry men. But although they realized that their only hope rested in entreaty, they could not forget that they were freeborn and Italian by birth. So, when their leader was asked in the Senate house

---

[27]The Teutons were from northern Germany. Marius defeated them in 102 B.C. The vestal virgins looked after the eternal fire of Rome in the temple of Vesta.

[28]Privernum was a city in Latium that rebelled against Rome in 330 B.C.

what punishment they deserved, he replied, "Whatever men deserve who think themselves worthy of freedom."

By these words he had practically taken up arms again and inflamed the minds of the Conscript Fathers, who were already quite exasperated. But the consul Plautius,[29] who sympathized with the people of Privernum, offered him a way of withdrawing his proud remark and asked him what sort of peace they would maintain with the Romans if they were released without punishment. But he said, with the most unwavering aspect, "If you offer us a good one, it will last forever; if you offer us a bad one, it will not last long." These words ensured that the conquered people were not just forgiven but were granted the rights and privileges of Roman citizenship.

2. 2. That is how a man from Privernum dared to speak up in the Senate. Even a consul, Lucius Philippus, did not hesitate to exercise the same freedom of speech against the same body.[30] Standing at the rostra, he criticized the Senate's laziness and said that he needed another Senate. He expressed no regret whatsoever for this remark. On the contrary, when Lucius Crassus, a man of the highest rank and greatest eloquence, complained about this remark in the Senate house, Philippus ordered his arrest.[31] But Crassus pushed the lictor away and said, "You are no consul in my eyes, since I am no senator in yours."

2. 3. Well, has free speech left the people alone and refused to attack them? No, it has attacked the people in the same way but found them equally tolerant. Gaius Carbo, a tribune of the plebs, was an extremist defender of the protest movement of Gracchus, which had recently been crushed; and he had also been the most violent agitator in these civil disturbances from the very beginning.[32] When Scipio Aemilianus was returning from the ruins of Numantia in a brilliant aura of glory, Carbo caught him almost at the city gates and brought him to the rostra.[33]

Carbo asked Scipio Aemilianus what he thought about the death of Tiberius Gracchus, since Scipio was married to Gracchus' sister.[34] Carbo hoped to add strength to the fire he had started by using the influence of this renowned man, and he had no doubt that Scipio would speak tenderly in memory of his murdered relative. But Scipio replied that Gracchus had been justifiably killed. When the assembly, urged on by the wild tribune, shouted violently against these words,

---

[29]Privernum was captured by the consul Gaius Plautius Decianus and his colleague in 329 B.C.

[30]Lucius Marcius Philippus (cos, 91 B.C.) wanted the reluctant Senate to crush the Italian movement that was demanding Roman citizenship (see 3:1,2). The Senate eventually agreed with him, and thereby drove the Italians into armed rebellion.

[31]The orator Lucius Licinius Crassus (cos, 95 B.C.) and many other senators had angered the consul Philippus by urging concessions to the Italians.

[32]Gaius Papirius Carbo (cos, 120 B.C.) was a tribune of the plebs in 130 B.C. He supported the reform movement of Tiberius Sempronius Gracchus (tribune of the plebs, 133 B.C.), who had been murdered by conservative senators.

[33]Scipio Aemilianus had destroyed the Spanish city of Numantia in 133 B.C. The rostra was the speaker's platform at the assembly place.

[34]Scipio Aemilianus was married to Sempronia, the sister of Tiberius Sempronius Gracchus.

Scipio said, "People should keep quiet if Italy is only their stepmother." They started grumbling at that, so he said, "I brought you here in chains, so you don't scare me, now that you are free."[35]

The entire people had been insulted and attacked once again by a single man, but—such is the regard paid to courage!—they remained silent. His own recent victory over Numantia, his father's victory over Macedonia, his grandfather's spoils gained from victories over Carthage, and the two kings, Syphax and Perseus, who had marched before their triumphal chariots with their necks in chains silenced the entire Forum at that time.[36] They did not grant him this silence through fear, but because their city and Italy had been released from many fears by the great deeds of the Aemilius and Cornelius families, so the Roman plebs was not free to criticize the free speech of Scipio.

2. 4. We should not, therefore, be so surprised that Pompey, a man of the highest prestige, had to tackle such free speech so often. But he won considerable respect from the way he calmly put up with insults from outrageous people of every kind. Gnaeus Piso was prosecuting Manilius Crispus, but he noticed that although Crispus was obviously guilty, he was getting away through the influence of Pompey.[37] Carried away by his youthful enthusiasm and his excitement at the prosecution, Piso made several serious charges against the powerful defender of Crispus. Pompey asked Piso why he did not prosecute him too, and Piso said, "Give me a guarantee that you will not wage a civil war against the Republic if you are prosecuted, and I shall at once send the jurymen to decide about your life rather than the life of Manilius."[38] So, during the same trial, Piso accused two men, Manilius by his prosecution, and Pompey by his frankness; and he made one accusation by having recourse to the law, and the other by his open statements— the only way he could accuse Pompey.

2. 5. Well, then, could there be free speech without Cato of Utica? No more than there could be Cato without free speech. When he sat on the jury in the case of a criminal and disgraceful senator, a statement by Pompey was presented that praised the accused and would no doubt have worked in his favor. Cato removed it from the court, citing a law that declared that senators were not allowed to use such support.[39] Cato's character made this action seem unremarkable: it might

---

[35]The remarks made by Scipio Aemilianus assume that the aristocratic patricians are the only real Romans, and that all plebeians are former slaves.

[36]Scipio's biological father, Lucius Aemilius Paullus Macedonicus, celebrated a triumph over King Perseus and the Macedonians in 167 B.C. His adoptive grandfather, Scipio Africanus, celebrated a triumph over the Carthaginians and King Syphax of Numidia in 201 B.C.

[37]Gnaeus Calpurnius Piso (cos, 23 B.C.) disliked Pompey, and Gaius Manilius Crispus (tribune of the plebs, 66 B.C.) was a loyal supporter of Pompey.

[38]After the second century B.C., people were exiled rather than executed. (The emperors brought the death penalty back.)

[39]Cato of Utica disliked both the accused Titus Munatius Plancus Byrsa (tribune of the plebs, 52 B.C.) and Pompey. Plancus was found guilty (51 B.C.).

have seemed daring in the case of another man, but in that of Cato, it was recognized as his usual self-assurance.

2. 6. When the consul Gnaeus Lentulus Marcellinus was complaining at a public meeting about the excessive power of Pompey the Great,[40] and the entire people were agreeing with him loudly and clearly, he said, "Applaud, my fellow citizens, applaud while it is still legal; soon you will not be allowed to do this with impunity." The power of an exceptional citizen was attacked by the criticism and complaints of this speaker and by the pitiful lamentations of the crowd.

2. 7. Pompey once had his leg tied up in a white bandage, and Favonius said to him, "It does not matter which part of the body you wear your crown on."[41] He used this little piece of cloth as an excuse to attack Pompey's royal powers. But Pompey did not change his face in any way and made sure people would not conclude from the delight on his face that he was glad to acknowledge his power, or from the anger on his face that he was forced to confess it.

Pompey was so forbearing that he allowed men of inferior rank and fortune to come up and attack him: from a whole host of examples, it will be more than enough to record two cases.

2. 8. Helvius Mancia of Formiae, the son of a former slave and a very old man himself, accused Lucius Libo before the censors.[42] During this dispute, Pompey the Great insulted his low rank and his age and said that Helvius had been sent up from the Underworld to accuse Libo.

Helvius replied, "You are not lying, Pompey; I do indeed come from the Underworld, and I come to accuse Lucius Libo. But while I was spending time in the Underworld, I saw Gnaeus Domitius Ahenobarbus there, covered in blood, and lamenting that he had been born into the highest family, had led a most blameless life, and had been a great patriot, but was cut down in the flower of his youth by your orders.[43]

"I saw, just as clearly, Marcus Brutus, who was easy to spot because he was torn to pieces by the sword, and he complained that this had happened to him first by your treachery and then by your cruelty.[44]

"I saw Gnaeus Carbo, who had eagerly defended you and your father's estate when you were a boy; Carbo was bound in the chains you had ordered to be put on him during his third consulship; and he swore that he had been murdered by

[40]Gnaeus Cornelius Lentulus Marcellinus was consul in 56 B.C. He disliked Pompey, who won the elections that year and was consul in 55 B.C.

[41]Marcus Favonius (praetor, 49 B.C.) was a supporter of Cato of Utica and shared his dislike for Pompey.

[42]Helvius Mancia accused Lucius Scribonius Libo (cos, 34 B.C.) before the censors in 55 B.C. Helvius disliked Pompey; Libo supported Pompey. Formiae was on the coast of southern Latium.

[43]Pompey killed Gnaeus Domitius Ahenobarbus, Marius' governor of Africa, in 81 B.C.

[44]Pompey killed Marcus Junius Brutus, a rebel legate in northern Italy, in 77 B.C.

[45]Pompey killed Gnaeus Papirius Carbo (cos, 85 B.C.) in Sicily in 82 B.C. (see 5:3,5). Carbo was consul for the third time in 82 B.C.

you against all notions of right and wrong, when he held the highest public office and you were just a Roman equestrian.[45]

"I saw the former praetor, Perperna, in the same condition and protesting in the same way, cursing your cruelty, and all those men with one voice cried out with indignation that although they had never faced a trial, they had been murdered by you, the juvenile executioner."[46]

Helvius was just a man from a small town, he still smelled of his father's slavery, he was a man of unbridled impetuosity and of unbearable pride, but he was allowed with impunity to recall the dreadful wounds of the civil wars, which had by this time been covered over with old scars. So it was at the same time very brave and very safe to criticize Pompey. But the even humbler status of the next person does not allow us to go on lamenting about this.

2. 9. Diphilus, an actor in tragedies, was performing at the Games of Apollo when he came to the line that contains the following statement: "It is to our sorrow that you are great." Diphilus spoke this line with his hands directed toward Pompey the Great, and when the people called him back several times for an encore, Diphilus, by repeating his gesture without the slightest hesitation, steadfastly accused Pompey of holding powers that were intolerable and excessive. He displayed the same impudence in the lines, "A time will come when you will bitterly lament that kind of superiority."[47]

2. 10. The mind of Marcus Castricius was also inflamed with frankness. When Castricius was holding public office at Placentia, the consul Gnaeus Carbo commanded him to issue a decree ordering the people of Placentia to hand over hostages to the consuls, but Castricius neither obeyed the head of state nor yielded before his great power.[48] And even when Carbo said he had many swords, Castricius replied, "I have many years." All those legions were amazed to see this tough relic of olden days. Carbo had very small grounds for venting his anger, and his victim had only a short period of life to lose, so Carbo's anger dwindled away.

2. 11. Servius Galba made a request that was full of impertinence when he had the nerve to speak to the divine Caesar in the following way,[49] after Caesar had accomplished his victories and was administering justice in the Forum: "Gaius Julius Caesar, I once guaranteed a debt for your former son-in-law, Pompey the Great, during his third consulship, and I am now being sued for it.[50] What should I do? Do I have to pay off his debt?" By openly and publicly criticizing Caesar for selling off the goods of Pompey, Galba deserved to be thrown out of the court. But Caesar's heart was softer than gentleness itself, and he ordered Pompey's debt to be paid from his own funds.

---

[46]Pompey killed Marcus Perperna Vento, a rebel legate in Spain, in 72 B.C.

[47]Diphilus made this remark in 59 B.C. at the Games of Apollo, which took place every July.

[48]Placentia (modern Piacenza) was a city in Aemilia (northern Italy). Gnaeus Papirius Carbo (cos, 85 B.C.) was consul in 82 B.C., the year Sulla marched on Rome.

[49]This incident occurred in 45 B.C. Servius Sulpicius Galba (praetor, 54 B.C.) had been a legate of Caesar in Gaul.

[50]Pompey was consul for the third time in 52 B.C. and was murdered in 48 B.C.

2. 12. Come now, how dangerously defiant Cascellius, the famous expert on civil law, was! No man's influence or prestige could force him to draw up a legal document for any gift or grant made by the triumvirs.[51] By his personal judgment, he declared that the rewards presented from their victory were completely against the law. When Cascellius spoke at length and with considerable frankness about current events, his friends kept advising him not to do that, but he replied that two things, which seem very bitter to most people, were giving him complete freedom: his old age and his lack of children.

Foreign Stories

2. ext. 1. A woman from a foreign nation joins these great men. She had been wrongly convicted by King Philip, who was drunk at the time.[52] She shouted out that she was appealing against the judgment, and when Philip asked her who she was going to appeal to, she said, "To Philip, but not until he is sober." He had been gaping stupidly, but she knocked his drunkenness out of him. By her determination, she forced him to come back to his senses, inspect her case more carefully, and make a more just decision. She had been unable to obtain justice so she got it by force, and she borrowed strength from her frankness rather than from her innocence.

2. ext. 2. The next story tells of frankness that was brave and witty too. There was a very old woman at Syracuse, and though everyone else was praying for the death of the tyrant Dionysius[53] because of the excessive harshness of his character and the unbearable burdens he imposed on them, she alone would go every day in the morning and beg the gods that Dionysius would be safe and live after her. When Dionysius discovered this, he was amazed at this undeserved good feeling toward him, so he summoned her and asked her why she was doing this, and what he had done to merit it. Then she said, "There is a definite logic to my behavior: when I was a young girl, we used to have a severe tyrant, and I wanted to be rid of him. But when he was killed, a much fiercer tyrant took over his fortress. I thought it essential that his tyranny should come to an end. But we started to have you as our third ruler, and you were even more oppressive than the previous ones. So I keep offering my own life on behalf of your safety, because if you were removed, an even worse man would take your place." Dionysius was too ashamed to punish her witty audacity.

2. ext. 3. There could have been a sort of marriage of brave hearts between those two women and Theodorus of Cyrene, because they were matched in courage, though they were quite different in their fates.[54] When King Lysimachus

---

[51]The triumvirs presented their cronies with the property of their victims in the massacres of 43 to 42 B.C. Aulus Cascellius must have been a praetor some time during their regime (43–33 B.C.).

[52]Philip II was king of Macedonia from 356 to 336 B.C.

[53]Dionysius I was tyrant of Syracuse from 405 to 367 B.C.

[54]Theodorus "the Atheist" was a fourth-century B.C. philosopher from Cyrene (modern Libya).

threatened him with death,[55] Theodorus said, "This is indeed a magnificent achievement of yours, since you have attained the power of the Spanish fly."[56] Enraged by this remark, the king ordered him to be crucified, and Theodorus said, "This may terrify your court officials, but to me it does not make any difference whether I rot down in the earth or up high."

Chapter 3. Severity

Preface

Our hearts will have to arm themselves with hardness while deeds of frightful and grim severity are related. We shall have to leave all our gentler sentiments aside and give our ears the chance to hear these harsh facts. Anger unleashed, unforgiving revenge, and various kinds of punishment will rush into view; they may be useful as bulwarks of the law, but they are the last things I would like to include among these quiet and peaceful pages.

Roman Stories

3. 1a. Marcus Manlius had driven the Gauls away from our citadel but was later thrown down off that citadel, because he had once bravely defended our liberty but then wickedly tried to crush it.[57] These were the words spoken before his rightful punishment: "You were Manlius in my judgment when you were driving the Senones in headlong flight; but after you started to imitate them, you became one of the Senones."

A provision that will always be remembered was included in his sentence: because of him, they decided to make it illegal for any patrician to live on the citadel or the Capitol, since his home had been in the place where the temple of Moneta can be seen today.[58]

3. 1b. The state burst out with equal indignation against Spurius Cassius.[59] The suspicion that he was aiming at despotism did him more damage than all the credit he gained from three magnificent consulships and two spectacular triumphs: the Senate and people of Rome were not just content with inflicting the death penalty on him; they also demolished his house on top of his dead body, so that he would

---

[55]Lysimachus was king of Thrace from 323 to 282 B.C.

[56]The Spanish fly (*cantharis*) was used in making poisons.

[57]Marcus Manlius Capitolinus (cos, 392 B.C.) drove the Senones (Gauls from northern Italy) away from the Capitol in 390 B.C. In 384 B.C. he attacked the practice of enslaving debtors, was tried for treason, and was thrown to his death from the Capitol.

[58]The temple of Juno Moneta on the Capitol was dedicated in 344 B.C.

[59]Spurius Cassius Vecellinus (cos, 502 B.C.) proposed redistributing public land in 485 B.C., was tried for treason, and was put to death (see 5:8,2).

be punished by the obliteration of his home; and on that spot they built a temple to Earth.[60] Formerly it had been the home of a madman; now it is a monument to scrupulous severity.

3. 1c. When Spurius Maelius dared to do the same thing, our country inflicted the same death penalty on him.[61] The site where his house had been was given the name of Aequimelium, so that the justice of his punishment would be renowned among posterity.[62] The ruins of the walls and roofs where the enemies of liberty lived reveals how much inborn hatred the ancients held in their hearts against such people.

This is why, after two very rebellious citizens, Marcus Flaccus and Lucius Saturninus, were put to death, their houses were destroyed right down to the foundations.[63] But after the site of Flaccus' home had been left vacant for a long time, it was decorated by Quintus Catulus with the spoils taken from the Cimbrians.[64]

3. 1d. Because of their high rank and great prospects, Tiberius and Gaius Gracchus were very successful in our state.[65] But because they had tried to undermine the stability of the state, their bodies were left without burial, and this final honor paid to every human being was denied to the sons of Gracchus and the grandchildren of Scipio Africanus.[66] In fact, even their friends were thrown to their deaths in prison,[67] so that nobody would wish to befriend enemies of the Republic.

3. 2. Publius Mucius, a tribune of the plebs, believed that he had the same rights as the Senate and people of Rome.[68] He burned all his fellow tribunes alive, because following the leadership of Spurius Cassius they had placed the liberty of all citizens in jeopardy by refusing to hold elections for the magistracies.[69] Certainly,

---

[60]The temple of Earth on the Esquiline hill was dedicated in 268 B.C.

[61]Spurius Maelius distributed free grain in 439 B.C. and allegedly wanted to be king.

[62]The Aequimelium was a market for sacrificial animals. Valerius interprets its name as meaning the just (*aequi*) punishment of Maelius (*Melium*).

[63]Marcus Fulvius Flaccus (cos, 125 B.C.) perished when the supporters of Gaius Sempronius Gracchus (tribune of the plebs, 123 B.C.) were massacred in 121 B.C. The populist Lucius Appuleius Saturninus (tribune of the plebs, 103 B.C.) was murdered in 100 B.C.

[64]Quintus Lutatius Catulus (cos, 102 B.C.) helped Marius defeat the Cimbrians (from Denmark) in 101 B.C.

[65]Tiberius Sempronius Gracchus (tribune of the plebs, 133 B.C.) and later his brother, Gaius Sempronius Gracchus (tribune of the plebs, 123 B.C.), were populist leaders. They perished in the general massacre of their supporters in 133 and 121 B.C., respectively.

[66]Their father was Tiberius Sempronius Gracchus (cos, 177 B.C.) Their mother, Cornelia, was the daughter of Scipio Africanus.

[67]The death chamber was in the basement of the prison, and was entered through a hole in its ceiling.

[68]Publius Mucius Scaevola was a tribune of the plebs in 486 B.C.

[69]The reformist Spurius Cassius Vecellinus (cos, 502 B.C.) was put to death in 485 B.C. (see 6:3,1b). The reformist tribunes burned to death by Mucius in 486 B.C. were military tribunes, not tribunes of the plebs.

nothing could be more self-assured than his severity: a single tribune dared to inflict that punishment on his nine colleagues, whereas those colleagues would have
been terrified to inflict it on one.

3. 3. So far, we have seen severity as the guardian and avenger of liberty; but it
is equally impressive in defending rank and discipline. The Senate handed Marcus
Claudius over to the Corsicans, because he had made a disgraceful peace treaty
with them.[70] When the enemy refused to take him, the Senate commanded that he
be put to death in the public prison; he had insulted the dignity of the empire just
once, but the Senate was a relentless avenger and showed its anger in so many
ways! It disavowed his actions, took away his freedom, ended his life, and disgraced
his dead body with the insult of imprisonment and the accursed indignity of the
Gemonian Steps.[71]

That man had deserved such punishment by the Senate. But Gnaeus Cornelius
Scipio, the son of Hispanus, suffered punishment even before he could deserve
it.[72] When he obtained the province of Spain by lot, the Senate decreed that he
could not go there, giving the reason that he did not know how to behave properly. So because of his dishonorable lifestyle, Cornelius, without even governing a
province, was all but convicted under the law against misgovernment.

Gaius Vettienus had cut off the fingers of his left hand so that he would not
have to fight in the Italian War,[73] but the severity of the Senate did not overlook
this. The Senate confiscated his property and decreed that he would be punished
with imprisonment for life. It made sure that since he had refused to sacrifice his
life honorably in battle, he would have to drag it out disgracefully in chains.

3. 4. The consul Manius Curius imitated the Senate's action when he was unexpectedly forced to conscript soldiers and none of the younger men responded to
his edict.[74] He put all the tribes into a lottery, and the Pollia tribe came out first.
He then ordered his attendants to pick the first name from the Pollia tribe out of
the urn and summon that person. When the young man did not respond, Curius
put his property up for sale by auction. When this news reached the young man,
he ran up to the consul's platform and appealed to the tribunes as a body. Then
Manius Curius first declared that the Republic had no need of a citizen who did
not understand obedience, and then he sold both the young man's goods and the
young man himself.

3. 5. Lucius Domitius was just as determined in laying down the law.[75] When
he was governor of Sicily, a boar of exceptional size was brought to him, and he
ordered the shepherd who had killed it to be brought before him. On questioning

---

[70]Marcus Claudius Clineas was sent as a legate to conquer Corsica in 236 B.C.

[71]The bodies of executed criminals were dumped on the Gemonian Steps, which led down
from the Capitol to the prison.

[72]Gnaeus Cornelius Scipio was a praetor in 109 B.C. but was not allowed to govern Spain.
His father was Gnaeus Cornelius Scipio Hispanus (praetor, 139 B.C.).

[73]The war between Rome and its Italian allies was fought from 91 to 89 B.C.

[74]Manius Curius Dentatus was consul and defeated King Pyrrhus of Epirus in 275 B.C.

[75]Lucius Domitius Ahenobarbus (cos, 94 B.C.) was governor of Sicily in 97 B.C.

the man who had killed the beast, and discovering that he had used a spear, Domitius had him crucified, because in order to stamp out the banditry that was destroying the province, he had issued an edict forbidding anyone to own a weapon. Someone might say that this was on the borderline between severity and savagery—the argument could go either way. But considerations of state policy do not allow us to judge that the governor was too harsh.

3. 6. That is how severely men were punished, but the same rigid severity was also used in punishing women. Horatius had just defeated the three Curiatius brothers in battle, and because of the nature of that combat, he had in effect defeated all the Albans.[76] He was returning home from that glorious battle when he saw his unmarried sister lamenting the death of her fiancé, Curiatius, rather more intensely than someone of her age should have done. Horatius killed her with the sword he had used to save his country, because he felt that her tears were far from innocent and must have arisen from a love that had gone too far. When he was brought before the people on account of this murder, his father defended him. The young woman's feelings had been too attached to the memory of her intended husband, so her brother punished her fiercely, and her father strongly supported that punishment.

3. 7. The Senate was equally severe when it ordered the consuls Spurius Postumius Albinus and Quintus Marcius Philippus to hold an investigation into those women who had abandoned chastity and joined the Bacchic cult.[77] Many of the women were found guilty by the consuls, and they were all put to death by their relatives in their homes. The disgrace of this scandal spread far and wide, but it was atoned for by the severity with which it was punished. If these women, by their disgraceful behavior, had caused such great embarrassment to our state, their heavy punishment won us equally great praise.

3. 8. Publilia had poisoned her husband, the consul Postumius Albinus, and Licinia did the same to her husband, Claudius Asellus, so the women were strangled by order of their relatives.[78] Those very severe men did not think there was any need to waste time on a long public trial since the crime was so obvious. They would have defended those women if they had been innocent, and likewise they were quick to punish them since they were guilty.

3. 9. The severity of those men drove them to revenge because of the serious nature of those crimes, but Egnatius Mecennius took revenge for a much more trivial reason.[79] He beat his wife to death with a cudgel simply because she had

[76]Under the legendary third king, Tullus Hostilius (672–641 B.C.), Rome settled a dispute with Alba by pitting the three Roman Horatius brothers against the three Alban Curiatius brothers. Marcus Horatius was the only survivor, so Rome won the dispute.

[77]Spurius Postumius Albinus and Quintus Marcius Philippus were consuls in 186 B.C. They initiated a bloodthirsty witch-hunt against the Bacchic cult. (See 1;3,1.)

[78]Publilia was accused of poisoning her husband, Lucius Postumius Albinus, when he was consul in 154 B.C. Licinia and Claudius Asellus have not been identified.

[79]Egnatius Mecennius supposedly lived in the days of Romulus, which was a way of saying that the rule against women drinking wine was a timeless Roman custom.

taken some wine. Nobody prosecuted him for doing this, and nobody even criticized him; everyone thought that Mecennius had set an excellent example by
punishing his wife in this way for violating the rules of sobriety. If any woman is
too fond of drinking wine, she definitely closes the door on all the virtues and
opens it to all kinds of mischief.

   3. 10. The stern pride of Gaius Sulpicius Galus as a husband was equally
harsh.[80] He divorced his wife because he discovered that she had gone around in
public with her head unveiled. His views were harsh, but there was some logic behind them. "If you want to be admired," he said, "the law allows you to display
your beauty to my eyes alone. You should buy cosmetics for my eyes alone; you
should be beautiful for them; they should be given an intimate knowledge of you.
If you display yourself elsewhere, you are provoking men for nothing, and you
will inevitably be subject to suspicion and accusations."

   3. 11. Quintus Antistius Vetus felt the same way, and he divorced his wife because he had seen her in a public place whispering some secret to a low-class freedwoman.[81] Antistius was offended not by full-grown immorality, but by immorality
that was, so to speak, still in its cradle and still being breast-fed. He wanted to forestall any wrongdoing rather than punish it.

   3. 12. We shall have to add Publius Sempronius Sophus to these men.[82] He humiliated his wife by divorcing her, though she had done nothing more than dare to
attend the games without his knowledge. This is how women were dealt with in
those days, so their minds stayed away from misbehavior.

Foreign Stories

   3. ext. 1. Although the entire world could learn a lesson from these stories of
Roman severity, we should not disdain to mention briefly some foreign cases. The
Spartans ordered the works of Archilochus to be removed from their country, because they felt it would be disgraceful and shameless to read them.[83] They did not
want the minds of their children to be corrupted by such reading, in case it would
do more harm to their morals than good to their minds. He was the greatest poet,
or certainly close to the top, but because he had used obscene abuse in tearing to
pieces a family he hated, the Spartans punished him by exiling his poetry.

   3. ext. 2. When Timagoras had to greet King Darius, he followed the Persian
custom and prostrated himself before the king.[84] For this the Athenians punished
him with death. They were angry that the humble groveling of this one citizen
had humiliated the glory of the entire city before the tyranny of Persia.

---

[80]Gaius Sulpicius Galus was consul in 166 B.C.

[81]Quintus Antistius and his wife have not been identified. Freedwomen were often prostitutes.

[82]Publius Sempronius Sophus was consul in 268 B.C.

[83]Archilochus of Paros lived in the seventh century B.C. and was noted for his abusive verses.

[84]Timagoras was sent as an envoy to Persia in 367 B.C. The king of Persia at that time was
Artaxerxes III, not Darius.

3. ext. 3. Cambyses showed unheard of severity in skinning the body of a corrupt judge, using the skin to cover a chair, and ordering the judge's son to sit on it when he was to give judgment.[85] He was a king and a barbarian, of course, but by his strange and dreadful punishment of this judge, he made sure that no judge would take bribes after that.

Chapter 4. Dignified Statements and Actions

Preface

A good large part of the glory won by famous men derives from their dignified statements and actions, and these are preserved by the eternal power of historical record. Since there is an abundant supply of such stories, I do not want to be too miserly nor again too lavish in handing them out. So let's take enough to satisfy our needs rather than overwhelm us.

Roman Stories

4. 1. When our country had been shattered by the defeat at Cannae,[86] the survival of the Republic was hanging on a very thin thread and depended on the loyalty of our allies. To make the hearts of our allies more loyal in supporting the Roman Empire, a majority of the senators voted to enroll the leaders of the Latins in their own order. Annius, a Campanian, even asserted that one of the consuls should be elected from Capua: that is how crushed and weak the spirit of the Roman Empire was. But then Manlius Torquatus,[87] the son of the man who had defeated the Latins in the famous battle by the river Veseris, [88] declared, in the loudest voice he could manage, that if any one of the allies dared to vote among the Conscript Fathers, he would kill him on the spot. The threats made by this one man restored its former vigor to the languishing spirit of the Romans and prevented Italy from rising up to demand equal citizen rights with us: vanquished by the weapons of the father and the words of the son, Italy backed down.

The Manlius in the next story was just as dignified.[89] Everyone voted that he should be given the consulship, but he refused it on the grounds that he had an eye

---

[85]Cambyses was king of Persia from 529 to 522 B.C. The judge's son, Otanes, later became an important general under the new dynasty of Darius I.

[86]Hannibal defeated the Romans at Cannae (in Apulia, eastern Italy) in 216 B.C.

[87]Titus Manlius Torquatus (cos, 235 B.C.) spoke out against allowing non-Romans to join the Senate in 216 B.C.

[88]Titus Manlius Imperiosus Torquatus (cos, 347 B.C.) defeated the Latins by the river Veseris (in Campania) in 340 B.C., but the Torquatus in 216 B.C. was his descendant not his son.

[89]This is actually the same Titus Manlius Torquatus (cos, 235 B.C.). He won the election in 211 B.C. but did not become consul in 210 B.C.

defect. When they all kept insisting, he said, "Citizens, you will have to find someone else to give this office to: because if you force me to exercise it, I won't be able to tolerate your morals, and you won't be able to endure my rule." His words as a private citizen were so weighty; how dignified his fasces as a consul would have been![90]

4. 2. Scipio Aemilianus was no less dignified either in the Senate house or at public meetings. His colleague as censor was Mummius, who was a nobleman but led a decadent lifestyle.[91] Speaking at the rostra, Aemilianus said that he would carry out his duties in accordance with the dignity of the Republic, whether his citizens had given him a colleague or not.

Scipio Aemilianus also spoke out when the consuls Servius Sulpicius Galba and Aurelius were arguing in the Senate about which of them should be sent to Spain against Viriathus, and a great dispute arose about this among the Conscript Fathers.[92] Everybody was eager to see which way Aemilianus would incline, but he said, "I think neither of them should be sent, because one of them has nothing, and the other is satisfied with nothing." Aemilianus felt that poverty and greed were equally bad guides in a command that was unlimited. By this statement, he ensured that neither was sent to that province.[93]

4. 3. Gaius Popillius was sent as an envoy by the Senate to Antiochus, to tell him to end his harassing war against Ptolemy.[94] When Antiochus came up to him and with an open spirit and friendly demeanor held out his right hand, Popillius refused to hold out his hand in turn. Instead, he handed him the document containing the decree of the Senate. When Antiochus read it, he said he would discuss it with his courtiers. Popillius was outraged that Antiochus would try to delay matters, so he used a rod to draw a line around the place they were standing in and said, "Before you leave this circle, you will have to give me a reply that I can bring back to the Senate."

You would have felt it was not an envoy that spoke, but that the Senate house itself was visibly present there. The king immediately declared that Ptolemy would have no further reason to complain about him, and it was only then that Popillius grasped his hand in a friendly way. What an effect can be produced by the curt dignity of a man's spirit and words! At one and the same moment, he intimidated the kingdom of Syria and saved the kingdom of Egypt.

4. 4. I can't say whether I would respect Publius Rutilius more for his words or for his deeds: there is an equally admirable power in both.[95] He was resisting an

---

[90]The fasces were bundles of sticks symbolizing the power of the state. Twelve fasces were carried before a consul.

[91]Scipio Aemilianus and Lucius Mummius Achaicus (cos, 146 B.C.) were censors in 142 B.C.

[92]Servius Sulpicius Galba and Lucius Aurelius Cotta were Consuls in 144 B.C. and both of them wanted to fight against the Spanish leader, Viriathus, in 143 B.C.

[93]Scipio Aemilianus arranged for his best friend and his brother to be sent to Spain in 143 B.C.

[94]Antiochus IV Epiphanes of Syria invaded Egypt in 170 B.C. and deposed King Ptolemy VI Philometor. The Senate sent Gaius Popillius Laenas (cos, 172 B.C.) as a special envoy to Egypt in 168 B.C.

[95]This is Publius Rutilius Rufus (cos, 105 B.C.).

unjust request made by a friend, and the friend said in high indignation, "What good is your friendship to me if you don't do as I ask?" Rutilius replied, "Well, what good is your friendship to me, if I have to act dishonorably because of it?"

His actions were in keeping with his words. He was put on trial because of the dissension between the orders rather than through any fault of his own,[96] but he did not wear old clothes, or take off his emblems as a senator, or reach his hands out in supplication to the knees of the jurymen, or say anything that would detract from the glory of his past career. He wanted this crisis to be a test of his dignity rather than an obstacle to it.[97]

Even when the victory of Sulla allowed him to return to his country, Rutilius stayed in exile rather than do something that might be against the laws. So it would have been much fairer if the title of "Fortunate" had been given to a man who was so impressive because of his character, than to one who had gone mad with military power: Sulla stole that title, but Rutilius earned it.[98]

4. 5. Marcus Brutus murdered his own fine qualities before he murdered the father of our country.[99] By that one deed, he threw all his virtues into the abyss and disgraced the memory of his name by a horrific blot, for which he could never atone. As Brutus was about to go into battle for the last time, some men said he should not fight, but he said, "I am going into battle with confidence: either all will be well today or I shall have nothing further to worry about." He took it for granted, of course, that he could neither survive without winning nor die without being released from all his worries.[100]

Foreign Stories

4. ext. 1. Now that I mention Marcus Brutus, it occurs to me that I should tell you about the dignified remark that was made against Decimus Brutus in Spain.[101] Almost all of Lusitania had surrendered to him, and Cinginnia was the only city of that nation that kept fighting stubbornly against him. When Decimus Brutus suggested leaving Cinginnia alone in exchange for payment, the city's inhabitants replied with one voice to the envoys of Brutus that their ancestors had given them swords to defend their city, not gold to buy their freedom from a greedy general.

---

[96]The two orders are the order of senators and the order of equestrians. (See equestrian and Senate, senator in the Glossary.)

[97]While he was serving as legate in Asia in 97 B.C., Rutilius prevented the equestrian tax companies from exploiting the Asians. An equestrian jury, resenting this interference by a senator, unfairly found him guilty of misgovernment in 92 B.C. (see 2:10,5).

[98]Sulla became dictator in 82 B.C. and took on the title "Fortunate" (*Felix*). Sulla sympathized with the senatorial order, but Rutilius refused to accept favors from a dictator.

[99]The "father of our country" is Caesar.

[100]Marcus Junius Brutus (the tyrannicide) was defeated at Philippi (in Macedonia) in 42 B.C. and took his own life.

[101]Decimus Junius Brutus Callaicus (cos, 138 B.C.) subdued Lusitania (modern Portugal) in 136 B.C.

It would no doubt have been better if the men of our nation had said this rather than heard it.

4. ext. 2. It was Nature that led the Spaniards onto this impressive path; Socrates, on the other hand, was the brilliant high point of Greek learning. When he had to plead his case in Athens, Lysias composed a defense speech for him to use in the court.[102] It was a humble and pleading speech, suited to the danger that threatened Socrates, but when Lysias read it out, Socrates said, "Please take it away: if I could be induced to deliver it, even in the remotest wilderness of Scythia,[103] I would be admitting that I deserved to be put to death." He was disgusted with the idea of living without self-respect, so he preferred to die like Socrates than survive like Lysias.[104]

4. ext. 3. Just as Socrates was the greatest in wisdom, Alexander was the greatest in warfare, and he made the following noble statement. Darius had already experienced Alexander's qualities in one or two battles, so he promised Alexander the part of his kingdom that went as far as the Taurus Mountains, and his daughter in marriage along with one million talents.[105] Parmenio said that if he were Alexander, he would take advantage of this offer. Alexander replied, "I would indeed take advantage of it, if I were Parmenio."[106] This was the proper answer for a man who had won two victories and deserved to get a third one, which is what happened.

4. ext. 4. That was the remark of a man with a proud spirit and fortunate circumstances. The following remark, which the Spartan envoys made to Alexander's father, revealed the tragic circumstances of their courageous spirit and was more to be admired than envied.[107] He was imposing intolerable burdens on their state, and they replied that if he persisted in giving them orders that were worse than death, then they would prefer death.

4. ext. 5. The following remark by a Spartan was certainly not lacking in dignity. He was a man of exceptional nobility and integrity, but he was defeated in an election for public office. He declared that it was a cause of great joy to him that his country had better men than he. By this statement, he made his defeat as honorable as the office he lost.

---

[102]Lysias was an Athenian speechwriter and a friend of Socrates.

[103]Scythia (modern Ukraine) was considered a wild and remote country.

[104]Socrates was put to death in 399 B.C.

[105]Alexander the Great of Macedonia was already in Syria when Darius III of Persia made him this offer in 332 B.C. The Taurus Mountains separated Asia Minor from Syria, so Darius was offering him all of Asia Minor. For talent, see money—Greek in the Glossary.

[106]Parmenio was Alexander's most trusted general.

[107]Philip II of Macedonia had invaded Sparta in 338 B.C. Sparta was the only Greek state that refused to join Philip's alliance in 337 B.C.

Chapter 5. Justice

Preface

It is now time to enter the sacred precincts of justice, where respect and religious regard are paid to fair and honest deeds; where prejudice gives way to shame, and greed to reason; where nothing is considered beneficial if it might be viewed as dishonorable. The highest and clearest model of justice among all nations is our own state.

Roman Stories

5. 1. When the consul Camillus was besieging Falerii,[108] a schoolteacher pretended to bring a large number of boys from noble families out for a walk but led them over to the Roman camp. If the boys had been held captive, there was no doubt that the people of Falerii would abandon their enthusiasm for fighting the war and surrender to our general. In spite of this, the Senate voted that the teacher be tied up, and that the boys be sent back to Falerii, beating him with rods all the way home. Although their walls could not be stormed, the hearts of the people of Falerii were won over by the justice of this action; defeated by kindness rather than by arms, they opened their gates to the Romans.

This city of Falerii was battered to pieces by its repeated rebellions and its constant defeats in battle, and it was finally forced to surrender to the consul Quintus Lutatius.[109] The Roman people wanted to take brutal action against the city, but Papirius by the consul's orders had written up the terms of its surrender.[110] When Papirius told the people that the citizens of Falerii had entrusted themselves not to the power of the Romans but to their good faith, the people kindly forgot their anger. They resisted the forces of hatred, which are usually difficult to overcome, and likewise the temptation of victory, which easily leads men on to uncontrolled abuse, because the people did not want to betray their standards of justice.

Under the leadership and auspices of Publius Claudius, the population of Cameria had been taken prisoner and auctioned off as slaves.[111] Even though the Roman people realized that their treasury was benefiting from the money, and that their territory was being increased by the land annexed, they still felt that the general's actions had not been quite honorable. So the people took great pains to find the prisoners and buy them back, granted them a place to live on the Aventine, and gave them back their landed property. The people also gave them money, not

---

[108]Marcus Furius Camillus (dictator, 396 B.C.) was a military consul in 394 B.C. when this incident occurred. Falerii was a city in southern Etruria.

[109]Falerii rebelled in 241 B.C. but surrendered to Quintus Lutatius Cerco (cos, 241 B.C.).

[110]Gaius Papirius Maso (cos, 231 B.C.) was a pontiff in 241 B.C.

[111]Cameria was a town in Latium. It was destroyed by the Romans in 502 B.C.

for a new town hall but for building shrines and offering sacrifices.[112] By their constant readiness to act justly, the people made it possible for the citizens of Cameria to be delighted with their defeat, since it brought them a new lease on life.

The stories I have told so far affected our own city area and the neighboring territories; the one that follows affected the entire world. Timochares of Ambracia promised the consul Fabricius that he would have Pyrrhus poisoned by his son, who was in charge of the king's drinks.[113] When this was reported to the Senate, it sent envoys warning Pyrrhus to take extra precautions against this kind of treachery. The Senate bore in mind that our city had been established by a son of Mars to make war with arms and not with poisons.[114] But the Senate withheld Timochares' name, acting justly in both cases, since it wished neither to set a bad precedent by killing an enemy in this way nor to betray someone who had meant well.

5. 2. Exceptional justice was seen in the simultaneous behavior of four tribunes of the plebs.[115] Lucius Atratinus had led our army into defeat at the hands of the Volscians near Verrugo, but these men along with the cavalry had rectified the situation.[116] When one of the other tribunes, Lucius Hortensius, prosecuted Atratinus before the people, these men swore at the rostra that they would wear mourning as long as their general was on trial.[117] These exceptional young men had defended him from danger with their blood and wounds, while he was a soldier; they could not bear to look on while they wore the emblems of their high office and he was forced to risk his life, now that he was a civilian. Moved by their sense of justice, the assembly forced Hortensius to give up his case; it behaved similarly in the story that follows.

5. 3. By carrying out too severe a censorship, Tiberius Gracchus and Gaius Claudius angered the greater part of our state, and Publius Rutilius, a tribune of the plebs, charged them with treason before the people.[118] In addition to the general outrage, he was personally incensed that they had ordered his relative Rutilius to demolish a wall that encroached on a public space. At the trial, most of the voting units of the first class found Claudius clearly guilty, but they all seemed to agree that Gracchus should be acquitted.[119] But Gracchus swore in a loud voice

[112]The Aventine hill was in the south of Rome. The people of Cameria got to keep their farmland and their religious traditions, but not their town hall and independence.

[113]Gaius Fabricius Luscinus (cos, 282 B.C.) was consul again in 278 B.C. during the war against King Pyrrhus of Epirus. Ambracia was a city in Epirus.

[114]The son of Mars is Romulus, the legendary founder of Rome.

[115]These tribunes of the Plebs in 422 B.C. had served during the previous year as cavalry officers under Gaius Sempronius Atratinus (cos, 423 B.C.).

[116]Atratinus was almost defeated by the Volscians (from southern Latium) in 423 B.C. (see 3:2,8). Verrugo was a Volscian fortress.

[117]Lucius Hortensius prosecuted Atratinus in 422 B.C.

[118]Gaius Claudius Pulcher (cos, 177 B.C.) and Tiberius Sempronius Gracchus (cos, 177 B.C.) were censors in 169 B.C., and Publius Rutilius was a tribune of the plebs in that year.

[119]For the voting system, see assembly—centuriate in the Glossary.

that if they reached an unfavorable verdict about his colleague, then he would join Claudius in undergoing the penalty of exile, since he was involved in the same actions. The fairness of this remark swept that entire storm away from the fortunes and lives of both men: the people acquitted Claudius, and Rutilius gave up his case against Gracchus.

5. 4. The entire body of tribunes won great praise for the following action. One of them, Lucius Cotta, relying of the inviolate nature of his office, refused to pay back his creditors;[120] but the entire group of tribunes decreed that if he did not pay back the money or give the name of someone who would guarantee the loan, they would support his creditors when they demanded payment. The tribunes considered it unfair that the dignity of the state should be used to cover up the dishonesty of a private person. The tribunes' sense of justice had found Cotta hiding behind the office of the tribune like a runaway slave hiding in a temple, and they dragged him out of there.[121]

5. 5. I shall turn to another equally famous action of the tribunes. Gnaeus Domitius, a tribune of the plebs, prosecuted Marcus Scaurus, the most prominent man in the state, before the people.[122] If fortune favored Domitius, he would win great fame by ruining this distinguished man; if he didn't quite succeed, he would still win great fame by attacking Scaurus. Domitius was burning with desire to destroy Scaurus when a slave of Scaurus came to him by night and promised that he would help Domitius' case by adding several serious charges against his master. In deciding how to view this wicked betrayal, Domitius was torn between acting like an enemy and acting like a real member of the Domitius family. Justice won out over hatred: he covered his ears, shut the betrayer's mouth, and had the slave brought at once to Scaurus. I won't say that this prosecutor should have been loved by the man he accused, but he certainly deserved Scaurus' respect! Because of his other virtues and because of this action, the people were happy to elect Domitius consul, censor, and chief pontiff.[123]

5. 6. Lucius Crassus proved his sense of justice by acting in the same way. He had been very bitter in his prosecution of Gaius Carbo, since Carbo was a great enemy of his.[124] But when a slave of Carbo's brought him a writing case containing several documents that could easily have destroyed Carbo, Crassus sent it back to Carbo just as it was with the seal intact and sent the slave back in chains too. Imagine how strong justice was among friends at that time, since we see that it had such force even among prosecutors and the men they accused.

5. 7. Sulla was eager to keep himself safe but he was even more eager to see Sulpicius Rufus destroyed, since Rufus, during his mad term as tribune, had harassed

---

[120]Lucius Aurelius Cotta (cos, 144 B.C.) was tribune of the plebs in 154 B.C.

[121]Abused slaves could hide safely in a temple.

[122]Gnaeus Domitius Ahenobarbus (cos, 96 B.C.) was a tribune of the plebs in 104 B.C. when he prosecuted Marcus Aemilius Scaurus (cos, 115 B.C.).

[123]Domitius was elected chief pontiff in 103 B.C., consul in 96 B.C., and censor in 92 B.C.

[124]Lucius Licinius Crassus (cos, 95 B.C.) prosecuted Gaius Papirius Carbo (cos, 120 B.C.) in 119 B.C. Even without the slave's evidence, Carbo was found guilty and took his life.

Sulla continuously.[125] But Sulla discovered that when Rufus had been put on his death list, he had hidden in his country home and had been betrayed by a slave.[126] So Sulla freed the murderous slave to keep the promise made in his edict, but he ordered him to be thrown at once from the Tarpeian Rock wearing the cap of liberty he had won by his crime.[127] Sulla was an arrogant victor in other respects, but he was very just in issuing this command.

Foreign Stories

5. ext. 1. I don't want people to think that I have forgotten the just behavior of other nations. Pittacus of Mytilene's fellow citizens owed so much to his good deeds, or else they trusted his character so much, that they voted to make him a tyrant.[128] He held that power for the duration of their war against Athens concerning the ownership of Sigeum.[129] When they won the war and made peace, he gave his power up immediately, even though the people of Mytilene begged him not to. But Pittacus did not want to remain master over his fellow citizens longer than the crisis of their state required. When his fellow citizens voted unanimously to offer him half of the territory they had won back, he refused to consider this offer, because he felt it would be disgraceful to lessen the glory of his merits by accepting so much plunder.

5. ext. 2. I have to tell you about the cleverness of one man to show up the justice of another man. Themistocles had thought up a very good plan and forced the Athenians to move onto their ships; he had expelled King Xerxes and his forces from Greece;[130] he was now restoring the ruins of his country to their former state; and through secret maneuvers he was developing its resources to make it the chief power in Greece. He then declared at an assembly that he had made special plans, and if fortune allowed them to come to fruition, no country would be greater or more powerful than the Athenian people. He could not, however, make his plans public, so he wanted them to give him a confidant to whom he could explain his plans in secret. They gave him Aristides.[131] Themistocles wanted to set on fire the Spartan fleet, which had withdrawn in its entirety to Gytheum, and once it was destroyed, the Athenians would have control over the seas.[132] When Aristides

[125]Sulla was consul, and Publius Sulpicius Rufus was a tribune of the plebs, in 88 B.C.

[126]Sulla made a death list of his main political opponents and rewarded their murderers.

[127]Sulla promised to free any slaves who betrayed their masters. Traitors were thrown from the Tarpeian Rock (the southern face of the Capitol).

[128]Pittacus was tyrant of Mitylene from 590 to 580 B.C. Mitylene was a city on the island of Lesbos (off the west coast of Asia Minor).

[129]Athens and Mytilene squabbled about the ownership of Sigeum (a city on the west coast of Asia Minor) throughout the first half of the sixth century B.C.

[130]Themistocles urged the Athenians to rely on their navy, and he defeated King Xerxes I of the Persia at the sea battle of Salamis in 480 B.C.

[131]Aristides "the Just" was sympathetic to the Spartans.

[132]Gytheum (on the south coast of the Peloponnese, in southern Greece) was the main naval base of the Spartans.

heard about this plan, he addressed his fellow citizens and told them that Themistocles had in mind a plan that was advantageous but completely unjust. At once, the entire assembly proclaimed that if it did not seem just, then it was of no advantage either, and it immediately ordered Themistocles to put an end to his scheme.

5. *ext. 3.* Nothing could be braver than the following acts of justice. Zaleucus had protected the city of Locri with the most beneficial and useful laws.[133] His son was found guilty on a charge of adultery, and in accordance with the law that Zaleucus himself had established, he should have had both his eyes gouged out. All the citizens, out of respect for the father, wanted to exempt the son from the rigors of the law, but Zaleucus resisted them for a long time. Finally, he was won over by the pleas of the people, so he gouged out one of his own eyes first, and then one of his son's, thereby leaving each of them with the ability to see. He carried out the punishment required by his own law, but with an admirable blend of justice, he divided himself between the roles of a merciful father and a strict lawmaker.

5. *ext. 4.* The justice of Charondas of Thurii was considerably more harsh and abrupt.[134] He went as far as using violence and bloodshed to control the turbulent assemblies of his fellow citizens, by passing a law that if any citizen came to an assembly with a sword, he would be put to death on the spot. A long time passed by, and Charondas was coming home from a distant farm wearing a sword. An assembly was called suddenly, and he went to it just as he was. The man who stood beside him pointed out that he had broken his own law, and Charondas said, "I shall carry it out too." At once he took his sword out and threw himself on top of it. He could have hidden his misdeed or defended it as a mistake, but he chose instead to pay the penalty at once, so that justice would not be cheated.

Chapter 6. Public Trust

Preface

As we visualize her image, the revered goddess of Trust shows us her right hand, the most definite guarantee of security for humankind. Every nation has experienced the power she has always exercised in our state, and we shall review it in a few stories.[135]

---

[133]Zaleucus created the law code of Locri Epizephyrii (in Bruttium, southern Italy) around 650 B.C.

[134]Charondas created the law code of Catana (on the east coast of Sicily) in the sixth century B.C. He had no connection with Thurii (in Bruttium, southern Italy), which was founded a century later.

[135]A temple to public trust (*fides publica*) was erected on the Capitol in 254 B.C.

Roman Stories

6. 1. When King Ptolemy appointed the Roman people as his son's guardian, the Senate sent Marcus Aemilius Lepidus, the one who was chief pontiff and held two consulships, to Alexandria to look after the boy.[136] This most distinguished and honorable man had shown integrity in serving the Republic in its political and religious affairs, and the Senate wanted him to carry out our responsibilities to these foreigners, so that nobody would feel they had placed their trust in our state without good reason. By its kind insistence, the Senate protected the royal cradle and honored it, so the boy Ptolemy was left uncertain whether he should take more pride in the good fortune of his father or in the grandeur of his guardians.

6. 2. The following is another splendid example of the good faith of the Romans. An enormous Carthaginian fleet had been defeated off Sicily, and its captains were disillusioned and started planning to ask for peace.[137] Hamilcar was one of them, and he said he would not dare to go to the consuls, because they might put him in chains, just as the Carthaginians themselves had done to the consul Cornelius Asina.[138] But Hanno was a better judge of Roman character, and he felt there was no reason to fear any such thing, so he went off with complete confidence to his meeting with the Romans. While Hanno was discussing the ending of the war with them, a military tribune told him that what happened to Cornelius could happen to him and it would serve him right. But both of the consuls ordered the tribune to be quiet and said, "Hanno, the good faith of our state frees you from that fear." The consuls became famous because they got an opportunity to capture an important enemy leader, but they became much more famous for refusing to do so.

6. 3. The Conscript Fathers showed equally good faith toward the same enemies in honoring the rights of envoys. During the consulship of Marcus Aemilius Lepidus and Gaius Flaminius,[139] the senators made special arrangements through the fetial priests[140] and ordered the praetor Marcus Claudius to hand Lucius Minucius and Lucius Manlius over to the Carthaginian envoys,[141] because the two men had physically abused these envoys. On this occasion, the Senate considered its own character rather than the character of the people it was doing this for.

6. 4. Scipio Africanus followed the Senate's example when a ship carrying a large number of illustrious Carthaginian men fell into his hands. He sent the ship

---

[136]Marcus Aemilius Lepidus (cos, 187 B.C.) stayed in Egypt from 201 to 199 B.C. Ptolemy V Epiphanes (king of Egypt, 221–180 B.C.) made the Roman people the guardian of the future king Ptolemy VI Philometor.

[137]The Carthaginian navy, under Hanno the Elder and Hamilcar, was badly defeated off Sicily in 256 B.C.

[138]Consul Gnaeus Cornelius Scipio Asina had been tricked and captured by the Carthaginians in 260 B.C.

[139]Marcus Aemilius Lepidus and Gaius Flaminius were consuls in 187 B.C.

[140]The fetial priests (*fetiales*) were responsible for the religious rituals involved in diplomacy. For example, they pronounced the ritual declaration of war.

[141]Marcus Claudius Marcellus (cos, 183 B.C.) had been a praetor in the previous year (188 B.C.).

away without harming it because the Carthaginians claimed they had been sent to him as envoys, though it was clear that they had falsely claimed the title of envoys simply to evade the present danger.[142] But Africanus preferred to have them cheat a Roman general's good faith rather than have people believe it was appealed to in vain.

6. 5. Let me also describe a deed of the Senate that cannot be omitted under any circumstances. Envoys were sent by the city of Apollonia to Rome, but a dispute arose, and two former aediles, Quintus Fabius and Gnaeus Apronius, physically abused the envoys.[143] When the Senate discovered this, it immediately got the fetial priests to surrender those men to the envoys. It also ordered a quaestor to accompany the envoys to Brundisium in case the relatives of the men being handed over might harm the envoys in some way.[144] Who would say that our Senate house was just a gathering of human beings rather than a temple of Good Faith? Our state has always generously displayed good faith, and it has likewise found it consistently displayed in the hearts of our allies.

Foreign Stories

6. ext. 1. After the tragic loss in Spain of the two Scipio brothers and two armies of Roman citizens,[145] the people of Saguntum were forced by the victorious army of Hannibal to withdraw inside the walls of their city.[146] When they were unable to ward off the Carthaginian attacks any longer, they gathered into the Forum the possessions that each person loved the most, put firewood around them, and set them alight. Then, rather than betray their alliance with us, they threw themselves onto this funeral pyre of their state and their society. I would be sure that the goddess Good Faith herself, who keeps a close watch on human affairs, must have looked very sad on that occasion, when she saw that those who honored her so steadfastly were doomed to such a tragic end by the unfair dictates of Fortune.

6. ext. 2. By maintaining their loyalty in the same way, the people of Petelia earned the same glorious honor.[147] Because they refused to betray our friendship, they were besieged by Hannibal, so they sent envoys to the Senate begging for help. But because of our recent defeat at Cannae, the Senate was unable to come to their aid.[148] It gave them permission to do whatever seemed most likely to ensure their survival, so they were free to embrace the friendship of the Carthaginians. Instead, they removed from their city the women and all those who were unsuited

---

[142]This incident occurred in 203 B.C. The ship was in fact carrying envoys back to Carthage.

[143]Quintus Fabius and Gnaeus Apronius had been aediles in 267 B.C. They insulted the envoys from Apollonia (a city on the east coast of the Adriatic) in 266 B.C.

[144]Brundisium (in Calabria, southern Italy) was the main harbor for travel eastward.

[145]The brothers Gnaeus Cornelius Scipio Calvus (cos, 222 B.C.) and Publius Cornelius Scipio (cos, 218 B.C.) died fighting in Spain in 211 B.C.

[146]Saguntum (on the east coast of Spain) was a Roman ally, but Hannibal captured it in 219 B.C. (not 211 B.C.—Valerius has mixed up the dates).

[147]Petelia was in Bruttium (southern Italy).

[148]Hannibal defeated the Romans at Cannae (in Apulia, southern Italy) in 216 B.C.

for battle because of their age, so that those in arms could endure the food shortage for a longer time. They defiantly manned their walls, and their entire state perished rather than in any way abandoning the respect they had for their alliance with Rome. So it was Hannibal's bad luck that he got to capture the loyal grave of Petelia rather than Petelia itself.[149]

Chapter 7. The Loyalty of Wives to Their Husbands

Roman Stories

7. 1. We must also touch on the loyalty of wives. Aemilia Tertia[150] was the wife of Scipio Africanus and the mother of Cornelia, who was herself the mother of the Gracchus brothers.[151] Aemilia Tertia was so affable and tolerant that she pretended not to notice when she learned that her husband had fallen for a young female slave of hers. She did not want a woman like herself to accuse a great man like Africanus, the conqueror of the world, of being unable to control his desires. She was so free of vindictiveness that when Africanus died she freed the slave and gave her in marriage to a freedman of hers.[152]

7. 2. When the triumvirs put Quintus Lucretius on their death list,[153] his wife, Turia, hid him between the ceiling and the roof over her bedroom, letting just one young female slave in on the secret. At great personal risk, Turia kept him safe from imminent death. Whereas other men on the death list went through great physical and mental agonies and barely escaped to foreign and hostile regions, her exceptional loyalty allowed him to stay safe in the bedroom and bosom of his wife.

7. 3. Sulpicia was strictly guarded by her mother, Julia, to prevent her from following her husband, Lentulus Cruscellio, to Sicily after the triumvirs had put him on their death list.[154] In spite of this, Sulpicia put on the clothes of a slave, secretly escaped with two female slaves and as many male slaves, and made her way to him. She allowed herself to be outlawed so that she could stay loyal to her husband, who had been outlawed.

---

[149]Petelia fell to Hannibal in 215 B.C.

[150]Aemilia Tertia was the youngest daughter of Lucius Aemilius Paullus (cos, 216 B.C.).

[151]Cornelia (see 4:2,3; 4:4,pref.; and 4:6,1) married Tiberius Sempronius Gracchus (cos, 177 B.C.). Her sons (the Gracchus brothers) were Tiberius Sempronius Gracchus (tribune of the plebs, 133 B.C.) and Gaius Sempronius Gracchus (tribune of the plebs, 123 B.C.).

[152]Scipio Africanus died at the end of 184 B.C.

[153]Quintus Lucretius Vespillo was a prefect in the Republican navy during 49 and 48 B.C. The triumvirs massacred their political opponents in 43 and 42 B.C.

[154]Lucius Cornelius Lentulus Cruscellio (praetor, 38 B.C.) escaped to Sicily in 42 B.C.

Chapter 8. The Loyalty of Slaves

Preface

It remains for me to record the loyalty of slaves toward their masters. Their loyalty is unexpected but all the more admirable for that very reason.

Roman Stories

8. 1. Marcus Antonius, the most famous public speaker in the days of our ancestors, was accused of sexual misconduct.[155] During the trial, his prosecutors persisted in demanding his slave for interrogation, because they claimed that this slave had carried a lamp for Antonius as he went to his sexual encounters. The slave was even then too young to have a beard, and as he was standing among the public, he saw that this line of argument would lead to his being tortured, but he did not try to evade torture.[156] In fact, when they got home, Antonius was deeply disturbed and troubled because of this, but the slave without prompting urged Antonius to hand him over to the jurymen to be tortured, assuring him that no word would escape from his mouth that would harm Antonius' case. And the slave showed extraordinary endurance in keeping his promise: he was torn to pieces with constant floggings, put on the rack, and burned with red-hot sheets of iron, but he kept his accused master safe and completely undermined the force of the prosecution's arguments. Fortune could justifiably be criticized for placing such a brave and loyal spirit in the body of a slave.

8. 2. Unluckily for the consul Gaius Marius, he was present when Praeneste tragically fell to its besiegers.[157] He had tried in vain to escape through a hidden tunnel, and then he made a suicide pact with Telesinus, but Telesinus only wounded him lightly with his sword. Marius' slave finished him off by running him through with a sword, because he wanted Marius to evade the cruelty of Sulla.[158] The slave realized, however, that there would have been great rewards in store for him if he handed Marius over to the victors alive.[159] By his timely service, this slave showed no less loyalty than those who protected the lives of their masters, because in this particular instance, it was kinder to kill Gaius Marius off than to keep him alive.

8. 3. The story that follows is equally splendid. To avoid falling into the hands of his enemies, Gaius Gracchus bared his neck so that his slave Philocrates could

---

[155]Marcus Antonius (cos, 99 B.C.) was accused of having sex with a vestal virgin in 113 B.C. (see 3:7,9).

[156]It was customary to interrogate slaves under torture.

[157]Gaius Marius (junior) was consul in 82 B.C. He made a last stand against Sulla in Praeneste. Pontius Telesinus was a friend of Marius (junior). Praeneste (modern Palestrina) was in Latium.

[158]Sulla marched on Rome and massacred his political enemies in 82 B.C.

[159]The slave would have won his freedom (but this was not definite—see 6:5,7).

behead him.[160] After Philocrates had beheaded him with one quick blow, he took the sword dripping with his master's blood and drove it through his own chest. Some authors say that the slave was called Euporus, but I am not going to argue about his name; what amazes me is the power of this slave's loyalty. If the young nobleman had imitated the slave's determination, he would have escaped imminent execution by his own merits rather than by those of his slave. As a result of Gracchus' behavior, the body of Philocrates was more honored in the grave than that of Gracchus.

8. 4. The next story tells of a different nobleman who was mad in a different way, but it tells of the same kind of loyalty. Pindarus had recently been freed by Gaius Cassius, and when Cassius was defeated at the battle of Philippi, Pindarus followed his former master's orders, killed him, and saved him from the mockery of his enemies.[161] Then Pindarus removed himself from the sight of his fellow men by taking his own life and did it in such a way that his dead body could not be found.

Which of the gods punished the dreadful crime of Cassius by paralyzing his wicked hand, which had burned with desire to kill the father of our country? Why did Cassius have to go down trembling before the knees of Pindarus so that he could evade the punishment he deserved for the assassination of our head of state, a punishment that our holy victory had decreed? It was you, of course, divine Caesar;[162] you got the revenge you deserved for your sacred wounds, by forcing the villain who betrayed you to beg for help from such a low quarter. Cassius was afflicted with such mental torment that he did not wish to stay alive, but he did not have the courage to end his life by his own hand.

8. 5. To these disasters I shall add the story of Lucius Plotius Plancus, the brother of the future consul and censor, Munatius Plancus.[163] When the triumvirs put Plotius on their death list, he hid in the region around Salernum.[164] But he had a refined lifestyle, and the smell of his perfume revealed the hiding place that could have saved his life. That was the clue that gave him away to the men who were hunting down wretched victims; with great care they sniffed out the secret room to which he had fled. These men had caught his slaves, while Plotius was still in hiding, and tortured them severely for a long time, but the slaves kept saying that they did not know where their master was. Plancus could not bear to have such loyal and exceptionally good slaves tortured any longer, so he came out into the open and offered his throat to the soldiers' swords. This competition in doing good to each other makes it difficult to decide whether the master was more worthy of having slaves who showed such unshakeable loyalty, or the slaves more

[160]Gaius Sempronius Gracchus (tribune of the plebs, 123 B.C.) perished in the general massacre of his supporters in 121 B.C.

[161]Gaius Cassius Longinus (the tyrannicide) committed suicide after being defeated at the battle of Philippi in 42 B.C.

[162]Caesar had been declared a god earlier in 42 B.C.

[163]Lucius Plotius Plancus (praetor, 43 B.C.) was murdered by order of the triumvirs at the end of 43 B.C. His brother, Lucius Munatius Plancus (cos, 42 B.C.), sided with the winners and had a successful political career.

[164]Salernum (modern Salerno) was on the coast of Campania.

worthy of having a master who was so fair and kind that he had to free them from the savagery of their interrogators.

8. 6. What extraordinary loyalty a slave of Urbinius Panapio possessed! When Panapio was put on the death list, some of his household slaves betrayed their master. The soldiers, receiving this information, came to his country house at Reate to kill him.[165] When his loyal slave discovered this, he exchanged clothes with him, and even exchanged rings, and secretly let Panapio out by a back door. The slave went to his master's bedroom, lay on the bed, and allowed himself to be killed as if he were Panapio.

The story of this deed may be a short one, but it offers lots of material for praise. If somebody imagines the soldiers bursting in suddenly, the locks of the door being smashed, their threatening voices, fierce looks, and gleaming swords, he will judge this matter properly, and he will realize that although you can quickly tell how one man was willing to die for another, it is not so easy for such a thing to happen. Panapio acknowledged how much he owed his slave by erecting an impressive monument to him and by testifying to his slave's loyalty in a grateful inscription.

8. 7. I would be satisfied with these stories on this topic, except that my admiration for the following deed forces me to tell one more story. When the triumvirs put Antius Restio on their death list, he saw that all his household slaves were preoccupied with looting and robbing, so he hid his escape as best he could and got away from his house in the middle of the night. There was one slave that he had punished by putting him in chains and branding him permanently with letters that completely disfigured his face. This slave noticed his secret escape with curiosity, followed his zigzagging tracks with well-meaning interest, crept up to him, and became his willing comrade. By this strange and dangerous act of kindness, the slave had reached the highest level of unexpected loyalty. The slaves who had enjoyed a happier lot in the home were focused on gain; this slave was only a shadow of himself after all his tortures, but he felt that the safety of the man who had punished him so brutally was his greatest priority. It would have been quite enough for him to have stopped being angry with his master, but he actually felt kindness toward him.

But the slave's goodwill did not end with this; he also used extraordinary cunning in saving his master's life. When he discovered that the soldiers, who were eager for blood, were catching up with them, he got his master out of the way. Then he built a funeral pyre, caught a poor old man, killed him, and put his body on the pyre. When the soldiers asked the slave where Antius was, he pointed to the pyre and said that his master was burning there as a punishment for his cruelty to him. Since his statement sounded plausible, they believed him. And that is how Antius managed to reach safety.

---

[165]The triumvirs put Urbinius Panapio on their death list in 43 B.C. Reate was a city in the Sabine region (central Italy).

Chapter 9. Changes in Character or Fortune

Preface

It can greatly increase people's spirit and confidence, and lessen their anxiety, when they see changes in the characters or fortunes of famous men, whether we consider our own circumstances or the personalities of those around us. If we consider the fortunes of others, we shall see that they can end up famous after starting in circumstances that are low and despised. So, is there any reason why we should not always think better of ourselves? We should remember that it is silly to condemn ourselves in advance to perpetual unhappiness, and to keep turning our uncertain hopes into certain despair, because even if our hopes are uncertain, it is always right to cherish them.

Roman Stories

9. 1. When he was a very young man, it was thought that Manlius Torquatus was mentally dull and obtuse.[166] His father, Lucius Capitolinus, was a very distinguished man,[167] and since the boy seemed useless for serving his home or the Republic, Capitolinus sent him off to the countryside to keep him busy with agricultural labor. But later when Capitolinus was put on trial, Torquatus freed him from the risk of being convicted;[168] when his own son was victorious in battle, Torquatus beheaded him with an axe because he had engaged with the enemy against his orders;[169] and Torquatus regaled our country with a splendid triumph after we had been exhausted by the Latin rebellions.[170] I suspect that fortune hid his youth in a cloud of contempt, so that the glory of his old age would shine out all the more splendidly.

9. 2. The gods wanted Scipio Africanus to be born so that people could conveniently see every aspect of virtue displayed in one man. But it is said that he spent the first years of his adolescence in loose living, and although those years were far from any suspicion of decadence, they were still too voluptuous for the trophies he won from the Carthaginians, or for his subjugation and conquest of Carthage.[171]

9. 3. In the days of the Second Punic War, Gaius Valerius Flaccus started off as a young man who was ruining himself with his decadent lifestyle. But the chief pontiff, Publius Licinius,[172] appointed him as a flamen to make it easier for him to give

---

[166]The young man was Titus Manlius Imperiosus Torquatus (cos, 347 B.C.).

[167]His father was Lucius Manlius Capitolinus Imperiosus (dictator, 363 B.C.).

[168]Torquatus defended his father in 362 B.C. (see 5:4,3).

[169]Torquatus put his own son to death in 340 B.C. (see 2:7,6).

[170]Torquatus celebrated his triumph over the Latins in 340 B.C.

[171]Scipio Africanus was a soldier by the age of seventeen (in 218 B.C.) and defeated Carthage in 202 B.C.

[172]Publius Licinius Crassus Dives (cos, 205 B.C.) was chief pontiff from 212 B.C. until his death in 183 B.C.

up his vices.[173] Valerius turned his mind to rituals and ceremonies and used religion to guide himself toward sober habits. He had earlier been a notorious example of decadent living, but later he turned out to be a model of propriety and holiness.

9. 4. Nobody was more disgraceful in his youth than Quintus Fabius Maximus, who won the title of Allobrogicus for himself and his descendants through his victory over the Gauls.[174] And in that era, our state had nobody more distinguished and respectable than him in his old age.

9. 5. Is anybody unaware that Quintus Catulus reached the highest level of prestige in a period when there was an exceptional number of very famous men? But if we were to turn back to his early days, we would find a great deal of self-indulgence and frivolity. But this did not prevent him from becoming the leading citizen of our country, from displaying his name on the pediment of the Capitol temple, or from courageously putting an end to the civil war that was developing with great momentum.[175]

9. 6. Up until the time he was elected quaestor, Sulla led a life that was corrupted with sexual indulgence, drinking, and an addiction to the theater. It is said that the consul Marius was annoyed that such a decadent quaestor was allotted to him while he had to wage a very difficult war in Africa.[176] But it was as if Sulla smashed and cast aside the barriers of vice that kept him back. Through his courage, he chained the hands of Jugurtha, crushed Mithridates, calmed the waves of the Social War, ended the tyranny of Cinna, and forced the man who had once disdained to have him as quaestor in Africa to flee to that very province as an outlaw and an exile.[177]

If one wished to consider these completely different and contradictory elements, and compare them carefully, one would think that there were two men in this one Sulla, a disgraceful young man and a mature adult whom I would have called brave, except that he himself preferred to be called fortunate.[178]

9. 7. By virtue of their repentance, these noblemen were brought to respect their true nature, but I shall now tell of individuals who dared to entertain hopes that were too high for people like them. Titus Aufidius controlled a tiny portion of the tax contract for Asia, but later he controlled all of Asia as its governor.[179]

[173]Gaius Valerius Flaccus was made the flamen (priest) of Jupiter in 209 B.C. He eventually became a praetor (in 183 B.C.).

[174]Quintus Fabius Maximus Allobrogicus defeated the Allobroges (in eastern Gaul) when he was consul in 121 B.C.

[175]When he was consul in 78 B.C., Quintus Lutatius Catulus restored the temple of Jupiter on the Capitol. He also put down a rebellion in 77 B.C. (see 2:8,7).

[176]Sulla was Marius' quaestor in Africa in 107 B.C.

[177]Sulla captured King Jugurtha of Numidia (in 105 B.C.); defeated Mithridates VI of Pontus (in 84 B.C.); and fought in the Social War against the Italians (90–89 B.C.). Lucius Cornelius Cinna (cos, 87 B.C.) was murdered by his own troops in 84 B.C., but Sulla did outlaw Marius in 88 B.C., and Marius had to flee to Africa.

[178]Sulla adopted the title of "Fortunate" (*Felix*) in 82 B.C. (see 6:4,4).

[179]Titus Aufidius (praetor, 67 B.C.) was an equestrian tax collector who left the world of business, joined the landed aristocracy, and became governor of Asia in 66 B.C. Collecting taxes in Asia was a very lucrative business.

And our allies did not resent obeying his fasces,[180] though they had seen him groveling before the tribunals of other governors. In fact, he behaved with great integrity and splendor. In this way he demonstrated that his former way of earning a living was to be blamed on Fortune whereas his present rise in status was to be attributed to his own character.

9. 8. Publius Rupilius did not even possess a tax contract in Sicily; he actually worked for tax contractors. He also had to save himself from utter destitution by offering his services to our allies.[181] But eventually all the Sicilians had to obey his laws when he was consul, and he put an end to their very difficult war against the pirates and runaway slaves.[182] I imagine that the harbors themselves (if mute objects could have any feelings) must have been amazed at the great changes in the status of this man: they had once observed him striving to make a daily living, and now they saw the same man making laws and commanding navies and armies.

9. 9. To this story of great advancement, I shall add a greater one. When Pompeius Strabo, the father of Pompey the Great, captured Asculum, he displayed Publius Ventidius, then a very young man, before the eyes of the people in his triumph.[183]

This is the Ventidius who later held a triumph in Rome over the Parthians, and through his triumph over the Parthians, he triumphed over the ghost of Crassus, whose body lay tragically on enemy soil. So the former captive who had been terrified by our prison now filled the Capitol with joyful crowds.[184]

Another extraordinary achievement of the same Ventidius is that he was elected praetor and consul in the same year.[185]

9. 10. Let us now consider the erratic nature of people's luck. Lucius Lentulus, a former consul, was ruined when he was convicted under the Caecilian law against misgovernment,[186] but later he was elected censor along with Lucius Censorinus.[187] Fortune tossed him from glory to disgrace and back again, turning his consulship into a conviction and his conviction into a censorship. She did not allow him to take pleasure in continual benefits or to complain at unending misfortunes.

---

[180]The fasces were bundles of sticks symbolizing the power of the state. They were carried before consuls, praetors, and governors.

[181]The Sicilians were Roman "allies."

[182]When Publius Rupilius was consul in 132 B.C. he finished off the First Slave War in Sicily (see 2:7,3 and 9:12,ext.1).

[183]Gnaeus Pompeius Strabo captured the Italian rebel city of Asculum (in Picenum, eastern Italy) when he was consul in 89 B.C.

[184]Publius Ventidius Bassus (cos, 43 B.C.) celebrated a triumph over the Parthians in 38 B.C. Marcus Licinius Crassus Dives (cos, 70 B.C.) had been defeated and killed by the Parthians in 53 B.C.

[185]Ventidius Bassus was a praetor in 43 B.C. and consul at the end of that year.

[186]Lucius Cornelius Lentulus Lupus (cos, 156 B.C.) was convicted in 154 B.C. The Caecilian law had just been passed in that year.

[187]Lentulus was a censor in 147 B.C. with Lucius Marcius Censorinus.

9. 11. Fortune also wanted to show her power in the case of Gnaeus Cornelius Scipio Asina. When he was consul, he was captured by the Carthaginians off the Lipari Islands and lost everything in accordance with the rules of war.[188] But then Fortune put on a happier face and helped him to win everything back, and he was even elected consul for a second time.[189] Who would have believed that he could have gone from the twelve axes of a consul to the chains of the Carthaginians?[190] And then again, who would have thought that he could have gone from Carthaginian chains to the emblems of the highest public office? But he did indeed change from consul to captive, and from captive to consul.

9. 12. Well, didn't his great sums of money make Crassus a byword for wealth? But later the same man's poverty branded him with the disgrace of bankruptcy, and his goods were sold off by his creditors since he could not pay them in cash. So he took it as a bitter insult when he walked around in poverty and was greeted as "Rich Man" by those who met him.[191]

9. 13. Quintus Caepio outdoes Crassus in the bitterness of his misfortunes. The splendor of his praetorship, the glory of his triumph, the honor of his consulship, and his priesthood as chief pontiff led to his being called the patron of the Senate.[192] But he ended his life in chains in the state prison, his body was torn to pieces by the grim hands of the executioner, and as it lay there on the Gemonian Steps, the entire Roman Forum gazed on it with horror.[193]

9. 14. Marius was constantly wrestling with Fortune, but he bravely endured all her attacks with his physical and mental stamina. When he was judged unworthy of political office at Arpinum,[194] he had the nerve to seek the quaestorship at Rome. After enduring many electoral defeats, he forced his way into the Senate house; he didn't just arrive there.[195] When he sought election as tribune and aedile, he experienced the same electoral humiliation in the Campus Martius, and when he was a candidate for the praetorship, he was the very last one to be elected, and he did not even keep this position without facing problems.[196] He was accused of electoral

---

[188]Gnaeus Cornelius Scipio Asina was consul in 260 B.C. when he was captured by the Carthaginians (see 6:6,2). The Lipari Islands were north of Sicily.

[189]Scipio Asina was consul again in 254 B.C.

[190]A consul was always accompanied by twelve lictors (attendants) carrying the fasces (a bundle of sticks symbolizing the power of the state). Each bundle had an axe attached to it, symbolizing the power to put a man to death.

[191]Publius Licinius Crassus Dives (cos, 205 B.C.) was the first member of his family to get the nickname "Rich Man" (*Dives*), but he went bankrupt.

[192]Quintus Servilius Caepio (cos, 106 B.C.) held all these offices except chief pontiff.

[193]Caepio was exiled (see 4:7,3), not executed, in 103 B.C. The bodies of executed criminals were dumped on the Gemonian Steps, which led down from the Capitol to the prison.

[194]Marius came from Arpinum, a small town in Latium.

[195]Roman aristocrats took it for granted that they would end up in the Senate; Marius was an outsider.

[196]Elections were held in the Campus Martius in Rome. Marius was a praetor in 115 B.C. but he was prosecuted for bribery that year.

bribery, and he only barely and with great difficulty managed to win an acquittal from the jury.

From that Marius, who was humiliated in Arpinum, dishonored in Rome, and rejected as a candidate, emerged the Marius who subdued Africa, who marched King Jugurtha before his chariot, who destroyed the armies of the Teutons and Cimbrians.[197] His two sets of trophies are still to be seen in our city; his seven consulships can still be read in our public records.[198] It was his destiny to be elected consul after enduring exile, and to publish a death list after being on one himself.[199] What could be more unreliable or more erratic than the status of this man? If you were to include him among the wretched, he would turn out to be the most wretched of all; if you were to include him among the fortunate, he would turn out to be the most fortunate of all.

9. 15. The virtuous qualities of Caesar paved a path to heaven for him, but while he was still a very young man and a private citizen, he traveled to Asia. He was intercepted by seafaring bandits near the island of Pharmacussa, and he bought his freedom for 50 talents.[200] Fortune wanted the most glorious star of our world to be paid for with this tiny sum of money in a pirate ship. So why should we make any further complaints against her, since she did not even spare those who were just as divine as she was? But his divine power avenged his ill-treatment: he captured the pirates immediately after and crucified them.[201]

Foreign Stories

9. ext. 1. We have told our own stories with eager attention: now let us tell some foreign stories in a more relaxed spirit. When Polemo was a young man in Athens, he abandoned himself to decadent living, and he delighted not only in its temptations but even in his own bad reputation. He got up from a party once, not only after sunset but even after sunrise, and as he was going back home, he noticed that the door of the philosopher Xenocrates was open.[202] Weighed down with drink, dripping with perfume, with garlands tied around his head, and wearing see-through clothes, he entered that man's schoolroom, which was packed with a crowd of learned men. This disgraceful entrance was not enough for Polemo; he sat there to belittle the renowned eloquence and brilliant teachings of Xenocrates with his drunken mockery.

---

[197]Marius defeated King Jugurtha of Numidia in 105 B.C., the Teutons (from northern Germany) in 102 B.C., and the Cimbrians (from Denmark) in 101 B.C.

[198]Marius celebrated a triumph over Jugurtha in 105 B.C. and a double triumph over the Teutons and Cimbrians in 101 B.C. He held seven consulships between 107 and 86 B.C.

[199]Marius was exiled in 88 B.C. and became consul in 86 B.C. He was put on Sulla's death list in 88 B.C. but returned to massacre his opponents in 87 B.C.

[200]Caesar was kidnapped in 75 B.C. Pharmacussa was an island off the west coast of Asia Minor.

[201]Caesar crucified the pirates in 74 B.C.

[202]Xenocrates was the head of Plato's Academy from 339 to 314 B.C.

They all became indignant, as was only natural, but the expression on Xenocrates' face did not change. He gave up the theme he was discussing and began to speak about restraint and self-control. His dignified words forced Polemo to come back to his senses. First Polemo took the garland off his head and threw it away; shortly afterward, he put his arm back inside his cloak; as time went on, he wiped the smirk of a partygoer off his face; and eventually he shook off his decadent attitude altogether. He was cured by the saving medicine of this one speech, and from being a disgraceful debauchee, he turned into a great philosopher. His mind wandered into vice for a short while; it did not make its permanent home there.[203]

9. ext. 2. I feel awkward about mentioning Themistocles' youth when I see that his father punished him by disowning him, or that his mother was forced to end her life by hanging herself because of her son's disgraceful behavior. And yet he later became the most famous man of the Greek nation, and he stood between Europe and Asia as a symbol of their hope and despair: for Greece he was the champion of her survival, for Asia he was a promise of victory.[204]

9. ext. 3. When Cimon was a child, everyone thought he was a fool; but when he grew up, the Athenians came to realize how beneficial his government was. He forced them to admit that they themselves had been guilty of folly in believing that he was a fool.[205]

9. ext. 4. In the case of Alcibiades, it was as if two fortunes shared him. The first one granted him extraordinary nobility, abundant riches, outstanding good looks, the enthusiastic support of his fellow citizens, the highest public offices, exceptional political influence, and a brilliant restless mind. The other one afflicted him with a legal conviction, exile, the sale of his property, poverty, the hatred of his country, and a violent death. Neither his good fortune nor his bad fortune was present throughout, but they were changeable and intertwined, like the current in a strait.[206]

9. ext. 5. Polycrates, the tyrant of Samos, was renowned for his excessive wealth, and the brilliance of his lifestyle inspired envy, not without reason.[207] Polycrates was able to achieve all his goals in a effortless manner; if he hoped for something, he got exactly what his heart desired; as soon as he made a prayer for something, he had to thank the gods for fulfilling it: for Polycrates, wanting something and being able to get it were identical. His expression changed only once, when he was jolted by a small bump of sorrow. This was when he deliberately threw his favorite ring into the sea so that he would not be completely inexperienced in misfortune. But

---

[203]Polemo became the head of Plato's Academy after Xenocrates died.

[204]Themistocles defeated the Persians at Salamis in 480 B.C. He was exiled in 472 B.C. and went to live in Persia in 464 B.C. The Greeks were afraid that Themistocles might conquer Greece for the Persians (see 5:3,ext.3 and 5:6,ext.3).

[205]Cimon dominated Athenian politics from 476 B.C. until his exile in 461 B.C.

[206]The Athenians had great hopes for Alcibiades, but he was very erratic. He went into exile in 415 B.C. and collaborated with the Spartans, who were at war with Athens. He returned briefly to Athens in 407 B.C. and was murdered by the Persians in 404 B.C. (see 1:7,ext.9).

[207]Polycrates was tyrant of Samos from 535 to 521 B.C.

he got it back at once, because someone caught a fish that had swallowed the ring. His happiness kept on its straight course of prosperity with all its sails spread out to the wind.

But Orontes, the governor of King Darius, crucified Polycrates on the highest peak of Mount Mycale,[208] and there the people of Samos could see his rotting limbs, his body covered with festering blood, and his decaying left hand, which had worn the ring that Neptune sent back to him through the fisherman. The people of Samos had been oppressed by the tyranny of Polycrates for a long time, so they gazed at this sight with free and happy eyes.

9. ext. 6. Dionysius inherited from his father a tyrannical regime over Syracuse and almost all of Sicily.[209] He had been the possessor of great riches, the commander of armies, the admiral of navies, and the master of cavalries, but in his later poverty, he had to teach the alphabet to little boys in Corinth. At the same time, because of the great changes in his life, he warned the grownups not to place too much trust in fortune, since he himself had changed from a tyrant to a schoolteacher.

9. ext. 7. The next story is that of King Syphax, who experienced similar injustice at the hands of Fortune.[210] On one side of him stood Scipio on behalf of Rome, and on the other stood Hasdrubal on behalf of Carthage, and both these men had come before his household gods to ask him to be their ally.[211] Syphax had reached such distinction that he could almost determine which of these very powerful nations would win. But after a short period of time had elapsed, he was put in chains and dragged off by the legate Laelius to his general, Scipio. Syphax had once sat on a royal throne and arrogantly accepted Scipio's handshake; now he humbly fell before his knees.[212]

What we call people's wealth and power are in fact very short-lived and fragile things, like a child's toys. They come to us suddenly, and they quickly disappear; they don't put down any roots, and they remain in no place and by no person; they are blown hither and thither by the unreliable gusts of fortune; they raise people on high, then they unexpectedly turn around, abandon them, and drown them miserably in a sea of disasters. So they should not be thought of or described as good things; by the bitterness of the evils they inflict on us, they double our desire for them, and in order to do this. . . .[213]

---

[208]Darius I made himself king of Persia in 521 B.C. Many supporters of the previous king were put to death, including Polycrates. Mount Mycale was on the west coast of Asia Minor, facing the island of Samos.

[209]Dionysius II, tyrant of Syracuse, was deposed in 344 B.C., and he spent the rest of his life in exile in Corinth.

[210]Syphax was king of western Numidia (in north Africa).

[211]In 206 B.C., Scipio Africanus and Hasdrubal, son of Gisgo, arrived in Numidia at the same time to win Syphax over. Scipio convinced him to join the Roman side.

[212]Syphax changed sides and joined the Carthaginians in 204 B.C. Gaius Laelius (cos, 190 B.C.) was a legate under Scipio Africanus and captured Syphax in 203 B.C.

[213]The end of Book 6 is missing.

BOOK SEVEN

Chapter 1. Good Fortune

Preface

We have told several stories about the fickleness of Fortune, but very few stories can be told about her being consistently well disposed. So it is clear that she is glad to inflict misfortunes but reluctant to bestow good fortune. But when that goddess forces herself to put aside her malicious nature, she piles up goods that are not only great and numerous but also permanent.

Roman Stories

1. 1. Let us see how she guided Quintus Metellus along through various stages of preferential treatment, from the first day he was born right up to the final time of his death. She never ceased to indulge him until he reached the highest peak of a happy life. She wanted him to be born in a city that ruled the world; she gave him the most noble parents; to this she added the rarest intellectual gifts and the physical strength to endure hardship; she found him a wife who was remarkable for her modesty and fecundity; she lavished on him the honor of a consul, the power of a general, and the glory of a splendid triumph;[1] she arranged that within the same period of time, he could see three of his sons consuls (and one of them was even a censor and celebrated a triumph), and the fourth son a praetor; and she enabled him to marry off his three daughters and hold their children in his arms.[2]

So many births, so many cradles, so many adult togas, so many marriage torches; a great abundance of public offices, military commands, and other causes for celebration; meanwhile, there was no funeral, no lamentation, no cause for sorrow. If you consider heaven itself, you will hardly find such circumstances there, since we hear the greatest poets asserting that the gods feel grief and sorrow in their hearts. His end was in keeping with the course of his life: Metellus lived to a ripe old age and ended with the gentlest kind of death among the kisses and embraces of those who were dearest to him; his sons and his sons-in-law carried his body through the city on their shoulders and placed him on his funeral pyre.

1. 2. His good fortune is famous; that of the next man is less well known but was rated above the splendor of the gods. Gyges was conceited about his kingdom

---

[1]Quintus Caecilius Metellus Macedonicus celebrated his triumph over the Macedonians in 146 B.C. and was consul in 143 B.C.

[2]Metellus died in 115 B.C. His eldest son, Quintus Caecilius Metellus Balearicus (cos, 123 B.C.), had celebrated a triumph over the Balearic Islands and had been a censor. All four sons became consuls eventually, and the daughters married into powerful political families.

of Lydia,[3] which abounded in riches and military power, so he came to Pythian Apollo to ask whether any mortal was more fortunate than he.[4] The god, speaking out from the hidden cave of his shrine, put Aglaus of Psophis ahead of him.[5] Aglaus was the poorest man in Arcadia, he was by then quite an old man, and he had never gone beyond the boundaries of his small property, being content with the produce of his little farm. The clairvoyance of Apollo's oracle did, of course, define the real goal of a happy life rather than an illusory goal. This explains the god's reply when Gyges insolently boasted of his fortune's splendor. The god commended a carefree cottage full of laughter rather than a grim court full of cares and worries, a small plot of land without any fear rather than the most fertile fields of Lydia filled with anxiety, one or two pairs of oxen that were easy to look after rather than armies and weapons and a cavalry that were a great burden and devoured money, and a small barn stocked with basic necessities that nobody would envy too much rather than treasures that were subject to treachery and greed from all sides. So, whereas Gyges wanted the god to support his silly notions, he learned instead where sound and lasting happiness lay.

Chapter 2. Wise Statements and Actions

Preface

Now I shall talk about the type of good fortune that depends entirely on the state of one's mind; it is not something one can acquire through prayers, because it arises in hearts that are gifted with wisdom and shines forth in intelligent statements and actions.

Roman Stories

2. 1. We have all heard how Appius Claudius would often say that it was better for the Roman people to be kept busy with drudgery than for them to enjoy free time.[6] He was not unaware how pleasant it is to be left in peace, but he realized that powerful empires had to be kept alert through constant activity if they were to attain excellence, and that they would collapse into decay if they were too quiet. And although "drudgery" has an ugly name, it certainly kept the character of our state in top condition, whereas peace, which has such a pleasant name, splattered it with countless vices.

2. 2. Scipio Africanus always claimed it was disgraceful to say "I hadn't thought of that" in military situations. This was, of course, because he felt that one should

---

[3]Lydia was a country on the east coast of Asia Minor. Gyges was its king from 687 to 652 B.C.
[4]Pythian Apollo was the name given to Apollo at his oracle in Delphi (in northern Greece).
[5]Psophis was in Arcadia (in southern Greece).
[6]Appius Claudius Caecus (cos, 307 B.C.) was the famous censor of 312 B.C.

test and scrutinize a plan before carrying out actions that require the use of armed force. He was absolutely right: it is impossible to undo a mistake once the violence of Mars takes over.[7]

Scipio also used to say that one should not engage with an enemy unless a suitable occasion arises, or one is forced to do so. This was equally intelligent, because it is the height of madness to let slip an opportunity of a successful engagement, while to refrain from battle when forced into circumstances that absolutely require battle produces the inevitable result of such disastrous cowardice. People who make such mistakes do not know how to take advantage of Fortune's favor in the first case, or to stand up to her insults in the second.[8]

2. 3. Quintus Metellus made a statement in the Senate that was both serious and profound.[9] After the defeat of Carthage,[10] he declared that he was not sure whether that victory would do more harm than good to the Republic, because although it had benefited us by restoring peace, it had done quite a lot of harm by removing Hannibal. When Hannibal had been marching through Italy, the dormant courage of the Roman people had been aroused; now that they had been deprived of their bitter rival, it was to be feared that they would go back to sleep again. So as far as he was concerned, having our houses burned, our fields destroyed, and our treasury exhausted was no worse than having the vitality of our former strength dwindle away.

2. 4. What about the very wise behavior of Gaius Fimbria, a former consul?[11] He was appointed judge in the case of Marcus Lutatius Pinthia, an excellent Roman equestrian who had made a legal guarantee to the plaintiff, that he, Pinthia, was an honorable man.[12] But Fimbria refused to give judgment in this case, because he would ruin the reputation of this highly regarded man, if he judged against Pinthia, or else he would be swearing that Pinthia was an honorable man, and that would imply an infinity of virtues.

2. 5. That was a story of intelligence shown in the courtroom; the next one will be a story of intelligence shown in a military campaign. When the consul Papirius Cursor was attacking Aquilonia[13] and wanted to engage the enemy in battle, the priest in charge of the sacred chickens told him that the auspices were excellent, though the sacred birds were not in fact favorable.[14] Papirius found out

---

[7]Mars was the war god, the ferocious god who drove people to blind rage and violence. Minerva was responsible for the discipline and tactics of warfare.

[8]Scipio Africanus was consistently successful in Spain (210–206 B.C.) and Africa (204–201 B.C.).

[9]Quintus Caecilius Metellus was consul in 206 B.C.

[10]The war against Hannibal ended in 201 B.C.

[11]Gaius Flavius Fimbria had been consul in 104 B.C.

[12]This legal guarantee was known as a *sponsio*. It was guaranteed by a sum of money that was paid to the legal opponent if the *sponsio* was false.

[13]In 293 B.C. Lucius Papirius Cursor was consul and captured Aquilonia, a city in Samnium (central Italy).

[14]The Romans predicted the future from the eating patterns of the sacred chickens (see auspices in the Glossary).

about the priest's deception, but he felt confident because a good omen had been
given to himself and the army, so he started to do battle. But he stationed the lying
priest in front of the battle line so that if the gods were angry, they would have
someone on whom to wreak their vengeance.

By chance, or perhaps by the providence of some god in heaven, the first spear
sent from the opposing army was aimed at the chest of the priest in charge of the
sacred chickens, and it knocked him to the ground, lifeless. When the consul discovered this, he attacked Aquilonia with complete confidence and captured it.
That is how quickly he discerned how a wrong done to a general should be
punished, how an offense against religion should be expiated, and how victory
should be grasped. He played the part of a strict man, a religious consul, and an
energetic general, and in one flash of genius, he quickly estimated the limits of
fear, the appropriate type of punishment, and the path to hope.

2. 6. Now I shall move on to the actions of the Senate. When it was sending
the consuls Claudius Nero and Livius Salinator out against Hannibal,[15] it saw that
although they were equal in merit, they were bitter enemies and always disagree-
ing with each other. So it paid the greatest attention to reconciling them, because
otherwise the two consuls might carry out the Republic's affairs very ineffectually
on account of their private disagreement. Unless people get on well together
when they hold the same office, they become more eager to obstruct their colleagues' work than to do their own work. Indeed, when intransigent hatred gets in
the way as they march out, they are more reliably hostile to each other than either
of them is to the enemy army.

These same men were prosecuted at the rostra by Gnaeus Baebius, a tribune of
the plebs, because they had exercised their censorship too harshly.[16] But the Senate
decreed that the censors should be exempted from defending their case, because it
wanted their high office to be free from any fear of prosecution, since censors should
demand explanations from others, not give explanations of their own behavior.

The next story tells of equal wisdom on the part of the Senate. When Tiberius
Gracchus, a tribune of the plebs, dared to propose his land law, the Senate punished him with death.[17] The same Senate made the excellent decision that the land
commission should allot land to the people in individual grants, in accordance
with the law of Gracchus.[18] In this way it simultaneously removed both the insti-
gator of a dangerous political movement and its cause.

Again, how intelligently the Senate behaved toward King Masinissa! It took advantage of his prompt and loyal assistance against the Carthaginians, and when it

[15]Gaius Claudius Nero (cos, 207 B.C.) and Marcus Livius Salinator (cos, 219 B.C.) were
consuls together in 207 B.C. during the Second Punic War.

[16]Nero and Salinator were very harsh and unpopular censors in 204 B.C. Gnaeus Baebius
Tamphilus (cos, 182 B.C.) was a tribune of the plebs in 204 B.C.

[17]Tiberius Sempronius Gracchus (tribune of the plebs, 133 B.C.) was murdered by a gang of
senators in 133 B.C. He had passed a law redistributing state-owned land.

[18]The land commission set up by Gracchus continued to give land to the poor after his
death.

observed that he was rather eager to expand his realm, it ordered a law to be passed that granted Masinissa complete freedom from the empire of the Roman people.[19] By this action, the Senate retained the goodwill of a man who deserved the best from it, and it also kept far from its doors the ferocious Mauritanians, Numidians, and other nations of that region, which never stay reliably at peace.[20]

Foreign Stories

2. ext. 1. I will not have enough time to tell national stories, since our empire has grown and maintained itself more by mental vigor than by physical strength. For the most part, therefore, I shall have to confine the intelligence of the Romans to silent admiration and give some space to foreign stories of this kind.

Socrates was like an earthly oracle of human wisdom,[21] and he felt that nothing further should be requested from the immortal gods than to grant us good things, because ultimately they know what is best for each person, whereas we usually request things in our prayers that it would be better for us not to get. Minds of mortals, you are indeed lost in the thickest darkness, you scatter your blind prayers on such a vast plain of error! You seek riches, which have been the ruin of many people; you long for public office, which has destroyed many people; you secretly think about royal power, which is often seen to end in misery; you reach out for splendid marriages, but although they sometimes bring glory, they just as frequently wreck families completely. So stop gaping after things that will bring you misfortune, as if they were the happiest things, and trust yourself completely to the judgment of the gods, because those who give favors so readily are also the best at choosing them.

Socrates also used to say that there was a quick and short road for those who wanted to attain glory: they would have to make sure that they would in fact be the type of people they wanted others to imagine they were. With this statement he clearly warned people to seize virtue itself rather than chase after its shadow.

When Socrates was asked by a young man whether he should take a wife or avoid marriage altogether, Socrates replied that whichever the young man did, he would regret it. "On the one hand," he said, "you will have loneliness, no children, the end of your family line, and an heir from outside your family; on the other, you will have constant worries, a continuous series of complaints, reproaches about the dowry, the annoying arrogance of your in-laws, the gossiping tongue of your mother-in-law, men who seduce the wives of others, and the uncertain future of your children." With his series of tough choices, Socrates did not allow the young man to think it was a matter of picking between two recipes for happiness.

---

[19]Masinissa, king of Numidia from 206 to 148 B.C., had been a Roman ally during the Second Punic War (218–201 B.C.) The Roman Senate allowed him to encroach on Carthaginian territory throughout the first half of the second century B.C.

[20]Mauretania (modern Morocco) and Numidia (modern Algeria) were in north Africa.

[21]Socrates was regarded as a philosopher's saint after his execution in 399 B.C. He had been sentenced to death for allegedly teaching atheism and corrupting the young.

When the Athenians were so wicked and mad as to pass their grim sentence against his life, Socrates took the cup of poison from the executioner's hand with a brave spirit and an unflinching expression. When he raised the cup to his lips, his wife, Xanthippe, kept shouting with tears and lamentations that an innocent man was being put to death. "Well, then," he said, "would you have thought it better if I had died a guilty man?" What boundless wisdom: it could not forget itself, even at the very end of his life!

2. ext. 2. Come, now, how clever it was of Solon[22] to judge that no one should be called happy while they were still alive, because right up to the last day of our lives we are subject to the vagaries of fortune! The funeral pyre enables a person to be called completely happy, since it prevents the onslaught of any further misfortunes.

When he saw one of his friends grieving bitterly, Solon led him to the top of the city and urged him to look all around at the houses below them. When he saw that his friend had done so, he said, "Now imagine how many sorrows there have been in these houses in the past, how many sorrows are afflicting them today, and how many sorrows will dwell there in ages to come; and stop complaining about normal human problems as if they afflicted you alone." With these consoling words, Solon showed that cities are pitiful playgrounds for human disasters.

Solon also used to say that if everybody gathered their problems into one place, they would all prefer to take their own problems back home rather than take up their fair share from the common heap of miseries. From this he deduced that we should not regard the things we have chanced to suffer as particularly and unbearably harsh.

2. ext. 3. When Bias' country, Priene, was invaded by the enemy,[23] all the people who had been allowed to escape unharmed by the savagery of warfare were running away, weighed down with heavy loads of valuables. Bias was asked why he was not bringing any of his goods with him, like everyone else, and he said, "I am indeed carrying my goods with me." For he was carrying them in his heart, not on his shoulders, and they were valued by the mind, not displayed before people's eyes. The things that remain inside the home of the mind cannot be destroyed by the violence of mortals or gods, and just as they are always there for us if we stay behind, they never desert us if we have to leave.

2. ext. 4. Plato's statement was restricted in its wording, but overpowering in its meaning, when he declared that the world would only be happy when philosophers began to rule, or rulers began to do philosophy.[24]

2. ext. 5. There was a king who had a very refined mind. They say that when he was offered the crown, he did not put it on his head at once. Instead, he held it, thought about it for a long time, and said: "You are an illustrious rag rather than a happy one! If someone were to consider seriously how many worries and dangers

---

[22]Solon created the Athenian law code in 594 B.C.

[23]Bias was a statesman of Priene (on the east coast of Asia Minor). Priene and the other Greek cities of Asia Minor were conquered by Persians in the 540s B.C.

[24]Plato, the Athenian philosopher of the fourth century B.C., makes this statement in Book 5 of the *Republic* (473c–d).

and sorrows come with a crown, he would not want to pick it up, even if he found it lying on the ground."

2. ext. 6. Well? Wasn't the reply of Xenocrates admirable![25] He was there when some men were gossiping maliciously, but he kept completely silent. One of them asked him why he alone was holding his tongue, and he said, "Because I have often regretted saying something, but I have never regretted keeping silent."

2. ext. 7. The advice of Aristophanes was also profoundly wise when he presented Pericles returning from the dead in a comedy and making the following prophecy to the Athenians:[26] that a lion should not be raised in the city, but if they did raise one, they would have to comply with its wishes. In this way Aristophanes warned them that young men of high noble birth and excitable character should be kept in check; that once they were fed on a diet of excessive popularity and extravagant self-indulgence, they could not be stopped from gaining power; and that it would be foolish and pointless to criticize the forces that you yourself had fostered.[27]

2. ext. 8. Thales also gave marvelous advice.[28] When he was asked whether human actions could escape the notice of the gods, he said, "Not even our thoughts can do this, so we ought to keep not just our hands pure but our minds too, and we should believe that the gods in heaven are aware of our innermost thoughts."

2. ext. 9. The following remark was no less wise. A father with only one daughter asked Themistocles[29] whether he should marry her off to a man who was poor but honorable or to a man who was rich but not well regarded. Themistocles said to him, "I would prefer a man without money, to money without a man." With this statement, he advised the foolish man to choose a son-in-law rather than a son-in-law's wealth.

2. ext. 10. Come, now, what an admirable letter Philip wrote![30] Alexander[31] had been trying to win the goodwill of some Macedonians by giving out money, and in his letter Philip criticized him as follows: "My son, what train of thought led you to this empty hope, that you would think men would stay loyal to you if you had forced them to become your friends with money?" As a father, he wrote this out of kindness, and as Philip, he wrote it from his own experience, since he had bought Greece rather than conquered it.[32]

[25]Xenocrates was the second head (339–314 B.C.) of the Academy, the school of philosophy founded by Plato in 387 B.C.

[26]The playwright Aeschylus (not the statesman Pericles) makes this remark in Aristophanes' *Frogs* (produced in 405 B.C.).

[27]The dangerous young nobleman in question was Alcibiades. See 3:1,ext.1 and 6:9,ext.4.

[28]Thales of Miletus was the first Greek philosopher. He lived in the sixth century B.C.

[29]Themistocles was the leading democratic politician in Athens from 493 B.C. until his exile in 472 B.C.

[30]Philip II was king of Macedonia from 356 to 336 B.C.

[31]Philip's son was Alexander the Great.

[32]Philip II was notorious for bribing people.

2. ext. 11. When Aristotle was sending his student Callisthenes off to Alexander,[33] he advised him to speak with Alexander either as seldom or as pleasantly as possible, presumably so that he would be safer through his silence or more pleasing through his conversation when the king was listening. But Callisthenes abused Alexander for being delighted when people bowed before him in the Persian way, though Alexander was himself a Macedonian, and in a well-meaning way, Callisthenes kept trying to call him back, against his will, to the Macedonian way. When Alexander ordered that he be put to death, Callisthenes regretted too late that he had neglected the lifesaving advice of Aristotle.[34]

Aristotle also used to say that you should not talk about yourself in either way, since it would be vain to praise yourself and foolish to abuse yourself. The following very practical advice also comes from Aristotle: we should imagine pleasures that are ending. He lessens their power by showing them in that light; he makes us visualize them when they have grown stale and filled us with regret, and so we become less eager to pursue them again.

2. ext. 12. Anaxagoras[35] showed no lack of intelligence when someone asked him who was a happy man and he said, "He will be none of those men you imagine to be happy, but you will find him among those you believe to be wretched." The happy man will not be overflowing with riches and political offices, but he will be a trustworthy and committed man, devoted to his small farm or to learning without ostentation; and he will be happier in his own private world than in public.

2. ext. 13. Demades also made a wise statement.[36] When the Athenians were refusing to grant divine honors to Alexander,[37] he said, "Make sure that while you are guarding heaven, you do not lose your own land."

2. ext. 14. How cleverly indeed Anacharsis used to compare laws with spiderwebs![38] Just as a web catches weaker creatures and lets the stronger ones get away, so the law oppresses the humble and the poor but does not bind the rich and powerful.

2. ext. 15. Nothing could be wiser than the following action taken by Agesilaus.[39] One night he discovered that a plot was being hatched against the state of Sparta, so he immediately repealed the laws of Lycurgus that forbade the punishment of any person without trial.[40] He arrested the guilty and put them to death, and immediately afterward he reinstated the laws. He provided for two things

---

[33]Callisthenes was Aristotle's nephew and a student of his. Callisthenes joined Alexander the Great of Macedonia in Bactra (modern Balkh in Afghanistan) in 327 B.C.

[34]Callisthenes refused to prostrate himself before Alexander and was put to death for plotting against the king later in 327 B.C.

[35]Anaxagoras of Clazomenae (on the west coast of Asia Minor) was a philosopher. He lived in Athens from 460 to 430 B.C.

[36]Demades was an Athenian politician in the fourth century B.C. He was pro-Macedonian.

[37]Alexander the Great of Macedonia demanded to be recognized as a god by the Greeks in 324 B.C.

[38]Anacharsis was a legendary sixth century sage from Scythia (modern Ukraine).

[39]Agesilaus II was king of Sparta from 399 to 360 B.C.

[40]The legendary Lycurgus created the law code of Sparta in the ninth century B.C.

simultaneously: his punitive action that saved the state was neither against the law nor obstructed by the law. Thus the laws had to disappear for a short while so that they could reappear forever.

2. ext. 16. I suspect that the advice of Hanno displayed the most exceptional intelligence.[41] Mago was announcing to the Carthaginian Senate how the battle of Cannae had turned out,[42] and to prove the extent of that victory, he poured out a pile of golden rings amounting to seven gallons in volume; these had been taken from our citizens who had been killed. Hanno asked Mago whether any of Rome's allies had deserted from Rome after this great defeat, and when he heard that nobody had gone over to Hannibal, he immediately advised them to send ambassadors to Rome to discuss peace terms. If Hanno's opinion had prevailed, Carthage would not have been defeated in the Second Punic War and destroyed in the Third.[43]

2. ext. 17. The Samnites also had to pay a heavy penalty for a similar mistake when they ignored advice from Herennius Pontius that would have saved them.[44] He surpassed all other Samnites in prestige and intelligence, and when he was asked by the soldiers and by their commander, his own son, what should be done with the Roman legions that were trapped in the Caudine Forks,[45] he replied that they should be sent home unharmed. When he was asked about the same matter again on the following day, he said that they should be wiped out. So, the Samnites should either earn the favor of their enemies by conferring a very great benefit or shatter their strength by inflicting a very heavy loss. But with unthinking folly, the victors rejected both pieces of good advice, and by sending our legions under the yoke,[46] they roused the Romans up to destroy them.

2. ext. 18. To all these great stories of wisdom, I shall add a minor one. When the Cretans want to use a really nasty curse against people they hate violently, they pray that those people will love bad habits. This restrained type of prayer guarantees them a revenge that has the most effective results. When people long for something that is bad for them and perversely give into that craving, their pleasure is right next to disaster for them.

---

[41]Hanno was an opponent of Hannibal's family and its anti-Roman policy.

[42]Mago was Hannibal's brother. Hannibal had defeated the Romans at Cannae in 216 B.C.

[43]The Second Punic War was from 218 to 201 B.C., and the Third Punic War from 149 to 146 B.C.

[44]Herennius Pontius was the wise father of Gaius Pontius, the Samnite commander.

[45]The Samnites (of central Italy) defeated the Romans at the Caudine Forks in 321 B.C.

[46]The Samnites humiliated the defeated soldiers by forcing them to crawl under a wooden bar called the yoke.

Chapter 3. Crafty Remarks or Actions

Preface

There is another type of action or statement that is a modification of wisdom, and it has acquired the name of craftiness. It reaches its goal only if it gathers strength from deception, and it wins praise by a secret path rather than on the open highway.

Roman Stories

3. 1. During the reign of Servius Tullius,[47] a cow of exceptional size and extraordinary beauty was born on the farm of a householder in the Sabine region.[48] The most reliable experts on oracles responded to this event by saying that the cow had been sent deliberately by the immortal gods, so that whoever sacrificed it to Diana on the Aventine, that person's country would attain mastery over the whole world.[49] The owner was delighted at this and drove the cow in great haste to Rome, where he set it in front of the altar of Diana on the Aventine, intending to sacrifice it and present the Sabines with control over the human race. When the priest of the temple learned about this, he presented his guest with a religious difficulty: the priest told the Sabine farmer that he could not kill the victim until he had washed himself in the water of the river nearby. While the Sabine went off in the direction of the river Tiber, the priest sacrificed the cow himself. By righteously tricking the Sabine out of the sacrifice, the priest made our city the mistress of countless states and nations.

3. 2. In this type of trickery, a foremost place should be granted to Junius Brutus.[50] He noticed that his uncle, King Tarquin, was eliminating every talented member of the nobility and that, among others, his own brother had been put to death because he was gifted with too lively an intelligence. So Brutus pretended that he himself was mentally defective, and by this deception he concealed his excellent qualities. He went off to Delphi with Tarquin's sons, for the king had sent them to Pythian Apollo[51] to honor the god with gifts and sacrifices. Brutus carried some gold as a gift for the god, but it was hidden in a hollow stick because he was afraid that it would not be safe for him to show his respect for the heavenly god through a public display of generosity. When the young men had carried out their father's instructions, they asked Apollo which of them he thought would rule in Rome. The god replied that the one who kissed his mother before the others

---

[47]Servius Tullius was the sixth king of Rome (578–535 B.C.).

[48]The Sabines lived in central Italy.

[49]Diana was the goddess of Latium, and her cult had recently been brought to the Aventine hill in Rome.

[50]Lucius Brutus (cos, 509 B.C.) was the nephew of Tarquin the Proud, the seventh and last king of Rome (535–510 B.C.).

[51]Pythian Apollo was the name given to Apollo at his oracle in Delphi (in northern Greece).

would have complete power over our city. Then Brutus pretended to fall by accident, but in fact he threw himself down deliberately and kissed the earth, because he realized it was the common mother of all men. The kiss that he cleverly gave to the goddess Earth brought liberty to our city and gave Brutus the first place in our list of consuls.[52]

3. 3. Scipio Africanus also resorted to the assistance of craftiness. He was leaving Sicily and heading for Africa, and he wanted to create a full cavalry unit of three hundred horsemen by enrolling some very brave Roman foot soldiers.[53] He couldn't equip them before the deadline, but although he was prevented from doing this by the constraints of time, he succeeded by a clever plan.[54] He had some young men drawn from all over Sicily with him, and these young men were very noble and very rich, but useless fighters. He ordered three hundred of them to get splendid weapons and excellent horses ready as quickly as possible, pretending that he was going to bring them off with him at once to attack Carthage. They obeyed his command promptly, but they were very worried at the thought of this dangerous war going on so far away. Scipio then proclaimed that he would exempt them from taking part in that campaign if they would agree to hand over their weapons and horses to his foot soldiers. The unwarlike and timid young men jumped at the opportunity and eagerly surrendered their equipment to our men. So our crafty commander saw to it that if this abrupt request seemed too demanding at first, it would soon be seen as a great favor, since it would relieve these Sicilians from their dreaded military service.

3. 4. I have to tell you the following story. The Senate appointed Quintus Fabius Labeo as arbitrator to settle a border dispute between Nola and Naples.[55] When he came to the place under dispute, he took each group aside and warned them that they should put aside their greed and agree to withdraw rather than advance. Moved by his prestige, each side did so, and a piece of territory was left empty in the middle. He established that the border should be where they themselves had marked it out, and he assigned the territory that was left over to the Roman people. Even though the people of Nola and Naples had been cheated, they were unable to complain, since his decision had been made in accordance with their own demarcation. Still, this new source of revenue had come to our state by a disgraceful type of trickery.

They also say that when Labeo had defeated King Antiochus in battle, he was supposed to get half the king's ships in accordance with the treaty they had made; but he cut all the king's ships in half and thereby deprived him of his entire navy.[56]

---

[52]Brutus was the first consul (in 509 B.C.).

[53]Scipio Africanus was consul in 205 B.C. and spent the year in Sicily, preparing for the invasion of Africa.

[54]The Senate refused to supply Scipio Africanus with regular troops or equipment, so he had to rely on volunteers and came up with this trick for equipping them.

[55]Quintus Fabius Labeo was consul in 183 B.C. Nola and Naples were cities in Campania (western Italy).

[56]Antiochus the Great of Syria was defeated by Scipio Asiaticus in 190 B.C., and Labeo was sent to destroy the king's navy in 188 B.C.

3. 5. We shall have to forgo denouncing Marcus Antonius.[57] He admitted that he deliberately had never written down a speech, because if something he said in an earlier legal case might harm someone he was defending in a later case, he could always claim that he had never said it. But he had a plausible excuse for his disgraceful behavior: on behalf of those who were risking their lives in court, he was prepared not only to use his eloquence but also to abuse his sense of honor.

3. 6. Sertorius found that Nature had been very generous to him. She endowed him with a strength of body that was matched by the intelligence of his mind. When Sulla published his death list, Sertorius was forced to become the leader of the Lusitanians.[58] His speeches were unable to convince the Lusitanians that they should avoid pitting their entire army against the Romans, but he brought them around to his point of view by means of a crafty trick. He stood two horses where they could be seen; one of these horses was very strong, while the other was very weak. Then he ordered a feeble old man to pluck off the strong horse's tail bit by bit, and he ordered a young man of exceptional strength to pluck off the weak horse's tail all at once. The two men followed his instructions. But whereas the young man wore himself out with his pointless efforts, the man who was feeble with old age accomplished his task. The barbarians assembled there wanted to know what the point in all of this was, and Sertorius explained that our Roman army was like a horse's tail: if someone attacked it little by little, they could defeat it; but anyone who tried to defeat it all at once would sooner concede defeat than inflict it. The people of this barbarous nation were rough and difficult to rule, and they had been rushing toward their own destruction, but although they rejected good advice with their ears, they did see its value with their eyes.

3. 7. Fabius the Delayer,[59] the man who made not fighting a form of winning, had in his camp a foot soldier of exceptional courage from Nola who was suspected of disloyalty, and a cavalryman from Lucania who carried out his duties energetically but was madly in love with a prostitute.[60] Fabius wanted to retain both of these good soldiers rather than punish them, so he concealed his suspicions about the foot soldier and bent the rules of military discipline a little from their proper form in the case of the cavalryman. Speaking from his platform, Fabius praised the foot soldier and rewarded him with every kind of honor, and this made the foot soldier transfer his affections from the Carthaginians back to the Romans; and Fabius allowed the cavalryman to buy the prostitute's freedom secretly, which made that cavalryman the most enthusiastic trooper we had.

[57]Marcus Antonius (cos, 99 B.C.), the grandfather of Antony, was a famous orator.

[58]Quintus Sertorius (praetor, 83 B.C.) was the governor of Nearer Spain in 82 B.C. when Sulla became dictator and massacred his political opponents. Sertorius refused to accept the new regime, assembled an army of Lusitanians (from modern Portugal), and held out in Spain for ten years.

[59]Fabius the Delayer commanded the Roman army against Hannibal for several years during the Second Punic War.

[60]Nola was a city in Campania (western Italy); Lucania was a region in southern Italy. The loyalty of the Italian allies to Rome was vital in the war against Hannibal.

3. 8. Now I shall come to those who saved their lives through trickery. When Marcus Volusius, a plebeian aedile, was put on the official death list,[61] he put on the clothes of a priest of Isis[62] and went on the roads and public highways begging for alms. This prevented the people he met from discovering who he really was, so he was protected by his trickery and reached the camp of Marcus Brutus.[63] What could be more pitiable than that a magistrate of the Roman people should be forced to lay aside the glory of his office, and to go through our city disguised in the robes of a foreign religion! People are too fond of their own lives or too eager to take the lives of another if they can endure such humiliations themselves or force others to undergo them!

3. 9. Sentius Saturninus Vetulo was in the same type of situation, but he found a more honorable way of evading death.[64] When he heard that his name had been posted on the death list of the triumvirs, he at once put on the insignia of a praetor and got some men to walk in front of him dressed up as lictors, attendants, and public slaves. He commandeered vehicles, demanded lodgings, cleared people out of his way, and acted like a magistrate so brazenly that in broad daylight he managed to keep his keen-eyed enemies completely in the dark. When he came to Puteoli,[65] he behaved as if he were on serious public business, and with complete cheek he commandeered some ships and made his way to Sicily, which at that time was the safest place of refuge for men on the official death list.[66]

3. 10. I shall add one more story on a lighter note before I turn to foreign ones. A man was very fond of his son, and when the son was on fire with a passion that was forbidden and dangerous, he wanted to hold the young man back from his insane lust, so he blended his natural indulgence as a father with a plan to save him. He asked his son to enjoy a permissible affair with a common prostitute before going on to the woman he was in love with. The young man yielded to his father's pleas, satisfied himself to his heart's content in a permissible way by sleeping with the prostitute, and lessened the force of his ill-fated passion. His feelings for the woman who was forbidden to him grew duller and slower, and he gradually got over his passion for her.

---

[61]Marcus Volusius was an aedile in 43 B.C. when he was put on the death list of Antony and Augustus.

[62]Isis, the Egyptian goddess, had a temple in Rome.

[63]Marcus Junius Brutus, the tyrannicide, was commanding the Republican army in Macedonia at the time.

[64]Sentius Saturninus Vetulo must have escaped in 43 B.C.

[65]Puteoli (modern Pozzuoli) was on the coast of Campania (western Italy).

[66]Pompey's son, Sextus Pompeius Magnus Pius, held out in Sicily from 43 to 35 B.C. and turned it into a safe haven for Republicans and other victims of the triumvirs.

Foreign Stories

3. ext. 1. Alexander, king of the Macedonians,[67] was warned by an oracle to order the execution of the first one that met him as he went outside the gate. A man driving an ass happened to be the first one to meet him, so Alexander ordered him to be taken away and put to death. The man asked him why he was being sentenced to death, since he was innocent and didn't deserve that, and Alexander told him about the words of the oracle in order to excuse his action. The man with the ass said, "If that's the way it is, my king, the oracle has sentenced another one to death: because the ass that I was driving ahead of me met you before I did." Alexander was delighted with his clever reply and also because he had been stopped from doing something wrong, so he seized the opportunity of upholding his religious scruples by killing an animal of little value. Alexander was a very clever man, but also a very kind one. The groom of the king in the next story was also very crafty.

3. ext. 2. When he had overthrown the disgraceful regime of the magi,[68] Darius took six of his helpers, who were of the same rank as he, and made a deal with these comrades who had carried out the glorious deed with him. They would sit on their horses at sunrise and ride them to a prearranged place, and the kingdom would belong to that man whose horse whinnied first in that place. His rivals relied on the favors of fortune, but Darius alone brought about the happy result he longed for by relying on the cunning of his groom, Oebaris. The groom stuck his hand into a mare's genitals, and when they came to the place, he put his hand to the nostrils of Darius' horse. Excited by the smell, the horse let out a whinny before all the others. When they heard it, the remaining six candidates for absolute power dismounted at once from their horses, and following the Persian custom, they prostrated themselves on the ground and hailed Darius as king.[69] What a great empire Darius had acquired by means of such a small trick!

3. ext. 3. The wisdom of Bias lasted longer among men than did his country, Priene, for his wisdom still lives on today, whereas his city is practically dead and only faint traces of it survive.[70] Bias used to say that in dealing with friends, people should remember that friendship can easily turn into the bitterest enmity. Perhaps this principle might seem to be too clever by far and to undermine sincerity, which is one of the great joys of friendship, but if you think about it more profoundly, you will discover that it is extremely useful.

3. ext. 4. The city of Lampsacus[71] was saved as a result of one clever trick: Alexander was proceeding eagerly toward its destruction[72] when he saw his former

---

[67]This is presumably Alexander the Great (king of Macedonia, 336–323 B.C.).

[68]Darius murdered Bardiya (king of Persia, 522–521 B.C.). Bardiya was supported by the magi (Persian priests).

[69]Darius I was king of Persia from 521 to 486 B.C.

[70]Bias of Priene was a statesman in the sixth century B.C. Priene (on the west coast of Asia Minor) was captured by the Persians in the 540s B.C.

[71]Lampsacus was on the northern coast of Asia Minor.

[72]Lampsacus was captured in 335 B.C. by Parmenio, the general of Alexander the Great of Macedonia.

teacher Anaximenes coming out of the city gates.[73] It was obvious that Anaximenes was going to plead with him to put aside his anger, so Alexander swore to him that he was not going to do what he wanted. Then Anaximenes said, "I want you to destroy Lampsacus." This quick-witted answer saved a famous city renowned since ancient times from the destruction marked out for it.

3. *ext. 5.* The cleverness of Demosthenes came to the rescue of an old woman in a remarkable way.[74] Two guests left a sum of money with her for safekeeping, on condition that she would return it to both of them at the same time. After some time had passed, one of the guests came completely disheveled as if his friend had died, and he tricked her into giving him all the money. Later, the other guest came along and started to demand the money he had left with her. The poor woman was in a fix, since she had absolutely no money and nobody to defend her, and she was already thinking about getting a rope and hanging herself. But Demosthenes came forward just in time as her defender. When he came to speak on her behalf, he said, "This woman is prepared faithfully to pay back the sum that was left with her, but unless you bring your friend here, she cannot do it, because, as you yourself kept insisting, this was the rule you had declared, that the money should not be given to one of you unless the other was also present."

3. *ext. 6.* The following story also reveals no lack of intelligence. There was a man in Athens who was hated by the entire people, and he had to plead his case before the people on a capital charge. So he suddenly began to seek election to the highest political office, not because he had any hopes of winning it, but because he wanted people to have a target for their first outburst of rage, which usually tends to be the harshest. The clever reasoning behind his plan did not let him down. At public meetings he was harassed by hostile shouting and frequent hissing from the entire audience, and he was disgraced by the humiliation of having the office denied to him. Shortly afterward, when his life was at stake in court, the same people were very merciful to him when they voted on his case. But if he had risked his life by coming before them when they were still thirsting for revenge, their ears would have been closed by their hatred, and they would not have listened to any part of his defense.

3. *ext. 7.* The cunning I have mentioned above was similar to the following clever trick. Hannibal had been defeated in a naval battle by the consul Duilius,[75] and he was afraid that he would be punished for losing his fleet, but he evaded retribution by the following trick. After the ill-fated battle, before any news of the defeat could reach home, Hannibal carefully prepared and instructed one of his friends and sent him to Carthage. When the friend entered the senate house of that country, he said, "Hannibal wants your advice: if a Roman commander

[73]Anaximenes of Lampsacus was a teacher of rhetoric and lived from 380 to 320 B.C.

[74]In addition to being a great political speaker, Demosthenes (who lived from 383 to 322 B.C.) also pleaded in a large number of law cases.

[75]Gaius Duilius was consul in 260 B.C. and defeated the Carthaginian navy under Hannibal, son of Gisgo, during the First Punic War. Hannibal's fears were justified, because he was crucified after another naval defeat in 258 B.C.

comes with a very large naval force, should he fight against him?" The entire senate shouted that there was no doubt that he should do so. Then the friend said, "Hannibal has fought, and he has been defeated." In this way he left them with no way of condemning that course of action, since they themselves had determined that it ought to have been carried out.

3. ext. 8. Hannibal played a similar trick.[76] Fabius the Delayer was making fun of the invincible power of Hannibal's army by the delaying tactics that saved us. Hannibal destroyed the farmland throughout Italy with fire and sword, but to make the Romans suspicious about the way Fabius was dragging out the war, he left the farm of only one person free from this kind of destruction, the farm of Fabius.[77] This pretended favor to Fabius would have worked to Hannibal's advantage if the tricky ways of Hannibal and the loyalty of Fabius had not been well known to the city of Rome.

3. ext. 9. The people of Tusculum were also saved by a clever plan.[78] Because of their constant rebellions, it served them right that the Romans wanted to destroy their city utterly. When our greatest commander, Furius Camillus, came with a mighty army to carry out this mission,[79] all the inhabitants of Tusculum marched out to meet him dressed in togas, and they very kindly presented him with food supplies and performed other peacetime duties for him. They allowed him to enter their city gates under arms and did not change their expression or manner. By preserving their peace of mind, they not only won the status of allies; they even got so far as to share citizenship with us. They had demonstrated a clever type of innocence, indeed, for they had discovered that it was better to conceal their fear with favors than to assert it in warfare.

3. ext. 10. Tullius, the commander of the Volscians, had a detestable plan.[80] He was burning with a great desire to wage war on the Romans. When he noticed that the morale of his soldiers had been undermined by several battles that went against them, and that they were consequently more eager for peace, he formed a treacherous scheme to push them where he wanted them to go. A great crowd of Volscians had come to Rome to see the games, and he told the consuls that he was very much afraid they might make a sudden attack. He warned the consuls to be particularly watchful and left the city at once. The consuls reported this matter to the Senate. Although there was no reason to be suspicious, the Senate was influenced by its respect for Tullius, and it decreed that the Volscians should leave before

---

[76]This is the famous Hannibal, who commanded the Carthaginian army throughout the Second Punic War (218–201 B.C.).

[77]Fabius the Delayer was appointed dictator in 217 B.C. after the Romans were defeated at Lake Trasimene. This was when Hannibal left Fabius' property intact.

[78]Tusculum (modern Frascati) was just south of Rome, in Latium.

[79]Marcus Furius Camillus (dictator, 396 B.C.) captured Tusculum in 381 B.C.

[80]Attius Tullius was a commander of the Volscians (in southern Latium) in the fifth century B.C.

nightfall.[81] Since the Volscians were angered by this insult, it was easy to drive them to rebellion. The cunning leader made it look as if his lie was well intentioned, and he deceived two nations at the same time: he fooled the Romans into insulting an innocent people, and the Volscians into getting angry with the victims of his deception.[82]

Chapter 4. Stratagems

Preface

There is an exceptional type of cunning that is far removed from any criticism, and since its operations cannot be accurately expressed by any Latin term, they are called by a Greek name, stratagems.

Roman Stories

4. 1. Tullus Hostilius had attacked Fidenae with all his military forces,[83] because even though the rise of our empire was still in its infant stages, the constant rebellions of Fidenae did not allow it to stay at rest. The trophies and triumphs we won over our neighbors increased our courage and led us to entertain even greater ambitions. Mettius Fufetius was the Alban commander,[84] and his loyalty to our alliance had always been dubious and under suspicion. He suddenly revealed his treachery on this battlefield. Mettius deserted his position on the flank of the Roman army and withdrew to a nearby hill. Instead of helping us, he waited out the battle so that he could trample on us after we were defeated or attack us after we had exhausted ourselves by winning.

There is no doubt that his behavior would have undermined the morale of our soldiers, since they would have seen that their enemies were attacking them and their allies were deserting them at the same time. Tullus made sure this would not happen: he spurred on his horse and dashing around to each group of soldiers, he declared that Mettius had withdrawn under his orders; as soon as Tullus gave the signal, Mettius would attack the army of Fidenae in the rear. By this clever use of his skill as a general, Tullus changed the anxiety of his men into confidence, and he filled their hearts with enthusiasm rather than fear.

---

[81]The Volscians were expelled from Rome during the Great Games of 489 B.C. The Great Games consisted of athletic events and military spectacles. They took place every September and honored the god Jupiter.

[82]The Volscians attacked Rome in 489 B.C. with the help of Gaius Marcius Coriolanus (see 5:2,1 and 5:4,1).

[83]Tullus Hostilius was the third king of Rome (673–642 B.C.). Fidenae was a town just north of Rome, in Latium.

[84]Mettius Fufetius was dictator of Alba Longa, the old religious center of Latium.

4. 2. I do not want to move away from our kings just yet. Sextus Tarquinius, the son of Tarquin, was indignant that his father's forces were unable to take Gabii by storm.[85] So he thought of a plan that would be more effective than armed force for capturing the city and adding it to the Roman Empire. He went off at once to Gabii, pretending that he was running away from his father's cruelty and beatings; he had marks from self-inflicted blows. He gradually won over the affections of every single citizen, seducing them with his carefully crafted flattering lies. As a result, he gained great power among them, and then he sent a friend to his father to tell him that he had everything under his control and to ask him what he would like to be done.

The old man's craftiness matched his young son's cleverness. Tarquin was absolutely delighted at this news, but he did not want to trust the messenger too much. So he said nothing in reply; instead, he took the messenger away to his garden and knocked off the heads of the biggest and tallest poppies with a stick. When his young son learned of his father's silence and his actions, he understood the cause of his silence and the meaning of his actions. He was well aware that he was being instructed to banish or put to death every outstanding citizen of Gabii. Once he had deprived the city of its best champions, he handed it over to Tarquin with its hands practically tied.

4. 3. Our ancestors came up with the following plan that was well though out and produced very favorable results. The Gauls had captured our city and were besieging the Capitol,[86] and they realized that their only hope of obtaining it lay in starving our people. But the Romans came up with a clever type of plan that deprived the Gauls of their only incentive in persevering: they started throwing loaves of bread from several places. The Gauls were amazed at this sight, and believing that our people had an unlimited supply of grain, they felt obliged to come to terms and give up their siege. Jupiter must certainly have pitied the courageous Romans at that time, when they had to find safety in trickery and when he saw them, in a time of great food shortage, throwing away the food that would have relieved the shortage. That is why he gave a happy ending to their scheme, which was as risky as it was cunning.

4. 4. Later, Jupiter also smiled favorably on the clever plans of our most outstanding commanders. Hannibal was mauling one part of Italy and Hasdrubal had invaded the other,[87] but the armies of these two brothers were not allowed to join together and put an unbearable burden on our already exhausted forces. They were prevented from doing so by the alert planning of Claudius Nero on the one hand, and by the renowned foresight of Livius Salinator on the other.[88] Nero had

---

[85]Sextus Tarquinius was the villainous son of Tarquin the Proud (king, 535–510 B.C.). Gabii was a town just east of Rome, in Latium.

[86]The Gauls captured the entire city of Rome, except the Capitol, in 390 B.C.

[87]Hannibal was in the south of Italy, and his brother Hasdrubal had invaded Italy from the north.

[88]Gaius Claudius Nero (cos, 207 B.C.) and Marcus Livius Salinator (cos, 219 B.C.) were consuls together in 207 B.C.

hemmed in Hannibal's army in Lucania,[89] and he made the enemy think that he was still there, because that is what the military situation required. In fact, he went off to bring aid to his fellow consul, completing the long journey with remarkable speed.

Salinator was in Umbria, intending to fight by the river Metaurus on the following day,[90] and he took Nero into his camp that night with the greatest secrecy. Salinator ordered his tribunes to take in Nero's tribunes, his centurions to take in Nero's centurions, his cavalry to take in Nero's cavalry, and his infantry to take in Nero's infantry. Without any commotion, he squeezed a second army into a space that could barely hold one. As a result, Hasdrubal did not know that he would have to battle against two consuls until he had already been utterly defeated by their courageous fighting.[91] So the Carthaginians, notorious throughout the world for being so crafty, were outwitted by the practical Romans. As a result, Hannibal was tricked by Nero and Hasdrubal by Salinator.

4. 5. Quintus Metellus should also be remembered for his mental ability. When he was a governor in Spain, he was fighting a war against the Celtiberians but his forces could not capture the city of Contrebia, the capital of that nation.[92] He considered several plans seriously for a long time and then found the path that would lead to the result he wanted. He used to start marching off with great vigor and then he would randomly turn toward one region or another: he used to occupy one mountain range, and shortly afterward he would move over to another one, and in the meantime neither his own men nor the enemy themselves knew what was the cause of his sudden, unexpected changes. When a very close friend of his asked him why he was pursuing such a sporadic and inconclusive kind of warfare, he said, "Don't ask! Because if I ever find out that my inner tunic knows what my plans are, I shall have it burned at once." How did his secret tactics turn out? What was their end result? After he had kept his own army in the dark and all the Celtiberians in confusion, he headed off in one direction, then suddenly turned around toward Contrebia and took the astonished city in a surprise attack. So if he had not forced his mind to consider such tricks, he would have had to sit with his army by the walls of Contrebia until he reached a ripe old age.

Foreign Stories

4. ext. 1. Agathocles, the king of Syracuse, was daringly clever.[93] When the Carthaginians had almost captured his entire city, Agathocles brought his army over to Africa, to dispel the panic and violence of their attack with the panic and violence of his own attack against them;[94] his plan was very effective. The

[89]Lucania was in the southwest of Italy.

[90]The river Metaurus was in Umbria (eastern Italy).

[91]Hasdrubal was killed in the battle.

[92]Quintus Caecilius Metellus Macedonicus (cos, 143 B.C.) was governor of Nearer Spain in 142 B.C. when he captured Contrebia. The Celtiberians lived in eastern Spain.

[93]Agathocles was king of Syracuse (on the east coast of Sicily) from 317 to 289 B.C.

[94]Agathocles crossed over to Africa and attacked Carthage from 310 to 308 B.C.

Carthaginians were astounded by his sudden arrival, and they were very glad to buy their own safety by leaving their enemy alone. They made an agreement that the Sicilians should withdraw their forces from Africa, and the Carthaginians should withdraw their forces from Sicily at the same time.[95] Well, what if he had kept fighting to defend the walls of Syracuse? Sicily would have been ruined by the misfortunes of war, and he would have left Carthage free to enjoy the benefits of peace without any cares. Now by waging the sort of warfare he had suffered from, and by attacking their resources rather than defending his own, he abandoned his kingdom with greater peace of mind and won it back with greater security.

4. ext. 2. Well, didn't Hannibal bring the army of the Roman people to such a tragic end at Cannae by entangling it in several clever traps, even before he started fighting?[96] First of all, he made sure that our army would have the sun and the wind against it, since the wind stirs up a lot of dust there. Then, while the battle was still going on, he ordered a part of his forces to run away deliberately; when a Roman legion broke off from the rest of our army to pursue them, he had the legion slaughtered by soldiers that he had positioned to ambush them. Finally, he arranged that four hundred of his horsemen would pretend to desert to our side and ask to see the consul. As is the custom when soldiers desert, the consul ordered them to lay down their weapons and go to the back of the battlefield. There they took out swords that they had hidden between their tunic and breastplate and cut the legs of the Romans as they were fighting. Such was the courage of the Carthaginians, laced with tricks and treachery and deception. Now it most clearly vindicates the courage of our outwitted men; we were cheated rather than defeated.

Chapter 5. Electoral Defeats

Preface

It will be useful to describe the way elections go at the Campus Martius,[97] because it will show men who are starting out on the road to political office how to endure unfavorable election results with greater fortitude. If they bear in mind the electoral defeats of very famous men, they will seek political office with their hopes undiminished but with greater intelligence and judgment; these beginning politicians will remember that it is not an outrage if all the people deny such an office to one individual, since individuals have often thought it proper to resist the will of all the people; and these starting politicians will know that they must seek office with patience if they cannot win it through influence.

[95]The peace treaty of 306 B.C. defined the Syracusan and Carthaginian spheres of influence in Sicily.
[96]Hannibal won the battle of Cannae in 216 B.C.
[97]The Campus Martius ("Plain of Mars") was a field between the city walls and the Tiber. Elections were held there.

Roman Stories

5. 1. Quintus Fabius Maximus was giving a banquet to the people in honor of his paternal uncle, Scipio Aemilianus.[98] Fabius asked Quintus Aelius Tubero to set up the dining room,[99] but Tubero put goatskins on cheap Carthaginian couches and set out Samian ware[100] rather than silver dishes. People were offended by his lack of taste, and although Tubero was considered a remarkable man in all other respects, and was helped by the reputation of his grandfather, Lucius Paullus, and of his maternal uncle, Scipio Aemilianus,[101] when he entered himself as a candidate in the elections for the praetorship, he walked away from the Campus humiliated by an electoral defeat. People always respected the self-restraint of his private life, but they cared greatly for outward show in public life. So the people of the city felt that it was not just the participants at one banquet but rather the entire city itself that had reclined on those skins, and they avenged their humiliation at that banquet when it came to casting their votes.

5. 2. Publius Scipio Nasica was the most glorious beacon of civil power.[102] As consul, he declared war on Jugurtha;[103] when the Idaean Mother moved from her Phrygian home to our hearths and altars, he welcomed her with reverend hands;[104] he crushed several destructive rebellions by the force of his prestige;[105] and under his leadership, the Senate won glory for several years.[106] When he was a young man, however, he was standing for election as curule aedile, and in the usual way of candidates, he vigorously shook hands with a man, whose hands were hardened by agricultural work, and as a joke he asked him whether he used to walk around on his hands.[107] People standing around heard this remark, and when it spread throughout the people, it resulted in an electoral defeat for Scipio. All the rural tribes felt that he had insulted them for being poor, and they unleashed their anger against his offensive joke. By forcing young noblemen to keep themselves free of

[98]Quintus Fabius Maximus Allobrogicus (cos, 121 B.C.) organized this banquet to commemorate the death of Scipio Aemilianus in 129 B.C.

[99]Quintus Aelius Tubero (land commissioner, 129 B.C.) was Fabius' first cousin.

[100]Samian ware was pottery from the island of Samos (off the west coast of Asia Minor).

[101]Tubero's mother, Aemilia (see 4:4,9), was the daughter of Lucius Aemilius Paullus (cos, 182 B.C.) and the sister of Scipio Aemilianus.

[102]Valerius Maximus has conflated four different generations of the Cornelius Scipio Nasica family in this story.

[103]Publius Cornelius Scipio Nasica Serapio (cos, 111 B.C.) declared war on Jugurtha.

[104]Publius Cornelius Scipio Nasica (cos, 191 B.C.) welcomed the stone of the Great Mother of the Gods in 204 B.C. (see 8:15,3).

[105]Publius Cornelius Scipio Nasica Serapio (cos, 138 B.C.) crushed the reform movement of Tiberius Sempronius Gracchus (tribune of the plebs, 133 B.C.) by resorting to murder, not "by the force of his prestige." See 3:2,17 and 5:3,2e.

[106]Publius Cornelius Scipio Nasica Corculum (cos, 162 B.C.) was leader of the Senate from 147 B.C. until his death in 141 B.C.

[107]Publius Cornelius Scipio Nasica Serapio (cos, 138 B.C.), the murderer of Tiberius Gracchus, made this offensive joke.

offensive behavior, our state turned them into great and helpful citizens; and by not allowing jokers to win public offices, it endowed these offices with the proper dignity and prestige.

5. 3. No such lapse was to be seen in the case of Lucius Aemilius Paullus, but he still was unsuccessful on several occasions when he sought the consulship. And yet, after he had worn out the Campus Martius with his electoral defeats, he reached the highest level of political power by getting elected twice as consul and also as censor.[108] His unfair defeats did not break his courage, they accentuated it; because these humiliations made his burning desire for the highest office even more intense as he went off to the elections. He had been unable to move the people by the splendor of his noble birth or his intellectual talents, but he won them over by his determination.

5. 4. A few sad friends escorted Quintus Caecilius Metellus back home when he was cast down by an electoral defeat and filled with sorrow and shame. But the entire Senate escorted him to the Capitol when he was happy and lively and celebrating his triumph over the so-called King Philip.[109] In the Achaean War, Lucius Mummius may have added the finishing touches to the war, but it was Metellus who did the greater part of the fighting.[110]

Could the people then have denied him the consulship, when he was soon about to give them Macedonia or set aside for them Achaea, their two most splendid provinces? They did, indeed, but this made him an even better citizen: he realized how diligently he would have to work during his consulship, since he saw how much work it took to obtain it.

5. 5. Who could be as outstanding, who could be as affluent as Sulla? He bestowed wealth and power lavishly, he repealed ancient laws and created new ones. But even he was humiliated by a defeat in the elections for praetorship in that very Campus that he would later be master of.[111] He would have received any kind of political office he requested if only one of the gods had revealed to the Roman people the shape and form of the power that would one day be his.

5. 6. But I must record a great injustice at our elections. Cato of Utica's character would have brought more distinction to the praetorship than its glory would have brought to the man himself, but on one occasion he was not able to get that office from the people. Their votes were close to madness, but they paid quite a heavy penalty for their mistake, because if they denied this office to Cato they were forced to grant it to Vatinius.[112] So if we want to judge the matter properly, Cato was not deprived of the praetorship; the praetorship was deprived of Cato.

---

[108]Lucius Aemilius Paullus was consul in 182 and 168 B.C. and censor in 164 B.C.

[109]Quintus Caecilius Metellus Macedonicus (cos, 143 B.C.) celebrated a triumph over Andriscus, who called himself King Philip of Macedonia, in 146 B.C.

[110]Metellus defeated the Achaeans in 146 B.C., but Lucius Mummius Achaicus (cos, 146 B.C.) got all the credit and celebrated a triumph over the Achaeans in 145 B.C.

[111]Sulla failed to get the praetorship in 94 B.C. He later became dictator (82–79 B.C.).

[112]Publius Vatinius (cos, 47 B.C.) was elected praetor in 55 B.C., having defeated Cato of Utica through bribery and violence.

Chapter 6. Necessity

Preface

The harsh laws and ferocious commands of hateful necessity have forced our own city and foreign nations to endure misfortunes that are hard to understand or even to hear about.

Roman Stories

6. 1. When the young men of our army had been worn out by several defeats during the Second Punic War, the Senate followed the proposal of the consul Tiberius Gracchus and decreed that slaves should be bought by the state to help keep the enemy away.[113] The tribunes of the plebs brought a law concerning this matter before the people, and a committee of three men was set up. This committee bought up twenty-four thousand slaves and put them under oath to do their duty with strength and courage, and to serve for as long as the Carthaginians would be in Italy, and then they sent the slaves off to the army. To add to the cavalry, 270 slaves were also bought from the Paediculi in Apulia.[114]

How great is the violence of bitter misfortune! Up to that time the state had disdained to have men without property in the army, even if they were of free birth,[115] and now it was taking men from slave quarters and collecting them from shepherds' huts, and it was including them in its army as a special reinforcement. A noble spirit must sometimes consider what is expedient and surrender to the power of fortune, because if you do not choose a plan that leads to safety but follow a path that looks good, you will have to come to a fall.

The defeat at Cannae shook our city so badly that, when the dictator Marcus Junius Pera was directing our Republic,[116] men had to tear down the weapons that had been put up in the temples and consecrated to the gods and use those weapons to fight with; boys who were still wearing the striped toga had to bear arms;[117] and we had to enlist six thousand men who had been enslaved for debt or sentenced to death. If these measures were viewed in themselves, they would be somewhat embarrassing; but if the force of necessity were brought into consideration too, they would seem to be defensive measures that were appropriate under the dreadful circumstances.

As a result of that same defeat, the Senate had to make the following reply to Otacilius, the governor of Sicily, and Cornelius Mammula, the governor of

---

[113]Tiberius Sempronius Gracchus (cos, 215 B.C.) was master of the horse (not consul) in 216 B.C., when the Senate decided it would have to enlist slaves.

[114]The Paediculi lived in Apulia (southeast Italy), near Cannae.

[115]See 2:3,1.

[116]Marcus Junius Pera (cos, 230 B.C.) was dictator in 216 B.C.

[117]Adult Roman men wore a plain white toga; boys wore a toga with a purple stripe along the edge.

Sardinia.[118] The governors had complained to the Senate that our allies were not supplying their fleets and armies with money or grain, and asserted that they themselves had no way of supplying them. The Senate replied that the treasury could not afford to spend money on faraway matters, so the governors would have to figure out some way of solving their great shortages. By this letter the Senate did nothing less than throw the tiller of the empire out of its hands. Sicily and Sardinia were the richest suppliers of our city, our bridgehead and mainstay in wartime, and they had been brought under our control with a great deal of sweat and blood. But, of course, when you, Necessity, gave your command, the Senate abandoned them with a few short words.

6. 2. The people of Casilinum were cut off by Hannibal's siege, and their food supplies were running out.[119] You, Necessity, forced them to remove leather straps used for tying things together, and to tear the hides from leather shields, soften the leather in boiling water, and eat it. What could be more pitiable than those people, if you were to consider the cruelty of their circumstances? What could be more loyal, if you were to consider their resilience? Rather than betray the Romans, they put up with eating that type of food, though they could see their rich fields and fertile plains stretching out before the city walls. Casilinum was right beside the Campanian city that eagerly welcomed the savage Carthaginians with all its delights, but the glorious courage of Casilinum lashed their treacherous eyes with this proof of its loyal friendship.[120]

6. 3. When three hundred men from Praeneste were loyally enduring the siege of Casilinum,[121] one of them happened to catch a mouse, but he chose to sell it for two hundred denarii rather than eat it himself to assuage his hunger. But, I believe, the providence of the gods assigned the seller and the buyer the end that each of them deserved: the miser died of hunger and was not allowed to enjoy the prize money from his parsimony; the man who did not mind spending money to save his life did indeed buy his food at a high price, but he did so under compulsion, and he survived.

6. 4. The civil war that the consuls Gaius Marius and Gnaeus Carbo were waging against Sulla was at a time when the goal was not victory for the Republic; instead, the Republic itself was the reward for victory.[122] By decree of the Senate, the gold and silver decorations of the temples were melted down so that the soldiers could be paid. That was a fine reason for plundering the immortal gods—to decide which party would satisfy its cruelty with a death list of its fellow citizens!

---

[118]Titus Otacilius Crassus and Aulus Cornelius Mammula had been praetors in 217 B.C. Both governors were rescued by loyal Roman allies.

[119]Casilinum was in Campania (western Italy). It fell after a long siege in 216 B.C.

[120]The treacherous Campanian city is Capua, which opened its gates to Hannibal in 216 B.C.

[121]Praeneste was in the north of Latium. Most of the soldiers defending Casilinum in 216 B.C. came from Praeneste.

[122]Sulla marched on Rome in 82 B.C. against the consuls of that year, Gaius Marius, junior (cos, 82 B.C.), and Gnaeus Papirius Carbo (cos, 85 B.C.).

It was not therefore the will of the Conscript Fathers but the fierce hands of horrible Necessity that put her pen to that decree.

6. 5. The army of the divine Caesar,[123] that is, the invincible right hand of that invincible commander, had cut Munda off.[124] He was running out of wood with which to build his siege ramp, so he piled up the dead bodies of the enemy soldiers and built the ramp up to the height he needed. Since he was short of wooden stakes, he made its palisade with spears and javelins. The teacher he had in this strange method of construction was Necessity.

6. 6. To this story recalling a heavenly father I must add one mentioning his divine son.[125] It seemed likely that Phraates, the king of Parthia,[126] would expand into our provinces, and the regions next to his empire were shaken by the sudden news that he was launching an attack. Such a shortage of food resulted in the area around the Bosporus that jars of oil went for 6,000 denarii each, and slaves were bartered for two gallons of grain. But Augustus took care of things and dispersed the bitter storm, for he was then free to look after the world.[127]

Foreign Stories

6. ext. 1. No such protection shone forth for the Cretans when they were besieged by Metellus and driven to the greatest deprivation.[128] It would be fairer for me to say that they tortured rather than assuaged their thirst by drinking their own and their pack animals' urine. In their terror at being defeated, they endured things that no conqueror would have forced them to endure.

6. ext. 2. When Scipio Aemilianus surrounded Numantia with a siege ramp and palisade, the people of that city had eaten up everything that could help them endure their hunger a bit longer, and finally they used human bodies as their food. This is why, after the city had been captured,[129] many of them were discovered carrying the limbs and members of people they had killed in their pockets. Necessity provided them with no excuse in this case: since they were free to die, it was not necessary for them to live at this price.

6. ext. 3. The revolting sacrilege of the inhabitants of Calagurris, who committed a similar crime, went even further than the savage defiance of the people of Numantia.[130] The inhabitants of Calagurris wanted to render the siege of Pompey

---

[123]Caesar was declared a god in 42 B.C.

[124]The Republicans made their last stand against Caesar at Munda (in southern Spain) in 45 B.C.

[125]The divine son is the emperor Augustus.

[126]Phraates IV was king of Parthia (modern Iran and Iraq) from 38 to 2 B.C.

[127]Augustus sent an army to intimidate Phraates IV in 20 B.C. Augustus was "free to look after the world" because he had by then killed off all his rivals at home.

[128]Lucius Caecilius Metellus Creticus (cos, 69 B.C.) besieged and captured several cities on Crete in 67 B.C.

[129]Scipio Aemilianus captured Numantia (in northern Spain) in 133 B.C.

[130]Calagurris was in northern Spain.

ineffective and remain steadfastly loyal to the ashes of their dead leader, Sertorius.[131] Since there was no longer any other creature left alive in their city, they had to make a wicked meal out of their own wives and children. In order to nourish their own flesh for a longer time by eating the flesh of their own ones, the young men of their army did not hesitate to pickle the wretched remains of the bodies in salt. They would have been fine specimens for someone to address on the battlefield, urging them to fight bravely for the lives of their wives and children!

Our great commander had to inflict punishment on these enemies rather than defeat, since they could bring him greater glory by being punished than by being defeated.[132] If we were to compare them on the grounds of savagery, these people would have outdone every kind of serpent and wild beast. Even for such animals, those sweet symbols of life are dearer than their own survival, but for the inhabitants of Calagurris they were lunch and dinner.

Chapter 7. Wills That Were Rescinded

Preface

Let us now devote some time to the business with which people take special care, since it is the last of their actions. Let us discuss wills that were made legally but then rescinded, wills that could have properly been rescinded but were upheld, and wills that transferred the honor of an inheritance to different people than the ones who were expecting it. I shall go through them in the order I have set out above.

Roman Stories

7. 1. A young man was serving as a soldier, and his father received a false notification from the army about the son's death. The father appointed other heirs and died afterward. After the young man had completed his military service, he headed home. Because of his father's mistake and the insolence of the new owners, he found himself locked out of his home: what could have been more shameless than those men? The young man had devoted the best years of his youth to the Republic, he had endured great hardship and many dangers, he could show the scars he had received from exposing his body to the enemy: but they were demanding that they should continue to possess his ancestral home, though they were useless burdens to the city. So as soon as he had put down his weapons, he was forced to fight a civilian battle in the Forum. And it was a bitter one: he argued before the centumvirate court for his father's property against these unscrupulous heirs. But

---

[131]Quintus Sertorius (praetor, 83 B.C.) had been supported by the Spaniards in his long rebellion (82–72 B.C.) against the Roman government (see 7:3,6).

[132]Pompey captured Calagurris in 72 B.C.

he came out on top in the verdict of every jury, and furthermore he won every juryman's vote.[133]

7. 2. Marcus Anneius (senior)[134] of Carseoli[135] had been an illustrious Roman equestrian,[136] and a similar thing happened to his son, who was adopted by Sufenas, the son's maternal uncle. The son rescinded the will of his biological father in the centumvirate court, because he had been bypassed in the will, and Tullianus, a friend of Pompey the Great, had been appointed heir in the will, which Pompey himself had witnessed. So in that court case, the son had to deal more with the influence of an extraordinary man than with the ashes of his father. Although these two things went against the son, he still held on to his father's property.

Lucius Sextilius and Publius Popillius were related by blood to Marcus Anneius (senior), and he had made them equal heirs with Tullianus,[137] but they did not dare to argue with a legal oath against the young man.[138] The power of Pompey the Great was exceptionally great at that time, and it could have encouraged them to stand by the words of the will,[139] and the heirs were also helped by the fact that Marcus Anneius (junior) had joined the family and sacred rites of Sufenas. But the bond created by birth is the closest one among human beings, and it overrode both the wishes of his father and the influence of a leading politician.

7. 3. Gaius Tettius (junior) was disinherited by his father when he was a baby, even though the baby's mother was Petronia, with whom Tettius (senior) had lived in marriage throughout his life. The divine Augustus ordered by decree that Tettius (junior) should come into his father's property, and in so doing Augustus acted in the spirit of the Father of the Fatherland.[140] Tettius (senior) had acted very unjustly in abandoning his duty as a father to his own son, born in his own house.

7. 4. Septicia was the mother of the Trachalus boys from Ariminum.[141] She was angry with her sons, and to insult them, she married a very old man, Publicius, when she herself was no longer able to bear children, and bypassed both of her

---

[133]The centumvirate court dealt with civil cases, especially wills. There were four separate juries in the court.

[134]I have added the words "junior" and "senior" in parentheses to help clarify the confusing situation in this and the following stories.

[135]Carseoli was in the Sabine region (central Italy).

[136]An equestrian was a member of the business elite (see Glossary).

[137]Marcus Anneius (senior) left his property to two distant relatives (Sextilius and Popillius) and a friend (Tullianus). From a strictly legal point of view, Marcus Anneius (junior) was now the son of Sufenas and had no right to the property of Marcus Anneius (senior). But the praetors tended to adjust the law in favor of the biological son, who wins out in this case.

[138]In a Roman court, a person could take a legal oath (*sacramentum*), guaranteeing that their version of the facts was correct. If their version was wrong, they had to pay a fine to the praetor.

[139]Pompey was the dominant figure in Roman politics from his consulship in 70 B.C. until his death in 48 B.C., so this legal dispute must date to that period.

[140]Augustus was proclaimed Father of the Fatherland (*Pater Patriae*) in 2 B.C.

[141]Ariminum (modern Rimini) was on the coast of Aemilia (northern Italy).

sons in her will. Her sons approached the divine Augustus, and he ruled against their mother's remarriage and her final arrangements: he ordered that the sons should inherit their mother's property, and since her remarriage had not been contracted for the sake of producing children, he forbade her husband to keep her dowry.[142]

If Equity herself were judging this case, could she have reached a fairer or more impressive verdict? You reject the sons you gave birth to, you marry when you are barren, you overturn the arrangements of your will because of your violent anger, and you are not ashamed to hand over the entire estate to a man whose body is almost laid out for his funeral and under whom you spread out your withered old body in bed. For behaving in this way, you were blasted by a thunderbolt from heaven that reached all the way down to you in hell.

7. 5. The decision reached by the city praetor, Gaius Calpurnius Piso,[143] was also outstanding: Terentius brought a complaint before him because he had raised eight sons to adulthood, and one of them, whom he had placed for adoption, had disinherited him. Piso gave Terentius possession of the young man's property and did not allow the heirs to take legal proceedings. Piso was obviously moved by the prestige of fatherhood, its gift of life, and its provision of education, but he was also affected by the number of sons standing around, because he saw that the seven brothers as well as their father had been wrongly disinherited.

7. 6. Well? What an impressive decree the consul Mamercus Aemilius Lepidus made![144] A man called Genucius, who was a gallus[145] of the Great Mother, had convinced the city praetor, Gnaeus Orestes,[146] that the property of Naevius Anius should be given back to him, since Genucius had received possession of that property in accordance with the will made out by Naevius himself. But Naevius was a freedman of Surdinus, so even though Naevius had made Genucius his heir, Surdinus appealed to Mamercus, and Mamercus overturned the praetor's ruling.[147]

He did so on the grounds that Genucius, by voluntarily castrating himself, should not be considered as belonging among men or women. This decree was worthy of Mamercus himself and of a leader of the senate,[148] and it stated that the tribunals of our magistrates should not be polluted by the obscene presence and disgusting voice of Genucius, under the pretense that he was seeking justice.

---

[142]A husband normally kept his wife's dowry if they were still married when she died, so Augustus was declaring that Septicia's second marriage was not valid.

[143]Gaius Calpurnius Piso (cos, 67 B.C.) was a praetor in 70 B.C.

[144]This case took place in 77 B.C., when Mamercus Aemilius Lepidus Livianus was consul.

[145]A gallus was a priest of the Great Mother of the Gods, and her priests had to castrate themselves.

[146]Gnaeus Aufidius Orestes (cos, 71 B.C.) was the city praetor in 77 B.C.

[147]Since Naevius Anius used to be the slave of Surdinus, and since his will in favor of Genucius was rescinded by the consul, the property of Naevius Anius went to his former master, Surdinus.

[148]Mamercus was appointed leader of the Senate in 70 B.C.

7. 7. Quintus Metellus acted much more severely as a city praetor than Orestes had done.[149] When Vecilius, a pimp, requested possession of the goods of Vibienus in accordance with the latter's will, Metellus denied this request. Being a very noble and dignified man, Metellus felt that the worlds of the Forum and the brothel should be kept apart. He did not want to condone the behavior of Vibienus, who had given away his fortune to a filthy brothel, or to grant Vecilius his rights as if he were an upright citizen, since Vecilius had cut himself off from every honorable walk of life.

Chapter 8. Wills That Were Upheld Although There Were Grounds for Rescinding Them

Preface

Let us be content with these cases of wills that were rescinded, and let us touch on wills that were upheld, even though there were grounds for rescinding them.

Roman Stories

8.1. How obvious and well known the madness of Tuditanus was! He scattered money among the general public, he dragged his toga after him in the Forum as if it were a tragic costume, while everyone looked on and laughed out loud, and he did many things similar to these. He appointed an heir in his will, and his nearest blood relative, Tiberius Longus,[150] tried in vain to have it overturned by the court of the spear.[151] The centumvirate jury felt that what was written in the will should get more consideration than who had written it.

8. 2. Tuditanus was mad throughout his life, but in the case of Aebutia, who had been the wife of Lucius Menenius Agrippa, it was her will that was full of insanity. Although she had two daughters, Plaetoria and Afronia, who were equally virtuous, she was led astray by the unsteadiness of her mind rather than influenced by any good or bad deed of either daughter, and made Plaetoria alone her heir; from her very large fortune, she also made a legacy of 20,000 sesterces to Afronia's children. Afronia did not want to argue with a legal oath against her own sister,[152] and she felt it was better to honor her mother's will by putting up with it than to

---

[149]Lucius Caecilius Metellus Creticus (cos, 67 B.C.) was a praetor in 74 B.C.

[150]These men belonged to the Sempronius family, so their names would be Sempronius Tuditanus and Tiberius Sempronius Longus.

[151]A spear was set up before the centumvirate court, which was therefore sometimes called the court of the spear.

[152]Afronia did not want to embarrass her sister by making a legal oath (*sancramentum*) and asserting her right to half the inheritance; in addition to losing half the inheritance, the sister would also be fined by the praetor for making a false assertion.

overturn it in a law court. She revealed how little she deserved such ill-treatment by the resignation with which she bore it.

8. 3. The behavior of Quintus Metellus makes that woman's delusions less surprising. Although lots of very famous men from the same family were thriving in our city, and the Claudius family, which was very closely tied to him by blood, was flourishing, he left Carrinas as his sole heir, but nobody questioned his will on account of this.[153]

8. 4. Pompeius Reginus, a man from the Transalpine region,[154] was bypassed in his brother's will. To prove his brother's injustice, he read out, before a large audience of both orders,[155] the two pages of his own will that had been recorded at the assembly place. In it, his brother was appointed heir to most of the estate, and was given an additional legacy of 15,000,000 sesterces. Reginus complained a great deal about it among his friends, who shared his sense of outrage, but as far as the court of the spear was concerned, he had to leave his brother's ashes in peace. And yet the heirs appointed by his brother were neither as close in blood as Reginus nor even close friends, but strangers of humble origin, so that his silence seemed outrageous and his preferring them offensive.

Wills That Appointed Heirs Contrary to General Expectations

8. 5. The following wills were equally lucky in avoiding censure, but I wonder whether they were more offensively immoral.

Quintus Caecilius achieved an honorable social rank and a very large fortune through the eager support and great kindness of Lucius Lucullus.[156] Caecilius always pretended that Lucullus was his only heir, and as he was dying he even handed his rings over to him,[157] but he adopted Pomponius Atticus in his will and left him the heir to all his property.[158] But the Roman people put a rope around his neck and dragged the corpse of this false and treacherous man through the streets. So the wicked man got the son and heir that he wanted but the funeral rites and burial that he deserved.

8. 6. Titus Marius of Urbinum[159] deserved the same kind of funeral. He started off at the lowest rank in the army, but through the kindness of his general, the di-

---

[153]Quintus Caecilius Metellus Nepos was consul in 57 B.C. His aunt and brother had married into the Claudius family. Gaius Carrinas was consul in 43 B.C.

[154]This region was Transalpine Gaul (modern France).

[155]The two orders are the order of senators and the order of equestrians.

[156]Quintus Caecilius was an equestrian, a member of the business elite (see Glossary). Lucius Licinius Lucullus Ponticus was consul in 74 B.C.

[157]By handing his signet ring over to Lucullus, Caecilius was implying that Lucullus was his heir.

[158]Caecilius adopted his nephew, Titus Pomponius Atticus, as his son and heir in his will.

[159]Urbinum was in Umbria (eastern Italy).

vine Augustus, he rose to the highest rank in the army, and from the ample rewards of this position he became a rich man.[160] Throughout his life he used to
proclaim that he was leaving his fortune to the man he had got it from, and even
on the day before he died he said the very same thing to Augustus himself. But at
the same time he did not even mention his name in the will.

8. 7. Lucius Valerius, who had the additional name of Heptachordus, found a
political enemy in Cornelius Balbus.[161] Balbus helped and advised others to harass
him with several private cases and finally arranged for someone to accuse him on a
capital charge.[162] But Valerius bypassed all his legal advisers and defenders and left
Balbus as his sole heir. Obviously some mental disorder had driven him astray: he
loved poverty, desired dangers, and begged and prayed for a legal conviction by
showing kindness to the people who was responsible for these things, and hatred to
the people who had defended him from these misfortunes.[163]

8. 8. Titus Barrus had experienced the loving spirit and generous friendship of
Lentulus Spinther,[164] and when Barrus was dying he handed his rings to Spinther
as if Spinther were his only heir, but he made him heir to nothing. What punishment his conscience must have inflicted on that disgusting man at that moment, if
indeed it has the powers it is believed to possess! He gave up his spirit while he was
thinking of his false and ungrateful scheme, but it was as if some torturer was perse-
cuting his mind from inside, because he was aware that his transition from life to
death would be hated by the gods above and cursed by the gods below.

8. 9. Marcus Popillius, a man of the senatorial order, had a very close friend
from childhood, Oppius Gallus. In accordance with their long-standing friendship,
Popillius, as he was dying, looked at Oppius very kindly and spoke to him in words
that showed his great love for him. Oppius was actually the only person out of the
many people sitting there that Popillius considered worthy of his last embrace and
kiss. In addition, he also gave his rings to Oppius, ostensibly so that Oppius would
not lose anything from the inheritance that in fact he would never possess.

Oppius was scrupulously honest, but he had been made a fool of and insulted
by his dying friend. He put the rings back in their box and had it sealed by those
present; then, though disinherited himself, he very honestly handed it over to his
friend's heirs. What could be more dishonorable or ill-timed than this joke? Popillius was a senator of the Roman people who had just left the Senate house; he was
a man who was soon to give up the pleasures of this life; but as death was weighing down his eyes, and his spirit was giving up its last breath, he picked out the
most sacred laws of friendship so he that he could mock them with a foolish joke.

---

[160]Augustus promoted Titus Marius socially to the status of an equestrian (which meant
providing him with a fortune of at least 400,000 sesterces).

[161]These two men were Lucius Valerius Flaccus "Heptachordus" (praetor, 63 B.C.) and
Lucius Cornelius Balbus (cos, 40 B.C.).

[162]Valerius had been governor of Asia in 61 B.C. and was tried for misgovernment in 59 B.C.

[163]Cicero had defended Valerius in 59 B.C.

[164]Publius Cornelius Lentulus Spinther was consul in 57 B.C.

BOOK EIGHT

Chapter 1. Why People Accused of Infamous Crimes Were Acquitted or Found Guilty

Preface

Now, to make it easier to bear with resignation the erratic ways of the law courts, let us tell of people who were victims of jealousy and the reasons they were acquitted or found guilty.

Acquittals

1. absol. 1.[1] Marcus Horatius was found guilty by King Tullus on the charge of murdering his sister, but he was acquitted when he appealed his case to the people.[2] The atrocious nature of the murder moved the king, while its motive influenced the people, since they felt that the young woman's premature love affair had been punished severely rather than criminally. So her brother's deed was absolved from harsh punishment, and he was able to get as much glory from the blood of a relative as he did from the blood of our enemies.

1. absol. 2. On that occasion the Roman people presented itself as a strict guardian of chastity; later, it presented itself as an unfairly lax judge. Servius Galba was being harshly denounced at the rostra by Libo, a tribune of the plebs,[3] because when Galba was governor he had killed a large group of Lusitanians in Spain after making a truce with them.[4] Cato the Censor was a very old man then, and he supported the tribune's charges in a speech that he recorded in his *Origins*.[5] The accused could raise no objection to defend himself against the charges, but he started weeping and asking the people to look after his own little children and the

---

[1]Valerius uses the Latin word *absoluti* (acquitted) to describe these legal cases, and that is why the abbreviation "absol." is used before the stories in this section. So the first story is 8:1,absol.1 (Book 8: Chapter 1, Acquittal 1).

[2]Tullus Hostilius was the third king of Rome (672–641 B.C.). After defeating the Curiatius brothers from Alba Longa, Marcus Horatius killed his own sister, because she had wept for one of the Curiatius brothers to whom she was engaged (see 6:3,6).

[3]Lucius Scribonius Libo (tribune of the plebs, 149 B.C.) prosecuted Servius Sulpicius Galba (cos, 144 B.C.) in 149 B.C.

[4]Galba had massacred eight thousand Lusitanians while he was governor of Farther Spain in 150 B.C.

[5]Cato the Censor wrote a work on Roman history called *Origins*.

son of Galus, a relative of his.[6] By this behavior he won the sympathy of the assembly, and although everyone had previously agreed that he was doomed, he ended up with almost no vote of guilty. That court was governed by pity rather than justice, and since it could not grant him an acquittal because of his innocence, it granted it to him out of consideration for his boys.

1. *absol. 3.* The story that follows fits in with the previous one. Feeling against Aulus Gabinius was running very high[7] when he was prosecuted by Gaius Memmius and placed at the mercy of the votes of the people.[8] His case seemed hopeless, because the prosecution was arguing its case fully, the arguments of the defense were unreliable, and the jury was very angry with Gabinius and eagerly demanded his punishment. So the jailer and the prison were constantly on his mind, when suddenly all these thoughts were dispelled by the intervention of Fortune in a benevolent mood. Sisenna, the son of Gabinius, was driven to distraction and threw himself at the feet of Memmius, begging for mercy, trying to find some remedy for their disaster in the very place where the whole force of the hurricane had burst out. With a fierce look on his face, the arrogant victor cast him aside, knocking the ring off his finger, and let him lie there on the ground for some time. This spectacle led Laelius, a tribune of the plebs,[9] to order the acquittal of Gabinius, and everybody agreed with him. It proved that people should not insolently abuse their good fortune, and that they should not be too readily dashed by bad fortune. This lesson will be equally clear from the next story.

1. *absol. 4.* I do not know whether Publius Claudius acted more unjustly toward our religion or our country, since he neglected the most ancient customs of our religion and lost the finest fleet of our country.[10] He was placed at the mercy of the angered people, and it was believed that there was no way he could escape his inevitable punishment, but by virtue of a sudden shower of rain he was saved from a conviction. The hearing was disrupted, and they decided not to start it all over again, since the gods seemed to have obstructed it. So a storm at sea had forced him to plead his case, and a storm from heaven had brought him an acquittal.

1. *absol. 5.* The same kind of assistance saved Tuccia, a vestal virgin who was accused of sexual immorality.[11] Her virginity had come under a cloud of suspicion but shone out in the end. With the clear conscience of the innocent, she had the courage to hope for an acquittal from a dangerous experiment: she picked up a sieve and said, "Vesta, if I have always kept my hands pure in performing your

[6]Galba's relative, Gaius Sulpicius Galus, had been consul in 166 B.C.

[7]Aulus Gabinius (cos, 58 B.C.) had been governor of Syria from 57 to 54 B.C. and had made himself unpopular with the equestrian tax companies.

[8]Gaius Memmius was a tribune of the plebs in 54 B.C., when he prosecuted Gabinius for treason.

[9]Decimus Laelius was a tribune of the plebs in 54 B.C.

[10]Publius Claudius Pulcher was consul in 249 B.C. He had thrown the sacred chickens into the sea and then lost most of the Roman fleet (see 1:4,3).

[11]Tuccia was tried for violating her vow of chastity in 230 B.C.

rites, grant that I may take water from the Tiber in this sieve and carry it to your temple." Nature itself gave way before the brave and rash promise made by this priestess.

1. absol. 6. Similarly, when Lucius Piso was accused by Gaius Claudius Pulcher of inflicting serious and intolerable wrongs on our allies,[12] he avoided the danger of certain ruin by a stroke of luck. At the very time that the negative votes were being cast against him, a sudden shower of rain fell down, and while he prostrated himself on the ground to kiss the feet of the jurymen, his mouth was filled with mud. The sight of this moved the entire court from severity to compassion and kindness. They felt he had already paid a harsh enough penalty to the allies, since he had been led to such a strait that he had been forced to throw himself down so humbly and raise himself up so shamefully.

1. absol. 7. I shall add the story of two men who were acquitted through the fault of their accusers. Marcus Flavius was brought on trial before the people by Gaius Valerius, an aedile.[13] When he had been found guilty by the votes of fourteen of the tribes, he shouted out that an innocent man was being ruined. Valerius replied in an equally loud voice that he did not care whether he was being ruined as an innocent man or a guilty one as long as he was being ruined. The violence of this remark presented his opponent with the votes of all the remaining tribes. Valerius had crushed his enemy into the ground, but when he was confident that his enemy was definitely finished, he raised him up again and lost his victory at the very moment of winning it.

1. absol. 8. Gaius Cosconius was accused under the Servilian law,[14] and because of his many obvious crimes, there was no doubt that he was guilty. But he saved himself by reciting before the court a poem of his accuser, Valerius Valentinus, in which Valerius had jokingly described in verse how he had seduced a young man in a striped toga and a young freeborn woman. The jurymen felt it would be unjust to let him walk away after winning the case, since he deserved not to defeat another but to be defeated himself. In this case Valerius was convicted by the acquittal of Consonius, rather than Consonius himself being set free.

1. absol. 9. I shall now touch on men who were ruined by their own crimes but were granted an acquittal as a favor to their famous relatives. Aulus Atilius Calatinus was charged with the disgraceful crime of betraying the town of Sora.[15] But in a few words, his father-in-law, Quintus Maximus, saved him from the imminent

---

[12]Lucius Calpurnius Piso Caesoninus (cos, 112 B.C.) died in 107 B.C. He must have been a governor in 111 B.C. and Gaius Claudius Pulcher (cos, 92 B.C.) probably prosecuted him on his return in 110 B.C.

[13]Gaius Valerius Potitus (cos, 331 B.C.) was an aedile in 329 B.C. He accused Marcus Flavius (tribune of the plebs, 327 B.C.) of seducing a married woman.

[14]The Servilian law against misgovernment was passed in 101 B.C. Gaius Cosconius (praetor, 89 B.C.) was governor of Illyria from 78 to 76 B.C.

[15]Sora was a Roman city in southern Latium that was captured twice by the Samnites (in 315 and 306 B.C.).

danger of a conviction.[16] Maximus declared that if he had discovered that Atilius was guilty of this crime, he would have ended his relationship with him. The people had almost made up their mind already, but they yielded to the judgment of this one man. They felt it would be unfair not to trust his testimony, since they remembered that they done well in trusting him with their armies during a very difficult period for the Republic.

1. absol. 10. Marcus Aemilius Scaurus was accused of misgovernment, and his defense in the case was doomed and pitiful.[17] The prosecutor said he had 120 men whose testimony he could legally use against him, but he would not object to his acquittal if Scaurus could name an equal number of people in his province from whom he had not taken anything. Scaurus could not even take advantage of this generous offer. But because of the ancient nobility of his family and the recent memory of his father,[18] he was acquitted.

1. absol. 11. But although the prestige of distinguished men could be very influential in protecting the accused, it was not quite so effective in destroying them; in fact, if it attacked them too harshly, it actually benefited men who were obviously guilty. Scipio Aemilianus prosecuted Cotta before the people.[19] Cotta's defense was undermined by his very serious crimes; but the trial was postponed seven times, and finally he was acquitted on the eighth hearing, because people were afraid that if he were convicted, it would be thought that their verdict was given as a favor to the exceptional status of his accuser. I imagine they said something like this to themselves: "If someone is seeking to deprive another man of his liberty, we do not want him to drag into the court his triumphs, trophies, spoils, and prows of captured ships. He should terrify our enemies, but he should not use the great sound of his glory to attack the life of a fellow citizen."

1. absol. 12. The jurymen behaved aggressively toward that extraordinary accuser, but they were kind to a man of far lower status who was put on trial. Calidius of Bononia[20] was caught at nighttime in the bedroom of a married man and had to defend himself against a charge of adultery. He emerged from those huge dangerous waves of disgrace by grabbing onto a very flimsy type of defense, a bit of wood from the shipwreck, so to speak. He claimed he had gone there because he was in love with a young male slave. The place was suspicious, the time was suspicious, the character of the wife was suspicious, and his own youthfulness was suspicious, but by confessing to his lust for the young male slave, he eluded the charge of adultery.

---

[16]Quintus Fabius Maximus Rullianus (cos, 322 B.C.) was a Roman leader during the Samnite Wars.

[17]Marcus Aemilius Scaurus (praetor, 56 B.C.) had been governor of Sardinia in 55 B.C. He was tried for misgovernment in 54 B.C. (see 3:6,7).

[18]His father was Marcus Aemilius Scaurus (cos, 115 B.C.), leader of the Senate from 115 B.C. until his death in 88 B.C.

[19]Scipio Aemilianus returned to Rome in 132 B.C. and prosecuted Lucius Aurelius Cotta (cos, 144 B.C.) shortly after that.

[20]Bononia (modern Bologna) was in Aemilia (northern Italy).

1. absol. 13. That story involved a minor matter, but the next story involves a much more serious one. The Cloelius brothers, who were born of a very illustrious family in Tarracina,[21] were defending themselves against the charge of murdering their father. Their father, Tiberius Cloelius, was killed while he was sleeping in his bedroom, and the brothers had been sleeping there in the other bed. No slave or free man was found against whom any suspicion of murder could be raised. The Cloelius brothers were acquitted for one reason alone: it was made clear to the jury that when the door was opened they were found still asleep. Sleep is the clearest proof of care-free innocence, and it rescued the wretched brothers. The jury decided that it was not naturally possible that they could have slept quietly beside the blood and wounds of their father if they had killed him.

Convictions

1. damn. 1.[22] We shall now briefly speak of those whose behavior before the trial did them more harm in arguing their case than their innocence could do them good.

After Scipio Asiaticus had celebrated a most splendid triumph over King Antiochus,[23] he was found guilty of taking bribes from the king.[24] Antiochus was master of all Asia and already stretching his conquering hands toward Europe, so I hardly imagine that he would have bribed Scipio to drive him back beyond the Taurus Mountains.[25] But although Scipio had led a completely blameless life and was far removed from any such suspicion, he was unable to resist the envy that dogged the famous titles granted to him and his brother.

1. damn. 2. Scipio Asiaticus was undone by the great splendor of his fortune, but Gaius Decianus,[26] a man of proven integrity, was ruined by his own words. He was prosecuting Publius Furius,[27] a man who led a most corrupt life, at the rostra, but in one part of his speech, he dared to denounce the murder of Saturninus.[28] As a result, Decianus did not secure the conviction of the accused, and on top of that he had to pay compensation to Furius.[29]

---

[21]Tarracina (modern Terracina) was on the south coast of Latium.

[22]Valerius uses the Latin word *damnati* ("convicted") to describe these legal cases, and that is why the abbreviation "damn." is used before the stories in this section. So the first story is 8:1,damn.1 (Book 8: Chapter 1, Conviction 1).

[23]Scipio Asiaticus celebrated his triumph over Antiochus the Great of Syria in 189 B.C.

[24]Scipio Asiaticus was prosecuted in 187 B.C. (see 3:7,1d) and again in 184 B.C. He was convicted at the second trial. See 5;3,2c.

[25]The Taurus Mountains separate Asia Minor from Syria. Scipio Asiaticus deprived Antiochus of all his territory in Asia Minor (see 4:1,ext.9).

[26]Gaius Appuleius Decianus was a tribune of the plebs in 98 B.C.

[27]Publius Furius had been a tribune of the plebs in 99 B.C.

[28]Decianus sympathized with Lucius Appuleius Saturninus (tribune of the plebs, 103 B.C.), who had been murdered by conservative senators at the end of 100 B.C.

[29]Decianus prosecuted Furius in 98 B.C., but Decianus had to go into exile in 97 B.C.

1. *damn*. 3. Similar circumstances ruined Sextus Titius.[30] He was innocent, and he was popular with the people because of the land law he proposed.[31] In spite of this, the entire assembly voted against him, because he had a picture of Saturninus in his home.[32]

1. *damn*. 4. Claudia must be added to these cases, because a wicked wish she made ruined her, even though she was innocent of the charge made against her. As she was coming back home from the games, she was jostled by the crowd, so she made a wish that her brother, who had caused great losses to our naval forces,[33] would come back to life, and that he would be elected consul several times so that he could get rid of the city's excess population by his ill-fated leadership.[34]

1. *damn*. 5. We can make a little digression, and move on to those who were attacked and unexpectedly convicted for the flimsiest of reasons.

The nocturnal committee men,[35] Marcus Mulvius, Gnaeus Lollius, and Lucius Sextilius, had arrived rather late to extinguish a fire that had broken out on the Sacred Way.[36] They were put on trial before the people by the tribunes of the plebs and convicted.

1. *damn*. 6. Similarly, Publius Villius, a nocturnal committee man, was prosecuted by Publius Aquillius, a tribune of the plebs, and lost his case before a court of the people, because he had been rather careless in performing the night watch.[37]

1. *damn*. 7. A court of the people was very harsh in punishing Marcus Aemilius Porcina. He was prosecuted by Lucius Cassius for building too high a holiday home in the region of Alsium, and the court imposed a heavy fine on him.[38]

1. *damn*. 8. We must not omit the conviction of a man who had fallen too much in love with his boyfriend. When they were in the country, he was asked by his boyfriend to have some tripe cooked for dinner. As there was no opportunity of buying beef in the neighborhood, the man killed a domestic ox and satisfied the boy's wishes. Because of this, the man had to face a trial before the people,

---

[30]Sextus Titius was a tribune of the plebs in 99 B.C.

[31]The land law of Titius was vetoed by his more conservative fellow tribunes.

[32]As in the previous story, a conservative jury punishes a supporter of Lucius Appuleius Saturninus (tribune of the plebs, 103 B.C.).

[33]Her brother Publius Claudius Pulcher (cos, 249 B.C.) lost a fleet during the First Punic War (see 1:4,3 and 8:1,absol.4).

[34]The aediles of the plebs fined Claudia for this misanthropic statement in 246 B.C.

[35]The nocturnal committee men (*triumviri nocturni*) were a committee of three men responsible for watching over the city of Rome at night.

[36]Marcus Mulvius, Gnaeus Lollius, and Lucius Sextilius were the nocturnal committee men in 241 B.C. The Sacred Way ran from the Velia hill down to the Forum.

[37]Publius Villius was a nocturnal committee man, and Publius Aquilius was a tribune of the plebs, in 211 B.C.

[38]When Lucius Cassius Longinus Ravilla (cos, 127 B.C.) was censor in 125 B.C., he fined Marcus Aemilius Lepidus Porcina (cos, 137 B.C.) for his extravagance. Alsium was on the coast of Etruria, just north of Rome.

though he would have been considered innocent had he not been born in so primitive an age.

Undecided Cases

1. amb. 1.[39] We shall now discuss those who had their lives placed in jeopardy but were neither convicted nor acquitted.

A certain woman was brought before the praetor Marcus Popillius Laenas,[40] because she had beaten her mother to death with a club. The jury did not vote either way, because it was abundantly clear that the daughter was driven to do this because her own children had been murdered with poison. Their grandmother had killed the children because she hated her own daughter, and the daughter had avenged their murder by murdering her own mother. The court's verdict was that the crime of the daughter did not deserve to be punished, and the crime of her mother did not deserve to be condoned.

1. amb. 2. When Publius Dolabella was ruling Asia as governor,[41] his mind wavered in the same kind of doubt. A married woman from Smyrna[42] killed her husband and her son when she discovered that they had killed a young man of wonderful character whom she had borne by a previous husband. When this mattered was reported to Dolabella, he referred the case to the Areopagus in Athens,[43] because he could not bear either to release a woman who had been guilty of two murders, or to punish a woman who was moved by a justifiable sense of grievance. The executive officer of the Roman people acted with consideration and kindness, but the judges of the Areopagus acted with no less wisdom. After investigating the case, they ordered the prosecutor and the accused to appear before them again one hundred years later. They were moved by the same feelings as Dolabella, but he avoided the insoluble problem of whether to convict or acquit her by transferring the case, they avoided the problem by postponing it.

[39]Valerius uses the Latin word *ambusti*, which literally means "half-burned," to describe these undecided legal cases in which the accused was neither acquitted and allowed to go away in raw innocence nor convicted and completely cooked by the legal system. That is why the abbreviation "amb." is used before the stories in this section. So the first story is 8:1,amb.1 (Book 8: Chapter 1, Undecided 1).

[40]Marcus Popillius Laenas (cos, 139 B.C.) was a praetor in 142 B.C.

[41]Publius Cornelius Dolabella was governor of Asia in 68 B.C.

[42]Smyrna was on the east coast of Asia Minor.

[43]The Areopagus was the law court for murder cases in Athens.

Chapter 2. Famous Private Cases

Preface

I shall add some private cases to these public trials. The equity of these cases will be able to delight the reader whereas a disorganized mass of such cases would annoy him.

Roman Stories

2. 1. Claudius Centumalus was ordered by the augurs[44] to lower the height of his house, which was on the Caelian hill,[45] because it was blocking their view when they were taking the auspices from the citadel. He sold the house to Calpurnius Lanarius without telling him what the college of augurs had demanded. The augurs forced Calpurnius to demolish the house, and he asked Marcus Cato, the father of the famous Cato,[46] to judge between him and Claudius on the following legal issue: What should Claudius in good faith do and give to Calpurnius? When Cato discovered that Claudius had deliberately concealed the command of the priests, he immediately judged against him and in favor of Calpurius. Cato acted with absolute fairness, because a man who sells something in good faith should neither exaggerate the benefits that will derive from it, nor conceal his knowledge of its drawbacks.

2. 2. The case I have mentioned was well known in its own era, but even the case I am going to speak of was not consigned to silence. Gaius Visellius Varro[47] was afflicted with a serious illness, and because he had had a sexual affair with Otacilia, the wife of Laterensis,[48] he allowed her to record in his books that she had advanced him 300,000 sesterces.[49] His plan was that if he died, she could demand that sum from his heirs. He wanted it to be a kind of legacy, but he disguised his generous payment for sexual pleasure by pretending it was a debt. But then, contrary to Otacilia's hopes, he escaped from that storm.

Otacilia was annoyed because Varro had not brought her hopes of gain to fruition by dying, so she suddenly changed from an obliging girlfriend and started acting openly as a profiteer and demanding the money. She had been trying to get at that money all along by using her own shameless impudence and Varro's worthless promise. Gaius Aquillius,[50] a man of great prestige and remarkable for his knowledge of civil law, was appointed to judge the matter, and he brought along

---

[44]See augur in the Glossary.

[45]The Caelian hill was southwest of the citadel (which was on the Capitol hill).

[46]Marcus Porcius Cato (tribune of the plebs, 99 B.C.) was Cato of Utica's father.

[47]Gaius Visellius Varro was an aedile in 59 B.C.

[48]The full name of Otacilia's husband was Marcus Juventius Laterensis.

[49]See money—Roman in the Glossary.

[50]Gaius Aquillius Gallus was a praetor in 66 B.C.

the leading men of the state to advise him; his intelligence and scruples led him to reject the woman's claims. But if Varro could have been convicted on this legal issue, but also released from his obligation to his opponent, I have no doubt that the judge would have been happy to penalize Varro's disgraceful and illicit sexual affair. Aquillius rejected Otacilia's legal trickery in this private case, but he left Varro's criminal adultery to be punished later by a public court.

2. 3. Marius behaved with great moral courage and in a way that suited the spirit of the army in a similar kind of case. Gaius Titinius of Minturnae[51] had knowingly taken Fannia as his wife, even though she had slept with other men, but then he divorced her and tried to deprive her of her dowry by accusing her of that. The couple got Marius to judge between them, and after he had held a public hearing, he took Titinius aside and warned him to give up his course of action and hand the dowry back to his wife. Marius tried to persuade him several times but in vain; the man forced him to pronounce judgment, so Marius ruled that the woman should pay a fine of one sesterce for her sexual immorality, and that Titinius should pay the entire value of the dowry. He explained beforehand that he was judging the case in this way because it was quite clear to him that Titinius had been scheming to get at Fannia's fortune, and this is why he had wanted to marry her in spite of her sexual immorality.

This is the same Fannia who later helped Marius in every way she could when he had been declared a public enemy by the Senate. He was covered in mud from the marsh they had dragged him out of, and he was brought to her house at Minturnae and held in custody there.[52] She bore in mind that if she had been declared sexually immoral, this was due to her own character, but if she had kept her dowry, this was due to the moral integrity of Marius.

2. 4. A lot of discussion arose from a court case in which a man was found guilty of theft, because although he had borrowed a horse as far as Aricia,[53] he had ridden it to a hill beyond that town. At this point, how could we not admire people's sense of honor in that era, when even such tiny breaches of propriety were punished?

---

[51]Minturnae was on the coast of Latium.

[52]When Sulla marched on Rome in 88 B.C., he declared Marius an outlaw. The people of Minturnae captured Marius and held him in Fannia's house, but they later repented and let Marius escape to Africa (see 1:5,5 and 2:10,6).

[53]Aricia was in Latium. It was the first stop after Rome on the highway to southern Italy.

Chapter 3. Women Who Pleaded Cases before Magistrates on Behalf of Themselves or Other People

Preface

We must not remain silent about the following women. The fact of their gender and the modesty of a married woman's dress were not strong enough to stop them speaking out in the Forum and in the courts.

Roman Stories

3. 1. Maesia from Sentinum[54] pleaded her own case when she was on trial before a court assembled by the praetor Lucius Titius and attended by a huge gathering of people.[55] She went through all the proper stages and points of her defense carefully and forcefully. She was acquitted at the preliminary hearing and almost unanimously. Because she had the heart of a man under the appearance of a woman, they called her Androgyne.[56]

3. 2. Carfania, the wife of Senator Licinius Buccio, loved to draw legal suits upon herself. She would always speak on her own behalf before the praetor, not because she had too few lawyers at her disposal, but because she had far too much impudence. So by her strange yelping in the Forum and her constant harassment of the courts, she became a notorious example of a woman who indulged in malicious prosecutions. In fact, if you wanted to condemn the shameless character of any woman, you would accuse her of being a Carfania. She lived on until the consulship of Caesar (his second one) and Publius Servilius:[57] the time when that monster came to an end, and not the time she came into existence, should be commemorated.

3. 3. When the married women as a group were burdened with a heavy property tax by the triumvirs, and no man would dare to come to their defense, Hortensia, the daughter of Quintus Hortensius,[58] pleaded the case of the women before the triumvirs with courage and success.[59] This reincarnation of her father's eloquence induced the triumvirs to waive most of the sum demanded from the women. Quintus Hortensius came back to life through his female offspring, and he inspired the words of his daughter.[60] If his male descendants had been prepared to follow her spirit,[61] the great legacy of Hortensian eloquence would not have ended abruptly with this single legal speech by a woman.

---

[54]Sentinum was in Umbria (eastern Italy).

[55]Maesia and the praetor Lucius Titius have not been identified.

[56]*Androgyne* is a Greek word meaning "man–woman."

[57]Caesar and Publius Servilius Isauricus were consuls in 48 B.C.

[58]Quintus Hortensius Hortalus (cos, 69 B.C.) was a famous Roman orator.

[59]Hortensia stood up to the triumvirs in 43 B.C.

[60]Hortensius had died in 50 B.C.

[61]His male descendants were failures (see 3:5,4 and 5:9,2).

Chapter 4. Interrogations

Preface

We must consider every aspect of the court system, so we must discuss interrogations in which the confessions were not believed or were trusted too readily.

Roman Stories

4. 1. Alexander, a slave of the banker Marcus Agrius, was accused of killing a slave belonging to Aulus Fannius. He was tortured by his own master because of this and boldly claimed that he had carried out the crime. So he was handed over to Fannius who had him put to death. A short time passed by and then the slave, who everyone thought had been murdered, came back home.[62]

4. 2. On the other hand, a different Alexander, who was the slave of Publius Atinius, was suspected of having murdered Gaius Flavius, a Roman equestrian. He was tortured six times but denied that he had anything to do with the crime. But it was just as if he had confessed to it. He was convicted by a jury and crucified by the prison manager Lucius Calpurnius.

4. 3. When Fulvius Flaccus was pleading his case, his slave Philippus, on whose evidence the entire case rested, was tortured eight times. But he did not let a single word fall that would implicate his master. Nevertheless, his master was convicted, though this man who was tortured eight times should have been a clearer proof of his master's innocence than eight men put to the torture at the same time.

Chapter 5. Witnesses

Roman Stories

5. 1. My next task is to record stories that relate to witnesses.

Gnaeus and Quintus Servilius Caepio were born of the same parents and went through every level of public office to reach the highest distinction;[63] similarly, the brothers Quintus and Lucius Metellus were former consuls and censors, and one of them had even held a triumph.[64] They all very eagerly gave testimony against

---

[62]Nothing further is known about any of the masters and slaves in this chapter.

[63]Gnaeus Servilius Caepio (cos, 141 B.C.) and Quintus Servilius Caepio (cos,140 B.C.) were brothers.

[64]These two were Quintus Caecilius Metellus Macedonicus (cos, 143 B.C.) and Lucius Caecilius Metellus Calvus (cos, 142 B.C.). Metellus Macedonicus celebrated a triumph over the Macedonians in 146 B.C. and was censor in 131 B.C.

Quintus Pompeius, the son of Aulus, who was on trial for misgovernment.[65] Their testimony was not disregarded, but Pompeius was acquitted. What went against them was the feeling that they might appear to have destroyed their enemy through their political power.

5. 2. The leader of the Senate, Marcus Aemilius Scaurus,[66] gave uncompromising testimony against Gaius Memmius, who was on trial for misgovernment; his testimony also cut Gaius Flavius to pieces when he was tried under the same law;[67] and when Gaius Norbanus had to face a public court on a charge of treason, Scaurus openly tried to destroy him.[68] But in spite of his influence, which made him very powerful, and his integrity, which nobody doubted, he was unable to destroy any of these men.

5. 3. Lucius Crassus[69] had as much power over juries as Aemilius Scaurus had over the Conscript Fathers. His career of powerful and effective eloquence ruled their verdicts, and he was the leading man in the Forum just as Scaurus was the leading man in the Senate house. But when he launched a thunderbolt of devastating testimony against Marcus Marcellus, who was on trial, his weighty attack turned out to be utterly ineffective.[70]

5. 4. Well, Quintus Metellus Pius, Lucius and Marcus Lucullus, Quintus Hortensius, and Manius Lepidus[71] testified against Gaius Cornelius, who was on trial for treason.[72] They not only jeopardized Cornelius' life but even demanded his death by claiming that the Republic could not survive if Cornelius were allowed to live! These glorious men of our state were, I am ashamed to record, driven back by the shield of our courts.

5. 5. Well, from his legal battles in the courts, Cicero won the highest honors and the most distinguished rank, but wasn't his testimony rejected in the very field of action of his eloquence? Cicero declared under oath that Publius Clodius had been visiting his house in Rome, whereas the only defense Clodius had against the

[65]The defendant, Quintus Pompeius (cos, 141 B.C.), had been governor of Nearer Spain (140–139 B.C.). He was prosecuted in 138 B.C. for taking bribes to make peace with the Spaniards.

[66]Marcus Aemilius Scaurus (cos, 115 B.C.) was leader of the Senate from 115 B.C. until his death in 88 B.C.

[67]Gaius Memmius was a praetor, and Gaius Flavius Fimbria was consul, in 104 B.C. They were both prosecuted after their term of office.

[68]Gaius Norbanus (cos, 83 B.C.) had been a tribune of the plebs in 103 B.C. He was blamed for a riot that year and eventually tried for treason in 94 B.C.

[69]Lucius Licinius Crassus (cos, 95 B.C.) was a famous orator.

[70]Marcus Claudius Marcellus was a praetor some time before 73 B.C.

[71]These men were influential conservative senators: Quintus Caecilius Metellus Pius (cos, 80 B.C.), Lucius Licinius Lucullus Ponticus (cos, 74 B.C.), Marcus Terentius Varro Lucullus (cos, 73 B.C.), Quintus Hortensius Hortalus (cos, 69 B.C.), and Manius Aemilius Lepidus (cos, 66 B.C.).

[72]Gaius Cornelius was a reformist tribune of the plebs in 67 B.C. His policies annoyed conservative senators, so they put him on trial for treason.

charge of sacrilege was that he had not been in Cicero's house.[73] Apparently, the jury preferred clearing Clodius on the charge of sexual immorality over clearing Cicero of the disgrace of perjury.

5. 6. All these witnesses were disregarded, but I shall tell of one man whose prestige was validated and influenced the court in a strange new way. Publius Servilius had been a consul and a censor, had celebrated a triumph, and had added the name of Isauricus to the titles of his ancestors.[74] As he was going by the Forum, he noticed that witnesses were being called to testify against a man on trial, so he took the stand as a witness and to the great amazement of the defense and the prosecution, he started to speak as follows:

"Gentlemen of the jury, this man is pleading his case today, and I do not know where he comes from, what kind of life he has led, or whether he is being accused rightly or wrongly: all I know is that he met me at a very narrow spot, when I was walking along the road to Laurentum,[75] but he refused to get off his horse. You yourselves will have to decide whether this has any relevance to your sacred duty as jurymen, but I felt it should not go unmentioned."

The jury barely listened to the other witnesses and found the defendant guilty. The eminence of Servilius and their profound indignation at the disrespect shown to him weighed heavily with the jury, and they were convinced that a man who did not know how to respect our leaders would readily commit any crime.

Chapter 6. People Who Committed Offenses but Punished Others for Similar Offenses

Preface

We must not allow people to stay hidden if they committed offenses but punished others for similar offenses.

Roman Stories

6. 1. Gaius Licinius, who was called Hoplomachus, requested the praetor to prevent his father from managing the family property, since his father was wasting it away; and Licinius actually got what he wanted. But shortly after the old man died, Licinius himself quickly ran through the large sum of money that was left by

---

[73]Publius Clodius Pulcher (aedile, 56 B.C.) had dressed up as a woman and taken part in a women's religious festival, in order to meet with and seduce Caesar's wife in 62 B.C. He was tried for sacrilege in 61 B.C. and acquitted, in spite of Cicero's testimony.

[74]Publius Servilius Vatia Isauricus (cos, 79 B.C.) celebrated a triumph over the Isaurians of Cilicia (on the south coast of Asia Minor) in 74 B.C. He was censor in 55 B.C.

[75]Laurentum was on the coast of Latium.

his father. He himself escaped being punished in turn, because he had chosen to waste his inheritance rather than produce an heir himself.

6. 2. Marius acted as a great citizen and saved the Republic by destroying Lucius Saturninus,[76] who used to display a cap of liberty as his military standard to urge the slaves to take up arms. But when Sulla and his army were attacking our city,[77] Marius himself raised the cap of liberty and resorted to the help of slaves. So by imitating the behavior that he himself had punished, he encountered a new Marius who would overthrow him.

6. 3. It was through the good offices of Gaius Licinius Stolo that the plebs were given the power to stand for the consulship.[78] He had also passed a law that nobody should possess more than three hundred acres of public land, but he himself bought six hundred acres, so to cover up his crime, he gave half the property to his son. He was prosecuted for this by Marcus Popillius Laenas and became the first victim of his own law.[79] Thus he showed that nobody should give a command that they are not prepared to carry out themselves.

6. 4. Quintus Varius, who was called Hybrida because of his doubtful right to Roman citizenship, was a tribune of the plebs,[80] and he got a law passed in spite of the veto of his fellow tribunes: it declared that men should be prosecuted if they maliciously induced the allies to take up arms.[81] This law caused great harm to the Republic, because it led to the Social War and later to a civil war.[82] But while he behaved like a dangerous tribune of the plebs rather than a sound citizen, his own law caught up with him by trapping him in its snares.[83]

[76]Marius was consul in 100 B.C. when he supported the Senate against his former ally, Lucius Appuleius Saturninus (tribune of the plebs, 103 B.C.).

[77]Sulla marched on Rome in 88 B.C. and declared Marius an outlaw.

[78]Gaius Licinius Stolo (cos, 364 B.C.) was a tribune of the plebs from 376 to 367 B.C., when his Licinio-Sextian laws were finally enacted. These laws required one consul to be a plebeian and forbade any person to possess more than three hundred acres of public land.

[79]Marcus Popillius Laenas (cos, 359 B.C.) prosecuted Licinius Stolo in 367 B.C.

[80]Quintus Varius Severus Hybrida was a tribune of the plebs in 90 B.C.

[81]His law was designed to prevent any politician from making concessions to the Italians (the "allies").

[82]The Italian allies were driven to rebellion, the Social War (90–89 B.C.), in order to assert their rights. Sulla's civil war against Marius started in 88 B.C. but was unrelated to the Social War or to Varius' law.

[83]Varius was condemned in 89 B.C. under his own law, which was then suspended.

Chapter 7. Enthusiasm and Dedication

Preface

Why should I hesitate to celebrate the effectiveness of dedication? Its confident spirit encourages those who serve in the army; it inspires people to fame in the Forum; it takes every activity to its trustworthy bosom and nurses it. Whatever wonderful things people do with their mind, with their hands, with their speech, dedication brings their activity to the height of glory. It is the most complete form of virtue, and the harder it grows, the stronger it becomes.

Roman Stories

7. *1.* When Cato the Censor was eighty-six years old, and his mind still retained its youthful vigor in defending the Republic, his enemies accused him of a capital crime.[84] He pleaded his own case, and as far as people could notice, his memory was not slower, the strength of his lungs was in no way diminished, and his speech suffered from no impediment. By constant and consistent dedication, he had maintained all his faculties in their original condition. In fact, right at the end of his long life, he spoke in defense of Spain against the charges made by Galba, a very eloquent speaker.[85]

Cato also wanted to study Greek literature—how late we can judge from the fact that he studied Latin literature only when he was quite an old man—and although he had already won great glory from his eloquence, he took care to become very learned in civil law also.

7. *2.* His amazing descendant, the Cato who is nearer to our times,[86] was so fired up with the love of learning that even in the Senate house, when the senators were assembling, he could not refrain from reading Greek books. His dedication showed that some people lack time and other people make time.

7. *3.* Terentius Varro lived as long as a human being could, but he lived even longer through his writings than through his actual years, which amounted to a century. On his deathbed, a life and also a series of extraordinary literary works came to an end.[87]

7. *4.* Livius Drusus was equally hardy.[88] Age deprived him of his strength and his eyesight, but he very kindly interpreted the civil law for ordinary people, and

---

[84]Cato the Censor was often prosecuted by his enemies. He was eighty-six years old in 149 B.C.

[85]Servius Sulpicius Galba (cos, 144 B.C.) treacherously massacred eight thousand Lusitanians who had surrendered to him in 150 B.C. (see 9:6,2). Galba was tried in 149 B.C., and Cato the Censor spoke out against him (see 8:1,absol.2). Galba was acquitted, and Cato died later that year.

[86]The "amazing descendant" is Cato of Utica.

[87]Marcus Terentius Varro was a polymath who wrote more than six hundred volumes. He lived from 116 to 27 B.C.

[88]Gaius Livius Drusus was a legal expert in the second century B.C.

wrote very useful books for those who wanted to learn about it. Nature may have been able to make him old, and Fortune may have been able to make him blind, but neither of them had the power to prevent him from exercising the strength and insight of his mind.

7. 5. Publilius, a senator, and Pontius Lupus, a Roman equestrian, were celebrated pleaders in their own day, and even after they went blind, they pursued their legal careers with the same dedication.[89] People came in even bigger crowds to hear these men. Some of the crowd were delighted by their talents, others were amazed by their persistence. Generally, people who suffer from such afflictions go into retirement, and they double their gloom by adding their own optional difficulties to the ones that fortune has forced upon them.

7. 6. During his consulship, Publius Crassus came to Asia to finish off the war against King Aristonicus.[90] He took such great care in acquiring a knowledge of the Greek language that he became fluent with every part and aspect of the five dialects into which it is divided. This completely won over the affections of our allies, because whatever dialect was spoken by anyone who appealed to his tribunal, Crassus would respond to them with a decree in their own dialect.

7. 7. Roscius should not be left out, as he was the most famous case of dedication to the stage.[91] When he faced the general public, Roscius never dared to make a single gesture that he had not practiced at home. So it was not his acting career that made Roscius famous, but Roscius who made acting famous. And he did not just win the admiration of the masses; he even became intimate with the leaders of the state. These are the rewards for a devotion to work that is conscientious, painstaking, and unceasing, so it is not inappropriate to include an actor among these stories honoring the greatest men.[92]

Foreign Stories

7. ext. 1. Since the dedication of the Greeks has greatly encouraged our own, it should get the reward it deserves in the Latin language.

The mere mention of the name of Demosthenes brings up the image of the greatest perfection in eloquence before the mind of the person who hears it.[93] When he was very young, he could not even pronounce the first letter of that art in which he wanted to excel,[94] but he tackled his speech defect with such vigor that nobody could pronounce it more clearly. Next, because his voice was very

---

[89]It is not known who these men were or when they lived.

[90]Publius Licinius Dives Crassus Mucianus (cos, 131 B.C.) fought against Aristonicus in 130 B.C. Aristonicus tried to prevent the Romans from annexing the province of Asia.

[91]Quintus Roscius Gallus was a famous comic actor. He died in 62 B.C.

[92]Most actors were slaves, and the acting profession was despised in ancient Rome. Actors could neither vote nor join the army.

[93]Demosthenes, the Athenian orator and statesman, lived from 383 to 322 B.C.

[94]Valerius means "r," the first letter of "rhetoric."

weak and unpleasant to listen to, he exercised it continually until it developed a rich sound that was pleasing to the ear.

He also suffered from a weakness of the lungs, but from exercise he borrowed the strength that his physical condition denied him: he would speak several lines of poetry in a single breath, and he would recite them while quickly running up a hill; he would stand where the land was met by shallow seawater and recite speeches against the noise of the crashing waves, so that he could train his ears to endure the noise of excited crowds. It is also said that he used to put pebbles in his mouth and speak out loud for a long time, so that his speech would be more quick and flowing when his mouth was empty. He battled against Nature and certainly came out on top, since he overcame her malice by the dogged determination of his willpower. So his mother gave birth to one Demosthenes, and his dedication gave birth to a new one.

7. *ext. 2.* I shall turn to a more ancient story about the results of dedication. Pythagoras started off his brilliant philosophical career when he was very young and filled with the desire to learn every kind of honorable activity. Nothing that is destined to reach its ultimate goal can do so without starting early and developing quickly.

Pythagoras went to Egypt and became familiar with the literature of that nation. He studied the records of its priests from ancient times and learned about the observations they had made over countless centuries. From there he went on to Persia and had himself trained in the very precise science of the magi,[95] who very kindly taught him about the movements of the constellations, the paths of the stars, and the force, characteristics, and effect of each one of them; his responsive mind absorbed all of this. Next he sailed to Crete and Sparta,[96] and after studying their laws and customs, he went to the Olympic Games.[97]

There he displayed his diverse abilities to the great admiration of all of Greece, and when he was asked what title they should give him, he said that was not a sage—because seven exceptional men had already won that title—but rather a lover of wisdom (which is called "philosopher" in Greek).[98] He went off to the part of Italy that was then called Greater Greece[99] and won approval for the results of his studies in most of its very prosperous cities. The citizens of Metapontum

---

[95]The magi were the priests of Persia.

[96]The island of Crete and the city of Sparta were famous for their regimented lifestyles.

[97]The Olympic Games were held every four years in the city of Olympia (in southern Greece).

[98]The title of sage or wise man (*sophos* in Greek) had already been given to the Seven Sages of Greece in the sixth century B.C., so Pythagoras modestly suggested that he should be called a lover of wisdom (*philo-sophos*) rather than a wise man (*sophos*).

[99]Greater Greece (*Magna Graecia*) was the name given to southern Italy, where there were many Greek cities. Pythagoras was born on the island of Samos (off the west coast of Asia Minor), but he moved to Croton (in Bruttium) around 530 B.C.

witnessed the burning of his funeral pyre,[100] and their eyes were full of veneration. Their city is more renowned and glorious as a monument to the ashes of Pythagoras than to the ashes of its own people.

7. *ext. 3.* Plato had the good fortune to have Athens as his country and Socrates as his teacher,[101] the place and the person that were the most intellectually creative, and he was also gifted with a divine supply of talent. He was already considered the wisest of all men, so wise indeed that people thought that Jupiter himself, if he came down from the heavens, could not have a more elegant or sumptuous style of speaking.

In spite of this, Plato traveled throughout Egypt to learn about its complicated geometrical calculations and its system of astronomical observation from the priests of that nation. At a time when enthusiastic young men were competing to get to Athens so that they could have Plato as their teacher, he himself was studying under Egyptian elders and traveling along the endless shores of the Nile and through its vast plains, its widespread exotic regions, and the twisting paths of its canals.

So I am hardly surprised that he went over to Italy, where he learned about the principles and teachings of Pythagoras[102] from Archytas at Tarentum,[103] and from Timaeus, Arion, and Echecrates at Locri.[104] He had to collect such a huge amount of learning from all over the place, so that he in turn could spread and extend it throughout the world. It is said that as he lay dying at the age of eighty-one, he had the mimes of Sophron under his pillow.[105] Even his very last hour was not devoid of scholarly activity.[106]

7. *ext. 4.* Democritus[107] could have been famous for his wealth, which was so great that his father was easily able to provide a banquet for the army of Xerxes.[108] But Democritus wanted to keep his mind free of distractions and to devote himself to studying learned works, so he retained a very small sum for himself and donated the rest of his fortune to his country. He stayed at Athens for many years, devoting every moment of his time to learning and to practicing a philosophical life. He lived unknown in that city, as he himself testifies in one of his books. My mind is overwhelmed with admiration for such dedication and now moves on to another story.

---

[100]In 510 B.C. Pythagoras moved to Metapontum (on the south coast of Lucania) where he ended his days.

[101]Plato was born in Athens in 429 B.C. Socrates was put to death in Athens in 399 B.C.

[102]Pythagoras, the sixth century philosopher, had moved to southern Italy in 530 B.C.

[103]Archytas of Tarentum (in Calabria, southern Italy) was a Pythagorean philosopher and a mathematician. He lived at the beginning of the fourth century B.C.

[104]Timaeus, Arion, and Echecrates were fourth-century Pythagoreans. Locri Epizephyrii was in Bruttium (southern Italy).

[105]Sophron of Syracuse was a fifth-century playwright.

[106]Plato lived from 429 to 347 B.C.

[107]Democritus was a philosopher in the fifth century B.C. He came from Abdera in Thrace.

[108]Xerxes I (king of Persia, 486–465 B.C.) would have passed through Abdera during his invasion of Greece (480–479 B.C.).

7. *ext. 5.* Carneades was a hardworking and long-serving veteran of philosophy.[109] He reached the age of ninety and did not stop studying philosophy until he stopped living. He had such a marvelous devotion to philosophical work that when he lay down to take a meal, he would get so absorbed in his thoughts that he would forget to reach his hand out toward the table. But Melissa, whom he kept as if she were his wife, balanced her obligation not to interrupt him during his research with her obligation to make sure he didn't starve and satisfied his needs with her own right hand. His only pleasure in life came from the mind alone, and he treated his body as a strange unnecessary container. Whenever he was going to have a discussion with Chrysippus,[110] he would flush his intestines out with a special medicine first,[111] to stimulate his mind and make it quicker at refuting his opponent. Dedication made such medicines tasty to men who wanted to win real glory.

7. *ext. 6.* What kind of enthusiasm should we imagine to have inflamed Anaxagoras?[112] He returned to his country after a long journey overseas and discovered that his property was abandoned: "I would not be saved," he said, "if it had not been destroyed." A statement that showed his attainment of complete wisdom! Because if he had devoted his time to developing his property rather than his mind, he would have stayed at home as the master of the family estate and would not have returned to it as the great Anaxagoras.

7. *ext. 7.* I could have said that Archimedes' dedication was rewarding if it had not spared his life and then taken it away.[113] When Marcellus captured Syracuse,[114] he realized that his victory had been delayed for a long time mainly due to the inventions of Archimedes. But Marcellus was delighted with the exceptional intelligence of this man and decreed that his life should be spared, believing that he would win as much glory by saving Archimedes as he had won by destroying Syracuse.

But Archimedes had his mind and his eyes glued to the ground where he was drawing diagrams when a soldier burst into the house to plunder it, drew his sword over Archimedes' head, and asked him who he was. Because he was so intent on finding the answer to his problem, Archimedes could not bring himself to tell his name. Instead, he covered the dust with his hands and said, "Please don't disturb my diagram." The victorious soldier felt that Archimedes was slighting his authority and killed him, so the blood of Archimedes disturbed the lines of his

---

[109]Carneades of Cyrene (in north Africa) was a skeptic philosopher from Plato's Academy (in Athens). He lived from 214 to 129 B.C.

[110]The philosopher Chrysippus of Soli (in Cilicia, on the south coast of Asia Minor) lived from about 280 to 204 B.C. He was the head of the Stoic school in Athens.

[111]The medicine was made from the hellebore plant; black hellebore made the patient go to the toilet, and white hellebore made the patient vomit.

[112]Anaxagoras was born in Clazomenae (on the west coast of Asia Minor) about 500 B.C. He lived in Athens from about 460 to 430 B.C.

[113]Archimedes, the great mathematician, was born in Syracuse around 287 B.C. and spent his life there.

[114]Archimedes was killed in 211 B.C. when Marcus Claudius Marcellus (cos, 222 B.C.) captured Syracuse.

diagram. This is how it came about that his life was spared and then taken away because of his enthusiasm.

7. *ext. 8.* It is widely known that when Socrates had reached an advanced age,[115] he started to devote his time to playing the lyre, feeling that it was better to learn this skill later than never. What an insignificant addition this was to the knowledge of Socrates! But the unremitting dedication of this man wanted to add the lowest branch of music to his great wealth of knowledge. Thus, while he felt that he was always poor when it came to learning, he made himself the richest man when it came to teaching.

7. *ext. 9.* But let us gather all our stories into one heap, as it were, of long and happy dedication. Isocrates composed his most famous book, the *Panathenaic Oration*, when he was ninety-four years old,[116] as he himself says, and it is a work filled with burning spirit. This makes it clear that the mind of a learned man retains its youthful vigor within his old limbs by virtue of his dedication. But even this piece of writing did not mark the end of his life; he was able to enjoy the admiration it won him for another five years.[117]

7. *ext. 10.* The vitality of Chrysippus reached the finishing post at an earlier age, but his life span was not short.[118] In his eightieth year he began the thirty-ninth volume of his *Logic*, and he left us a work that is argued with great precision. He was so eager to hand over the achievements of his great mind, and he put so much work and attention into this task, that you would need to live a long time to gain a thorough knowledge of everything he wrote.

7. *ext. 11.* The goddess Dedication herself looked up to you, Cleanthes,[119] as you worked so hard to get your fill of philosophy, and struggled so persistently to pass it on to others. She saw you when you were a young man, as you saved yourself from destitution by working at night getting water from wells, while in the daytime you were free to learn the philosophy of Chrysippus.[120] She saw you teaching your students with great care up till your ninety-ninth year. You spent an entire century doing the work of two men, and made it difficult for others to decide whether you should be praised more as a student or as a teacher.

---

[115]Socrates was seventy years old when he was put to death in 399 B.C.

[116]Isocrates, the Athenian orator and teacher, was born in 436 B.C. He wrote the *Panathenaic Oration* in 346 B.C.

[117]Isocrates delivered his *Panathenaic Oration* at the Panathenaic festival of 342 B.C. He died in 338 B.C.

[118]The philosopher Chrysippus of Soli (in Cilicia on the south coast of Asia Minor) lived from about 280 to 207 B.C. He was the third head of the Stoic school in Athens.

[119]Cleanthes of Assos (on the west coast of Asia Minor) lived from 331 to 232 B.C. He was the second head of the Stoic school.

[120]Chrysippus of Soli (in Cilicia on the south coast of Asia Minor) lived from about 280 to 207 B.C. Valerius has confused the historical order of the heads of the Stoic school of philosophy: Zeno (304–264 B.C.), Cleanthes (264–232 B.C.), and Chrysippus (232–207 B.C.). Cleanthes was Zeno's student, and Cleanthes did not learn philosophy from Chrysippus; he taught Chrysippus.

7. ext. 12. Sophocles also had a glorious competition with Nature;[121] he was as kind in displaying his marvelous works to her as she was generous in granting him the time to complete them. He almost reached his hundredth year, and just when he was about to pass away in death, he wrote *Oedipus at Colonus*.[122] This play alone could have snatched the prize for glory from all the poets who worked in this genre. Iophon,[123] the son of Sophocles, did not want posterity to be unaware of this, so he inscribed the fact I have just mentioned on his father's tomb.

7. ext. 13. The poet Simonides himself boasts that he directed recitals of his poems and entered poetic competitions in his eightieth year.[124] It was not wrong for him to derive such pleasure from his talent for so long, since he was destined to give such pleasure to all future generations.

7. ext. 14. In his own poetry Solon describes the great dedication that inspired him.[125] There he explains that as he grew old, he learned something new every day. He proved this on the last day of his life. His friends were sitting beside him and they were discussing some matter among themselves. Death was already drawing near, but he raised his head, and they asked him why he had done this. He replied, "I will die only after I find out what you are talking about." Idleness would certainly have disappeared from the human race if people had the same spirit when they entered this life as Solon had when he left it.

7. ext. 15. How dedicated Themistocles was![126] Even though he was worried about the most serious matters, he still memorized the names of all his fellow citizens. When he had been banished most unjustly from his country he was forced to seek refuge with Xerxes,[127] whom he had thoroughly defeated shortly before this. Before he entered the king's presence, he made himself familiar with the Persian language. He wanted to earn the king's approval by hard work and to address his royal ears in tones that would be personal and familiar.

7. ext. 16. Two kings divided between them these two types of praiseworthy dedication shown by Themistocles. Cyrus learned the names of all his soldiers,[128] and Mithridates learned the languages of the twenty-two nations that were under his rule.[129] Cyrus wanted to address his soldiers without someone to remind him, and Mithridates wanted to address the people he ruled without an interpreter.

---

[121]Sophocles lived from 496 to 406 B.C.

[122]*Oedipus at Colonus* was produced after Sophocles' death in 401 B.C.

[123]Iophon was also a playwright.

[124]Simonides of Ceos (an island in the Aegean Sea) lived from 556 to 468 B.C.

[125]Solon, the Athenian statesman and poet, lived from about 640 B.C. to about 560 B.C.

[126]Themistocles was the leading democratic politician in Athens from 493 B.C. until his exile in 472 B.C.

[127]Themistocles had defeated Xerxes I of Persia at Salamis in 480 B.C. He did not go to Persia until 464 B.C., when Xerxes I was dead and Artaxerxes I was king.

[128]Cyrus the Great was king of Persia from 555 to 530 B.C.

[129]Mithridates VI was king of Pontus from 120 to 63 B.C.

Chapter 8. Leisure

Preface

Leisure seems to be the complete opposite of dedication and enthusiasm, so it should definitely be put right next to them: not the type of leisure that makes energy disappear, but the type that revives it. The first type is to be avoided even by idle men, but even energetic men should occasionally demand the second type. In this way, the idle would not live a completely useless life, and the energetic would take a timely break from their work and become invigorated for further work.

Roman Stories

8. 1. That famous pair of real friends, Scipio and Laelius,[130] were joined together by ties of affection and by their shared pursuit of every virtue. They went along the path of a busy life at the same speed, and they also got together to give their minds a rest. It is well known that they used to wander around on the seashore at Caieta and Laurentum,[131] picking up seashells and pebbles. Lucius Crassus said that he often heard this from his father-in-law, Scaevola,[132] who was the son-in-law of Laelius.

8. 2. This Scaevola,[133] who is the most reliable witness of their quiet relaxation, is said to have been an excellent ballplayer. It was obviously his custom to relax his mind with this pastime when he was worn out by his legal work. It is said that he sometimes used to take time off to play board games when he had spent a long time carefully organizing laws for his fellow citizens and ceremonies for his gods. He behaved like Scaevola in serious matters and like an ordinary human being in his free time, because nature does not allow a man to stay at work all the time.

Foreign Stories

8. ext. 1. Socrates realized this, and no part of wisdom was hidden from him. That is why he was not embarrassed when Alcibiades saw him playing with his little boys with a reed between his legs.[134]

8. ext. 2. Homer, that poet of heavenly talent, felt the same way, because he had Achilles play songs on the lyre with his violent hands, so that the hero would relax his martial strength with this gentle peacetime relaxation.[135]

---

[130]Gaius Laelius Sapiens (cos, 140 B.C.) was a friend of Scipio Aemilianus.

[131]Caieta and Laurentum were on the coast of Latium.

[132]Lucius Licinius Crassus (cos, 95 B.C.), the famous orator, had married the daughter of Quintus Mucius Scaevola the Augur (cos, 117 B.C.). See 4:5,4.

[133]Quintus Mucius Scaevola the Augur was consul in 117 B.C. and augur from the 130s B.C. until his death in 88 B.C.

[134]Alcibiades was the erratic Athenian leader who lived from about 450 to 404 B.C. His friendship damaged Socrates' reputation.

[135]Homer has Achilles playing the lyre at *Iliad* 9: 186–9.

Chapter 9. How Great the Power of Eloquence Is

Preface

Even though we know that the power of eloquence is supreme, it is still appropriate for us to discuss it under its own stories, so that its strength will be fully attested.

Roman Stories

9. 1. After the kings were expelled, the plebeians had a dispute with the patricians.[136] The plebeians armed themselves and sat down by the banks of the river Anio[137] on a hill that is called Sacred.[138] The condition of the Republic was not just out of shape but positively miserable, as the other body parts were cut off from the head by this destructive disagreement. If the eloquence of Valerius had not come to the rescue,[139] the prospects of our great empire would have dwindled away almost at the moment of its birth. The people were foolishly delighted with their new and unaccustomed freedom, but he brought them around to a better and more useful attitude and put them under the power of the Senate; in other words, he joined the city to the city. Anger, confusion, and armed force surrendered to his eloquent words.

9. 2. Eloquence also restrained the swords of Marius and Cinna[140] as they madly longed to shed the blood of their fellow citizens. These savage leaders sent some soldiers to murder Marcus Antonius,[141] but the soldiers were mesmerized by his words, and although they had already drawn their swords and were waving them about, they put them back in their scabbards without bloodshed. When the soldiers went off, Publius Annius[142]—he was the only one who had stayed in the entrance and had not witnessed the eloquence of Antonius—carried out his cruel orders with ferocious obedience. How eloquent must we imagine Antonius to have been, if not even his enemies could bear to kill him once they had allowed his voice to reach their ears?

9. 3. The divine Caesar was the perfect high point of heavenly divinity and human talent. He accurately described the power of eloquence in the speech he

---

[136]The first secession of the plebs to the Sacred Mount took place in 494 B.C.

[137]The river Anio flowed into the Tiber just north of Rome.

[138]The Sacred Mount (*Mons Sacer*) was three miles outside of Rome.

[139]Publius Valerius Publicola (cos, 509 B.C.) had died in 503 B.C. The plebs were enticed back to the city by Agrippa Menenius Lanatus (cos, 503 B.C.). See 4:4,2.

[140]Lucius Cornelius Cinna (87 B.C.) and Marius (cos, 107 B.C.) massacred their political enemies in 87 B.C.

[141]Marcus Antonius (cos, 99 B.C.) was a famous orator.

[142]Publius Annius was a military tribune in 87 B.C.

made when he prosecuted Gnaeus Dolabella,[143] where he said that Gaius Cotta's[144] arguments for the defense had undermined the prosecution's great case. This was the complaint our greatest master of eloquence made against eloquence.

Having mentioned Caesar, there could not be any greater national story for me to add, so we must move on to foreign ones.

Foreign Stories

9. ext. 1. It was said that Peisistratus was such a powerful orator that the Athenians gave him royal power after being captivated by a speech of his,[145] in spite of the fact that the great patriot Solon was arguing against Peisistratus.[146] Solon's arguments were sounder, but those of Peisistratus were expressed more skillfully. As a result, this state, which was normally very intelligent, chose servitude over liberty.

9. ext. 2. Pericles was gifted with wonderful talents by nature,[147] and he perfected them with great eagerness under the guidance of Anaxagoras,[148] and that is how he imposed the yoke of servitude on the free shoulders of Athens. He drove and turned that city as he pleased, and even when he spoke against the wishes of the people, his words were no less pleasant and democratic. So although the malicious voice of Old Comedy[149] was eager to attack his power, it still admitted that a charm sweeter than honey hung on the lips of that man, and it declared that he left a kind of bee sting in the minds of those who had heard him.

It is said that a very old man was present at the first public speech that the young Pericles made, and that this old man had in his youth heard the aged Peisitratus making a speech, so he could not prevent himself from exclaiming that they had better beware of that citizen, because Pericles' speech was very similar to the one made by Peisistratus. The old man was not mistaken either in his judgment of Pericles' eloquence or in his prediction about Pericles' character. What difference was there between Peisistratus and Pericles, apart from the fact that the former had tyrannical power backed by armed force and the latter had tyrannical power without it?[150]

---

[143]Gnaeus Cornelius Dolabella (cos, 81 B.C.) had been governor of Macedonia from 80 to 77 B.C. Caesar prosecuted him for misgovernment in 77 B.C.

[144]Gaius Aurelius Cotta (cos, 75 B.C.) secured Dolabella's acquittal.

[145]Peisistratus seized power for the first time in 561 B.C.

[146]Solon had created the Athenian law code in 594 B.C. He went into exile when Peisistratus became tyrant of Athens and died shortly afterward.

[147]Pericles dominated Athenian politics from about 460 B.C. until his death in 429 B.C.

[148]Anaxagoras of Clazomenae was a philosopher who lived in Athens from about 460 B.C. to 430 B.C.

[149]Old Comedy is the name given to the type of comedy produced in Athens during the fifth century B.C. This comedy included a lot of political satire.

[150]Peisistratus was a dictator who relied on armed force, but the Athenians were perfectly free to vote Pericles out of office.

9. ext. 3. What power do we imagine the Cyrenaic philosopher Hegesias exercised through his eloquence?[151] He portrayed the misfortunes of life in such a way that when this miserable picture had entered the hearts of his audience, it filled many of them with the desire to take their own lives. For this reason King Ptolemy prevented him from giving any more lectures on this topic.[152]

Chapter 10. How Much Importance Lies in Proper Enunciation and Appropriate Physical Gestures

Preface

Proper enunciation and appropriate physical gestures are the chief things that enhance eloquence. When eloquence is supplied with these, it affects people in three ways: eloquence itself captures their minds, it hands over their ears to be charmed by enunciation, and it hands over their eyes to be charmed by gesture.

Roman Stories

10. 1. The proof of this notion must be shown in the case of famous personalities. Gaius Gracchus was a young man who was more fortunate in his eloquence than in his objectives.[153] Although he could have upheld the Republic successfully, his fiery temperament wickedly chose to throw it into confusion instead. Whenever he would speak before the people, he would have a slave trained in the art of music behind him. This slave would secretly mark the correct tempo of his delivery on an ivory whistle and hurry him up when he was too slack, or restrain him when he was speaking more quickly than he should. The fieriness and violence of his speech made Gracchus incapable of paying attention or judging his own tempo properly.

10.2. Quintus Hortensius[154] believed that everything depended on graceful physical gestures, and he put almost more effort into working on them than into pursuing eloquence itself. So you could not have told whether people came more eagerly to hear him or to look at him, because the appearance of the orator suited his words, and his words in turn suited his appearance. It is well known that our most accomplished stage actors, Aesopus and Roscius,[155] would often join the audience when he was pleading a case, so that they could study the gestures he used in the Forum and transfer them to the stage.

---

[151]The Cyrenaic school taught that pleasure was the goal of life. Hegesias lived around 300 B.C.

[152]Ptolemy I Soter was king of Egypt from 323 to 285 B.C.

[153]Gaius Sempronius Gracchus (tribune of the plebs, 123 B.C.) was murdered by his conservative opponents in 121 B.C.

[154]Quintus Hortensius Hortalus (cos, 69 B.C.) was a famous orator.

[155]Aesopus acted in tragedies, and Quintus Roscius Gallus acted in comedies. They were famous in the early first century B.C.

10. 3. In the speech he delivered on behalf of Gallius,[156] Cicero showed how much importance lies in the two things we are discussing. He attacked the prosecutor, Marcus Calidius,[157] because Calidius claimed he could prove his case with witnesses, written statements, and slave interrogations, and show that the accused had procured poison to use against him, but in spite of this, Calidius kept speaking with a relaxed expression and an apathetic voice, and in an easygoing style. Cicero simultaneously exposed this rhetorical defect and used it as an argument on behalf of the accused, summarizing his entire line of reasoning as follows: "Would you be acting in this way, Marcus Calidius, if you weren't making the whole thing up?"

Foreign Stories

10 ext. 1. Demosthenes agreed with Cicero's judgment.[158] When someone asked him what the most effective device in speaking was, he replied, "Acting." When he was asked what the second and third most effective devices were, he gave the same answer, thereby acknowledging that he owed almost everything to this device.

Aeschines[159] was, therefore, quite right in his words to the Rhodians. He had left Athens because of a humiliating defeat in the courts and gone off to Rhodes. At the request of the state of Rhodes, he first delivered his speech against Ctesiphon and then Demosthenes' speech in defense of Ctesiphon, speaking in a very clear and pleasant voice.[160] They were all amazed at the eloquence of each work but slightly more by the speech of Demosthenes, and Aeschines said, "What if you had heard the man himself?"

Aeschines was a great orator and had recently been a bitter opponent of Demosthenes, but he greatly respected the power and spirit of his enemy as a speaker and proclaimed that he was not really worthy to read out his speeches, because he knew from experience the fierce power of his eyes, the terrible impact of his face, the sound of his voice, which varied to suit each word, and the effect of his bodily gestures. So even if nothing could be added to his work, a great part of Demosthenes is still absent from the works of Demosthenes, because they are read rather than heard.

[156]This is Quintus Gallius (praetor, 65 B.C.).

[157]Marcus Calidius (praetor, 57 B.C.) accused Gallius of trying to poison him in 67 B.C.

[158]Demosthenes, the Athenian orator and statesman, lived from 383 to 322 B.C.

[159]Aeschines was politically opposed to Demosthenes.

[160]In 330 B.C. Aeschines had attacked Ctesiphon, an ally of Demosthenes, in a speech called *Against Ctesiphon*. Demosthenes defended Ctesiphon in a speech called *On the Crown*.

Chapter 11. How Great the Results of the Liberal Arts Can Be

Preface

When we consider their results, it will be seen that the liberal arts give people pleasure, and it will also be immediately clear what a useful development they were. Since their results are worth recording, they will now be displayed conspicuously, and the work that went into achieving those results will not be without its reward.

Roman Stories

11. 1. Sulpicius Galus was very enthusiastic about studying every type of learned work and thereby did a great service to the Republic. He was a legate under Lucius Paullus in the war against King Perseus,[161] and on one clear night there was a sudden eclipse of the moon. Our army was terrified, regarding this as a sinister omen, and lost its confidence about engaging with the enemy. Galus gave a very learned lecture about the arrangement of the heavens and the nature of the constellations, and he sent the men back to the battlefield in high spirits. So it was Galus' knowledge of the liberal arts that paved the way to the famous victory of Paullus, because if Galus had not vanquished the panic of our soldiers, our general could not have vanquished our enemies.

11. 2. Spurinna's expertise in interpreting warnings from the gods turned out to be more accurate than the city of Rome would have wanted it to be.[162] He had warned Caesar to be careful during the following thirty days because they would be fateful for him, and the last of these days was the ides of March.[163] By chance the two of them met in the house of Domitius Calvinus,[164] where they were paying their respects to Domitius, and Caesar said to Spurinna, "Don't you know that the ides of March have come already?" And Spurinna replied, "Don't you know that they have not yet gone by?" One of them had cast fear aside, as if the dangerous period had passed; the other felt that even the last part of that period was not free of danger. If only the diviner had been mistaken in his augury, rather than the father of our country mistaken in his confidence.

Foreign Stories

11. ext. 1. Let us examine some foreign stories. There was a sudden eclipse of the sun at Athens, and the city was covered with a strange darkness. People felt

---

[161]Lucius Aemilius Paullus (cos, 182 B.C.) defeated King Perseus of Macedonia in 168 B.C. Gaius Sulpicius Galus (cos, 166 B.C.) was his legate in 168 and 167 B.C.

[162]Spurinna was a diviner (see Glossary).

[163]The ides were originally the day of the full moon. In March, they came on the 15th. Caesar was assassinated on March 15, 44 B.C.

[164]Gnaeus Domitius Calvinus (cos, 53 B.C.) was one of Caesar's supporters.

very anxious, believing that this was a heavenly warning foretelling their own destruction. Pericles[165] appeared in public and gave them a lecture on everything he had learned from his teacher Anaxagoras relating to the courses of the sun and the moon.[166] He did not allow his fellow citizens to be terrified any longer by such empty fears.

11. ext. 2. How much respect do we imagine that King Alexander paid to the arts, since he wanted to be painted by Apelles alone and sculpted only by Lysippus?[167]

11. ext. 3. The Vulcan in Athens that was created by the hands of Alcamenes captivates those who see it.[168] In addition to all the other marks of consummate artistry that it displays, they especially admire the fact that it stands upright but delicately reveals a trace of his hidden limp under his garment. It is not emphasized as a defect, but it is discretely displayed as a recognizable characteristic peculiar to this god.

11. ext. 4. Praxiteles placed his marble statue of Vulcan's wife,[169] which almost seemed to breathe, in her temple on Cnidos.[170] The beauty of this statue exposed it to the sexual embrace of a certain man. This makes it easier to excuse the mistake of the stallion when he saw a picture of a mare and had to whinny, or the dogs that are excited and start barking when they see a picture of a dog, or the bull that was filled with desire and mated with the bronze cow in Syracuse, since he was aroused by the extraordinary likeness. Why should we be surprised if animals devoid of reason are deceived by artistic works, when we see that a man was driven to sacrilegious lust by the shape of a mute statue?

Certain Things Cannot Be Achieved by Art

Foreign Stories (continued)

11. ext. 5. Although Nature often allows art to imitate her powers, she sometimes leaves art behind, and lets it get exhausted in pointless efforts. The hands of that great artist, Euphranor,[171] learned this to his cost. When he was painting the twelve gods in Athens,[172] he painted the figure of Neptune in the most exceptional and majestic colors he could, and he intended to make Jupiter's portrait even more

---

[165]Pericles was the democratic leader of Athens from 460 to 429 B.C.

[166]Anaxagoras of Clazomenae lived in Athens from 460 to 430 B.C. His skepticism about the divinity of the sun and the moon led to his expulsion from Athens in 430 B.C.

[167]Alexander the Great was king of Macedonia from 336 to 323 B.C. Apelles was a fourth-century painter, and Lysippus was a sculptor in bronze.

[168]Alcamenes worked as a sculptor between 440 and 400 B.C.

[169]Praxiteles was a sculptor in marble of the fourth century B.C. Vulcan's wife is Venus, the Roman name for the Greek goddess Aphrodite.

[170]The Aphrodite of Cnidos (an island off the west coast of Asia Minor) was considered the masterpiece of Praxiteles.

[171]Euphranor of Corinth worked as a painter from 370 to 330 B.C.

[172]Euphranor decorated the Stoa of Zeus in Athens with three paintings, one of which was this painting of the twelve gods.

venerable. But he had used up all his powers of invention in the previous work, so his later efforts were unable to produce the result he intended.

11. ext. 6. Well? That other painter, who is equally famous, was depicting the tragic sacrifice of Iphigenia,[173] and he showed all the men standing around the altar, Calchas looking sad, Ulysses mourning, and Menelaus lamenting, but he showed Agamemnon covering his face with his cloak.[174] Did he not admit thereby that his art could not express the bitterness of Agamemnon's enormous grief? So his picture was moist with the tears of the seer and the friend and the brother, but he left it to the spectator's feelings to judge what the father's grief was like.

11. ext. 7. I must add another story about the art of painting. An artist of exceptional talent had devoted a lot of work to depicting a horse that was coming back from its exercise. The painting almost looked alive. He wanted to add the foam coming from the horse's nostrils, but this great artist was completely worn out and frustrated for a long time by this tiny task. He was burning with indignation, so he took a sponge that happened to be there beside him, soaked with all his colors, and threw it at his painting, wanting to destroy the entire work. Fortune made him aim the sponge at the horse's nostrils, so it carried out the painter's wishes. In this way, art did not have the power to depict something, but chance imitated it successfully.

Chapter 12. Each Person Is the Best Practitioner and Teacher of His Own Profession

Preface

We should have no doubt that each person is the best practitioner and teacher of his own profession, and a few stories should draw our attention to this.

Roman Stories

12. 1. Quintus Scaevola was our most famous and reliable oracle when it came to law.[175] But whenever he was consulted about land repossessed by the state, he would refer his clients to Furius and Cascellius,[176] because they had dedicated themselves to this branch of the law. His behavior did not undermine his own authority but rather highlighted his modesty when he confessed that this matter

---

[173]This painting was the work of Timanthes.

[174]The seer, Calchas, sacrificed Iphigenia, the daughter of Agamemnon, at the beginning of the Trojan War. Menelaus was Agamemnon's brother; Ulysses is the Roman name for Agamemnon's friend, Odysseus.

[175]Quintus Mucius Scaevola the Pontiff (cos, 95 B.C.) wrote the first treatise on private law.

[176]Numerius Furius was an equestrian; Aulus Cascellius had bought up confiscated properties belonging to victims of Sulla.

could be explained better by men who had become experts by dealing with it on a daily basis. The wisest teachers of their profession are the ones who judge their own expertise modestly, and that of others shrewdly.

Foreign Stories

12. ext. 1. The same attitude was found in the very learned mind of Plato. Some men who had contracted to build a holy altar tried to get him to discuss its shape and form, but he ordered them to go to Euclid,[177] the geometrician, yielding to his knowledge, or rather specialization.

12. ext. 2. Athens boasts of its arsenal, and not without reason. It is worth seeing as a work of architecture because of its expensive elegance. It is well known that its architect, Philo,[178] explained his plans for the building so eloquently in the theater that those well-educated people rewarded his eloquence with no less praise than they granted for his skill as an architect.

12. ext. 3. There is also the wonderful remark of the artist,[179] who was content to have his work criticized by a cobbler as far as the sandal and its straps were concerned, but when the cobbler started to discuss the leg of his statue, the artist told him not to go above the sole.

Chapter 13. Old Age

Preface

In our stories of dedication to work earlier in this book,[180] we have seen several famous men who persevered to a very advanced old age. But old age should be set apart and given its own chapter, because we would not want to deprive anyone of an honorable mention if they have been blessed with exceptional favors by the immortal gods. We would also like to supply props, so to speak, for our hope of a long life, and by relying on these props, we should become more cheerful as we look back to happy stories from the old days. Our confidence will continually reassure us about the peace and quiet of our era, a time that is more fortunate than any previous age, as we see that the life of the leader[181] who keeps us all safe is extended to the longest period possible for a human being.

---

[177]Euclid, the famous mathematician, lived from about 325 to 250 B.C. Plato, who died in 347 B.C., never knew him.

[178]Philo of Eleusis built the arsenal at the Piraeus (the harbor of Athens) in the fourth century B.C.

[179]This artist was Apelles of Colophon (in the west of Asia Minor), a painter of the fourth century B.C. (see 8:11,ext.2).

[180]Book 8, Chapter 7.

[181]The leader is the emperor Tiberius.

Roman Stories

13. 1. Marcus Valerius Corvus reached the age of one hundred. There was a span of forty-six years between his first and his sixth consulship,[182] but his physical strength remained intact, and he was able to take on the most spectacular public duties as well as the most demanding work on his own farmlands. He was a marvelous example both as a citizen and as a family man.

13. 2. Metellus had an equally long span of life, and four years after holding office as consul, when he was a very old man, he was elected chief pontiff.[183] For the next twenty-two years he supervised all our rituals without ever stumbling over the words as he read out the prayers or letting his hand shake as he performed the sacrifices.

13. 3. Fabius the Delayer performed his priestly duties as an augur for sixty-two years, though he was already middle-aged when he obtained this office.[184] If you put these two time periods together, they would easily add up to a century.

13. 4. What could I say about Marcus Perperna?[185] He outlived everyone he had summoned to the Senate when he was consul; and out of the Conscript Fathers he had chosen when he was censor with Lucius Philippus,[186] he saw only seven left alive. He had outlived the entire distinguished order.[187]

13. 5. I would have measured the life of Appius in terms of his disability, because he spent countless years afflicted by blindness,[188] but although he was burdened with this misfortune, he courageously ruled over four sons, five daughters, a vast clientele, and also the Republic itself. Even when he was already worn out by his life, he had himself carried into the Senate house on a stretcher, so that he could prevent the ratification of the disgraceful peace treaty with Pyrrhus.[189] Could anyone call him blind? It was he who forced our country to see what was honorable when our country was too blind to see it.

13. 6. In the case of several women, it is clear that their lives were no shorter, but it will be enough for me to mention some of them briefly: Livia, the wife of Rutilius,[190] reached the age of 97; Terentia, the wife of Cicero, reached the age of 103;[191] Clodia, the wife of Aufilius, whose fifteen sons died before her, reached the age of 115.

---

[182]Marcus Valerius Maximus Corvus (cos, 348 B.C.) held six consulships between 348 and 299 B.C.

[183]Lucius Caecilius Metellus (cos, 251 B.C.) was chief pontiff from 243 B.C. (four years after he was consul for the second time in 247 B.C.) until his death in 221 B.C.

[184]Fabius the Delayer was an augur from 265 B.C. until his death in 203 B.C.

[185]Marcus Perperna (cos, 92 B.C.) lived from 148 to 49 B.C.

[186]Perperna was censor in 86 B.C. with Lucius Marcius Philippus (cos, 91 B.C.).

[187]Many of Perperna's fellow senators had been murdered by Marius or Sulla.

[188]Appius Claudius Caecus (cos, 307 B.C.) was supposedly struck blind after his censorship in 312 B.C. (see 1:1,17).

[189]Appius opposed peace with King Pyrrhus of Epirus in 280 B.C.

[190]Publius Rutilius Rufus was consul in 105 B.C.

[191]Terentia married Cicero in 77 B.C. They divorced in 46 B.C.

Foreign Stories

13. ext. 1. To these cases I shall add two kings whose longevity was very beneficial to the Roman people. Hiero, the ruler of Sicily, reached the age of ninety.[192] Masinissa, the king of Numidia, exceeded even this, as the length of his reign measured sixty years, so that he was more remarkable than any other person for the toughness of his old age.[193] What Cicero writes about him in the book he wrote on old age[194] is well known: no matter how much it rained or how cold it was, he could never be induced to cover his head. They also say that he would stand still on the same spot for several hours, and he would not move one step until he had worn out the younger men with this endurance test. If he had to do some sedentary work, he would often spend the entire day on his throne without turning his body to either side. He would also lead his armies on horseback, usually riding by day and night without a break. He had learned to carry out these tasks as a young man, but he did not give any of them up so as to spend his old age in greater comfort. In sexual matters, he was always very active, and when he was over eighty-six years old, he produced a son who was named Methymnus. His country was an empty desert when he inherited it, but by constantly working to cultivate it, he left it a grain-producing land.

13. ext. 2. Gorgias of Leontini,[195] who taught Isocrates[196] and several other men of great brilliance, was a very fortunate man by his own reckoning. When he was 107 years old, someone asked him why he wanted to stay alive for so long, and he said, "Because I have nothing to say against my old age." What could be longer or happier than his lifetime? He was already starting off his second century, and he did not find anything to complain of in the new one, nor did he leave behind anything he had to complain of in the old one.

13. ext. 3. The Pythagorean philosopher Xenophilus of Chalcis was two years younger, but he was no less happy. He died, as the musician Aristoxenus says,[197] in the glory of having attained the highest philosophical wisdom without ever experiencing any human misfortune.

13. ext. 4. Arganthonius of Cadiz[198] ruled for so many years that his reign was as long as a normal human life span. He ruled his country for eighty years, and he succeeded to the throne when he was forty years old. The historians who record this are very reliable. Asinius Pollio,[199] no small figure in Roman literature, records

---

[192]Hiero II was king of Syracuse from 269 to 215 B.C.

[193]Masinissa was king of Numidia (modern Algeria) from 209 to 148 B.C.

[194]Cicero mentions Masinissa in *De Senectute* 10:34.

[195]Gorgias of Leontini (in eastern Sicily) lived from 485 to 375 B.C. He was a great orator and teacher of rhetoric.

[196]His student Isocrates, the famour Athenian orator, lived from 436 to 338 B.C.

[197]Aristoxenus of Tarentum lived from 376 to 322 B.C.

[198]Arganthonius was king of Tartessus in Spain in the seventh century B.C.

[199]Gaius Asinius Pollio (cos, 40 B.C.) was a Roman historian and a poet; he lived from 76 B.C. to A.D. 5.

in the third book of his history that Arganthonius reached the age of 130, and Pollio himself was no trivial example of hardy longevity.

13. ext. 5. Similar cases make the number of years reached by King Arganthonius less surprising. Herodotus writes that the Ethiopians live for more than 120 years;[200] Ctesias reports the same thing about the Indians;[201] and Theopompus says that Epimenides of Cnossus lived for 157 years.[202]

13. ext. 6. Hellanicus[203] says that some people from the nation of the Epii, which is a part of Aetolia,[204] reach the age of two hundred. Damastes[205] endorses this, and states furthermore that a man from that nation called Litorius, who was very strong and exceptionally tall, accumulated three hundred years.

13. ext. 7. Alexander,[206] in the book he wrote about the region of Illyria, states that a man called Dando survived to the age of five hundred without growing old in any way. Xenophon[207] was much more generous, as we read in his *Voyage around the Coast*: he grants a life span of eight hundred years to a king of the Latmians' island. And so as not to make the king's father feel unwanted, he attributes a life span of six hundred years to him.

Chapter 14. The Desire for Glory

Preface

Where does glory come from? What are its characteristics? How should it be acquired? Would it be better to ignore it, since it is not necessary for virtue? These are questions to be answered by people who are deeply concerned with examining issues of this kind, and who happen to have a gift for eloquently describing their acute observations. But I am content to match agents with their actions, and actions with their agents in this work, so with a few appropriate stories, I shall try to show how great the desire for glory tends to be.

---

[200]Herodotus is the famous historian of fifth century Greece. He records this in his *Histories* 3:23.

[201]Ctesias of Cnidos lived during the fourth century B.C. He was a doctor at the Persian court and wrote a history of the Persian empire.

[202]Theopompus of Chios lived during the fourth century B.C. Epimenides was a prophet from Cnossus (on the island of Crete) around 600 B.C. who supposedly went into a trance when he was a boy and woke up 57 years later.

[203]Hellanicus of Lesbos was a historian and lived from 480 to 395 B.C.

[204]Aetolia was in northern Greece.

[205]Damastas was a fifth-century geographer.

[206]Alexander Polyhistor of Miletus lived from 105 to 40 B.C.

[207]Xenophon of Lampasacus was a geographer in the second century B.C.

Roman Stories

14. 1. Scipio Africanus wanted to place a statue of the poet Ennius among the tombs of the Cornelius family, because he felt that his own achievements had been made famous by the poet's talent.[208] Scipio did, of course, realize that as long as the Roman Empire flourished, and Africa lay at the feet of Italy, and the citadel of the Capitol remained the pinnacle of the entire world, the memory of his family could not be extinguished. But he considered it a matter of great importance that the light of literature had shone over his deeds also. Africanus was a man who deserved to be publicized by Homer rather than by a rough and unpolished poet.

14. 2. Decimus Brutus,[209] who was a famous commander in his own day, adopted a similar respectful attitude to the poet Accius.[210] Brutus was delighted that Accius sought his friendship and was so ready to praise him, so he decorated the entrance to the temple that he had consecrated from the spoils of his victory with the verses of this poet.[211]

14. 3. Not even Pompey the Great was immune to this craving for glory. Because Theophanes of Mytilene had written about his achievements,[212] Pompey, while addressing his army, presented Theophanes with Roman citizenship.[213] Although this was a very generous reward in itself, Pompey followed it up with a detailed speech that was heard by many people. Thus Pompey made sure that nobody would doubt that he was repaying a favor rather than conferring one.

14. 4. Sulla did not direct his attention toward any writer, but when King Bocchus handed over Jugurtha to Marius,[214] Sulla so passionately wanted all the glory for himself that he had this handing over engraved on the signet ring he used.[215] And however great he may have become later, he never despised even the slightest trace of glory.

14. 5. After these stories about generals, I must add one about an ordinary soldier's desire for glory. When Metellus Scipio was distributing military awards to men who had performed exceptional services,[216] Titus Labienus suggested to him that he should present golden armbands to one brave horseman.[217] Metellus Scipio

---

[208]Scipio Africanus was a friend of the epic and tragic poet Quintus Ennius, who lived from 239 to 169 B.C.

[209]Decimus Junius Brutus Callaicus was consul in 138 B.C.

[210]Lucius Accius, the tragic poet, lived from 170 to 86 B.C.

[211]Brutus defeated the Callaeci of Spain in 137 B.C.

[212]Theophanes of Mytilene was a politician and a historian.

[213]Pompey made Theophanes a Roman citizen in 62 B.C.

[214]King Bocchus of Mauretania (modern Morocco) surrendered King Jugurtha of Numidia (modern Algeria) to Marius in 105 B.C.

[215]Sulla was Marius' quaestor and carried out the final negotiations for the handing over of Jugurtha.

[216]Quintus Caecilius Metellus Pius Scipio Nasica (cos, 52 B.C.) was in command of the Republican army in Africa from 47 to 46 B.C.

[217]Titus Labienus (tribune of the plebs, 63 B.C.) was a legate in the army of Metellus Scipio.

said he could not do this, because the honor of the army would be disgraced by rewarding someone who had recently been a slave, so Labienus himself presented the horseman with a large amount of gold from the booty taken from the Gauls. Metellus Scipio did not put up with this quietly. He said to the horseman, "You will have this as a gift from a rich man." When the horseman heard this, he threw the gold at the feet of Labienus and hung his head. But when he heard Scipio saying, "Your general presents you with these silver armbands," he went away jumping with joy. There is no one so humble that he cannot be touched by the charm of glory.

14. 6. Sometimes even famous men have tried to win glory from the most trivial achievements. What was the objective of Gaius Fabius,[218] a most noble citizen, when he did the paintings on the walls in the temple of Security, which had been dedicated by Gaius Junius Bubulcus,[219] and then signed his name on them? This and none other was the one honor that his family, so famous for its consulships and priesthoods and triumphs, had so far failed to acquire. His mind was devoted to this low pastime, and whatever kind of work it was that he produced, he did not want it to be passed over in silence. He was, no doubt, following the example of Phidias, who included a self-portrait on the shield of Minerva in such a way that if it were removed, the structure of the entire work would collapse.[220]

Foreign Stories

14. ext. 1. But if Fabius was so taken up with the idea of imitating foreigners, it would have been much better for him to copy the intensity of Themistocles.[221] They say that Themistocles was tormented and goaded on by other men's achievements, and that he spent sleepless nights because of this. When people asked him why he was wandering around in public at that hour, he replied, "Because the trophies of Miltiades will not let me sleep."[222] It was indeed Marathon that drove him on with its secret torches to make Artemisium and Salamis so famous, those names that produced such glory for the navy.[223]

Once when Themistocles was going to the theater, he was asked whose voice he would enjoy hearing the most, and he said, "The voice of the man who would sing best about my achievements." O, the sweetness of glory! (I almost said "the boastful sweetness of glory"!)[224]

---

[218]Gaius Fabius Pictor was an artist but belonged to the aristocratic Fabius family.

[219]Gaius Junius Bubulcus Brutus (cos, 317 B.C.) dedicated the temple of Security (*Salus*) on the Quirinal hill in 302 B.C.

[220]Phidias finished the cult statue of Athena (Roman Minerva) in the Parthenon temple of Athens by 432 B.C.

[221]Themistocles led the Athenians during the Persian invasion of 480 B.C.

[222]Miltiades had commanded the Athenian army that won the battle of Marathon in 490 B.C.

[223]Themistocles fought an indecisive battle at Artemisium (on the north coast of Euboea) and defeated the Persians completely at Salamis in 480 B.C.

[224]There is a pun on glory (*gloria*) and boastful (*gloriosus*) in the Latin.

14. ext. 2. Alexander's heart had an insatiable longing for glory.[225] When his friend Anaxarchus told him,[226] following the authority of his teacher Democritus,[227] that there were innumerable worlds, Alexander said, "Alas, poor me, because so far I have not even gained possession of one!" To possess the world was too inglorious for this man, though the world is great enough to serve as the home of all the gods.

14. ext. 3. I shall add a story about Aristotle's thirst for acquiring glory, which was similar to the burning desire of that youthful king. Aristotle had presented his books on the art of rhetoric to Theodectes, so that this student of his could publish them as his own work.[228] Later, Aristotle was annoyed that the authorship of this work should be attributed to another writer, so in a different book that he published under his own name, when he was discussing some issues involving rhetoric, he added that he had discussed these issues more clearly in the books of Theodectes.[229] If I were not held back by my respect for Aristotle's great and wide-ranging knowledge, I would have said that he was the kind of philosopher who should have been handed over to a more high-minded philosopher for the improvement of his character.

But glory is not ignored even by those who try to induce others to despise it. After all, those writers always take good care to put their own names on their books. So although they ostensibly make light of glory, they still run after it by asserting their right to be remembered. But in spite of their hypocrisy, such as it is, they are far easier to deal with than people who, in their pursuit of eternal fame, do not hesitate to win notoriety through criminal actions.

14. ext. 4. I wonder whether Pausanias should be mentioned above all other men of this kind. He asked Hermocles how he could suddenly become famous, and Hermocles replied that if Pausanias murdered some illustrious man, then the glory of that man would also spread over him. Immediately thereafter, Pausanias murdered Philip, and he did indeed get what he wanted, because he made himself as famous to future generations for this murder as Philip was for his goodness.[230]

14. ext. 5. The desire for glory in the following case was sacrilegious. There was a man who wanted to burn down the temple of Diana in Ephesus[231] so that when this beautiful work of art was destroyed, his name would spread throughout the entire world. He revealed his mad scheme after he was put on the rack. The

---

[225]Alexander the Great of Macedonia was thought to have conquered the entire world.

[226]The philosopher Anaxarchus of Abdera lived from 380 to 320 B.C.

[227]Democritus of Abdera believed that the universe is composed of many worlds.

[228]Theodectes was actually Aristotle's predecessor, not his student, and Aristotle wrote a summary of Theodectes' work on rhetoric.

[229]Aristotle was referring to his summary of Theodectes; he was not claiming that the original book of Theodectes was his own work.

[230]Pausanias murdered King Philip II of Macedonia in 336 B.C. His real motive was that Philip refused to punish a man who had sexually abused Pausanias.

[231]Herostratus burned down the temple of Artemis (Roman Diana) in Ephesus in 356 B.C.

Ephesians made a wise decision and decreed that all evidence of this repulsive man's existence should be wiped out, but the very eloquent and talented Theopompus included the man's name in his historical work.[232]

Chapter 15. Marvelous Honors That Were Given to Certain People

Preface

We shall bring joy to good-natured souls by displaying in full view the marvelous honors that have been deservedly given to certain people. It must be considered equally good to look upon the rewards of virtue and upon the accomplishments of virtue. Nature itself makes us happy when we see people striving for honor with such effort and winning it in such a gratifying manner. At this point my mind immediately rushes eagerly toward the imperial palace, our most generous and honored temple, but it would be better to restrain myself, because when someone has an ascent into heaven open before him,[233] even the greatest honors that can be paid to him on this earth are far less than he deserves.

Roman Stories

15. 1. Scipio Africanus was granted a consulship before the legal age limit,[234] because the army had urged the Senate by letter that this should be done. So you would not know whether his authorization by the Conscript Fathers or his recommendation by the soldiers brought him more glory: the toga[235] appointed Scipio, and the army demanded Scipio, as our commander against the Carthaginians.

It would take a long time to recount the extraordinary honors that were given to him during his lifetime, because there were lots of them, and it would not be necessary, since we have already mentioned most of them. So I shall add an exceptional honor that he holds to this very day. He has a statue located in the main chamber of the temple of Jupiter Best and Greatest.[236] Whenever there is a funeral

---

[232]The historian Theopompus of Chios lived from 378 to 320 B.C.

[233]Caesar and Augustus had been deified, so it was only natural for Valerius to assume that a similar ascent to heaven would be granted to the emperor Tiberius. The Senate, however, refused such divine honors on the death of Tiberius.

[234]Scipio Africanus was elected consul in 205 B.C. when he was only thirty years old. The legal age limit was forty-two, but this rule did not become law until 180 B.C.

[235]The toga was the symbol of civilian life, so when Valerius says "the toga," he means the civilian Senate.

[236]The temple of Jupiter Best and Greatest was on the Capitol hill in Rome.

to be held in the Cornelius family, the statue is taken from there, so for that family alone the Capitol serves as their living room.[237]

15. 2. In the same way, of course, the statue of Cato the Censor is removed from the Senate house for funerals in his family. How grateful the senatorial order is! It wanted that senator who had done so much for the Republic almost to live forever with the senators. Cato was rich in every aspect of virtue, and he was great by his own merits rather than by the kindness of fortune. It was Cato's advice rather than Scipio's military command that first destroyed Carthage.[238]

15. 3. We come across a rare type of honor in the case of Scipio Nasica.[239] On the advice of Pythian Apollo, the Senate wanted the goddess it had brought from Pessinus to be welcomed by Nasica's hands into his own home,[240] although he was not even a quaestor yet. The Senate had been told by the oracle that this service to the Mother of the Gods should be performed by our most upright man. Read through the list of all our consuls, imagine all our triumphal chariots, but you will not find anything more splendid than moral superiority.

15. 4. The Scipio family keeps supplying us with glorious deeds to commemorate. When Scipio Aemilianus was only a candidate for the aedileship, the people elected him consul instead.[241] When he went to the Campus to support the candidacy of his brother's son, Quintus Fabius Maximus,[242] for the quaestorship, the people once against escorted him home as consul.[243] The Senate twice gave him a province without making him go through the lottery, giving him Africa the first time, and then Spain.[244] These honors were given to a man who was not ambitious as a citizen or as a senator, as is made clear not only by his strict way of life but also by his death, which was a result of a secret plot.[245]

15. 5. The gods and also his fellow citizens made Marcus Valerius famous for two remarkable things: when he was fighting in hand-to-hand combat against a Gaul, the gods sent a crow down to fight for him;[246] and though he was only

---

[237]Images of ancestors were displayed in the living room (*atrium*) of an aristocratic Roman house and were taken out for funeral processions.

[238]Cato the Censor kept urging the Senate to destroy Carthage up until his death in 149 B.C. Scipio Aemilianus destroyed Carthage in 146 B.C.

[239]Publius Cornelius Scipio Nasica was consul in 191 B.C.

[240]Scipio Nasica welcomed the black stone of the Mother of the Gods, which was brought from Pessinus (in Galatia, central Asia Minor) to Rome in 204 B.C.

[241]Scipio Aemilianus was elected consul for 147 B.C. and given Africa as his province.

[242]Scipio Aemilianus helped his nephew, Quintus Fabius Maximus Allobrogicus (cos, 121 B.C.), during the election campaigns of 135 B.C.

[243]Scipio Aemilianus was consul (for the second time), and his nephew was quaestor, in 134 B.C. They worked together in Spain.

[244]Normally, governors were assigned their provinces by lottery.

[245]Scipio Aemilianus died suddenly in 129 B.C. (see 4:1,12 and 5:3,2d).

[246]Marcus Valerius Maximus Corvus (cos, 348 B.C.) was a military tribune in 349 B.C. when the miracle of the crow occurred. His last name, Corvus, means "crow."

twenty-three years old, his fellow citizens presented him with the consulship.[247] This family of ancient origin and the highest reputation preserved the first honor by taking on the extra name Corvinus ("of the crow"). In addition to this great glory the family also has the honor of his consulship, and it boasts that he was so young and that this was the first of many consulships for him.[248]

15. 6. The glory of Quintus Scaevola, who was the colleague of Lucius Crassus in the consulship, was quite impressive too.[249] He governed Asia so conscientiously and bravely that the Senate issued a decree stating that all public officials going to that province in the future should use Scaevola as their example and model in carrying out their duties.[250]

15. 7. The seven consulships and the two distinguished triumphs of Marius are closely associated with a remark made by Scipio Aemilianus.[251] Right up to the day of his cremation, Marius danced with joy because of this remark. At that time, Marius was serving in the cavalry at Numantia under the command of Scipio Aemilianus,[252] and someone happened to ask Scipio during a banquet whether the Republic would ever have as great a general if anything should happen to Scipio himself. Turning to Marius, who was reclining above him, Scipio said, "Perhaps this man." It is almost impossible to judge whether the prediction made by this man of supreme ability clearly foresaw the rise of the able Marius or effectively inspired it. That banquet in the army anticipated all the splendid banquets throughout our city that would honor Marius later. After the news reached the city at nightfall that Marius had wiped out the Cimbrians,[253] there was nobody who did not pour a libation to Marius during their prayers at dinner, treating him as if he were one of the immortal gods.[254]

15. 8. The distinguished and extraordinary honors that were showered on Pompey shout out at us from the literary works that commemorate those honors, some showing enthusiastic admiration and others grumbling with jealousy. When he was just a Roman equestrian, he was sent as governor to Spain to fight against Sertorius,[255] and he was given equal power with the leading man of the state,

---

[247]Marcus Valerius was consul for the first time in 348 B.C.

[248]Marcus Valerius was consul six times between 348 and 299 B.C.

[249]Quintus Mucius Scaevola the Pontiff was consul in 95 B.C., along with the famous orator, Lucius Licinius Crassus.

[250]Scaevola was governor of Asia in 97 B.C.

[251]Marius held seven consulships between 107 and 86 B.C. He celebrated a triumph over King Jugurtha of Numidia in 104 B.C. and another triumph over the Cimbrians and Teutons in 101 B.C.

[252]Marius served under Scipio Aemilianus at the siege of Numantia in Spain (134–133 B.C.).

[253]At a battle in northern Italy, Marius defeated the Cimbrians (from Denmark) in 101 B.C. and was hailed as Rome's savior.

[254]A libation was a drink offering poured in honor of the gods.

[255]From 77 to 71 B.C., Pompey was governor of Nearer Spain, where he fought against the rebel Roman governor, Quintus Sertorius (praetor, 83 B.C.).

Metellus Pius.[256] Before he had even started on any public office, he celebrated two triumphs.[257] He started his career as a magistrate with the highest office in the state.[258] By decree of the Senate, he held his third consulship alone.[259] He celebrated one great triumph over Mithridates, over Tigranes and over many other kings too, over a vast number of states and nations, and over the pirates.[260]

15. 9. The voice of the Roman people almost elevated Quintus Catulus to the stars.[261] When he stood at the rostra and asked the people, since they had persisted in entrusting everything to Pompey, in whom they would place their hopes if some sudden chance event took Pompey away, they shouted back with one voice, "In you." The power of their respect and esteem was amazing, since in the space of two syllables it equated Catulus with Pompey and with those honors of his that I mentioned.

15. 10. Cato of Utica's landing on the banks of the Tiber, when he came back from Cyprus with the king's fortune, can also be seen as memorable.[262] As he disembarked from his ship, the consuls, the other high public officials, the entire Senate, and the Roman people were all there to pay their respects, and they rejoiced not because the fleet had brought them this great weight of gold and silver, but because it had brought Cato back safe.

15. 11. I suspect that Lucius Marcius might be the greatest example of extraordinary honors.[263] He was only a Roman equestrian, but our two armies, devastated by the deaths of Publius and Gnaeus Scipio[264] and by the victory of Hannibal,[265]

---

[256]Quintus Caecilius Metellus Pius (cos, 80 B.C.) was governor of Farther Spain from 79 to 71 B.C.

[257]Pompey celebrated his triumph over Spain at the end of 71 B.C. He also crushed the remains of the army of Spartacus (but he did not literally celebrate a triumph over Spartacus).

[258]Pompey's first political office was his consulship in 70 B.C.

[259]Pompey was consul without any colleague in 52 B.C. This was the only time such a thing had happened in the history of the Republic.

[260]Pompey celebrated a great triumph in 61 B.C. for his victories over the pirates (67 B.C.), King Mithridates VI of Pontus (66 B.C.), and King Tigranes II of Armenia (66 B.C.).

[261]Quintus Lutatius Catulus (cos, 78 B.C.) was an opponent of Pompey.

[262]Cato of Utica was sent as a quaestor to annex Cyprus in 58 B.C. Ptolemy, king of Cyprus from 80 to 58 B.C., had committed suicide, and Cato returned to Rome with the king's treasure in 56 B.C.

[263]Lucius Marcius Septimius was a military tribune in the army of the Scipio brothers in 211 B.C.

[264]Publius Cornelius Scipio (cos, 218 B.C.) and his brother Gnaeus Cornelius Scipio Calvus (cos, 222 B.C.) were defeated and killed in Spain in 211 B.C.

[265]Hannibal did not defeat the Scipio brothers, but Valerius may be referring to the traumatic Roman defeat at Cannae in 216 B.C.

chose him to be their commander.[266] At that time their chances of survival had come to a critical point, and there was no room left for politics.[267]

15. 12. It is only right that to our commemoration of great men we should add Sulpicia, the daughter of Servius Paterculus and wife of Quintus Fulvius Flaccus.[268] The committee of ten had examined the Sibylline Books,[269] and the Senate consequently decreed that a statue of Venus Changer of Hearts be consecrated to the goddess, so that the minds of unmarried girls and mature women would easily change from lust to modesty. They chose one hundred out of all the married women, then chose by lottery ten out of these, and then these ten women were to decide who was the most virtuous woman: Sulpicia was chosen above all the others because of her chastity.

Foreign Stories

15. ext. 1. Since some remarkable foreign stories can be examined without detracting from the prestige of Rome in any way, we shall now turn to them.

Pythagoras[270] received such great veneration from his students that they felt it was morally wrong to raise a discussion about anything they had learned from him. In fact, if they were challenged to justify his teachings, they would simply reply, "He said it himself." This was a great honor, but it affected only his school.

Entire cities, however, voted to honor him in the following ways. With exceptional eagerness, the people of Croton asked him to allow their Senate, which consisted of one thousand members, to adopt his political theories.[271] The people of Metapontum, an exceptionally prosperous state, venerated him continually, and after his death they made his house a shrine of Ceres.[272] During that city's heyday, the goddess was honored in memory of that man, and that man was honored in the cult of the goddess.

15. ext. 2. Gorgias of Leontini surpassed all the men of his era in his knowledge of learned works,[273] so much so that he was the first person who dared to

---

[266]An equestrian was a member of the business elite (see equestrian in the Glossary). An equestrian was considered inferior to a senator, and military commanders were always senators.

[267]The Senate was not too pleased with the army's choice, but the soldiers did not have time to worry about that (see 2:7,15).

[268]Her father's full name was Servius Sulpicius Paterculus. Her husband, Quintus Fulvius Flaccus, was consul four times between 237 and 209 B.C.

[269]The committee of ten were in charge of the prophecies of the Sibylline Books (see committee of ten and Sibyl in the Glossary).

[270]Pythagoras of Samos, the famous philosopher and mathematician, lived during the sixth century B.C.

[271]Pythagoras lived in Croton from 530 to 510 B.C.

[272]Pythagoras moved to Metapontum in 510 B.C. and died there.

[273]Gorgias of Leontini (in eastern Sicily) lived from about 485 to 375 B.C. He traveled throughout Greece teaching rhetoric.

challenge his audience to pick any topic they would like to hear him lecture on. All of Greece set up a statue of solid gold to him in the temple of Apollo at Delphi, whereas it had set up only gilded statues to all other men until that time.

15. ext. 3. The Greek nation was also unanimous in its eagerness to honor Amphiaraus.[274] It gave the place where he had been buried the form and status of a temple and started the custom of taking oracles from it.[275] His ashes enjoy the same honor that is paid to the Pythian tripod,[276] to the bronze cauldron at Dodona,[277] and to the spring of Ammon.[278]

15. ext. 4. Berenice received no common honor, since of all women, she alone was allowed to be a spectator at an athletic event.[279] This was when she had escorted her son, Eucles, to the Olympic Games, where he was going to compete.[280] Berenice herself was the daughter of an Olympic champion, and her brothers, who had won the same honor, walked by her side.

[274]Amphiaraus was a prophet and one of the legendary seven heroes who attacked Thebes.

[275]At the shrine of Amphiaraus in Oropus (in Boeotia, in central Greece), the future was revealed through dreams.

[276]At Delphi, the prophetess of Apollo (the Pythia) sat on a tripod and spoke in a trance.

[277]At Dodona, the future was revealed by the clanging of bronze cauldrons hanging in the oak grove.

[278]The oracle of Jupiter Ammon was in the Libyan desert.

[279]Apart from the priestess of Demeter, no woman was allowed to attend the Olympic Games.

[280]A man from Rhodes called Eucles won the boxing match at the Olympics in 396 B.C., but his mother's name was Kallipateira.

BOOK NINE

Chapter 1. Self-indulgence and Sexual Indulgence

Preface

Self-indulgence is an attractive vice, so it is much easier to criticize it than to avoid it. But let's include it in our work, not to give it any honor but to make it face up to its true nature and repent. And let's include sexual indulgence with it, because it arises from the same vicious source. The two vices should not be separated, whether we condemn them or amend them, since they are connected through an identical flaw of the mind.

Roman Stories

1. 1. Gaius Sergius Orata was the first person to build baths heated from below. The cost started off small, but eventually he paid for what was almost an ocean of hot water over his furnace. He also invented his own private sea, presumably so that his gluttony would not be subject to the whims of Neptune. He diverted the seawater into inlets, and he trapped various shoals of fish there, separating them from each other with dams. No storm, however savage it might be, could prevent Orata's tables from having an abundant variety of dishes. With his widespread and tall buildings, he encroached on the shores of the Lucrine Lake,[1] which had been deserted up until then, so that he could enjoy shellfish that were even fresher.

When he encroached too greedily on state-owned waters, he got involved in a legal dispute with Considius, who was renting them from the state. During this case, Lucius Crassus,[2] who was arguing against Orata, said that his friend Considius was wrong in thinking that Orata would have to do without oysters if he moved away from the lake; because even if Orata was not allowed to get them from the lake, he could always find them on his roof tiles.

1. 2. The tragic actor Aesopus[3] should definitely have had his son adopted by Orata rather than leaving him as heir to his own property, because the young man's self-indulgence was not just ruinous; it was actually insane. It is well known that he paid outrageous prices for little songbirds that were high in demand because of their singing and served them up for dinner, instead of figpecker birds,[4]

---

[1]The Lucrine Lake was a lagoon at the fashionable resort of Baiae, and it was famous for its oysters.

[2]This is Lucius Licinius Crassus (cos, 95 B.C.), the famous orator.

[3]Aesopus acted in tragedies during the first century B.C.

[4]Figpeckers were considered a delicacy, but Orata goes out of his way to serve songbirds for dinner instead.

and that he used to dissolve very expensive pearls with vinegar and sprinkle them on his drinks. It was as if his enormous inheritance were some kind of cumbersome burden that he wanted to get rid of as quickly as possible.

Some have followed the philosophy of these two men, of the first old man or the second younger one, but they have stretched their hands out even farther: no vice ends where it began. This is why people have fish brought to them from the shores of the ocean, why their savings have been wasted on their cuisine, and why they have invented the pleasure of eating and drinking their property away.

1. 3. The end of the Second Punic War and the defeat of King Philip of Macedonia[5] encouraged our city to adopt a more self-indulgent lifestyle. At that period, the married women had the nerve to besiege the home of the Brutus brothers,[6] because these men were ready to veto the repeal of the Oppian law,[7] but the women wanted it repealed. This law did not allow women to wear multicolored clothes, possess more than half an ounce of gold, or travel by carriage within a mile of the city unless they were going to a sacrifice. The women got what they wanted, and this law, which had been in force continuously for twenty years, was repealed.

The men of that era did not foresee what kind of society the stubborn determination of that unusual gathering would lead to, or where this insolence that was more powerful than the law would end up. If their minds could have seen women's fashions, which come up with something new and more expensive every day, they would have resisted the stampede toward self-indulgence at the very beginning. But why should I go on talking about women any longer? Their intellectual weakness and their inability to aspire to serious work induce them to devote all their efforts to paying more attention to their appearance. But I see that even men of previous eras, though renowned for their reputation and intelligence, fell into this sidetrack that was unknown to our old-fashioned self-denial. And this should be clear from a dispute that occurred between two men from those old days.

1. 4. Gnaeus Domitius had a disagreement with his colleague, Lucius Crassus,[8] and criticized him for having pillars of Hymettian marble in the portico of his house.[9] At once Crassus asked him what he would evaluate his own house at, and Domitius answered, "Six million sesterces."[10] "How much less," Crassus said, "do you think it would be, if I cut down ten of your shrubs?" "Three million sesterces less," said Domitius. Then Crassus said, "Which of us is more self-indulgent: I, who bought ten pillars for one hundred thousand sesterces, or you, who paid a sum of

[5]The Second Punic War ended in 201 B.C., and Philip V of Macedonia was defeated in 197 B.C.

[6]Marcus Junius Brutus (cos, 178 B.C.) and his brother Publius Junius Brutus (praetor, 180 B.C.) were tribunes of the plebs in 195 B.C. and wanted the Oppian law to remain in force.

[7]The Oppian law was passed in 215 B.C. as a special war measure, and it was repealed in 195 B.C. because of the women's protest movement.

[8]Gnaeus Domitius Ahenobarbus (cos, 96 B.C.) and Lucius Licinius Crassus (cos, 95 B.C.), the famous orator, were censors in 92 B.C.

[9]Mount Hymettus was near Athens.

[10]See money—Roman in the Glossary.

three million sesterces for the shade of ten shrubs?" This conversation had forgotten about Pyrrhus and was heedless of Hannibal;[11] it was already jaded with our enormous overseas revenues! And yet how much more restrained was the affluence they introduced than the buildings and groves of the centuries that followed! But those men chose to bequeath to posterity the self-indulgence they had created themselves, rather than to preserve the self-restraint they had inherited from their forefathers.

1. 5. Metellus Pius was our leading statesman in his own day, but what was he up to when he permitted his hosts to celebrate his arrival in Spain by offering incense on their altars?[12] Or when he would gaze with pleasure on his walls, which were covered with tapestries that King Attalus might have owned?[13] When he would allow elaborate shows to take place in the intervals of his enormous banquets? When he would attend banquets wearing clothes embroidered with palm leaves, and golden crowns would come down from the ceiling and land on his head, as if he were a god? And where did those things happen? Not in Greece or in Asia, where austerity itself might be corrupted by the local self-indulgence; they occurred in a dangerous and belligerent province, at the very moment when our most bitter enemy, Sertorius, was terrorizing the Roman armies with the sight of his Lusitanian forces attacking them.[14] That is how much the Numidian campaigns of his own father had vanished from the memory of Metellus.[15] It is clear, therefore, how quickly self-indulgence can overtake a man; in his youth, Metellus had seen old-fashioned morality, but his old age marked the beginnings of our new morality.

1. 6. A similar change occurred in the Curio family, since our Forum witnessed the father's dignified severity,[16] and the son's debt of sixty million sesterces, which he had illegally contracted by disgracefully abusing our young noblemen.[17] Thus, at the same period and in the same family, two different eras lived together, one that was very frugal and one that was utterly abandoned.

1. 7. What self-indulgence and sexual indulgence emerged during the trial of Publius Clodius![18] The accused was clearly guilty on the charge of sacrilegious adultery, but Clodius did not give cash to the trial jury in exchange for his acquit-

---

[11]The Romans fought against King Pyrrhus of Epirus from 280 to 275 B.C. and against Hannibal from 218 to 201 B.C.

[12]Quintus Caecilius Metellus Pius (cos, 80 B.C.) was governor of Farther Spain from 79 to 71 B.C.

[13]King Attalus III of Pergamum discovered the art of weaving cloth from gold.

[14]Quintus Sertorius (praetor, 83 B.C.) was a rebel governor. The Lusitanians (who lived in modern Portugal) supported him, and he held out against the Roman government from 82 to 72 B.C.

[15]His father was Quintus Caecilius Metellus Numidicus (cos, 109 B.C.), who had fought against King Jugurtha of Numidia (modern Algeria) from 109 to 107 B.C.

[16]The father, Gaius Scribonius Curio, was consul in 76 B.C. and censor in 61 B.C.

[17]The son, also called Gaius Scribonius Curio, was a tribune of the plebs in 50 B.C. Antony was allegedly one of his sexual partners.

[18]Publius Clodius Pulcher (aedile, 56 B.C.) was tried for sacrilege in 61 B.C., because he had dressed up as a woman and infiltrated a festival restricted to women, in order to seduce Caesar's wife.

tal; instead, he procured nights of pleasure with ladies and young noblemen for the jury at enormous expense. In this disgraceful scandal involving so many aspects, you would not know whom to hate the most: the man who thought up this form of corruption, the young men and women who allowed their sexual morality to be used as a down payment for a perjured verdict, or the jurymen who sold their religious duty for sexual pleasure.

1. 8. An equally scandalous party was arranged by Gemellus, a tribune's messenger. Although Gemellus was of free birth, his occupation was a low one, and his lifestyle was almost that of a slave. He organized this party for the consul Metellus Scipio[19] and the tribunes of the plebs, which was a great embarrassment to our state. He set up a brothel in his home and prostituted Mucia and Flavia there, both of whom were well known because of their fathers and husbands, and also Saturninus, a boy from the nobility. How could their bodies have endured such a disgrace and become the playthings of drunken lust! That party should have been punished, not attended, by the consul and the tribunes!

1. 9. The sexual indulgence of Catiline was particularly criminal: carried away by his insane love for Aurelia Orestilla, he saw that there was only one thing that was preventing them from being joined in marriage; so he poisoned his son, who was his only child and already an adult. Then he used his son's funeral pyre to light his marriage torch and presented his own childlessness as a wedding gift to his new wife. Afterward he behaved as a citizen in the same spirit in which he had behaved as a father, but he paid the penalty to the ghost of his son and to the fatherland he had attacked so wickedly.[20]

Foreign Stories

1. ext. 1. The self-indulgence of the Campanians benefited our state greatly. Hannibal was invincible militarily, but Campania entangled him with its allurements[21] and handed him over to be defeated by the Roman army. He was a most energetic leader and his army had great morale, but with its lavish feasts, flowing wine, sweet-smelling perfumes, and wild sexual delights, Campania lured Hannibal's army to pleasure and sleep. The ferocity of the Carthaginians was finally broken and shattered when Seplasia Street and Alba Road started to be their camp.[22] What then could be more disgusting than these vices, what indeed could be more destructive? Because of them, courage wears away, victories grow faint, glory falls asleep and changes into disgrace, and mental and physical strength break down, so that you would wonder whether it should be considered more dangerous to be captured by your enemies or by these vices.

[19]Quintus Caecilius Metellus Pius Scipio Nasica was consul at the end of 52 B.C.

[20]Catiline's rebellion started in 63 B.C. He was killed in battle in 62 B.C.

[21]Campania (in western Italy) sided with Hannibal and welcomed the Carthaginians from 216 to 211 B.C.

[22]These were streets in Capua, the capital of Campania. Seplasia Street was famous for its perfumes.

1. ext. 2. These vices brought heavy and embarrassing defeats upon the city of Volsinii.[23] It used to be a rich city, it used to be governed by morality and the law, it used to be considered the capital of Etruria; but after it succumbed to self-indulgence, it fell into an abyss of injustice and disgrace and was subjected to a most outrageous tyranny by its slaves. At first, very few of the slaves dared to enter its senatorial order, but soon they controlled the entire republic. They commanded that wills be drawn up to suit their wishes, they forbade freeborn men to have parties or to assemble together, and they married the daughters of their masters. Finally, they passed a law that they could with impunity have sex with widowed and married women, and that no young woman could marry a freeborn man unless one of the slaves had first enjoyed her virginity.[24]

1. ext. 3. Well, Xerxes flaunted his royal wealth far too much,[25] and he took such delight in self-indulgence that he issued an edict offering a prize to anyone who discovered a new type of pleasure. But while he was completely absorbed in his pleasures, what a disaster he turned out to be for his vast empire![26]

1. ext. 4. King Antiochus of Syria was no better as an example of self-restraint.[27] His army imitated his blind and mindless self-indulgence. Most of the soldiers had golden studs in the soles of their sandals, they provided themselves with silver pots in which to cook, and they put up tents that were decorated with embroidered figures. They presented a welcome prey for a greedy enemy rather than any real obstacle for an energetic army to overcome.[28]

1. ext. 5. The life of King Ptolemy was merely an appendix to his vices, and this is why he was called "Potbelly."[29] What could be worse than his depravity? His elder sister was married to their brother, and he forced her to marry himself.[30] Later he raped her daughter and then divorced his wife so that he would be free to marry this niece.[31]

1. ext. 6. The people of Egypt behaved just like the rulers of their nation. When they marched out of their city walls under the leadership of Archelaus[32] to

[23]Volsinii was in Etruria (western Italy).

[24]The people of Volsinii called in the Romans to overthrow the regime of the slaves in 264 B.C.

[25]Xerxes I was king of Persia from 486 to 465 B.C.

[26]The disaster was Xerxes' unsuccessful invasion of Greece (480–479 B.C.).

[27]Antiochus VII Sidetes was king of Syria from 138 to 129 B.C.

[28]Antiochus fought unsuccessfully against the Parthians, who had conquered the eastern part of Syria.

[29]Ptolemy VIII Euergetes "Physcon" was king of Egypt from 145 to 116 B.C. *Physcon* means "potbelly."

[30]His brother, Ptolemy VI Philomator, had been king of Egypt from 180 to 145 B.C. The sister and wife of the two kings was Cleopatra II.

[31]The young woman he raped, Cleopatra III, was the daughter of his brother, Ptolemy VI Philomator, and his sister, Cleopatra II.

[32]Archelaus led the Egyptians in their rebellion (58–55 B.C.) against King Ptolemy XII Neos Dionysus.

fight against Aulus Gabinius,[33] they were ordered to build a fence and a ditch around their camp, but they shouted with one voice that public funds should be used to contract that work out. As a result, their minds were so weakened by pleasure that they could not stand up to the high spirits of our army.

1. ext. 7. The masses in Cyprus were, however, even more effeminate. Their queens[34] used to climb into their chariots using Cypriot women placed on top of each other as a stairs, so that they would have a soft place to step on, and the Cypriots were content to put up with this. If Cypriot men had been real men, they would have preferred to lose their lives than to humor such decadent whims.

Chapter 2. Cruelty

Preface

The combination of self-indulgence and sexual indulgence has a lecherous face, eyes that are fixed on their latest desire, and a spirit that thrives on decadent living and flits through the feelings aroused by different enticements. Cruelty, on the other hand, has a frightening manner, a ferocious appearance, a violent temper, and a terrifying voice, and it is brimming all over with threats and bloodthirsty commands. To keep silent about it is only to encourage it: What limit will cruelty impose on itself, indeed, if we do not even use the reins of criticism to restrain it? In short, if it has the power to induce fear, we have the power to respond with hatred.

Roman Stories

2. 1. Nobody can adequately praise or condemn Sulla, because while he was on the path to victory, he acted like Scipio to the Roman people, but once he had acquired it, he acted like Hannibal.[35] He had admirably defended the privileges of the nobility, but he cruelly flooded the entire city and every part of Italy with rivers of our citizens' blood.[36]

Four legions[37] from the opposite side had trusted his word, but he had them all beheaded in the state guest house in the Campus Martius,[38] as they begged for mercy, appealing in vain to his treacherous promises. Their pitiful cries for help

---

[33]Aulus Gabinius (cos, 58 B.C.) restored Ptolemy XII Neos Dionysus to the throne of Egypt in 55 B.C.

[34]The Cypriot monarchy came to an end in 58 B.C. when the Romans conquered the island.

[35]Scipio is Scipio Africanus, who defeated Hannibal in the Second Punic War.

[36]Sulla marched on Rome and massacred his political enemies in 82 B.C.

[37]Four legions would be about twenty thousand men.

[38]The Campus Martius ("Plain of Mars") was a large field by the Tiber. The state guest house was built there in 435 B.C. for Roman officials and foreign ambassadors.

reached the ears of the terrified city, and the Tiber, which could barely manage such a burden, was forced to carry their bodies, mutilated by the sword, in its bloodstained waters.

Five thousand men from Praeneste were lured outside the walls of their city,[39] because Publius Cethegus assured them of their safety.[40] When they threw down their weapons and lay flat on the ground, Sulla had them killed immediately and had their bodies scattered over the countryside. He entered in the public records that he had slaughtered 4,700 people in accordance with his edict ordering this frightful massacre; apparently he did not want the memory of so glorious an achievement to fade away.

Sulla was not content to exercise his savagery against those who had fought against him; he also hunted down peace-loving citizens with the help of his nomenclator[41] and added them to his death list simply because they had large fortunes. He also unleashed his sword against women, as if he could not be properly satiated with the slaughter of men. Here is another indication of his insatiable savagery: he wanted the decapitated heads of his unfortunate victims to be brought into his presence while they almost still had their normal facial expression and breath, so that he could gorge his eyes on them, since he was not allowed to gorge his mouth on them.

How cruelly indeed he behaved toward the praetor Gratidanus![42] In full view of the mob, Sulla dragged him to the tomb of the Lutatius family[43] and did not take his life until he had gouged his wretched eyes out and smashed every part of his body in turn. It seems even to me that the things I am telling are scarcely believable; but when Marcus Plaetorius fainted during this execution of Gratidanus, Sulla put him to death immediately.[44] He punished the new crime of pity; for him it was a criminal action to look askance at his own criminal actions.

But perhaps he had mercy on the spirits of the dead at least? Not at all; even if Sulla later became Marius' enemy, he had once been his quaestor,[45] but Sulla dug up his ashes and scattered them in the river Anio.[46] Behold the kinds of actions he felt would entitle him to be called "Fortunate"![47]

[39]Praeneste (modern Palestrina) was a city in Latium. Gaius Marius (junior), son of the famous Marius, made a last stand in Praeneste.

[40]Publius Cornelius Cethegus was a legate in Sulla's army in 82 B.C.

[41]A nomenclator was a slave who memorized the names of socially important people and reminded his master of their names whenever his master met them.

[42]Marcus Marius Gratidanus had been a praetor in 85 and 84 B.C.

[43]Sulla had Gratidanus mutilated and killed at the tomb of the Lutatius family to avenge the murder of Quintus Lutatius Catulus (cos, 102 B.C.) by the supporters of Marius in 87 B.C.

[44]Marcus Plaetorius was a senator.

[45]Sulla had been the quaestor of Marius in Numidia from 107 to 105 B.C.

[46]The Anio flows into the Tiber just north of Rome.

[47]Sulla took on the extra name "Fortunate" (Felix) when he made himself dictator in 82 B.C. From then on, his full name was Lucius Cornelius Sulla Felix.

2. 2. Nevertheless, Marius lessens our outrage at Sulla's cruelty. Marius also unleashed his anger in horrible ways as he pursued his enemies obsessively.[48] He butchered Lucius Caesar,[49] a former consul and censor, with disgraceful savagery, and what is more, he did this at the tomb of a despicable troublemaker; this was a misfortune that the Republic still had to undergo, that Lucius Caesar would die to appease the ghost of Varius.[50] The victories of Marius[51] were hardly worth that much; Marius forgot them, and he earned more condemnation for his behavior at home than praise for his achievements in war.

After Marcus Antonius was beheaded,[52] Marius, who was at a banquet, joyfully kept the head in his hands for a long time, revealing the absolute arrogance of his spirit and his words. He allowed the sanctity of his table to be polluted with the blood of a renowned citizen and orator, and he even embraced Publius Annius,[53] who brought the head, even though Annius was covered with bloodstains from the recent killing.

2. 3. Damasippus did not have a reputation to lose, so his memory can be subjected to a more open attack.[54] By his orders, the heads of the leaders of our state were thrown in with the heads of sacrificial victims, and the headless trunk of Carbo Arvina was carried around attached to a gibbet.[55] This reveals either how much power an evil man holding the praetorship could wield, or how little power the dignity of the Republic could have.

2. 4. Munatius Flaccus was more enthusiastic than justifiable in the way he defended Pompey's cause.[56] When our general, Caesar,[57] trapped him behind the walls of Ategua in Spain, and the city was put under siege, Flaccus revealed his savage cruelty through a ferocious kind of madness. He slaughtered all the citizens of that city who, he felt, were inclined toward Caesar, and threw them down from the city walls. He called out the names of the men who were in the opposite camp so that they could witness the deaths of their wives, and then he murdered the women and also children resting in their mother's arms. While their parents looked on, he dashed some infants to the ground and threw others down onto spears. These things are unbearable even to hear of, but they were carried out under the orders of a Roman

---

[48]When Marius took over Rome in 87 B.C., he massacred his political enemies.

[49]Lucius Julius Caesar had been consul in 90 B.C. and censor in 89 B.C.

[50]Quintus Varius Severus Hybrida had been a tribune of the plebs in 90 B.C.

[51]Marius had defeated King Jugurtha of Numidia (106 B.C.), the Teutons of Germany (102 B.C.), and the Cimbrians of Denmark (101 B.C.).

[52]This is Marcus Antonius (cos, 99 B.C.), the famous orator (see 8:9,2).

[53]Publius Annius was a military tribune in 87 B.C.

[54]Lucius Junius Brutus Damasippus was a praetor in 82 B.C. and executed the political enemies of Gaius Marius (junior).

[55]Gaius Papirius Carbo Arvina had been a praetor in 83 B.C.

[56]Lucius Munatius Flaccus was the Republican prefect in Ategua in 45 B.C. Pompey himself had been murdered in 48 B.C.

[57]Caesar besieged and captured Ategua in 45 B.C.

and by the hands of Lusitanians. Flaccus was protected by the support of that nation and kept resisting divine power with insane stubbornness.

Foreign Stories

2. ext. 1. We shall now turn to stories that are equally sad but cause no embarrassment to our state. The Carthaginians cut off the eyelids of Atilius Regulus and locked him into a contraption that had sharpened spikes sticking inward from its sides.[58] Lack of sleep and the prolonged and continuous agony killed him. He suffered a type of torture that he did not deserve but was typical of the people who invented it.

The Carthaginians showed the same type of cruelty against soldiers of ours whom they had overpowered in a naval battle. They placed the soldiers on the ground under their ships and crushed them to death as the heavy hulls went over them. This strange kind of death was designed to satisfy the savagery of those barbarians, who would later violate the sea itself with the ships that they had polluted by this disgusting crime.

2. ext. 2. The courage of their leader, Hannibal, lay for the most part in savagery. He led his army across a river,[59] making a bridge out of Roman bodies. He wanted Earth to witness the evil progress of the Carthaginian land forces just as Neptune had witnessed the evil progress of their sea forces. Hannibal would wear down prisoners of war by making them carry heavy loads over long distances, and then he would cut their toes off and leave them behind. If he brought some of them to his camp, he would form them into pairs, usually of brothers or relatives, and force them to fight duels with each other. His thirst for blood was not satisfied until he had reduced all those men to one final winner. Our Senate acted with justifiable hatred, therefore, though his punishment came rather late, when they forced Hannibal to take his own life after he had become a refugee at the court of King Prusias.[60]

2. ext. 3. The Senate's action against King Mithridates was, indeed, equally justifiable. By means of one letter, he put to death eighty thousand Roman citizens, who were businessmen settled throughout the cities of Asia.[61] He splattered the gods of hospitality in this great province with their blood, which was shed unjustly but would not go unavenged. He died in great agony, because his body resisted the poison he took, but he finally forced his spirit to succumb.[62] At the same time,

---

[58]Marcus Atilius Regulus was tortured to death by the Carthaginians in 255 B.C., during the First Punic War.

[59]The manuscripts give the river's name as Gellus, but there is no such river. Some editors have suggested that the correct name of the river might be Vergellus or Cerbalus.

[60]Hannibal was exiled from Carthage in 195 B.C. The Romans ordered King Prusias I of Bithynia to hand him over in 183 B.C., but Hannibal committed suicide instead.

[61]Mithridates VI of Pontus had ordered the massacre of all Roman citizens in the province of Asia in 88 B.C.

[62]Mithridates committed suicide in 63 B.C. after his son and his subjects rebelled against him.

he atoned for the crosses on which he had crucified his friends, following the advice of his eunuch, Gaurus. He was lecherous in humoring this man and evil in the commands he gave.

2. ext. 4. The savagery of his nation makes the cruelty of the Thracian king, Zisemis, the son of Diogyris, less remarkable.[63] The madness of his savagery, however, makes his cruelty worth telling. He did not consider it wrong to cut men in two while they were alive, or to make parents eat the bodies of their children.

2. ext. 5. Ptolemy Potbelly[64] makes a second appearance here. Shortly before, he appeared as a disgusting example of sexual madness;[65] now he must be mentioned again among the most exceptional cases of cruelty. What could be more ferocious than the following behavior? He had a son named Memphites from Cleopatra, who was both his sister and his wife. The boy had a noble appearance and excellent prospects, but Potbelly ordered him to be put to death in his presence; then he had his head and feet cut off, wrapped in a cloak, and placed in a box. He sent this as a birthday present to the boy's mother, pretending that he had nothing to do with the sorrow he was inflicting on her. But he was no less fortunate, because they were both childless now, and he made everyone pity Cleopatra and hate him.

Exceptional cruelty always bursts out in blind fury like this whenever it tries to derive reassurance from its own power. When Potbelly noticed how much hatred his country felt toward him, he found a remedy for his fears in further crimes and decided to make his reign more secure by murdering ordinary people. He positioned his soldiers around a gymnasium that was full of young men and set it on fire; he then killed everyone in it, some being put to the sword and others being burned to death.

2. ext. 6. Ochus, who was later called Darius,[66] had been a member of the conspiracy that had eliminated the seven magi,[67] and he was bound by the most sacred oath known to the Persians. He had sworn not to kill any other conspirator through poison, the sword, violence, or starvation. So he thought up a more cruel form of death that would enable him to kill them without breaking his religious obligation. He built high walls around a place and filled it with ashes; then he placed a wooden beam jutting out over this pit. He sat the other conspirators on this beam and generously supplied them with food and drink. Finally they grew drowsy with sleep and fell down into the treacherous pile of ashes.[68]

---

[63]Zibelmios is the correct name of "Zisemis." He was king of Thrace around 150 B.C. His father, Diegylis (the correct name of "Diogyris") had been murdered, and Zibelmios avenged his death with great brutality.

[64]Ptolemy VII Euergetes "Physcon" ("Potbelly") was king of Egypt from 145 to 116 B.C.

[65]For the earlier account, see 9:1,ext.5.

[66]Darius II Ochus was king of Persia from 424 to 404 B.C.

[67]Valerius has confused King Darius I, who killed the magi (see 3:2,ext.2), with King Darius II Ochus.

[68]King Darius II Ochus killed his enemies in this way. They smothered to death in a deep pile of ashes.

2. ext. 7. The cruelty of the other Ochus, who was called Artaxerxes,[69] was more open and more revolting. He took his sister Atossa, who was also his mother-in-law, and buried her alive head first. He left his father's brother along with more than one hundred of his sons and grandsons in an empty courtyard and had them speared to death. They had not provoked him by doing anything wrong, but he saw that they had the greatest reputation for honesty and courage among the Persians.

2. ext. 8. The state of Athens was moved by a similar kind of jealousy to issue a decree unworthy of its glorious reputation. It decreed that the thumbs of the young men of Aegina be cut off so that this nation with its powerful fleet would not be able to compete with Athens in naval power.[70] I cannot recognize Athens when it borrows a cure for its fears from cruelty.

2. ext. 9. Another savage man was the famous inventor of the bronze bull. Victims were shut up inside it, a fire was lit under it, and they were forced to die after a long torture hidden from sight as their cries came out like the bellowing of a bull. Otherwise their screams, coming out with the sound of a human voice, might appeal to the pity of the tyrant Phalaris.[71] Because its inventor wanted the unfortunate victims to find no pity, he deservedly broke in his revolting masterpiece and was the first person to be shut up inside it.[72]

2. ext. 10. Even the Etruscans showed no lack of ferocity in thinking up punishments.[73] They would tie the bodies of living people face to face with corpses, squeezing them tightly together, in such a way that each part of their body would be tied to the corresponding part of the corpse. Then they would let them rot away together, harshly torturing both the living and the dead.

2. ext. 11. They acted just like those barbarians who, they say, slaughter cattle, remove the intestines and organs, and then force human beings into the carcass in such a way that only their heads stick out. To make the punishment last all the longer, they prolong the victim's miserable life with food and drink, until decay sets in and the victim is eaten alive by the creatures that are produced inside rotting carcasses.

So let's complain against the nature of the universe, because it has wanted to expose us to the harsh afflictions of ill health. And let's be disappointed, because the resilience of the gods has been denied to human beings. And yet mortals themselves have been driven by cruelty to invent so many tortures for each other.

---

[69] Artaxerxes III Ochus was king of Persia from 358 to 335 B.C.

[70] Aegina (an island between Athens and the Peloponnese) was the traditional enemy of Athens. The Athenians conquered Aegina in 457 B.C.

[71] Phalaris was tyrant of Agrigentum (on the south coast of Sicily) in the sixth century B.C.

[72] Phalaris decided to test out the new torture machine by using it on its inventor.

[73] Virgil attributes this torture to the mythical Etruscan tyrant, Mezentius, at *Aeneid* 8: 485–88.

Chapter 3. Anger and Hatred

Preface

Anger and hatred also give rise to great waves of emotion in the human heart, anger being quicker to rush ahead and hatred being more tenacious in its desire to do harm. Each one is a feeling full of confusion and never acts violently without torturing itself, because when it wants to inflict pain, it feels pain itself, being troubled by the bitter worry that its vengeance may not be effective. But there are very clear images of the special properties of these vices, because the gods themselves wanted us to notice these images in the violent words or actions of famous people.

Roman Stories

3. 1. When Livius Salinator was leaving the city to fight against Hannibal,[74] Fabius the Delayer warned him not to go onto the battlefield before he discovered what the strength and morale of the enemy forces were. Livius replied that he was not going to give up his first chance of fighting, and when Fabius asked him why he wanted to engage the enemy so quickly, Livius said, "Because I want to be as quick as possible in winning glory by defeating the enemy, or in getting pleasure by killing off my fellow citizens." His words at that time were torn between anger and courage: anger because he remembered his unjust condemnation,[75] courage because he was eager for the glory of a triumph. But I wonder whether the person who spoke these words was the same man who won such a victory.

3. 2. This is how far the goads of anger drove a man of high spirits, who was used to battle; Gaius Figulus, on the other hand, was a very gentle man, renowned for his quiet study of the civil law,[76] but the goads of anger made him forget all his intelligence and self-restraint. He was burning with resentment at his defeat in the consular elections, especially when he recalled that the consulship had been granted twice to his father.[77] On the day after the elections, when many people came to consult him, he sent them all away after asking them, "How is it that you know how to consult me, but you don't know how to elect me as consul?" His words were strong, and rightly so. Still it would have been somewhat better if he had not spoken them. Who in their right mind could get angry with the Roman people?

3. 3. We should not approve of the following men, even though the splendor of their noble births covered up their behavior. They were offended when Gnaeus

---

[74]Marcus Livius Salinator (cos, 219 B.C.) was consul again in 207 B.C. during the war against Hannibal.

[75]Livius had been convicted of mishandling the war against Demetrius of Pharos (which was fought in 219 B.C.) and retired from public life for ten years.

[76]Gaius Marcius Figulus was a praetor in 130 B.C.

[77]His father, also called Gaius Marcius Figulus, had been consul in 162 and 156 B.C.

Flavius won the praetorship,[78] simply because he had come originally from a very poor family. Taking off their golden rings and removing the bridle ornaments from their horses, they threw them away and showed their inability to control their rage in what was almost an act of public mourning.

3. 4. This is how individuals or small groups were moved to anger against the entire people: the masses were moved to anger against their leading politicians and military commanders in the following way. Manlius Torquatus brought back a splendid and glorious victory over the Latins and the Campanians to our city.[79] The older people celebrated joyfully and went out to welcome him, but none of the younger men went to meet him, because he had beheaded his own young son for fighting too bravely against his orders.[80] They pitied a young man of their own age who had been punished too harshly. I am not defending their behavior; I am simply showing the force of their anger, which had the power to create divisions in our united state between the two generations and their emotions.

3. 5. The power of anger is so great that it once immobilized the entire cavalry of the Roman people. They had been sent by the consul Fabius to pursue enemy forces, and they could safely and easily have destroyed the enemy, but then they remembered that Fabius had prevented the passage of the land law,[81] and they did not move.

Public anger also harmed Appius.[82] His father had struggled to preserve the privileges of the Senate and had bitterly attacked the rights of the plebs.[83] This antagonized the men Appius was commanding and made them turn their backs to the enemy in a deliberate flight, because they did not want to win a triumph for their general.[84]

How often anger has been the victor over victory! It refused to congratulate Torquatus for his victory, it deprived Fabius of the finest part of his victory, and it forced Appius to give up his victory entirely and accept defeat instead.

3. 6. See now, how violently anger reacted in the hearts of the entire Roman people when they voted that the temple of Mercury should be dedicated by Marcus Plaetorius, a senior centurion[85] They deliberately bypassed the consuls: Appius,

---

[78]Gnaeus Flavius was elected curule aedile (not praetor) in 304 B.C. He was descended from a former slave.

[79]Titus Manlius Imperiosus Torquatus was consul in 340 B.C. when he defeated the Latins and Campanians.

[80]See 2:7,6.

[81]Caeso Fabius Vibulanus was consul in 481 B.C. when his infantry (not his cavalry) refused to pursue the defeated Aequians (from the Sabine region, in central Italy). Fabius had opposed land reforms in 484 B.C.

[82]Appius Claudius Crassus Inregillensis Sabinus was consul in 471 B.C.

[83]His father, Appius Claudius Sabinus Inregillensis, was very harsh to debt-ridden plebeians when he was consul in 495 B.C.

[84]The soldiers fled deliberately, when the Volscians (from southern Latium) attacked, and deprived Appius Claudius Crassus Inregillensis Sabinus (cos, 471 B.C.) of his victory.

[85]Marcus Plaetorius dedicated the temple of Mercury on the Aventine hill in 495 B.C.

because he had opposed measures to rescue them from their debt problems, and Servilius, because although he had taken up their cause, he had fought for it half-heartedly.[86] Can you deny the effectiveness of anger, when it induces people to choose a common soldier over the highest officers of the state?

3. 7. Anger did not just trample on the highest officers of the state; it also drove those officers themselves to act insanely. Quintus Metellus had almost completely conquered the two parts of Spain, first as consul and then as governor,[87] but he discovered that his enemy, the consul Quintus Pompeius, was being sent to succeed him.[88] So he dismissed all the soldiers who wanted to finish their military service; he gave a leave of absence to anyone who asked for it, without questioning their reasons or setting a time limit; he removed the guards from the granaries and let them be robbed easily; he had the bows and arrows of the Cretans broken up and thrown in the river; and he forbade everyone to feed the elephants. His actions satisfied his whims, but they undid the glory of his splendid achievements, and he lost the triumph he deserved, because he had been stronger in overcoming our enemies than in overcoming his own anger.

3. 8. What about Sulla? By giving in to this vice, did he not shed a lot of other people's blood and finally pay for it with his own?[89] He was burning with indignation in Puteoli,[90] because its town councilors had promised him funds for the rebuilding of the Capitol,[91] but the leader of that colony,[92] Granius, had made delays in paying the money. Sulla got worked up into such a temper and shouted so uncontrollably that he injured his lungs and vomited up his last breath in a mixture of blood and threats. He did not succumb to old age, as you might expect from a man who was starting his sixtieth year, but to his uncontrollable rage, which had fed on the misfortunes of our Republic. So it is uncertain which ended first, Sulla or his bad temper.[93]

Preface to Foreign Stories[94]

I do not like digging up stories about obscure people, and on the other hand it embarrasses me to harp on the failings of great men. But if I am to remain true to

---

[86]Appius Claudius Sabinus Inregillensis and Publius Servilius Priscus Structus were consuls in 495 B.C.

[87]Quintus Caecilius Metellus Macedonicus was consul in 143 B.C. and governor of Nearer Spain in 142 B.C.

[88]Metellus was replaced by the consul Quintus Pompeius in 141 B.C.

[89]Sulla massacred his political opponents in 82 B.C.

[90]Puteoli (modern Pozzuoli) was on the coast of Campania, near Naples.

[91]The Romans started rebuilding the temple of Jupiter on the Capitol in 78 B.C.

[92]A colony was a city inhabited by Roman citizens. After 89 B.C., when all Italians became Roman citizens, the distinction was no longer relevant for Italian cities.

[93]Sulla died in 78 B.C.

[94]This is the only Preface to Foreign Stories in Valerius. This paragraph is cited as 9:3,ext.praef. (ext.praef. is the abbreviation for *externa praefatio,* "foreign preface") .

my goals, I am obliged to include every exceptional story. My personal wishes must give way before my task, for I am well aware that although I enjoy celebrating glorious deeds, it is my inescapable duty to speak of other deeds.

Foreign Stories

3. ext. 1. Alexander's bad temper almost snatched his heavenly reward away from him.[95] What prevented him from reaching the heavens if not his throwing Lysimachus to a lion,[96] running Clitus through with a spear,[97] and ordering the death of Callisthenes?[98] Alexander was defeated by anger, and he made up for his three great victories by unjustly murdering three of his own friends.[99]

3. ext. 2. How violent was the hatred that Hamilcar nursed against the Roman people! He looked at his four sons, who were only boys, and declared that he was raising four lion cubs to destroy our empire.[100] It would have been ideal if these offspring turned against their own country and destroyed it. And that is exactly what happened!

3. ext. 3. One of those sons was Hannibal, who quickly followed in his father's footsteps. When Hamilcar was getting ready to bring his army over to Spain and was making a sacrifice for the crossing, Hannibal, who was nine years old, grasped the altar and swore that as soon as he was old enough, he would be the most bitter enemy of the Roman people.[101] By constantly pestering his father, Hannibal forced Hamilcar to allow him to serve in the war that was looming ahead.

Hannibal wanted to show how much hatred Rome and Carthage felt for each other, so he kicked the ground with his foot to raise a cloud of dust, and he said that the war between them would end when one of the cities was reduced to dust.

3. ext. 4. Hatred had such power over the heart of a boy, but it was equally powerful in the heart of a woman. Semiramis, the queen of Assyria,[102] was busy with arranging her hair when it was announced to her that Babylon had rebelled.

---

[95]This is Alexander the Great of Macedonia, who became a god (this was his "heavenly reward").

[96]Alexander did not kill Lysimachus; in fact, he died before him. Lysimachus was king of Thrace from 323 to 282 B.C.

[97]Alexander murdered his friend Clitus in a drunken rage while they were at a banquet in Maracanda (modern Samarkand in Uzbekistan) in 327 B.C. See 7:2,ext.11.

[98]Aristotle's nephew, Callisthenes, refused to prostrate himself before Alexander, and was put to death for treason in Bactra (modern Balkh in Afganistan) in 327 B.C.

[99]Alexander fought against King Darius III of Persia in a campaign that lasted from 334 to 330 B.C. and defeated him in three great battles.

[100]Three of Hamilcar Barca's sons (Hannibal, Hasdrubal, and Mago) commanded Carthaginian armies during the Second Punic War (218–201 B.C.) Nothing is known about a fourth son.

[101]Hamilcar Barca made Hannibal swear eternal enmity to Rome when the two of them set out in 237 B.C. to conquer Spain and make it part of the Carthaginian empire.

[102]Semiramis is the Roman name for Sammu-ramat, a queen of Assyria in the ninth century B.C.

Leaving the rest of her hair undone, she ran off at once to sack the city, and she did not rearrange her hair until she had brought that great city under her control again. This is why a statue was erected to her in Babylon depicting her as she was when she rushed off in a hurry to wreak vengeance on the city.

Chapter 4. Avarice

Preface

Avarice will be dragged out too. It searches for hidden profit and greedily devours an obvious prey. The pleasure of ownership does not make it happy; the desire for gain makes it miserable.

Roman Stories

4. 1. Somebody in Greece forged a will in the name of Lucius Minucius Basilus, an extremely rich man.[103] To win support for his forgery, he included the most powerful men in our state, Marcus Crassus and Quintus Hortensius,[104] as heirs in the will, even though Minucius was unknown to them. The will was obviously a forgery, but the two men were greedy for the money and did not refuse to benefit from the other man's crime. How lightly I mentioned such a great crime! These men were the light of the Senate and the glory of the Forum. They should have punished this crime, but they were enticed by the prospect of dishonest gain and used their prestige to cover up the crime.

4. 2. Greed displayed even greater powers in the case of Quintus Cassius.[105] While he was in Spain, he caught Silius and Calpurnius red-handed.[106] They were carrying daggers and were going to murder him, but he made a deal with them, took 5,000,000 sesterces[107] from Silius, 6,000,000 from Calpurnius, and let them both go free. You would wonder whether he would have been happy to offer his throat to them if they had offered him double the amount.

4. 3. But avarice dominated the heart of Lucius Septimuleius above all other men. Although he was a close friend of Gaius Gracchus,[108] he brought himself to cut off his friend's head and carry it throughout the city stuck on a spear, simply

---

[103]Lucius Minucius Basilus was a military tribune under Sulla in 86 B.C.

[104]Marcus Licinius Crassus (cos, 70 B.C.) was the political partner of Caesar and Pompey. Quintus Hortenius Hortalus (cos, 69 B.C.) was a famous orator.

[105]Quintus Cassius Longinus was a tribune of the plebs in 49 B.C. He fought for Caesar in Spain in 48 B.C.

[106]Their full names were Quintus Silius and Calpurnius Salvianus.

[107]See money—Roman in the Glossary.

[108]Gaius Sempronius Gracchus (tribune of the plebs, 123 B.C.) perished in the general massacre of his supporters in 121 B.C.

because the consul Opimius had proclaimed that he would pay for its weight in gold.[109] There are some people who claim that he hollowed out part of the head and filled it with molten lead, to make it heavier. Gracchus may have been a trouble-maker, and his death was a good warning to others, but his client's wicked hunger for money should not have gone so far in greed as to commit such a crime against a man who was already dead.

Foreign Stories

4. ext. 1. The avarice of Septimuleius deserves our hatred, but you would have to laugh at the avarice of Ptolemy, the king of Cyprus.[110] With obsessive miserli-ness, he had amassed a huge fortune, but he saw that it would lead to his death. So he loaded all his money onto ships and went off to the deep sea intending to scuttle the fleet when he felt ready, and to deprive his enemies of their booty. But he could not bring himself to sink his gold and silver, so he brought it back home to be a prize for his killer. Without a doubt, this man did not own his wealth; he was owned by his wealth. In name he was king of an island, but in spirit he was a mis-erable slave to money.

Chapter 5. Haughty and Outrageous Behavior

Roman Stories

5. 1. We shall also expose haughty and outrageous behavior. The consul Mar-cus Fulvius Flaccus, who was the colleague of Marcus Plautius Hypsaeus,[111] was introducing very damaging laws for the Republic granting citizenship to others and allowing those who did not want to change their citizenship the right of ap-peal to the people.[112] He could barely be compelled to go to the Senate house; then, when some senators warned him and others begged him to give up his plans, he did not even answer them. It would be thought that a consul had a tyrannical nature if he acted toward a single senator in this way, but Flaccus had behaved like this to show his contempt for the prestige of that entire distinguished order.

5. 2. The prestige of the Senate was also attacked with great insolence by Mar-cus Drusus, a tribune of the plebs.[113] He considered it a minor detail to have the consul Lucius Philippus[114] grabbed by the throat and thrown so violently into

---

[109]Lucius Opimius (cos, 121 B.C.) crushed the movement of Gaius Gracchus.

[110]Ptolemy, the last king of Cyprus, reigned from 80 B.C. until 58 B.C. He committed sui-cide in 58 B.C. when the Romans annexed Cyprus.

[111]Marcus Fulvius Flaccus and Marcus Plautius Hypsaeus were consuls in 125 B.C.

[112]The people whom Flaccus wanted to benefit were the Italians.

[113]Marcus Livius Drusus was a tribune of the plebs in 91 B.C.

[114]Lucius Marcius Philippus was consul in 91 B.C.

prison that blood poured from his nostrils. Drusus had this done simply because the consul had dared to interrupt him while he was addressing a public meeting. Furthermore, Drusus ordered one of his own personal clients rather than one of his official attendants, to do this.[115] But Drusus went even further, and when the Senate sent for him to come to the Senate house, he said, "Why doesn't the Senate come instead to the Hostilius Senate house,[116] which is near the rostra—in other words, to me?" I am disgusted to add what happened next: the tribune ignored the orders of the Senate, the Senate obeyed the words of a tribune.

5. 3. How arrogant the behavior of Pompey was! As he was coming out of the bath, Hypsaeus,[117] who had been accused of electoral bribery,[118] threw himself down at his feet. Hypsaeus was a noble and a friend of his, but Pompey left him lying there after crushing him with this insulting remark: he replied that Hypsaeus would achieve nothing apart from delaying Pompey's banquet.[119] Even though Pompey had this remark on his conscience, he was able to dine at peace with himself.

But when his father-in-law, Metellus Scipio,[120] fell foul of the laws that Pompey himself had passed, Pompey was not ashamed to ask the jury, even in the Forum itself, to acquit Scipio as a favor to him, even though many other illustrious men were put on trial and ruined. Thus he jeopardized the stability of the Republic for the pleasures of his marriage bed.

5. 4. A party given by Antony was equally disgusting for what he did and said there. He was a triumvir then,[121] and the head of a senator, Caesetius Rufus, was brought to him. The other guests turned away, but Antony ordered that the head be brought closer, and he looked at it carefully for a long time. Everybody was waiting to see what he would say, and he said, "I didn't even know this one." A haughty confession to make about a senator, an outrageous one to make about a man he had murdered.[122]

---

[115]If he had ordered an official attendant to attack the consul, the action of Drusus might have seemed vaguely legal; but by abusing his personal contacts and getting a client to do it, Drusus made it clear that he was settling a private grudge.

[116]The Senate met in several places, but the main Senate house was the Hostilius Senate house (*Curia Hostilia*) in the Forum.

[117]Publius Plautius Hypsaeus (praetor, c. 55 B.C.) had been an unsuccessful candidate for the consulship during the election campaign of 52 B.C.

[118]Pompey had enacted laws against electoral bribery and violence when he was consul in 52 B.C.

[119]The Romans bathed just before dinner.

[120]Pompey had married Caecilia, the daughter of Quintus Caecilius Metellus Pius Scipio Nasica (cos, 52 B.C.). Metellus Scipio had been involved in electoral violence, but Pompey made sure that all charges were dropped.

[121]Antony and his fellow triumvirs massacred their political opponents in 43 and 42 B.C.

[122]Antony's wife, Fulvia, wanted the house of Caesetius Rufus, and that is why he was murdered.

Foreign Stories

5. ext. 1. That is quite enough about our own people: now let us add some foreign stories. The courage and good fortune of King Alexander made him grow arrogant in three obvious stages. He looked down on Philip, and claimed that Jupiter Hammon was his father;[123] he grew tired of Macedonian customs and society, so he took up Persian ways of dressing and behaving;[124] he rejected his status as a human being and strove to become a god.[125] He had no qualms about denying his father, his country, and his humanity.

5. ext. 2. Haughty and outrageous behavior is embodied in the name of Xerxes. How arrogantly he acted, even though he was within his rights, when he summoned all the leaders of Asia just as he was about to declare war on Greece.[126] "I did not want people to think," he said, "that I was only acting on my own initiative, so I brought you together here. But remember that it is your duty to obey me rather than persuade me." This would have been arrogant, even if he had the good fortune to return to his palace as a conqueror; but he suffered such a humiliating defeat that you would wonder whether his words were more arrogant or stupid.

5. ext. 3. Hannibal was elated with his success at the battle of Cannae,[127] and he would not receive any of his fellow citizens in his camp, or respond to any of them except through a go-between. He even insulted Maharbal,[128] who had said in a loud voice, in front of Hannibal's tent, that he had planned things so that Hannibal would be dining on the Capitol in Rome within a few days. That is how far apart good fortune and self-restraint live from each other.

5. ext. 4. There was a sort of competition in arrogance between the senates of Carthage and Campania. The Carthaginian senators would bathe in separate baths from the plebs, and the Campanian senators would use a different forum. It is clear from the speech written by Gaius Gracchus against Plautius[129] that this custom was maintained at Capua for a long time.

[123]Philip II of Macedonia was the father of Alexander the Great. In 331 B.C. Alexander visited the oracle of Jupiter Hammon in the Libyan desert, where he was told that the god recognized him as his son.

[124]When Alexander was in Bactra (modern Balkh in Afghanistan) in 327 B.C., he started insisting that people should prostrate themselves before him in the Persian fashion.

[125]In 324 B.C., Alexander demanded that the Greek republics should recognize him as a god.

[126]King Xerxes I of Persia came to Sardis (in western Asia Minor) in 481 B.C. to plan his invasion of Greece.

[127]Hannibal defeated the Romans at Cannae (in Apulia, southern Italy) in 216 B.C.

[128]Maharbal was Hannibal's cavalry commander.

[129]Gaius Sempronius Gracchus (tribune of the plebs, 123 B.C.) was a great orator. Marcus Plautius Hypsaeus was consul in 125 B.C.

Chapter 6. Treachery

Preface

A hidden and insidious vice, treachery, must now be dragged out of its hiding place. Its most effective devices are lies and deception, and its success lies in the commission of some crime. It becomes sure of itself when it entangles the credulous in its wicked snares, and it does as much harm to the human race as sincerity does good. So, it should get as much criticism as sincerity gets admiration.

Roman Stories

6. 1. During the reign of Romulus,[130] Spurius Tarpeius was in charge of the citadel. His unmarried daughter went outside the city walls to get water for ritual purposes, where Tatius[131] bribed her to let armed Sabines go with her into the citadel. They agreed that as her reward, she would get what they had on their left hands. The Sabine soldiers, in fact, wore armbands and rings that were made of gold and very heavy. When the Sabine soldiers captured the citadel, the girl asked them for her reward. They crushed her to death under their shields, which was in keeping with their promise, because they had been carrying these shields on their left hands. We should not condemn them, because their action brought her immediate punishment for her wicked treachery.

6. 2. Servius Galba was also a man of the greatest treachery.[132] He called together the people of three Lusitanian states as if he wished to discuss matters that would be in their interest; but instead, he picked out eight thousand of the best of their young men, and he removed their weapons, slaughtered some of them, and sold the others into slavery. His treachery made the magnitude of his crime even worse than the heavy losses he inflicted on these barbarians.

6. 3. Gnaeus Domitius came from a very noble family and was a man of high spirits,[133] but his excessive desire for glory drove him to treachery. He was enraged with Bituitus, the king of the Arverni, because even though Domitius himself was still in the province, Bituitus had urged his own people and the Allobroges[134] to seek the protection of Quintus Fabius,[135] who was to succeed Domitius. Domitius summoned Bituitus, pretending that he wanted to enter negotiations, and gave him a hospitable welcome, but then he put Bituitus in chains and had him sent to Rome

---

[130]Romulus was the legendary first king of Rome (753–716 B.C.).

[131]Titus Tatius was king of the city of Cures (in the Sabine region, central Italy).

[132]Servius Sulpicius Galba (cos, 144 B.C.) was governor of Farther Spain in 150 B.C. when he massacred the Lusitanians (in modern Portugal).

[133]Gnaeus Domitius Ahenobarbus was consul in 122 B.C.

[134]The Arverni lived in southern Gaul (modern Auvergne), and the Allobroges lived in eastern Gaul (modern Savoy).

[135]Quintus Fabius Maximus Allobrogicus was consul in 121 B.C.

by ship. The Senate could not approve of his action, but it did not want to rescind it, because if Bituitus was sent back to his country, he might start the war all over again. So it banished Bituitus to Alba,[136] where he could be kept under guard.

6. 4. The murder of Viriathus[137] involves two charges of treachery: against his friends, because it was their hands that killed him, and against the consul Quintus Servilius Caepio,[138] because he organized this crime and promised that its perpetrators would not face punishment. Caepio did not deserve his victory; he bought it.

Foreign Stories

6. ext. 1. But we must examine the very fountainhead of treachery. The Carthaginians had benefited from the excellent services of Xanthippus, the Spartan,[139] during the First Punic War, and it was with his help that they had captured Atilius Regulus.[140] The Carthaginians pretended that they were bringing Xanthippus home; but instead, they drowned him in the sea. What were they aiming at in committing such an enormous crime? Was it that they did not want their partner in victory to survive? He lives on in spite of them and is a reproach against them, since they could easily have left him unharmed without diminishing their glory in any way.

6. ext. 2. Hannibal urged the inhabitants of Nuceria to come, carrying two garments each, out of their city, which was defended by impregnable walls; but then he smothered them in the steam and smoke of their baths. He used the same method to get the senators of Acerrae to come outside their city walls, and then he threw them into some deep wells.[141] Hannibal was pretending to fight a war against the Roman people and Italy, but was he not, in fact, fighting a more bitter war against trust itself, rejoicing in lies and deception as if they were glorious techniques? Were it not for this, he would have left behind a memorable name for himself, but because of his treachery, he made it doubtful whether he should be remembered as a great man or an evil one.

---

[136]Alba Longa was near Rome, in Latium.

[137]Viriathus, the leader of Lusitania (modern Portugal), had been consistently successful against the Romans from 146 B.C. until his treacherous murder in 140 B.C.

[138]Quintus Servilius Caepio was consul in 140 B.C.

[139]Xanthippus was a Spartan commander in the Carthaginian army during the First Punic War.

[140]Xanthippus defeated Marcus Atilius Regulus (cos, 267 B.C.) in Africa in 255 B.C.

[141]Hannibal captured the Campanian cities of Nuceria and Acerrae in 216 B.C.

Chapter 7. *Violence and Rioting*

Roman Stories

7. *1.* We must now discuss violent acts and riots, both in civilian and military life. Lucius Equitius, who went around pretending to be the son of Tiberius Gracchus,[142] illegally stood for election as a tribune with Lucius Saturninus.[143] Marius was holding his sixth consulship at the time,[144] and he put Equitius in the state prison. The people wrenched off the locks of the prison, put Equitius up on their shoulders, and carried him around with high-spirited enthusiasm.

7. *2.* The people tried to stone to death the censor Quintus Metellus,[145] because he refused to accept the census return in which Equitius described himself as the son of Gracchus.[146] Metellus asserted that Tiberius Gracchus had only had three sons: one of them had died while serving in the army in Sardinia, the second had died as an infant in Praeneste,[147] and the third, who was born after his father's death, had died in Rome; so it would not be right for him to let some unknown beggar sneak into this glorious family. But this was a period when the impulsive mob had been roused up and was attacking—what impudence and presumption!—the consulship and the censorship and was disturbing its leaders with every kind of effrontery.

7. *3.* That riot was just mad, but the next one was bloody too. Nunnius was seeking election against Saturninus,[148] and nine tribunes had already been elected, so there was just one place left for these two candidates. The people first used force to chase Nunnius into a private house; then they dragged him out and killed him. The murder of this most upright citizen was intended to give a most repulsive man the opportunity of winning political office.

7. *4.* The panic felt by creditors burst into flames against the city praetor, Sempronius Asellio,[149] in an unbearable manner. He had taken up the cause of those who were in debt, and the creditors were roused up against him by Lucius

[142]Lucius Equitius claimed to be the son of Tiberius Sempronius Gracchus (tribune of the plebs, 133 B.C.).

[143]Lucius Equitius and Lucius Appuleius Saturninus (tribune of the plebs, 103 B.C.) won the elections in 100 B.C., but they were murdered before they could take office at the end of the year.

[144]Marius was consul for the sixth time in 100 B.C.

[145]Quintus Caecilius Metellus Numidicus (cos, 109 B.C.) was censor in 102 B.C.

[146]See 9:7,1.

[147]Praeneste (modern Palestrina) was in Latium.

[148]Aulus Nunnius was murdered during the election campaign of 101 B.C., and Lucius Appuleius Saturninus (tribune of the plebs, 103 B.C.) was elected as tribune of the plebs for 100 B.C.

[149]Aulus Sempronius Asellio was the city praetor in 89 B.C.

Cassius,[150] a tribune of the plebs. As Asellio was performing a sacrifice in front of the temple of Concord, the creditors forced him to run away from the altars and leave the Forum. They found him wearing his official striped toga,[151] hiding in a small shop, and tore him to pieces.

Mutinies by Roman Soldiers

7. mil. Rom. 1.[152] The plight of our Forum was horrible, but if you turn to the army, you would feel an equally great indignation. Under the Sulpician law,[153] the province of Asia was assigned to Marius, who was then a private citizen, so that he could wage war on Mithridates.[154] Marius sent his legate, Gratidius,[155] to the consul Sulla[156] to take over the legions, but the soldiers murdered Gratidius. They were doubtless annoyed that they were being forced to change from the command of the chief executive officer to that of a man who was occupying no public office. But who could tolerate it that soldiers would correct the resolutions of the plebs by murdering a legate?

7. mil. Rom. 2. In that case, the army had acted with great violence on behalf of the consul, but in the following case, it acted against the consul. Sulla's colleague, Pompeius Rufus,[157] followed the Senate's orders and dared to go off to the army of Pompeius Strabo, who remained in command of his army against the wishes of the state.[158] The soldiers were bribed with the inducements presented by their ambitious commander, and when Pompeius Rufus was starting to perform a sacrifice, they attacked him and slaughtered him like a sacrificial victim. By letting this great crime go unpunished, the Senate confessed that it could not stand up to its own army.

7. mil. Rom. 3. Another army used violence in the cause of evil. Gaius Carbo[159] was the brother of the Carbo who had held three consulships.[160] Army discipline had collapsed because of the civil wars, so Gaius Carbo tried to restore it in a

---

[150]Lucius Cassius was a tribune of the plebs in 89 B.C.

[151]Roman magistrates wore a toga with a red stripe along its edge.

[152]Valerius uses the Latin words *milites Romani* (Roman soldiers) to describe these stories about army mutinies, and this is why the abbreviation "mil. Rom." is used before the stories in this section. The first story in this section would be 9:7,mil.Rom.1 (Book 9: Chapter 7, Roman soldiers 1).

[153]Publius Sulpicius Rufus (tribune of the plebs, 88 B.C.) passed the Sulpician law transferring Asia from Sulla to Marius.

[154]Rome was starting its first war (88–84 B.C.) against King Mithridates VI of Pontus.

[155]Marcus Gratidius was an army legate in 88 B.C.

[156]Sulla was consul in 88 B.C.

[157]Quintus Pompeius Rufus was consul with Sulla in 88 B.C.

[158]Gnaeus Pompeius Strabo (cos, 89 B.C.) was still in command of the army he had used in fighting against the Italians.

[159]Gaius Papirius Carbo was a legate in Sulla's army when he was murdered in 80 B.C.

[160]Gnaeus Papirius Carbo had been consul in 85, 84, and 82 B.C.

rather harsh and rigid manner. The army took his life, thinking it better to be disgraced by a great crime than to change their warped and disgusting ways.

Chapter 8. Reckless Behavior

Preface

The impulses toward reckless behavior are also sudden and violent. When people's minds are stricken by them, they are unable to see dangers to themselves or judge other people's actions fairly.

Roman Stories

8. 1. How reckless it was of Scipio Africanus to cross over from Spain to Syphax[161] in two quinqueremes,[162] since he was risking his own safety as well as that of his country on the unreliable heart of a single Numidian! So for one brief moment, the outcome of a most important matter depended on whether Syphax would become Scipio's murderer or his prisoner.[163]

8. 2. The dangerous undertaking of Caesar, even though it was taken care of by the gods, can hardly be told without mental horror. He was getting impatient because his legions were crossing so slowly from Brundisium to Apollonia,[164] so he pretended he was not feeling well and left his dinner party, disguised his majestic appearance in the clothes of a slave, boarded a ship, went down the river Aoüs, and headed for the entrance to the Adriatic in the middle of a fierce storm.[165] He ordered the ship to sail toward the open sea immediately, and it was only after he had been tossed around for a long time by strong waves crashing against him, that he finally yielded to external circumstances.

8. 3. Come, now, how accursed was the rash behavior of our soldiers in the following case! Aulus Albinus was an exceptional citizen because of his noble birth, his character, and his tenure of every political office.[166] Because of false and groundless suspicions, he was stoned to death in the camp by his soldiers, and what

---

[161]Scipio Africanus went to north Africa and won Syphax over to the Roman side in 206 B.C. Syphax was a king of Numidia (modern Algeria).

[162]A quinquereme was a warship.

[163]Syphax later joined the Carthaginians and was ultimately defeated and captured by Scipio Africanus in 203 B.C. But Scipio Africanus was not thinking of making Syphax prisoner in 206 B.C.

[164]Caesar's army was crossing from Brundisium (on the coast of Calabria) to Apollonia (on the coast of Illyria) in 48 B.C.

[165]Caesar was already in Apollonia, which was on the river Aoüs, in 48 B.C. He wanted to go back across the Adriatic to see what was delaying his troops in Brundisium.

[166]Aulus Postumius Albinus (cos, 99 B.C.) was an army legate in 89 B.C.

goes beyond all indignation, his soldiers denied their commander the opportunity of defending himself, even though he begged and pleaded with them.

Foreign Stories

8. ext. 1. I am not so surprised, therefore, that the pitiless and savage heart of Hannibal gave a harmless helmsman no chance to defend himself. As Hannibal was heading back from Petelia to Africa with his fleet,[167] he came to the straits.[168] Hannibal could not believe that Italy and Sicily were separated by so small a distance, so he thought that the man who was setting their course had betrayed him, and he killed him. Later, when he had examined the true circumstances more carefully, he pardoned the man, though at this stage the only thing he could do for this innocent man was to give him an honorable burial. His statue looks down from his high tomb onto the narrow and choppy sea, and being in full view of those who sail in and out of the strait, it reminds them about the story of Pelorus[169] and the recklessness of the Carthaginians.

8. ext. 2. The state of Athens was reckless to the point of insanity, when it tried all ten of its generals on a capital charge.[170] The generals were coming back after a splendid victory, but the state put them to death, simply because they had been unable to bury the bodies of their dead soldiers, being prevented by the wild sea conditions. The state punished them for what they were forced to do, whereas it should have honored their courage.

Chapter 9. Mistakes

Preface

Mistakes are very close to reckless behavior, because they do an equal amount of harm, but it is easier to forgive them. Mistakes do not involve deliberate wrongdoing; they are caused by false notions. If I tried to describe how widespread their effect is on the human heart, I would be guilty of the very vice I am talking about. So we shall discuss just a few of these blunders.

---

[167]Hannibal left Italy to defend Carthage in 203 B.C. Petelia was on the east coast of Bruttium (southern Italy).

[168]The straits of Messina are between Italy and Sicily.

[169]Pelorus was at the northeastern tip of Sicily, on the straits of Messina. Valerius believes the story that it was called after Hannibal's pilot, who was also named Pelorus. Hannibal was sailing clockwise around the toe of Italy.

[170]The ten Athenian generals had defeated the Spartan navy at the Arginusae Islands (off the west coast of Asia Minor) in 406 B.C. See 3:8,ext.3.

Roman Stories

9. 1. Gaius Helvius Cinna,[171] a tribune of the plebs, was heading back home from the funeral of Caesar. The people tore him to pieces because they mistakenly thought they were attacking Cornelius Cinna.[172] They were furious with Cornelius Cinna because, although he was related by marriage to Caesar,[173] he had made a disloyal speech at the rostra against him after Caesar was viciously murdered. The people went so far in their mistaken belief that they carried the head of Helvius Cinna stuck on a spear around Caesar's pyre, thinking that it was the head of Cornelius Cinna. What a tragic victim Helvius Cinna was to his own sense of duty and to the mistaken belief of others!

9. 2. A mistaken belief held by Gaius Cassius made him punish himself.[174] While the outcome of the battle being fought by four armies at Philippi was still uncertain, and unclear to the commanders themselves, Cassius sent a centurion[175] called Titinius during the night to observe how things stood with Marcus Brutus.[176] Titinius made lots of detours on the way, because it was so dark that he could not distinguish whether he was going toward the enemy or his fellow soldiers, so he came back to Cassius rather late. Cassius assumed that he had been intercepted by the enemy, and that everything had now come under their control, so he quickly ended his life, though it was the enemy camp that had been captured instead, and the troops of Brutus were for the most part safe.

The courage of Titinius should not be passed over in silence. For a while he could not take his eyes away, amazed at the unexpected sight of his commander lying there dead; then he burst into tears and said, "Even if I was unwittingly the cause of your death, general, this deed should still not go unpunished, so you must accept me as your comrade in death." Standing over the lifeless body, he stuck his sword all the way to the hilt into his own throat. The pair of victims lay there, mingling their blood; Titinius was a victim of his sense of duty, and Cassius was a victim of his mistaken belief.

9. 3. But I wonder whether a mistaken belief harmed the household of Lars Tolumnius, king of Veii, above all the others.[177] He had a lucky throw of the dice, and as a joke he said to his opponent, "Kill them!" Envoys from Rome happened to drop in at that moment, and his guards, misunderstanding his words, changed his joke into a command and killed the envoys.

[171]Gaius Helvius Cinna was a tribune of the plebs in 44 B.C. and a strong supporter of Caesar.

[172]Lucius Cornelius Cinna (praetor, 44 B.C.) had supported the tyrannicides.

[173]Caesar had married Cornelia, the sister of Cornelius Cinna. Cornelia had died in 69 B.C.

[174]The Republican army led by Gaius Cassius Longinus (the tyrannicide) was defeated by Antony at Philippi (in Macedonia) in 42 B.C.

[175]See centurion in the Glossary.

[176]Cassius did not realize that Marcus Junius Brutus (the tyrannicide) had led his army to victory over Augustus and captured the enemy camp.

[177]Lars Tolumnius was king of Veii (in Etruria, just north of Rome) when Veii fought against Rome in 438 B.C.

Chapter 10. Revenge

Preface

The stings of revenge are bitter, but they are also just. People move quickly when they have been provoked to revenge and want to repay the pain they have felt. There is no point in discussing this too much.

Roman Stories

10. 1. Marcus Flavius, a tribune of the plebs,[178] raised the matter of Tusculum before the people, claiming that the Tusculans had instigated the people of Velitrae and Privernum to rebel.[179] The Tusculans came shabbily dressed with their wives and children as suppliants to Rome, and as a result all the other tribes voted to spare them. The tribe of Pollia alone judged that the grown men should be flogged and beheaded with an axe in public, and that the remaining crowd, which had been incapable of fighting, should be sold into slavery. Because of this, the Papiria tribe, which was later dominated by the Tusculans after they had been granted Roman citizenship,[180] never elected any candidate from the Pollia tribe to public office. It did not want any public office to go to the Pollia tribe by means of its votes, since that tribe had done everything in its power to deprive the Tusculans of life and liberty.

10. 2. Both the Senate and the general consensus of all our citizens approved of the following act of revenge. Hadrianus had oppressed the Roman citizens who lived in Utica under his mean-spirited regime,[181] and for this reason they had burned him alive. No investigation was held in our city about the matter, and no complaint was registered.

Foreign Stories

10. ext. 1. There were two queens whose vengeance became famous. Tomyris ordered that Cyrus be beheaded and his head put in a leather bag filled with human blood.[182] This was her way of denouncing his insatiable thirst for blood, and at the same time she was punishing him for the death of her son.

---

[178]Marcus Flavius was a tribune of the plebs in 327 B.C., and again in 323 B.C., when he denounced the Tusculans before the people.

[179]Tusculum (modern Frascati), Velitrae, and Privernum were cities in the hills of Latium near Rome. They had taken part in the Latin revolt (340–338 B.C.).

[180]The Tusculans had already been granted Roman citizenship in 338 B.C.

[181]Gaius Fabius Hadrianus (praetor, 84 B.C.) had been a supporter of Marius. Hadrianus stayed on as governor of Africa from 84 B.C. until the inhabitants of Utica killed him in 82 B.C.

[182]Tomyris was a queen of Scythia (modern Ukraine), and Cyrus the Great of Persia died fighting her people in 530 B.C.

Berenice was very upset when Laodice treacherously murdered her son,[183] so she armed herself, mounted her chariot, and hunted down Caeneus, the royal servant who had carried out this cruel deed. Berenice had tried in vain to get him with her spear, but she managed to knock him down by throwing a rock at him. Then she drove her horses over his body, rode through the middle of the enemy forces, and made her way to the house where she thought the body of her murdered boy was hidden.[184]

10. ext. 2. It is hard to judge whether the vengeance that overtook Jason of Thessaly,[185] as he was preparing to go to war against the king of Persia, was justified. Taxillus, the master of a gymnasium,[186] complained that he had been beaten by some of his young men, and Jason allowed him to get 300 drachmas from each of them, or to inflict ten blows of the rod on each of them. Taxillus inflicted the second punishment, and the young men who were beaten killed Jason, basing their revenge on the mental distress they had suffered rather than the physical pain. But this small insult to the pride of these freeborn men destroyed people's expectations of a great event, since the Greeks had placed great hopes in Jason, believing that he might achieve as much as Alexander actually did.[187]

Chapter 11. Shameless Remarks and Evil Deeds

Preface

Since we are investigating both the good things and the bad things about our human existence, using stories to illustrate each one, we must now record shameless remarks and evil deeds.

Roman Stories

11. 1. Where should I begin rather than with Tullia?[188] Her story is the oldest one in time, horrible in its guilt, and almost monstrous in its telling. She was going in her carriage when the man who drove the team jerked at his reins and stopped.

---

[183]Berenice was the second wife, and Laodice was the first wife, of Antiochus II Theos (king of Syria, 261–246 B.C.). After Antiochus died, Laodice murdered Berenice's son to make sure that her own son would be king.

[184]Laodice later murdered Berenice.

[185]Jason of Pherae was murdered in 370 B.C. He had made Thessaly a major power in northern Greece.

[186]Almost every city had its public gymnasium where young men were trained in sports and philosophy. The gymnasium was an essential part of the Greek educational system.

[187]After Jason's death, Macedonia started to dominate Greece, and eventually Alexander the Great conquered the Persian empire.

[188]Tullia was the daughter of Servius Tullius (king of Rome, 578–535 B.C.).

She demanded the reason for this sudden stop, and when she learned that the body of her murdered father, Servius Tullius, was lying there, she ordered her driver to drive the carriage over the body, so that she could get more quickly into the arms of her father's killer, Tarquin.[189] Her utterly amoral and disreputable haste disgraced her with eternal infamy, and the street itself with the name of Crime Street.[190]

11. 2. Gaius Fimbria's deed and remark were not quite as dreadful as hers, but both his deed and his remark were outrageous, if we consider them by themselves.[191] Fimbria arranged for Scaevola to be murdered during the funeral of Marius, but he later discovered that Scaevola had recovered from his wound,[192] so he built up a case against him before the people. Fimbria was asked what he could say against this man who could not be adequately praised for the integrity of his character, and he replied that he was going to denounce him because he had not allowed the weapon to enter his body properly. What unrestrained madness! Our failing Republic should have groaned to hear it.

11. 3. When Cicero said in the Senate that Catiline had started a conflagration,[193] Catiline replied, "I realize that, and if I cannot extinguish it by water, I shall do so by demolition." What else should we think but that he was driven by the pangs of his guilty conscience and was putting himself on trial for the treason he was planning?

11. 4. The mind of Magius Chilo was driven astray by madness. Caesar had granted Marcus Marcellus his life,[194] but Chilo took it with his own hand. Chilo was an old friend of Marcellus and had been his comrade in Pompey's army, but he was annoyed that Marcellus preferred some other friends to him. As Marcellus was traveling back to our city from Mytilene, where he had fled, Chilo stabbed him with a dagger in the port of Athens.[195] Immediately afterward Chilo went on to murder the source of his insanity.[196] Chilo was an enemy to friendship, he obstructed the kindness of a god, and he cruelly undermined the public-spirited religious sentiment that had spared the life of a renowned citizen.

11. 5. It might seem impossible to go beyond such cruelty, but the horrifying murder that Gaius Toranius committed on his father surpassed it. He followed the party of the triumvirs,[197] and when his father, a distinguished former praetor, was

---

[189]Tullia's husband was Tarquin the Proud, the last king of Rome (534–510 B.C.).

[190]The Latin name for the street was *Sceleratus Vicus*.

[191]Gaius Flavius Fimbria was an army legate in 86 B.C., the year Marius died.

[192]Quintus Mucius Scaevola the Pontiff (cos, 95 B.C.) survived until 82 B.C.

[193]Catiline plotted his rebellion when Cicero was consul in 63 B.C.

[194]Marcus Claudius Marcellus (cos, 51 B.C.) had strongly opposed Caesar. Marcellus was pardoned by Caesar in 46 B.C.

[195]Magius Chilo accompanied Marcellus on his way home from Mytilene (on the island of Lesbos, off the west coast of Asia Minor) in the summer of 45 B.C., but they had an argument when they reached Athens.

[196]Chilo killed himself immediately after stabbing Marcellus.

[197]The triumvirs massacred their political opponents in 43 and 42 B.C.

put on their death list,[198] some centurions came searching for him. Toranius told them where his father was hiding, how old he was, and what were the physical characteristics by which they could recognize him. The old man was more worried about his son's safety and progress than about the short time he himself had yet to live, so he started asking the soldiers whether his son was safe and whether his generals were pleased with him. One of the soldiers replied, "You were pointed out to us by that son you love so much, and you will be killed by our actions and by his treachery." With that, he stuck his sword through the old man's chest. The unfortunate man fell dead, more wretched because of the man who had brought about his murder than because of that murder itself.

11. 6. The same bitter ending fell to the lot of Lucius Villius Annalis.[199] He was going to the Campus for his son's election to the quaestorship[200] when he discovered that he had been put on the death list, so he went off and hid in the house of a client. But the criminal behavior of his evil young son saw to it that the client's loyalty would not save the father. He led the soldiers on his father's trail and handed him over, so that they could kill his father in his presence.[201] He killed his father twice over, first by planning the murder and then by looking on at it.

11. 7. When Vettius Salassus was put on the death list, his ending was also a very bitter one. He was in hiding, and what should I say? Did his wife hand him over to death, or did she kill him herself? Is someone's crime all that much lighter if the only thing they did not do was carry it out in person?

Foreign Stories

11. ext. 1. The following crime will be described with calmer feelings, since it is a foreign one. Scipio Africanus was putting on a gladiator show in memory of his father and paternal uncle in New Carthage.[202] Two royal princes whose father had recently died marched into the arena.[203] They declared that they would fight each other for the throne, and that they hoped their duel would make Scipio's show more glorious. Scipio suggested to them that they decide which of them ought to be king by using words rather than swords. The older one was beginning to heed Scipio's advice, but the younger one placed his hopes in his physical

---

[198]The father, also called Gaius Toranius (usually spelled Turranius), had been a praetor in 44 B.C. and was one of the first victims of the triumvirs.

[199]The father, Lucius Villius Annalis, had been a praetor around 58 B.C.

[200]The son was campaigning in 43 B.C. and was elected as aedile (not quaestor) for 42 B.C.

[201]The father was murdered in 43 B.C.

[202]The Scipio brothers, Publius Cornelius Scipio (cos, 218 B.C.) and Gnaeus Cornelius Scipio Calvus (cos, 222 B.C.), had died fighting in Spain in 211 B.C. Scipio Africanus was the son of Publius, and he commemorated their deaths in 206 B.C. New Carthage (modern Cartagena) was on the east coast of Spain.

[203]The Spanish combatants were cousins, not brothers.

strength and persisted in his madness.[204] The duel began, and the one who was more stubbornly amoral was punished with death by the verdict of Fortune.

11. ext. 2. Mithridates behaved much more wickedly, in that he did not fight with a brother for his father's kingdom;[205] he fought a war against his father himself for royal power.[206] I really wonder how he found any men to help him in this conflict or dared to call on the gods for help.

11. ext. 3. Why should we be amazed at the following story, as if it were something unusual for such nations? Sariaster plotted against his father, Tigranes, the king of Armenia,[207] and made a pact with his friends that they should all draw blood from their right hand and then suck each other's blood. I could hardly bear it if someone arranged such a bloodthirsty pact, even to save his father's life.

11. ext. 4. But why should I criticize these evil deeds and harp on those ones, when I see that every crime is outdone by one great evil plot to assassinate our father?[208] My feelings are sincere rather than violent, but they force me to denounce this crime with every mental impulse and with a strong sense of outrage. When a man has destroyed the ties of friendship[209] and attempted to bury the human race in bloodshed and darkness, how could any writer find words that would be strong enough to send that evil man into the depths of hatred he deserves?

You were more ferocious than the most brutal, savage barbarians.[210] Did you really think that you could possibly snatch the reins of the Roman Empire from the benevolent hands of our emperor and father? Could the world have survived if you had achieved your mad goals?

Our city was once captured by the Gauls;[211] on the infamous day of Allia, three hundred men from a famous family perished;[212] the two Scipio brothers were de-

---

[204]The deceased king was the father of the younger combatant.

[205]Mithridates VI was king of Pontus from 120 to 63 B.C. He was only eleven years old when his father was murdered.

[206]Mithridates murdered his mother and brother in the struggle for his father's throne, but never fought against his father. Valerius may be thinking of his son Pharnaces II who rebelled against Mithridates VI and drove him to suicide in 63 B.C.

[207]Tigranes II was king of Armenia from 95 to 55 B.C. His son, Sariaster (usually spelled Zariadres), rebelled against him.

[208]Valerius is talking about the plot of Lucius Aelius Sejanus to assassinate Tiberius and make himself emperor. This recent event that shocked the Roman world occurred when Valerius was finishing his book in A.D. 31.

[209]Tiberius trusted Sejanus and had made him consul along with Tiberius himself in A.D. 31.

[210]Valerius never mentions Sejanus by name. His feelings are deeply hurt by the horrifying thought that anyone could think of murdering Tiberius.

[211]The Gauls captured Rome in 390 B.C.

[212]On July 18, 390 B.C., the Gauls defeated the Romans at the river Allia (about ten miles from Rome, in Latium). July 18 was known as the day of Allia and was marked as a black day on the Roman calendar every year. On July 18, 477 B.C., three hundred members of the Fabius family died fighting against Veii (in Etruria, western Italy).

feated in Spain;[213] there was Lake Trasimene, Cannae,[214] and the insane civil wars that flowed with our own blood.[215] But you wanted to recreate and surpass these disasters with the mad schemes you furiously devised.

But the watchful gods were alert, the stars retained their power, our altars, sacred couches, and temples were protected by the active presence of the gods; no force that should have looked out for the life of our august emperor and for our country allowed itself to relax its attention. Above all else, the founder and guardian of our security took care, in his divine foresight, that his exceptional achievements would not come to nothing in the destruction of the entire world.[216] That is why peace is with us, the laws prevail, and people keep to the honest paths of private and public service.

But the man who violated the ties of friendship and tried to undermine all these things has been crushed along with his entire family by the power of the Roman people. Even in the Underworld, if they actually allowed him in there, he is getting the punishment he deserves.

Chapter 12. Unusual Deaths

Preface

The condition of our human existence is especially affected by our first and last day, because a great difference is made by the circumstances in which it starts off, and the ending with which it concludes. This is why we decide that a man has been truly happy only if he has had the good fortune both to begin his life auspiciously and to leave it peacefully. During the period in between, according to how Fortune steers the tiller, we sometimes sail in troubled waters, and at other times we sail in calm waters. But life never fulfills our expectations, because we spend most of our time making eager wishes and waste most of our time behaving irrationally. If you wanted to have a good life, you could make even a very short life more than enough for you, by outdoing the number of your years with the quantity of your achievements. Otherwise, what would be the point in enjoying a lazy stay here, since you would be dragging out your life rather than making it worthwhile? But I do not want to digress any more, so I shall talk about those who have been taken away by an unusual type of death.

---

[213]Publius Cornelius Scipio (cos, 218 B.C.) and Gnaeus Cornelius Scipio Calvus (cos, 222 B.C.) died fighting against the Carthaginians in Spain in 211 B.C.

[214]Hannibal defeated the Romans at Lake Trasimene (in Etruria, western Italy) in 217 B.C. and at Cannae (in Apulia, eastern Italy) in 216 B.C.

[215]The civil wars lasted from 49 to 31 B.C.

[216]Tiberius grew suspicious of Sejanus and had him put to death later in A.D. 31.

Roman Stories

12. 1. Tullus Hostilius was struck by lightning and burned up along with his entire house.[217] This was a strange blow of fate, since it so happened that the leader of our city was taken away in the city itself, and his countrymen could not even give him the last honors of a funeral. The fire from heaven arranged matters in such a way that the very same building served as his royal palace, his funeral pyre, and his tomb.

12. 2. It hardly seems credible that joy could have the same power to take someone's life away as a stroke of lightning, but it did have that power. When the news of the defeat at Lake Trasimene arrived,[218] one woman at her own doorstep came across her son, who had survived, and she died as she embraced him; another was sitting sadly at home because she had wrongly been told that her son had died, and at the first sight of him when he came back, she dropped dead. What a strange kind of accident! Their grief had not killed them, but their joy did. But I am not so surprised, since they were women.

12. 3. The consul Manius Juventius Thalna was the colleague of Tiberius Gracchus when Gracchus was holding his second consulship.[219] While Thalna was making a sacrifice in Corsica, which he had recently subdued, he received a letter announcing that the Senate had decreed a thanksgiving to the gods in his honor. While he was focusing his attention on reading this letter, he began to feel faint, collapsed in front of the altar fire, and lay dead on the ground. What else should we think but that he was killed off by too much joy? There's the kind of man to whom the destruction of Numantia or Carthage should have been entrusted![220]

12. 4. Quintus Catulus was a commander of considerably higher spirits,[221] and the Senate had made him a partner with Marius in his triumph over the Cimbrians.[222] But the end of Catulus was rather violent, since this same Marius ordered his death because of the civil wars. Catulus had recently repainted his room with white-wash, so he brought the room to a great heat with a huge fire and killed himself by shutting himself up inside. This dreadful action forced upon Catulus was a very great disgrace to the glory of Marius.[223]

12. 5. Lucius Cornelius Merula, a former consul and a flamen of Jupiter,[224] also perished in the same storm that afflicted the Republic.[225] He did not want to

[217]Tullus Hostilius was king of Rome from 672 to 641 B.C. According to Roman legend, his palace was struck by lightning because he had performed rituals incorrectly.

[218]The Romans were defeated by Hannibal at Lake Trasimene (in Etruria) in 217 B.C.

[219]Manius Juventius Thalna and Tiberius Sempronius Gracchus (cos, 177 B.C.) were consuls together in 163 B.C.

[220]Scipio Africanus destroyed Numantia (in Spain) in 133 B.C. and Carthage in 146 B.C.

[221]Quintus Lutatius Catulus and Marius were consuls in 102 B.C.

[222]Marius and Catulus defeated the Cimbrians (from Denmark) in 102 B.C.

[223]Catulus committed suicide when Marius and his supporters seized Rome in 87 B.C.

[224]A flamen was a chief priest (see flamen in the Glossary).

[225]Lucius Cornelius Merula (cos, 87 B.C.) was put on trial when Marius and his supporters took over in 87 B.C., and he committed suicide.

be subjected to the derision of the arrogant victors, so he slit his veins in the shrine of Jupiter to evade the shameful death that had been set for him. The ancient fireplace was drenched with the blood of its own priest.

12. 6. The departure of Herennius Siculus from this life was bitter but high-spirited. He had served as a diviner to Gaius Gracchus and had also been a close friend of his, and he was being brought to prison for this reason.[226] He smashed his head against the doorpost of the prison, collapsed at the very entrance to that place of shame, and gave up his life when he was just one step away from a public execution and the hand of the executioner.

12. 7. A similar impulse brought about the suicide of Gaius Licinius Macer, a former praetor[227] who was the father of Calvus. He was on trial for misgovernment and while the jury's votes were being counted, he went up to the balcony. When he saw that Cicero, who was presiding over the court,[228] was taking off his official striped toga, Macer sent someone to tell Cicero that he had ended his life, not after he was found guilty, but when he was still on trial, so his property could not be auctioned off by the state. Macer happened to have a handkerchief in his hand, and at once he stuffed it into his mouth and down his throat, and by smothering himself he forestalled his punishment. When Cicero heard about this, he passed no sentence against him. By his father's unusual type of death, an orator of illustrious talent was saved from the loss of his inheritance and from the disgrace of a criminal conviction in his family.[229]

12. 8. Macer's death was a brave one, but the death of the following men was quite ridiculous. Cornelius Gallus, a former praetor, and Titus Etereius, a Roman equestrian, died while having sex with boys. But what is the point in making fun of their death, since it was not their sexual indulgence but the fragility of the human condition that ended their lives? The end of our life can be brought about by all kinds of unexpected causes, some of which hardly deserve to be called our final destiny, since they occur at the time of death, rather than causing our deaths.

Foreign Stories

12. ext. 1. There are foreign deaths that are also worth noting. Foremost among them is the death of Comas, who is said to have been the brother of the great bandit chieftain, Cleon.[230] He was brought before the consul Publius Rupilius at Henna,[231] a city that the bandits had held but was now brought back under our control. When Comas was interrogated about the strength and goals of the runaway slaves, he asked for some time to collect his thoughts. He covered his

---

[226]The supporters of Gaius Sempronius Gracchus (tribune of the plebs, 123 B.C.) were massacred in 121 B.C.

[227]Gaius Licinius Macer had been a praetor in 68 B.C.

[228]Cicero was the praetor responsible for misgovernment cases in 66 B.C.

[229]Macer's son, Gaius Licinius Calvus, was a well-known poet and orator.

[230]Cleon led the rebel slaves during the First Slave War in Sicily (135–132 B.C.).

[231]Publius Rupilius (cos, 132 B.C.) crushed the slave rebellion. Henna was in central Sicily.

head, went down on his knees, and smothered himself. He was in the very hands of the guards and in the presence of our highest executive officer, but he died in enviable peace.

Let wretched people, who are better off dead than alive, torture themselves with fearful and anxious questions, trying to figure out how they should end their lives. Let them sharpen a sword, mix poisons together, grab a noose, and look around for great heights as if there were any need for great preparations or ingenious efforts to break the union between body and soul, which depends on such a flimsy tie. Comas did not need any of these things; he found a way of ending his life by simply keeping his breath inside his chest. We should not strive too hard to hold onto this good called life, because our possession of it is insecure, and it can vanish away at the slightest touch of force.

12. ext. 2. The end of the poet Aeschylus was not self-inflicted, but it is worth recording because of its strange circumstances.[232] He was staying in a city in Sicily, and he went outside its walls and sat down in a warm spot. An eagle was carrying a tortoise above him, and it was deceived by the sheen of his head—for he had no hair left—and thinking it was a rock, the eagle dashed the tortoise onto it, so that it could eat the meat once the shell was broken. That blow wiped out the founder and beginner of a more powerful type of tragedy.

12. ext. 3. It is said that Homer's death also was an unusual one.[233] It is believed that he died of grief on the island of Ios[234] because he was not able to answer a riddle that the fishermen asked him.

12. ext. 4. Euripides ended in a considerably more horrible way.[235] He had been at a banquet offered by King Archelaus in Macedonia,[236] and was going back to the home of a friend with whom he was staying, when he was torn to pieces by the guard dogs and died. Such a great genius did not deserve this cruel fate.

12. ext. 5. The deaths of the following illustrious poets were unworthy of their characters and works. Sophocles was already a very old man and had entered a tragedy for a competition. He spent a long time worrying how the doubtful voting would turn out, and when he finally won by a single vote, his joy brought about his death.[237]

12. ext. 6. Philemon was carried off by the violence of his excessive laughter.[238] He got some figs, and when they were right in front of him, an ass started eating them, so he shouted to his slave to drive the ass away. The slave arrived after the ass had already eaten all the figs, so Philemon said, "Since you were so late, you might as well give the ass my wine too." And at once he followed his witty remark with

[232]Aeschlus died at Gela (on the south coast of Sicily) in 456 B.C.

[233]Homer lived and died at the end of the eighth century B.C.

[234]Ios was one of the Cycladic Islands in the Aegean Sea.

[235]Euripides went to Macedonia in 408 B.C. and died there in 406 B.C.

[236]Archelaus was king of Macedonia from 413 to 399 B.C.

[237]Sophocles died in Athens in 406 B.C.

[238]Philemon was a writer of comedies who lived from 361 to 263 B.C.

laughs that made him breathe in and out too quickly, and the jerkiness of his breathing overwhelmed his elderly throat.

12. ext. 7. Pindar was in a gymnasium with the boyfriend in whom he took special delight, and he lay his head on the boy's lap and fell asleep.[239] They did not realize he had died until the master of the gymnasium was trying to lock the place up and tried to wake him in vain. I would definitely believe that the same kindness of the gods granted him such great fluency as a poet and such a peaceful ending to his life.

12. ext. 8. The same thing happened to Anacreon.[240] He had outlived the normal human lifespan, and he preserved the flimsy and delicate health he was left with by sucking the juice of dried grapes. But one grape seed got lodged in his dry throat and killed him.

12. ext. 9. I shall add the following stories, because their subject matter and the deaths they describe are similar. Milo of Croton[241] was walking along the road when he saw in a field an oak tree that was being split with wedges. Confident in his strength, he went up to it, put his hands in the gap, and tried to split the tree in two. The wedges sprang out, the tree returned to its natural form, and it caught his hands. In spite of all his victories in the gymnasium, he was trapped, and he was torn to pieces by wild animals.

12. ext. 10. A storm forced the athlete Polydamas[242] to enter a cave, but there was a sudden huge rush of water that made its roof disintegrate and collapse. All his friends escaped the danger by running away, and he stayed behind alone, trying to support the collapsing mass on his shoulders. But the weight was too much for any human body, and he was crushed to death. So the shelter he had sought from the rain became his tomb after this insane effort.

These men can prove to us that excessive physical strength weakens our mental capacity. It is as if Nature refuses to spoil us with both these gifts, and that it would go beyond human happiness for the same man to be both exceptionally strong and exceptionally wise.

Chapter 13. The Craving to Survive

Preface

But since we have mentioned both accidental and manly departures from this life, as well as a few reckless ones, we shall now add some cowardly and effeminate deaths for you to consider. By the very fact of comparing them, it will be obvious

---

[239]Pindar died in Argos (in southern Greece) in 438 B.C.

[240]The poet Anacreon of Teos lived during the sixth century B.C.

[241]Milo of Croton was a famous athlete who lived during the sixth century B.C.

[242]Polydamas came from Skotussa in Thessaly (northern Greece). He won the pentathlon at the Olympics in 408 B.C.

that it is sometimes not only much braver but also much wiser to choose death over life.

Roman Stories

13. 1. Manius Aquillius could have died in glory, but he disgracefully chose instead to become the slave of Mithridates.[243] Wouldn't someone be right in saying that he deserved execution in Pontus rather than military command in Rome? His behavior turned his private disgrace into a public embarrassment.

13. 2. Gnaeus Carbo is also a great disgrace to Latin history. During his third consulship he was brought to execution by Pompey's orders in Sicily.[244] In tears, he humbly begged the soldiers to let him relieve his bowels before he died, but he really wanted to enjoy the wretched light of day a little longer. He kept delaying there until they had to behead him while he was squatting in that disgusting place. When you tell such a disgraceful story, the very words struggle with themselves. They are opposed to silence, because this story should not be hidden, but they are not favorable to speech, because it is distasteful to tell this story.

13. 3. What about Decimus Brutus?[245] With such great disgrace he bought a few wretched minutes of life! Antony had sent Furius to kill him, and when Brutus was caught by Furius, he did not just pull his neck away from the sword; when he was warned to present his neck bravely, he even swore in the following words: "I swear by my life, I will do it." Oh, what a miserable way of delaying death! Oh, what a stupid way of backing up a promise! O irrational pleasure in holding on to life—it is you who inflict this madness and defeat the rational way of thinking, which teaches us to love life but not to fear death.

Foreign Stories

13. ext. 1. You also forced Xerxes to burst into tears on behalf of the young men in his army from all over Asia, because they would all be dead within a century.[246] It seems to me that he was ostensibly saddened by the condition of others, but he was truly lamenting his own, and he was more fortunate in the greatness of his power than in the depth of his understanding. What person of even average intelligence would lament that he was born a mortal?

---

[243]Manius Aquillius was an army legate in 88 B.C. when he was defeated by King Mithridates VI of Pontus. The usual story is that he was captured and killed by Mithridates.

[244]Gnaeus Papirius Carbo (cos, 85 B.C.) was consul for the third time in 82 B.C. He was put to death by Pompey, who was the governor of Sicily in that year.

[245]Decimus Junius Brutus Albinus (the tyrannicide) was put to death in 43 B.C. (see 4:7,6).

[246]Xerxes I was king of Persia from 486 to 465 B.C. He wept when he saw his great army crossing from Asia into Europe in 480 B.C.

What Extraordinary Precautions Were Adopted by People Who Were Suspicious of Their Servants.

Foreign Stories (continued)

13. ext. 2. I shall now discuss people who were suspicious of others and adopted extraordinary precautions for themselves. I shall begin not with the most miserable person but with a man who was believed to be one of the very few exceptionally fortunate men.

King Masinissa[247] placed little faith in the hearts of men, so he protected his life by surrounding himself with guard dogs. What good was it to have such a widespread empire? What good was it to have such a large number of children? What good was it, in the end, to enjoy the friendship of Rome, which was reinforced by such tight bonds of affection, if he thought that nothing could be more effective in guarding these things than the barking and biting of his dogs?

13. ext. 3. Alexander[248] was less happy than this king, because his heart was tormented by love and also by fear. He was possessed by an unbounded love for his wife, Thebe, but when he was coming to her in his bedroom after a banquet, he would order a barbarian covered with Thracian tattoos to march in front of him with sword drawn. He would not dare to go into the bed until it had been carefully examined by his bodyguard. The gods must have been angry with him and devised this punishment for him, that he could control neither his desire nor his fear. But the woman who caused his fear was also the woman who ended it: Thebe was angry with Alexander for keeping a mistress and killed him.

13. ext. 4. Come, now, what a long story there is to tell about the torments endured by Dionysius, the tyrant of Syracuse![249] This is how he spent his reign of thirty-eight years. He sent his friends away, replaced them with men from the most ferocious nations and with very strong slaves chosen from the households of rich men, and trusted them to keep him safe. He was also distrustful of barbers, so he taught his daughters how to shave his face. But when they started to approach adulthood, he did not dare to trust even them with a blade in their hands, so he ordered them to singe his beard and his hair with red-hot walnut shells.

He felt no safer as a husband than as a parent. He tied himself by marriage with two women at the same time, Aristomache of Syracuse and Doris of Locri,[250] but he would never go to sleep with either of them until she had been searched. He even had the bed in his room surrounded by a wide ditch, as if the bed were an army camp. He would retire to his bed by crossing a wooden bridge, but only after his guards had locked the door of the bedroom from the outside, and he himself had also carefully locked it with a bolt from the inside.

---

[247]Masinissa was king of Numidia (modern Algeria) from 209 to 148 B.C.

[248]Alexander was king of Pherae (in Thessaly) from 369 to 357 B.C.

[249]Dionysius I was tyrant of Syracuse from 405 to 367 B.C.

[250]Locri Epizephyrii was on the south coast of Bruttium (southern Italy).

Chapter 14. Physical Resemblance

Preface

People who are endowed with profound learning have subtle discussions about resemblances between faces or entire bodies. Some of them follow one view and think that such resemblances depend on descent and blood relationship, and they find strong evidence in the example presented by other animals, which are nearly always similar to their parents. Others say that this is not a fixed law of nature, and that the appearance of mortals depends on the random circumstances of their conception, and that is why good-looking parents often have ugly children, and strong ones have weakly children. Since this question is a controversial one, we shall tell a few stories about striking resemblances between unrelated people.

Roman Stories

14. 1. Vibius, a man of free birth, and Publicius, a freed slave, were so similar to Pompey the Great that if they changed their social status, Pompey could have been greeted as one of them and one of them could have been greeted as Pompey. It is certainly the case that wherever Vibius or Publicius would go, everybody would turn around to look at them, and each person would remark how much these lowly men resembled that most distinguished citizen.

14. 2. This joke played by chance came to Pompey almost by inheritance. His father[251] looked so much like his cook, Menogenes, that this man, who was a great soldier and ferociously proud, could not prevent people from calling him by that low-class name.

14. 3. Cornelius Scipio was a young man of exceptionally noble birth, and he had more than enough famous surnames from his own family,[252] but he had the slave name of Serapio forced on him by the general public, because he looked so much like a sacrificial attendant who had this name. Neither the integrity of his character nor respect for the death masks of his ancestors could protect him from having this insult thrown at him.

14. 4. Lentulus and Metellus were colleagues in a very highborn consulship,[253] but they were practically seen on the stage because of their resemblance to two actors. Lentulus got the name of Spinther from one of the actors who played second roles, and if Metellus had not already received the name of Nepos ("playboy") because of his behavior, he would have been called Pamphilus, an actor who played third roles, because it was said that he looked exactly like him.

14. 5. Although Marcus Messalla was a former consul and censor,[254] and Curio

---

[251]Pompey's father was Gnaeus Pompeius Strabo (cos, 89 B.C.).

[252]His full name was Publius Cornelius Scipio Nasica Serapio (cos, 138 B.C.).

[253]Publius Cornelius Lentulus Spinther and Quintus Caecilius Metellus Nepos, who came from very aristocratic families, were consuls together in 57 B.C.

[254]Marcus Valerius Messalla Niger was consul in 61 B.C. and censor in 55 B.C.

had held every high political office,[255] they had the names of actors forced upon them. Messalla got the name of Menogenes because of his facial appearance, and Curio got the name of Burbuleius because his gait was similar.

These national stories should be more than enough, since their main characters are outstanding men and the stories are well known to everyone.

Foreign Stories.

14. ext. 1. It is said that a man called Artemon, who was the same age and also a member of the royal family, was very similar to King Antiochus.[256] When she had killed Antiochus, the king's widow, Laodice,[257] wanted to hide her crime, so she placed Artemon in the bed and pretended that he was the king and that he was sick. Then she allowed all the people to come in, and she deceived them with his voice and his face which were so similar to the king's. So they all believed that the dying Antiochus had commended Laodice and her children to them.

14. ext. 2. Hybreas of Mylasa was an orator of flowing and arousing eloquence,[258] but the eyes of all Asia practically identified him as the brother of a slave from Cyme[259] who used to sweep up the dirt in a gymnasium: they were almost identical in the appearance of their faces and of the rest of their bodies.

14. ext. 3. There was a cheeky man, and it is well known that he was very similar to the governor of Sicily. The governor said he was amazed that this man could resemble him so closely, since his father had never gone to that province, and the fellow said, "But my father went to Rome." His mother's reputation had been insulted by the governor's joke, so he avenged the insult by casting suspicion on the governor's mother instead. He showed more daring than was suitable for someone who was subjected to the governor's rods and axes.

Chapter 15. People Who Were Born Very Low but Tried to Insinuate Themselves into Glorious Families by Lying

Preface

That sort of risqué insolence was bearable and affected only one person. But the following type of insolence cannot be tolerated in any way, and it quite obviously poses a threat both to private citizens and to the state.

---

[255]Gaius Scribonius Curio was consul in 76 B.C. and censor in 61 B.C.

[256]Antiochus II Theos was king of Syria from 261 to 246 B.C.

[257]Laodice was the first wife of Antiochus. She murdered his second wife, Berenice, along with Berenice's son, and thereby ensured the succession of her own son. (See 9:10,ext.1.)

[258]Hybreas came from Mylasa in Caria (western Asia Minor) and lived in the first century B.C.

[259]Cyme was a city on the west coast of Asia Minor.

Roman Stories

15. 1. I shall leave aside Equitius, that monster from Firmum in Picenum, as I have already told his story in a previous part of this book.[260] He claimed that Tiberius Gracchus was his father, and although this was an obvious lie, he was protected by the folly of the rioting mob and the great power of the tribunes.[261]

Herophilus, an eye doctor, was so brazen in claiming Marius, who had been a consul seven times,[262] as his grandfather, that several colonies of veteran soldiers and some splendid municipalities, as well as almost all the trade guilds, adopted him as their patron. In fact, when Caesar had defeated the young Gnaeus Pompeius in Spain[263] and welcomed the crowds into his gardens, Herophilus, who was standing between the next two columns, was greeted with almost equally great enthusiasm by an equally large crowd. If the power of the divine Caesar had not stood up to this shameful whirlwind, the Republic might have received as great a wound as it had from Equitius.

Herophilus was banished from Italy by a decree of Caesar, but after Caesar had been welcomed into heaven, Herophilus came back to the city and had the nerve to make plans for killing the senators. On these grounds he was put to death by order of the Fathers, and in prison he paid the overdue penalty for possessing a mind that was ready to concoct every type of crime.[264]

15. 2. Not even the most excellent divine power of Augustus was immune to this type of insult when he was still ruling the earth. There surfaced a man who dared to lie that he had been born from the womb of the emperor's most glorious and blameless sister, Octavia.[265] He claimed that he had, however, been handed over to another man, because he was very weak physically, and that he had been raised by that man as his own son, while that man's son had been put in his place instead. He obviously wanted our most sacred family to be deprived of its reputation for legitimate descent and at the same time to be disgraced by the polluting presence of a low and false offspring. But while he was voyaging with his sails full of insolence toward the highest degree of outrage, he was chained to the oar of a government trireme by order of Augustus.[266]

---

[260]The story of Lucius Equitius is told at 9:7,1 and 9:7,2.

[261]Equitius was supported by Lucius Appuleius Saturninus (tribune of the plebs, 103 B.C.).

[262]Marius had been consul seven times between 107 and 86 B.C.

[263]Gnaeus Pompeius Magnus (the son of Pompey the Great) was defeated and killed at the battle of Munda (in southern Spain) by Caesar in 45 B.C.

[264]Herophilus led the mob that worshiped Caesar after his assassination, and he was put to death by Antony, who feared him as a rival.

[265]Octavia's only son, Marcus Claudius Marcellus, died in 23 B.C.

[266]A trireme was a warship. The imposter in this story was enslaved and spent the rest of his life rowing a trireme. By describing the imposter metaphorically as a ship sailing toward outrage, Valerius is suggesting that his literal punishment suited his imaginary schemes.

15. 3. There was also a man who claimed that he was the son of Quintus Sertorius;[267] but no force could compel the wife of Sertorius to recognize the man.

15. 4. What about Trebellius Calcha? How earnestly he insisted that he was Clodius (junior)![268] Indeed, when he sued for the inheritance of Clodius (senior), he was so popular when he entered the centumvirate court[269] that the hysteria of the people hardly left any opportunity for a just and fair verdict. In spite of this, the oath taken by the jury in that court did not give way before the false claims of the plaintiff or the violence of the plebs.

15. 5. A man behaved much more boldly and burst into the house of Gnaeus Asinius Dio during the regime of Sulla.[270] He kicked Dio's son out of the house and kept shouting that he himself, not the other man, was Dio's son. But after the fair-minded rule of Augustus restored the Republic from the violence of Sulla's regime, and a just leader was at the helm of the Roman Empire, this man ended his life in the state prison.[271]

Foreign Stories

15. ext. 1. When Augustus was presiding over the Republic,[272] he cut short the folly of a woman in Mediolanum who persisted in a similar lie.[273] She said that she was Rubria, and that people were wrong in thinking that she had died in a fire. She claimed Rubria's property, even though she was in no way related to her, and she had excellent witnesses from that region and won the support of the emperor's friends. But the steadfastness of Augustus could not be overcome, and her wicked schemes came to nothing.

15. ext. 2. There was a barbarian who claimed the throne of Cappadocia by pretending, because of his remarkable resemblance, to be Ariarathes, though it was clearer than day that Ariarathes had been killed by Antony.[274] The imposter was supported by the gullible states and nations of almost the entire East, but Augustus forced this man who was madly threatening our empire to pay the proper penalty.[275]

[267]Quintus Sertorius (praetor, 83 B.C.) was a supporter of Marius, and a governor of Nearer Spain. He held out against the Roman government until he was murdered in 72 B.C.

[268]Publius Clodius Pulcher (aedile, 56 B.C.) was murdered in 52 B.C. The imposter was pretending to be his son, who was also called Publius Clodius Pulcher (see 3:5,3).

[269]The centumvirate court dealt with wills and inheritance cases.

[270]Sulla was dictator from 82 to 79 B.C.

[271]Augustus "restored the Republic" in 27 B.C.

[272]Augustus was emperor from 27 B.C. to A.D. 14.

[273]Mediolanum (modern Milan) was in Transpadana (in northern Italy).

[274]Ariarathes X Eusebes Philadelphus was king of Cappadocia from 42 B.C. until 36 B.C., when he was killed by Antony.

[275]The new king of Cappadocia (Archelaus, 36 B.C.–A.D. 17) was a client-king of Augustus, which is why Augustus supported him against rival claimants.

GLOSSARY

aedile Four aediles were responsible for the upkeep of the city of Rome. Aediles held office for one year. Two of the aediles were plebeian aediles. The other two were curule aediles and had to come from a patrician familiy. See also patrician, plebeian.

Africa The province of Africa included modern Tunisia and part of Libya.

ancestral death mask (*imago*) Aristocratic Roman families kept the death masks of their ancestors on display in the living room. The public offices held by each ancestor were recorded under his mask.

Antony Marcus Antonius (cos, 44–34 B.C.; triumvir 43–33 B.C.) was the partner and rival of Augustus after Caesar's death.

as (plural = asses) See **money—Roman.**

Asia The province of Asia included the western part of modern Turkey.

Asia Minor Asia Minor, which means "smaller Asia," covered the same area as modern Turkey.

assembly—centuriate The centuriate assembly elected magistrates and enacted laws. Citizens could also appeal to the centuriate assembly if they had been convicted in a law court. Citizens voted by their voting unit, so this assembly was weighted in favor of the upper classes. See also **units—voting**.

assembly—tribal The tribal assembly was summoned by a magistrate and could make laws. All citizens could attend and they voted by tribe. See also **plebs—assembly, tribe**.

augur An augur was a Roman priest who was an expert in taking the auspices—that is, interpreting the will of the gods from the behavior of birds. See also **auspices.**

Augustus Gaius Julius Caesar Augustus (cos, 43–33 B.C., 31–23 B.C., A.D. 5; triumvir 43–33 B.C.; emperor, 27 B.C.–A.D.14) dominated the Roman world after Caesar's death and eventually became its first emperor.

auspices "Taking the auspices" was the science of observing the flight patterns of birds or the eating patterns of sacred chickens and interpreting the will of the gods from them.

Caesar Gaius Julius Caesar (cos, 59–48 B.C. 46–44 B.C.; dictator, 49–44 B.C.) conquered Gaul (modern France), made himself dictator, and defeated Pompey and the Republicans.

Catiline Lucius Sergius Catilina (praetor, 68 B.C.) organized a rebellion against the Roman government in 63 B.C.

Cato of Utica Marcus Porcius Cato Uticensis (praetor, 54 B.C.) was the hero of the Republicans in their struggles against Caesar and Augustus. He committed suicide in 46 B.C. rather than live under a dictatorship.

Cato the Censor Marcus Porcius Cato (cos, 195 B.C.) was notorious for his rigid puritanism and patriotism. He was censor in 184 B.C.

censor Two censors were elected every five years to hold a census. They could punish people for moral lapses (such as extravagance or sexual misconduct) by demoting them to a lower social class, depriving them of their vote, or (in the case of senators) expelling them from the Senate.

centurion   A centurion was similar to a modern sergeant. It was the highest rank an enlisted soldier could reach. He commanded a unit (*centuria*). See also **unit—army**.

Cicero   Marcus Tullius Cicero (cos, 63 B.C.) was a famous politician and writer.

citizens without property   The poorest Roman citizens were known as citizens without property. They were officially called *capite censi* (men counted by head) or *proletarii* (reproducers), because their only social function was to be counted and to produce children.

cohort   A cohort was a subdivision of a legion. There were ten cohorts in a legion, each consisting of six units.

college   A college was a group of public officials or priests. So the college of tribunes would be the whole group of tribunes, and the college of augurs would be the whole group of augurs.

committee of ten   The committee of ten men for making sacrifices (*quindecimviri sacris faciundis*) were in charge of the Sibylline Books at Rome. See also **sibyl**.

Conscript Fathers   The term *Conscript Fathers* means senators, because senators were originally the heads (fathers) of aristocratic families, or important men who were not the heads of such clans but were enrolled (conscript) into the Senate. See also **Patrician, Senate.**

consul   The consul (abbreviation = cos) was the chief executive officer in Rome, roughly equivalent to a president except that there were two of them. The consuls commanded the army, called meetings of the Senate, and executed the Senate's decrees. They held office for one year and were then sent to govern a province. See also **governor**.

cos   Abbreviation for consul. In this book, when placed after someone's name, it refers to the first consulship held (most Romans held only one consulship). The date of the first consulship also gives an indication of a man's age, because a consul had to be at least forty-two years old. See **consul.**

denarius   (plural = denarii) See **money—Roman.**

dictator   A dictator was appointed for six months during an emergency and overrode all other government officials. Sulla and Caesar were unusual and unconstitutional in holding permanent dictatorships.

diviner   (*haruspex*, plural *haruspices*) The term *haruspex* literally means an "entrail watcher." A diviner was an expert in ascertaining the will of the gods by examining the inner organs of animals that had been sacrificed. This science originated in Etruria.

drachma   See **money—Greek.**

emperor   The title of emperor was a completely illegal and unconstitutional one used by the tyrant Augustus and his successors to describe their absolute power. The word *imperator* simply means general, but it was this military position that gave the "emperors" their power. The "emperor" combined the power of several Roman officials. He commanded the army, as general; supervised the state religion, as chief pontiff; controlled all the provinces, as supreme governor; and could veto any law, as tribune. See also **king.**

equestrian   The equestrians were the business elite of the Roman Empire. They alone could get government contracts, including the very profitable contracts to collect taxes in the various provinces.

Fabius the Delayer   Quintus Fabius Maximus Verrucosus (cos, 233 B.C., 228 B.C., 215 B.C., 214 B.C., 209 B.C.) helped to defeat Hannibal and win the Second Punic War (218–201 B.C.) with his delaying tactics.

flamen   A flamen was the chief priest of a particular god. The flamen of Mars, for example, would be responsible for the cult of Mars. There were fifteen flamens.

general   The general (*imperator*) was usually a consul. Sometimes both consuls acted as joint generals.

governor   Each province of the Roman Empire was ruled by a governor. Consuls and praetors who had just finished their term of office were appointed as governors by the Senate.

imperator   See **general; emperor.**

king   The monarchy was abolished by the Romans on the February 24, 509 B.C. It was reintroduced by the tyrant Augustus under the title of "emperor." See also **emperor.**

king of sacrifices   (*rex sacrorum*) The king of sacrifices was appointed to carry out rituals that had formerly been restricted to the kings of Rome and therefore required the presence of a "king."

legate   A legate commanded a legion or assisted the general in doing so.

legion   A division of the Roman army. There were twenty-five of them throughout the entire empire in the time of Augustus.

magistrate   A magistrate was any of the major elected government officials: censor, consul, praetor, aedile, or quaestor. They were usually men from a relatively small number of aristocratic families.

The term *magistrate* was not applied to tribunes of the plebs, because their duty was to protect ordinary people from the magistrates and act as a counterbalance to their power.

Marius   Gaius Marius (cos, 107 B.C., 104–100 B.C., 86 B.C.) defeated King Jugurtha of Numidia (modern Algeria), the Cimbrians (from Denmark), and the Teutons (from Germany). He massacred his political opponents during the civil war against Sulla.

master of the horse   Whenever a dictator was appointed, a master of the horse was also appointed to serve as his second-in-command.

military tribune   Six military tribunes assisted the legate in commanding a legion.

mina   See **money—Greek.**

money—Greek   The obol was a copper coin, but there were smaller coins that were fractions of an obol. The silver drachma was worth six obols and roughly equivalent to the Roman denarius. An unskilled laborer earned a drachma a day.

When dealing with large sums of silver money, the Greeks used the terms mina (one hundred drachmas) and talent (six thousand drachmas), but there was no such thing as a mina or talent coin. Equivalences:

6 obols = 1 drachma. 100 drachmas = 1 mina. 60 minas = 1 talent.

money—Roman   The as was a small copper coin, but there were also smaller coins which were fractions of the as. A sextans ("sixth"), for example, was a small coin worth a sixth of an as.

Four asses were equivalent to one sesterce. The sesterce was a large copper coin, and an unskilled laborer earned four sesterces per day.

There was also a silver coin, the denarius, which was worth four sesterces, but even when dealing with large sums of money, the Romans usually calculated in terms of sesterces, or even asses. Equivalences:

4 asses = 1 sesterce. 4 sesterces = 1 denarius.

nonvoting citizen (*aerarius,* "copper man") People were demoted to the class of nonvoting citizen by the censors as a punishment.

patrician A patrician was a member one of the old aristocratic families that dated back to the time of the kings (before 509 B.C.). See also **Conscript Fathers**.

plebs, plebeian The word *plebs* means "the masses," and the plebeians were the poorer classes in Rome. In 494 B.C. they formed their own political organization, the assembly of plebs, and elected their own leaders, the tribunes of plebs. The term "plebeian" was also applied to all Romans who were not patricians, but "conscript" Senators from nonpatrician families were not poor men. See also **aedile, Conscript Fathers, patrician, plebs—assembly, tribune of the plebs**.

plebs—assembly The assembly of the plebs was summoned by a tribune of the plebs and could make laws. Only plebeian citizens attended, and they voted by tribe. See also **assembly—tribal, tribe, tribune of the plebs**.

Pompey Gnaeus Pompeius Magnus (cos, 70 B.C.) conquered western Asia and later led the Republicans against Caesar.

pontiff A pontiff was an official in charge of organizing the state religion in Rome. There were sixteen pontiffs, led by the chief pontiff. One of the chief pontiff's most important and difficult functions was to organize the calendar of religious festivals.

praetor The praetors were judges. They held office for one year, after which they were sent to govern a province. See also **governor**.

prefect A prefect was an officer commanding one of the auxiliary forces in the Roman army: allied soldiers in the army, a troop of horsemen in the cavalry, or a fleet in the navy.

prison manager (*triumvir capitalis*). There were three prison managers in Rome: "the Committee of Three Men for Executions." They were responsible for prisons and executions.

Punic The name Punic is another word for Carthaginian. It is used when speaking of the great wars between Rome and Carthage: the First Punic War (264–241 B.C.); the Second Punic War, also called the War against Hannibal (218–201 B.C.); and the Third Punic War, in which the Romans destroyed Carthage (149–146 B.C.).

quaestor The quaestors were in charge of government finances. A quaestor always accompanied a general to look after army supplies. Quaestors held office for one year.

Scipio Aemilianus Gaius Cornelius Scipio Aemilianus Africanus (cos, 147 B.C., 134 B.C.) destroyed Carthage in 146 B.C. and completed the conquest of Spain by destroying Numantia in 133 B.C.

Scipio Africanus Gaius Cornelius Scipio Africanus (cos, 205 B.C., 194 B.C.) defeated Hannibal in the Second Punic War (218–201 B.C.).

Scipio Asiaticus Lucius Cornelius Scipio Asiaticus (cos, 190 B.C.) was the brother of Scipio Africanus. Together, they defeated King Antiochus the Great of Syria in 190 B.C.

Senate, senator There were six hundred men in the Roman Senate, and they remained there for life. Every magistrate was eligible to be a senator, subject to space being available. The censors would enroll enough new senators every five years to bring the number of senators up to six hundred. The Senate discussed policy, issued decrees, declared war, and negotiated peace treaties.

sesterce See **money—Roman**.

sibyl   A prophetess who was inspired by the god Apollo and predicted the future. The most famous sibyl operated in Cumae. One of the sibyls of Cumae gave the famous Sibylline Books (a collection of prophecies) to the last king of Rome, Tarquin the Proud (534–510 B.C.).

slaves   Slaves had no legal rights and could be abused with impunity. If a Roman citizen freed a slave, the slave was regarded as a member of his family and automatically became a Roman citizen.

Sulla   Lucius Cornelius Sulla Felix (cos, 88–80 B.C.; dictator, 82–79 B.C.) defeated king Mithridates VI of Pontus. After his civil war against Marius, Sulla massacred his political opponents and made himself dictator.

talent   See **money—Greek.**

tribe   Roman territory (which after 89 B.C. included all of Italy) was divided into thirty-five tribal areas. Each tribe had one electoral vote in the tribal assembly and the assembly of the plebs. See also **assembly—tribal, plebs—assembly.**

tribune of the plebs   The ten tribunes protected the rights of ordinary Romans. They could veto any law or action by the government that violated those rights. They could also enact laws through the assembly of the plebs, or the tribal assembly (see **assembly—plebeian, assembly—tribal**). Tribunes held office for one year.

triumvir   The term *triumvir* literally means a member of any three-man committee, but it usually refers to the Committee of Three Men for Reorganizing the Republic (*Triumviri Rei Publicae Constituendae*). These three men—Octavian (who later became the emperor Augustus), Antony, and Lepidus—initiated a reign of terror in Rome (43–42 B.C.) during which they massacred their political opponents. The triumvirs remained in power from 43 to 33 B.C. See also **Antony, Augustus.**

tyrannicide   Tyrannicides were people who killed a tyrant, especially the Republicans who killed Caesar in 44 B.C.

unit—army   An army unit (*centuria*) usually consisted of about sixty men. There were sixty units in a legion. Each unit was commanded by a centurion. See also **centurion.**

unit—voting   The Roman social classes were divided into voting units at meetings of the centuriate assembly. Each voting unit (*centuria*) had one electoral vote. Since the upper classes had a larger number of voting units, they could always outvote the lower classes in any election. See also **assembly—centuriate.**

THEMATIC GUIDE

What follows is a very incomplete list of some topics that I found interesting. I hope it will be useful for teachers of Roman history who might like to use this work as a sourcebook. The topics include some strange absences, which reflect the prejudices of Valerius and his society. For example, there are several stories about what he considers to be good brothers (see Good brother under the heading "Parents and Children"), but almost none about sisters, good or bad.

The references to Valerius consist of numbers in the following format: 1:2,3. The first number refers to a book; the second number (after the colon) refers to a chapter; and the last number (after the comma) refers to a Roman story. If the last number has the abbreviation "ext.," it is a foreign story. Otherwise, it is a Roman story. The abbreviation "praef" refers to the preface at the beginning of each chapter.

Examples: 1:2,3 = Book 1: Chapter 2, Roman Story 3
              1:2,ext.3 = Book 1: Chapter 2, Foreign Story 3
              1:2,praef. = Book 1: Preface to Chapter 2

In Book 8, Chapter 1, Valerius has several stories about law cases. These have special abbreviations: damn. = conviction; absol.= acquittal; and amb. = undecided case.

Example: 8:1,absol.2 = Book 8: Chapter 1, acquittal 2.

In Book 9, Chapter 7, Valerius has several Roman Stories on the topic of violence and rioting. These are followed by stories about mutinies in the Roman army, which are abbreviated as mil.Rom.

Example: 9:7,mil.Rom.2 = Book 9: Chapter 7, Mutiny by
              Roman Soldiers 2.

Finally, in Book 9, Chapter 3, Valerius has the unique heading "Preface to Foreign Stories," abbreviated as ext.praef.

The main thematic headings are in the following order:

Religion
Parents and Children
Marriage
Women
Slaves

Friendship
Personal Behavior
The People
The Army
The Empire

Religion

Foreign cults welcomed
1:1,1 (general); 1:8,2 (Aesculapius); 1:8,3 (Juno Regina)

Foreign cults rejected
1:3,entire chapter

Books banned
1:1,12 (book burned); 4:3,6 (philosophy denounced); 6:3,ext.1 (book banned)

Religion mocked
1:1,ext.3 (Dionysius robs temple); 1:4,3 (consul drowns sacred chickens); 1:8,ext.8 (philosopher mocks oracle); 3:7,ext.6 (Hannibal mocks diviner)

Disaster inevitable
1:4–8, entire chapters

Prophecy evaded
1:4,5 (Metellus saves statue); 1:4,ext.2 (Deiotarus evades building collapse); 1:5,5 (Marius evades execution); 1:7,1 (Augustus evades capture); 1:7,ext.3 (Simonides evades shipwreck); 1:8,ext.7 (Simonides evades building collapse)

Parents and Children

Good father
1:1,20 (Flaccus dies on death of sons); 2:4,5 (Valesius and his sick children); 5:7,entire chapter (father loves son); 5:9,entire chapter (father defends worthless son); 6:5,ext.3 (Zaleucus takes on son's punishment); 7:3,10 (father helps son in love); 8:8,ext.1 (Socrates plays with his boys)

Bad father (ill-treats son)
5:4,3 and 6:9,1 (Capitolinus exploits loyal son); 5:8,entire chapter (father puts son to death); 9:1,9 (Clodius murders son); 5:10,entire chapter (father ignores son's death and carries on with his work)

Bad father (ill-treats daughter)
6:1,2–4 and 6 (kills daughter for lack of chastity)

Good mother
9:12,2 (mother dies with joy); 1:8,4 (Veturia persuades son not to attack Rome)

Bad mother
7:7,4 (Septicia remarries and disowns sons)

Good son
5:2,1 and 5:4,1 (Coriolanus obeys mother); 5:2,7 (Metellus helps father's benefactor); 5:4,2 (Scipio Africanus saves father in battle); 5:4,ext.7 (Italian saves father in battle); 5:4,3 (Manlius Torquatus defends brutal father); 5:4,4 (Marcus Cotta attacks father's enemy); 5:4,5 (Gaius Flaminius obeys father); 5:4,ext.2 (Cimon pays for father's funeral); 5:4,ext.4 (sons carry parents); 5:4,ext.5 (Scythians defend ancestral graves); 5:4,ext.6 (mute son cries out); 5:7,ext.1 and 2 (son overwhelmed by father's affection)

Bad son
5:9,entire chapter (son hates father); 9:11,5 and 6 (son betrays father to assassin); 9:11,ext.2–3 (prince plots against father)

Good daughter
5:4,6 (vestal virgin defends father); 5:4,7 and 5:4,ext.1 (daughter breast-feeds imprisoned parent)

Good brother
5:5, entire chapter

Bad brother
6:3,6 and 8:1,absol.1 (Horatius kills sister); 9:11,ext.1 (Spanish princes fight)

Marriage

Duty to marry
2:9,1 (men should marry); 7:2,ext.1 (perhaps men should not marry)

Divorce
2:1,4 (first divorce in Rome); 2:1,6 (reconciliation); 2:9,2 and 6:3,10–12 (divorce for frivolous reasons); 8:2,3 (Titinius tries to divorce wife for money)

Good husband
4:6,1 (Tiberius Gracchus devoted to wife)

Bad husband
6:3,9 (Egnatius Mecennius kills drunk wife); 8:1,amb.2 (husband murders stepson); 9:1,ext.5 (King Ptolemy VIII forces Cleopatra II into marriage and rapes her daughter)

Good wife
4:6,ext.2–3 and 6:7,2–3 (wife helps endangered husband); 8:7,ext.5 (Melissa nurtures philosopher); 8:15,12 (Sulpicia honored for chastity)

Widow
4:6,4 and 4:6,ext.1 (widow distressed by husband's death); 2:1,3 and 4:3,3 (widow refuses to remarry); 2:6,14 (suttee); 3:2,15 and 4:6,5 (widow kills herself); 8:13,6 (widows live long lives)

Widower
4:6,2 and 3 (widower kills himself)

Adultery
6:1,13 (husband punishes wife's lover); 6:7,1 (wife tolerates cheating husband); 8:1,absol.12 (husband catches wife's lover); 8:2,2 (mistress wants legacy); 9:13,ext.3 (wife kills cheating husband)

Women

Rules
2:1,2 (sit up at meals); 2:1,5 (no touching, no wine); 8:15,ext.4 (forbidden to attend Olympics)

Religion
1:1,6, 1:1,7, 1:1,10, 6:1,praef., 8:1,absol.5 (vestal virgins); 1:8,4 and 5:2,1 (Feminine Fortune); 6:3,7 (Bacchic cult)

Rape
4:3,1 (Scipio does not rape a captive); 6:1,1 (Lucretia's suicide after rape); 6:1,ext.1 and 3 (suicide to avoid rape); 6:1,ext.2 (woman kills rapist); 9:1,ext.2 (slaves rape free women)

Rebellion
2:5,3 and 6:3,8 (poison husbands); 8:3,entire chapter (women lawyers); 9:1,3 (protest movement)

Slaves

Loyal slave
3:3,ext.7 (Spanish slave avenges master); 6:8,entire chapter (slave helps outlawed master); 7:6,1 (slaves fight for Rome); 8:4,3 (slave refuses to betray master)

Disloyal slave
6:5,5–7 (slave betrays master to political enemy)

Slave ill-treated
1:7,4, 6:1,3, 8:4,1, 8:4,2 (executed); 6:1,6 and 6:1,9 (sexually abused); 8:4,1 and 8:4,2 (tortured)

Rebellion
2:7,3 and 9 and 9:12,ext.1 (Sicily); 9:1,ext.2 (Volsinii)

Friendship

Happiness of friends
1:8,ext.17 (Epicureans); 4:7,7 (Laelius and Scipio Aemilianus; Agrippa and Augustus); 4:7,ext.2 (Hephaestion and Alexander the Great, Valerius and Sextus Pompeius); 8:8,1 (Laelius and Scipio Aemilianus)

Face death for friend
3:2,ext.9 (princess); 4:7,1 and 2 (Gracchus brothers); 4:7,5 (against Cinna); 4:7,4 and 6 (Republicans); 4:7,ext.1 (against Dionysius)

Personal Behavior

Control sexuality
4:3,1–3 (Romans); 4:3,ext.1–3 (Greeks); 4:5,ext.1 (Etruscans)

Heterosexual relationships
3:5,3 and 9:1,7 (Clodius); 6:1,4 (man killed for kissing); 6:1,13 (adulterers punished); 7:7,7 (pimp disinherited); 8:1,absol.8 (seducer loses law case); 9:1,8 (aristocratic female prostitute); 9:1,9 (Catiline)

Male homosexual relationships
3:5,4 and 9:1,8 (aristocratic male prostitute); 3:8,ext.4 (man resists boyfriend); 6:1,7 and 8:1,damn.8 (seducer convicted); 6:1,9 (slave owner convicted) 6:1,10–12 (army seducer punished); 8:1,absol.12 (seducer acquitted); 9:12,8 (men die while having sex)

Resist money and luxury
2:5,5 (simple food); 2:5,6 (hardy life); 2:6,1 (Spartan); 2:9,4 (silver); 2:9,5 (banquets); 4:3,4–14 (simple lifestyle); 4:3,ext.4 (Diogenes); 4:4,entire chapter (poverty of ancient Romans); 9:1,1–5 (luxury goods)

Hard work
2:6,3 and 4 (Athens); 7:2,1–2 (Rome)

Do not reveal feelings when in danger
2:2,5 (abusive crowd); 3:2,7 (Gauls); 3:3,1 (Etruscan captors); 3:3,2 (Illyrian captors); 3:3,ext.1 (fire); 3:3,ext.2–5 (philosophers); 3:3,ext.6 (Hindu ascetics); 3:8,2 (Carthaginians); 6:4,5 (civil war); 7:2,ext.1 (Socrates); 7:3,ext.9 (Tusculans)

Do not reveal feelings in misfortunes
3:7,ext.5 (humiliating job); 4:1,13 and 4:1,ext.3 (exile); 5:10,entire chapter (death of son); 6:4,ext.5 and 7:5,3 (defeat at elections)

Dignity
2:10,1, 2:10,ext.2, 3:7,8, 6:4,4, 6:4,ext.2, 8:1,absol.9, 8:5,6 (in law court); 2:10,8 (Cato in theater); 3:7,1d and 1e (Scipio in Senate); 3:7,11 and 3:7,ext.1–4 (professional pride of artists); 4:5,4 (Crassus canvassing)

Suicide
2:6,7–8 (euthanasia); 3:2,13–15, 3:2,ext.8, 9:9,2 (defeated in battle); 4:7,2, 9:12,4–7, 9:12,ext.1 (evade execution); 5:8,3–4 (son driven to suicide by father); 8:9,ext.3 (hear gloomy lecture)

The People

Snobbery
2:3,1 (men without property are not included in the people); 2:4,3, 4:5,1, 9:5,ext.4 (senators segregated from ordinary people); 2:5,2 and 9:3,3 (contempt for plebeian officials); 3:1,2 and 6:4,1 (contempt for Italians); 3:7,3, 6:2,3, 7:5,2; 8:1,damn.4 (contempt for ordinary Romans)

Reform movements
early Republic: 2:5,4 and 8:9,1 (strikes); 5:4,5, 5:8,2, 6:3,1b, 6:3,2 (land reform); 6:3,1a, 9:3,6, 9:7,4 (debt cancellation); 6:3,1c (free grain)

late Republic: 1:4,2, 2:8,7, 5:3,2e, 5:3,2f, 5:3,2g, 6:2,3, 6:3,1d, 7:2,6 (Gracchus brothers); 2;3,1, 8:6,2, 9:15,4 (Marius); 3:2,18, 8:1,damn.2–3, 8:6,2, 9:7,3 (Saturninus); 9:7,1–2 (Equitius, see Gracchus Brothers); 9:5,2, (Livius Drusus); 3:5,3 and 9:15,4 (Clodius)

Opposition to powerful men
Foreign: 3:2,ext.6 and 5:6,ext.2 (Thirty at Athens); 7:2,ext.11 and 7:2,ext.13 (Alexander the Great); 5:4,ext.3, 6:2,ext.1–3; 8:9,ext.1 (other foreign leaders)

Roman: 3:1,2 and 3, 3:8,5, 6:4,4 (Sulla); 3:2,13–15, 5:7,2, 6:2,11 (Caesar); 6:2,4–9 (Pompey); 6:2,12 (triumvirs); 4:3,14, 6:2,10, 9:3,4–7 (other Roman leaders)

The Army

Discipline
2:3,2 and 3, 2:6,2, 2:7,ext.2 (training); 2:7,1 and 2, 7:3,7, 9:7,mil.Rom.3 (morale); 6:3,3–4 and 7:3,3 (draft evaded); 9:7,mil.Rom.1–3 and 9:8,3 (mutinies)

Punishment
2:7,3–5, 2:7,7–9, 2:9,7 (humiliated); 2:7,11 (mutilated); 2:7,12–14, 2:7,6, 2:7,8, 5:8,3–5, 6:9,1 (executed)

Triumphs
2:8,entire chapter, 3:6,5, 5:2,5 and 6, 5:4,6, 5:5,2, 5:7,1

The Empire

Roman treatment of Italians
3:1,2, 6:2,1, 6:4,1, 9:5,1 (Italian rights); 3:2,ext.1 and 3:8,1 (massacre of disloyal Campanians); 7:2,ext.16 (Italian loyalty to Rome)

Roman treatment of provincials
2:2,3 (imposition of Latin); 3:2,ext.7, 6:4,ext.1, 7:6,ext.1–3 (siege); 6:3,5 (ruthless laws); 8:1,absol.2 and 9:6,2 (massacre)

Roman behavior in civil wars
3:8,7 and 9:13,2–3 (execution of prisoners); 5:3,3–5, 6:2,8, 9:2,1–3, 9:5,4 (execution of political opponents); 7:3,8 and 9 (victims escape); 9:2,1 (massacre of four legions by Sulla); 9:2,1 (massacre of people of Praeneste); 9:2,4 (massacre of people of Ategua)

Enemy treatment of Romans
6:6,ext.2 and 7:6,2–3 (siege); 9:2,ext.1 and 2 (execution of prisoners); 9:2,ext.3 and 9:6,ext.2 (massacre of civilians)